Linux 3D Graphics Programming

Norman Lin

Wordware Publishing, Inc.

Library of Congress Cataloging-in-Publication Data

Lin, Norman.
    Linux 3D graphics programming / by Norman Lin.
      p. cm.
    Includes bibliographical references and index.
    ISBN 1-55622-723-X (pbk.)
    1. Computer graphics. 2. Linux. 3. Three-dimensional display systems. I. Title.

    T385 .L556   2001
    006.6'93--dc21
                                            00-69314
                                                CIP

Printed in the United States of America

ISBN 1-55622-723-X
10 9 8 7 6 5 4 3 2
0103

All inquiries for volume purchases of this book should be addressed to Wordware Publishing, Inc., at the above address. Telephone inquiries may be made by calling:

(972) 423-0090

Contents

Preface

"3D graphics" is a term that anyone involved with computers has heard and seen; modern programs of all kinds increasingly use 3D graphics. Similarly, the term "Linux" has worked its way into everyday usage; the free, zero cost, open source, and community-developed Linux operating system is a significant player in the ongoing OS wars, and shows no signs of slowing down.

Only very recently, however, have we begun to see the terms "3D graphics" and "Linux" combined in the same sentence. The suitability of Linux for learning and programming 3D graphics appears to be less well known, or a closely guarded secret. I hope this book helps to change that. Linux is an excellent and enjoyable environment for interactive 3D graphics programming.

For a programmer—and I assume you are one if you are reading this book—3D graphics is one of the most challenging and rewarding of problem domains. Programmers in all fields grapple daily with abstract concepts requiring powerful mental visualization skills. With 3D graphics programming, the abstract concepts move into the realm of the concrete. You see the results of your effort, and with interactive programs, your creations appear to come alive in the most realistic way technology can produce—in 3D. All programmers know the satisfaction that comes with an elegant solution to a difficult problem. Such inherent satisfaction for a job well done is immeasurably greater with 3D graphics programs, because the reward also comes in the form of a breathtaking, animated 3D world—a believable universe conceived and brought to life by the programmer, a masterpiece of technical and visual synergy. The visual and creative rewards offered by 3D graphics programming are among the highest any field can offer.

Creating 3D programs requires a programming environment. As an absolute minimum, you need an editor, a compiler, and some standard libraries; a debugger is also practically indispensable. In general, programming 3D graphics demands more; you need image manipulation programs to create texture maps and generate common palettes, 3D modeling programs to generate 3D worlds and objects, language-parsing utilities to convert between file formats, and libraries to abstract some areas of the problem domain such as hardware accelerated rasterization.

All of these tools and more are available at no cost, and mostly with source code, for the Linux system. On other platforms, you must literally pay thousands of dollars just to get started programming 3D graphics: a compiler, a 3D modeler, and of course the operating system itself must all be purchased or licensed—assuming, of course, that you wish to legally use the software as opposed to illegally copying it. Under Linux, you can legally get all of this for free.

The low cost of 3D graphics development under Linux opens up this exciting realm to many creative, innovative, but financially limited individuals who otherwise might never get involved with 3D graphics. Students, universities, schools, hobbyists, and amateurs are but a few of the groups for whom Linux represents an economically attractive environment to explore professional 3D graphics.

But this low cost does not imply that Linux is just a toy system for starving students—indeed, nothing could be further from the truth! Linux is renowned for its power, stability, and flexibility in rigorous production environments. Linux workstations have been used to create professional graphics for Hollywood special effects and commercial 3D games. The freely available development and modeling tools are first-rate—literally some of the best software available at any price. Linux is absolutely a viable and proven production platform for professional programs.

Linux represents a new, open, and economical model of software development and distribution—one that has proven itself in practice. I am continually surprised and excited by the quality of software appearing for Linux and the new possibilities it opens. I hope that through this book you, too, will get a sense for the exciting and infinite possibilities that Linux and 3D graphics have to offer.

Acknowledgments

In addition to my parents, Forest and Vicki Lin, I would like to thank the following individuals who directly or indirectly played a role in the completion of this book. Thanks go to my brother Tony, who persuaded me to download and try out the game *Doom*, an experience which convinced me that interactive 3D graphics on the PC was finally possible. Special thanks also to Stan Hall, who provided encouragement and advice even when it seemed that the book might not see the light of day.

Solveig Haring and Margit Franz were kind enough to provide me with Internet access and a cup of coffee for some of the longer nights in the computer lab. Ton Roosendaal provided some very interesting insights into Blender and 3D graphics in general. My work colleagues Horst Hörtner, Werner Pankart, Klaus Starl, and Thomas Wieser were all supportive and understanding during those times when work on the book required absence from the office. Andreas Jalsovec and Dietmar Offenhuber gave me insight into some of the nuances of 3D modeling. Renate Eckmayr, Viju John, Azita Ghassemi, Manfred Grassegger, Ulrike Gratzer, Andrea Groisböck, Jogi and Reni Hofmueller, Angelika Kehrer, Astrid Kirchner, Dietmar Lampert, Christine Maitz, Paula McCaslin, Bernd Oswald, Gabi Raming, Regina Webhofer, and other individuals too numerous to mention all expressed interest upon hearing that I was writing this book, and gave me much needed inspiration and motivation.

Professor Deborah Trytten got me started on the right track in 3D graphics during my studies at the University of Oklahoma. Kevin Seghetti carefully read and checked the text for technical accuracy and provided many valuable suggestions. Thanks also to everyone at Wordware Publishing: Wes Beckwith, Kellie Henderson, Beth Kohler, Martha McCuller, Denise McEvoy, Paula Price, and everyone behind the scenes. Special thanks goes to Jim Hill, who shared my enthusiasm about the book and was key in actually getting this project out the door.

Last but not least, I would like to thank the countless individuals around the world involved with the creation and maintenance of the freely available, high quality, open source GNU/Linux operating system and tools.

Introduction

Welcome, reader! I am glad to have you along, and hope that you are as excited as I am about Linux and interactive 3D graphics programming. Take your time and enjoy the following few pages as we leisurely discuss the goals and contents of this book.

This book is the first volume of a two-volume work on interactive 3D graphics programming under Linux. First, let's look at the two-volume work as a whole; then, we'll look more specifically at the contents of this volume.

Taken as a whole, the two-volume work aims to provide you with the knowledge, code, and tools to program top-notch, object-oriented, real-time 3D games and interactive graphics applications for Linux, which can also easily be ported to other platforms. By working through both volumes, you will learn to use the most important techniques, tools, and libraries for Linux 3D graphics: portals, OpenGL/Mesa, Xlib, 3D hardware acceleration, collision detection, shadows, object-oriented techniques, and more. We also cover the often neglected topic of 3D modeling, illustrating in detail how to use the professional 3D modeling package Blender, included on the CD-ROM, to create animated 3D models and portal worlds for use in our interactive 3D programs.

This first volume, titled simply *Linux 3D Graphics Programming*, covers the basics of Linux programming and 3D polygonal graphics. Broadly, this encompasses the following major topics: Linux programming tools, the X Window System, rasterization, hardware acceleration, Mesa and OpenGL, 3D-to-2D projection, coordinate systems, vectors, matrices, transformations, arbitrary camera orientation, 3D polygonal objects, simple hidden surface removal, object-oriented design, and creation of basic 3D models using the program Blender. Summaries of each chapter in this volume appear later in this section. The second volume, titled *Advanced Linux 3D Graphics Programming*, covers more advanced techniques needed for realistic display of larger datasets often used in interactive 3D environments. Topics in the *Advanced* volume include: advanced rendering and animation techniques for 3D polygons (3D morphing, texture mapping, light mapping, fog), the creation of more sophisticated 3D models with Blender (including jointed figures animated with inverse kinematics), importing such models from Blender into our programs, hidden surface removal (portals, BSP trees, octrees, *z*-buffer), non-graphical issues relevant to interactive environments (special effects, collision detection, digital sound, TCP/IP networking, particle systems), and tutorials on using advanced 3D content development systems under Linux (Game Blender and World Foundry). In both volumes, sample programs are provided, both in the text and on the CD-ROM, that illustrate the concepts.

The field of interactive 3D graphics programming under Linux is a very exciting area due mainly to two parallel developments: the explosion of 3D graphics applications and the widespread acceptance of Linux in all areas of computing, including 3D graphics. Furthermore, 3D graphics has always been an inherently challenging and exciting field, and Linux has always been an inherently exciting operating system for programmers due to its open source nature and freely available tools.

Goals of This Text

This text has several objectives.

A primary goal of this text is to give you a solid understanding of the fundamental concepts involved in interactive 3D graphics programming. Such an understanding not only enables you to write your own 3D programs, libraries, and games under Linux, but also gives you the knowledge and confidence you need to analyze and use other 3D graphics texts and programs. In the open source world of Linux, understanding fundamental concepts is indeed important so that you can understand and possibly contribute to the common pool of knowledge and code. Furthermore, learning fundamental 3D graphics concepts also enables you to understand and effectively use sophisticated 3D applications and libraries such as 3D modelers and OpenGL. After completing this book, you will have a firm grasp on the theoretical and technical issues involved with 3D graphics programming.

 TIP This intentional emphasis on the foundations prepares you for the *Advanced* volume or for further independent study.

A second goal of this text is to give you plenty of hands-on experience programming 3D graphics applications under Linux. It is one thing to understand the theoretical mechanics of an algorithm; it is another to actually implement, debug, and optimize that same algorithm using a particular set of programming tools. Small standalone programs are scattered throughout this text to demonstrate key 3D graphics concepts. It is often easy to lose sight of the forest for the trees, particularly in the complicated world of 3D graphics. Standalone sample programs address this problem by concisely illustrating how all the necessary components of a 3D program "fit together." They reduce the intimidation that often accompanies the study of large, complicated programs, giving you confidence in developing and modifying complete 3D programs under Linux.

A third goal of this text is to help you develop and understand the techniques for creating a reusable 3D application framework or library. In addition to the standalone programs mentioned above, the book also develops a series of generally reusable C++ library classes for 3D graphics, called the l3d library. This C++ library code follows an object-oriented approach, relying heavily on virtual functions, (multiple) inheritance, and design patterns. In this manner, the developed library classes are usable as is but still open for extension through subclassing. Each chapter builds upon the library classes developed in previous chapters, either adding new classes or combining existing classes in new ways. The new concepts in each chapter are implemented via new classes or subclasses which add exactly the new functionality, instead of a time-consuming and wasteful complete reimplementation via cut-and-paste which is "similar but different" and not reusable. A constant search for abstract classes, including such less-than-obvious behavior classes as rasterizer, pipeline, and event dispatcher, yields code that is extremely flexible and modular, running on a variety of platforms including Linux, Microsoft Windows, and DOS, with and without hardware acceleration through a Mesa/OpenGL back end. Through subclassing, the library classes can be adapted to work with virtually any hardware or software platform or API. The techniques used to develop the 3D library classes illustrate both valuable 3D abstractions and generally applicable object-oriented techniques.

A fourth goal of this text is to demonstrate the excellence of the Linux platform as a graphics programming environment. For a programmer, Linux is a dream come true—all of the source code is available, all of the operating system features are enabled, a large number of excellent first-rate software development tools exist, and it is all freely available, being constantly tested and improved by thousands of programmers around the world. Linux empowers the programmer with open source, open information, and open standards. Given this outstanding basis for development, it is no wonder that programmers in every conceivable application area—including 3D graphics—have flocked to Linux. This has created a wealth of 3D libraries, tools, and applications for Linux. Linux is therefore an outstanding software development platform with powerful 3D tools and software—an ideal environment for learning and practicing 3D graphics programming.

A final, personal goal of this text, and the main reason I am writing this book, is to impart to you a sense of the excitement that 3D graphics programming offers. You, the 3D programmer, have the power to model reality. You control every single z-buffered, Gourad-shaded, texture-mapped, perspective-correct, dynamically morphed, 24-bit, real-time pixel on the flat 2D screen, and amazingly, your painstakingly coded bits and bytes merge to form a believable 3D world. And by working under Linux, you are no longer held back by a lack of tools or software. It's all out there—free for download, and top quality. Linux software gives you the tools you need to realize your 3D ideas.

Organization of the Book and the Code

This text follows a bottom-up organization for the presentation order of both concepts and program code. This bottom-up organization serves two purposes: pedagogical and practical.

Seen pedagogically, a bottom-up approach means first covering fundamental concepts (such as 2D graphics) before proceeding to more complex subjects (3D to 2D projection, 3D polygons, 3D objects, and complete interactive 3D worlds). This is a fully natural progression which deals with computer graphics at ever-increasing levels of abstraction. Seen practically, a bottom-up approach means that simple C++ classes are developed first, with later, more complicated examples literally "building upon" the foundation developed earlier through the object-oriented mechanism of inheritance. This ensures compilable, executable code at each level of abstraction which is incrementally understandable and extensible. Every chapter has complete, executable sample programs illustrating the concepts presented.

The bottom-up organization has a rather far-reaching impact on the structure of the code in general. The principal goal I had in mind when structuring the code for the book was that all parts of a class presented within a chapter should also be explained within that same chapter. While in some cases it was not practically feasible to fulfill this requirement completely, in most cases the chosen code and chapter structure does allow understanding a class as fully as possible within the context of the current chapter, with minimal references to future chapters. The second most important goal for the code was to reuse as much code as possible from previous chapters, typically through subclassing, thus truly illustrating how more complex 3D concepts literally, at the code level, build upon simpler concepts. To achieve these goals, the overall design of the code relies heavily on indirection through virtual functions, even in fairly time-critical low-level routines such as accessing elements of a list. The presence of so many virtual functions allows for a rather clean, step-by-step, bottom-up, incrementally understandable presentation of the code. The design is also very flexible; new concepts can be implemented through new subclasses, and behavior can be swapped out at run time by plugging in new concrete classes.

But as is always the case in computer science, there is a tradeoff between flexibility and performance. The code design chosen for the book is not absolutely as fast as it could be if all the virtual function calls were eliminated; of course, eliminating virtual function calls leads to reduced flexibility and increased difficulty extending the code later. Still, the code performs well; it achieves 30+ frames per second with software rendering on a Pentium II 366 in a 320×240 window with 24-bit color, and 30+ frames per second in 1024×768 with Voodoo3 hardware acceleration. In spite of its definite educational slant, it is fast enough for real use. Again, this is one of the great things about doing 3D programming in the 21st century: a straightforward, educationally biased code structure can still be executed fast enough by consumer hardware for real-time, interactive 3D environments. Real-time 3D no longer forces you to wrestle with assembly or to have access to expensive dedicated graphics workstations. If you know how to program in C++, and you understand the geometrical concepts behind 3D graphics, you can program real-time 3D graphics applications using free tools under Linux.

Let's now look at the organization of the text itself.

Chapter 1 provides an overview of 3D graphics programming under Linux and reviews the available tools, trends, and programs. We also write a simple Linux program that displays a window, with the goal of familiarizing ourselves with the entire process of editing, compiling, and running C++ programs under Linux.

Chapter 2 explains 2D screen access under Linux, since the foundation of traditional 3D graphics is the presentation of images that appear to be 3D on a 2D screen. This chapter first gives a few practical examples of 2D graphics under the X Window System and illustrates object-oriented techniques for developing reusable code. Basic 2D theory is then covered, including discussion of pixels, colors, and 2D screen coordinates. Along the way, we develop reusable library classes for 2D graphics, separating abstraction from implementation. Sample programs illustrate the use of the developed library classes.

Chapter 3 discusses 2D rasterization. We look at the algorithms necessary to draw lines and polygons using individual pixels of the 2D screen. We also discuss convexity, clipping, and sub-pixel correction, all of which complicate 2D rasterization. Finally, we examine hardware acceleration with the Mesa library and present new subclasses implementing hardware acceleration.

Chapter 4 lays the theoretical foundation for understanding what 3D graphics are all about: fooling the eye into seeing 3D objects on a 2D computer screen. This chapter examines in detail the processes of vision, visual perception, and light rays. By understanding these subjects, we understand how the eye can be tricked into seeing a 3D image where only a 2D image exists. We write a "fake" 3D program using a parallax effect, and explain the "3D effect" in terms of perceptual concepts. We then discuss the problems with the sample program's simple-minded approach to 3D graphics, all of which stem from the lack of a formal model for displaying arbitrary 3D data realistically on a 2D screen.

Chapter 5 solves the problems of Chapter 4 by developing the mathematical formulas necessary for specifying and projecting arbitrary 3D points onto a 2D plane. We redevelop the example 3D program in a more general, mathematically correct way. We also cover 3D coordinate systems, 3D points, 3D vectors, and operations on 3D vectors. Furthermore, we see how to use point projection to project entire polygons from 3D into 2D, thereby creating 3D polygonal graphics. Library classes are developed for all of these concepts.

Chapter 6 serves a number of purposes. First, it explains the idea of transformations as a manipulation of a 3D point. Second, it justifies the use of matrices to store transformations. Matrix math can generate a certain aura of mystique or skepticism for new 3D programmers or for those unfamiliar with the use of matrices in graphics. The justification for matrices is followed by a series of C++ classes which implement the necessary matrix operations. The chapter then shows the matrix form of three important transformations: translation, rotation, and scaling of a 3D point. We demonstrate the power of combining transformations through three practical examples: specification of an arbitrary camera location and orientation, rotation about an arbitrary axis (sometimes called "*Descent*-style" camera rotation, in honor of one of the first PC games incorporating this technique in real time), and local rotation and scaling. We also discuss some of the general properties of matrices which are useful for 3D graphics.

Chapter 7 justifies and implements the use of 3D polygons to model individual 3D objects and entire 3D worlds in computer memory. We also look at basic hidden surface removal, which allows for a correct display of complex polygonal objects. We discuss how to clip objects against arbitrary planes in 3D, which is needed for some advanced visible surface determination algorithms covered in the *Advanced* volume. All of these techniques are implemented in C++ classes.

Chapter 8 introduces Blender, a free and powerful 3D modeling and animation package for Linux (included on the CD-ROM). The information in the previous chapters gives us the code to create visually realistic polygonal 3D images, but we still need interesting 3D data to display. Creating this data is the role of a 3D modeler. We review the extensive features of Blender and then create, step by step, a basic spaceship model. This 3D model is then imported and displayed in a 3D program.

Chapter 9 briefly introduces a number of advanced topics, all covered in the *Advanced* volume. These topics include 3D morphing, more advanced algorithms for visible surface determination (portals, BSP trees), texture mapping, lighting and light mapping, special visual effects (particle systems, billboards), and non-graphical elements often used in interactive 3D graphics programs (collision detection, sound, Newtonian physics).

The Appendix provides installation instructions for the CD-ROM, an explanation of fixed-point math, information on porting the graphics code to Windows, and a list of useful references, both in electronic (WWW) and in print form. Notations in brackets, such as [MEYE97], are detailed in the "References" section of the Appendix.

The CD-ROM contains the Linux operating system, C++ software development tools, freely available Linux 3D libraries and applications, the Blender 3D modeling and animation suite, all sample code from the book, and a series of animated videos illustrating some of the more difficult-to-visualize 3D concepts discussed in the text (such as the transformation from world space to camera space). In other words, the CD-ROM contains a complete learning and development environment for 3D programming and modeling.

Reader and System Requirements

This book requires you to have a working Linux installation up and running with the XFree86 server for the X Windows System on an IBM PC or compatible system with a Pentium or better processor. If you don't yet have Linux installed, you can install the Linux distribution included on the CD-ROM or download Linux for free from the Internet (see the Appendix). Installing Linux is no more difficult than installing other common PC operating systems, such as Microsoft Windows. A 3D graphics card with Mesa drivers is necessary for the hardware-accelerated demonstration programs, although the code will also run acceptably fast without hardware acceleration. If your graphics card is supported by the new XFree86 4.0 Direct Rendering Infrastructure, you can also link the code with the DRI's OpenGL library to achieve hardware accelerated rendering in a window.

In order to effectively read this book, you should have a working knowledge of the following:

- Executing programs from the command line under Linux
- Finding, loading, editing, and saving text files under Linux
- Manipulation of windows under the X Window System (dragging, resizing, switching among, minimizing, maximizing, etc.)
- The concepts of "compiling" and "linking" programs (the exact Linux commands are described later)
- Basic to intermediate concepts of the C++ language (bit manipulation, classes, virtual functions, multiple inheritance)
- Basic data structures and algorithms (pointers, linked lists, binary trees, recursive traversal, binary search)
- Basic high school mathematics (geometry, trigonometry, linear algebra)

In essence, this means that you should have programmed in C++ before, and that you should have basic familiarity with using Linux and the X Window System.

 NOTE If you need to brush up on some of the above topics, have a look at the references, both online and in book form, presented in the Appendix.

Even if you are an absolute newcomer to Linux, don't despair. Linux comes with a variety of online documents which can help you with installation and basic file and directory manipulation. Many of these documents are on the CD-ROM; see the Appendix for details.

Typographical Conventions Used in This Book

The following typographical conventions are used in this book.

- Program code, class names, variable names, function names, filenames, and any other text identifiers referenced by program code or the operating system are printed in a `fixed-width font`.

- Commands or text to be typed in exactly as shown are printed in **boldface**.

- Key sequences connected by a plus (+) sign (such as Ctrl+C) mean to hold the first key while typing the second key.

Chapter 1

Introduction to 3D Graphics and Linux

During the course of the 15th century, great painters of the Renaissance grew very excited about a new discovery that was sweeping the artistic world. This new discovery, now termed *linear perspective*, allowed painters to portray their visions with striking realism—realism that drew viewers into the painting with the feeling of depth. Closer objects appeared larger, farther objects appeared smaller, parallel lines converged on the horizon, and it all was done with convincing, mathematical precision. Through the use of perspective, two-dimensional pictures could finally faithfully capture the elusive third dimension. The art world was changed forever.

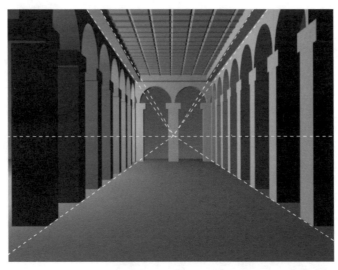

Figure 1-1: A Renaissance-style image illustrating linear perspective and the convergence of parallel lines on the horizon.

The field of computer graphics has experienced a similar revolution. Barely a decade ago, text interaction was still a standard means for communicating with computers. Graphics, on those computers supporting them, generally merely enhanced text-based applications by drawing accompanying 2D pictures or graphs. As graphics capabilities became common on more computers, graphical user interfaces began to replace command-line interfaces, until completely graphical operating systems became widely available. Correspondingly, programming languages incorporated 2D graphics features, or could be linked with 2D graphics libraries.

As soon as 2D graphics capabilities were available, enthusiastic computer scientists combined their knowledge of linear perspective with these 2D graphics capabilities to create so-called 3D graphics. The display on the screen was of course still 2D (although even this has changed in recent years), yet through perspective, the images appeared to exist and move convincingly in 3D.

The problem was one of computational speed. 3D graphics requires many mathematical computations; the more realistic the image, the more computations needed. Early consumer PCs simply did not have the raw power needed to display interactive 3D graphics. Computing just one reasonably realistic image could take minutes—far too slow for interactive displays. Thus, interactive 3D graphics was only a reality on expensive, high-end computers, which are far out of the reach of the average consumer or the average programmer.

But at long last, today, interactive 3D graphics has become widespread. The ever-increasing computational power of personal computers has reached such a stage that the average consumer's PC can now display real-time, interactive, animated 3D graphics—indeed, complete immersive 3D environments. Compiler technology has also matured to such a level that a straightforward implementation of 3D graphics concepts in a high-level language yields acceptable real-time performance. 3D graphics has become accessible to both the consumer and the programmer.

The proliferation of 3D computer graphics implies increasingly that successful software must incorporate 3D graphics. Though most evident in the computer games industry, this trend also affects other software areas: business and scientific software often allow some form of 3D data visualization; WWW browsers allow 3D navigation through virtual worlds written in VRML; word processors even offer built-in 3D drawing functions with controllable lighting and perspective parameters. The consumer has come to expect 3D graphics in modern software of all kinds.

Figure 1-2: 3D graphics comes to the personal computer. Here, one of the 3D figures for this book is being prepared using a free Linux 3D modeling package, Blender. A few years ago, it would have been impossible to run such a computationally demanding 3D application on a normal, consumer-level PC.

Apart from consumer expectation, there is another, perhaps ultimately more compelling reason to program 3D graphics: it's just plain fun. 3D graphics programmers have the unique privilege of seeing stunning animated displays as a result of their long hours of coding. However complicated or intricate 3D graphics might seem at times, it's important not to lose sight of the "fun" aspect!

Why Linux

Linux is an excellent and perhaps unsurpassed environment for learning, programming, and producing 3D graphics. Two good examples from the late 1990s include the heavy use of Linux machines in producing the graphics for the movie *Titanic*, and the appearance of commercial games for the Linux platform (*Quake* from id software is but one example). Let's examine more closely why Linux makes such a good environment for 3D graphics programming.

Linux is Free and Open

Linux is a freely available, open source operating system. The operating system and most of the available software are released under a free software license, typically the *GNU General Public License*, abbreviated *GPL*. The accompanying CD-ROM contains the text of the GPL; Figure 1-3 shows a portion of the license. The GPL ensures the availability of source code for the licensed product and for all derivative works. In practice, this means that a vast amount of Linux software is available and will remain available free of charge and with source code.

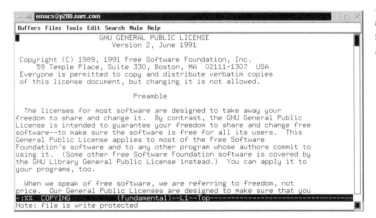

Figure 1-3: An excerpt from the GNU General Public License.

Linux therefore offers the 3D graphics programmer a low-cost, open source platform. Freely available compilers and graphical debuggers make real software development possible, and the availability of source code for 3D applications allows you to study and learn from others' code. You might expect the available 3D graphics source code to be limited to small example programs written by individuals. Though many examples fall into this category, larger scale 3D programs are also available with source code for study. This includes blockbuster games from a few years ago, such as *Descent*, *Doom*, and *Quake*, all of which are now available with source code and free of charge for the Linux platform.

NOTE   As with any other software license, you should read the GPL carefully and make sure that you understand your rights and obligations. Also note that not all Linux software is licensed under the GPL; always read the license agreement for the particular software package in question.

Linux is Powerful

Linux is sometimes viewed as the operating system for "power users." Its tools are no different: they are powerful and efficient. Let's take a quick glance at some of the powerful tools Linux offers the 3D graphics programmer:

- gcc: Fully featured optimizing C++ compiler. Features include support for various dialects of C and C++, configurable debugging and optimization, inline assembly, cross compilation, several processor targets, and front ends for compiling other computer languages.
- gprof: Code profiler. Various reports and graphs illustrate how much time was spent in particular routines, which routines called which others, or how often a particular source code line was executed.
- gdb: Text-mode debugger. All typical debugger features are supported: setting breakpoints, single stepping, stack tracing, dynamic inspection, and alteration of data.
- xxgdb: Graphical interface to the debugger gdb. Through xxgdb most functions may be invoked via the mouse, and source code is displayed in its own window with breakpoint.
- Blender: Professional 3D modeling and animation package.
- rcs: Revision control system for tracking changes to individual files.
- cvs: Concurrent version control system fulfilling the same role as rcs, but allowing multiple developers to simultaneously make changes to the same file; often used for projects which have a modifiable source code repository accessible through the Internet.
- Aegis: Change management system built on top of a version control system; used for tracking problem reports and changes to sets of files.
- Emacs: Multi-file editor with interfaces to compiler, debugger, version control, and more.

Linux has the powerful tools needed to do serious, professional 3D graphics programming—tools for everything from version control to code profiling to 3D modeling. These tools often surpass their commercial counterparts that cost thousands of dollars. With the right tools, you can concentrate on the task at hand: programming interactive 3D graphics.

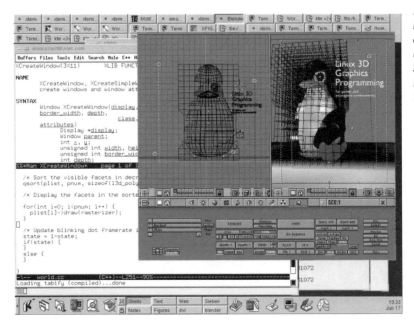

Figure 1-4: A typical desktop under Linux, using the X Window System (X) and the K Desktop Environment (KDE).

Linux is Compatible

The open source nature of Linux development implies that programmers must eventually agree upon some standards to support: libraries, languages, protocols, and so on. The many standards supported in Linux ensure long-term compatibility with a wide range of other systems and programs.

Some of these standards include:

- C++: This is a standardized, widespread, object-oriented language. The GNU/Linux C++ compiler gcc is available on a large number of platforms, including 68000-based Linux systems, Microsoft Windows, DOS, and even some console game systems. The availability of the same C++ compiler for all of these systems allows C++ programs developed under Linux to run on a wide range of platforms with a minimum of code change. In fact, the 3D graphics programs in this book can also be made to compile and run under Windows and DOS; see the Appendix for details.

- Mesa and OpenGL: OpenGL is a standardized, widespread library for interfacing to 2D and 3D graphics hardware. Mesa is a free library written by Brian Paul, which, in practice, is source-code compatible with OpenGL. (Mesa is not an "officially" licensed OpenGL implementation, since the official licensing and conformance testing process costs money, which programmers working for free cannot be expected to pay.) Under Linux, Mesa offers support for hardware acceleration on 3DFX cards, and support for other high-performance 3D hardware has just become available through the Direct Rendering Infrastructure, which is part of XFree86 4.0. OpenGL or Mesa implementations are also available for Microsoft Windows and DOS.

■ VRML: VRML, the Virtual Reality Modeling Language, is an object and scene description language widely used in WWW pages. The free 3D modeler Blender can import and export VRML files.

By supporting these 3D graphics standards, Linux allows the 3D graphics programmer to remain compatible with several platforms. This compatibility allows for easier porting of programs and exchange of data.

Linux is Contemporary

Linux 3D graphics is constantly evolving. Today, this means support for hardware acceleration and the development of standardized APIs. Current examples include Mesa's support for 3DFX hardware acceleration, and SGI's release of the Performer scene graph library for Linux. In the future, this will probably mean increased support for true 3D input and display devices and further development of 3D operating system interfaces to replace the 2D desktop metaphor. Whatever the future may hold, this much is certain: the 3D graphics community does not stand still, and neither does the Linux community. The open source, distributed development philosophy ensures that Linux can keep up with the most current 3D graphics developments, whether these developments are in the form of ideas, algorithms, software, or hardware.

A Survey of 3D Graphics Under Linux

Under Linux, programming 3D graphics—or programming any real system, for that matter—requires a different approach than on commercial systems. With commercial systems, you typically pay a software vendor for an operating system license and a compiler license. You then read the compiler manuals to see what libraries and operating system features are available, and program your application based on the features that the operating system, the compiler, and its libraries offer. You build your systems based on the building blocks you buy or license from your software vendor.

Linux software development is radically different. As mentioned earlier, the operating system itself has been released under an open source license, in this case the GPL. The GPL requires that the source code to the product, and all derivative products, always be available to everyone. Most software available under Linux also falls under either the GPL or a similar open source license (notable non-GPL but open source products include XFree86 and the Qt graphics library used by the K Desktop Environment, KDE—though the legal status of Qt was just recently changed). This unique approach to software development means that you as a programmer literally determine what features the operating system, the compiler, and available software libraries have to offer. The entire environment was programmed by programmers like you, and must be extended in the future by you or programmers like you. It is a radical concept, but one that works amazingly well in practice due in no small part to the communication possibilities offered by the growing Internet.

This means, however, that there is no official ruling body which will tell you what functions or libraries are "officially supported." You must decide for yourself which resources are available under Linux to help you get your job done. In our case, this job is 3D graphics.

Figure 1-5 summarizes graphically the important concepts and libraries relevant to Linux 3D graphics programming. Linux 3D graphics programming, like many other programming endeavors, can be viewed and carried out at various layers of abstraction. In the figure, the topmost layer is the most abstract; the bottommost, the least abstract. In between are various libraries and concepts which allow your 3D application (top layer) to ultimately create the hardware signals necessary to display a 3D image on the monitor (bottom layer). The arrows in the figure represent possible communications between layers. (The solid and dotted lines represent which concepts are emphasized or not emphasized in this book, respectively, and have no technical significance.) Notice that a particular layer may not only communicate with the layer immediately beneath it, but may also bypass the immediately underlying layer to communicate more directly, and thereby more quickly, with lower layers. Bypassing a lower layer, though, means that the higher layer must do the bypassed layer's work as well—usually in a faster, more specific, and less general way than the lower layer would have done. The higher the layer, the more choices must be made as to which underlying layers should be used, and which not. This is what makes the figure, and the practical side of 3D programming, complex.

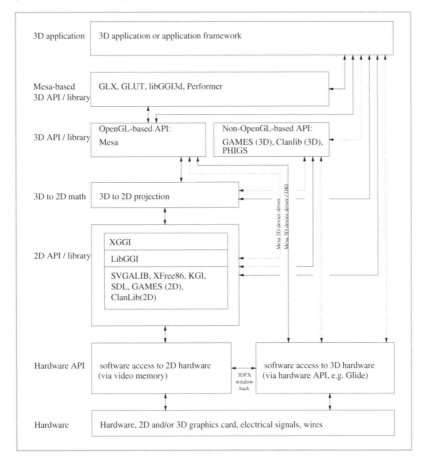

Figure 1-5: Libraries for Linux 3D graphics programming.

Let's now take a closer look at some of the available 3D tools and libraries under Linux. We first cover projects that are relatively stable, continue with a list of developing projects, and close with a list of "dead" projects. As you read the following sections, you may want to refer to Figure 1-5 in order to keep the overall structure in mind.

 NOTE The following sections are not exhaustive, but do provide a representative view of 3D graphics development under Linux at the time of this writing. Again, the open source model requires you to inform yourself about trends in this area, but at the same time gives you the freedom to choose and the power to change. The Appendix lists some useful Internet resources for Linux and 3D graphics, where you can inform yourself about the latest happenings.

Stable Ideas, Projects, and Libraries

The following list provides an overview of some of the stable and well-established ideas, projects, and libraries related to 3D graphics programming under Linux.

- 2D/3D theory: There are no two ways about it—you <u>must</u> understand the geometric and mathematical theory behind 2D and 3D graphics in order to do any sort of serious 3D graphics programming. Rest assured, after completing this book, you will indeed have a firm understanding of this theory. Coordinate systems, mappings, perspective projection, vectors, matrices, and intersections are but a few of the fundamental topics which every 3D programmer, and you too, must know by heart. This theory is the very foundation of every 3D program ever written and is the area where the most exciting new discoveries can be made. Know the theory, and the rest is just implementation.

- Hardware: A basic understanding of hardware display technology and raster displays is essential to programming graphics of any kind.

- X Window System/XFree86: The X Window System forms the primary display environment under Linux. It provides a device-independent, network-transparent interface to graphics hardware. XFree86 is one freely available implementation of the X Window System. Programs may draw into a window by using functions provided by X.

- Mesa: Mesa is a free graphics library written by Brian Paul, with a syntax identical to that of the standard graphics library OpenGL. Programs using Mesa can take advantage of hardware acceleration in a platform-independent way.

- GLUT: The OpenGL Utility Toolkit is a free library, written by Mark Kilgard, which is built on top of OpenGL and which makes the implementation of certain frequently occurring OpenGL operations much simpler. GLUT is compatible with Mesa.

- Blender: Blender is a freely available professional 3D modeling and animation package which has been used to produce 3D graphics in commercial production environments. Its advanced features include keyframe animation, motion curves, inverse kinematics, and lattice deformation—to name just a few.

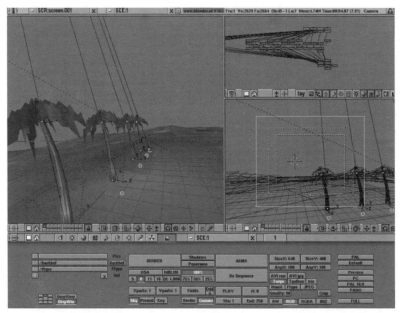

Figure 1-6: Blender, a professional 3D modeling and animation package. Blender is included on the CD-ROM accompanying this book.

Developing Ideas, Projects, and Libraries

The following sections provide an overview of some of the significant development efforts taking place in the field of Linux 3D graphics. These represent works in progress, projects to which you may eventually wish to contribute.

Developing APIs

The following list summarizes some of the important developing APIs (application programming interfaces) relevant to Linux and 3D graphics programming. These libraries are in various stages of development, some more usable than others. You should check the WWW pages of these libraries (provided in the appendix) for more details.

- SDL: The Simple DirectMedia Layer (SDL) is a 2D frame buffer, audio, and input API. SDL works on a number of operating systems including Linux.

- GGI: The General Graphics Interface (GGI) aims to develop a portable 2D (ggi2D) and 3D API (ggi3D) offering Linux graphics developers an alternative to the "SVGALIB or X" decision for graphics ouptut. GGI has both a kernel part, KGI, which interfaces at a low level to the OS, and a user part such as XGGI. GGI does not replace X; X is a window system, GGI is a graphics interface. Mesa can direct its output to 2D GGI devices.

- GAMES: The GNU Animation and Multimedia Entertainment System is an object-oriented 2D, sprite, 3D, and sound API for multimedia and games applications.

- ClanLib: ClanLib is a gaming library planning to offer 2D and 3D graphics, image, sound, and networking routines.

3D Applications with Source

The following list summarizes some important 3D applications available with source code for the Linux system. These applications illustrate a variety of techniques for 3D graphics programming and most are being actively extended. You might eventually want to contribute to these projects.

- *Descent:* The game *Descent* is a commercial, indoor, portal-based 3D game whose source has been released and ported to Linux.

- *Doom: Doom* was one of the first games with real-time texture mapping for PCs, utilizing special restrictions on game geometry to speed up texture mapping. Its source has also been released and ported to Linux.

- *Golgotha:* This is a mostly complete game from crack.com which unfortunately was not completed. Instead of letting the source code and numerous graphics and music files go to waste, crack.com released it all to the public for study and use.

- *Obsidian:* This is an Internet, multi-player, client-server virtual reality system, currently being developed under an open source model.

- *Crystal Space:* This is a portal-based engine aiming to become a general purpose gaming system, currently being developed under an open source model.

- *Flight Gear:* This is an open source flight simulator project for PCs with hardware acceleration.

- *World Foundry:* The World Foundry system is an open source, complete 3D game production environment with advanced physics, camera, and scripting systems, allowing an extremely rich variety of virtual worlds to be created with little or no additional programming. Originally used to produce commercial games for Windows and the Sony PlayStation, World Foundry is now being ported to Linux.

 NOTE I personally have helped with porting the World Foundry system to Linux. This is one of the most enticing features of an open source development model: if a project interests you, and if you know enough about the subject, nothing stops you from jumping in and helping. As mentioned in the introduction, one of the major goals of this book is to give you a solid enough foundation and broad enough perspective on Linux 3D graphics so that you too can participate in or even initiate your own open source 3D projects.

3D Modelers

The following list summarizes some of the many 3D modeling programs available under Linux that are in various stages of development.

- amapi: Modeler with a tool-based interface and various deformation and mesh editing capabilities.

- sced, sceda: Constraint-based scene editor, allowing linking of objects based on "constraints" (somewhat similar in effect to inverse kinematics). Support for Computational Solid Geometry (CSG).

- Midnight Modeler: CAD-like modeler with tools for generating and deforming meshes. Command-line and menu-based interface.

- 3DOM: Open source 3D modeler.
- ac3d: Shareware modeler with multiple simultaneous views.

None of these modelers currently matches Blender's flexibility and power (introduced in the section titled "Stable Ideas, Projects, and Libraries"). For this reason, we cover Blender in this book; Chapter 8 goes into more detail about the specifics of using Blender to create models and portal worlds.

Dead Ideas, Projects, and Libraries

Not all software projects enjoy great success or even long life. The following list describes some previously potentially promising but now essentially dead ideas, projects, and libraries relating to Linux 3D graphics.

- SVGALIB: This library provides direct access routines for displaying graphics on SVGA video cards. The main problems are that SVGALIB programs don't interface well with X, and that not all video cards are supported—fewer video cards than are supported by XFree86, for instance. SVGALIB historically played an important role in early Linux graphics programming because it offered a working, fast graphics solution. However, due to the problems mentioned above, it is no longer as important as it once was. The future lies with X and 3D hardware acceleration integrated into the X server (covered in the next section).

- X3D-PEX/PEX/PHIGS: The Programmers Hierarchical Interface Graphics System, PHIGS, is an ANSI 3D graphics standard which never really enjoyed great acceptance. PEX, or the PHIGS Extension to X, was an extension to the X Window System to incorporate PHIGS functions. PHIGS is basically dead; OpenGL and the OpenGL Extension to X (GLX) have taken its place.

Other Ideas, Projects, and Libraries

Outside of "stable," "developing," and "dead," there are also some other important trends in Linux 3D graphics which go beyond the scope of this book but which deserve mentioning.

- VRML/Java/Java 3D: The Virtual Reality Modeling Language is a scene description language which also offers facilities for user interaction. Java programs can interface with VRML worlds, making VRML an attractive language for WWW-based 3D applications. Java 3D is a high-level, scene graph API in Java intended for more direct programming of platform-independent 3D applications (notice that VRML is fundamentally a "modeling language," whereas Java 3D aims to be a high-performance programming API). The main problem with WWW-based Java and VRML applications is the speed of the network connection. Linux VRML browsers (such as VRWave and FreeWRL) already exist.

 NOTE A *scene graph* is a data structure storing the various components of a 3D scene and the relationships among these components. That Java 3D is a scene graph API means that it provides application programmers access to a data structure representing the 3D scene, rather than requiring the programmer to define his own data structures to manipulate the 3D scene. The higher-level access at the scene graph level means that application programmers can focus on higher-level issues, but also constrains programmers to work within the scene graph structure as provided by the API.

■ Non-interactive 3D graphics: A number of packages exist for doing non-interactive, photorealistic 3D graphics under Linux. Some of the important packages in this area include POVRay, the Persistence of Vision Raytracer, and BMRT, the Blue Moon Rendering Tools, which implement the Renderman specification.

Scope of This Book, Revisited

The introduction covered in detail the goals and contents of this book. Given the survey of Linux 3D graphics just presented, we can now understand the book's scope in a new context: we focus on stable ideas, projects, and libraries dealing with real-time Linux 3D graphics programming. These are also the solid arrows in Figure 1-5. Toward the end of the book and in the advanced volume we also discuss some of the developing trends and provide a list of WWW addresses that often contain information about new developments.

Let's Talk About X

The graphics programs we write under Linux will display their output under the X Window System. So, let us now examine the X Window System in more detail to understand at a high level how the system works. As mentioned in the introduction, you should already be familiar with basic usage of the X Window System; the following discussion is primarily from a programmer's point of view, not necessarily a user's.

The X Window System, as mentioned earlier, is the usual display environment under Linux. If you have used other operating systems, you may be slightly confused by this terminology. What is meant by "usual display environment"? Let's first look at Linux itself: Linux is a variant of the Unix operating system, and provides access to services such as files, directories, processes, hardware, and network connections. Unlike some other operating systems, Linux does not dictate a particular display environment. You can, for instance, productively run Linux in an 80x25 text console. A Linux-based WWW server often does exactly this. For graphics programming, you can either try to access the video hardware directly, or you can go through a graphical display environment. But regardless of what your program does, the operating system itself is separate from any graphical display environment.

That understood, the usual graphical display environment under Linux is, in fact, the X Window System, also called simply "X" or "X11." (The term "X Windows" is to be avoided, since it incorrectly suggests a relationship to a proprietary operating system of a similar name and often causes confusion.) The particular implementation of the X Window System most commonly used on Linux systems is XFree86, so named because its target processor family is the Intel x86 family.

Definition of X: A Client-Server System

So, what exactly is X?

X is a distributed, hardware-independent windowing system developed at MIT. X is based upon a *client-server* model. An *X server* controls access to the video hardware and runs on the computer which is physically connected to the monitor. Applications, also called *X clients*, connect to an X server and send a request to the X server to display something, such as a point, rectangle, circle, or bitmap image, which then appears on the X server's screen. X clients can also send requests to the X server to access the server's video hardware in other ways, such as to change a color palette (which we define in Chapter 2). Since it is a windowing system, X handles the display as being composed of *windows* (a rectangular area of the display capable of receiving input and displaying output). Under X, windows may be hierarchically arranged and may overlap.

 NOTE From a programming point of view, a window is not necessarily the same as the informal concept of an application window. For instance, one application window might contain three buttons and a text entry field. Each button and the edit field might be a separate window, all hierarchically existing as children of the main window. Typically, each application window in reality contains several child windows. You cannot tell just by looking how many child windows a particular window has, since a child window does not necessarily have any visible delineating border.

An important component of X is its *network transparency*: X clients do not need to be running on the same machine as the X server. If you are encountering this concept for the first time, its full impact might not yet be clear. Network transparency means that any machine, running any operating system, can connect to an X server and display graphics on its screen. You can think of an X server as a sort of universal monitor on which any program (which understands the X protocol) can display graphics. For this reason, some vendors produce inexpensive *X terminals*, which contain nothing more than a monitor, a network card, and an X server in firmware. Such X terminals simply need to be connected to a network and can immediately display graphics coming from any program (any X client) reachable via the network—in the case of the Internet, this means worldwide. As a personal anecdote, I used to use a low-cost X terminal to display graphics coming from a Cray supercomputer located hundreds of miles away in a different scientific computing center. Furthermore, dozens of other users were doing the same thing at the same time, each with their own X terminal, located in various laboratories throughout the world. Here, each X terminal is an X server controlling access to its own monitor; the Cray in this case runs several X clients, each X client requesting to display graphics on the X server from the user who started the X client. (If you are particularly devious, you can try to start an X client requesting to display its output on a different X server than your own, which is sometimes desirable but usually viewed as a security risk, for which reason this is usually disabled by default.)

The terms "X server" and "X client" are often confusing to newcomers to X, because of the pervasive notion that "the computer running the application is the server." This notion is too narrow: in general, a server controls usage of particular resources. In the Cray example above, the Cray may therefore be viewed as the application server, controlling usage of the Cray CPU. The X server is <u>always</u> the machine physically connected to the target monitor. The X server serves requests for display on the target monitor. In other words, from an X viewpoint, your machine is the X server, the application program is the X client, and the machine running the application program is irrelevant (network transparency).

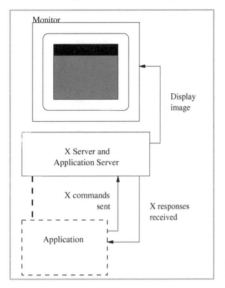

Figure 1-7: X on a single-user system.

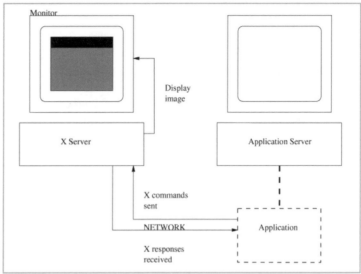

Figure 1-8: X in a network environment.

 NOTE   Even when the X server and client are on the same machine, the communication still takes place via the same mechanism, namely, network sockets. The client is thus isolated from the server and generally does not know whether the display is local or not.

The X programs we write in this book will be X clients, which, like all X clients, contact an X server to do the actual graphics display. Thankfully, we don't need to write an X server, because that has already been done for us by the XFree86 team. The XFree86 X server is a stable and freely available X server supporting a wide range of video cards on PCs using the Intel x86 processor family. XFree86 undergoes active development and improvement. Lately, much work has gone into integrating hardware acceleration into the X server. Let's examine this topic a bit more closely.

Hardware Acceleration and X Servers

One current field of development in the area of Linux X servers is the ongoing work to integrate 3D hardware acceleration into the X server. In order to understand the significance of this development, let us first examine what hardware acceleration is, what the difficulties are, and some current hardware acceleration projects.

What is Hardware Acceleration?

The term "hardware acceleration" generally refers to the use of additional hardware components to offload processing which would otherwise need to be done in the main CPU, thereby freeing the main CPU for other tasks. Hardware acceleration is therefore a form of parallelism, where the additional hardware and the CPU perform different processing tasks simultaneously. One of the oldest examples of hardware acceleration is the now-ubiquitous FPU, or floating-point unit, which performs time-consuming floating-point operations in a special processor, thereby freeing the CPU for other calculations.

In 3D graphics, hardware acceleration more specifically refers to hardware which performs computations specific to 3D graphics. In this way, image quality and/or speed may be improved.

To understand what 3D hardware can accelerate, we need to understand what 3D graphics programs, in general, do. Covering this in detail is the subject of the rest of the book. For now, here is a broad generalization of typical processing which 3D programs do, also called a *3D pipeline*. You are not yet expected to fully understand all terms below, such as culling, polygons, or camera space. These terms are all defined in due course in the coming chapters.

1. Objects in the 3D world or scene are processed. This means updating the position of any moving objects and coarse culling (rejection) of objects which are deemed to be invisible for the current camera position (i.e., objects behind the camera or outside of the view frustum).
2. Polygons (more specifically, just their corner points or vertices) belonging to the remaining objects are rotated and transformed into so-called camera space, finer culling of individual polygons is performed, and surviving polygons are projected into screen space for display.
3. Pixels for each remaining polygon are computed and displayed. Depending on the type of surface detail applied to the polygon, there may be a lot of computation done for each pixel: lighting, texture mapping, fog, antialiasing, z-buffering, and so forth.

The 3D pipeline is executed for each frame (image) to be displayed, where the number of frames per second for interactive programs is usually anywhere from 10 to 60 or more.

Figures 1-9 through 1-11 illustrate the pipeline graphically. Here, a viewer is looking at a scene containing several cubes, only two of which are visible. The viewer's location is represented by the sphere located at the left of the figures. The large truncated pyramidal shape with its apex at the camera is the *view frustum*, which represents the portion of the world visible to the camera. The figures show object-level, polygon-level, and pixel-level operations, respectively.

Notice that for each object, we have several polygons, and for each polygon, we have several pixels. Thus the amount of processing at each stage in the pipeline (objects, polygons, and pixels) increases by an order of magnitude or more.

 NOTE An "order of magnitude" is a difference that is a factor of ten.

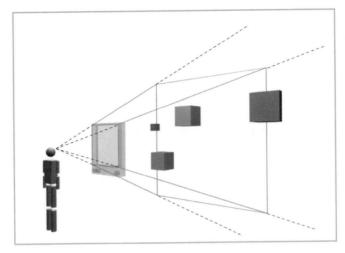

Figure 1-9: Object-level processing. All objects are first updated. Then, based on the camera position, only the two cube objects in the center of the picture are retained. Other objects are culled.

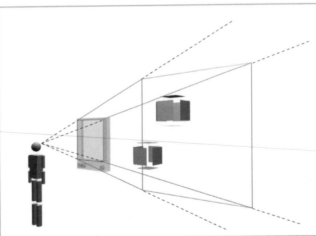

Figure 1-10: Polygon-level processing. For the surviving objects, the visible polygons or potentially visible polygons are computed and retained. Other polygons are culled. Here, only the polygons facing the camera will be retained, a technique called back-face culling.

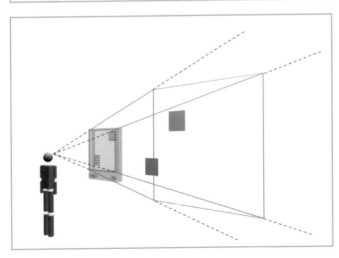

Figure 1-11: Pixel-level processing. Pixels for all surviving polygons are computed and displayed on the screen, which is located in the diagram between the camera (left) and the objects (right). Notice the large number of pixels displayed for each polygon.

In the last stage, at the pixel level, we have the most time-consuming operations: hundreds of thousands or even millions of operations must be performed per frame. Therefore, this stage was the first to be accelerated in consumer-level 3D graphics hardware. 3D hardware acceleration at this level is also called *hardware-accelerated rasterization*. Such hardware takes over the most numerous and time-consuming pixel-for-pixel operations required when drawing polygons to the screen. Hardware acceleration on consumer-level 3D graphics hardware (under $1,000) typically supports hardware-accelerated rasterization.

The next step is to move polygon-level operations into 3D hardware. This already exists on high-end ($50,000) graphics workstations, and has recently started to become available for consumer-level PCs. For instance, MMX is a fixed-point math coprocessor which can operate on multiple scalars simultaneously. This accelerates 3D geometry by allowing effectively more 3D calculations to be performed in less time than with the main CPU.

Object-level operations will also, eventually, be moved into common consumer-level 3D hardware. Hardware acceleration at the polygon and object level is also called *hardware-accelerated geometry*, because the hardware assumes the responsibility for mathematically manipulating the higher-level geometrical description of the world, as opposed to the lower-level pixel-based view of rasterization hardware.

NOTE   Notice that hardware acceleration, which is most important at the lowest (pixel) level, cooperates with software-based culling schemes, which are most important at the highest (object) level. Hardware accelerates the pipeline from the bottom up; software culling accelerates the pipeline from the top down. You can think of this as "cull what you can, accelerate what you can't." The companion book *Advanced Linux 3D Graphics Programming* discusses culling schemes.

Integrating Hardware Acceleration into X

We have seen that the X Window System forms the primary display environment under Linux. It is therefore vital that Linux 3D hardware somehow interface with X. The fundamental difficulty is that X by default views the underlying graphics hardware as being 2D. There are various solutions to this problem.

The oldest solution was that of 3Dfx graphics cards: the 3D hardware is physically separate from the 2D hardware and is not controlled by or even known to X. This allows for full-screen accelerated 3D graphics through a special driver, but not accelerated graphics within an X window. The next solution was then a hack to copy the image from the 3D card into an X window, which is slower than full-screen mode (since copying the entire image into an X window is a time-consuming process), but still faster than non-accelerated rendering. Finally, the newest and most promising approach is to extend the X server and the Linux kernel to communicate directly with the 3D hardware.

3Dfx Hardware Acceleration

The company 3Dfx manufactures variants of the Voodoo chipset, which are used in a number of 3D accelerator cards. The earliest cards were 3D-only cards, designed to work in cooperation with an existing 2D card. The library Glide (from 3 Dfx) forms the programmer's interface to the

Voodoo hardware, offering functions for sending 3D data directly to the chips. Daryll Straus wrote the Linux version of Glide, thereby making accelerated 3D under Linux a reality. David Bucciarelli then wrote a Glide device driver for Mesa, another important achievement which allowed normal Mesa programs using standard OpenGL commands to take advantage of 3Dfx hardware acceleration. For these reasons, 3Dfx hardware has historically been the best supported 3D hardware under Linux.

One reason that 3Dfx hardware works well under Linux is that it is a physically separate card. Full-screen accelerated programs can be started from within the X Window System without crashing or otherwise disturbing the X server. The normal X display takes place on the 2D graphics card, while the full-screen 3D accelerated application switches the monitor to use the 3D card for display. In fact, it is possible to use two completely separate monitors with 3Dfx hardware: one for the normal 2D display and one for the hardware-accelerated 3D display. The 3D hardware is completely separate from the 2D hardware, and thus causes no problems with the 2D hardware or the X server.

Of course, full-screen isn't always desirable—this is why windowing systems were invented in the first place. While full-screen mode might be most effective for a 3D game, this is not necessarily the case for a less immersive 3D program, such as a 3D Modeler. We often want both the speed provided by 3D hardware acceleration and the convenience of display within a window.

To address this need for 3Dfx cards, a special "trick," called the *in-window hack*, used the separate 3Dfx card to render the image, then did a memory copy of the image from the 3Dfx card into an X window. This is not nearly as fast as full-screen rendering, because the memory copy is slow, but is in most cases faster than pure Mesa software rendering. Also, you can't really run more than one accelerated application at once. If you try this, the applications will fight for use of the 3D card, creating a somewhat amusing flickering effect among the windows as the competing images from each application are sent to the card.

While the first generation of 3Dfx hardware provides a working solution, which for a long time was the only working solution, a more general approach is needed for integrating hardware acceleration and windowed display under X.

GLX: The OpenGL Extension to X

We have seen that one fundamental problem is that X views display hardware as being 2D. 3Dfx hardware works well because it is separate and left alone by X, but this makes true integration into the windowing system difficult. A more direct approach is to extend the X server itself to understand a more sophisticated concept of display system.

GLX is one such X extension. (PEX, as mentioned in the "dead projects" section, was another which is no longer of great significance today.) GLX is the OpenGL extension to the X protocol, allowing OpenGL commands to be communicated to a server directly. The X server then communicates with the 3D hardware.

Though it was originally not open source, Silicon Graphics has since released the source code to their reference implementation of GLX. This makes the creation of a fully working and compliant Linux GLX implementation much easier, and is a major step in realizing accelerated X servers making use of 3D hardware.

Accelerated X Servers of the Future

Hardware acceleration of the future will use GLX to communicate Mesa (OpenGL) commands to a newer form of X server which can communicate through a software infrastructure with underlying 3D hardware. At the time of this writing, two major projects are currently underway to create such software infrastructures for communication with the 3D hardware. These projects are DRI, the Direct Rendering Infrastructure from Precision Insight Inc., and MLX, the Mesa-Linux kernel-X server project from SuSE. The goals of these projects are essentially the same: to allow multiple simultaneous applications to use 3D hardware acceleration under X. There are a number of architectural questions raised by such goals (related to context switching and synchronization with the X server), and it will be interesting to see which ideas from these two projects eventually flow into the mainstream. Currently, both projects have working demonstrations in the form of patched X servers with hardware drivers for a small number of 3D cards.

The latest news on this front at the time of this writing (March 2001) is that the DRI has been integrated into the newest version of XFree86 4.0, and currently offers in-window acceleration for a number of 3D graphics cards. The DRI has more or less established itself as the current standard for 3D acceleration in an X window under Linux. For those cards not yet supported by the DRI, you might be able to find Linux drivers in the Utah-GLX project (`http://utah-glx.sourceforge.net`)—a separate effort with goals similar to those of the DRI, and which will eventually be integrated into the DRI.

Summary of Hardware Acceleration

Let's take a step back and summarize the preceding hardware acceleration projects. 3Dfx hardware acceleration works today, and has historically been the best supported Linux 3D hardware. Future hardware acceleration focuses on a tighter integration with X. Originally this meant a patched X server with drivers for your particular 3D card, but the recent release of XFree86 4.0 with the DRI provides a more robust solution supporting a wide range of 3D hardware.

But what impact does hardware acceleration have on 3D programming? How can we write programs which will take advantage of hardware acceleration, when the field is in a constant state of flux?

The answer, in a word, is OpenGL. For Linux, this means Mesa, the free OpenGL-like library. OpenGL is a standard, and the projects involving hardware acceleration all focus on using OpenGL as the interface to the hardware. So, for Linux 3D programming, "hardware acceleration" can currently be equated with "Mesa." This makes our lives much easier. To take advantage of hardware acceleration, we simply use Mesa routines where appropriate and don't worry about the underlying hardware acceleration infrastructure. Chapter 2 provides a detailed example of this.

Having completed our introductory X education, let's now try writing a simple X program under Linux.

"Hello, Linux": A Sample Program

This section introduces you to compiling and debugging C++ programs under Linux. The goal is to familiarize you with the software development tools by entering, compiling, executing, and debugging a simple program which displays an empty window under X. This is perhaps somewhat less than spectacular, but it's at least a start.

First, you should install the software on the CD-ROM. The Appendix provides instructions to get the software up and running on your Linux system. The software includes development tools (such as the compiler and debugger), the Mesa graphics library, the Blender 3D modeling and animation package, and all of the sample programs in the book. After installing the software, you are ready to get started programming.

Start the X server, enter a command shell, and verify that the `DISPLAY` and `L3D` environment variables are set correctly. If you don't know how to do this, see the Appendix. From the command shell, you can start all other applications.

NOTE   From now on, if not otherwise specified, it will be assumed that you have started the X server, have started a command shell, have verified that the `DISPLAY` and `L3D` environment variables are set correctly, and know how to activate the window containing the command shell. For all commands intended to be passed to the operating system (also called *shell commands*), you should activate the window containing the command shell, type the command to be executed, and press **Enter** to execute the command.

Entering the Sample Program

We first edit the program using a text editor. This immediately raises the question, which editor?

Two of the most common editors under Linux are vi and Emacs. If you have seriously used any Unix system before, you will almost certainly have extensively used one or both of these editors. For those new to Linux and not familiar with these editors, a brief description follows.

The Vi and Emacs Editors

Vi is a single file text editor with keystroke commands designed to minimize typing. Vi has the advantage of being small, fast, powerful, and available on almost all systems. Once you learn the commands, you can perform text editing tasks (replacement, indentation, deleting and moving text) extremely quickly in vi. I used to (and sometimes still do) race other programmers with text editing tasks, each of us using the text editor of our own choice. I would almost always win with vi, simply because I know the vi commands by heart, and because the vi philosophy minimizes keystrokes—even going so far as to place commonly used keys on the touch-typist's "home row" (the row containing the keys A-S-D-F) to maximize potential speed. There is no menu to invoke, no mouse to click; you press a key, and the command is done. Vi's disadvantages, however, also stem from this "speed above all" philosophy; its keystroke-based interface is admittedly cryptic with a steep learning curve. Furthermore, vi is primarily aimed at editing one single text file; while editing more than two files at once is technically possible, it is extremely inconvenient using vi. Editing binary files with vi is generally not possible.

NOTE   It has been proved, so I am told, that the expressive power of vi's commands (including simple keyboard macros) is equivalent to that of a Turing machine, meaning effectively that any computational problem can be solved through vi commands! This is amazing when one considers that vi has no "programming language" as such. This means that, theoretically, you could write an X server, the Linux operating system, or 3D graphics programs using only vi commands.

Emacs is a multiple-file, multiple-window, extensible editor for text and binary files. Emacs has literally no limits and is the most powerful editor available on any system, period. You might think this statement exaggerated, but it is not: Emacs is programmatically extensible, which means that its functionality can be infinitely extended through new program modules, with a power and flexibility exceeding that of simple plug-in or macro-based systems. Furthermore, a very large number of useful modules (packages) do in fact exist, either built-in or available for download. As a small example of the unmatched integrated functionality which Emacs offers, here are some of its features: multiple simultaneous editing of text and binary files, automatic syntax highlighting for scores of languages, symbol completion, multiple windows, interfaces to compilation, version control, and debugging systems, multi-byte character set support, class browser, symbolic and numeric math, directory browser, keyboard macros, desktop save, file differencing, shell interface, calendar, diary, web browser, mail and USENET news reader, fully remappable keyboard bindings, typesetting modes, and emulation of other editors. Emacs is often viewed as one of the shining examples of the excellent software that can be developed under the open source model.

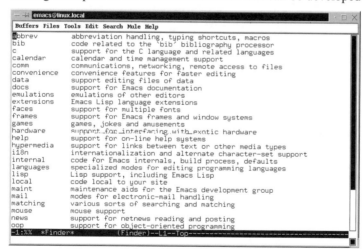

Figure 1-12: A partial list of some of the categories of available Emacs packages.

With all of this power, Emacs also has a bit of a learning curve. However, for a while now, Emacs has provided a drop-down menu system which makes learning much simpler. Furthermore, Emacs has an extensive online help system. Taking the time to learn Emacs will be paid off by higher productivity while programming.

The following sections describe how to start and use the Emacs editor to enter the program. For simple text editing, Emacs is fairly intuitive to use—the normal arrow, cursor movement, and text deletion keys act as expected and are all that is required.

NOTE Although Emacs has a lot of integrated functionality, we will not concentrate on this aspect, instead using Emacs simply to edit text. Other commands, even if they are integrated into Emacs, will be entered in a normal command shell. This doesn't force you to use Emacs if you don't want to—for instance, if you already know how to use another text editor and wish to use it to edit the program code. If you are interested in learning more about the integrated features of Emacs, simply start using it and read the online documentation, which includes a hands-on tutorial section. I personally learned Emacs exactly this way—just by using it regularly and by working through the extensive online documentation.

Basic Editing with Emacs

After this brief excursion into text editors, we are now ready to start Emacs.

1. Enter a command shell.

2. Type **cd $L3D/source/app** to change to the directory containing the sample programs. If you receive the error "No such file or directory," then either the software is not correctly installed or the L3D variable is not set correctly. See the Appendix for installation instructions.

3. Type **emacs** and press **Enter**. A new Emacs window opens:

```
emacs@p200.narc.com

Buffers Files Tools Edit Search Mule Help
Welcome to GNU Emacs, one component of a Linux-based GNU system.

Get help           C-h  (Hold down CTRL and press h)
Undo changes       C-x u      Exit Emacs         C-x C-c
Get a tutorial     C-h t      Use Info to read docs   C-h i
Mode-specific menu   C-mouse-3 (third button, with CTRL)
('C-' means use the CTRL key.  'M-' means use the Meta (or Alt) key.
If you have no Meta key, you may instead type ESC followed by the character.)

If an Emacs session crashed recently, type M-x recover-session RET
to recover the files you were editing.

GNU Emacs 20.2.1 (i386-suse-linux, X toolkit)
 of Tue Aug  4 1998 on neumann
Copyright (C) 1997 Free Software Foundation, Inc.

GNU Emacs comes with ABSOLUTELY NO WARRANTY; type C-h C-w for full details.
You may give out copies of Emacs; type C-h C-c to see the conditions.
Type C-h C-d for information on getting the latest version.

-:--  *scratch*      (Lisp Interaction)--L1--C0--All---------------------
For information about the GNU Project and its goals, type C-h C-p.
```

Figure 1-13: Emacs immediately after starting.

If you do not see a new Emacs window but instead see a text-based Emacs program within the same window, then you have not set the DISPLAY environment variable correctly (as described in the Appendix). To correct this, you should:

1. Press **Ctrl+x**, **Ctrl+c** to quit the text-based Emacs program. You should now again be in the command shell.

2. Type **export DISPLAY=localhost:0.0** and press **Enter**.

3. Type **emacs** and press **Enter** to restart Emacs in a separate window.

 NOTE For key sequences connected by a plus (+) sign (such as Ctrl+C), hold the first key while typing the second key.

Next, open the sample file `hello/hello.cc` in the sample programs directory. In the Emacs window:

1. Press **Ctrl+x**, **Ctrl+f** to "Find" (i.e., open or create) a file. Notice the words "Find file:" and the current pathname at the bottom of the screen.

2. Press **Tab**, **Tab** to display a completion list. The first Tab tries to complete any partially entered string you have entered; the second Tab displays a list of possible completions. Notice the completion window which appears, and the subdirectory `hello`.

Figure 1-14: Emacs automatically provides a completion list.

3. Type **hel** and press **Tab**. Notice that Emacs completes this automatically to the subdirectory `hello`, the first entry matching "hel." Then type / to complete the directory name.

4. Press **Tab**, **Tab** to again display a completion list. Notice the completion window again appears and displays the contents of the subdirectory `hello`.

5. Type **hello.c** and press **Tab**. Notice that Emacs completes this automatically to the full filename `hello.cc`.

6. Press **Enter** to accept the filename. Emacs opens and displays the file. The source code is automatically highlighted in color if your copy of Emacs has been so configured. To manually toggle the syntax highlighting, press **Alt+x**, type **font-lock-mode**, and press **Enter**.

```
— emacs@p200.narc.com                                    · □ ×
 Buffers Files Tools Edit Search Mule C++ Help
#include <X11/Intrinsic.h>
#include <X11/Xlib.h>
#include <stdio.h>

#define SCREEN_XSIZE 320
#define SCREEN_YSIZE 200
#define BITS_PER_BYTE 8

main() {
  Visual *vis;           // X11: Visual (visual info about X server)
  Display *dpy;          // X11: Display (connection to X server)
  Window w;              // X11: Window

  // establish connection to X server

  dpy = XOpenDisplay(NULL);

  // create and map (display) an X window for output

  vis = DefaultVisual(dpy,0);
  w = XCreateWindow(dpy,                     // display
-:--  hello.cc          (C++)--L1--C0--Top-------------------------------
Loading cc-mode (compiled)...done
```

Figure 1-15: Emacs after opening the file `hello.cc`.

If you make a mistake while entering an Emacs command, press **Ctrl+g** to cancel the command. You might need to press **Ctrl+g** multiple times, depending on the command you are canceling. If you ever get completely lost, press **Ctrl+x**, **Ctrl+c** to quit Emacs and try again.

NOTE To create a new file, follow exactly the same procedure described above, but enter the new filename instead of entering "hello.cc." Emacs notices that the file does not yet exist and creates a new file upon saving.

The contents of the file `hello.cc` are shown in Listing 1-1.

NOTE The code listings in this book have been automatically reformatted so that extraneous comments do not appear in the printed source listings. These comments, however, are useful if you wish to change or debug the code, so they do appear in the code on the CD-ROM. Therefore, the actual code you see in Emacs when you open the source files will likely contain some extra comment lines which you do not see in the printed listings here.

Listing 1-1: `hello.cc`

```c
#include <stdio.h>
#include <X11/Intrinsic.h>
#include <X11/Xlib.h>
//- empty line
#define SCREEN_XSIZE 320
#define SCREEN_YSIZE 200

main() {
  Display *dpy;
  //- establish connection to X server

  dpy = XopenDisplay(NULL);

  //- create and map (display) an X window for output

  Visual *vis;
  Window w;
  vis = DefaultVisual(dpy,0);
  w = XCreateWindow(dpy,                        //- display
                    DefaultRootWindow(dpy),     //- parent
                    100, 100,                   //- x, y position
                    SCREEN_XSIZE, SCREEN_YSIZE, //- width, height
                    0,                          //- border width
                    CopyFromParent,             //- depth (we use max. possible)
                    CopyFromParent,             //- visual class (TrueColor etc)
                    vis,                        //- visual
                    0, NULL);                   //- valuemask, window attributes
  XStoreName(dpy, w, "hello");

  XMapWindow(dpy, w);

  XSelectInput(dpy, w, KeyPressMask);

  XEvent event;
  char ch;
  KeySym keysym;
  XComposeStatus xcompstat;

  while(1) {
```

```
if(XCheckWindowEvent(dpy,w,KeyPressMask,&event)) {
  XLookupString(&event.xkey, &ch, 1, &keysym, &xcompstat);
  switch(ch) {
    case 'q': {
        exit(0);
      }
  }
  }
 }
}
```

Let's now make a few changes to the file to familiarize ourselves with editing in Emacs. In the Emacs window:

1. Press the arrow keys, **PgUp**, and **PgDn** to scroll through the text. Notice that the cursor moves and the text scrolls in a completely usual manner. Press **Home** and **End** to go to the beginning and end of file, respectively.

2. Move the cursor to the beginning of the line containing the text "empty line."

3. Press **Del** several times until the entire line has been erased.

4. Type the following text: // **sample comment**.

5. Move the cursor to the space between the words "sample" and "comment."

6. Type the text **new**. Notice that the text is inserted at the cursor position and by default does not overwrite the following text.

7. Save the file by pressing **Ctrl+x**, **Ctrl+s**.

8. Close the file (more precisely, the editing buffer containing the file) by pressing **Ctrl+x**, **k**, **Enter**. The "k" stands for "kill buffer," and the final Enter confirms the choice of which buffer to kill, which is by default the current buffer.

You may exit Emacs by pressing **Ctrl+x**, **Ctrl+c**. However, during a programming session, it is useful to leave Emacs itself open, and to open and close individual files as needed.

We now have enough knowledge of Emacs to open, edit, and save files. There are many more Emacs commands available—enough to fill a book. Since this book is on 3D graphics and not on Emacs, we won't go into further detail about the myriad of Emacs commands. I do, however, encourage you to explore the online documentation available from within Emacs itself. The best place to start is the online tutorial.

 TIP In Emacs, press **Ctrl+h**, **t** to invoke the online tutorial.

Compiling and Linking the Sample Program

We use a utility called make to compile and link our program. The make utility searches for a file called `Makefile`, reads compilation rules from the Makefile, and executes the proper commands to compile and link the programs (or *targets*) listed in the Makefile. A Makefile is therefore simply a description of how to compile a particular program or library.

The general compilation process under Linux is identical to that of other systems. In the first phase, compilation, a *compiler* translates the source code files written by a programmer into *object files*. Under Linux, the C++ compiler is g++ (which calls the C compiler gcc with special C++

parameters). By convention, C++ source files have `.cc` as the filename extension; object files, `.o`. In the second phase, linking, a *linker* binds the object files with one another and possibly with a number of external libraries, resolves all inter-module dependencies which can be statically determined, and creates an executable program file. Under Linux, the C linker is ld; the C++ linker, g++. Finally, at run time, dynamic module dependencies, known as *shared libraries*, *shared object files*, or *.so files*, are loaded during program execution by the dynamic linker and loader, ld.so.

For complicated programs, there is a large number of source, object, and executable files—all possibly in different directory hierarchies. The compilation process must find all of the input files and create all of the output files in the right places. Manually specifying all of this information during every compilation is unmanageable. The make utility addresses this problem by automating program compilation and collecting compilation information once and for all in Makefiles.

Overview of Makefiles

A *Makefile* is a non-procedural description of how to compile a program. Similar to a script file or a batch file, a Makefile in effect does nothing other than execute a series of commands in sequential order (ignoring some parallelizing variants of make). But unlike a script file, the contents of a Makefile do not explicitly list the commands in the order to be executed. Instead, a Makefile is ordered based on rules and dependencies. A *rule* states how to generate a particular file; for instance, an object file is created by calling the gcc compiler on the corresponding C++ file, and an executable file is created by calling the linker on the corresponding object files. A *dependency* states which other files are needed to create a particular file; for instance, the executable `hello` file depends on the existence of the `hello.o` object file. The idea of rules and dependencies is that make can save compilation time by reusing existing object files from previous compilations instead of recompiling everything every time. Make checks the dependencies, and only executes a command to create a target if the target does not already exist or is older than its dependents.

 CAUTION Incorrect Makefile dependencies can lead to linking of old object files and to segmentation faults at run time. If in doubt, recompile everything by manually deleting all object files.

Determining dependencies, though, is a very tricky subject indeed. If your Makefile dependencies are not 100% correct, then make will sometimes reuse an old object file when it should actually recompile the file. Such reuse of old object files can lead to segmentation faults at run time, because of changes in structure or class definitions which have propagated to some but not all object files. There are tools to automatically generate Makefile dependencies, but unfortunately, even these sometimes make mistakes! At least, this had been my experience while developing a system for compilation under Linux, Windows, and DOS. In this case, the automatic dependencies intermittently failed on one of these three platforms, leading intermittently to segmentation faults. For this reason, the more complicated Makefiles in this book always recompile everything (by removing all object files beforehand), which is slower but always correct. If you wish to investigate the more efficient usage of Makefiles, only recompiling files when absolutely necessary, see the manual entry for the `makedepend` command, and be aware that mysterious segmentation faults at run time may be due to incorrect dependencies. When in doubt, recompile everything.

We use Makefiles primarily to save us effort during compilation. Often, we need to pass specific flags or `#define` directives to the compiler, and pass several long object filenames and library names to the linker. With a Makefile, we write the compilation rules once, and every time thereafter we simply type **make**.

The Makefile for the `hello` application looks as follows:

```
LD = g++
LDFLAGS = -L/usr/X11R6/lib -lX11 -lXt -lm
CPPFLAGS = -O3

hello: hello.o
        $(LD) $(LDFLAGS) $^ -o $@
```

Let's first run the make process, then analyze the Makefile.

Compiling the Program with Make

To compile the program using make:

1. Enter a command shell.
2. Type **cd $L3D/source/app/hello** and press **Enter**.
3. Type **ls** and press **Enter**. Notice that the only files in the current directory are `hello.cc` and `Makefile`.
4. Type **make** and press **Enter**. Notice the compilation and linking commands which are printed to the screen and executed. Wait until the command prompt appears again.
5. Type **ls** and press **Enter**. Notice that the new files `hello.o` (object file) and `hello` (executable program) have been created by the make process.

 NOTE You can compile your program from within Emacs. Press **Alt+x**, type **compile**, and press **Enter**. Then, type the compilation command **make** and press **Enter**. Emacs changes the current directory to be the directory of the source file and executes the command you entered. Error and warning messages are displayed in a separate Emacs window, allowing you to simultaneously view the compile messages and your source code. See the online info documentation for more information.

 TIP Makefiles usually have the filename Makefile. However, you can tell make to use a differently named Makefile by specifying the flag `-f [filename]`.

Compiling the Program Manually

After typing make, the following commands are printed on screen and are executed:

```
g++  -O3  -c hello.cc -o hello.o
g++ -L/usr/X11R6/lib -lX11 -lXt -lm hello.o -o hello
```

To demonstrate that make has simply executed these commands and only these commands, let's execute these commands manually. In the command shell from the previous section:

1. Type **rm hello hello.o** and press **Enter** to remove the executable and object files created by the previous make process.

2. Type the first command that was executed by make: **g++ -O3 -c hello.cc -o hello.o**, and press **Enter**. This calls the gcc compiler to create the object file `hello.o` from the source file `hello.cc`. Wait for the command to complete.

3. Type **ls** and press **Enter** to verify that the file `hello.o` has been created.

4. Type the second command that was executed by make: **g++ -L/usr/X11R6/lib -lX11 -lXt -lm hello.o -o hello**, and press **Enter**. This calls gcc to link the object file `hello.o` with the necessary libraries to create the executable program `hello`. Wait for the command to complete.

5. Type **ls** and press **Enter** to verify that the file `hello` has been created.

As a final experiment, now type **make** again and press **Enter**. The following message appears:

```
make: 'hello' is up to date.
```

Make has noticed that the target file `hello` already exists, and is newer than its dependent file `hello.o`. Therefore, nothing needs to be done, and make accordingly does nothing.

 NOTE This Makefile, since it is so simple, did not delete the existing object files before recompilation. It is for exactly this reason that make found the old object files and decided that nothing needed to be done.

Analysis of Makefile

Let's now take a closer look at the Makefile to understand its structure. The Makefile's contents, once again, are as follows:

```
LD = g++
LDFLAGS = -L/usr/X11R6/lib -lX11 -lXt -lm
CPPFLAGS = -O3

hello: hello.o
        $(LD) $(LDFLAGS) $^ -o $@
```

The first line sets the variable named LD to be g++, instead of the standard ld. The variable LD—which is written $(LD) when its value is being read—signifies the name of the program used as the linker. We change the linker to be g++ instead of ld because we are writing C++ programs and thus use g++ as a C++ linker.

The second line lists the flags passed to the linker. We include the X11 directory (with the flag -L/usr/X11R6/lib), and link in the X11 library (-lX11), the Xt Intrinsics library (-lXt), and the math library (-lm).

The third line lists the flags passed to the C++ compiler. Here, we pass -O3, which optimizes the program for speed, at the cost of space.

The next line states that the executable file `hello` depends on the file `hello.o`. Below this line is the rule for making `hello` once all of its dependencies exist. Assuming `hello.o` exists, we invoke the linker (designated by $(LD) $(LDFLAGS)) on all dependent object files (designated by $^) to create the target file `hello` (designated by -o $@).

CAUTION   The rules line(s) should begin with a Tab character, not spaces.

NOTE   `$^` and `$@` are *automatic variables* which have special meanings in Makefiles. A list of all internal variables and their meanings appears under the entry for make in the online info documentation (described later in this chapter, and invoked with command `info.`).

At this point, you should be wondering, "but where do we call the gcc compiler to compile `hello.cc` into `hello.o`?" Until now, we have said that program `hello` requires `hello.o` to be present, but we have not said where `hello.o` comes from. Of course, we as programmers know that the object file `hello.o` should be compiled from the `hello.cc` source file. This is actually also an *implicit rule*, which is internally known to the make program. Make knows of several ways to make a `.o` file, and one of the ways is to look for a corresponding `.cc` file. This rule is so common that it has been built into make and we do not need to specify it explicitly. Since the file `hello.cc` is indeed present in the current directory, make realizes that it should invoke the rule to create a `.o` file from a `.cc` file. What exactly is this rule? According to the online info documentation, the rule is to invoke `$(CXX) -c $(CPPFLAGS) $(CXXFLAGS)`. Notice that the variable `CPPFLAGS` appears in this implicit rule, which is exactly the reason that the flags set in `CPPFLAGS` get passed on to the compiler during compilation. The variable `CXX` signifies by default the gcc C++ compiler, and the variable `CXXFLAGS` allows further compilation flags to be set. (The actual compilation command which appeared above, g++, simply calls the gcc compiler with certain C++ specific flags.)

NOTE   If you wish to see exactly what rules make is trying to execute, type **make -d**. This starts make in debug mode and is useful for understanding the machinery behind make.

Complicated Makefiles for large projects (millions of lines of code over thousands of source files) can literally span scores of pages. I used to have the pleasure of debugging such Makefiles on a regular basis, where the `-d` flag, mentioned above, was invaluable. The Makefiles in this book will not be nearly this complicated, but it is worth knowing that make can handle very large projects.

All of the programs in this book come with Makefiles, so you normally need only type **make** to compile the sample programs. Detailed instructions for compiling all of the code at once appear in the Appendix.

For your own programs, you may also wish to use Makefiles. In this case, you can use the sample Makefile above as a template. You will probably also want to look at some of the more complicated Makefiles for the other sample programs in this book which illustrate the use of multiple targets, multiple dependencies per target, and multiple commands per target.

Executing the Sample Program

After compiling the program as described above, execute the sample program as follows. In the command shell from the previous section:

1. Type **hello** and press **Enter**. The program window appears. (Some distributions of Linux by default do not allow you to execute files in the current directory. If this is the case with your

system, you must type **./hello** to execute the program.) Try moving the window by dragging its title bar with the mouse, or try resizing the window, and observe the results.

2. Type **q** in the program window to quit.

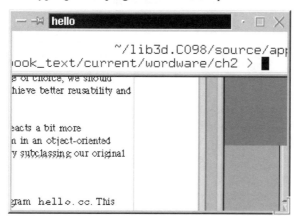

Figure 1-16: Output from the sample program `hello`. Exact output on your system will not be identical to this figure, for reasons covered in Chapter 2.

A detailed explanation of the workings of this program must wait until the next chapter; for now, it is enough that we have edited, compiled, and executed the program. Now let's cover every programmer's favorite topic: debugging.

Debugging the Sample Program

Life would be great if all programs followed the simple progression "edit, compile, execute." Our programs would work perfectly the first time and we could spend our evenings musing about Turing machines or NP-complete problems.

In reality, of course, we programmers spend our evenings hunched over the keyboard trying to find that elusive "bug," caffeinated drink and Kung-Pao chicken close at hand. While not absolutely necessary, a debugger is usually an extremely useful tool for serious bug tracking and real software development. Naturally, Linux has had good debuggers for some time now.

A debugger is a controlled execution environment for a program. It allows you to step through the source code one instruction at a time to see what line in your source file is currently being executed. You can set *breakpoints*, which signal the debugger to stop execution at a certain point in the source code. A debugger also allows dynamic inspection and alteration of data, eliminating or greatly reducing the need for `printf`-type statements littered throughout the code just to inspect data, and which can themselves be a source of errors.

 NOTE With the relatively recent industry acceptance of object-oriented programming paradigms, the importance of tracing data flow, rather than control flow, has increased. This is because the very notion of object orientation centers around the class, which is an abstract data type. The flow of control or execution in object-oriented designs tends to be less centralized, because good object-oriented designs yield architectures which can be easily recombined to form new solutions to problems. Enabling such recombination means that an object-oriented design should generally not be based on a sequential, step-by-step view of the problem domain, but rather on a data-centered view, trying to find relevant domain abstractions as classes. In terms of debugging, this means that understanding the data within objects and the ways in which it is transformed—in other words, understanding data flow—is at least as important as understanding the control flow.

The classical Linux debugger is gdb, the GNU Debugger. The gdb is a freely available text-based debugger which offers all typical debugger features. While fully functional, gdb is somewhat less than comfortable to use. When stepping through a complicated series of function calls, it is important to visualize the context of the current operation within the framework of the program. With a text-mode debugger, this is somewhat difficult, because we typically only see one line of the program at a time—the line currently being executed. While we can easily display the surrounding context, we must invoke an extra command to do so. This distracts from the main debugging task.

For this reason, graphical front ends to gdb have been developed. These graphical front ends still use gdb as the core debugger, but have a much more comfortable interface. For instance, they automatically switch to the appropriate source file, positioning the cursor on the current line. This allows a much more fluid debugging process which does not interrupt the train of thought.

NOTE Emacs, not surprisingly, has an integrated and easy-to-use interface to gdb. To invoke it, press **Alt+x**, type **gdb**, and press **Enter**. See the online info documentation for more information.

To use a debugger, we must compile the program with debugging information included in the object file. For this, we change the compilation flags to include the debugging flag -g. To do this:

1. Open the Makefile in Emacs.
2. Use the arrow keys to move the cursor to the beginning of the line containing the text "CPPFLAGS."
3. Press **Ctrl+k** to delete the contents of the current line.
4. Type **CPPFLAGS=-g**.
5. Save the Makefile: **Ctrl+x**, **Ctrl+s**.
6. Close the buffer containing the Makefile: **Ctrl+x**, **k**, **Enter**.
7. Enter a command shell, type **cd $L3D/source/app/hello**, and press **Enter**.
8. Type **rm *.o** and press **Enter** to remove all old object files. The old object files did not contain any debugging information.
9. Compile the program again by entering **make**. Notice that the -g flag appears in the compilation command instead of the -O3 which appeared previously. Wait for the command to complete.
10. Start the graphical debugger by typing **xxgdb hello** and pressing **Enter**.

NOTE Under the Debian Linux distribution included on the CD-ROM, you must be logged in as the root user (who has all access rights to the system) in order to be able to run xxgdb. This is apparently due to an unusual default configuration of access rights.

The xxgdb debugger appears as shown in Figure 1-17 on the following page.

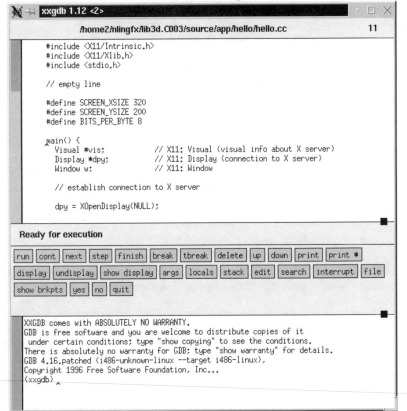

Figure 1-17: The xxgdb debugger.

The xxgdb window is divided into three sub-windows. A sub-window is active and can receive keyboard input only when the mouse cursor is on top of it.

The top window shows the current source file. Notice that the caret (the position of the cursor in a non-active window, shown as "^") appears on the first function name, `main`. During debugging, if a function in another file is called, xxgdb displays the new file automatically. The scroll bar on the left or the arrow keys scroll the window.

The middle window contains a number of buttons for executing debugger functions. Some of these buttons only work if an item is highlighted in the top section of the window. For instance, you cannot use the Print button (which displays the value of a variable) unless you have already highlighted a variable. Other buttons, such as the Continue button, require no highlighted items.

The bottom window shows debugger output and also allows direct input of debugger commands via the keyboard. The scroll bar or the arrow keys scroll the window.

Let's now set a breakpoint and single step through the program to familiarize ourself with the use of xxgdb.

1. Left-click the word **main** in the top section of the window. Notice that the word "main" becomes highlighted.

2. Left-click the **Break** button in the middle section of the window. This sets a breakpoint at the symbol highlighted in the top section of the window. Notice the command `break main` in the bottom section of the window, the message verifying the setting of the breakpoint, and the red hand icon in the left margin of the top section. This icon graphically represents the breakpoint's location. The breakpoint appears at the first executable line below the clicked line, which in this case is a few lines later.

3. Move the mouse cursor on top of the bottom section of the window to activate it. Type **run** and press **Enter**. Alternatively, you can left-click the Run button in the middle section of the window.

4. Wait a few moments for the program to initialize. Notice the blue arrow which then appears in the left margin of the top section, and the message "Breakpoint 1, main()" in the middle and bottom sections of the window. The blue arrow signifies that the statement is about to be executed.

5. Inspect data as follows. Left-click the word **dpy** in the top window, left-click the **Print** button, and notice the output in the bottom section: "$1 = (Display *)0x0." This indicates that the value of the variable `dpy` is currently NULL. This makes sense, since the current line has not yet been executed.

6. Left-click the **Step** button, wait a few moments until the blue arrow reappears, and notice that the blue arrow now appears next to the following instruction.

7. Again, left-click the word **dpy** in the top window, left-click the **Print** button, and notice the output in the bottom section: "$2 = (Display *)0x804d7a0." (The exact hexadecimal address will be different on your machine.) This indicates that the variable `dpy` now has a particular value as a result of the instruction just executed.

8. Left-click the **Cont** button to continue program execution normally.

9. Left-click on the application window to activate it and press **q** to end the program. Notice the message "Program exited normally" in the xxgdb window.

We have just worked through the most important functions of xxgdb: setting a breakpoint, examining data, single stepping through instructions, and resuming execution. You might also want to try single-stepping through the entire program; simply keep on left-clicking Step instead of Cont.

To summarize the most important features of xxgdb:

■ The window is divided into three sub-windows: source, buttons, and output/command. A sub-window is active only when the mouse cursor is positioned on top of it.

■ Left-clicking an item in the top window highlights it for later use. Left-clicking a button activates the function, using the highlighted item if appropriate.

■ The Break button sets a breakpoint, Print examines data, Step steps to the next instruction in the program, and Cont continues execution after a breakpoint.

■ All button commands can also be entered in the output/command window as text commands, which are passed directly to the underlying text debugger.

The Text Debugger—Not Just for Masochists

It's worth noting that in some cases, using the text debugger gdb is actually more convenient than using a graphical interface. This is particularly the case if your program crashes in such a way that the stack is corrupted and gdb no longer knows where the program execution stopped.

If the program crashes in this way, then to find the offending statement, you must find the error just before it occurs; after execution of the offending statement, it is in this case too late—the debugger will no longer be able to print out the location where execution stopped because of the corrupted stack. This is one of the classical, rather annoying problems with debugging: needing to find an error without having any idea where it is.

In this case, you typically set a breakpoint at a statement which you know is executed before the error can possibly have occurred. You then execute the program and wait until this breakpoint is reached. Then, you single step through the program until the error occurs, observing as you go along where the program crashes.

With a graphical debugger, such a continuous step-through operation might require hundreds of mouse clicks on the Step button. With the text-mode debugger, you can enter the step command just once, and simply press **Enter** to execute the last command again. So, by holding down the **Enter** key, you can very quickly step through the program execution one step at a time, with each line being printed as it is executed. Eventually your program will crash and gdb will not allow execution of any further instructions. At this point you simply scroll back through the text (using the scroll bar on your shell window) to see the last instruction that was executed before gdb stopped.

Although you can use the same trick within xxgdb (remember, the bottom window in xxgdb is a direct interface to the underlying debugger), it is much slower than the plain gdb interface, because xxgdb must find and display the source file for each line it executes. If you enter several single step instructions in a row, by first clicking Step then pressing Enter several times in the bottom xxgdb window, xxgdb will only be able to step through the program at a very slow rate because it must always find, load, and display the associated source file after every instruction. (In fact, as I write this now, xxgdb is still churning away in the background doing exactly this.) With the text-based gdb, you can step through hundreds of lines in just a few seconds, and scroll back in the window to see a chronological log of which statements were executed in which order.

To summarize, a graphical debugger such as xxgdb is useful for interactive debugging of selected, detailed parts of your program, where you must carefully inspect several variables at each step of execution and visualize the context of each operation within its source file. The text debugger gdb is useful when you have no idea where the error is occurring and want to step very quickly through large blocks of code until the program crashes.

Both xxgdb, and the underlying text debugger gdb, have entries in the online manual.

NOTE I find that using the Emacs interface to gdb is the most convenient way of debugging a program, since I can develop, compile, execute, and debug all within Emacs. It is worth noting, however, that recently a number of fancier graphical debuggers and even IDEs (integrated development environments) have appeared for Linux. Some of these include DDD, Code Crusader, and Code Medic.

Getting Online Help

We have referred a number of times to the "online manual" and the "online info documentation." Let's take a closer look at these and other documentation which Linux offers the programmer.

Linux has a staggering amount of online information available. By "online," we mean accessible in electronic form from your system. This does not mean "online" in the network sense of the word; that is, you don't need to download this information off of the Internet. It's all already available and installed on a standard Linux system.

It cannot be emphasized enough how vital this online information is to the Linux programmer. You can learn a lot just by reading other people's code and looking up the online documentation for the functions used. In this way, you learn of the existence of a function, its specification, and its idiomatic use in a certain context.

The information in this book does not, and should not, replace the online manual. The online documentation is an excellent reference for specific details of particular functions, but often lacks a broader perspective. For this reason, this book aims to provide this broader perspective, describing the general purpose and context of a function and leaving the details of exact bytes or parameters to the copious online documentation. This book and the online documentation thus complement one another and should be seen as addressing needs at two different levels.

The Online Manual "man"

The most important online reference available to the Linux programmer is the online manual. The online manual refers collectively to all documentation accessible to the Linux system via the command man. The online manual, also called the *man pages*, covers countless numbers of utilities, programs, and functions useful to the programmer.

The online manual is divided into a number of sections. These sections are:

1. Executable programs or shell commands
2. System calls (functions provided by the kernel)
3. Library calls (functions within system libraries)
4. Special files (usually found in /dev)
5. File formats and conventions e.g., /etc/passwd
6. Games
7. Macro packages and conventions e.g., man(7), groff(7)
8. System administration commands (usually only for root)
9. Kernel routines [non-standard]

In practice, you usually do not need to know what section of the manual a particular entry is in, since this is only important if identically named entries appear in different sections of the manual. In this case, you would need to specify which section of the manual you want (see below).

There are two main ways of using the online manual. The first is if you know the exact name of the function, utility, or program you want information on. The second is if you need to do a keyword search on the manual entries.

If you know the exact name of the manual entry, simply type **man [entry]**, where [entry] is the name of the function, utility, or program. For instance, type **man XCreateWindow** and press **Enter**. The text in Figure 1-18 appears. Press **Space** to scroll through the text of the manual entry, and press **q** to quit.

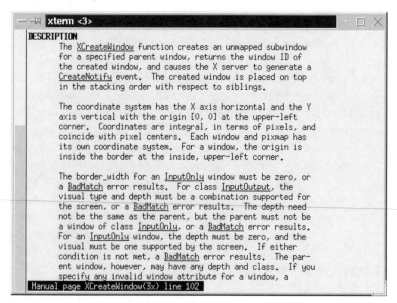

Figure 1-18: Manual entry for XCreateWindow.

The manual entry contains a detailed, complete specification of the XCreateWindow function. Standard C library functions, X functions, and Linux system functions all have similarly complete entries in the online manual.

If you do not know the exact name of the manual entry for which you are looking, you should invoke man as follows: type **man -k [entry]**. The "-k" stands for keyword search. For instance, let's say you wanted to read up on the X Visual structure. Type **man -k visual** and press **Enter**. On my system, the following list appears:

```
GetVisual (3)            - translate from string to visual
SetVisual (3)            - change visual characteristics of window
Tk_GetVisual (3)         - translate from string to visual
Tk_SetWindowVisual (3)   - change visual characteristics of window
GetVisual (3)            - translate from string to visual
SetVisual (3)            - change visual characteristics of window
Tk_GetVisual (3)         - translate from string to visual
Tk_SetWindowVisual (3)   - change visual characteristics of window
XGetVisualInfo (3x)      - obtain visual information and visual structure
XMatchVisualInfo (3x)    - obtain visual information and visual structure
```

```
XVisualIDFromVisual (3x) - obtain visual information and visual structure
XVisualInfo (3x)         - obtain visual information and visual structure
pnmindex (1)             - build a visual index of a bunch of anymaps
```

This list displays the name of the manual entry, the manual section number in parentheses, and a brief description. You can then refer to the specific manual page by using the first form of the man command described above.

In the rare event that two or more entries with identical names appear under different sections of the manual, you need to specify which entry in which section you want. In this case, simply type **man [section] [entry]**, where [section] is the desired section number of the manual.

For more information on the online manual itself, can you guess where you need to look? That's right: the online manual. Type **man man** and press **Enter** to see the manual entry on the manual itself.

 TIP   Emacs offers an integrated interface to the online manual. Press **Alt+x**, type **man**, and press **Enter**. Then, enter the manual entry and press **Enter**. The manual page is displayed in a separate window within Emacs.

The Online Info Documentation

Many programs, in addition to or instead of the manual entries, have entries in the so-called "info" or "TeXinfo" documentation. Info offers an Emacs-like hypertext interface with hierarchically arranged nodes of information. The primary advantage of info over man pages is the hierarchical organization. Extremely comprehensive documentation, such as the documentation for the gcc compiler, is better viewed online as a hierarchy of information which can be read a page at a time, rather than as a linear mass of text.

Info, like Emacs, has a built-in tutorial. Type **info**, press **Enter**, and press **h** to invoke the info documentation and start the tutorial. It takes about 10 minutes to complete.

When you first invoke info, you see the top level of the information hierarchy. This typically lists just a few pages of entries which have info documentation. Since the information is hierarchically arranged, each entry may eventually correspond to many commands; thus, the total amount of information available is more than it may seem at first.

The most important keystroke commands within info are as follows:

- h: Invoke the tutorial.
- q: Quit to the shell.
- Arrow keys: Scroll the screen.
- Enter: Go down one level in the hierarchy, to the node (menu) underneath the cursor. Selectable nodes are marked with an asterisk (*).
- n: Go to the next node at the same level in the hierarchy.
- p: Go to the previous node at the same level in the hierarchy.
- u: Go up one level in the hierarchy.
- l: Go to the last-visited node.

Again, you can learn more by going through the online tutorial.

TIP Yes, Emacs also has an integrated interface to the info documentation. Invoke it by pressing **Alt+x**, **info**, **Enter**.

Other Ways of Finding Information

There are a few other methods of finding information on a Linux system which deserve mention. This section covers some of these methods.

Searching header files is always an informative, if somewhat low-level, way of finding and hopefully understanding structure and class definitions. The header files are usually located in `/usr/include` or `/usr/local/include` and have the file extension `.h`. You can search through the header files with a command such as `grep` or `find`.

The GNU "binutils" offer routines for manipulating binary files. This is useful to find which library file contains a particular function. For instance, if you are calling a function in your code and get a linker error that the function could not be found, you have most likely not specified the required library name on the linker command line in the Makefile. The question is, which library contains the function? You can use the `nm` command, part of the binutils, on a library file (ending with extension `.a` or `.so`) to determine its contents. This can help you find the exact library file containing a function you need. Library files are usually located in `/usr/lib`, `/usr/local/lib`, `/lib`, and `/usr/X11/lib`. You can also use the `find` command to search for other `.a` or `.so` library files on your system.

The HOWTO files are a collection of files describing answers to common "how-to" questions. Most HOWTO files tend to deal more directly with hardware or configuration issues rather than programming issues, but the information can be useful for programming in certain areas. The HOWTO files are usually located in `/usr/doc/howto`.

Summary

Linux and 3D graphics is a winning combination because of the power, price, and openness of Linux, and because of the 3D graphics revolution. In this chapter, we looked at available Linux libraries and tools for doing 3D graphics. We then defined the X Window System and discussed 3D hardware acceleration with X. We familiarized ourselves with the practical side of Linux programming by writing a simple program, compiling it, and debugging it. Finally, we looked at some of the online documentation available to the Linux programmer.

With this experience, we are now ready to dive into writing Linux applications in earnest. The next chapter explores how to access the 2D screen under Linux. The 3D graphics we create in later chapters must eventually appear on the screen, so it is natural that we first discuss screen access.

Chapter 2

Accessing the Screen

Overview

This chapter explains screen access under Linux. Most consumer PCs have one graphics card and one flat, 2D screen. Therefore, 3D graphics programs, such as the ones we write in this book, must ultimately display their results on this single 2D screen. In this chapter, we look at the terminology, techniques, and program code for initializing and creating some elementary output on the 2D screen. The next chapter covers rasterization algorithms which build on the ideas in this chapter to draw specific images on the screen.

This chapter begins by looking at 2D graphics programming under Linux by using Xlib directly. We then abstract the Xlib concepts to illustrate the development of reusable graphics classes, called l3d. We extend and build upon these l3d classes throughout the rest of this book.

 TIP We also continue to build upon the l3d library in the companion book, *Advanced Linux 3D Graphics Programming*. The l3d library is available on the CD-ROM and for download from the Internet; see the Appendix for more information.

This chapter covers the following concepts:

- Object-oriented, event-driven programming with the X Window System
- Graphics display and event handling under X
- Development and use of reusable graphics classes, called l3d
- Coordinate systems in 2D

X Programming

We begin this chapter by writing some sample programs which display windows and respond to user input under X. The 2D code and the object-oriented techniques developed in the following sections form the theoretical and practical basis for the graphics code in the rest of the book.

The Role of X

Before going into the details of X programming, let us first briefly consider X's role in graphical applications under Linux.

At a basic level, one goal of computer graphics is to display images on a *screen*. We use the term "screen" to denote a number of related but slightly different concepts. Generally, the term "screen" describes either the entire physical display area or the logical display area into which the operating system allows a program to write graphics data. The context determines the usage. If we say that a program writes to the "screen," we usually mean that it actually writes to a small portion of the physical screen in a windowing system, and that the rest of the physical screen is occupied by other applications. On the other hand, if we say "part of the screen," we usually mean "part of the entire display area." Also, the X Window System uses the term "screen" to denote a monitor number when dealing with multiple-monitor displays.

Physically, the display monitor of your computer translates the electrical signals from the video card into visible patterns of light. In the early days of computer graphics, applications typically had exclusive access to the video memory (and often to the entire computer). A graphics application would write directly to video memory, which the hardware would directly interpret and display on the monitor. As a result, graphics applications typically took over the entire physical display area, a practice also called *full-screen mode* (Figure 2-1).

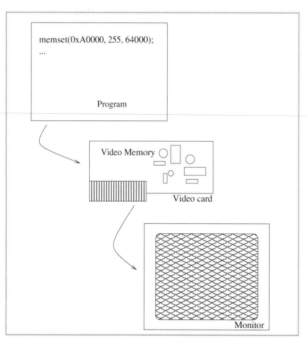

Figure 2-1: Full-screen, direct access to video hardware.

The emergence of multi-tasking operating systems changed the nature of this practice. Programs no longer had exclusive access to all computer resources, including the display. The operating system regulated access to all shared resources and prevented programs from directly accessing the resource (Figure 2-2). In the case of the screen, a *windowing system* was given the responsibility of controlling access to the video memory. The windowing system allowed each application to use a portion of the physical video memory, called a *window,* for its display purposes. This system allowed multiple graphical applications to run simultaneously, all sharing one physical screen.

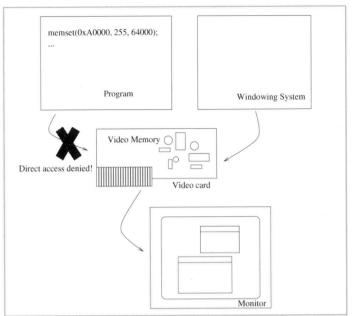

Figure 2-2: Windowing system controls access to video hardware

The windowing system forms a middle layer between the application and the video hardware. Graphics applications can, in general, no longer directly access the video hardware but instead direct requests to the windowing system to display images within the application's window (Figure 2-3).

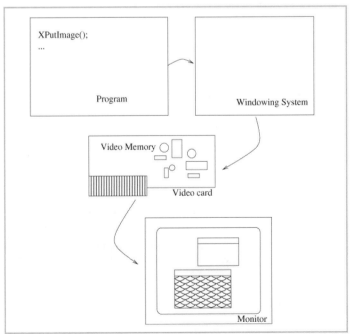

Figure 2-3: Access to screen through window manager

The introduction of a windowing system between the application and the video hardware imposes a slight performance penalty. In general, we have to live with this performance hit, since well-behaved graphics programs must be able to function within windows. It cannot be expected that every graphics application should always be allowed to have complete access to the entire display, refusing to coexist with other running graphical applications. The performance problem, however, is not as limiting as it might at first seem. The efforts to incorporate 3D hardware acceleration into the X Window System, described in the last chapter, have yielded high-performance X architectures. With faster 3D hardware and an efficient X interface, the performance penalty imposed by going through X becomes negligible.

A well-designed program will, however, isolate application code from the underlying screen access code. An application should only access a screen as a logical output device through an abstract C++ class interface. This allows the application to display its output on a variety of physical screens—for instance, on an unaccelerated window under X, full-screen using hardware acceleration, or on a window using another operating system such as Microsoft Windows.

NOTE An *abstract class* is one which has at least one pure virtual function and cannot be instantiated. A *concrete class* is one which is not abstract, though it may descend from an abstract class. Abstract classes are the key to good object-oriented design, since they represent characteristic, fundamental abstractions of the problem domain independent of "irrelevant" details. The "irrelevant" details are implemented within derived concrete classes by overriding the pure virtual functions, but users of the class who go through the abstract interface will remain compatible for all variants, past and future, of the abstract class. The requirement for this to work is that the abstract class truly be a general, characteristic classification of all possible past and future variants of the data type represented by the class, thereby allowing the future flexibility and compatibility through subclassing. Finding the appropriate abstract classes is equivalent to identifying or defining the fundamental, universal abstractions in the problem domain, and is one of the most difficult parts of object-oriented design.

Thus, from the application's point of view, its display is directed to a logical output device which we will call the "screen." In reality, the screen will usually be a window which has been allocated by a windowing system and which only uses up part of the physical display, but this fact is hidden from the application program so that the program may be configured (even at run time) to use different physical output devices.

Under the older Linux operating system, "direct access" to video memory was often done through a graphics library called SVGALIB. This library, as we saw in Chapter 1, is more or less outdated. The X Window System now regulates access to the video hardware.

Therefore, with the exception of full-screen hardware-accelerated graphics, when we use the term "screen" we are actually referring to a display window created under the X Window System. Let us now see how we create windows under X, then see how to display images in the window.

Structure of an X Program

The X Window System, like other windowing systems, is an *event-driven system* which notifies individual windows of events of interest, thereby allowing the window to respond accordingly. For instance, pressing a key when a window is active would automatically (through the windowing system) send a keypress event to the window. The application code for this window would then notice the event and call a function to respond to the event; such an event-handling function is called a *callback function*. The calling of the appropriate function in response to an event is called *event dispatching*.

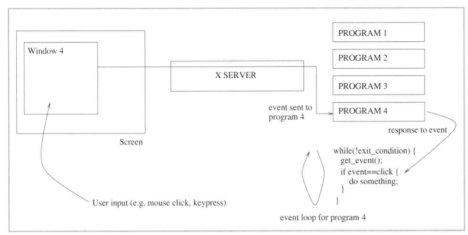

Figure 2-4: Structure of an X program.

Programming the X Window System is a very broad area of expertise; volumes have been written on the subject. For the purposes of this book, we won't delve too deeply into the intricacies of X, but will instead simply focus on X as a mechanism for displaying windowed 2D images. (This alone is complicated enough!) 3D graphics, as will be explained in Chapter 4, also ultimately reduces to 2D images.

Let us begin by examining the typical structure of an X program; in the next section, we then deal specifically with displaying graphics. In pseudocode, a typical X application would look as follows:

```
create_window();
ask_to_be_notified_of_interesting_events();
while(1) {
 if event_pending_for_window() {
    dispatch_event(); // call callback function
 }
}
```

The program is nothing more than a classical event-polling loop. We have an infinite loop which waits for an event to occur, then reacts to that event. In most cases, some particular event, such as typing q or clicking on a Quit button, will eventually cause the program to exit the event-polling loop and terminate execution.

With this understanding, we can now make a detailed analysis of the sample program `hello` from the previous chapter, which created a simple window under X. The program's code is shown here again, in Listing 2-1.

Listing 2-1: `hello.cc`

```cpp
#include <stdio.h>
#include <X11/Intrinsic.h>
#include <X11/Xlib.h>
//- empty line
#define SCREEN_XSIZE 320
#define SCREEN_YSIZE 200

main() {
  Display *dpy;
  //- establish connection to X server

  dpy = XopenDisplay(NULL);

  //- create and map (display) an X window for output

  Visual *vis;
  Window w;
  vis = DefaultVisual(dpy,0);
  w = XCreateWindow(dpy,                       //- display
                    DefaultRootWindow(dpy),    //- parent
                    100, 100,                  //- x, y position
                    SCREEN_XSIZE, SCREEN_YSIZE, //- width, height
                    0,                         //- border width
                    CopyFromParent,            //- depth (we use max. possible)
                    CopyFromParent,            //- visual class (TrueColor etc)
                    vis,                       //- visual
                    0, NULL);                  //- valuemask, window attributes
  XStoreName(dpy, w, "hello");

  XMapWindow(dpy, w);

  XSelectInput(dpy, w, KeyPressMask);

  XEvent event;
  char ch;
  KeySym keysym;
  XComposeStatus xcompstat;

  while(1) {
    if(XCheckWindowEvent(dpy,w,KeyPressMask,&event)) {
      XLookupString(&event.xkey, &ch, 1, &keysym, &xcompstat);
      switch(ch) {
        case 'q': {
            exit(0);
          }
      }
    }
  }
}
```

Xlib, the X Toolkit, and the Xt Intrinsics

The program `hello.cc` begins by including the header files we need to do X programming:

```
#include <stdio.h>
#include <X11/Intrinsic.h>
#include <X11/Xlib.h>
```

Every C programmer is familiar with `stdio.h`, the header file for the standard input/output library, but the X header files may be new to you. The exact location for these files is `/usr/include/X11/Intrinsic.h` and `/usr/include/X11/Xlib.h`. You might want to glance at the contents of these files to get an idea of what you are including.

 TIP The location for #include files appearing within angle brackets (< >) is the pathname within the brackets prefaced by `/usr/include` or `/usr/local/include`. These directories are the standard include file directories for a Linux system.

The X files in our case don't contain secret government information, but rather function and structure definitions for the Xlib library and for the X Toolkit. Xlib is a low-level C library for controlling output to and input from windows on an X server. The X Toolkit is a higher-level collection of functions for programming X, and is divided into two parts: the Xt Intrinsics and a widget set. The functions in the Xt Intrinsics allow applications to create user interfaces by combining user interface components, called widgets. Figure 2-5 illustrates graphically the relationship between Xlib, the Xt Intrinsics, and a widget set.

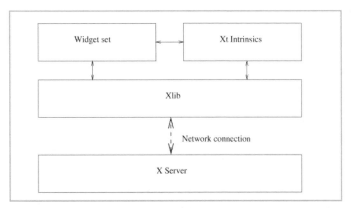

Figure 2-5: Libraries used by a typical X application.

It should now be clear exactly which header files we have included: `Xlib.h` contains the Xlib declarations; `Intrinsic.h` contains the Xt Intrinsics declarations. We don't use any widget set in this program (since it doesn't have any user interface), so we correspondingly do not include any widget header file.

 NOTE In contrast to other windowing systems, it is theoretically possible to write an X application without using any X library at all. This is because the X server protocol is defined at the byte level of network packets. An X client could therefore directly open a TCP/IP network connection to the X server, and manually send, receive, and decode packets of bytes in order to control the display on the X server. This would, however, be absurdly complicated, but it is useful to know that, technically speaking, the X libraries are a convenience, not a necessity.

Next, we define some constants for the screen size:

```
#define SCREEN_XSIZE 320
#define SCREEN_YSIZE 200
```

Connecting to the X Server

Since X is a client-server system, and since our programs are all X clients, we must connect to the X server in order to create a window and display graphics on the screen. `hello.cc` declares the variable `dpy`, which represents a pointer to an X `Display` structure. The display represents the connection between our application program (the X client) and the X server (connected to the monitor).

```
Display *dpy;
```

The connection between client and server might be a TCP/IP network connection in the case of a true client-server setup, where the X server and the X client are located on two physically separate machines. With a local setup, where the X server and the X client are located on the same machine, the connection will be done through some local interprocess communication protocol.

Let's take a glance at the definition of the `Display` structure. This is located in `/usr/include/X11/Xlib.h`:

```
/*
 * Display datatype maintaining display specific data.
 * The contents of this structure are implementation dependent.
 * A Display should be treated as opaque by application code.
 */
#ifndef XLIB_ILLEGAL_ACCESS
typedef struct _XDisplay Display;
#endif
```

As seen in the structure definition, we don't need to—and should not—know more about the internals of the `Display` structure, since its contents are implementation specific and not guaranteed to remain constant among implementations or versions of XFree86. This is a typical example of the object-oriented technique of *information hiding*, where users of a particular class or structure are protected from the inevitable changes which sooner or later will occur. By treating the `Display` structure as opaque, we are guaranteed that our program will continue to compile and function even in the face of changes to the internal representation of the `Display` structure.

NOTE This particular example of information hiding is somewhat extreme, since the `Display` structure is completely opaque; as users of this structure, we do not have access to any part of it. More generally, a class in an object-oriented design will expose a public interface to the outside world, which must be a relatively stable foundation upon which users of the class (called *client classes*) can build. The internal workings of the *supplier class* (the class being used by the client class) are much more volatile and therefore "hidden" in the private sections of the supplier class. These sections may be changed without affecting client classes, since the compiler prohibits client classes from accessing the private members of a supplier class, aborting compilation with an error message. This guarantees the public/private separation at the lowest level. One of the most difficult decisions for object-oriented designs is deciding which parts of the class declaration should be made public, and which private. A complete answer to this question exists, but is rather theoretical in nature, being based upon class theory and the theory of abstract data types (ADTs) [MEYE97]. Briefly summarized, the idea is that it must be impossible to write a client class whose correctness depends in any way on the

private declarations of the supplier class. In other words, correctness of the clients of a particular supplier class must be formally provable using only the public declarations of the
supplier class.

With the dpy variable declared, we can establish a connection to the X server by using the
XOpenDisplay function:

```
dpy = XOpenDisplay(NULL);
```

A complete description of this function appears in the online manual. Hopefully you have already
taken the time to read through some of the entries in the man pages. If not, here is the complete
manual entry for XOpenDisplay:

```
XOpenDisplay(3X11)        XLIB FUNCTIONS        XOpenDisplay(3X11)


    NAME
            XOpenDisplay, XCloseDisplay - connect or disconnect to X
            server

    SYNTAX
            Display *XOpenDisplay(display_name)
                  char *display_name;

            XCloseDisplay(display)
                  Display *display;

    ARGUMENTS
            display    Specifies the connection to the X server.

            display_name
                       Specifies the hardware display name, which
                       determines the display and communications domain
                       to be used.  On a POSIX-conformant system, if
                       the display_name is NULL, it defaults to the
                       value of the DISPLAY environment variable.

    DESCRIPTION
            The XOpenDisplay function returns a Display structure that
            serves as the connection to the X server and that contains
            all the information about that X server.  XOpenDisplay
            connects your application to the X server through TCP or
            DECnet communications protocols, or through some local
            inter-process communication protocol.  If the hostname is
            a host machine name and a single colon (:) separates the
            hostname and display number, XOpenDisplay connects using
            TCP streams.  If the hostname is not specified, Xlib uses
            whatever it believes is the fastest transport.  If the
            hostname is a host machine name and a double colon (::)
            separates the hostname and display number, XOpenDisplay
            connects using DECnet.  A single X server can support any
            or all of these transport mechanisms simultaneously.  A
            particular Xlib implementation can support many more of
            these transport mechanisms.

            If successful, XOpenDisplay returns a pointer to a Display
            structure, which is defined in <X11/Xlib.h>.  If XopenDis-
            play does not succeed, it returns NULL.  After a success-
            ful call to XOpenDisplay, all of the screens in the dis-
            play can be used by the client.  The screen number speci-
```

fied in the display_name argument is returned by the
DefaultScreen macro (or the XDefaultScreen function). You
can access elements of the Display and Screen structures
only by using the information macros or functions. For
information about using macros and functions to obtain
information from the Display structure, see section 2.2.1.

The XCloseDisplay function closes the connection to the X
server for the display specified in the Display structure
and destroys all windows, resource IDs (Window, Font,
Pixmap, Colormap, Cursor, and GContext), or other
resources that the client has created on this display,
unless the close-down mode of the resource has been
changed (see XSetCloseDownMode). Therefore, these windows, resource IDs, and other resources should never be
referenced again or an error will be generated. Before
exiting, you should call XCloseDisplay explicitly so that
any pending errors are reported as XCloseDisplay performs
a final XSync operation.

XCloseDisplay can generate a BadGC error.

SEE ALSO
        AllPlanes(3X11), XFlush(3X11), XSetCloseDownMode(3X11)
        Xlib - C Language X Interface

NOTE From now on, you are encouraged to look up the manual entries for the functions described in the text.

Notice that we passed NULL as the parameter to XOpenDisplay. As documented in the man page, this uses the default display.

Having now established the connection to the X server, we can create a window on the X server's display.

Creating and Mapping the Window

The next thing `hello.cc` does is create a window. Two variables are declared for this purpose: one to store so-called "visual" information, and one for the window itself:

```
Visual *vis;
Window w;
```

The definition for the Visual structure is in `/usr/include/X11/Xlib.h`:

```
/*
 * Visual structure; contains information about colormapping possible.
 */
typedef struct {
        XExtData *ext_data;     /* hook for extension to hang data */
        VisualID visualid;      /* visual id of this visual */
#if defined(__cplusplus) || defined(c_plusplus)
        int c_class;            /* C++ class of screen (monochrome, etc.) */
#else
        int class;              /* class of screen (monochrome, etc.) */
#endif
        unsigned long red_mask, green_mask, blue_mask;  /* mask values */
        int bits_per_rgb;       /* log base 2 of distinct color values */
        int map_entries;        /* color map entries */
} Visual;
```

The `Visual` structure definition is quite simple and well commented. It deals with the color structure of the X server. We return to this topic shortly, in the section titled "X Server Depth and Visual Class." For now, we only need to know the visual so that we may create the window, since the window creation function requires a visual as a parameter.

The other variable we have declared is from type `Window`. Its declaration, in `/usr/include/X11/X.h`, is as follows:

```
typedef unsigned long XID;
typedef XID Window;
```

A Window is therefore nothing more than an integer identifier.

The first step is to ask the X server for the default visual of the screen, by using the `DefaultVisual` macro:

```
vis = DefaultVisual(dpy,0);
```

With the display from the previous step and the visual now known to us, we have enough information to create the window. The `XCreateWindow` function creates a window on a particular display. `hello.cc` calls this function as follows:

```
w = XCreateWindow(dpy,                         //- display
                  DefaultRootWindow(dpy),      //- parent
                  100, 100,                    //- x, y position
                  SCREEN_XSIZE, SCREEN_YSIZE,  //- width, height
                  0,                           //- border width
                  CopyFromParent,              //- color depth (we use max. possible)
                  CopyFromParent,              //- visual class (TrueColor etc)
                  vis,                         //- visual
                  0, NULL);                    //- valuemask, window attributes
      XStoreName(dpy, w, "hello");
```

The `XCreateWindow` function takes a number of parameters, only a few of which need further explanation. In particular, the parameters labeled `parent`, `color depth`, `visual class`, `valuemask`, and `window attributes` deserve mention.

The `parent` parameter specifies the *parent window* for the window about to be created. As mentioned in Chapter 1, windows under X are hierarchically arranged. The parent window is the immediate ancestor of the child window in the hierarchy. In our case, we have specified that the parent window is to be the *root window*, which is the window at the very top of the hierarchy that encompasses the entire physical screen.

The `color depth` parameter and the `visual class` parameter work closely together to specify the number and type of colors available to the window. We cover this in more detail in the section titled "X Server Depth and Visual Class." In our case, we specify these parameters as `CopyFromParent` which simply copies the values from the parent window. The `valuemask` and `window attributes` parameters are used together to toggle specific creation options of the window. The `valuemask` is interpreted bit-wise and is specified as a logical OR of the desired options. The valid options are listed in the man page and cover such options as the cursor for the window or which events should be passed to the window. The `window attributes` parameter points to a structure of type `XSetWindowAttributes`, which specifies the data needed by the options activated through the `valuemask`. For now, we do not specify any particular window attributes.

The next line calls XStoreName, which simply associates a text string with the window. This text string typically appears in the title bar of the window to assist the user in identifying and finding windows. (We say "typically appears" because this behavior is dependent upon the window manager being used.)

After calling XCreateWindow, the window has been allocated in memory but is not yet visible. To display the window, we must map it by calling XMapWindow:

```
XMapWindow(dpy, w);
```

Receiving X Events

hello.cc calls the XSelectInput function to request notification for certain types of input events. Specifically, we ask X to inform us of keypress events, which are generated whenever a key is pressed within our window:

```
XSelectInput(dpy, w, KeyPressMask);
```

The constant KeyPressMask, along with other masks for watching other events, are defined in /usr/include/X11/X.h. The list of all event masks is as follows:

```
/******************************************************************
 * EVENT DEFINITIONS
 ******************************************************************/

/* Input Event Masks. Used as event-mask window attribute and as arguments
   to Grab requests.  Not to be confused with event names.  */

#define NoEventMask                     0L
#define KeyPressMask                    (1L<<0)
#define KeyReleaseMask                  (1L<<1)
#define ButtonPressMask                 (1L<<2)
#define ButtonReleaseMask               (1L<<3)
#define EnterWindowMask                 (1L<<4)
#define LeaveWindowMask                 (1L<<5)
#define PointerMotionMask               (1L<<6)
#define PointerMotionHintMask           (1L<<7)
#define Button1MotionMask               (1L<<8)
#define Button2MotionMask               (1L<<9)
#define Button3MotionMask               (1L<<10)
#define Button4MotionMask               (1L<<11)
#define Button5MotionMask               (1L<<12)
#define ButtonMotionMask                (1L<<13)
#define KeymapStateMask                 (1L<<14)
#define ExposureMask                    (1L<<15)
#define VisibilityChangeMask            (1L<<16)
#define StructureNotifyMask             (1L<<17)
#define ResizeRedirectMask              (1L<<18)
#define SubstructureNotifyMask          (1L<<19)
#define SubstructureRedirectMask        (1L<<20)
#define FocusChangeMask                 (1L<<21)
#define PropertyChangeMask              (1L<<22)
#define ColormapChangeMask              (1L<<23)
#define OwnerGrabButtonMask             (1L<<24)
```

XSelectInput is not the only way to request event notification. We could have achieved the same effect at window creation time by specifying these parameters in the valuemask and window attributes parameters passed to XCreateWindow. We would have declared and initialized a variable to hold the window parameters:

```
XSetWindowAttributes a;
a.event_mask = KeyPressMask;
```

We then would have passed the values `CWEventMask, &a` as the last two parameters to `XCreateWindow`.

Notice that if you do not specify `KeyPressMask` in either the window attributes or through `XSelectInput`, the program will not respond to keyboard events at all. Indeed, any event type for which you do not request notification will not be sent to your window.

Responding to X Events

The last part of `hello.cc` is an event loop which checks for keypress events and responds to them. For this, we use the `XCheckWindowEvent` function, which searches for any pending events corresponding to the given window and event mask. If `XCheckWindowEvent` finds an event, it returns it in an `XEvent` structure, which you specify as the last parameter of the function call. Other routines which search for relevant events are `XNextEvent`, `XPeekEvent`, `XWindowEvent`, `XCheckWindowEvent`, `XMaskEvent`, `XCheckMaskEvent`, `XCheck-TypedEvent`, and `XCheckTypedWindowEvent`. These routines differ in the way that they look for events, whether or not they leave the event on the queue, and whether or not they *block*, or wait until a matching event can be found. The following list summarizes the available event checking routines:

- `XNextEvent`: Removes and returns the first event from the queue. Blocks if no events could be found.
- `XPeekEvent`: Returns but does not remove the first event from the event queue. Blocks if no events could be found.
- `XWindowEvent`: Searches for, removes, and returns an event matching a particular window and event mask. Blocks if no matching events could be found.
- `XCheckWindowEvent`: Searches for, removes, and returns the first event matching a particular window and event mask. Does not block. Returns TRUE if an event could be found, FALSE otherwise.
- `XMaskEvent`: Searches for, removes, and returns an event matching a particular event mask. Blocks if no matching events could be found.
- `XCheckMaskEvent`: Searches for, removes, and returns the first event matching a particular event mask. Does not block. Returns TRUE if an event could be found, FALSE otherwise.
- `XCheckTypedEvent`: Searches for, removes, and returns the first event matching a particular type. Does not block. Returns TRUE if an event could be found, FALSE otherwise.
- `XCheckTypedWindowEvent`: Searches for, removes, and returns the first event matching a particular window and event type. Does not block. Returns TRUE if an event could be found, FALSE otherwise.

By using one of the event functions above, we receive an `XEvent` structure as a result (assuming some matching event could be found). The `XEvent` contains detailed information about the particular event which occurred; the application program then extracts this information out of the event and responds accordingly. The `XEvent` structure, defined in `Xlib.h`, is actually a union of several structures, with a type field to distinguish the actual type of the event (i.e., which element of the union we should access).

```
/*
 * this union is defined so Xlib can always use the same sized
 * event structure internally, to avoid memory fragmentation.
 */
typedef union _XEvent {
        int type;                    /* must not be changed; first element */
        XAnyEvent xany;
        XKeyEvent xkey;
        XButtonEvent xbutton;
        XMotionEvent xmotion;
        XCrossingEvent xcrossing;
        XFocusChangeEvent xfocus;
        XExposeEvent xexpose;
        XGraphicsExposeEvent xgraphicsexpose;
        XNoExposeEvent xnoexpose;
        XVisibilityEvent xvisibility;
        XCreateWindowEvent xcreatewindow;
        XDestroyWindowEvent xdestroywindow;
        XUnmapEvent xunmap;
        XMapEvent xmap;
        XMapRequestEvent xmaprequest;
        XReparentEvent xreparent;
        XConfigureEvent xconfigure;
        XGravityEvent xgravity;
        XResizeRequestEvent xresizerequest;
        XConfigureRequestEvent xconfigurerequest;
        XCirculateEvent xcirculate;
        XCirculateRequestEvent xcirculaterequest;
        XPropertyEvent xproperty;
        XSelectionClearEvent xselectionclear;
        XSelectionRequestEvent xselectionrequest;
        XSelectionEvent xselection;
        XColormapEvent xcolormap;
        XClientMessageEvent xclient;
        XMappingEvent xmapping;
        XErrorEvent xerror;
        XKeymapEvent xkeymap;
        long pad[24];
} Xevent;
```

The valid values for the type field are defined in X.h:

```
/* Event names.  Used in "type" field in XEvent structures.  Not to be
confused with event masks above.  They start from 2 because 0 and 1
are reserved in the protocol for errors and replies. */

#define KeyPress         2
#define KeyRelease       3
#define ButtonPress      4
#define ButtonRelease    5
#define MotionNotify     6
#define EnterNotify      7
#define LeaveNotify      8
#define FocusIn          9
#define FocusOut        10
#define KeymapNotify    11
#define Expose          12
#define GraphicsExpose  13
```

```
#define NoExpose            14
#define VisibilityNotify    15
#define CreateNotify        16
#define DestroyNotify       17
#define UnmapNotify         18
#define MapNotify           19
#define MapRequest          20
#define ReparentNotify      21
#define ConfigureNotify     22
#define ConfigureRequest    23
#define GravityNotify       24
#define ResizeRequest       25
#define CirculateNotify     26
#define CirculateRequest    27
#define PropertyNotify      28
#define SelectionClear      29
#define SelectionRequest    30
#define SelectionNotify     31
#define ColormapNotify      32
#define ClientMessage       33
#define MappingNotify       34
#define LASTEvent           35      /* must be bigger than any event # */
```

 NOTE The use of a type field is generally frowned upon in object-oriented designs, since the mechanism of inheritance is used to specify subtypes in a much safer and more flexible way. Nothing prevents us, for instance, from accidentally changing the type field or accessing the wrong member of the union. Manipulation of types through type fields cannot be checked for validity by the compiler, in contrast to a class-based approach. The idea of "class as type" is therefore central to object orientation in strongly typed languages. The reason X uses a type field is quite simple: X is written in the C language, which unlike C++ has no true support for object-oriented mechanisms such as inheritance.

In the case of keyboard events, the returned event is of type KeyPress, corresponding to the member xkey in the XEvent structure. xkey is of type XKeyEvent, which is defined as follows:

```
typedef struct {
        int type;               /* of event */
        unsigned long serial;   /* # of last request processed by server */
        Bool send_event;        /* true if this came from a SendEvent request */
        Display *display;       /* Display the event was read from */
        Window window;          /* "event" window it is reported relative to */
        Window root;            /* root window that the event occured on */
        Window subwindow;       /* child window */
        Time time;              /* milliseconds */
        int x, y;               /* pointer x, y coordinates in event window */
        int x_root, y_root;     /* coordinates relative to root */
        unsigned int state;     /* key or xbutton mask */
        unsigned int keycode;   /* detail */
        Bool same_screen;       /* same screen flag */
} XKeyEvent;
typedef XKeyEvent XKeyPressedEvent;
typedef XKeyEvent XKeyReleasedEvent;
```

The returned event contains detailed information about which key was pressed, and where, when, and how it was pressed. We could decode all of this information manually, but we don't have to. X provides a convenient function to decode keypress events: XLookupString. We use this function to extract keypress information out of the event structure, and only respond to the q key, which ends the program. The event loop in `hello.cc` looks as follows:

```
XEvent event;
char ch;
KeySym keysym;
XComposeStatus xcompstat;

while(1) {
  if(XCheckWindowEvent(dpy,w,KeyPressMask,&event)) {
    XLookupString(&event.xkey, &ch, 1, &keysym, &xcompstat);
    switch(ch) {
      case 'q': {
        exit(0);
      }
    }
  }
}
```

TIP Remember that all of these X functions have entries in the online manual.

We've now covered all of the important topics relevant to a basic X program. The sample program `hello` is not much more complicated than the pseudocode presented at the beginning of the discussion. There are a few extra variables and parameters, but the overall structure is quite simple.

Critique of the Sample Program

You may have noticed that the window created by the program `hello` is not truly empty, but instead seems to contain the contents of the window lying "underneath" it. On my computer, the image looks like Figure 2-6. Exactly what you see depends on your particular video card, since the X server handles video memory differently for different cards.

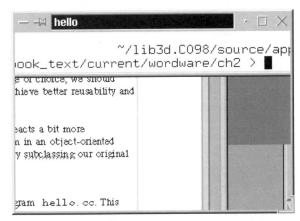

Figure 2-6: The window created by the sample program is not empty, but instead appears to contain "leftover" graphics from another window.

The reason for the strange window contents is simple: we did not explicitly specify that the window should be drawn. This means that the background is not even empty, but is instead completely undefined. In particular, each window under X is always responsible for drawing itself when requested to do so. This request comes, as you might have guessed, in the form of an event—specifically, a so-called expose event. This request was indeed sent to our sample program, but our program did not watch for this event and therefore never even knew about the request.

Another thing you have probably noticed about `hello.cc` is that the code is about as non-object-oriented as can be. Since this book uses C++ as the language of choice, we should make use of the object-oriented features of the C++ language to achieve better reusability and extendibility of our program modules.

Let us now rewrite the program so that it is better structured and reacts a bit more intelligently to events. We will first restructure the original program in an object-oriented (class-based) fashion, then implement an improved event handler by subclassing our original application class.

An Object-Oriented Rewrite

Listings 2-2 through 2-11 are an object-oriented rewrite of the program `hello.cc`. This code is located in directory `$L3D/source/app/hello_oo`.

Listing 2-2: `ch2_app.h`

```
#ifndef __CH2_APP_H
#define __CH2_APP_H

#include <stdio.h>

class ch2_app {
  protected:
    virtual void create_window(void) = 0;
    virtual void ask_to_be_notified_of_interesting_events(void) = 0;
    virtual void event_loop(void) = 0;

  public:
    virtual ~ch2_app(void) {};
    virtual void execute(void);
};
#endif
```

Listing 2-3: `ch2_app.cc`

```
#include "ch2_app.h"

void ch2_app::execute(void) {
  create_window();
  ask_to_be_notified_of_interesting_events();
  event_loop();
}
```

Listing 2-4: `ch2_app_x.h`

```
#ifndef __CH2_APP_X_H
#define __CH2_APP_X_H
#include "ch2_app.h"
#include <X11/Intrinsic.h>
#include <X11/Xlib.h>

class ch2_app_x : public ch2_app {
  protected:
    const static int screen_xsize = 320;
    const static int screen_ysize = 200;
    Visual *vis;
```

```
        Display *dpy;
        Window w;

        void create_window(void);
        void ask_to_be_notified_of_interesting_events(void);
        void event_loop(void);

     public:
     virtual ~ch2_app_x(void) {};
   };
   #endif
```

Listing 2-5: `ch2_app_x.cc`

```
#include "ch2_app_x.h"
#include <stdio.h>

void ch2_app_x::create_window(void) {

  dpy = XopenDisplay(NULL);

  vis = DefaultVisual(dpy,0);
  w = XcreateWindow(dpy,
                    DefaultRootWindow(dpy),
                    100, 100,
                    screen_xsize, screen_ysize,
                    0,
                    CopyFromParent,
                    CopyFromParent,
                    vis,
                    0, NULL);

  XMapWindow(dpy, w);
}

void ch2_app_x::ask_to_be_notified_of_interesting_events(void) {
  XSelectInput(dpy, w, KeyPressMask);
}

void ch2_app_x::event_loop(void) {
  XEvent event;
  char ch;
  KeySym keysym;
  XComposeStatus xcompstat;

  while(1) {
    if(XCheckWindowEvent(dpy,w,KeyPressMask,&event)) {
      XLookupString(&event.xkey, &ch, 1, &keysym, &xcompstat);
      switch(ch) {
        case 'q': {
            exit(0);
          }
      }
    }
  }
}
```

Listing 2-6: `ch2_appfactory.h`

```
#ifndef __CH2_APPFACTORY_H
#define __CH2_APPFACTORY_H

#include "ch2_app.h"

class ch2_appfactory {
  public:
    virtual ch2_app *create(void) = 0;
};

#endif
```

Listing 2-7: `ch2_appfactory_x.h`

```
#ifndef __CH2_APPFACTORY_X_H
#define __CH2_APPFACTORY_X_H

#include "ch2_appfactory.h"

class ch2_appfactory_x : public ch2_appfactory {
    ch2_app *create(void);
};
#endif
```

Listing 2-8: `ch2_appfactory_x.cc`

```
#include "ch2_appfactory_x.h"
#include "ch2_app_x.h"

ch2_app *ch2_appfactory_x::create(void) {
  return new ch2_app_x;
}
```

Listing 2-9: `ch2_factorymanager.h`

```
#ifndef __CH2_FACTORYMANAGER_H
#define __CH2_FACTORYMANAGER_H
#include "ch2_appfactory.h"

class ch2_factorymanager {
  public:
    static ch2_appfactory *appfactory;
    void choose_factories(void);
};

#endif
```

Listing 2-10: `ch2_factorymanager.cc`

```
#include "ch2_factorymanager.h"

#include "ch2_appfactory_x.h"

ch2_appfactory *ch2_factorymanager::appfactory = 0;

void ch2_factorymanager::choose_factories(void) {
  int i;

  printf("Which Appfactory should create your application?");
  printf("1. Appfactory creating the simple X app");

  scanf("%d", &i);
```

```
      switch(i) {
        case 1: {
            appfactory = new ch2_appfactory_x;
          };
          break;
      }
    }
```

Listing 2-11: `ch2_hello.cc`

```
    #include "ch2_factorymanager.h"

    main() {
      ch2_app *application;
      ch2_factorymanager fm;

      fm.choose_factories();
      application = fm.appfactory->create();
      application->execute();
    }
```

Figure 2-7 illustrates the class hierarchy for these files. The notation used in the class diagram is similar to UML, the Unified Modeling Language. The following list explains the diagrammatical conventions.

■ A class is represented by a rectangle with three sections. From top to bottom, these sections are: class names, class attributes (variables), and class methods (functions).

■ A line without an arrowhead between two classes indicates a component relationship. A component relationship relates two classes: the containing class, marked with a pound sign (#), and the contained class, not marked with a pound sign. The numbers on each side of the component relationship indicate the cardinality of the relationship. The label on the component relationship indicates the name of the member variable within the containing class. An asterisk before the component relationship name indicates that a pointer to the component object, rather than the component object itself, is stored.

■ The solid arrows indicate inheritance relationships and are labeled with the text "is_a."

For instance, the class `ch2_factorymanager` contains a variable named `appfactory` (the label on the component relationship). This variable is a pointer (indicated by the asterisk in the label) to an object of type `ch2_appfactory` (the contained class, indicated by the lack of a pound sign on that side of the relationship). The cardinality of the relationship is 1:1—that is, one object of type `ch2_factorymanager` has a pointer to exactly one object of type `ch2_appfactory`. Furthermore, the class `ch2_appfactory_x` inherits from class `ch2_appfactory`, indicated by the "is_a" arrow.

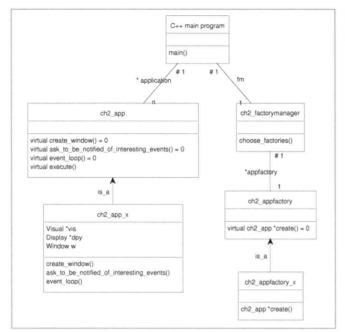

Figure 2-7: Class diagram for sample program `ch2_hello.`

To compile the code, follow the same instructions as before. Change to the source directory by typing **cd $L3D/source/app/hello_oo** and pressing **Enter**. Type **make** and press **Enter**. After successful compilation, type **ch2_hello_oo** and press **Enter** to execute the program. Notice the new question which appears:

```
Which Appfactory should create your application?
1. Appfactory creating the simple X app
```

The section titled "Factory Design Pattern" discusses the concept of an application factory in detail. For now, type **1** and press **Enter**. Notice that the program then does exactly the same thing as `hello.cc`—it creates an empty window with undefined contents. Press **q** to exit the program.

Program `ch2_hello_oo` illustrates a number of important object-oriented techniques that will be used throughout the rest of this book. Therefore, understanding the design techniques used is very important and the subject of the following sections.

An Abstract Application Class

Let us begin with the class `ch2_app` (files `ch2_app.h` and `ch2_app.cc`). This is an abstract class, as defined earlier, since it has at least one pure virtual function. This class represents the general structure of an event-driven application. The function `execute` starts execution of the application. Notice that the code for `execute` calls, quite logically, the following three functions in order:

```
void ch2_app::execute(void) {
  create_window();
  ask_to_be_notified_of_interesting_events();
  event_loop();
}
```

All of these function calls are purely virtual. This means that the ch2_app class cannot function as it is, but must be subclassed to "fill in the blanks" left by the virtual functions. What the abstract class does is define that an execution of an event-driven program consists of the three steps listed above. In the original discussion of event-driven programs, we said that exactly these three steps formed the general structure of all event-driven programs. We have therefore captured the essence of the problem domain clearly and concisely within this abstract class.

CAUTION If you use polymorphic assignment, make sure your destructors are virtual.

Notice that the destructor for ch2_app is virtual, since we will be using polymorphic assignments, and destructor calls should also be virtual in this case. Without a virtual destructor, the compiler would call the destructor based upon the type of the pointer, not the type of the object pointed to. In other words, resolution of a destructor call in the face of polymorphic assignment takes place in the same manner as resolution of any other function call with polymorphic assignment.

A Concrete Application Class

The next class of interest is ch2_app_x, which is derived from class ch2_app. This class defines an event-driven application implemented under the X Window System. Notice that nothing in the abstract ch2_app class is in any way dependent on X; there is not a single #include of an X header file. Only in the ch2_app_x descendant do we introduce platform-specific code. Accordingly, ch2_app_x includes the X header files and defines the protected variables necessary for windowed display under X: the visual, the display, and the window. Finally, class ch2_app_x overrides the pure virtual functions declared in ch2_app: create_window, ask_to_be_notified_of_interesting_events, and event_loop.

In other words, ch2_app_x fills in the spaces left open by the abstract ch2_app class, and in particular, fills in these spaces with X-specific code. Class ch2_app_x, therefore, is a concrete class, one of many possible concretely realized implementations of the abstract ch2_app concept. Class ch2_app_x can be instantiated and used at run time, whereas ch2_app cannot; an attempt to create an object of type ch2_app would cause the linker to abort with an error message that the virtual table for class ch2_app could not be resolved. (Try it.)

The code in class ch2_app_x is the same as appeared in hello.cc—the only difference is that the code has been logically restructured to fit within the three-step framework provided by the abstract class. This is an important property of object-oriented designs: they tend to restructure designs into abstract frameworks representing the problem domain.

Factory Design Pattern

The next few classes are factory classes that represent an important design pattern in object-oriented architectures: the so-called *abstract factory pattern*. A *design pattern* is an architectural combination of classes in a particular way which solves a recurring type of problem occurring in object-oriented designs. *Design Patterns: Elements of Reusable Object-Oriented Software* [GAMM95] was the milestone publication which introduced this object-oriented technique in a coherent manner for the first time. The key thing to understand about design patterns is that a number of classes must cooperate in a particular way to solve a particular type of problem. The specification of the roles of the classes and the communication between them, which is applicable in a broad range of contexts, forms a design pattern.

The *factory design pattern* is something like a "virtual constructor." The idea is that instead of creating an object directly (via the C++ operator `new`), we ask some other object, called the factory, to create an object for us and return a pointer to the newly created object. What is the advantage of such an apparently roundabout scheme?

The advantage is that by going through a factory, the program requesting the object only needs to maintain an abstract class pointer to the object being created. The factory creates a concrete object (indeed, only concrete objects can be created at all), but returns a pointer of the more general, less specific abstract type. This means that the factory can be extended to create new types of concrete objects, without needing to modify the main program.

Consider the following analogy. Assume you are a carpenter, and that you need to build a ladder to climb on your roof. You actually don't care too much for building ladders; you just want to reach your roof to get your job done. The process of building your own ladder is analogous to creating an object directly with the C++ operator `new`. That is to say, if you want to build your own ladder, you must specifically know everything about the ladder to create it: the material, the spacing between the rungs, the length of the ladder, and so forth. If you only know how to build one type of ladder, say a wooden ladder, and one day decide that you need a metal ladder, you must learn to build a metal ladder. In a similar manner, a program which directly creates objects using the C++ `new` operator must know, specifically, the exact class of the object being created, even though this knowledge might distract from the main task of the program. If, in the future, the program needs to be modified to work with new kinds of objects, the code of the main program must be changed to invoke `new` on the new class, just as the carpenter needing new metal ladders must first learn how to create metal ladders.

The factory analogy extends to the carpenter as follows: instead of building your own ladder to climb on the roof, you call up a ladder factory and tell them, "give me a ladder." Depending on what factory you call, they might give you a wooden ladder, a metal ladder, with wide or narrow spacing between the rungs, extendable or not, and so on. But you as the carpenter no longer need to know, or care, about the exact fabrication process or even what kind of ladder you receive. All you know and care about is that you are getting a "ladder" which fulfills your specifications and with which you can do your job. The exact type of ladder and its creation are unknown to you; you only deal with the ladder factory.

The reasoning is the same with software factories and the factory design pattern. A class requesting object creation through a factory does not want to be burdened by knowing the exact concrete type (i.e., the exact concrete class) of the objects being created by the factory; its only condition is that the returned object belong to a particular abstract class. The carpenter doesn't care if the ladder is wooden or metal (the concrete class); he only cares about the fact that it is a ladder (the abstract class).

Moving object creation into an external factory object eliminates the dependency between the main program (or more generally the client class) and the myriad of possible concrete classes which the factory might produce. The factory can be extended to create new kinds of objects without even needing a recompile of the client class. Plug-in architectures, which have become quite popular recently for programs such as WWW browsers, also use a similar scheme: the browser cannot possibly anticipate the different kinds of plug-ins which might be plugged into the browser, yet through a factory the browser can indeed request creation of some plug-in object without knowing its concrete type.

An Application Factory and Factory Manager

In the case of our program `ch2_hello_oo`, the factory creates an application object conforming to a `ch2_app` abstract interface. The abstract factory class is therefore called `ch2_appfactory`—it is an application factory, which creates an application object. The object creation function is, surprisingly enough, the `create` function. Notice that `create` returns an abstract pointer to a `ch2_app` object, <u>not</u> a concrete pointer to a `ch2_app_x` object:

```
class ch2_appfactory {
  public:
    virtual ch2_app *create(void) = 0;
};
```

We then create a concrete factory, which, concretely speaking, returns objects of type `ch2_app_x`. This factory is implemented in class `ch2_appfactory_x`. Notice that the `create` function of this concrete factory actually creates an object of the concrete type `ch2_app_x`, yet returns a pointer of abstract type `ch2_app`. This is called *upcasting* and is a form of type-safe polymorphic assignment, where a pointer of one type points to an object of a different (but related) type.

```
ch2_app *ch2_appfactory_x::create(void) {
  return new ch2_app_x;
}
```

Some class in the program must know about the existence of this concrete factory; otherwise, there is no possible way any part of the program could ever use it. That is to say, some class, eventually, has to actually create the concrete factory so that it may be used by other classes, albeit through an abstract interface. Managing the concrete factory or factories is the role of the factory manager class, `ch2_factorymanager`. This class is a singleton class, which means that it will be created once during program execution. This single instance is declared in the main program, in the new version of `ch2_hello.cc`:

```
main() {
  ch2_app *application;
  ch2_factorymanager fm;
```

The `ch2_factorymanager` class has a static member `appfactory` which points to the actual application factory that the main program will call in order to receive its application object. This appfactory is initialized by the factory manager's `choose_factories()` method, which interactively asks the user which factory he wants to use. This information could also be read out of a configuration file or set to a default value.

```
fm.choose_factories();
```

Execution of the Main Program

As we just saw, the first thing the main program does is create a factory manager and ask it (through the user) to select the appropriate application factory. Having chosen an application factory, the next step is for the main program to ask the factory to create an application. We don't know and don't care what kind of application, because we know that we have already selected the right factory and that the factory will give us the proper type of object.

```
application = fm.appfactory->create();
application->execute();
}
```

Finally, once we have our application object, we call `execute` on it to start. This is a virtual function call, since we have no idea what kind of application lies behind the abstract interface. But we know that it is an application, and we know therefore that it must support the `execute` method. We call it, the virtual function call is resolved through the virtual function table, and execution begins in the `execute` method of the concrete class, which we, in this case, know to be `ch2_app_x` (since that is the only factory we have defined so far).

The `execute` method of `ch2_app_x` has not been overridden, so the version from `ch2_app`, the ancestor class, is called. From here, the three-step process, which we already described above, begins: `create_window`, `ask_to_be_notified_of_interesting_events`, and `event_loop`.

You might find it useful to step through this program with the debugger. Set a breakpoint on the `main` function and single step through every instruction. Figure 2-8 illustrates the execution order of the program graphically. Each oval represents an object (not a class) at run time. The numbered arrows represent the order of function calls within the program. To summarize the entire execution process, based on Figure 2-8:

1. The main program object asks the factory manager to choose the appropriate factories.
2. The factory manager creates, via the `new` operator, the appropriate concrete appfactory, in this case of type `ch2_appfactory_x`.
3. The main program asks the newly created appfactory to create an application.
4. The appfactory creates, via the `new` operator, an application of type `ch2_app_x`.
5. The main program asks the newly created application, fresh from the factory, to begin execution.
6. The application's `execute` method first asks the application (i.e., itself) to create a window.
7. The application's `execute` method next asks the application to take the necessary steps to be notified in case of interesting events.
8. The application's `execute` method finally asks the application to enter its event loop.

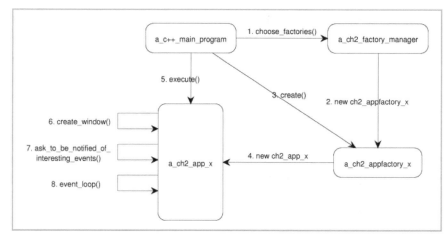

Figure 2-8:
Run-time order of function calls among objects for sample program `ch2_hello_oo`

Object-Oriented: Is It Worth It?

If this is your first encounter with design patterns or the general indirection techniques achievable through virtual functions, your head might be spinning at this point. You might wonder if such techniques are really worth the apparent extra effort they incur. Let's consider the alternative for a moment.

In this example, we used a factory design pattern to move creation of the application object out of the main program. It would have been very tempting indeed to have allowed the main program to directly create the concrete `ch2_app_x` object itself. But by doing this, we would have infected the main program with a physical dependency (in the form of an `#include`) on the `ch2_app_x.h` file. We would have forever tied our application code to the concrete `ch2_app_x` class. Suppose that we then write a new descendant of the abstract `ch2_app` class, which implements the event loop under a completely different operating system, say Microsoft Windows. (Indeed, the Appendix discusses how to do exactly this.) We then have a problem—our main program is physically tied to the `ch2_app_x` class because of the `#include`. The main program will not even compile under Microsoft Windows, which does not have the X include files. We would have to have conditional compilation statements in the main program—if X11, then include the `ch2_app_x` header file, otherwise include the `ch2_app_windows` file. Similar type-based conditional statements would litter our code as well—if X11, then do this; if Windows, then that. The problem gets even worse. Any new variation of the abstract class requires extending all of the conditional compilation and execution statements. From personal experience, I can say that maintaining such code over a period of years becomes a programmer's worst nightmare.

We solve this once and for all by moving all platform-specific code—that is, all concrete or non-abstract code—into subclasses in separate files. The abstract class simply contains placeholders, in the form of virtual functions, for those functions which will be implemented in a platform-specific way in the concrete subclasses. We then ensure that our main program only directly uses the abstract class, and not any concrete class. In this way the program is kept at a higher level of abstraction, can be compiled on a variety of platforms, and can be extended with minimal impact through subclassing. Through virtual function calls, the proper platform-specific code is called at run time. The hard part is finding that abstract class in the first place, i.e., recognizing that an abstraction exists or can be justified.

The problems which object-oriented design addresses might appear insignificant with small example programs of a few hundred lines. But exactly these problems—and the solutions offered by object orientation—become absolutely critical with programs consisting of thousands, tens of thousands, or even hundreds of thousands or millions of lines of code, developed by different people over several years. Object orientation is currently one of the most effective weapons that software architects have to combat the number one enemy of software development: complexity.

To check if your object-oriented design is really as modular as you think it is, try making all of your source and object files read-only, with the `chmod` command. Then create a new concrete subclass implementing your new functionality. See how many existing files you need to change—this will be evident because to change a file, you must first make it writable again. If you find that you have to change more than a few files, your concrete classes have probably infected your main program too greatly. While a few extra `#include` dependencies on concrete classes might seem harmless, they very quickly destroy the extensibility and reusability of the class, especially in other contexts. Trying to port the code at an early stage to another operating system is also a good test (though not necessarily comprehensive) of system modularity.

Creating modular object-oriented architectures requires a different perspective on programming. It requires a search for abstractions, for underlying fundamental characteristics of the problem at hand. The sequential step-by-step execution of "the main program" is secondary. You need to look beyond the immediate problem for more general abstractions. You need to constantly ask yourself, "how can the functionality of my program be seen as operations on some abstract data type? Do these operations generally characterize all possible variants of the abstracted data type? If I were to use this code in a different environment, would my abstractions still be valid?"

Abstraction, indirection, virtual functions, abstract classes, concrete classes, factories, design patterns—these are some of the object-oriented techniques which we use for the code throughout this book. Through such techniques we will develop graphics classes which work with and without hardware acceleration, under Linux and Microsoft Windows. The object-oriented perspective on software construction might seem a bit awkward at first, but it is worth it, and it does yield architectures that are much more resilient to change than traditional function-oriented programs.

Introduction to XImages

The previous program, while better structured, still suffers from the same technical shortcoming as the first: its display is undefined because it does not respond to X events. The next program corrects this. It displays a black background and prints in real time all events being sent to the window. It is quite instructive to see exactly what events X is sending to the window and when—when the mouse pointer moves, when the window loses or gains focus, when a key is pressed, when part of the window is exposed, and so forth.

This program has three goals: to illustrate extension of existing code through subclassing, to illustrate basic use of XImages, and to reinforce the event-handling concepts by displaying in real time all events.

A Practical Example of OO Reuse

The code for this program is in directory `$L3D/source/app/hello_oo_event`. The code in this directory is not complete in and of itself, but rather uses the classes from the previous program and extends them by adding new classes. This is a key goal of object-oriented software: instead of copying heaps of source code and destroying carefully created structures in the original code with new specializations, we leave the original code untouched and build upon it with new derived classes.

The Makefile is the key to the practical side of this reuse process. To reuse the original source and object files in another project located in another directory, the compiler and linker need to be able to find the original files. In our case, the original directory is `hello_oo` and the new directory is `hello_oo_event`. The Makefile for the new project is located in `hello_oo_event`, and contains specific compiler and linker flags referring to the original `hello_oo` directory. The new Makefile is shown in Listing 2-12.

Listing 2-12: The Makefile for the `hello_oo_event` program
References to the old hello_oo directory, which are necessary so that the original code may be reused, are underlined.

```
OLDDIR_OO = ../hello_oo

LD = gcc
LDFLAGS = -L/usr/X11/lib -lg++ -lX11 -lXt -lm
CPPFLAGS = -g -I$(OLDDIR_OO)

ch2_hello_oo_event:\
  $(OLDDIR_OO)/ch2_hello.o\
  $(OLDDIR_OO)/ch2_app.o\
  $(OLDDIR_OO)/ch2_app_x.o\
  $(OLDDIR_OO)/ch2_appfactory_x.o\
  ch2_factorymanager.o \
  ch2_app_xevent.o \
  ch2_appfactory_xevent.o
        $(LD) $(LDFLAGS) $^ -o $@
```

The first line in the Makefile defines a (string) variable named `OLDDIR_OO`, containing the name of the original directory. Then, the line with `CPPFLAGS`, which indicates the flags to be passed to the C++ compiler, includes the directive `-I$(OLDDIR_OO)`. This indicates that header files during compilation should also be searched for in this directory. Finally, the dependency lines for the Makefile indicate that the object files containing the classes we want to reuse are also located in the original directory, indicated by the `$(OLDDIR_OO)` preceding the object file name. For the newly created or changed source files, we want to use the new files, and therefore do not specify `$(OLDDIR_OO)` on the dependency line. In this particular example, we are reusing four object files, containing four classes, exactly as is from the previous example. We changed slightly the original class `ch2_factorymanager`, located in file `ch2_factorymanager.cc`, and compiled into object file `ch2_factorymanager.o`. Since we changed this class, we don't specify `$(OLDDIR_OO)` on the dependency line, so that our new version is compiled and linked. The other two object files, `ch2_app_event.o` and `ch2_appfactory_xevent.o`, correspond to source files containing completely new classes, so naturally these must also come from the new directory.

When you compile this program (as usual, simply with make), you will notice that none of the object files in the old directory need to be recompiled. Thus, code reuse at the programming language level (through inheritance) also translates directly into object-file reuse at the linker level. This means that the new directory contains exactly the new code. All of the old code we reused appears, unchanged and in its pristine state, in the original directory. "Reused code" is therefore really "reused" and not "copied." This makes maintenance easier; instead of needing to maintain the original and copied versions of the code, you can physically treat the new code and the old code as separate modules.

 TIP If you find that it is impossible for you to extend a program by creating new subclasses, instead requiring you to copy the original source code into a new file and to modify the original source code directly, you almost certainly do not have an object-oriented design.

The following list summarizes the theoretical side (source code level) and practical side (file-system level) of object-oriented code reuse:

- At the source code level, we do reuse a class either by declaring a new class inheriting from the original class (the inheritance relationship), or by creating an instance of the original class as is and using its features in a new context (the client relationship, not illustrated above). We don't copy the source code from the old class into a new class.

- At the file-system level, we do reuse a class by physically compiling and linking the program with the original class's header, source, and object files. We don't copy the original class's files and modify the copied file.

- At the source code level, the technical mechanisms allowing for code reuse are virtual functions and inheritance. Through inheritance, a derived class reuses (inherits) all the attributes and functions of the ancestor class. Through virtual functions, a derived class can selectively redefine specific parts of the original class, in a type-compatible way, without needing access to its source code. Through new declarations in the derived class, the derived class can offer new features not present in the ancestor class. Through object-oriented C++ mechanisms we thus achieve code reuse, selective code adaptation, and code extension, all without modifying the original source code.

- At the file-system level, the technical mechanisms allowing for code reuse are search directives for the compilation and linking commands, located in the makefile.

 NOTE Code reuse through inheritance is called the *inheritance relationship* between classes and represents a type-compatible form of reuse: instances of classes of the derived type may be assigned to variables of the ancestor type. Another form of reuse is the *client relationship* and simply entails creating an instance of an existing class, the supplier class, and reusing its features (its functions and variables) in a new context to perform a new job. However, a client class simply reusing the features of a supplier class will not, in general, be type compatible with the supplier class—although it could be, if both classes inherited (possibly through multiple inheritance) from a common ancestor class.

Running the New Subclassed Program

After compilation of the new subclassed program, the executable file named `ch2_hello_oo_event` is created. Execute the program as follows.

1. Type **ch2_hello_oo_event** and press **Enter**.

2. Notice the new appfactory which appears in the list at program start. Previously, only one factory was listed, but now two appear. Remember: our main program file, `ch2_hello.o`, has not been changed at all and was linked from the original object file in the original directory, yet we have introduced new behavior indirectly into the unchanged main program by supplying a new factory. This is very difficult or tedious to achieve with non-object-oriented designs.

```
Which Appfactory should create your application?
1. Appfactory creating the simple X app
2. Appfactory creating the simple X app with event display
```

3. Type **2** and press **Enter**. This creates an instance of the new application class (described in detail in the next section). Notice the messages which appear in the shell window. The first few lines display information about the X display. Then follows a list of all X events received by the program.

```
max depth of display 24
bytes per pixel: 4
Vis is TrueColor
lsb first
Event type PropertyNotify
Event type PropertyNotify
Event type PropertyNotify
Event type ReparentNotify
Event type PropertyNotify
Event type ConfigureNotify
Event type PropertyNotify
Event type PropertyNotify
Event type PropertyNotify
Event type PropertyNotify
Event type PropertyNotify
Event type MapNotify
Event type VisibilityNotify
Event type Expose
Event type PropertyNotify
Event type PropertyNotify
Event type FocusIn
```

4. Notice the new window which appears. See Figure 2-9. The background is black, not undefined as previously, and a status line in the window displays the same event messages which appear in the shell window.

5. Move the mouse cursor within the window. Notice the event messages that are generated, and that the string "hello!" is printed underneath the mouse cursor.

6. Press some random keys (avoiding the key **q**) in the window. Notice the event messages that are generated. Notice that keys such as Shift or Alt by themselves also generate events.

7. Type **q** to quit the program.

Figure 2-9: The subclassed `hello_oo_event` *program, which displays X events in real time on a black XImage background.*

This program provides a good illustration of event-based programming under X by showing all of the many events that a typical X window can receive. If you are new to event-based programming, you may be surprised at the large number of events which are generated, all automatically and transparently by the X Window System.

Let us now see exactly what new classes we have added to the program, and how they respond to X events in a better way than the original program, which silently ignored most events.

New Classes

Figure 2-10 shows the updated class diagram for the new classes we have created. Listings 2-13 through 2-17 contain the code for the new classes.

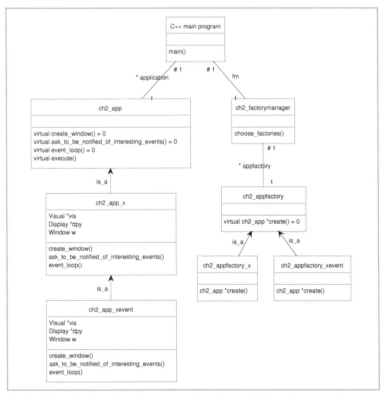

Figure 2-10: Updated class diagram with new event-handling classes.

Listing 2-13: `ch2_appfactory_xevent.h`

```
#ifndef __CH2_APPFACTORY_XEVENT_H
#define __CH2_APPFACTORY_XEVENT_H

#include "ch2_appfactory.h"

class ch2_appfactory_xevent : public ch2_appfactory {
    ch2_app *create(void);
};

#endif
```

Listing 2-14: `ch2_appfactory_xevent.cc`

```
#include "ch2_appfactory_xevent.h"
#include "ch2_app_xevent.h"

ch2_app *ch2_appfactory_xevent::create(void) {
  return new ch2_app_xevent;
}
```

Listing 2-15: `ch2_app_xevent.h`

```
#ifndef __CH2_APP_XEVENT_H
#define __CH2_APP_XEVENT_H

#include "ch2_app_x.h"

class ch2_app_xevent : public ch2_app_x {
  protected:
    char *screen;
    XImage *ximg;
    int depth, bytespp, scanline_pad;

    const char *event_name(int type) const;
    void create_window(void);
    void ask_to_be_notified_of_interesting_events(void);
    void event_loop(void);

  public:
    virtual ~ch2_app_xevent(void);

};

#endif
```

Listing 2-16: `ch2_app_xevent.cc`

```
#include "ch2_app_xevent.h"
#include <stdio.h>

const char *ch2_app_xevent::event_name(int e_type) const {
  static char text[80];

  switch (e_type) {

      //- event types from X11.h

    case KeyPress : sprintf(text, "KeyPress"); break;
    case KeyRelease : sprintf(text, "KeyRelease"); break;
    case ButtonPress : sprintf(text, "ButtonPress"); break;
    case ButtonRelease : sprintf(text, "ButtonRelease"); break;
    case MotionNotify : sprintf(text, "MotionNotify"); break;
```

```
      case EnterNotify : sprintf(text, "EnterNotify"); break;
      case LeaveNotify : sprintf(text, "LeaveNotify"); break;
      case FocusIn : sprintf(text, "FocusIn"); break;
      case FocusOut : sprintf(text, "FocusOut"); break;
      case KeymapNotify : sprintf(text, "KeymapNotify"); break;
      case Expose : sprintf(text, "Expose"); break;
      case GraphicsExpose : sprintf(text, "GraphicsExpose"); break;
      case NoExpose : sprintf(text, "NoExpose"); break;
      case VisibilityNotify : sprintf(text, "VisibilityNotify"); break;
      case CreateNotify : sprintf(text, "CreateNotify"); break;
      case DestroyNotify : sprintf(text, "DestroyNotify"); break;
      case UnmapNotify : sprintf(text, "UnmapNotify"); break;
      case MapNotify : sprintf(text, "MapNotify"); break;
      case MapRequest : sprintf(text, "MapRequest"); break;
      case ReparentNotify : sprintf(text, "ReparentNotify"); break;
      case ConfigureNotify : sprintf(text, "ConfigureNotify"); break;
      case ConfigureRequest : sprintf(text, "ConfigureRequest"); break;
      case GravityNotify : sprintf(text, "GravityNotify"); break;
      case ResizeRequest : sprintf(text, "ResizeRequest"); break;
      case CirculateNotify : sprintf(text, "CirculateNotify"); break;
      case CirculateRequest : sprintf(text, "CirculateRequest"); break;
      case PropertyNotify : sprintf(text, "PropertyNotify"); break;
      case SelectionClear : sprintf(text, "SelectionClear"); break;
      case SelectionRequest : sprintf(text, "SelectionRequest"); break;
      case SelectionNotify : sprintf(text, "SelectionNotify"); break;
      case ColormapNotify : sprintf(text, "ColormapNotify"); break;
      case ClientMessage : sprintf(text, "ClientMessage"); break;
      case MappingNotify : sprintf(text, "MappingNotify"); break;
      case LASTEvent : sprintf(text, "LASTEvent"); break;
  }

  return text;
}


ch2_app_xevent::~ch2_app_xevent(void) {
  if(screen) {delete [] screen; }
}


void ch2_app_xevent::create_window(void) {
  XPixmapFormatValues *pixmap_formats;
  int i, count;
  const int bits_per_byte = 8;

  //- establish connection to X server

  dpy = XopenDisplay(NULL);

  //- find deepest pixmap format allowable

  pixmap_formats = XListPixmapFormats(dpy, &count);
  for(i=0, depth=0; i<count; i++) {
    if(pixmap_formats[i].depth > depth) {
      depth      = pixmap_formats[i].depth;
      bytespp    = pixmap_formats[i].bits_per_pixel / bits_per_byte;
      scanline_pad = pixmap_formats[i].scanline_pad;
    }
  }
  Xfree(pixmap_formats);
  printf("max depth of display %d", depth);
```

```
    printf("bytes per pixel: %d", bytespp);

    //- print out some information about the visual

    vis = DefaultVisual(dpy,0);
    switch(vis->c_class) {
      case PseudoColor: printf("Vis is pseudocolor");break;
      case StaticColor: printf("Vis is StaticColor");break;
      case GrayScale: printf("Vis is GrayScale");break;
      case StaticGray: printf("Vis is StaticGray");break;
      case DirectColor: printf("Vis is DirectColor");break;
      case TrueColor: printf("Vis is TrueColor");break;
    }

    //- create and map the window using max. possible depth

    w = XCreateWindow(dpy, DefaultRootWindow(dpy), 100, 100,
                      screen_xsize, screen_ysize,
                      0,
                      depth, CopyFromParent, vis,
                      0, NULL);
    XStoreName(dpy, w,"hello_oo_event");
    XMapWindow(dpy, w);

    //- create XImage and offscreen buffer

    screen = new char[screen_xsize*screen_ysize*bytespp];

    if (ImageByteOrder(dpy) == LSBFirst ) {
      printf("lsb first");
    }else {
      printf("msb first");
    }

    ximg = XCreateImage(dpy, vis, depth,
                        Zpixmap,
                        0,
                        screen,
                        screen_xsize, screen_ysize,
                        scanline_pad,
                        0);

  XSetForeground(dpy, DefaultGC(dpy, 0), ~0);
  XSetBackground(dpy, DefaultGC(dpy, 0), 0);
}

void ch2_app_xevent::ask_to_be_notified_of_interesting_events(void) {
  XSelectInput(dpy, w, 0x00FFFFFF ^ PointerMotionHintMask);
}

void ch2_app_xevent::event_loop(void) {
  XEvent event;
  char ch;
  KeySym keysym;
  XComposeStatus xcompstat;

  int mouse_x, mouse_y;
  while(1) {
    XNextEvent(dpy, &event);
    char event_text[80];
```

```
              sprintf(event_text, "Event type %s                ", event_name(event.type));
              printf("%s", event_text);

          switch(event.type) {
            case KeyPress: {
                XLookupString(&event.xkey, &ch, 1, &keysym, &xcompstat);
                switch(ch) {
                  case 'q': {
                      exit(0);
                    }
                }
              }
              break;

            case MotionNotify: {
                printf("x %d y %d", event.xmotion.x,event.xmotion.y);
                mouse_x = event.xmotion.x;
                mouse_y = event.xmotion.y;

                XEvent e;
                e.type = Expose;
                e.xexpose.send_event = TRUE;
                e.xexpose.display = dpy;
                e.xexpose.window = w;
                e.xexpose.x = e.xexpose.y = e.xexpose.width = e.xexpose.height =
                                          e.xexpose.count = 0;

                XSendEvent(dpy, w, TRUE, ExposureMask, &e);
              }
              break;

            case Expose: {
                if(event.xexpose.count==0) {
                  XPutImage(dpy, w, DefaultGC(dpy,0), ximg,
                          0,0,0,0,  /* source x,y; destination x,y */
                          screen_xsize, screen_ysize);

                  XDrawString(dpy, w, DefaultGC(dpy, 0), mouse_x, mouse_y, "hello!", 6);
                }
              }
              break;
          }

        XDrawImageString(dpy, w, DefaultGC(dpy, 0), 50, 50, event_text,
                      strlen(event_text));
        }
    }
```

Listing 2-17: The changed ch2_factory_manager.cc

```
#include "ch2_factorymanager.h"

#include "ch2_appfactory_x.h"
#include "ch2_appfactory_xevent.h"

ch2_appfactory *ch2_factorymanager::appfactory = 0;

void ch2_factorymanager::choose_factories(void) {
  int i;

  printf("Which Appfactory should create your application?");
```

```
        printf("1. Appfactory creating the simple X app");
        printf("2. Appfactory creating the simple X app with event display");

        scanf("%d", &i);

        switch(i) {
          case 1: {
              appfactory = new ch2_appfactory_x;
            };
            break;

          case 2: {
              appfactory = new ch2_appfactory_xevent;
            };
            break;
        }
      }
```

Referring to the class diagram, it should be clear what we have done: we have added a new class `ch2_app_xevent`, derived from class `ch2_app_x`. We have also added a new application factory class, `ch2_appfactory_xevent`, which descends directly from class `ch2_appfactory` and is responsible for creating objects of type `ch2_app_xevent`. We have made a minor change to the factory manager to allow selection of the new factory. This is the only change we made to the original source code and is indeed minimal.

The new factory class requires little explanation, as its function is exactly the same as the existing factory class, only returning a different kind of application object. The new application class is where the improved event handling takes place. Let's take a closer look at the functions defined in the `ch2_app_xevent` class.

X Server Depth and Visual Class

The first routine which is called is `ch2_app_xevent::create_window`. This routine begins as usual by connecting to the X server with `XOpenDisplay`. Then, we call `XListPixmapFormats` to obtain a list of image formats supported by the X server. The image formats are returned as a list of `XPixmapFormatValues` structures, which is defined as follows.

```
    typedef struct {
        int depth;
        int bits_per_pixel;
        int scanline_pad;
    } XpixmapFormatValues;
```

The reason we need to query the server in this way is that we are going to create a black background image to fill the window. In order to create any sort of image, we need to know some details about how the image is to be stored so we know how much memory to allocate. In particular, we need to know how many bits to allocate for each pixel in the image. A *pixel* is the smallest physically addressable element of an image; the section "Picture Elements—Pixels" covers this in more detail.

The number of bits per pixel, returned in the `bits_per_pixel` member of the structure, is also known as the *color depth* or simply *depth* of the image. If we consider the 2D area of an image to be its width and height, we can imagine the color as being an additional dimension, thus leading to the concept of color "depth." The greater the depth, the more colors can be displayed and the higher the potential image quality.

The depth of an image sent to an X server must be supported by the X server; otherwise, the results will probably be unrecognizable. This is why we ask the server, through `XListPixmapFormats`, which image depths are supported.

As described in the Appendix, you control the depth of the X server by specifying extra parameters to the `startx` command. For instance, **startx -- -bpp 32** starts the X server with 32 bits per pixel (bpp), while **startx -- -bpp 8** starts with 8 bits per pixel. Your video hardware and your X server configuration determine the maximum depth supported. You can use the `xdpyinfo` command to find out what depth(s) your X server supports.

Because our application program can't know beforehand the depth of the X server, it has to be flexible enough to query the X server for its depth and configure itself accordingly. `ch2_app_xevent` chooses the maximum depth supported by the X server, and then uses the depth information to calculate the correct number of bytes to allocate for an empty (black) image. For an X server with 8 bits per pixel, we have to allocate one byte for every pixel in the display. For an X server with 32 bits per pixel, we have to allocate four bytes (32 bits divided by 8 bits per byte) for every pixel in the display.

Alternatively, we could have chosen to only support one depth, for instance 8 bits per pixel, aborting the program if the X server does not support exactly this depth. Some programs do this, but it is rather frustrating to have to shut down the X server and start it in another depth just to run a program. It is a bit more difficult to make a program which adaptively supports multiple depths, but this makes the user's life easier.

After querying the supported depths, the `ch2_app_xevent` program also prints out some information about the types of visuals supported by the X server. (Remember, a "visual" describes a color structure supported by an X server.) The "type" of visual is called its *class*. The following six visual classes are supported by X, as defined in `X.h`.

```
/* Display classes  used in opening the connection
 * Note that the statically allocated ones are even numbered and the
 * dynamically changeable ones are odd numbered */

#define StaticGray          0
#define GrayScale           1
#define StaticColor         2
#define PseudoColor         3
#define TrueColor           4
#define DirectColor         5
```

We mentioned earlier, in the discussion of `XCreateWindow`, that the depth and visual class work closely together to specify the number and type of colors available to the window. We can now understand this more precisely. With a depth of N bits per pixel, the visual class determines how these N bits for each pixel are used to display a color on the screen. The following list describes the meaning of each visual.

▪ StaticGray: The N bits for each pixel are interpreted as an index into a static grayscale colormap with 2^N entries.

▪ GrayScale: The N bits for each pixel are interpreted as an index into a dynamically changeable grayscale colormap with 2^N entries.

- StaticColor: The N bits for each pixel are interpreted as an index into a static colormap with 2^N entries.

- PseudoColor: The N bits for each pixel are interpreted as an index into a dynamically changeable colormap with 2^N entries.

- TrueColor: The N bits for each pixel are divided into R bits for red, G bits for green, and B bits for blue, where R+G+B = N. The R, G, and B bits map statically to 2^R, 2^G, and 2^B red, green, and blue intensities, respectively.

- DirectColor: The N bits for each pixel are divided into R bits for red, G bits for green, and B bits for blue, where R+G+B = N. The R, G, and B bits are interpreted as indices into a dynamically changeable red, green, and blue colormap, respectively.

Note that most colors can be defined as a combination of intensities of red, green, and blue; those which cannot (such as some pastel colors) form only a small part of the color spectrum and are ignored in the RGB color model.

A *colormap*, also sometimes called a *color palette*, is simply a table containing color values. When a colormap is used, we refer to a color by its index within the colormap. In other words, instead of saying, "the color with red intensity 128, green intensity 64, and blue intensity 96," we might say, "the color at location 25 in the colormap." Colormapped color models are also called *indexed* or *paletted* color. We usually use a colormap when the video hardware physically cannot display more than a certain number of colors at once. The X color model allows for both static and dynamic colormaps. With a static colormap, the color of each entry is predefined; with a dynamic colormap, each entry may be individually set by the application program.

The most common visuals you will probably encounter are 8-bit PseudoColor (256 simultaneous arbitrary colors), 16-bit TrueColor (65,536 simultaneous colors), and 24-bit TrueColor (16,777,216 simultaneous colors, though a typical display does not have that many pixels).

After retrieving the visual and maximum depth from the server, the `ch2_app_xevent` program creates and maps a window with this visual and depth. The next step is to create an empty background image compatible with the visual and depth.

Graphics and Double Buffering with XImages

Our first program, `hello.cc`, did not respond to requests that the window redraw itself (the expose event). Indeed, the program did not draw anything at all.

To correct this, `ch2_app_xevent` creates an empty image to fill the window, and draws this when requested. This image is of type `XImage`.

An XImage is an off-screen graphics image which can be copied to the screen with the function `XPutImage`. An XImage stores the image in a region of memory which is allocated by and accessible to the application program. Therefore, modifying the image data for an XImage simply requires setting the appropriate bytes in the memory region used by the XImage, then calling `XPutImage` to display the changes on-screen.

The idea of making image changes off-screen then copying them to the screen is called *double buffering*; the copying of the off-screen image to the screen is sometimes called *blitting* (from the phrase "bit block transfer," yielding the infinitive which only a computer scientist could invent, "to blit"). The alternative to double buffering is a drawing scheme which directly and immediately updates the display after every drawing operation. The reason we use double buffering is to reduce flickering. We perform all drawing operations invisibly off-screen; then, when the entire image has been prepared, we copy the finished image as quickly as possible to the screen with a single function call. Updating the screen after every drawing operation would allow the user to see the partial image as it is still being drawn, which causes flickering and is visually very distracting.

NOTE A *pixmap* is another X structure which stores an off-screen image, similar to an XImage. However, the image data for a pixmap cannot be accessed directly, but must instead be manipulated through Xlib functions (XDrawLine, XDrawPoint, XDrawRectangle, XDrawArc, and so forth). This is too slow for interactive displays, where every single pixel must be updated for each new image. Also, it is possible to use Xlib functions to draw directly to a visible window, in which case the window is updated immediately. This, too, is not ideal for interactive displays due to the flickering effect mentioned above.

For now, we just create an image, but don't fill it with any data. ch2_app_xevent first allocates the off-screen image data for the XImage as follows:

```
screen = new char[screen_xsize*screen_ysize*bytespp];
```

Notice that the total number of bytes to be allocated must be multiplied by the number of bytes per pixel, which we determined earlier (in the form of bits per pixel, which we divide by 8 to get bytes per pixel) by querying the X server.

With the off-screen image data (also called the *off-screen buffer* or the *frame buffer*) allocated, we can then create the XImage itself:

```
ximg = XCreateImage(dpy, vis, depth,
               Zpixmap,
               0,
               screen,
               screen_xsize, screen_ysize,
               scanline_pad,
               0);
```

The first three parameters to XCreateImage specify the display, visual, and depth. The next parameter will for our purposes always be the constant ZPixmap. This parameter specifies the ordering of bits for each pixel in the image. ZPixmap specifies that each byte in the image data corresponds to at most one pixel. (The other option would be to allow the individual bits of each byte to correspond to different pixels.) The fifth parameter specifies the number of pixels to ignore at the beginning of each line; we set this to zero. The sixth parameter is a pointer to the off-screen buffer which we just allocated. The seventh and eighth parameters specify the dimensions in pixels of the image. The scanline_pad parameter indicates that one horizontal line in the image is a multiple of this many bits long; we use the same value which we received from the X server earlier with the XListPixmapFormats function. The last parameter specifies the number of bytes per line in the image; if the image data is continuous in memory (which for the programs in this book will always be the case), then we can set this parameter to zero and let the function automatically compute this value itself.

The last thing that ch2_app_event::create_window does is set the foreground and background color for future drawing operations. These are used by the text output functions.

Requesting Notification for All Events

The next function which is called in the `ch2_app_event` class is the function `ask_to_be_notified_of_interesting_events`. We use `XSelectInput` with a mask consisting of all 1s in the lower 24 bits. We use 24 bits because according to the X header files, all event masks are currently defined in the lower 24 bits. We explicitly exclude one event type, `PointerMotionHintMask`, because this interferes with continuous tracking of `PointerMotion` events.

Since the application has specified 23 of the 24 possible event masks, all of these events will be reported to the window.

Visual Event Display

The next function which is called in the `ch2_app_event` class is the function `event_loop`. The event loop begins by taking the next event out of the queue with `XNextEvent`. We then have a case statement which handles the event based upon its type.

If the event was a keypress event, we check if it was q and if so, exit.

If the event is a motion notify event, we know that the mouse pointer just moved. We store the current location for later use, and then generate an expose event to force the window to redraw itself. We do this by declaring a variable of type `XEvent`, initializing its fields as required for an expose event, and sending this message to the window with `XSendEvent`.

If the event is an expose event, we check to see if this is the last of a series of expose events, by seeing if the `number` parameter is zero. An expose event, which is a request for a window to redraw itself, need not apply to an entire window; it might only apply to part of a window. Applications that want to optimize redrawing will only redraw that part of the window which is specified in the expose event. For our application, we won't optimize at this level, instead redrawing the entire image. In general, 3D programs must regenerate the entire image every time the screen is updated anyway. In any case, once we decide that this expose event is one which needs acting upon—one with zero as the `number` parameter—we do two things: we copy our empty XImage to the screen, ensuring a blank background, and then we draw the string "hello!" underneath the mouse cursor, the position of which we saved during the last motion notify event.

The `XPutImage` function copies the XImage to the window; the `XDrawString` function draws a text string to the window. Both of these functions have quite simple parameter lists requiring no further explanation. The only parameter of note to both of these functions is the third parameter, which specifies the graphics context, abbreviated GC. A *graphics context* is a context for doing graphics operations; it stores "global parameters" which then apply to all graphics operations occurring within this context. These parameters include such things as line width, foreground color, background color, fill patterns, fonts, and so on. You can think of a GC as a saveable set of parameters for graphics operations. Since we aren't using any built-in drawing functions, instead manipulating the XImage data directly, we don't need to allocate or manipulate our own GC. We just use the default GC of the display.

The last thing that the event loop of class `ch2_app_event` does is draw a string in the window displaying the type of the event just received. The helper function `event_name` converts the event type code to a string.

Summary

This program, subclassed from the previous one, displayed all events received by the window in real time. Its techniques introduced us to XImages by creating an empty XImage and copying it into the window on an expose event. Creating an XImage requires us to ask the X server about the supported depths, so that we know how many bits per pixel to allocate for the image data. The visual class of the X server determines how the bits for each pixel are interpreted to form a color. The data of an XImage may be changed by directly manipulating the bytes in an off-screen buffer.

The next thing we would like to do is display graphics in the XImage.

Displaying Graphics in XImages

As we saw earlier, an XImage stores an off-screen graphical image in a region of memory accessible to the application program. The last program didn't put any data into the off-screen buffer, which is why the background was empty. Let's try putting some data into the buffer and see what happens.

Random Dots

Our first experiment will be to put completely random data into the buffer. Listings 2-18 through 2-22 illustrate the program changes necessary. The source code for this program is in directory $L3D/source/app/hello_oo_image, and the class diagram appears in Figure 2-11.

Listing 2-18: ch2_appfactory_ximage.h

```
#ifndef __CH2_APPFACTORY_XIMAGE_H
#define __CH2_APPFACTORY_XIMAGE_H

#include "ch2_appfactory.h"

class ch2_appfactory_ximage : public ch2_appfactory {
    ch2_app *create(void);
};

#endif
```

Listing 2-19: ch2_appfactory_ximage.cc

```
#include "ch2_appfactory_ximage.h"
#include "ch2_app_ximage.h"

ch2_app *ch2_appfactory_ximage::create(void) {
  return new ch2_app_ximage;
}
```

Listing 2-20: ch2_app_ximage.h

```
#ifndef __CH2_APP_XIMAGE_H
#define __CH2_APP_XIMAGE_H

#include "ch2_app_xevent.h"

class ch2_app_ximage : public ch2_app_xevent {
  protected:
    void event_loop(void);
    void ask_to_be_notified_of_interesting_events(void);
```

```
    public:
      virtual ~ch2_app_ximage(void) {};

};

#endif
```

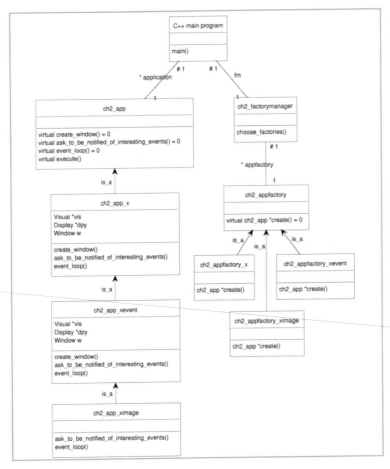

Figure 2-11: Class diagram for `hello_oo_image`.

Listing 2-21: ch2_app_ximage.cc

```
#include "ch2_app_ximage.h"
#include <stdio.h>
#include <stdlib.h>

void ch2_app_ximage::ask_to_be_notified_of_interesting_events(void) {
  XSelectInput(dpy, w, KeyPressMask);
}

void ch2_app_ximage::event_loop(void) {
  XEvent event;
  char ch;
  KeySym keysym;
```

```
    XComposeStatus xcompstat;

    int mouse_x, mouse_y;
    while(1) {
      if (XCheckWindowEvent(dpy, w, KeyPressMask, &event)) {
        XLookupString(&event.xkey, &ch, 1, &keysym, &xcompstat);
        switch(ch) {
          case 'q': {
              exit(0);
            }
        }
      }

      int i,j,k;
      char *c;
      c = screen;
      for(i=0; i<screen_xsize; i++) {
        for(j=0; j<screen_ysize; j++) {
          for(k=0; k<bytespp; k++) {
            *c++ = rand() % 255;
          }
        }
      }

      XPutImage(dpy, w, DefaultGC(dpy,0), ximg,
                0,0,0,0,  /* source x,y; destination x,y */
                screen_xsize, screen_ysize);
    }
}
```

Listing 2-22: The changed `ch2_factorymanager.cc`

```
#include "ch2_factorymanager.h"

#include "ch2_appfactory_x.h"
#include "ch2_appfactory_xevent.h"
#include "ch2_appfactory_ximage.h"

ch2_appfactory *ch2_factorymanager::appfactory = 0;

void ch2_factorymanager::choose_factories(void) {
  int i;

  printf("Which Appfactory should create your application?");
  printf("1. Appfactory creating the simple X app");
  printf("2. Appfactory creating the simple X app with event display");
  printf("3. Appfactory creating the random dots app");

  scanf("%d", &i);

  switch(i) {
    case 1: {
        appfactory = new ch2_appfactory_x;
      };
      break;

    case 2: {
        appfactory = new ch2_appfactory_xevent;
      };
      break;
```

```
    case 3: {
        appfactory = new ch2_appfactory_ximage;
    };
    break;
  }
}
```

The new application factory and the updated factory manager should look quite familiar to you now. As usual, the new application class, in this case ch2_app_ximage, is where the action is.

The new class ch2_app_ximage descends from the existing ch2_app_ximage class, overriding the event notification and event loop. The window creation and XImage initialization remain the same. (It is for this reason, incidentally, that the title bar of the window for this program still displays the name of the previous program; the window creation, which includes setting the title text, is inherited from the previous program's class.)

In the event notification routine ask_to_be_notified_of_interesting_ events, we again revert to only monitoring keypress events. Monitoring events we are not inter- ested in creates unnecessary communication between the server and the application, resulting in poorer performance.

You might think that we still need to monitor expose events, but in this particular case we do not, because in the main loop, after we look for an event to process (with XCheckWindowEvent), we update and copy the XImage to the screen. This takes place regard- less of whether any event occurred or not. Therefore, our application is pushing images as fast as it can to the display, even in the absence of any events, and does not need to worry about expose events: another image will be generated within a fraction of a second anyway.

The following code from class ch2_app_ximage updates and copies the image to the screen:

```
int I,j,k;
char *c;
c = screen;
for(i=0; i<screen_xsize; i++) {
  for(j=0; j<screen_ysize; j++) {
    for(k=0; k<bytespp; k++) {
      *c++ = rand() % 255;
    }
  }
}

XPutImage(dpy, w, DefaultGC(dpy,0), ximg,
          0,0,0,0,  /* source x,y; destination x,y */
          screen_xsize, screen_ysize);
```

First we initialize the pointer c to point to the beginning of the off-screen image data which we allocated earlier and connected with the XImage. We then have three nested for loops which iter- ate through all bytes in the image. The for loops iterate along the width, height, and depth of the image, respectively. In the innermost loop, we set the current byte of the image to a random value and increase the pointer to point to the next byte in the image.

Compile and run the program. Type **3** and press **Enter** to select the new application factory for this program. Notice that a window appears and is filled with a randomly changing pattern of dots. Press **q** to quit.

Figure 2-12: The output of program
hello_oo_image, which displays random dots in
an XImage.

A Word on Animation

Although simple, this program illustrates a fundamental animation technique: draw off-screen, copy to screen, repeat. Our "drawing" in this case simply consists of filling the buffer with random dots, but the random pattern of dots changes every frame. (A *frame* is simply a single image in an animated sequence of images.) Since the image is changed and displayed several times a second, we see a moving pattern reminiscent of television static.

The exact same technique is used for 2D or 3D animation: we draw our complete 2D or 3D scene in an off-screen buffer, then copy this image to the screen to make it visible. While the image is visible, we draw the next frame, and display it as soon as it is ready. We repeat this process for the duration of the program.

Summary

Now we're starting to see some practical results. We have an application which creates an X window, queries the X server for allowable image depths, creates an off-screen image of the correct depth, directly manipulates the bytes in the image, copies this image to the screen, animates the image in real time, and responds to user events. This is a lot indeed. We've overcome the first hurdle and have created a fully functional X program under Linux.

However, so far, we have either created no image at all or created a completely random image. Both of these tasks are similarly easy because they do not require us to understand exactly how the order of bytes in the image memory corresponds to the physical pixel order on the screen. We simply fill the entire buffer, but have no idea which bytes correspond to which pixels on-screen. The next section discusses controlling individual pixels in the image. We also begin with the development of generally reusable graphics classes which will be reused throughout the book.

Picture Elements—Pixels

Up to this point, we have fairly casually referred to "pixels" as they relate to 2D images. We have used the concept of "pixel" somewhat loosely in reference to "bytes per pixel" and the "pixels" making up an XImage. It's now time to take a closer look at exactly what pixels are, since we must control them exactly in image memory to create graphics.

Physically, images on a 2D raster display consist of a 2D, evenly spaced grid of individually controllable rectangular picture elements, called *pixels*. This grid is also called a *raster*, hence the term "raster graphics." A pixel is the smallest individually addressable visible element of an image on a raster display. In particular, "individually addressable" means "addressable by the video hardware"—in other words, a pixel is the smallest element of an image which can be controlled by the hardware.

Each pixel is the same size as other pixels, and may be assigned a color (in the case of color displays), an intensity level (in the case of gray-level displays), or an on/off status (in the case of monochrome displays). We may say that pixels are "set" or "on" if they have been assigned a visible color or intensity value. We say that pixels are "unset" or "off" if they have been assigned a color or intensity which is the same as the background color (e.g., black). Figure 2-13 illustrates a sample line drawing and its approximation on a raster display. Each shaded box represents a set pixel. Pixels can only form a discrete approximation to an image, but the finer the grid of pixels, the more accurate the image.

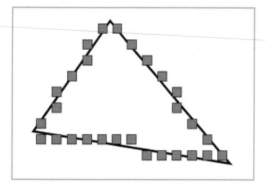

Figure 2-13: Pixels form an approximation to an image.

2D Pixel Coordinates

In general, a *coordinate system* provides a unique way of identifying *points*, or locations in space. In particular, a *2D pixel coordinate system* allows specifying physical pixel locations on the screen. (In this case, by "screen" we mean the logical display device, which for our current purposes is a window under X.) The 2D pixel coordinate system, by definition, exactly covers the number of pixels which may be displayed on the screen—no more and no less.

NOTE The term *coordinate space*, or simply *space*, describes the same concept as a coordinate system. We may thus say "a 2D pixel coordinate system," "2D pixel coordinates," "a 2D pixel coordinate space," or "2D pixel space" interchangeably.

Since computer screens and windows are flat and rectangular, being oriented in a normal upright position (as opposed to, for instance, standing on a corner), it makes sense to refer to pixels in relation to horizontal (x) and vertical (y) axes. A pixel may then be uniquely identified by its position along the x and y axes, which is written in the form of a coordinate pair (x,y). In order for a coordinate pair (x,y) to have any meaning, we must define a coordinate system which specifies how values of x and values of y should be interpreted. There are two main coordinate systems we can use for specifying pixels: 2D Cartesian coordinates and "reversed-y" coordinates.

2D Cartesian Coordinate System

The 2D Cartesian coordinate system, which you may recall from high school geometry, is illustrated in Figure 2-14. In this coordinate system, two perpendicular (or *orthogonal*) coordinate axes, the x axis and the y axis, specify horizontal and vertical positions. Values of x increase as they move towards the right, and values of y increase as they move upwards. Given a coordinate pair of the form (x,y), the corresponding pixel is found by starting at the origin, whose coordinates are (0,0), and moving x pixels horizontally and y pixels vertically. This coordinate system is a "natural" system, in that it corresponds to the "natural" way we usually measure sizes or distances. For instance, rulers (in Western cultures) are marked with digits from left to right, with the larger numbers representing larger horizontal distances appearing towards the right. This corresponds to the left-to-right ordering of values along the x axis in 2D Cartesian coordinates. Furthermore, when we speak of "height" in everyday usage, we expect that an item 10 cm "higher" than another item extends 10 cm upwards above the shorter item. This corresponds to the bottom-to-top ordering of values along the y axis in 2D Cartesian coordinates. Display systems which implement 2D Cartesian coordinates usually place point (0,0) at the lower left of the physical screen. All pixels in the display thus have coordinates in the shaded portion of the diagram.

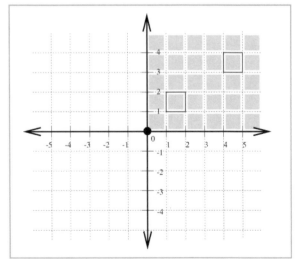

Figure 2-14: Cartesian coordinate system. Shaded area represents region visible on-screen. Pixels at (1,1) and (4,3) are highlighted.

Reversed-y or 2D Screen Coordinate System

Figure 2-15 illustrates a similar coordinate system, but with the *y* axis "reversed." That is, values of *y* increase as they move downwards, in contrast to the standard 2D Cartesian coordinate system. Values of *x* still increase as they move towards the right, just as in the normal Cartesian system. Graphics systems which implement this coordinate system usually place the point (0,0) at the upper left of the screen. All pixels in the display thus have coordinates in the shaded portion of the figure. This system is somewhat unnatural in the vertical direction, because larger values of *y*, which correspond to larger height values, grow downward, instead of upward as in standard 2D Cartesian coordinates.

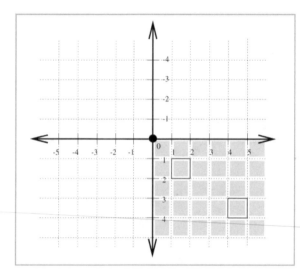

Figure 2-15: Reversed-y coordinate system. Pixels at (1,1) and (4,3) are highlighted.

The reversed-*y* coordinate system is the more commonly used system to specify pixel coordinates, and is the one we use for this book. The reason for this is mainly due to the fact that the 2D grid of pixels is often physically a linear sequence of bytes in memory representing the rows of pixels from the top down (as discussed in the next section). The "top down" ordering implies the reversal of *y* orientation. We will assume from now on when we refer to physical screen coordinates that we are using this reversed-*y* coordinate system, and we will refer to this as the 2D pixel coordinate system.

Byte-to-Pixel Correspondence

As far as we are concerned, we manipulate bytes in an off-screen buffer to control pixels; this off-screen buffer is attached to an XImage and may be displayed by calling `XPutImage`. A relevant question then is: "how do the bytes in an XImage's image data map to the actual pixels forming the image?"

NOTE The XFree86 DGA extension, which we cover briefly later in this chapter, allows direct access to the video memory as the video hardware sees it. This physical video memory is very often <u>not</u> linearly arranged. This is why we specifically phrased the question above in relation to XImage image data; in general, there is no single definitive way for mapping a set of bytes onto a set of pixels.

With an XImage in ZPixmap format, the answer is relatively simple. The 2D grid of pixels in the image is treated as a *linear sequence* of pixels, starting at the upper left-hand corner of the image, traversing all pixels from left to right in the first line, then continuing with the leftmost pixel of the second line, finally ending up at the last pixel in the lower right-hand corner of the image. Given this pixel ordering, the bytes in the image data are then mapped to the pixels in the image in this same order.

There are two complications we must consider. First, multiple bytes may map to just one pixel, and second, we must somehow interpret the bits that make up one pixel.

The first problem is that multiple bytes may map to one pixel. With 8-bit depths, we conveniently have one byte (i.e., 8 bits) per pixel, a situation which is easy to understand and implement. The problem arises with greater display depths. As with scuba diving, increased depth means more problems but also increased beauty. The greater visual quality possible with greater color depths implies that the color information for one pixel cannot be stored in one single byte, and that pixel plotting routines must deal with a variable number of bits (and thus bytes) per pixel. With a 32-bit color depth, for instance, we need 4 bytes per pixel. Figures 2-16 and 2-17 illustrate the correspondence between bytes in memory and pixels for display depths of 8 and 32 bits, respectively.

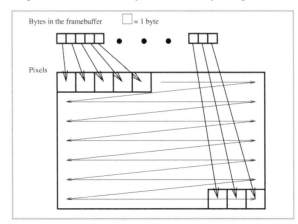

Figure 2-16: Correspondence between bits and pixels, with a depth of 8 bits per pixel.

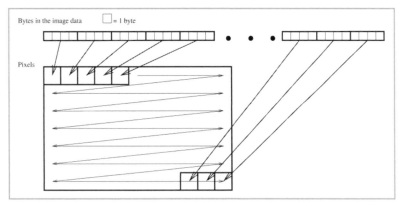

Figure 2-17: Correspondence between bits and pixels, with a depth of 32 bits per pixel.

The following formula maps a pixel location to offset image memory to the first byte associated with the pixel. Given a pixel located in row x and column y of the image:

Equation 2-1 $offset = (x + (width * y)) * bytes\_per\_pixel$

The width of the image in pixels is represented by *width*; the number of bytes per pixel, by *bytes_per_pixel* (which must be a positive integer value). This formula assumes that the leftmost row and the topmost column are labeled zero, that the x axis increases to the right, and that the y axis increases downward. These are exactly the conditions describing the 2D pixel coordinate system discussed previously. The linear arrangement of pixels, the fact that the first pixel corresponds to the upper-left corner of the image, and the use of a reversed-y pixel coordinate system yield the intuitive formula presented above. (With a Cartesian pixel coordinate system, we would need to reverse the y orientation by subtracting the y value from the image height.)

So now we know which bytes correspond to which pixels. The next question is, what data do we put into these bytes to give a pixel a certain color?

Colors and XImages

The second problem mentioned above is the interpretation of the bits making up a pixel. With the above formula and the *bytes_per_pixel*, we can figure out exactly which bytes in the image buffer correspond to a particular pixel. But what values do we assign to this byte or these bytes to make a color appear?

We actually already addressed this question earlier during our discussion of X visual classes. The visual class determines the interpretation of the bits making up each pixel.

Indexed, Colormapped, or Paletted Color

If the visual is StaticGray, GrayScale, StaticColor, or PseudoColor, then the bits of the pixel are interpreted as being an index into a colormap. As mentioned earlier, this is called indexed, colormapped, or paletted color.

There may be multiple bytes per pixel. If so, then the pixel value is obtained by interpreting all bits of all bytes in least-significant-byte first (LSBFirst) order. Expressed as a formula, this means that for all bytes of a pixel, the LSBFirst value is computed as follows:

Equation 2-2 $$final\_value = first\_byte+$$
$$256 * second\_byte+$$
$$65536 * third\_byte+$$
$$16777216 * fourth\_byte$$

With only one byte per pixel, we ignore the *second_byte*, *third_byte*, and *fourth_byte* terms; with two bytes per pixel, we ignore the *third_byte* and *fourth_byte*; with three bytes per pixel, we ignore the *fourth_byte*; with four bytes per pixel, we use all four terms.

 NOTE To be completely portable, we would theoretically have to question this byte order assumption. The ImageByteOrder macro provided by Xlib indicates whether the bits are to be interpreted LSBFirst (also called little endian) or MSBFirst (also called big endian).

However, it's a pretty safe bet that on x86-based Linux machines running XFree86, the byte order will be little endian.

The final value of each pixel is then used as an index into a colormap. The colormap is simply a table containing a specific color for each index. We need to create a colormap and fill it with colors before we can use it. Under X, the general process of creating a colormap is as follows:

1. Create a colormap with the XCreateColormap function.
2. Allocate empty color cells for the colormap with the XAllocColorCells function.
3. For each empty entry within the colormap, declare a temporary variable of type XColor, fill the XColor variable with the appropriate RGB values, and call XAllocColor and XStoreColor to enter this color into the colormap.

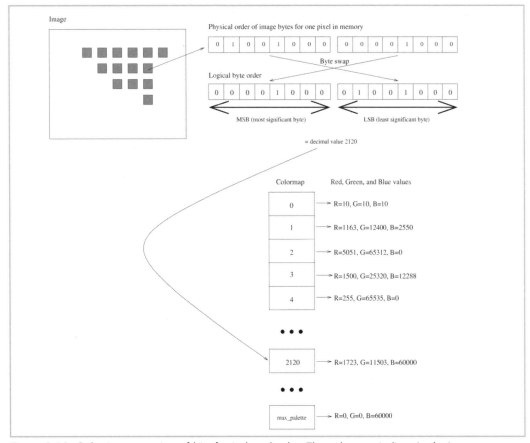

Figure 2-18: Color interpretation of bits for indexed color. The colormap indices in the image are computed by taking all bytes corresponding to one pixel and using the LSBFirst rule. These colormap indices are then looked up in the colormap to determine the final red, green, and blue color values.

 NOTE   The red, green, and blue values in the XColor structure are always specified in the range 0 (lowest intensity) to 65535 (highest intensity); the X server then scales these RGB values to the actual red, green, and blue values needed by the video hardware.

4. After initializing all entries within the colormap, assign it to your window with `XSetWindowColormap`.

The class `l3d_screen_x11`, presented in the section titled "Developing Reusable Graphics Classes," illustrates this process in source code.

TrueColor and DirectColor

For TrueColor and DirectColor visuals, the bits for each pixel are divided into red, green, and blue components. We have to determine which bits are responsible for red, green, and blue. Unfortunately, this is a rather confusing issue, because of logical and physical bit orders. Let's see how this works.

X provides the function `XMatchVisualInfo` function to find and return extra information about a particular visual. The information is returned in an `XVisualInfo` structure. For TrueColor and DirectColor visuals, the `XVisualInfo` structure contains three members of interest: `red_mask`, `green_mask`, and `blue_mask`, each of type `unsigned long`. For the matching visual structure, these fields contain the bit masks necessary to access the red part of the pixel, the green part of the pixel, and the blue part of the pixel.

The confusing part is that these masks assume a most-significant-byte first order (MSBFirst), while the XImage (on Linux x86 systems) stores the bytes in least-significant-byte first order (LSBFirst). Thus, to correctly interpret the bit masks, we have to swap the byte order.

An example will make this clear. Let's say your X server is running at 16 bits per pixel. After querying the visual with `XMatchVisualInfo`, we would obtain values such as the following:

```
red_mask = 63488
green_mask = 2016
blue_mask = 31
```

Let's see what these numbers are in binary. To do this we can use the command line calculator `bc` as follows:

1. Type **bc** and press **Enter**.
2. Notice the welcome message. Type **obase=2** and press **Enter** to set the output number base to be base 2 (binary).
3. Type **63488**, the decimal value of the red mask, and press **Enter**.
4. Notice the output 1111100000000000.
5. Type **2016**, the decimal value of the green mask, and press **Enter**.
6. Notice the output 11111100000.
7. Type **31**, the decimal value of the blue mask, and press **Enter**.
8. Notice the output 11111.
9. Press **Ctrl+D** to quit.

Notice that these bit masks define different, contiguous, non-overlapping positions of bits within the 16 bits of color depth we have available. If we denote the bits in the red mask by "r," the green mask by "g," and the blue mask by "b," we would obtain the following result:

```
r r r r r g g g g g g b b b b b
```

We have 5 bits of red resolution, 6 bits of green, and 5 bits of blue. This is often called "565 RGB." We interpret the red bits, green bits, and blue bits separately. Within the red bits, for instance, we have 5 bits and can thus specify $2^5 = 32$ shades of red, where 0 is the least intense and 31 the most. For the green bits, we can specify $2^6 = 64$ shades of green, with 0 being the least intense and 63 the most intense. Finally, for the blue bits, we again have $2^5 = 32$ shades of blue, from 0 to 31. This gives a total of $32 * 64 * 32 = 65536$ possible combinations of red, green, and blue—in other words, 65,536 possible colors.

Each section of bits is interpreted in normal binary fashion, with the leftmost bits being more significant than the rightmost bits. For instance, to specify a color with red=10, green=20, and blue=30, we would first convert these values to binary:

```
red = 10 = 1010 in binary
green = 20 = 10100 in binary
blue = 30 = 11110 in binary
```

We then fill the red bits into the 5 bits for red, the green bits in the 6 bits for green, and blue bits in the 5 bits for blue, padding each section on the left with 0s if needed:

```
r r r r r g g g g g g b b b b b
0 1 0 1 0 0 1 0 1 0 0 1 1 1 1 0
```

So far, so good. The problem is that these 16 bits of color resolution are too much to fit in one byte, so they are divided into two bytes as follows:

```
Byte 1: r r r r r g g g
Byte 2: g g g b b b b b
```

Notice that the green values have been split across a byte boundary. For our example of red=10, green=20, and blue=30, the bytes would then look as follows:

```
Byte 1: r r r r r g g g
        0 1 0 1 0 0 1 0

Byte 2: g g g b b b b b
        1 0 0 1 1 1 1 0
```

The confusing part (if you are not already confused!) is that byte 2, the least significant byte, is stored first in memory, followed by byte 1. So, in memory, the values look like this:

```
Byte 1: g g g b b b b b
        1 0 0 1 1 1 1 0

Byte 2: r r r r r g g g
        0 1 0 1 0 0 1 0
```

So, you see that the byte order in memory must be reversed in order to use the bit mask returned by XMatchVisualInfo. Whenever we write pixels to memory, we must take this byte-swapping into account. What makes the situation even more enjoyable is that each particular color depth has its own red mask, green mask, and blue mask, since the total number of color bits is different in each case.

Fortunately, we can encapsulate this rather confusing calculation once and for all within a class, so that we can then just say "draw this pixel, with this color" and be assured that the right bits get set.

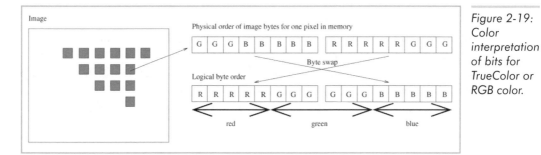

Figure 2-19:
Color
interpretation
of bits for
TrueColor or
RGB color.

Developing Reusable Graphics Classes: l3d Library

As we just saw in the preceding discussion of colors and XImages, X programming can be a bit tedious at times. Just plotting a single pixel requires us to know the image depth, the RGB masks, and whether the visual is based on an indexed or a TrueColor model. And plotting a pixel in an XImage is only the beginning. We want to develop much more advanced graphics routines—incorporating shading, texture mapping, hardware acceleration, and other interesting effects—all of which fundamentally rely upon plotting pixels in particular colors at particular locations on a screen. It is absolutely vital that we create a solid, understandable, and extendable foundation so that more advanced graphics routines don't need to worry about the infinitude of irrelevant and distracting implementation details such as window creation, event monitoring, byte swapping, RGB masks, or color depths. Without a solid foundation, we'll never be able to program advanced graphics routines; they would quickly become far too complicated if they had to take care of every single implementation detail themselves.

Starting now, we will therefore be developing some library classes which encapsulate all of the graphics concepts we have discussed so far and which will be useful throughout the rest of this book. In fact, these classes are useful beyond the scope of this book, since good object-oriented designs yield classes which can be used in a variety of situations.

NOTE Recall at the beginning of this chapter we said that we would first look at Xlib programming, then abstract the Xlib concepts into a more general framework. This more general framework is the l3d library presented and used in the following sections.

If you've cast even a fleeting glance at the sample code, you will have noticed that all of the classes so far have begun with the prefix ch2_. This indicates that these classes, while very possibly being reused within the current chapter, are generally illustrative in nature and are not completely fit as is for general-purpose use. The library classes, in contrast to the chapter-specific classes, all begin with the prefix l3d_, which stands for "library 3d."

The developed l3d classes strictly separate the abstraction (plotting a pixel) from the implementation (setting particular bits in an XImage using RGB masks obtained from an XVisualInfo structure). As you have probably guessed, this is accomplished through use of an abstract class specifying the abstraction, and a concrete class for the X implementation. A different derived, concrete class can implement the same abstraction using hardware acceleration (illustrated in Chapter 3) or a different operating system (discussed in the Appendix).

Sample Program Using l3d

Before looking at the l3d code itself, let's first look at a sample program which uses l3d. This will give you a practical perspective on the code before looking at the following sections, which go into more detail on the inner workings of the classes. For the most part, the library classes don't introduce many new ideas; we have already covered most of the important technical issues related to 2D programming under X and Linux.

The next sample program is called `drawdot` and illustrates usage of the l3d library classes in order to move a green dot around the screen, thereby forming a simple drawing program. Significantly, this is the first program where we draw a pixel at a specific location and with a specific color. This program works with visuals of any color depth and in both TrueColor or indexed color modes. This is no mean feat—as we saw earlier, calculation of pixel position and pixel contents is all quite complicated due to the multitude of possible color depths and color models. These complicated calculations have all been encapsulated in easy-to-use classes. Incidentally, as we see later, the program not only works with "normal" X windows, but also can use shared-memory or hardware-accelerated output devices.

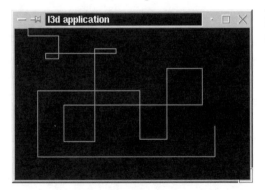

Figure 2-20: Output from sample program drawdot.

Listing 2-23: `drawdot.cc`

```
#include <stdlib.h>
#include <stdio.h>

#include "../lib/tool_2d/screen.h"
#include "../lib/tool_os/dispatch.h"
#include "../lib/raster/rasteriz.h"
#include "../lib/tool_2d/scrinfo.h"
#include "../lib/system/factorys.h"


//————————————————————————————
//-
//- STEP 1: CHOOSE THE FACTORIES
//-
```

```
//————————————————————

void choose_factories(void) {
  factory_manager_v_0_1.choose_factories();
}

//————————————————————
//-
//- STEP 2: DECLARE A PIPELINE SUBCLASS
//-
//————————————————————

class my_pipeline : public l3d_pipeline {
  protected:
    l3d_rasterizer_2d_imp *ri;
    l3d_rasterizer_2d *r;

    int x, y, dx, dy;
    unsigned long color;

  public:
    l3d_screen *s;
    my_pipeline(void);
    virtual ~my_pipeline(void);

    void key_event(int ch);   //- from dispatcher
    void update_event(void);  //- from dispatcher
    void draw_event(void);    //- from dispatcher
};

my_pipeline::my_pipeline(void) {
  s = factory_manager_v_0_1.screen_factory->create(320,200);
  ri = factory_manager_v_0_1.ras_2d_imp_factory->create(320,200,s->sinfo);
  r = new l3d_rasterizer_2d(ri);

  s->sinfo->ext_max_red =
    s->sinfo->ext_max_green =
      s->sinfo->ext_max_blue = 255;

  s->sinfo->ext_to_native(0, 0, 0); //- allocate background color
  color = s->sinfo->ext_to_native(0, 255, 128);
  s->refresh_palette();

  x = y = dx = dy = 0;
}

my_pipeline::~my_pipeline(void) {
  delete s;
  delete ri;
  delete r;
}

void my_pipeline::key_event(int ch) {
  switch(ch) {
    case 'h': dx=-1; dy=0; break;
    case 'l': dx=1; dy=0; break;
    case 'j': dx=0; dy=1; break;
    case 'k': dx=0; dy=-1; break;
    case ' ': dx=0;dy=0; break;
    case 'q': {
```

```
        exit(0);
      }
  }
}

void my_pipeline::update_event() {
  x += dx;
  y += dy;

  if(x < 0) x = 0;
  if(x > s->xsize-1) x = s->xsize-1;
  if(y < 0) y = 0;
  if(y > s->ysize-1) y = s->ysize-1;
}

void my_pipeline::draw_event(void) {
  r->draw_point(x,y, color);
  s->blit_screen();
}

main() {
  choose_factories();

  l3d_dispatcher *d;
  my_pipeline *p;

  //——————————————————————————
  //-
  //- STEP 3: CREATE A DISPATCHER
  //-
  //——————————————————————————

  d = factory_manager_v_0_1.dispatcher_factory->create();

  //——————————————————————————
  //-
  //- STEP 4: CREATE A PIPELINE
  //-
  //——————————————————————————

  //- plug our custom behavior pipeline into the dispatcher
  p  = new my_pipeline();

  //——————————————————————————
  //-
  //- STEP 5: START DISPATCHER
  //-
  //——————————————————————————

  d->pipeline = p; //- polymorphic assignment
  d->event_source = p->s;
  d->start();

  delete d;
  delete p;
}
```

 NOTE Notice that this program is rather short and declares only one class. This is because the l3d library has already declared several useful classes to simplify application programs.

First, let's look at compiling the program, since the programs using l3d have a slightly different directory structure. Then, we look at the structure program itself. Finally, we discuss the l3d classes themselves.

The source code for the sample program is located in directory `$L3D/source/app/drawdot`. In contrast to the other sample programs we have seen so far, the source and binary files are located in different directory trees. The next section discusses this in detail. For now, compile and run the program as follows:

1. Compile the l3d library: type **cd $L3D/source/app/lib**, press **Enter**, type **make -f makeall.lnx**, and press **Enter**. Notice that this Makefile has a different filename than the standard name of "`Makefile`"; therefore we specify the `-f` flag to tell the `make` command which file is the Makefile.

2. Change to the source directory for `drawdot`: type **cd $L3D/source/app/drawdot** and press **Enter**. Compile `drawdot`: type **make -f makeall.lnx** and press **Enter**.

3. Change to the binaries directory: type **cd $L3D/binaries/linux_x/float/app/drawdot** and press **Enter**.

4. Notice the object and executable files from the compilation process are placed in the corresponding binary directory. Type **drawdot** and press **Enter** to run the program.

5. Notice the question, "which configuration?" Type **1** for now to select a normal X11 window, and press **Enter**.

6. Notice the empty, black window which appears. Type **l**. Notice the green line which moves from left to right across the very top of the display, and that the line continues moving after you release the key.

7. Type **j**. Notice that the green line moves downward.

8. Control the movement of the line with the following keys: **h** to move left, **l** to move right, **j** to move down, **k** to move up, and **Space** to stop movement.

9. Type **q** to end the program.

Having now successfully executed the program, let's now take a look at the organization of the l3d directory structure, then examine the `drawdot` program itself.

l3d Directory Structure

The library classes and the applications using them follow a different directory structure than that of the sample programs we have looked at so far. Up until now, the source and binary files for the programs were in the same directory. By contrast, the library classes and applications using the library classes are split into separate source and binary directory trees.

The reason we split the source files and binary files into two separate trees is that the same source code can be compiled on a number of different platforms. Keeping the binary files, which vary from platform to platform, in the same directory as the source files, which remain the same, leads to a rather chaotic organization. While chaos theory is a rich and fascinating field of scientific study, we don't necessarily want to organize our directory structure on this basis. Splitting source and binary directories allows for a neater multi-platform directory structure.

Specifically, the following directory structure is used:

- $L3D/source$: All source files.
- $L3D/source/util$: Non-C++ source files (preprocessing scripts, etc.).
- $L3D/source/app$: C++ source files related directly to 3D applications.
- $L3D/source/app/lib$: C++ source for the l3d library classes.
- $L3D/source/app/[program\_name]$: C++ source for example programs. A few simple programs (such as the ones we have seen until now) place the binary files in the source directory, but most programs place them in the binaries directory.
- $L3D/binaries/linux\_x$: Linux binary files compiled for the X Window System.
- $L3D/binaries/linux\_x/fixed$: Linux binary files compiled with fixed-point math (a topic covered in more detail in the Appendix). Subdirectory structure is the same as that under the float subdirectory.
- $L3D/binaries/linux\_x/float$: Linux binary files compiled with floating-point math. This is the primary output directory for binary files.
- $L3D/binaries/linux\_x/float/app/lib$: Linux floating-point binary files for the l3d library.
- $L3D/binaries/linux\_x/float/app/[program\ name]$: Linux floating-point binary files for example programs.

The Makefiles automatically place the binary files in the corresponding binary directory. You typically invoke **make -f makeall.lnx** in the source directory for an application program, which then compiles all of the Linux binaries and places them in the appropriate binaries directories.

NOTE Remember, the Appendix provides instructions on how to compile all of the sample programs at once. The preceding discussion is primarily to give you an idea of the directory structure and the reasoning behind it.

To summarize, then, the source files for the l3d library are in $L3D/source/app/lib$, and the source files for the sample programs are all in $L3D/source/app$. The primary binaries are in $L3D/binaries/linux\_x/float/app$.

Fundamental l3d Concepts

Let's now turn our attention to the exact workings of the drawdot program, since it illustrates compactly many key ideas of the l3d library.

The drawdot program can be broken up into five steps, which are representative of programming with l3d. In fact, these steps are representative of event-based programming in general, on a variety of platforms, as evidenced by the fact that the following scheme also can be applied to event-driven programs under various operating systems.

The five steps are as follows.

1. *Choose the proper factories* for three classes: the screen, the rasterizer implementation, and the event dispatcher.
2. *Declare a pipeline subclass.* The pipeline must directly or indirectly ask the factory to create a screen and a rasterizer implementation (typically in the pipeline constructor). Override the

abstract pipeline methods to allow your program to respond to events, to update itself, and to draw to the screen using the rasterizer implementation.

3. *Create a dispatcher*, by using the factory.

4. *Create a pipeline.* Your pipeline should in its constructor ask the factory to create a screen and a rasterizer implementation, and store these objects locally. Connect the pipeline and the screen to the dispatcher.

5. *Start the dispatcher.* The dispatcher enters an event loop, extracts events from the screen, and calls your pipeline periodically to allow your pipeline to do its work, respond to input, and draw to the screen.

Let's examine each step in detail to understand the general l3d structure within the context of the sample `drawdot` program. This serves two goals: first, to understand the general l3d structure, and second, to understand the specific functions called by `drawdot` in order to draw to the screen. Then, we will take a look at the l3d classes themselves, which we build upon throughout the book to incorporate increasingly advanced and reusable 3D graphics concepts.

Step 1. Choose the Proper Factories

The first step in writing an l3d application is to choose the proper factories for the program. This is done by calling the `choose_factories` function defined in the so-called "factory manager." We encountered this concept earlier: to localize object creation and free applications from needing to know specific details of concrete classes, we used the factory design pattern. The factory manager is the central location where all concrete factories, globally visible to the entire program, are accessible. The following line chooses the factories within the factory manager:

```
factory_manager_v_0_1.choose_factories();
```

 NOTE The class name has the suffix `v_0_1` to represent the fact that this is the first version of the factory manager. In a later chapter, we subclass this first version of the factory manager to create a new factory manager which manages more factories. This is an example of how subclassing can provide a historical record of program development, within the source code itself.

Choosing the factories essentially means customizing, at run time, all customizable behavior which then takes effect for the duration of the program. In particular, the l3d factory manager manages three factories:

1. A screen factory, producing objects corresponding to the abstract interface `l3d_screen`. Class `l3d_screen` represents the physical output device—a window under X11, a full-screen hardware-accelerated window using Mesa, or even a DIBSection under Microsoft Windows.

2. A rasterizer implementation factory, producing objects corresponding to the abstract interface `l3d_rasterizer_2d_imp`. Class `l3d_rasterizer_2d_imp` represents a particular implementation of 2D *rasterization* concepts. We use the term "rasterizer" to denote a software interface to a rasterizer implementation. A rasterizer implementation, then, is a particular hardware or software component which draws 2D graphics primitives (triangles, lines, dots) into a frame buffer. Two important types of rasterizer implementations

are software rasterizer implementations, which write directly into an off-screen buffer, and hardware rasterizer implementations, which use specialized, faster functions for hardware-accelerated pixel operations. See Chapter 3 for details on rasterization.

3. A dispatcher factory, producing objects corresponding to the abstract interface l3d_dispatcher. Class l3d_dispatcher represents a generalized event dispatcher in a particular operating system environment. Under X, the dispatcher intercepts X events within a window's event loop and passes them on transparently to our application. Using hardware acceleration with Mesa, the dispatcher works within the event framework provided by Mesa and GLUT, again forwarding events in a transparent way to our application. Under another operating system, the dispatcher would need to call any OS-specific routines necessary to capture and forward events.

All of these factories represent system-specific information: the output device, the rasterizer implementation, and the event dispatcher. Therefore, by choosing the factories, we are essentially dynamically configuring the program to use the desired run-time environment. In our case, the factory manager simply asks the user which factories should be used, but more sophisticated solutions are also possible. We could, for instance, have an auto-detect routine which searches for the existence of particular hardware, and which, depending on whether or not it finds it, configures the factory to create the appropriate software component accordingly.

Step 2. Declare a Pipeline Subclass

The second step in writing an l3d application is to declare a pipeline subclass. A *pipeline* is simply a sequence of operations on data. The main loop in a game or graphics program is typically called the pipeline. Therefore, the pipeline contains, directly or indirectly, your application's main data and functionality.

We say "directly or indirectly" because the pipeline might do nothing other than create another object, to which it then delegates the main program's responsibility. In such a case, the pipeline is not directly responsible for the application's data and functionality, but instead merely serves as an interface between the dispatcher and the object actually doing the real work. We see this in Chapter 7, where an l3d_world class manages an entire 3D world.

The pipeline does not <u>control</u> execution of the program. Instead, it <u>responds</u> to events. The abstract l3d_pipeline class provides a set of virtual event functions, which are automatically called by an event dispatcher (class l3d_dispatcher, covered in the next section). By declaring a subclass of l3d_pipeline, you can override the virtual event functions to provide specific responses to specific events, without needing to know how or when these functions are invoked.

In particular, an l3d_pipeline subclass should do three things:

1. Directly or indirectly create and store a screen object, a rasterizer implementation object, and a rasterizer object. This is typically done in the constructor. The first two objects, the screen and rasterizer implementation, must be created by using the already chosen factories. The third object, the rasterizer itself, is directly created via the C++ operator new, since the rasterizer itself contains no platform-specific dependencies. (Such dependencies are all in the rasterizer implementation, not the rasterizer.)

2. Declare internal variables, functions, and objects to store the current state of the virtual world.

3. Override the `l3d_pipeline` virtual event functions to handle input, update internal objects, and draw output to the screen. Handling input and updating internal objects are both done by using data structures specific to the application program. Drawing output to the screen is done by using the screen, rasterizer, and rasterizer implementation objects created in the constructor.

The first responsibility of an `l3d_pipeline` subclass is easy to understand. The pipeline represents the application. The application should display interactive graphics on the screen. We therefore create and store a screen object, representing the output device, and a rasterizer implementation, representing a strategy for drawing graphics to the screen. The rasterizer itself presents a high-level interface to rasterization functionality, implemented by the low-level tools offered by a rasterizer implementation. Again, remember that a rasterizer implementation can be either a software rasterizer implementation, directly manipulating bytes in an off-screen frame buffer, or a hardware rasterizer implementation, calling hardware API functions to instruct the hardware to draw the graphics for us. Therefore, through the rasterizer, rasterizer implementation, and screen, our program has an interface to screen and screen-drawing functionality.

NOTE Theoretically, the screen object could also be created outside of the pipeline. (The following discussion also applies to the rasterizer and rasterizer implementation objects.) There is no technical reason why the screen absolutely must be created within the pipeline constructor. In practice, though, this would make little sense. Consider this: the pipeline represents the entire application logic. Creating a screen outside of the pipeline would also mean needing to destroy the screen outside of the pipeline. This would imply some sort of a "higher-level" layer of functionality which creates and destroys objects the pipeline needs in order to function. This would only make sense if the screen object often needed to be used outside of the context of the pipeline, at this "higher-level" layer. Given the current premise that the pipeline is the application, a higher-level layer makes no sense. Therefore, in the current architecture, there is no reason to move management of the screen object outside of the pipeline.

The second responsibility of an `l3d_pipeline` subclass, declaring data, is also intuitive. Since it represents the application, the pipeline subclass must contain all data necessary for maintaining and updating the current state of everything within the virtual world. This might include such things as the current positions and velocities for objects of interest, energy levels for spaceships, the prevailing wind velocity, or anything else being modeled. All of this data is stored within the `l3d_pipeline` subclass in the form of member variables or objects.

The third and final responsibility of an `l3d_pipeline` subclass is to override virtual event functions to respond to events. An `l3d_pipeline` subclass can override any of the following virtual functions declared in `l3d_pipeline`:

```
void key_event(int ch); //- from dispatcher
void update_event(void); //- from dispatcher
void draw_event(void);   //- from dispatcher
```

The `key_event` function is automatically called whenever a key is pressed in the application window. The function is called with a parameter indicating the ASCII value of the key pressed, thereby allowing the application to respond to the particular key pressed.

The `update_event` function is automatically called whenever the application is allowed to update itself. You can think of your program as being a giant clockwork, with everything happening at each tick of the clock. This event function represents one "tick" in your program. At this point you update the internal variables storing the positions of various objects, update velocities, check for collisions, and so on.

 TIP The calling frequency of `update_event` is not necessarily guaranteed to be constant. That is to say, the amount of physical time which elapses between successive calls may be slightly different. For accurate physical simulations, where velocities or other physical quantities should be updated based on time, we can store an internal variable recording the value of the system clock the last time that `update_event` was called. We can then compare the current system clock to the value of the variable to determine how much physical time has elapsed, and update the time-dependent quantities accordingly. The companion book *Advanced Linux 3D Graphics Programming* contains examples of this sort of code.

The `draw_event` function is called whenever the application is allowed to draw its output to the screen. This function typically will be called immediately after `update_event`, but this does not necessarily have to be the case. In other words, the updating of the virtual world and the drawing of the virtual world can be thought of as two separate threads of control, which are usually but not necessarily synchronized.

With this general understanding of a pipeline's structure (creation of screen, storage of variables, and response to events), we can take a closer look at the particular details of the pipeline in the `drawdot` program.

The constructor for the `drawdot` pipeline takes care of the first responsibility of an `l3d_pipeline` subclass: creation of screen, rasterizer implementation, and rasterizer objects. In the constructor, we first ask the screen factory to create a screen and the rasterizer implementation factory to create a rasterizer implementation. We then create a rasterizer which uses the created rasterizer implementation. The member variables `s`, `ri`, and `r` represent the screen, rasterizer implementation, and rasterizer, respectively.

The constructor also takes care of the second responsibility of an `l3d_pipeline` subclass: management of data representing our virtual world. In our case, our virtual world consists of a single pixel (a humble start). The following member variables are declared and initialized to keep track of the dot's status: `color`, `x`, `y`, `dx`, and `dy`. Variables `x`, `y`, `dx`, and `dy` represent the dot's current horizontal and vertical positions and velocities, and are all initialized to zero. The variable `color` represents the dot's current color, and is specified as follows. First, we logically define the maximum red, green, and blue values to be 255. Then, we specify a color of (0, 255, 128), which means a red intensity of 0, a green intensity of 255, and a blue intensity of 128, all being measured in relation to the logical maximum of 255 which we just set. Finally, we convert this RGB color to a "native" color appropriate for the current screen's color depth and color model. The conversion is done via an object of type `l3d_screen_info`, which encapsulates the complicated color calculation discussed earlier. The color conversion function is called `ext_to_native`, as it changes a color from an "external" RGB format into a format "native" to the XImage.

The `drawdot` pipeline then overrides the `key_event`, `update_event`, and `draw_event` methods to respond to events. This fulfills the third and final responsibility of an `l3d_pipeline` subclass, responding to events.

The `key_event` for the `drawdot` pipeline checks if any one of the directional keys was pressed, and updates the `dx` and `dy` variables, representing the horizontal and vertical velocities, accordingly.

The `update_event` for the `drawdot` pipeline adds the velocities to the positional variables, and makes sure the position stays within the bounds of the screen. In other words, $x \mathrel{+}= dx$ and $y \mathrel{+}= dy$.

The `draw_event` for the `drawdot` pipeline first calls the `draw_point` routine of the rasterizer, which then forwards the request to the rasterizer implementation to draw a pixel at a particular point in a particular color. Remember that the drawing occurs off-screen (double buffering). The pixel color must be specified in "native" format for the current color depth and color model. We already computed and stored this color earlier by using the function `l3d_screen_info::ext_to_native`. After plotting the point, we call `blit_screen` to cause the off-screen graphics to be copied to the screen.

Let us summarize the main idea behind the pipeline. A pipeline represents the main functionality of an application and is subclassed from `l3d_pipeline`. An `l3d_pipeline` subclass has three responsibilities: creating screen-access objects, declaring world data, and responding to events. Creating screen-access objects (screen, rasterizer implementation, and rasterizer) allows access to the screen and screen-drawing functions. Declaring world data allows the program to keep track of the state of all objects in the virtual world. Responding to events is how the pipeline responds to input (through `key_event`), updates the virtual world (through `update_event`), and draws to the screen (through `draw_event`, using the previously created screen-access objects).

The pipeline does not need to worry about how or when events occur; it merely responds to them. The pipeline's virtual event functions are thus called from an outside source. This outside source is the *dispatcher*.

Step 3. Create a Dispatcher

The third step in writing an l3d application is to create an event dispatcher object. The event dispatcher serves as an interface between an event source and an event receiver. The event receiver in our case is the pipeline. The event source is a window created under a specific event-driven windowing system. The role of the dispatcher is to receive events from the system-specific window, and to call the appropriate pipeline functions to allow the pipeline to respond to the events.

The whole idea is to isolate the pipeline (i.e., your application logic) from the details of the underlying event generating mechanism. This way, the pipeline's logic can focus exclusively on application-specific responses to events, without needing to know exactly how the windowing system generates and transmits events. The dispatcher handles all the messy details of event capturing and translates this into a clean, simple, virtual function call to the pipeline. This allows your pipeline to work on a variety of platforms, with a variety of event generating mechanisms.

The event dispatcher must be created using the factory chosen in step 1. This is because the dispatcher represents system-specific code, and should thus be created through an abstract factory.

Step 4. Create a Pipeline

The fourth step in creating an l3d application is to create your pipeline object. This step is easy. Having already declared and defined an `l3d_pipeline` subclass, which fulfills the three pipeline responsibilities (creating screen-access objects, declaring world data, and overriding event-handling functions), we simply create the pipeline directly with the C++ `new` operator. This in turn invokes the pipeline's constructor, which creates the screen, rasterizer implementation, and rasterizer objects.

At this point, the application is ready to respond to events. We just need to pump events to the pipeline in order to allow it to respond to input, update itself internally, and draw to the screen. To start the entire event process, we start the dispatcher.

Step 5. Start the Dispatcher

The fifth step in writing an l3d application is to start the dispatcher. We must do three things:

1. Assign a pipeline to the dispatcher.
2. Assign an event source to the dispatcher.
3. Call `start`.

A moment's reflection makes it clear why the two assignments are necessary. The dispatcher takes events from the event source, interprets them minimally, and calls the appropriate pipeline virtual event function to allow the pipeline to respond. The `pipeline` member of the dispatcher object is set to the pipeline which we just created. The `event_source` member of the dispatcher object is set to the screen object created in the pipeline's constructor—in other words, the screen (in our case the X window) is the source of events. With these two member variables set, the dispatcher can then begin to extract events from `event_source` and pass them on to `pipeline`—a process set in motion by calling `start`.

Summary of Fundamental l3d Concepts

The five-step process presented above is typical of l3d programs. First, you choose the proper factories to configure the program to its environment. Then, you declare a pipeline representing your application and its data. You create an instance of the pipeline, which in turn creates screen, rasterizer implementation, and rasterizer objects. You "plug in" this pipeline into an event dispatcher. Your application pipeline responds to events from the dispatcher by filling in the blanks left by the virtual functions `key_event`, `update_event`, and `draw_event`. The application pipeline draws to the screen by using the screen, rasterizer implementation, and rasterizer objects it created within its constructor. This forms a complete, interactive, event-driven, hardware-independent graphics program.

Having understood the sample l3d program, we are now ready to look at the specific l3d classes in a bit more detail.

Overview of l3d Classes

Let us first consider, at a very high level, the roles of the l3d library classes we are about to discuss in the following sections. This overview will help keep the class descriptions, found in the following sections, in perspective. Again, the classes do not really introduce any concepts we have not already covered. They do, however, reorganize the concepts into general, reusable, abstract classes.

The main application is subclassed from `l3d_pipeline`. The `l3d_dispatcher` takes events from an `l3d_event_source` and automatically calls the appropriate event-handling routines in `l3d_pipeline`. Class `l3d_dispatcher_x11` is the X specific dispatcher.

Class `l3d_screen` is subclassed from `l3d_event_source`, and represents an output device into which an `l3d_rasterizer_2d_imp` (next paragraph) can draw. The screen, under this model, must also be able to provide event notification to other objects, which is the role of the parent class `l3d_event_source`. Class `l3d_screen_x11` is a screen under X, in the form of an X window with an `XImage` in it.

Class `l3d_rasterizer_2d` represents a high-level interface to 2D rasterization concepts; class `l3d_rasterizer_2d_imp` represents a low-level implementation of 2D rasterization functions using either software or hardware. Class `l3d_rasterizer_2d` uses `l3d_rasterizer_2d_imp` to do its work. Class `l3d_rasterizer_2d_sw_imp` is a software rasterizer implementation.

Class `l3d_screen_info` provides the rasterizer implementation with information about the screen which is necessary in order to perform rasterization. The `ext_to_native` function transparently converts arbitrary RGB colors into the native bit format required by the screen—regardless of the color depth and color model. The `light_native` and `fog_native` methods apply a light or a fog factor to a particular color in native format, altering the color appropriately. Class `l3d_screen_info_rgb` handles information about screens based upon a direct RGB color specification, while class `l3d_screen_info_indexed` handles information about screens based upon an indexed color model. Class `l3d_screen_info_indexed` also manages a palette of RGB colors, which is simply a dynamically allocated array containing entries of type `l3d_rgb`.

Class `l3d_factory_manager_v_0_1` is the factory manager which centrally manages all factories for the entire program. One global instance of this class is automatically created, with the name `factory_manager_v_0_1`. An application chooses its factories through variable `factory_manager_v_0_1`.

An X application using l3d will follow the five-step process illustrated by `drawdot`: choose factories, declare pipeline subclass, create dispatcher, create pipeline, start dispatcher. The factories are chosen by calling `factory_manager_v_0_1.choose_factories`. For now, the chosen factories will be of types `l3d_dispatcher_factory_x11`, `l3d_screen_factory_x11`, and `l3d_rasterizer_2d_sw_imp_factory`. This means that the dispatcher (`l3d_dispatcher_x11` knows how to handle X events, and that the screen (`l3d_screen_x11`) knows how to communicate with and display XImages on the X server. Drawing into the XImage's off-screen buffer is done by using a 2D, software rasterizer implementation (`l3d_rasterizer_2d_sw_imp`).

NOTE Later, we see how to use hardware-accelerated rasterizer implementations and shared memory screen factories. So, the preceding paragraph is not a hard-and-fast rule dictating which classes will always be used by an X application using l3d; it merely illustrates a typical structure based on the concepts we have seen so far.

Source Code Walk-through of l3d Classes

With the preceding overview of the l3d classes we are about to cover, we can now dive head-first into the source code of the classes themselves. Remember, you have already seen everything which is about to be presented, just in a less general form.

The following sections describe in detail each l3d class we use in this chapter. We first describe the general type of data represented by the class, and mention where we first encountered the concept within our previous discussions. Then we list the meaning of each member variable and function within the class. Each class is presented with its complete source code. When several classes work together, a class diagram is presented after the description of the last class, illustrating the relationships among the classes. At the end, a class diagram is presented for all l3d classes discussed so far.

When reading the following sections, you may find it useful to refer to the preceding overview of the l3d classes and to the concluding class diagram to keep everything in perspective.

Abstracting an Event-Driven Graphics Application: l3d_Pipeline

The class `l3d_pipeline` is an abstract class representing your application. As we saw earlier, you subclass from `l3d_pipeline` to create your application, and must fulfill three responsibilities: creating the screen-access objects, declaring world data, and responding to events.

We first saw this concept in the sample program `hello_oo`, which used an abstract application class.

Member variable `done` is a flag indicating that the pipeline has finished its processing completely; in other words, the application should exit. This variable is initially set to zero, and is typically set to one somewhere within `key_event` as a response to the user pressing some key to exit the application pipeline. This variable's value is checked by the event dispatcher object.

Listing 2-24: `pipeline.h`

```
#ifndef __PIPELINE_H
#define __PIPELINE_H
#include "../tool_os/memman.h"

class l3d_pipeline {
  public:
    int done;
    l3d_pipeline(void) {done = 0; }
    virtual void draw_event(void) {};
    virtual void update_event(void) {};
    virtual void key_event(int c) {};
};

#endif
```

Abstracting Event Generation: l3d_Event_Source

Class l3d_event_source is an empty class whose sole purpose is to indicate that any class derived from this class is capable of serving as an event source for an l3d_dispatcher object. A class will inherit, possibly multiply inherit, from l3d_event_source if it is usable as a source of events. Class l3d_screen inherits from l3d_event_source.

We first saw this concept in the sample program hello_oo, which directly monitored the X window to check for events (in ask_to_be_notified_of_interesting_events and event_loop). Class l3d_event_source is a recognition of the more general concept of any object—not just an X window—capable of generating events which need to be monitored.

Listing 2-25: ev_src.h

```
#ifndef __EV_SRC_H
#define __EV_SRC_H
#include "../tool_os/memman.h"

class l3d_event_source {
};


#endif
```

Abstracting the Event Dispatching Loop: l3d_Dispatcher

The class l3d_dispatcher is an abstract class representing an event dispatching mechanism. It extracts events from an underlying event generating mechanism and translates these into virtual function calls on a pipeline, thereby allowing the pipeline to respond to events.

We first saw this concept in program hello_oo, which directly had a loop in the main application class which extracted and dispatched events from an X window (in the overridden function event_loop). Class l3d_dispatcher is a recognition of the more general concept of an event dispatching mechanism, which can be subclassed to provide support for event dispatching on a variety of platforms other than Linux and X (e.g., Linux and Mesa, or Microsoft Windows and a Windows window). This is an example of the *strategy design pattern*, in which an algorithm (in this case the event loop) is turned into a class of its own; this allows more flexibility than the approach originally taken in hello_oo, where a virtual function had to be overridden to define the event dispatching strategy. A virtual function approach requires a new application subclass if the event dispatching strategy changes (the inheritance relationship); a strategy approach simply requires connecting the unchanged application subclass with a new event dispatching strategy (the client relationship).

Listing 2-26: dispatch.h

```
#ifndef _DISPATCH_H
#define _DISPATCH_H
#include "../tool_os/memman.h"

#include "../tool_2d/screen.h"
#include "../pipeline/pipeline.h"
#include "ev_src.h"

class l3d_dispatcher {
  public:
```

```
    l3d_pipeline *pipeline;
    l3d_event_source *event_source;

    virtual void start(void) = 0;
};

class l3d_dispatcher_factory {
  public:
    virtual l3d_dispatcher *create(void) = 0;
};

#endif
```

The variable `pipeline` points to the pipeline which should be called when particular events occur.

The variable `event_source` points to the object which generates events in a system-specific way. In our case, `event_source` is an `l3d_screen` object.

The method `start` sets the event loop in motion, calling the appropriate pipeline virtual functions when relevant events from the `event_source` occur.

Figure 2-21 illustrates the relationship among the abstract classes `l3d_pipeline`, `l3d_dispatcher`, and `l3d_event_source`.

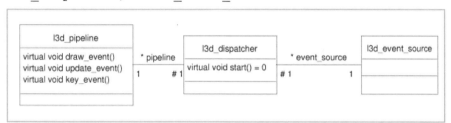

Figure 2-21: Class diagram for event-related classes.

A Dispatcher for X: l3d_Dispatcher_X11

The class `l3d_dispatcher_x11`, subclassed from `l3d_dispatcher`, represents a dispatcher specific to the X Window System.

As with the parent class `l3d_dispatcher`, we first saw this concept in program `hello_oo`.

Listing 2-27: `dis_x11.h`

```
#ifndef _DIS_X11_H
#define _DIS_X11_H
#include "../tool_os/memman.h"

#include <X11/Intrinsic.h>
#include <X11/Xlib.h>
#include "dispatch.h"
#include "../tool_2d/sc_x11.h"

class l3d_dispatcher_x11 : public l3d_dispatcher {
  public:
    void start(void);
};

class l3d_dispatcher_factory_x11 : public l3d_dispatcher_factory {
```

```
    public:
      l3d_dispatcher *create(void) {
        return new l3d_dispatcher_x11;
      }
};

#endif
```

Listing 2-28: `dis_x11.cc`

```
#include "dis_x11.h"
#include "../tool_os/memman.h"

void l3d_dispatcher_x11::start(void) {
  XEvent event;
  char ch;
  KeySym keysym;
  XComposeStatus xcompstat;
  l3d_screen_x11 *screen;

  screen = (l3d_screen_x11 *)event_source;
  {
    while(!pipeline->done) {
      if(XCheckWindowEvent(screen->dpy,screen->w,KeyPressMask,&event)) {
        XLookupString(&event.xkey, &ch, 1, &keysym, &xcompstat);
        pipeline->key_event(ch);
      }

      pipeline->update_event();
      pipeline->draw_event();
      XSync(screen->dpy, False);
    }
  }
}
```

The method `start` is overridden and interprets the `event_source` as an object of type `l3d_screen_x11`. It extracts the display and window variables from the X11 screen, checks for keyboard events with `XCheckWindowEvent`, and translates these into a virtual function call on the pipeline. It also immediately calls `update_event` and `draw_event` on the pipeline for every iteration through the event loop, meaning that these events occur as quickly as the operating system allows. Finally, we call `XSync` to make sure that the output is really displayed to the screen; otherwise, the X server might queue up events, including display requests, causing an indeterminate delay before the output is actually visible within the X window. Calling `XSync` guarantees that the output is immediately visible.

Abstracting Control of the Screen: l3d_Screen

The classes `l3d_screen` and `l3d_screen_info` work closely together to control and provide access to the display hardware.

The class `l3d_screen` is an abstract interface to a display device. A screen is responsible for the creation, setup, and display of the data which has been plotted to the screen. However, the screen is not responsible for doing the plotting itself. In other words, the screen is a "dumb" display device. It can show itself, initialize a color palette, and so forth, but it does not know how to draw polygons, lines, dots, or anything else. The screen is simply a passive display device which other objects can use as a target to draw into. In particular, the `l3d_rasterizer` class handles plotting (rasterization) tasks, manipulating data within the screen.

We first saw this concept in program `hello_oo_image`, which directly used an XImage as a screen to display a random pattern of dots. Class `l3d_screen` is a recognition of the more general concept of a screen as a generalized output device—not just an X Window with an XImage. The application program uses a screen through the abstract `l3d_screen` interface, and is therefore not tied to any particular display device.

Listing 2-29: `screen.h`

```
#ifndef __SCREEN_H
#define __SCREEN_H
#include "../tool_os/memman.h"

#include "../geom/polygon/polygon.h"
#include "si_rgb.h"
#include "si_idx.h"
#include "../tool_os/ev_src.h"

class l3d_screen : public l3d_event_source {
  protected:
  virtual void wait_vtrace(void) {};
    virtual void close_screen(void) {};
    l3d_two_part_list<l3d_coordinate> *vwin_vlist;
    int bufsize;
  public:
    l3d_screen(int xsize, int ysize);
    virtual ~l3d_screen(void);
    int xsize, ysize;
    l3d_polygon_2d *view_win;
    l3d_screen_info *sinfo;

    virtual void refresh_palette(void) {};
    virtual void open_screen(void)=0;
    virtual void blit_screen(void)=0;
};

class l3d_screen_factory {
  public:
    virtual l3d_screen *create(int xsize, int ysize)=0;
};

#endif
```

Listing 2-30: `screen.cc`

```
#include <stdlib.h>
#include "screen.h"
#include "../tool_os/memman.h"

l3d_screen::l3d_screen(int xsize, int ysize) {

  this->xsize = xsize; this->ysize = ysize;

  //- initialize view-window to a rectangle

  vwin_vlist = new l3d_two_part_list<l3d_coordinate> ( 4 );

#define BORDER 3
  (*vwin_vlist)[0].transformed.set(int_to_l3d_real(BORDER),
                                   int_to_l3d_real(BORDER),
                                   int_to_l3d_real(0),
```

```
                                        int_to_l3d_real(0));
    (*vwin_vlist)[1].transformed.set(int_to_l3d_real(xsize-BORDER),
                                     int_to_l3d_real(BORDER),
                                     int_to_l3d_real(0),
                                     int_to_l3d_real(0));
    (*vwin_vlist)[2].transformed.set(int_to_l3d_real(xsize-BORDER),
                                     int_to_l3d_real(ysize-BORDER),
                                     int_to_l3d_real(0),
                                     int_to_l3d_real(0));
    (*vwin_vlist)[3].transformed.set(int_to_l3d_real(BORDER),
                                     int_to_l3d_real(ysize-BORDER),
                                     int_to_l3d_real(0),
                                     int_to_l3d_real(0));
    view_win = new l3d_polygon_2d(4);
    view_win->vlist = &vwin_vlist;

    (*(view_win->ivertices)) [view_win->ivertices->next_index()].ivertex = 0;
    (*(view_win->ivertices)) [view_win->ivertices->next_index()].ivertex = 1;
    (*(view_win->ivertices)) [view_win->ivertices->next_index()].ivertex = 2;
    (*(view_win->ivertices)) [view_win->ivertices->next_index()].ivertex = 3;
    view_win->init_clip_ivertices();
}

l3d_screen::~l3d_screen(void) {

    //- Close the physical screen
    close_screen();

    delete vwin_vlist;
    delete view_win;

}
```

The variables xsize and ysize represent the horizontal and vertical size of the screen (window) in pixels.

The variable bufsize represents the number of bytes in the off-screen buffer.

The variables view_win and vwin_vlist represent the clip window of the screen.

The method open_screen performs any initialization necessary to display the screen for the first time.

The method blit_screen copies the off-screen buffer onto the visible screen.

The method close_screen performs any shutdown operations necessary when a graphics display on the screen is finished.

The method refresh_palette applies only to indexed color modes. It makes sure that the palette we have defined for our application is made known to the operating system and/or hardware. You must call refresh_palette whenever you wish any changes made to the palette to take effect; this implies that you must call refresh_palette at least once in your program if you wish the program's colors to display correctly under an indexed color mode. Calling refresh_palette when the program is running in a non-indexed color mode has no effect.

The method wait_vtrace is not used under X. Under other operating systems, this routine would wait for the so-called "vertical retrace," a period of time which lasts for a fraction of a second and which occurs when the video hardware has just finished drawing one frame on the monitor. By performing operations such as blit_screen during the vertical retrace, we can try to copy our off-screen image on-screen when the video hardware is between frames, thereby eliminating flickering. In multi-tasking operating or windowing systems such as Linux and X, there is no real way to wait for the vertical trace, since it is the windowing system which ultimately controls the visibility of graphics. Furthermore, hardware acceleration makes this issue mostly irrelevant.

Abstracting Relevant Screen Attributes: l3d_screen_info

The class l3d_screen_info is an abstract interface to screen information. We define screen information as follows: any information which an external class needs to know about a screen object in order to be able to work with that screen. Class l3d_screen_info encapsulates the vital statistics about a screen and makes them available through a clean, easy interface.

We first saw this concept in the discussion of colors and XImages, where we observed that the bytes making up a pixel and their interpretation depend on the color depth and color model of the underlying X server. Class l3d_screen_info is a recognition of the more general concept that external users of a screen need to access such "screen information" in order to do anything useful with the screen.

Listing 2-31: scrinfo.h

```
#ifndef _SCRINFO_H
#define _SCRINFO_H
#include "../tool_os/memman.h"

#define MAX_LIGHT_LEVELS 255
#define NUM_LIGHT_LEVELS (MAX_LIGHT_LEVELS+1)

class l3d_screen_info {
  public:
    int ext_max_red, ext_max_green, ext_max_blue;
    char bytes_per_pixel;
    virtual unsigned long ext_to_native(int red, int green, int blue)=0;
    virtual ~l3d_screen_info(void) {};

    virtual void compute_light_table(void)=0;
    virtual void compute_fog_table(void)=0;
    virtual void light_native(unsigned char *pcolor, int intensity)=0;
    virtual void fog_native(unsigned char *pcolor, int intensity)=0;

    virtual void set_color(unsigned long col ) {};

    unsigned char *p_screenbuf;

};

#endif
```

The method ext_to_native converts an RGB color, specified in an external format, to a long integer value representing the proper color in "native" format for the screen associated with this l3d_screen_info object. This is a great convenience indeed. The tedious calculation of pixel bits based upon color depth and color model is all hidden behind the function ext_to_native. This function takes as parameters a red, green, and blue value, and returns an unsigned long integer with the color in native format. This native color can then be dumped directly into the off-screen buffer.

The variables `ext_max_red`, `ext_max_green`, and `ext_max_blue` set the maximum logical red, green, and blue intensities which will be passed to the `ext_to_native` function. The idea is that you define your own custom, external maximum red, green, and blue values to any convenient value (e.g., 255). Then, you call `ext_to_native` with red, green, and blue values within this range. The function `ext_to_native` then scales the red, green, and blue values to the proper RGB value appropriate for the screen's color depth and color model. In the case of indexed color, `ext_to_native` allocates a palette entry for the specified RGB color.

The variable `bytes_per_pixel` represents the number of bytes per pixel for the screen.

The variable `p_screenbuf` is a pointer to the off-screen image data. This is used by software rasterizer implementations, which draw pixels directly into the off-screen buffer.

The method `set_color` is a placeholder for a call to a hardware color-setting routine. By default this routine does nothing. In the case of a Mesa screen, we must call an OpenGL function (`glIndexi` or `glColor4f`) to set the current color; therefore, in `l3d_screen_info` descendants for Mesa, we override this function.

The abstract method `compute_light_table` computes a so-called "lighting table" for all possible colors in the screen. We haven't encountered the concept of a lighting table yet, but the idea is very simple. Assume we have an arbitrary color specified by red, green, and blue intensities. An interesting question is, given this particular color, what is the same color at a different intensity? This question arises because the color of an object typically is a constant, but the intensity of light falling on it might not be. Therefore, it makes sense to define colors independent of intensity (e.g., a box is red), and to compute a final display color as a combination of color and light intensity (in the sun with a light intensity of 255, the box is bright red; in shadow, with a light intensity of 15, the box is dark red). Let us define intensity to be an integer from 0 to 255, with 0 being the lowest, darkest intensity, and 255 being the highest, brightest intensity. (The `#define` `MAX_LIGHT_LEVELS` controls the brightest intensity in the program code.) A lighting table is simply a 2D lookup table of colors and intensities. Along one axis, we specify the desired color. Along the other axis, we specify the desired intensity. The corresponding entry in the table is the desired color at the desired intensity. Using such a lighting table allows us to display any color at any intensity. This is very useful when applying lighting effects: we can define the colors of an object any way we want, compute a dynamic light intensity, then use the lighting table to combine the known color and the computed intensity to give a final, appropriately lighted color to be displayed on-screen. The companion book *Advanced Linux 3D Graphics Programming* discusses lighting algorithms, light maps, and lighting tables in more detail, including working code examples.

The abstract method `compute_fog_table` computes a so-called *fog table* for all possible colors in the screen. The concept of a fog table is very similar to that of a lighting table. Whereas a lighting table computed the various intensities of a color from completely black to the normal intensity, the fog table computes intensities of a color from normal intensity to completely white. A lighting table fades from black (intensity of 0) up to the normal color (intensity of 255). A fog table, on the other hand, fades from the normal color intensity (fog of 0) up to completely white (fog of 255). Increasing values of fog cause the color to wash out and appear whiter, as if the color were disappearing into a thick white fog. With a fog table, we look up the desired color on one axis, and the desired fog factor on the other axis. The corresponding entry in the table is the desired color with the desired fog factor applied. Note that a fog table does not need to fade to pure white, but can instead fade to gray or another color entirely.

The abstract method `light_native` changes the intensity of a pixel, stored in native screen format and pointed to by parameter `pcolor`, based on the `intensity` parameter and the pre-computed lighting table. The original color in `pcolor` is looked up in the lighting table with the specified intensity, and is then overwritten in memory with the new, lighted color.

The abstract method `fog_native` changes the intensity of a pixel, stored in native screen format and pointed to by parameter `pcolor`, based on the `intensity` parameter and the pre-computed fog table. The original color in `pcolor` is looked up in the fog table with the specified intensity, and is then overwritten in memory with the new, fogged color.

NOTE It might appear tempting to merge `l3d_screen_info` into the `l3d_screen` class itself. After all, isn't screen information part of the screen itself? The problem appears when we try to subclass the screen. Screen information can be handled fundamentally in two different ways: as RGB (TrueColor) or as indexed color. Similarly, screens themselves come in a variety of sorts: X11 screens, Mesa screens, Windows screens, DOS screens. If screen information and the screen were merged into one class, we would have the unpleasant situation of having several sorts of each screen: an X11 RGB screen, an X11 indexed screen, a Mesa RGB screen, a Mesa indexed screen, a Windows RGB screen, a Windows indexed screen, a DOS RGB screen, a DOS indexed screen. Extending the class hierarchy with a new information type or a new screen type becomes a major headache. This situation is sometimes called a *nested generalization* and indicates that the class should be split into two. For this reason, we keep the screen information separate, in its own `l3d_screen_info` class hierarchy. The `l3d_screen` is also separate, in its own `l3d_screen` class hierarchy. We can then, at run time, mix and match screen information types and screen types freely, without the multiplicative explosion of classes which would have resulted had we combined `l3d_screen_info` and `l3d_screen` into one class.

Screen Information for TrueColor: l3d_screen_info_rgb

The class `l3d_screen_info_rgb`, subclassed from `l3d_screen_info`, represents screen information for X TrueColor visuals or other color models based upon a direct specification of red, green, and blue pixel values.

We first saw this concept in the discussion of colors and XImages, for TrueColor visuals under X.

Listing 2-32: `si_rgb.h`

```
#ifndef _SI_RGB_H
#define _SI_RGB_H
#include "../tool_os/memman.h"

#include "scrinfo.h"

class l3d_screen_info_rgb : public l3d_screen_info {
  private:
```

```
      int *red_light_table, *green_light_table, *blue_light_table,
      *red_fog_table, *green_fog_table, *blue_fog_table;
  public:
    l3d_screen_info_rgb(unsigned long red_mask, unsigned long green_mask,
                        unsigned long blue_mask, char bytes_per_pixel, char bytes_per_rgb);
    virtual l3d_screen_info_rgb::~l3d_screen_info_rgb(void);

    char bytes_per_rgb;
    unsigned long red_mask, green_mask, blue_mask;
    int red_shift, green_shift, blue_shift,
    red_max, green_max, blue_max;
    void compute_color_resolution();

    unsigned long ext_to_native(int red, int green, int blue);
    void compute_light_table(void);
    void compute_fog_table(void);
    void light_native(unsigned char *pcolor, int intensity);
    void fog_native(unsigned char *pcolor, int intensity);

};

#endif
```

Listing 2-33: `si_rgb.cc`

```
#include "si_rgb.h"
#include "../system/sys_dep.h"
#include "../tool_os/memman.h"

l3d_screen_info_rgb::l3d_screen_info_rgb(unsigned long red_mask, unsigned
  long green_mask, unsigned long blue_mask, char bytes_per_pixel,
  char bytes_per_rgb)
{

  this->red_mask = red_mask;
  this->green_mask = green_mask;
  this->blue_mask = blue_mask;
  this->bytes_per_pixel = bytes_per_pixel;
  this->bytes_per_rgb = bytes_per_rgb;

  //- initial reasonable default values for external max rgb values; these
  //- can be overridden just before actually reading rgb values from an
  //- external source
  ext_max_red = 255;
  ext_max_green = 255;
  ext_max_blue = 255;

  compute_color_resolution();

  red_light_table = new int[(red_max+1)*NUM_LIGHT_LEVELS];
  green_light_table = new int[(green_max+1)*NUM_LIGHT_LEVELS];
  blue_light_table = new int[(blue_max+1)*NUM_LIGHT_LEVELS];
  red_fog_table = new int[(red_max+1)*NUM_LIGHT_LEVELS];
  green_fog_table = new int[(green_max+1)*NUM_LIGHT_LEVELS];
  blue_fog_table = new int[(blue_max+1)*NUM_LIGHT_LEVELS];

  compute_light_table();
  compute_fog_table();
}

l3d_screen_info_rgb::~l3d_screen_info_rgb(void) {
```

```
      delete [] red_light_table;
      delete [] green_light_table;
      delete [] blue_light_table;
      delete [] red_fog_table;
      delete [] green_fog_table;
      delete [] blue_fog_table;
  }

void l3d_screen_info_rgb::compute_color_resolution(void) {
   int red_mask_tmp=red_mask,
                 green_mask_tmp=green_mask,
                             blue_mask_tmp=blue_mask;

   for(red_shift=0;
       (red_mask_tmp & 0x01) == 0 ;
       red_shift++, red_mask_tmp>=1);
   for(red_max=1;
       (red_mask_tmp & 0x01) == 1 ;
       red_max*=2, red_mask_tmp>=1);
   red_max--;

   for(green_shift=0;
       (green_mask_tmp & 0x01) == 0 ;
       green_shift++, green_mask_tmp>=1);
   for(green_max=1;
       (green_mask_tmp & 0x01) == 1 ;
       green_max*=2, green_mask_tmp>=1);
   green_max--;

   for(blue_shift=0;
       (blue_mask_tmp & 0x01) == 0 ;
       blue_shift++, blue_mask_tmp>=1);
   for(blue_max=1;
       (blue_mask_tmp & 0x01) == 1 ;
       blue_max*=2, blue_mask_tmp>=1);
   blue_max--;

}

unsigned long l3d_screen_info_rgb::ext_to_native(int red,
    int green, int blue)
{
  unsigned long red_rescaled, green_rescaled, blue_rescaled;

  red_rescaled = red * red_max / ext_max_red;
  green_rescaled = green * green_max / ext_max_green;
  blue_rescaled = blue * blue_max / ext_max_blue;

  return (red_rescaled<red_shift)
         | (green_rescaled<green_shift)
         | (blue_rescaled<blue_shift);

}

void l3d_screen_info_rgb::compute_light_table(void)
{
  int i,c;
  int *tableptr;

  tableptr = red_light_table;
```

```
    for(c=0; c<=red_max; c++) {
      for(i=0; i<NUM_LIGHT_LEVELS; i++) {
        *tableptr++ = c * i / MAX_LIGHT_LEVELS;
      }
    }
    tableptr = green_light_table;
    for(c=0; c<=green_max; c++) {
      for(i=0; i<NUM_LIGHT_LEVELS; i++) {
        *tableptr++ = c * i / MAX_LIGHT_LEVELS;
      }
    }
    tableptr = blue_light_table;
    for(c=0; c<=blue_max; c++) {
      for(i=0; i<NUM_LIGHT_LEVELS; i++) {
        *tableptr++ = c * i / MAX_LIGHT_LEVELS;
      }
    }
  }

  void l3d_screen_info_rgb::compute_fog_table(void)
  {
    int i,c;
    int *tableptr;

    tableptr = red_fog_table;
    for(c=0; c<=red_max; c++) {
      for(i=0; i<NUM_LIGHT_LEVELS; i++) {
        *tableptr++ = c + (int) (((float)i/MAX_LIGHT_LEVELS)*(red_max - c));
      }
    }
    tableptr = green_fog_table;
    for(c=0; c<=green_max; c++) {
      for(i=0; i<NUM_LIGHT_LEVELS; i++) {
        *tableptr++ = c + (int) (((float)i/MAX_LIGHT_LEVELS)*(green_max - c));
      }
    }
    tableptr = blue_fog_table;
    for(c=0; c<=blue_max; c++) {
      for(i=0; i<NUM_LIGHT_LEVELS; i++) {
        *tableptr++ = c + (int) (((float)i/MAX_LIGHT_LEVELS)*(blue_max - c));
      }
    }
  }

  void l3d_screen_info_rgb::light_native(unsigned char *pcolor,
                                         int intensity)
  {

    unsigned char *c2 = pcolor;

    register int p;
    unsigned long color=0;
    unsigned long color_shift = 0;
    for(p=0; p<bytes_per_rgb; p++) {
      color += (*c2++) < color_shift;
      color_shift += BITS_PER_BYTE;
    }
    for(p=bytes_per_rgb; p<bytes_per_pixel;p++) {c2++; }

    unsigned long r = (color & red_mask) > red_shift;
```

```
  unsigned long g = (color & green_mask) > green_shift;
  unsigned long b = (color & blue_mask) > blue_shift;

  color =
    (red_light_table[r*NUM_LIGHT_LEVELS+intensity] <red_shift) |
    (green_light_table[g*NUM_LIGHT_LEVELS+intensity] <green_shift) |
    (blue_light_table[b*NUM_LIGHT_LEVELS+intensity] <blue_shift);

  {
    register int i;
    unsigned long mask = 255;
    char shift = 0;

    for(c2-=bytes_per_pixel, i=0; i<bytes_per_pixel; i++) {
      *c2 = (color & mask) > shift;
      c2++;
      mask <= BITS_PER_BYTE;
      shift += BITS_PER_BYTE;
    }
  }
}

void l3d_screen_info_rgb::fog_native(unsigned char *pcolor,
                                     int intensity)
{

  unsigned char *c2 = pcolor;

  register int p;
  unsigned long color=0;
  unsigned long color_shift = 0;
  for(p=0; p<bytes_per_rgb; p++) {
    color += (*c2++) < color_shift;
    color_shift += BITS_PER_BYTE;
  }
  for(p=bytes_per_rgb; p<bytes_per_pixel;p++) {c2++; }

  unsigned long r = (color & red_mask) > red_shift;
  unsigned long g = (color & green_mask) > green_shift;
  unsigned long b = (color & blue_mask) > blue_shift;

  color =
    (red_fog_table[r*NUM_LIGHT_LEVELS+intensity] <red_shift) |
    (green_fog_table[g*NUM_LIGHT_LEVELS+intensity] <green_shift) |
    (blue_fog_table[b*NUM_LIGHT_LEVELS+intensity] <blue_shift);

  {
    register int i;
    unsigned long mask = 255;
    char shift = 0;

    for(c2-=bytes_per_pixel, i=0; i<bytes_per_pixel; i++) {
      *c2 = (color & mask) > shift;
      c2++;
      mask <= BITS_PER_BYTE;
      shift += BITS_PER_BYTE;
    }
  }

}
```

The constructor takes as parameters a red mask, a blue mask, a green mask, and a bytes-per-pixel specification. The masks are bit masks indicating which bit positions specify the red, green, and blue parts of the color. These bit masks are the same as those obtained from an `XVisualInfo` structure, discussed earlier. The constructor calls its own helper routine `compute_color_resolution` to compute the `shift` and `max` variables, discussed next.

The variables `red_shift`, `green_shift`, and `blue_shift` represent the number of bits by which we must left-shift a color value in order to place it in the red, green, or blue portion of the color specification.

The variables `red_max`, `green_max`, and `blue_max` represent the maximum red, green, and blue values which may be specified for the given color depth.

The overridden method `ext_to_native` uses the `mask`, `shift`, and `max` variables to scale the externally specified RGB values to lie within the range of the native RGB values.

The variables `red_light_table`, `green_light_table`, and `blue_light_table` are pointers to the light tables: one for each component of the RGB color. The variables `red_fog_table`, `green_fog_table`, and `blue_fog_table` are pointers to the fog tables: one for each component of the RGB color. It would have been equally possible to make one huge table for light values and one huge table for fog values; this would, however, require `(red_max+1)*(green_max+1)*(blue_max+1)*MAX_LIGHT_LEVELS` total entries in each table—a staggeringly large number. By splitting the tables into separate red, green, and blue components, we have a total requirement of only `((red_max+1)+(green_max+1)+(blue_max+1))*MAX_LIGHT_LEVELS` entries.

The overridden method `compute_light_table` computes the red, green, and blue light tables separately. The computation for each color component is identical. Each color (red, green, or blue) has an intrinsic, unlit color value going from 0 to `xxx_max`, where xxx is red, green, or blue. For each intrinsic, unlit color value, we then compute 256 (which is the constant `MAX_LIGHT_LEVELS+1`) lighted intensities of this color. The lighted colors start at 0, which is completely black and corresponds to intensity 0, and progress all the way up to the intrinsic unlit value, which is as bright as possible and corresponds to intensity 255 (`MAX_LIGHT_LEVELS`).

The overridden method `compute_fog_table` similarly computes the red, green, and blue fog tables separately. For all three tables, for each intrinsic, non-fogged color value, we then compute 256 (which is the constant `MAX_LIGHT_LEVELS+1`) fogged intensities of this color. The fogged colors start at the intrinsic, non-fogged color value, which corresponds to fog factor 0, and progress all the way up to completely white, which washes out all traces of the original color and corresponds to the maximum fog factor of 255 (`MAX_LIGHT_LEVELS`).

The overridden method `light_native` changes the intensity of a pixel, pointed to by parameter `pcolor`, based on the `intensity` parameter and the pre-computed lighting table. First, we decode the original color in `pcolor`, by extracting the bytes one by one, and split the color into its separate red, green, and blue components by using the appropriate bit masks. Then, we use the value of each color component (red, green, and blue) and the `intensity` parameter to perform a lookup in the corresponding red, green, or blue lighting table. We then take these lighted, and still separate, red, green, and blue values, combine them back into one single RGB color value, and write the new lighted RGB color value back to the same memory location as the original color.

The overridden method `fog_native` changes the intensity of a pixel, pointed to by parameter `pcolor`, based on the `intensity` parameter and the pre-computed fog table. As with the method `light_native`, we first split the original color into red, green, and blue; perform a lookup in the fog tables for each component and the fog factor; combine the separated fogged red, green, and blue values back into one RGB color; and finally write the RGB color back to memory.

Screen Information for Indexed Color: l3d_screen_info_indexed

The class `l3d_screen_info_indexed`, subclassed from `l3d_screen_info`, represents screen information for X PseudoColor visuals or other color models based upon an indexed or paletted color model.

We first saw this concept in the discussion of colors and XImages, for PseudoColor visuals under X.

Listing 2-34: `si_idx.h`

```
#ifndef _SI_IDX_H
#define _SI_IDX_H
#include "../tool_os/memman.h"

#include "scrinfo.h"

struct l3d_rgb {
  int red, green, blue;
};

class l3d_screen_info_indexed : public l3d_screen_info {
    int *light_table;
    int *fog_table;

  public:
    l3d_screen_info_indexed(int palette_size, int max_red, int max_green, int max_blue);
    virtual ~l3d_screen_info_indexed(void);

    int palette_size;
    l3d_rgb *palette;
    int get_palette_size(void) {return palette_size; }
    int palette_num_used;
    int palette_max_red, palette_max_green, palette_max_blue;
    unsigned long ext_to_native(int red, int green, int blue);
    void compute_light_table(void);
    void compute_fog_table(void);
    void light_native(unsigned char *pcolor, int intensity);
    void fog_native(unsigned char *pcolor, int intensity);
};

#endif
```

Listing 2-35: `si_idx.cc`

```cpp
#include "si_idx.h"

#include <stdio.h>
#include <values.h>
#include "../tool_os/memman.h"

l3d_screen_info_indexed::l3d_screen_info_indexed(int palette_size,
    int max_red, int max_green, int max_blue)
{

  this->palette = new l3d_rgb[palette_size];
  this->palette_size = palette_size;
  this->palette_num_used = 0;

  this->palette_max_red = max_red;
  this->palette_max_green = max_green;
  this->palette_max_blue = max_blue;

  this->bytes_per_pixel = 1;

  light_table = new int[palette_size * NUM_LIGHT_LEVELS];
  fog_table = new int[palette_size * NUM_LIGHT_LEVELS];

  //- initial reasonable default values for external max rgb values; these
  //- can be overridden just before actually reading rgb values from an
  //- external source
  ext_max_red = 255;
  ext_max_green = 255;
  ext_max_blue = 255;

}

l3d_screen_info_indexed::~l3d_screen_info_indexed() {
  delete [] palette;
  delete [] light_table;
  delete [] fog_table;
}

unsigned long l3d_screen_info_indexed::ext_to_native(int red,
    int green, int blue)
{
  int i;
  unsigned long result=0;
  int found = 0;

  int red_scaled = red*palette_max_red / ext_max_red,
                   green_scaled = green*palette_max_green / ext_max_green,
                                  blue_scaled = blue*palette_max_blue / ext_max_blue;

  for(i=0; i<palette_num_used && !found; i++) {
    if (    (palette[i].red == red_scaled)
         && (palette[i].green == green_scaled)
         && (palette[i].blue == blue_scaled) )
    {
      found = 1;
      result = i;
    }
  }
```

```
  if ( !found ) {
    if (palette_num_used >= palette_size) {
      printf("palette overflow; generate common palette for all textures");
      result = 0;
    }
    else {
      palette[palette_num_used].red = red_scaled;
      palette[palette_num_used].green = green_scaled;
      palette[palette_num_used].blue = blue_scaled;
      result = palette_num_used;
      palette_num_used++;
    }
  }

  return result;
}

void l3d_screen_info_indexed::compute_light_table(void)
{
  int c,i;
  int unlit_r, unlit_g, unlit_b;
  int lit_r, lit_g, lit_b;

  int *tableptr;
  tableptr = light_table;

  for(c=0; c<palette_num_used; c++) {
    unlit_r = palette[c].red;
    unlit_g = palette[c].green;
    unlit_b = palette[c].blue;

    for(i=0; i<=MAX_LIGHT_LEVELS; i++) {
      lit_r = unlit_r * i / MAX_LIGHT_LEVELS;
      lit_g = unlit_g * i / MAX_LIGHT_LEVELS;
      lit_b = unlit_b * i / MAX_LIGHT_LEVELS;

      int existing_c;
      int closest_existing_c=0;
      int smallest_distance=MAXINT;
      int squared_distance=0;
      for(existing_c=0; existing_c < palette_num_used; existing_c++) {
        squared_distance =
          (palette[existing_c].red - lit_r) *
          (palette[existing_c].red - lit_r)
          +
          (palette[existing_c].green - lit_g) *
          (palette[existing_c].green - lit_g)
          +
          (palette[existing_c].blue - lit_b) *
          (palette[existing_c].blue - lit_b) ;

        if(squared_distance < smallest_distance) {
          closest_existing_c = existing_c;
          smallest_distance = squared_distance;
        }
      }

      if(squared_distance > 300
          && palette_num_used < palette_size)
      {
```

```
          palette[palette_num_used].red = lit_r * palette_max_red / ext_max_red;
          palette[palette_num_used].red = lit_g * palette_max_red / ext_max_red;
          palette[palette_num_used].red = lit_b * palette_max_red / ext_max_red;
          closest_existing_c = palette_num_used;

          palette_num_used++;
        }

      *tableptr++ = closest_existing_c;

    }
  }
}

void l3d_screen_info_indexed::compute_fog_table(void)
{
  int c,i;
  int unlit_r, unlit_g, unlit_b;
  int lit_r, lit_g, lit_b;

  int *tableptr;
  tableptr = fog_table;

  for(c=0; c<palette_num_used; c++) {
    unlit_r = palette[c].red;
    unlit_g = palette[c].green;
    unlit_b = palette[c].blue;

    for(i=0; i<=MAX_LIGHT_LEVELS; i++) {
      lit_r = unlit_r + (int) (((float)i/MAX_LIGHT_LEVELS)*
              (palette_max_red - unlit_r));
      lit_g = unlit_g + (int) (((float)i/MAX_LIGHT_LEVELS)*
              (palette_max_green - unlit_g));
      lit_b = unlit_b + (int) (((float)i/MAX_LIGHT_LEVELS)*
              (palette_max_blue - unlit_b));

      int existing_c;
      int closest_existing_c=0;
      int smallest_distance=MAXINT;
      for(existing_c=0; existing_c < palette_num_used; existing_c++) {
        int squared_distance =
          (palette[existing_c].red - lit_r) *
          (palette[existing_c].red - lit_r)
          +
          (palette[existing_c].green - lit_g) *
          (palette[existing_c].green - lit_g)
          +
          (palette[existing_c].blue - lit_b) *
          (palette[existing_c].blue - lit_b) ;

        if(squared_distance < smallest_distance) {
          closest_existing_c = existing_c;
          smallest_distance = squared_distance;
        }
      }

      *tableptr++ = closest_existing_c;

    }
  }
}
```

```
    }

    void l3d_screen_info_indexed::light_native(unsigned char *pcolor, int intensity)
    {
      *pcolor = light_table[ (*pcolor) * NUM_LIGHT_LEVELS + intensity ];
    }

    void l3d_screen_info_indexed::fog_native(unsigned char *pcolor, int intensity)
    {
      *pcolor = fog_table[ (*pcolor) * NUM_LIGHT_LEVELS + intensity ];
    }
```

The variable `palette` is a dynamically allocated array of red, green, and blue color entries (of type `l3d_rgb`).

The variables `palette_size` and `palette_num_used` keep track of the total size and the currently used entries within the palette.

The variables `palette_max_red`, `palette_max_green`, and `palette_max_blue` store the maximum allowable red, green, and blue intensities in each palette entry. These are used as a reference in mapping the palette entries to the actual color range needed by the underlying windowing or hardware system.

The overridden method `ext_to_native` returns a palette index corresponding to the RGB color. First, it scales the specified RGB value to lie within the RGB range supported by the palette. It then searches to see if the specified RGB value can be found in the palette. If so, then the color has already been used before, and the index of the already-allocated palette entry is returned. If not, the color has not yet been used, a new palette entry is allocated for the new RGB color, and the new index is returned. If the palette is full (i.e., no new entries can be allocated), an error message is printed indicating palette overflow. It is the responsibility of the calling routine to ensure that palette overflow does not occur. Typically, the allocated colors come from external image files, and palette overflow at run time can be avoided by using a preprocessing tool on all image files to generate a common palette for all images, thereby ensuring that all image files and therefore all allocated colors do not overflow the palette size. The companion book *Advanced Linux 3D Graphics Programming* discusses texture mapping, palettes, and common palette generation in more detail.

The variable `light_table` is pointer to the single light table; since a palette typically has no more than 256 entries, we do not need to split the light table into red, green, and blue components as we did with class `l3d_screen_info_rgb`. The variable `fog_table` is a pointer to the fog table.

The overridden method `compute_light_table` functions similarly to its counterpart in class `l3d_screen_info_rgb`, but with the added restriction that only `palette_size` colors are available for use. For each entry in the palette, we extract the corresponding true red, green, and blue color components. We then compute the light intensity for this color exactly as in class `l3d_screen_info_rgb`, for all intensities from 0 to `MAX_LIGHT_LEVELS`, where 0 corresponds to black and `MAX_LIGHT_LEVELS` corresponds to the intrinsic unlit color. This is then the desired color entry which should be referenced in the light table for this particular color and intensity. But, we must work within the restrictions of the palette; we cannot have all the colors we want. We therefore search the existing palette color entries for the entry which is nearest to the desired entry. The nearest entry is the existing palette entry whose red, green, and blue values have the smallest squared distance from the desired red, green, and blue values (this is the well-known "least-squares" method). After finding the nearest match in the palette, we then have two possibilities. First, it is possible that all palette entries have already been allocated to other colors—in this case, we cannot allocate any new colors, and must accept the nearest match which we found, no matter how close or far it is to the actual desired color. We therefore enter the palette index of the nearest match into the light table. On the other hand, it might be the case that the palette still has some free entries into which we can allocate new colors. In this case, we see how close the nearest existing match was. If it was "near enough" to the desired color, then we just go ahead and accept the nearest match; however, if the nearest match was substantially different from the desired color, then we allocate a new entry in the palette, assign the exact desired color to the new palette entry, and finally enter the new palette index into the light table. The criteria for deciding how near "near enough" must be is arbitrary; in the code, this is currently set to be any squared distance less than 300. Note that this `compute_light_table` method should only be called after all other palette entries, for the main colors used by the program, have been allocated. Otherwise, the light table computation may, as we just saw, reserve some palette entries for its computed light values, meaning that fewer or perhaps no other palette entries will be available for use by the program if other colors are needed.

The overridden method `compute_fog_table` functions identically to `compute_light_table`, except that it accesses the fog table, and computes the desired color based on the fog factor going from the normal intensity to pure white.

The overridden method `light_native` changes the intensity of a pixel, pointed to by parameter `pcolor`, based on the `intensity` parameter and the pre-computed lighting table. The pixel being pointed to is an index into a palette. We simply use this palette index and the desired intensity to perform a look-up in the light table. The entry we find in the light table is also a palette index, pointing to the nearest match in the palette for the original color at the desired intensity. Then, we just write this nearest-match palette index back into the memory pointed to by `pcolor`.

The overridden method `fog_native` changes the intensity of a pixel, pointed to by parameter `pcolor`, based on the `intensity` parameter and the pre-computed fog table. It functions identically to the `light_native` method, merely using the fog table instead of the light table.

A Screen Under X: l3d_screen_x11

The class `l3d_screen_x11`, subclassed from `l3d_screen`, represents a screen under the X Window System, in the form of a window using an XImage for graphics display.

As with the parent class `l3d_screen`, we first saw this concept in program `hello_oo_image`, which directly used an XImage in an X window as an output device. Concrete class `l3d_screen_x11` is a recognition of the fact that an X window is only one particular concrete type of screen, but does not necessarily characterize all abstract types of screens which our application program may use in the future.

Listing 2-36: sc_x11.h

```
#ifndef __SC_X11_H
#define __SC_X11_H
#include "../tool_os/memman.h"

#include "screen.h"
#include <X11/Intrinsic.h>
#include <X11/Xlib.h>

class l3d_screen_x11 : public l3d_screen {
  protected:
    Visual *vis;
    Colormap cmap;
    unsigned char *buffer;
    GC gc;
    int depth, bytespp, scanline_pad;
    unsigned long* col_cells;

    void close_screen(void);
  public:
    XImage *ximg;
    virtual XImage *create_ximage(void);
    virtual void create_buffer(void);

    Display *dpy;
    Window w;
    l3d_screen_x11(int xsize, int ysize);
    virtual ~l3d_screen_x11(void);
    void refresh_palette(void);
    void open_screen(void);
    void blit_screen(void);
};

class l3d_screen_factory_x11 : public l3d_screen_factory {
  public:
    l3d_screen *create(int xsize, int ysize) {
      l3d_screen_x11 *s;
      s = new l3d_screen_x11(xsize,ysize);

      s->create_buffer();
      s->ximg = s->create_ximage();

      return s;
    }
};

#endif
```

Listing 2-37: sc_x11.cc

```
#include "sc_x11.h"
#include <stdlib.h>
#include "../tool_os/memman.h"

l3d_screen_x11::l3d_screen_x11(int xsize, int ysize) :
    l3d_screen(xsize,ysize)
{

  XPixmapFormatValues *pixmap_formats;
  int i, count;
```

```
dpy = XopenDisplay(NULL);

pixmap_formats = XListPixmapFormats(dpy, &count);
for(i=0, depth=0; i<count; i++) {
  if(pixmap_formats[i].depth > depth) {
    depth        = pixmap_formats[i].depth;
    bytespp      = pixmap_formats[i].bits_per_pixel / BITS_PER_BYTE;
    scanline_pad = pixmap_formats[i].scanline_pad;
  }
}
Xfree(pixmap_formats);
printf("max depth of display %d", depth);
printf("bytes per pixel: %d", bytespp);

bufsize = xsize * ysize * bytespp;

vis = DefaultVisual(dpy,0);
w = XcreateWindow(dpy,
                  DefaultRootWindow(dpy),
                  100, 100,
                  xsize, ysize,
                  0,
                  depth,
                  CopyFromParent,
                  vis,
                  0, NULL);
XStoreName(dpy, w, "l3d application");
XMapWindow(dpy, w);

switch(vis->c_class) {

    XVisualInfo vi;
    int result;

  case PseudoColor:
    result=
      XMatchVisualInfo(dpy, DefaultScreen(dpy), depth, PseudoColor, &vi);
    if(result) {
      printf("visual is PseudoColor (indexed),");
      printf("colormapsize %d,", vi.colormap_size);
      printf("bits per rgb %d",vis->bits_per_rgb);

      col_cells = new unsigned long[vi.colormap_size];
      sinfo = new l3d_screen_info_indexed(vi.colormap_size,
                                         (1<vis->bits_per_rgb)-1,
                                         (1<vis->bits_per_rgb)-1,
                                         (1<vis->bits_per_rgb)-1);
      printf("is indexed");
    }else {
      printf("no information for PseudoColor visual");
    }

    break;

  case TrueColor:
    result=
      XMatchVisualInfo(dpy, DefaultScreen(dpy), depth, TrueColor, &vi);
    if(result) {
      printf("visual is TrueColor, %d bytes per pix, %d bytes per rgb",
             bytespp,
```

```
                    vi.depth / BITS_PER_BYTE);
        col_cells = NULL;
        sinfo = new l3d_screen_info_rgb(vis->red_mask,
                                        vis->green_mask,
                                        vis->blue_mask,
                                        bytespp,
                                        vi.depth / BITS_PER_BYTE);
    }else {
      printf("Couldn't get visual information, XmatchVisualInfo");
      exit(-1);
    }
    break;

  case StaticColor: printf("unsupported visual StaticColor");break;
  case GrayScale:   printf("unsupported visual GrayScale");break;
  case StaticGray:  printf("unsupported visual StaticGray");break;
  case DirectColor: printf("unsupported visual DirectColor");break;
  }

  XSelectInput(dpy, w, KeyPressMask);
  gc = DefaultGC(dpy, DefaultScreen(dpy));

}


l3d_screen_x11::~l3d_screen_x11(void) {
  delete sinfo;
  XdestroyImage(ximg);
  if(col_cells) delete [] col_cells;
  XcloseDisplay(dpy);
}


inline void l3d_screen_x11::blit_screen(void) {
  XPutImage(dpy, w, gc, ximg,
            0,0,0,0,  /* source x,y; destination x,y */
            xsize, ysize);
}


void l3d_screen_x11::open_screen(void) {
}


void l3d_screen_x11::close_screen(void) {

}


void l3d_screen_x11::refresh_palette(void) {

  l3d_screen_info_indexed *si;
  if ((si = dynamic_cast<l3d_screen_info_indexed *>(sinfo))) {

    int idx;

    cmap = XCreateColormap(dpy, w, vis, AllocNone);

    XAllocColorCells(dpy, cmap, TRUE, NULL, 0, col_cells,
                     (int)pow(2.0, (double)depth));

    for(idx=0; idx<si->palette_size; idx++) {
      XColor xcolor;

      xcolor.pixel = idx;
```

```
        xcolor.red = (int) (( (float)si->palette[idx].red /
                              si->palette_max_red ) * 65535);
        xcolor.green = (int) (( (float)si->palette[idx].green /
                                si->palette_max_green ) * 65535);
        xcolor.blue = (int)( ( (float)si->palette[idx].blue /
                               si->palette_max_blue ) * 65535);
        xcolor.flags = DoRed | DoGreen | DoBlue;
        XAllocColor(dpy, cmap, &xcolor);
        XStoreColor(dpy, cmap, &xcolor);
      }
      XSetWindowColormap(dpy, w, cmap);
    }


  }

  XImage *l3d_screen_x11::create_ximage(void) {
    return XCreateImage(dpy, vis, depth,
                    Zpixmap,
                    0,
                    (char *)buffer,
                    xsize, ysize,
                    scanline_pad,
                    0);


  }

  void l3d_screen_x11::create_buffer(void) {
    buffer = new unsigned char [xsize*ysize*bytespp];
    sinfo->p_screenbuf = buffer;
  }
```

The variables dpy, w, vis, and GC store the X display, window, visual, and graphics context, respectively.

The variable ximg points to the XImage used for graphics display.

The variable buffer points to the memory allocated for the off-screen buffer, used by the XImage.

The variables cmap and col_cells are internally used for specification and storage of an X colormap, used only for visuals based on an indexed color model.

The variables depth, bytespp, and scanline_pad represent information about the supported image format of the X window.

The constructor creates and maps the X window, allocates an off-screen buffer, creates an l3d_screen_info object corresponding to the window's color depth and model, and requests event notification for the window.

The overridden method blit_screen calls XPutImage to copy the off-screen image into the window.

The overridden method refresh_palette transfers the platform-independent palette stored in the l3d_screen_info_indexed object into the X colormap. The Xlib functions XCreateColormap, XAllocColorCells, XAllocColor, XStoreColor, and XSetWindowColormap are used to set the X colormap.

The method create_buffer allocates off-screen memory for the XImage. It also stores a pointer to this memory in the l3d_screen_info object. This does not take place automatically in the constructor for reasons discussed in the next paragraph.

The method `create_ximage` creates the XImage that is used to display the graphics. This is a virtual function and is not called within the constructor because subclasses might call a different routine to create an XImage. In particular, the shared-memory extension allows creation of a faster, shared-memory XImage, in which case we override the `create_ximage` virtual method—a technique which would not work if the XImage had already been created within the constructor. The factory, which is responsible for creating `l3d_screen_x11` objects, calls the virtual `create_buffer` and `create_ximage` functions, thereby correctly initializing the object.

 NOTE In general, virtual functions called from within a constructor don't work.

Figure 2-22 illustrates the class diagram for the screen-related classes.

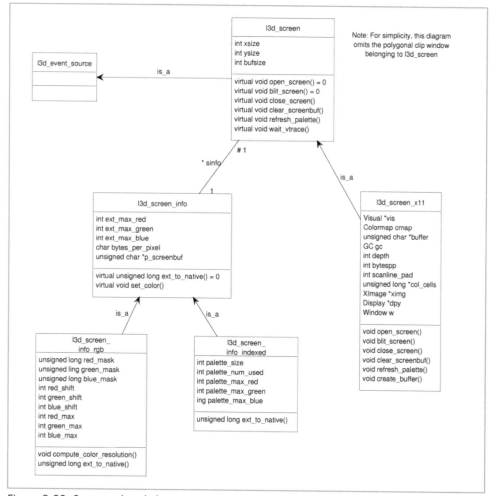

Figure 2-22: Screen-related classes.

Abstracting the Rasterizer: l3d_rasterizer_2d

The class `l3d_rasterizer_2d` represents a 2D, double-buffered rasterizer—a subsystem capable of drawing 2D geometric primitives on a double-buffered raster output device. The class does not do any of the rasterization work itself, but instead relies on a rasterizer implementation (covered in the next section) to provide a "toolkit" of functions which the rasterizer then calls.

We first saw this concept in the discussion of byte-to-pixel correspondence, where we manually used a formula to calculate which bytes in an off-screen buffer correspond to a pixel at a particular location. At that point, we implicitly assumed that the main application program directly manipulates the bytes in an off-screen buffer, thereby assuming full responsibility for rasterization concepts (such as plotting a pixel) and their implementation (calculating the byte-to-pixel correspondence and setting the bytes according to the color depth and color model). Class `l3d_rasterizer_2d` is a recognition of the more general concept of a rasterizer interface, which allows access to abstract rasterization concepts. The rasterizer interface allows drawing not only of individual pixels, but also of groups of pixels forming geometric primitives, such as lines and polygons.

 NOTE Separating the rasterizer and the rasterizer implementation is an example of the generally applicable *bridge design pattern*, where an abstraction and its implementation are two separate classes. This allows for the class hierarchies for the abstraction and the implementation thereof to vary and be refined independently, avoiding the multiplicative explosion of classes discussed earlier (nested generalizations). This technique is also referred to as using a *handle*.

Listing 2-38: `rasteriz.h`

```
#ifndef __RASTERIZ_H
#define __RASTERIZ_H
#include "../tool_os/memman.h"

#include "../tool_2d/scrinfo.h"

class l3d_polygon;
class l3d_polygon_2d_flatshaded;

class l3d_rasterizer_2d_imp {
  protected:
    int xsize, ysize;
    l3d_screen_info *sinfo;
  public:
    l3d_rasterizer_2d_imp(int xs, int ys, l3d_screen_info *si);
    virtual ~l3d_rasterizer_2d_imp(void) {};

    virtual void clear_buffer(void);
    virtual void draw_point( int x ,
                             int y ,
                             unsigned long col );
    virtual void draw_line( int x0 ,
                            int y0 ,
                            int x1 ,
                            int y1 ,
                            unsigned long col );
```

```
           virtual void draw_polygon_flatshaded( const l3d_polygon_2d_flatshaded
                                                   *p_poly );
};

class l3d_rasterizer_2d {
  protected:
    l3d_rasterizer_2d_imp *imp2d;

  public:
    l3d_rasterizer_2d(l3d_rasterizer_2d_imp *i) {
      imp2d = i;
    }
    virtual ~l3d_rasterizer_2d(void) {}

    virtual void clear_buffer(void)
   {imp2d->clear_buffer(); }

    virtual void draw_point( int x ,
                             int y ,
                             unsigned long col )
   {imp2d->draw_point(x,y,col); }

    virtual void draw_line( int x0 ,
                            int y0 ,
                            int x1 ,
                            int y1 ,
                            unsigned long col )
   {imp2d->draw_line(x0,y0,x1,y1,col);}

    virtual void draw_polygon_flatshaded( const l3d_polygon_2d_flatshaded
                                            *p_poly )
   {imp2d->draw_polygon_flatshaded(p_poly); }
};

class l3d_rasterizer_2d_imp_factory {
  public:
    virtual l3d_rasterizer_2d_imp *create(int xs, int ys, l3d_screen_info *si)=0;
};

#include "../geom/polygon/polygon.h"
#include "../geom/polygon/p_flat.h"

#endif
```

Listing 2-39: `rasteriz.cc`

```
#include "rasteriz.h"
#include "../tool_os/memman.h"

l3d_rasterizer_2d_imp::l3d_rasterizer_2d_imp
(int xs, int ys, l3d_screen_info *si)
{
  xsize=xs; ysize=ys; sinfo=si;
}

void l3d_rasterizer_2d_imp::clear_buffer(void)
{}

void l3d_rasterizer_2d_imp::draw_point( int x ,
                                        int y ,
```

```
                                      unsigned long col )
  {}

void l3d_rasterizer_2d_imp::draw_line( int x0 ,
                                       int y0 ,
                                       int x1 ,
                                       int y1 ,
                                       unsigned long col )
  {}

void l3d_rasterizer_2d_imp::draw_polygon_flatshaded
( const l3d_polygon_2d_flatshaded
  *p_poly )
  {}
```

The variable `imp2d` is a pointer to a 2D rasterizer implementation object, which provides the rasterizer with a toolkit of system-specific functions for directly manipulating the underlying raster display hardware.

Notice the absence of an off-screen buffer pointer in the rasterizer class. The rasterizer does not need to and in fact cannot provide the rasterizer implementation with an off-screen buffer. This is because the rasterizer implementation might be a hardware rasterizer implementation, where direct access to the frame buffer might not be possible or desirable. Therefore, the rasterizer implementation itself must worry about whether the off-screen buffer exists in main memory directly accessible to the program, or whether the off-screen buffer is only accessible through hardware API functions of a dedicated hardware rasterization subsystem.

The method `clear_buffer` clears the off-screen buffer by asking the rasterizer implementation to do so. Clearing the off-screen buffer erases any image in the buffer, making it completely empty. We often do this before drawing to the off-screen buffer, since otherwise the "leftover" contents from the last frame still remain within the buffer. One exception to this is if we always update every pixel in the screen every frame, in which case clearing the off-screen buffer is unnecessary and a waste of time. This situation is indeed the case with indoor portal-based environments (discussed and implemented in the companion book *Advanced Linux 3D Graphics Programming*).

The method `draw_point` draws a point in the off-screen buffer by asking the rasterizer implementation to do so. The parameters specify the location and color of the point, where the color is specified in native screen format, as supplied by `l3d_screen_info::ext_to_native`.

The method `draw_line` draws a line of pixels in the off-screen buffer by asking the rasterizer implementation to do so. The parameters specify the location of the starting and ending points, and the color is specified in native screen format, as supplied by `l3d_screen_info::ext_to_native`. We have not used `draw_line` yet; it is described in Chapter 3.

The method `draw_polygon_flatshaded` draws a single-colored (flat-shaded) polygon, filled with identically colored pixels, in the off-screen buffer by asking the rasterizer implementation to do so. The parameter is a polygon object. We have not used `draw_polygon_flatshaded` or polygon objects yet; they are introduced in Chapter 3.

A Rasterizer Implementation: l3d_rasterizer_2d_imp

The class `l3d_rasterizer_2d_imp` represents an implementation of the tools necessary for a 2D rasterizer to do its work, and is called a *rasterizer implementation*. A rasterizer implementation is an abstract class, and is subclassed to provide concrete rasterizer implementations for specific software or hardware platforms.

As with the related class `l3d_rasterizer_2d`, we first saw this concept in the discussion of byte-to-pixel correspondence. While the related class `l3d_rasterizer_2d` represents an interface to 2D rasterizer functionality, the class `l3d_rasterizer_2d_imp` represents an interface to an <u>implementation of</u> 2D rasterizer functionality. This rasterizer implementation can (in subclasses) be based upon either hand-coded software algorithms or an API to hardware-accelerated rasterization functions.

The code for class `l3d_rasterizer_2d_imp` is in the previously shown Listings 2-38 and 2-39; the code for the rasterizer and the (abstract) rasterizer implementation are in the same files.

The variable `sinfo` points to an object of type `l3d_screen_info`. Through the `sinfo` pointer, the rasterizer implementation can obtain all the information it needs about the target display device in order to draw into it.

The variables `xsize` and `ysize` store the horizontal and vertical dimensions of the off-screen buffer in pixels.

The abstract method `clear_buffer` is a placeholder for a routine to clear the off-screen buffer. This method is overridden in descendants with the actual system-specific implementation code.

The abstract method `draw_point` is a placeholder for a routine to draw a point in the off-screen buffer. This method is overridden in descendants with the actual system-specific implementation code.

The abstract method `draw_line` is a placeholder for a routine to draw a line in the off-screen buffer. This method is overridden in descendants with the actual system-specific implementation code. Drawing lines in software is covered in Chapter 3.

The method `draw_polygon_flatshaded` is a placeholder for a routine to draw a single-colored (flat-shaded) polygon in the off-screen buffer. This method is overridden in descendants with the actual system-specific implementation code. Drawing polygons in software is covered in Chapter 3.

A Software Rasterizer Implementation: l3d_rasterizer_2d_sw_imp

The class `l3d_rasterizer_2d_sw_imp`, derived from class `l3d_rasterizer_2d_imp`, represents a rasterizer implementation implemented in software (as opposed to hardware).

As with the parent class `l3d_rasterizer_2d_imp`, we first saw this concept in the discussion of byte-to-pixel correspondence. The calculation of the bytes corresponding to a pixel and setting these bytes in order to display geometric primitives are all operations typical of software rasterization implementations, but not necessarily of hardware rasterizer implementations. This is the reason that such byte and pixel calculations take place only in the concrete l3d_rasterizer_2d_sw_imp subclass, which represents a software rasterizer implementation, and not in the abstract ancestor class l3d_rasterizer_2d_imp, which represents a more abstract concept of a software or hardware rasterizer implementation.

NOTE The following code implements in software two functions which we have not yet seen in any example programs: drawing a line and drawing a flat-shaded polygon. For now, just skip these functions; we return to them in Chapter 3, which discusses rasterization in detail.

Listing 2-40: ras_sw.h

```
#ifndef __RAS_SW_H
#define __RAS_SW_H
#include "../tool_os/memman.h"

#include "rasteriz.h"
#include "math.h"
#include "../system/sys_dep.h"

class l3d_rasterizer_2d_sw_imp :
    virtual public l3d_rasterizer_2d_imp
{
  protected:
    unsigned char *address_of_point(int x, int y);
    void draw_point_at_paddress(unsigned char **a, unsigned long col);

  public:
    l3d_rasterizer_2d_sw_imp(int xs, int ys, l3d_screen_info *si);
    void clear_buffer(void);
    void draw_point(int x, int y, unsigned long col);
    void draw_line(int x0, int y0, int x1, int y1, unsigned long col);
    void draw_polygon_flatshaded(const l3d_polygon_2d_flatshaded *p_poly);
};

class l3d_rasterizer_2d_sw_imp_factory :
    public l3d_rasterizer_2d_imp_factory
{
  public:
    l3d_rasterizer_2d_imp *create(int xs, int ys, l3d_screen_info *si);
};

inline unsigned char *l3d_rasterizer_2d_sw_imp::address_of_point(int x, int y)
{
  return sinfo->p_screenbuf +(x + (y*xsize)) * sinfo->bytes_per_pixel;
}

inline void l3d_rasterizer_2d_sw_imp::draw_point_at_paddress
(unsigned char **p, unsigned long col)
{
  register int i;
  unsigned long mask = MAX_BYTE;
  char shift = 0;

  for(i=0; i<sinfo->bytes_per_pixel; i++) {
    **p = (col & mask) > shift;
    (*p)++;
    mask <= BITS_PER_BYTE;
    shift += BITS_PER_BYTE;
  }
```

```
}

inline void l3d_rasterizer_2d_sw_imp::draw_point
(int x, int y, unsigned long col)
{
  unsigned char *p = address_of_point(x,y);
  draw_point_at_paddress(&p, col);
}


#endif
```

Listing 2-41: `ras_sw.cc`

```
#include "ras_sw.h"
#include "../system/sys_dep.h"
#include <string.h>
#include <stdlib.h>
#include "../tool_os/memman.h"

l3d_rasterizer_2d_imp * l3d_rasterizer_2d_sw_imp_factory::create
(int xs, int ys, l3d_screen_info *si)
{
  return new l3d_rasterizer_2d_sw_imp(xs,ys,si);
}


l3d_rasterizer_2d_sw_imp::l3d_rasterizer_2d_sw_imp
(int xs, int ys, l3d_screen_info *si)
    : l3d_rasterizer_2d_imp(xs,ys,si)
{
}


void l3d_rasterizer_2d_sw_imp::clear_buffer(void) {
  memset(sinfo->p_screenbuf, 0x00, (size_t)xsize*ysize*sinfo->bytes_per_pixel);
}


void l3d_rasterizer_2d_sw_imp::draw_line(int x0, int y0,
    int x1, int y1, unsigned long col)
{
  l3d_real fx,fy,m;
  int x,y,tmp,dx,dy;

  dx = x1 - x0;
  dy = y1 - y0;

  if(abs( ABS_CAST dx) > abs( ABS_CAST dy)) {//- a "mostly horizontal" line
    //- ensure (x0,y0) is horizontally smaller than (x1,y1)
    if(x1<x0) {tmp=x0;x0=x1;x1=tmp; tmp=y0;y0=y1;y1=tmp;}
    fy = int_to_l3d_real(y0);
    m = l3d_divrr( int_to_l3d_real(dy), int_to_l3d_real(dx) );
    for(x=x0; x<=x1; x++) {
      draw_point(x,
                 SW_RAST_Y_REVERSAL(ysize,
                                    l3d_real_to_int
                                    (fy+float_to_l3d_real(0.5))),
                 col);
      fy = fy + m;
    }
  }//- mostly horizontal line
  else {//- mostly vertical line
    //- ensure (x0,y0) is vertically smaller than (x1,y1)
    if(y1<y0) {tmp=x0;x0=x1;x1=tmp; tmp=y0;y0=y1;y1=tmp;}
```

```
      fx = int_to_l3d_real(x0);
      if( !(int_to_l3d_real(dy) )) return; //- degenerate: line is just a point
      m = l3d_divrr( int_to_l3d_real(dx), int_to_l3d_real(dy) );
      for(y=y0; y<=y1; y++) {
        draw_point(l3d_real_to_int(fx+float_to_l3d_real(0.5)),
                   SW_RAST_Y_REVERSAL(ysize,y),
                   col);
        fx = fx + m;
      }
  }//- mostly vertical line
}

void l3d_rasterizer_2d_sw_imp::draw_polygon_flatshaded
(const l3d_polygon_2d_flatshaded *p_poly)
{
  l3d_real x0,y0,x1,y1,x2,y2,x3,
  left_x_start,left_y_start,left_x_end,left_y_end,left_dx,left_x,leftedge,
  right_x_start,right_y_start,right_x_end,right_y_end,right_dx,right_x,rightedge;
  int left_ceily_start, left_ceily_end,
  right_ceily_start, right_ceily_end, scanline;
  l3d_real top_y, bottom_y;
  int point_on_right=0;
  int left_idx, right_idx, top_y_idx, bottom_y_idx;

  int clipleftedge, cliprightedge;
  int maxy_upper, iceil_y0, iceil_y1, iceil_y2;

  int i;

  //- convenience macro for accessing the vertex coordinates. Notice
  //- that we access the clipped vertex index list (not the original),
  //- and the transformed coordinate (not the original). This means
  //- we draw the clipped version of the transformed polygon.
  #define VTX(i) ((**(p_poly->vlist))[ (*(p_poly->clip_ivertices))[i].ivertex ].transformed)

  //------------------------------------------
  //- STEP 1: Find top and bottom vertices
  //------------------------------------------

  top_y = VTX(0).Y_;
  top_y_idx = 0;
  bottom_y = top_y;
  bottom_y_idx = top_y_idx;
  for(i=0; i<p_poly->clip_ivertices->num_items; i++) {

    if(VTX(i).Y_ < top_y) {
      top_y = VTX(i).Y_;
      top_y_idx = i;
    }
    if(VTX(i).Y_ > bottom_y) {
      bottom_y = VTX(i).Y_;
      bottom_y_idx = i;
    }
  }

  left_idx = top_y_idx;
  right_idx = top_y_idx;

  //------------------------------------------
  //- STEP 2: Create empty left edge
```

```
//————————————————————————
left_x_start = VTX(top_y_idx).X_;
left_y_start = VTX(top_y_idx).Y_;
left_ceily_start=iceil(left_y_start);
left_ceily_end=left_ceily_start;


//————————————————————————
//- STEP 3: Create empty right edge
//————————————————————————
right_x_start=left_x_start;
right_y_start=left_y_start;
right_ceily_start=left_ceily_start;
right_ceily_end=right_ceily_start;


//————————————————————————
//- STEP 4: Loop from top y to bottom y
//————————————————————————
scanline = left_ceily_start;

while(scanline < ysize) {

   //————————————————————————————
   //- STEP 5: Find next left-edge of non-zero height (if needed)
   //————————————————————————————
   while( left_ceily_end - scanline <= 0 ) {
     if (left_idx == bottom_y_idx) return;   //- done
     left_idx    = p_poly->next_clipidx_left
                  (left_idx, p_poly->clip_ivertices->num_items);
     left_y_end= VTX(left_idx).Y_;
     left_ceily_end = iceil(left_y_end);

     if(left_ceily_end - scanline) { //- found next vertex
        //————————————————————————
        //- STEP 5a: Initialize left-x variables
        //————————————————————————
        left_x_end= VTX(left_idx).X_;
        left_dx = l3d_divrr(left_x_end-left_x_start,left_y_end-left_y_start);
        left_x = left_x_start +   //- sub-pixel correction
                 l3d_mulrr(int_to_l3d_real(left_ceily_start)-left_y_start , left_dx);
     }else { //- did not find next vertex: last failed end = new start
        left_x_start = VTX(left_idx).X_;
        left_y_start = VTX(left_idx).Y_;
        left_ceily_start = iceil(left_y_start);
     }
   }


   //————————————————————————
   //- STEP 6: Find next right-edge of non-zero height (if needed)
   //————————————————————————
   //- if needed, find next right-edge whose ceily_end > current scanline
   //- this is a while and not an if, as desribed above...
   while(right_ceily_end - scanline <= 0 ) {
     if (right_idx == bottom_y_idx) return;   //- done
     right_idx = p_poly->next_clipidx_right
                  (right_idx,p_poly->clip_ivertices->num_items);
     right_y_end=VTX(right_idx).Y_;
     right_ceily_end = iceil(right_y_end);
     if(right_ceily_end - scanline) { //- found next vertex
        //————————————————————————
        //- STEP 6a: Initialize right-x variables
```

```
      //————————————————————————————
      right_x_end=VTX(right_idx).X_;
      right_dx =
        l3d_divrr(right_x_end-right_x_start,right_y_end-right_y_start);
      right_x = right_x_start +  //- sub-pixel correction
                l3d_mulrr(int_to_l3d_real(right_ceily_start)-right_y_start , right_dx);
    }else { //- did not find next vertex: last failed end = new start
      right_x_start = VTX(right_idx).X_;
      right_y_start = VTX(right_idx).Y_;
      right_ceily_start = iceil(right_y_start);
    }
  }


  //- clamp edge values to screen
  if (left_ceily_end > ysize) left_ceily_end = ysize;
  if (right_ceily_end > ysize) right_ceily_end = ysize;


  //————————————————————————————
  //- STEP 7: Loop until left and/or right edge is finished
  //————————————————————————————
  while ( (scanline < left_ceily_end) && (scanline < right_ceily_end) ) {
      clipleftedge = iceil(left_x);
#ifdef FIXED_POINT_MATH
      //- due to numerical inaccuracy with fixed-point math we also
      //- perform this (otherwise unnecessary) check here to clamp the
      //- edge values to the screen borders
      clipleftedge = (clipleftedge < 0) ? 0 : clipleftedge;
#endif
      cliprightedge = iceil(right_x);

#ifdef FIXED_POINT_MATH
      //- due to numerical inaccuracy with fixed-point math we also
      //- perform this (otherwise unnecessary) check here to clamp the
      //- edge values to the screen borders
      cliprightedge = (cliprightedge > xsize) ? xsize : cliprightedge;
#endif

#ifdef FIXED_POINT_MATH
      //- due to numerical inaccuracy with fixed-point math we also
      //- perform this (otherwise unnecessary) check here to clamp the
      //- edge values to the screen borders
      if( (left_x<int_to_l3d_real(xsize   )) && (right_x>int_to_l3d_real(0))
          &&  (clipleftedge <= cliprightedge) && (scanline>0) )
#endif
      {

        //————————————————————————————
        //- STEP 8: Draw horizontal span
        //————————————————————————————
        for(register char unsigned *pix =
            address_of_point(clipleftedge,
                             SW_RAST_Y_REVERSAL(ysize,scanline));
          pix < address_of_point(cliprightedge, scanline);
          )
        {
          draw_point_at_paddress(&pix, p_poly->final_color);
        }
      }


      //————————————————————————————
```

```
//- STEP 9: Increase y, and step x-values on left and right edges
//-----------------------------------
scanline++;
left_x += left_dx;
right_x += right_dx;
}


//-----------------------------------
//- STEP 10: Continue loop, looking for next edge of non-zero height
//-----------------------------------

//- for the left and/or right segment(s) which just completed drawing
//- initialize xxx_start = xxx_end, to begin next segment. xxx_end is
//- then searched for in the next iteration (the while() loops)
if ( left_ceily_end - scanline <= 0 ) {
  left_x_start=left_x_end;
  left_y_start=left_y_end;
  left_ceily_start=left_ceily_end;
}
if ( right_ceily_end - scanline <= 0 ) {
  right_x_start=right_x_end;
  right_y_start=right_y_end;
  right_ceily_start=right_ceily_end;
}
}
}
}
#undef VTX(i)
```

The private method `address_of_point` returns the memory address in the off-screen buffer of the first byte corresponding to the pixel at the given location. The formula which is used was presented earlier, in the discussion of byte-to-pixel correspondence. Notice that this function uses the `sinfo` object (of type `l3d_screen_info`) to find out the display depth and the address of the first byte in the off-screen buffer.

The private method `draw_point_at_paddress` draws a pixel with a specified color at a particular address in the off-screen buffer. As parameters it takes a pointer to the first address to be drawn to (obtainable via the `address_of_point` function) and a color specified in native format (obtainable via the `l3d_screen_info::ext_to_native` function). The function places the bytes from the color parameter into the off-screen buffer in the proper order, and increments the pointer variable in the calling function to point to the next pixel in the off-screen buffer. This way, plotting a series of horizontally adjacent pixels only requires one call to `address_of_point` and a series of repeated calls to `draw_point_at_paddress`. Calling both `address_of_point` and `draw_point_at_paddress` for every single pixel to be drawn would be wasteful and unnecessarily slow. When drawing filled polygons (covered in Chapter 3), we often need to draw series of horizontally adjacent pixels (called horizontal *spans*), and will thus follow the strategy of calling `address_of_point` once and `draw_point_at_paddress` several times for each horizontal span.

The overridden method `clear_buffer` uses the `memset` function to set all bytes in the off-screen buffer to zero, thereby clearing the screen. Recall, we need to clear the off-screen buffer before drawing a new frame, since otherwise the contents from the previous frame will still be in the buffer. The exception to this rule is if every pixel in the buffer is updated every frame.

The overridden method `draw_point` uses the `address_of_point` and `draw_point_at_paddress` functions to find and fill the correct bytes in the off-screen buffer corresponding to the desired pixel. As mentioned above, calling both `address_of_point` and `draw_point_at_paddress` is unnecessarily slow if we are drawing a series of horizontal span of pixels, so the function `draw_point` is only used if we are drawing a single point to the screen.

The overridden method `draw_line` uses a software algorithm to draw pixels lying on a line between the given endpoints. The algorithm used is covered later in Chapter 3, which deals with the topic of software rasterization.

The overridden method `draw_polygon_flatshaded` uses a software algorithm to draw pixels lying within a polygon specified by the given polygon object. The algorithm used, as well as the polygon class itself, is covered in Chapter 3.

Figure 2-23 illustrates the class diagram for rasterization-related classes.

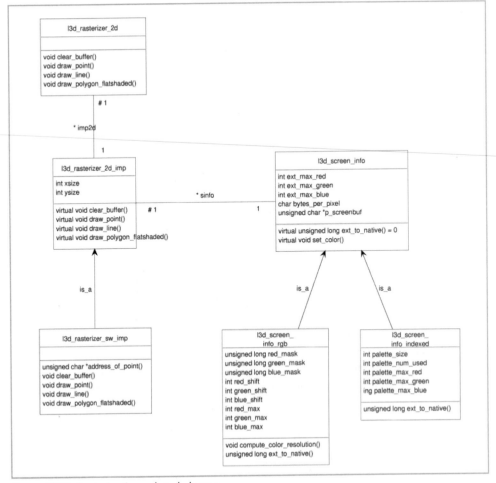

Figure 2-23: Rasterization-related classes.

Choosing the Concrete Factories

The class `l3d_factory_manager` represents the factory manager which contains all factories that any class might need in the entire program. Whenever an object requests object creation through "a factory," this factory is to be found in the central factory manager.

We first encountered this concept in sample program ch2_hello_oo, which used an application factory to create the main application object, thereby shielding the program logic from the underlying concrete application type. (We also discussed at length the idea behind the abstract factory design pattern, using a carpenter analogy.)

Listing 2-42: `factorys.h`

```
#ifndef __FACTORYS_H
#define __FACTORYS_H
#include "../tool_os/memman.h"

#include "../tool_2d/screen.h"
#include "../raster/rasteriz.h"
#include "../tool_os/dispatch.h"

class l3d_factory_manager_v_0_1 {
  public:
    l3d_factory_manager_v_0_1(void);
    virtual ~l3d_factory_manager_v_0_1(void);
    int should_delete_factories;
    l3d_screen_factory *screen_factory;
    l3d_rasterizer_2d_imp_factory *ras_2d_imp_factory;
    l3d_dispatcher_factory *dispatcher_factory;

    int choose_factories(void);
};

extern l3d_factory_manager_v_0_1 factory_manager_v_0_1;

#endif
```

Listing 2-43: `factorys.cc`

```
#include "factorys.h"

#include "../tool_os/dis_x11.h"
#include "../tool_os/dis_mesa.h"
#include "../tool_2d/sc_x11.h"
#include "../tool_2d/sc_x11sh.h"
#include "../tool_2d/sc_mesa.h"
#include "../raster/ras_sw.h"
#include "../raster/ras_mesa.h"
#include <stdio.h>
#include "../tool_os/memman.h"

l3d_factory_manager_v_0_1 factory_manager_v_0_1;

l3d_factory_manager_v_0_1::l3d_factory_manager_v_0_1(void) {
  screen_factory = NULL;
  ras_2d_imp_factory = NULL;
  dispatcher_factory = NULL;
  should_delete_factories=1;
}
```

```
l3d_factory_manager_v_0_1::~l3d_factory_manager_v_0_1(void) {
  if(should_delete_factories) {
    if(screen_factory) {
      delete screen_factory;
      screen_factory = NULL;
    }
    if(ras_2d_imp_factory) {
      delete ras_2d_imp_factory;
      ras_2d_imp_factory = NULL;
    }
    if(dispatcher_factory) {
      delete dispatcher_factory;
      dispatcher_factory = NULL;
    }
  }
}

int l3d_factory_manager_v_0_1::choose_factories(void) {
  char input[80];
  int i;

  printf("which configuration?");
  printf("1. Software X11");
  printf("2. Software X11 with SHM extension");
  printf("3. Mesa (with 3DFX h/w accel if installed with Mesa)");
  gets(input);
  sscanf(input,"%d", &i);
  switch(i) {
    case 1:
      screen_factory = new l3d_screen_factory_x11;
      ras_2d_imp_factory = new l3d_rasterizer_2d_sw_imp_factory;
      dispatcher_factory = new l3d_dispatcher_factory_x11;
      break;
    case 2:
      screen_factory = new l3d_screen_factory_x11_shm;
      ras_2d_imp_factory = new l3d_rasterizer_2d_sw_imp_factory;
      dispatcher_factory = new l3d_dispatcher_factory_x11;
      break;
    case 3:
      screen_factory = new l3d_screen_factory_mesa;
      ras_2d_imp_factory = new l3d_rasterizer_2d_mesa_imp_factory;
      dispatcher_factory = new l3d_dispatcher_factory_mesa;
      break;
  }
  return i;
}
```

The variable `screen_factory` is a pointer of abstract type `l3d_screen_factory`, which polymorphically points to an actual concrete screen factory. Concrete screen factories (such as `l3d_screen_factory_x11`) are declared in the same files as the concrete screens themselves (such as `l3d_screen_x11`). External objects requesting screen creation do so through the abstract `screen_factory` pointer, which then gets connected at run time to the correct concrete screen factory. The screen factory then returns a concrete screen object through an abstract pointer of type `l3d_screen`.

The variable `ras_2d_imp_factory` is a pointer of abstract type `l3d_rasterizer_2d_imp_factory`, which polymorphically points to an actual concrete rasterizer implementation factory. Concrete rasterizer implementation factories (such as `l3d_rasterizer_`

`2d_sw_imp_factory`) are declared in the same files as the concrete rasterizer implementations themselves (such as `l3d_rasterizer_2d_sw_imp`). External objects requesting creation of a rasterizer implementation do so through the abstract `ras_2d_imp_factory` pointer.

The variable `dispatcher_factory` is a pointer of abstract type `l3d_dispatcher_factory`, which polymorphically points to an actual concrete dispatcher factory. Concrete dispatcher factories (such as `l3d_dispatcher_factory_x11`) are declared in the same files as the concrete dispatchers themselves (such as `l3d_dispatcher_x11`). External objects requesting creation of a dispatcher do so through the abstract `dispatcher_factory` pointer.

The method `choose_factories` interactively asks the user which factories should be chosen, and creates the appropriate concrete factories, assigning them to the factory variables listed above. The concrete factories are created directly with the C++ `new` operator. The interactive user query could be replaced with an automatic hardware detection routine or conditional compilation statements which create the proper concrete factories. Conditional compilation statements would be required if the different concrete factories require different, incompatible header files in order to be compiled at all.

Global variable `factory_manager_v_0_1` is a global instance of the factory manager. An application chooses its factories at startup time through the global variable `factory_manager_v_0_1`. Thus, the factory manager class is a singleton class, which is instantiated only once in the entire program.

Notice that this is the only l3d class which directly manipulates the concrete factories by their class name, and which includes the header files for the concrete factories. All other users of the factories always go through an abstract factory interface, and do not include the header files for the concrete factories. This is the whole point of the abstract factory: to completely isolate the application from the underlying concrete types to allow for future extension of code without any change of original code (as we saw illustrated in the `hello_oo_event` example).

Summary of l3d Classes Covered So Far

Figure 2-24 illustrates all classes covered up to this point. Study the previously presented `drawdot` program to keep a practical perspective on the use of the l3d classes, and remember the general five-step process for creating l3d applications.

Generally, the main part of an l3d program will only directly deal with the pipeline, screen, and rasterizer classes. Your application is the pipeline; it draws to the screen using the rasterizer.

With one exception, all of the l3d classes presented above implement concepts which we already covered in the previous sections. Again, this is an important property of object-oriented designs: they organize or reorganize code in terms of relevant abstractions.

The "one exception" we mentioned above is the `l3d_rasterizer_2d_sw_imp` class. In this class, we presented routines for drawing pixels, lines, and flat-shaded polygons. While we have already looked at drawing individual pixels (in the earlier discussions of byte-to-pixel correspondence and colors in XImages), we have not yet discussed drawing lines and polygons. This is the topic of the next chapter: rasterization.

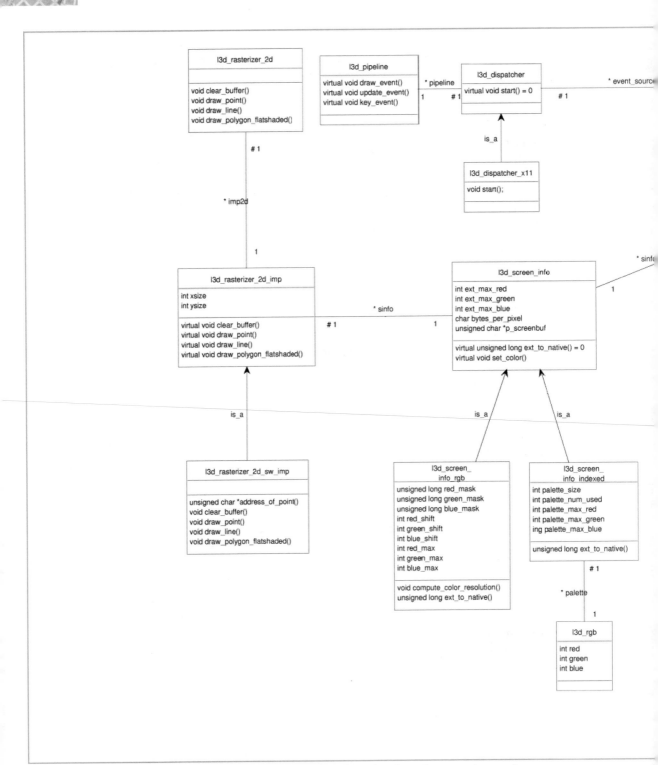

Figure 2-24: Class diagram for all l3d classes covered so far, plus a few from the upcoming sections.

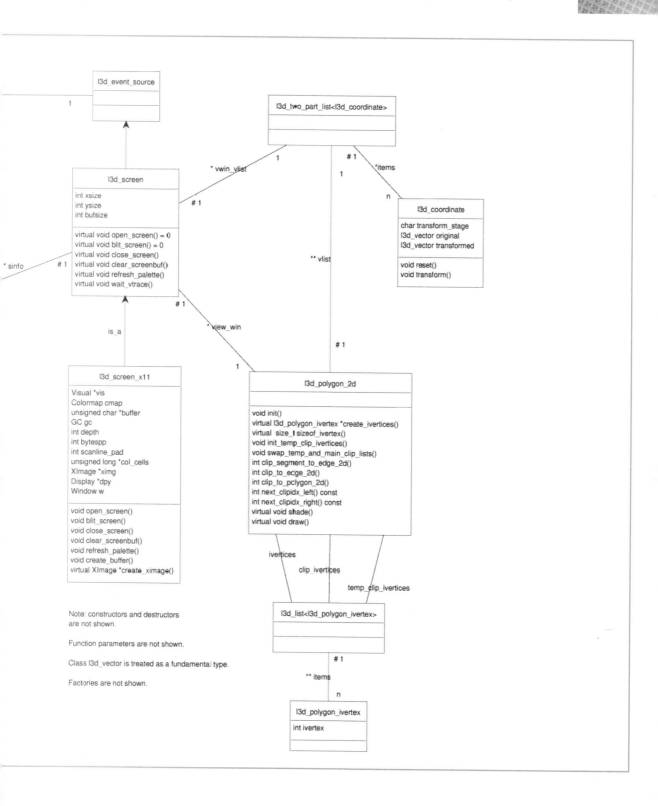

l3d_event_source

1

l3d_two_part_list<l3d_coordinate>

l3d_screen

int xsize
int ysize
int bufsize

virtual void open_screen() = 0
virtual void blit_screen() = 0
virtual void close_screen()
virtual void clear_screenbuf()
virtual void refresh_palette()
virtual void wait_vtrace()

* vwin_vlist

1

1

1

1

*items

1

n

l3d_coordinate

char transform_stage
l3d_vector original
l3d_vector transformed

void reset()
void transform()

* sinfo

** vlist

is_a

1

* view_win

1

l3d_screen_x11

Visual *vis
Colormap cmap
unsigned char *buffer
GC gc
int depth
int bytespp
int scanline_pad
unsigned long *col_cells
XImage *ximg
Display *dpy
Window w

void open_screen()
void blit_screen()
void close_screen()
void clear_screenbuf()
void refresh_palette()
void create_buffer()
virtual XImage *create_ximage()

1

l3d_polygon_2d

void init()
virtual l3d_polygon_ivertex *create_ivertices()
virtual size_t sizeof_ivertex()
void init_temp_clip_ivertices()
void swap_temp_and_main_clip_lists()
int clip_segment_to_edge_2d()
int clip_to_edge_2d()
int clip_to_polygon_2d()
int next_clipidx_left() const
int next_clipidx_right() const
virtual void shade()
virtual void draw()

Note: constructors and destructors
are not shown.

Function parameters are not shown.

Class l3d_vector is treated as a fundamental type.

Factories are not shown.

ivertices

clip_ivertices

temp_clip_ivertices

l3d_list<l3d_polygon_ivertex>

1

** items

n

l3d_polygon_ivertex

int ivertex

Summary

In this chapter, we covered accessing the 2D screen under Linux under the X Window System. We looked at the following topics:

- Creation of windows under X and X event handling
- XImages and animated, double-buffered graphics
- X visuals, color depths, color models, and pixel formats
- Object-oriented techniques such as inheritance, virtual functions, design patterns, factories, and handles
- Design of an object-oriented graphics library, l3d

We therefore have a theoretical and practical foundation for flexibly accessing the 2D screen under Linux. The next chapter deals with 2D graphics, which we need for 3D graphics. In particular, we look at the rasterization of 2D lines and polygons, both in pure software as well as in a hardware-accelerated environment.

Chapter 3

2D Rasterization

Overview

This chapter discusses 2D rasterization and related issues. Rasterization, as we touched on in the previous chapter, is the process of rendering geometric primitives onto a raster display composed of pixels. Chapter 2 showed us how to initialize a screen under Linux and how to light individual pixels with specific colors. In this chapter, we look at algorithms to draw groups of pixels—in particular, lines and filled polygons. Drawing polygons is an important and frequently occurring operation in 3D graphics programs. Indeed, Chapter 7 returns to the topic of polygons, and extends the ideas to 3D.

Geometric primitives rendered to the screen may be larger than the screen itself, which introduces the need for clipping the primitives to fit within the display. This chapter therefore discusses a few approaches to clipping. Also, rasterization may be carried out either purely in software or with the help of dedicated graphics hardware. This chapter discusses and implements both. We use the Mesa library to realize hardware-accelerated rasterization under Linux. In the process, we also learn about Mesa and OpenGL programming in general.

This chapter covers the following concepts:

- Software rasterization of dots, lines, and polygons
- Clipping polygons in 2D
- Vertex animation and morphing of polygons
- Basic Mesa/OpenGL programming
- Hardware acceleration using Mesa and 3DFX

The sample programs in this chapter illustrate working code to draw lines and polygons on the 2D screen using l3d classes.

 NOTE From now on, it is assumed that you already know how to compile and run the sample programs, so we won't devote any more space to these issues. Chapter 2 contains several step-by-step examples of compiling and running individual programs, and the Appendix contains instructions for compiling all the example programs in the book at once.

Software Rasterization

In Chapter 2, we saw the sample program `drawdot`, which uses the l3d library. We also looked at the structure of l3d programs, and at the structure of the l3d library itself. In this process, we saw how the rasterizer and rasterizer implementation objects in the l3d library form an interface to and implementation of rasterization services (the bridge design pattern).

Although we discussed the structure of the l3d rasterization classes in the previous chapter, what we didn't discuss were the actual rasterization algorithms appearing in the software rasterizer implementation class. That is the purpose of this section: to describe in detail the software rasterization algorithms used in the l3d library.

The term *software rasterization* refers to the use of algorithms in software to draw geometric primitives into a frame buffer. The alternative to software rasterization is hardware rasterization, where dedicated hardware provides functions for drawing primitives more quickly than is possible through software.

The l3d class dealing with software rasterization, initially presented in Chapter 2, is `l3d_rasterizer_2d_sw_imp`. The l3d classes distinguish between the rasterizer itself, which is a description of (or equivalently, an interface to) rasterizer functionality, and the rasterizer implementation, which is one particular way of realizing the functionality described by the rasterizer. A software rasterizer implementation implements algorithms to set the appropriate pixels corresponding to a geometric primitive.

By "geometric primitive," we mean a point, line, or polygon. (Don't worry if you don't yet have a solid idea of what a "polygon" is; we define this below, in the section titled "Rasterizing Flat-shaded Polygons.") Therefore, a software rasterizer implementation takes a specification of a point, line, or polygon, and sets the corresponding pixels within the frame buffer to produce a rasterized image of the specified primitive.

If you have done some 2D graphics programming before, you might question the need for a software rasterizer implementation. After all, as noted in Chapter 1, practically all modern operating systems offer some sort of a library for drawing 2D primitives to the screen. Is it really necessary to do this work ourselves?

The answer to this question used to be a clear-cut "yes," but the appearance of hardware acceleration on the PC scene has changed this slightly. Let's first view the situation historically, assuming no hardware acceleration, then see what role hardware acceleration plays.

In the absence of hardware acceleration, there are two compelling reasons to do your own rasterization instead of relying on an external library provided by the OS or your compiler: speed and flexibility. Typically, a ready-made, general-purpose 2D drawing library (such as the 2D drawing functions provided by Xlib) will be slower than a specialized routine, might not support double buffering, and will almost certainly not offer any provision for per-pixel operations necessary for high-quality 3D graphics such as smooth shading or texture mapping. For these reasons, interactive, high-quality 3D programs have historically done their own rasterization. At first, it might seem to be a rather mind-boggling proposition that the CPU actually can be fast enough to compute each and every single pixel in each image, several times a second. However, the situation becomes understandable when we realize that setting a pixel by hand is equivalent to setting bytes in memory, as opposed to calling an API function with its associated function-call overhead. Calling a function thousands of times per frame to set a pixel is intolerably slow (due to the push and pop activity of the run-time stack); on the other hand, setting bytes in memory thousands of times per frame is acceptably fast. Recall, this is why we chose XImages as the display medium of choice: we can directly access the bytes and do not need to go through functions to manipulate pixels. (We actually do have a pixel-plotting function in the rasterizer implementation, but it is declared inline and therefore incurs no function-call penalty at run time.)

That software rasterization outperforms a ready-made API was a general truth until 3D hardware acceleration appeared. With hardware acceleration, API function calls get translated into hardware instructions. If a single function call can then set thousands of pixels at once, the overhead of the single function call is outweighed by the drastically increased speed of the entire rasterization operation in hardware. Furthermore, 3D hardware acceleration also provides support for specifying texture mapping, smooth shading, and other parameters necessary for high-quality 3D graphics. Accelerated hardware can also perform many more operations which are typically too time-consuming for software rasterizer implementations, such as z-buffering, blending, or filtering.

If hardware acceleration provides such advantages, why bother with software rasterization? There are three reasons. First, the l3d library is designed such that it can use either software or hardware rasterization; we do not lose any flexibility by implementing software rasterization. Second, not everyone has hardware acceleration—laptop, notebook, palmtop, or embedded computer devices often do not have any sort of 3D hardware acceleration. Third, understanding rasterization concepts is important for a well-rounded understanding of 3D graphics. Without an understanding of rasterization, the hardware API becomes a magical black box which somehow mysteriously draws polygons. I believe it would be a great hinderance to a 3D programmer not to understand how rasterization works. There is something very enlightening and satisfying about knowing exactly how and why every single pixel on the display is generated.

Rasterizing Dots

Rasterizing a dot means drawing one pixel. To do this in software, we need to calculate the address of the pixel in the frame buffer, and fill the byte or bytes corresponding to the pixel with the correct values for the desired color. We already discussed this topic in Chapter 2 (in the discussions of byte-to-pixel correspondence and colors in XImages), so the l3d methods for rasterizing a dot are only briefly described here.

The method `address_of_point` calculates the memory address of a pixel within the frame buffer, given the pixel's (x,y) coordinates:

```
inline unsigned char *l3d_rasterizer_2d_sw_imp::address_of_point(int x, int y)
{
  return sinfo->p_screenbuf +(x + (y*xsize)) * sinfo->bytes_per_pixel;
}
```

The method `draw_point_at_paddress` takes a pointer to a pointer to a memory address (typically initially calculated by the method `address_of_point`) and a color specification. The exact format of the color specification depends on the bit depth of the screen and can be computed by using the method `l3d_screen_info::ext_to_native`, as we saw in Chapter 2.

The method `draw_point` then draws the specified color into the pixel at the specified address, and updates the pointer to point to the next horizontally adjacent pixel in the frame buffer. In this manner, we can plot groups of horizontally adjacent pixels (called *spans*) without needing to invoke the code in `address_of_point` for every pixel in the horizontal span. As we see later in this chapter, we draw polygons by drawing a vertical stack of horizontal spans.

```
inline void l3d_rasterizer_2d_sw_imp::draw_point_at_address
(unsigned char **p, unsigned long col)
{
  register int I;
  unsigned long mask = MAX_BYTE;
  char shift = 0;

  for(i=0; i<sinfo->bytes_per_pixel; i++) {
    **p = (col & mask) > shift;
    (*p)++;
    mask <= BITS_PER_BYTE;
    shift += BITS_PER_BYTE;
  }
}
```

The method draw_point takes an (x,y) location and a color as parameters. It then plots a pixel with the specified color at the specified (x,y) location. It merely calls the above two methods in order.

```
inline void l3d_rasterizer_2d_sw_imp::draw_point
(int x, int y, unsigned long col)
{
  unsigned char *p = address_of_point(x,y);
  draw_point_at_paddress(&p, col);
}
```

Rasterizing Lines

Rasterizing a line means drawing a set of pixels which lie on the line segment between two given endpoints specified in pixel coordinates. In reality, we will rarely need to draw lines for the programs in this book, but the function is provided for completeness.

There are several ways to approach the problem of drawing a line. We will use the most geometrically intuitive approach, called the *incremental algorithm*.

NOTE The incremental algorithm (also sometimes called a *digital differential analyzer* or *DDA algorithm*) is in practice not the most accurate method for drawing lines. We can define "accuracy" to mean always drawing the pixels which are closest to the mathematically "true" line segment between the two specified points. Bresenham's algorithm and the midpoint algorithm are two approaches for drawing the most "accurate" lines possible. These algorithms are a bit less geometrically intuitive, and rely upon an error term and a decision variable to incrementally choose the next "correct" pixel as they step across the line in pixel space.

The idea behind the incremental algorithm is as follows. Let us name the coordinates of the starting point (x_0, y_0), and those of the ending point (x_1, y_1). We first calculate the slope of the line, called m:

Equation 3-1
$$m = \frac{\Delta y}{\Delta x} = \frac{y_1 - y_0}{x_1 - x_0}$$

We then use the slope-intercept form of the line:

Equation 3-2 $y_i = mx_i + B$

B represents the y-intercept of the line, which is the coordinate along the y axis where the line intercepts it. For each pixel x_i between x_0 and x_1, we then use the above slope-intercept formula to compute the appropriate value of y_i. We then plot the pixel at (x_i, y_i), though we must first round the value of y_i to an integer pixel coordinate before plotting it, since in general the slope-intercept formula will generally yield a y coordinate with a fractional part.

The above algorithm can be made more efficient by realizing the following:

Equation 3-3 $y_{i+1} = mx_{i+1} + B = m(x_i + \Delta x) + B = (mx_i + B) + m\Delta x = y_i + m\Delta x$

In other words, we now have an incremental way of determining the next y value, y_{i+1}, based upon the current y value, y_i. The next y value is the current y value plus the slope times the x stepping increment $?x$. Since we want to draw all pixels within the line, we will step by single pixels, and $?x = 1$. The formula then becomes:

Equation 3-4 $y_{i+1} = y_i + m$

This means that the next value of y is the current y plus the slope. The first y value is set to y_0; the first x value is set to x_0. We step in the x direction from x_0 to x_1, incrementing y and plotting pixels as we go.

The catch is that the above logic only works as is for lines with a slope less than or equal to one (i.e., lines which are more horizontal than vertical). The implicit assumption of the previous equation is that y is a function of x. For lines with a slope greater than one, stepping in the x direction yields vertical gaps in the line, because y is no longer a function of x (in the discrete domain of pixels). In fact, x is a function of y in this case. This simply means that we need to reverse the roles of x and y in the above equation, computing an inverse slope, stepping in the y direction, and increasing x each time by the inverse slope.

With this knowledge, understanding the `l3d_rasterizer_2d_sw_imp::draw _line` function is straightforward. We first decide if the line is mostly horizontal or mostly vertical, compute the slope or inverse slope as appropriate, and step in whole pixels along one axis while moving by the slope or inverse slope along the other axis.

```
void l3d_rasterizer_2d_sw_imp::draw_line(int x0, int y0,
    int x1, int y1, unsigned long col)
{
    l3d_real fx,fy,m;
    int x,y,tmp,dx,dy;

    dx = x1 - x0;
    dy = y1 - y0;

    if(abs( ABS_CAST dx) > abs( ABS_CAST dy)) {//- a "mostly horizontal" line
        //- ensure (x0,y0) is horizontally smaller than (x1,y1)
        if(x1<x0) {tmp=x0;x0=x1;x1=tmp; tmp=y0;y0=y1;y1=tmp;}
        fy = int_to_l3d_real(y0);
        m = l3d_divrr( int_to_l3d_real(dy), int_to_l3d_real(dx) );
        for(x=x0; x<=x1; x++) {
            draw_point(x,
```

```
                    SW_RAST_Y_REVERSAL(ysize,
                                       l3d_real_to_int
                                       (fy+float_to_l3d_real(0.5))),
                 col);
      fy = fy + m;
    }
  }//- mostly horizontal line
  else {//- mostly vertical line
    //- ensure (x0,y0) is vertically smaller than (x1,y1)
    if(y1<y0) {tmp=x0;x0=x1;x1=tmp; tmp=y0;y0=y1;y1=tmp;}
    fx = int_to_l3d_real(x0);
    if( !(int_to_l3d_real(dy)) ) return; //- degenerate: line is just a point
    m = l3d_divrr( int_to_l3d_real(dx), int_to_l3d_real(dy) );
    for(y=y0; y<=y1; y++) {
      draw_point(l3d_real_to_int(fx+float_to_l3d_real(0.5)),
                 SW_RAST_Y_REVERSAL(ysize,y),
                 col);
      fx = fx + m;
    }
  }//- mostly vertical line
}
```

The macro SW_RAST_Y_REVERSAL performs, if necessary, a reversal of the *y*-axis orientation. Whether this is necessary or not is determined at compile time; depending on the target system (Linux or Windows, for instance) this macro is defined differently. In the case of Linux, this macro returns the passed-in *y* value. When compiling for Windows, this macro effectively reverses the orientation of the *y* axis by returning the value of the expression (*ysize–y*), where *ysize* is the vertical size of the screen. The reason for the necessity of this macro is that systems can map the frame buffer memory to the physical display differently. On many systems (e.g., Linux using XImages in ZPixmap format), the first byte of the frame buffer represents the upper-left corner of the screen, and increasing memory addresses in the frame buffer represent positions which are successively further to the right and downward on the physical display. This organization corresponds to the left-to-right, top-to-bottom operation of the electron gun in a CRT display, and also corresponds to the natural left-to-right, top-to-bottom reading order we are used to in English. Other systems (e.g., Microsoft Windows using device-independent bitmaps) map the bytes in the frame buffer so that they start at the lower-left corner of the image, and move to the right and upward as memory addresses increase. This corresponds to a left-to-right, bottom-to-top organization of image memory.

The only other thing of note in the draw_line function is the use of the type l3d_real, and a few functions for dealing with this type. Let's take a brief look at the purpose and workings of the l3d_real type.

Real Numbers in l3d: Type l3d_real

Until now, we have only used integer variables in our computations. We have dealt with pixels and bytes, both of which are discrete values and can be addressed completely with integers.

For the incremental line algorithm, however, we for the first time need a fractional value: the slope of an arbitrary line will generally be a fractional value. For this, we introduce the type l3d_real.

The purpose of the l3d_real type is to allow all computations using real values to be performed using either floating- or fixed-point arithmetic. *Floating-point arithmetic* is done by using the C type float, and for good real-time performance requires a hardware floating-point unit. *Fixed-point arithmetic* requires no floating-point unit in hardware, and simulates fractional values with integers by multiplying the fractional value so that the fractional part moves into the integer part. The Appendix covers this in more detail.

By using l3d_real any time we want a real value, we can configure our code at compile time to use either fixed- or floating-point math. For now, there are four rules you need to know for using variables of type l3d_real:

1. Type conversions. A variable of type l3d_real can be converted to and from an integer or floating-point value through the macros l3d_real_to_float, l3d_real_to_int, float_to_l3d_real, and int_to_l3d_real. Furthermore, a variable of type l3d_real can be converted to and from a fixed-point number through the macros l3d_real_to_fixed and fixed_to_l3d_real.

2. Addition and subtraction. Variables of type l3d_real may be added to and subtracted from other variables types of l3d_real with the normal plus (+) and minus (–) operators. Addition and subtraction with variables of any other type must first use one of the type conversion macros to convert the variable of the other type to l3d_real.

3. Multiplication and division. Variables of type l3d_real can be multiplied or divided by variables of type l3d_real or of type int only. Such multiplications or divisions must use one of the following macros, all of which return a type of l3d_real: l3d_mulrr (multiplies an l3d_real by an l3d_real), l3d_mulri (multiplies an l3d_real by an int), l3d_divrr (divides an l3d_real by an l3d_real), and l3d_divri (divides an l3d_real by an int).

4. Other functions. The iceil function returns the integer ceiling of (i.e., the smallest integer larger than) an l3d_real. ifloor returns the integer floor of (the largest integer smaller than) an l3d_real. The function l3d_sqrt returns an l3d_real representing the square root of the given l3d_real argument.

 NOTE Ordinarily, we should make l3d_real a class, with the above functions (or more precisely, macros) being member operations on the class. Unfortunately, in this one particular case, we cannot do this, because the entire reason for using fixed-point math is performance; the subtle overheads introduced by making l3d_real a class are too great. Type l3d_real forms the very basis for all mathematical operations in our 3D programs, of which there are thousands or millions per frame. See the Appendix for a more detailed discussion of the performance issues involved and a detailed answer as to why we (unfortunately) cannot make l3d_real a class.

If we choose to use floating-point math (at compile time via a #define), then the l3d_real macros are defined as shown in Listing 3-1. Notice that the macros do nothing other than call the ordinary cast, multiplication, or division operators.

Listing 3-1: An excerpt from `sys_dep.h`, illustrating the definitions of the `l3d_real` macros

```
typedef float l3d_real;
#define l3d_real_to_float(m) (m)
#define float_to_l3d_real(f) ((float)(f))
#define l3d_real_to_int(m)    ((int)(m))
#define int_to_l3d_real(i)    ((float)(i))
#define l3d_mulrr(a,b) (a)*(b)
#define l3d_mulri(a,b) (a)*(b)
#define l3d_divrr(a,b) (a)/(b)
#define l3d_divri(a,b) (a)/(b)
#define iceil(x) ( (int)ceil((double)(x)) )
#define ifloor(x) ( (int)floor((double)(x)) )
#define l3d_sqrt(x)  ( float_to_l3d_real(sqrt(l3d_real_to_float(x))) )
#define l3d_real_to_fixed(f) float2fix(f)
#define fixed_to_l3d_real(f) fix2float(f)
```

If we choose to use fixed-point math (again, at compile time via a `#define`), then the `l3d_real` macros are defined quite differently, applying the somewhat arcane rules for fixed-point math to simulate real-valued computations using purely integer arithmetic. Again, the Appendix covers this in more detail; for now, you just need to know how to properly use the `l3d_real` types, and know that by doing so, your code will be able to use either fixed- or floating-point math with no changes.

An unfortunate consequence of using the `l3d_real` macros for multiplication and division is that this leads to somewhat awkward code. For instance, the following computation with floating-point values:

```
x = a * ( ( b + c ) / d )
```

would need to be expressed with `l3d_real` types as:

```
x = l3d_mulrr( a , l3d_divrr( b + c , d ) )
```

The multiplication and division must therefore be realized as nested macro invocations. Notice, however, that no macro invocation is necessary for the addition of b and c, since addition and subtraction of `l3d_real` types can be done with the normal addition and subtraction operators.

Returning to the subject of the current section, rasterization, the `draw_line` function uses `int_to_l3d_real` and `l3d_divrr` to compute the real-valued slope (or inverse slope) of the line from the given integer coordinates.

Rasterizing Flat-shaded Polygons

Rasterizing a polygon means drawing the set of pixels that lie inside of a polygon. A *polygon* is the area contained within a closed, connected series of line segments. See Figure 3-1. Informally, you can think of polygons as flat, finite surfaces with straight edges. In 2D and 3D graphics, drawing a polygon is one of the most frequently occurring operations. Typically, an entire 3D world consists of polygons (albeit in 3D, not in 2D, as we see in Chapter 7).

For various reasons, complex or concave polygons (those which intersect themselves or which have "dents" or "holes") are computationally expensive to process. Therefore, almost all graphics programs (including l3d and OpenGL) restrict themselves to simple, convex polygons. It should be noted, however, that a complex or concave polygon can be decomposed into a series of simple, convex polygons, which is called *tessellation*. Figure 3-2 illustrates some various kinds of polygons and tessellation.

NOTE A test to see if a polygon is convex is to draw a line between every pair of vertices in the polygon. If all such lines lie within the interior of the polygon, then the polygon is convex; otherwise, it is concave or complex. You can also use the "rubber band rule": if you were to stretch an imaginary rubber band around the polygon, the rubber band would touch every edge of the polygon, if the polygon is convex. Otherwise, the polygon must have dents or holes, and is therefore not convex.

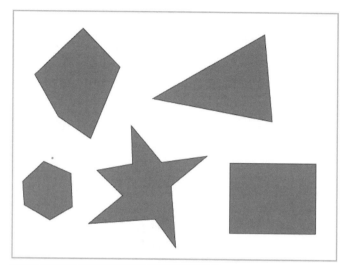

Figure 3-1: Polygons.

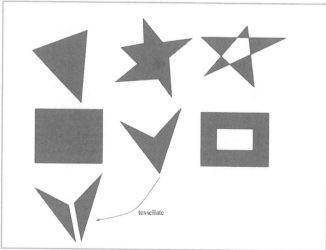

Figure 3-2: Convex, concave, and complex polygons. (Left, middle, and right, respectively.)

We may specify a polygon by choosing an arbitrary endpoint of any one of the lines as a starting point, and then specifying the endpoints of the line segments in clockwise or counterclockwise order. This is shown in Figure 3-3.

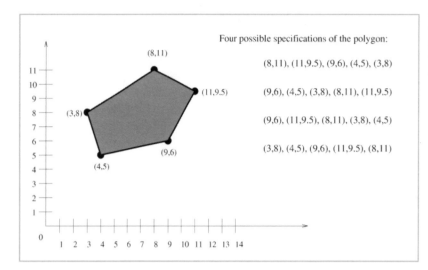

Figure 3-3: A polygon and some possible specifications.

We will use the clockwise ordering convention to specify polygon points. The points defining a polygon are called *vertices* (singular *vertex*).

Though polygons are one of the most widely used means of modeling worlds in computer graphics, other methods exist as well. Some are based on *curves*, where points may then define control points through which curves or curved surfaces must pass. Some are based on *spatial occupancy*, where we explicitly define all points belonging to the figure (*voxels,* short for volume pixels, are an example of this). Due to their simplicity and ease of processing (in hardware as well), polygons are still the main building block of most 3D models used in interactive applications.

Before discussing the rasterization of polygons, let us first discuss their storage in memory. This is not as simple as it might seem because we want to create a general, flexible, extendable polygon structure which we can reuse later for 3D graphics (see Chapter 7). This requires a bit of forethought and some less-than-obvious data structures. After laying down the structure of a polygon class, we then discuss the actual polygon rasterization algorithm.

Specifying Coordinates

To specify a polygon, we first need to specify its coordinates. Specifying coordinates is done through two classes: l3d_point and l3d_coordinate.

Listing 3-2: point.h

```
#ifndef __POINT_H
#define __POINT_H
#include "../../tool_os/memman.h"

#include <math.h>
#include <stdio.h>
#include "../../system/sys_dep.h"

class l3d_point {
  public:
```

```
    l3d_point(void);
    l3d_point(l3d_real a0, l3d_real a1, l3d_real a2, l3d_real a3);
    l3d_point(int a0, int a1, int a2, int a3);
    l3d_point(const l3d_point &right);
    const l3d_point &set(l3d_real a0, l3d_real a1, l3d_real a2, l3d_real a3);
    const l3d_point  &set(int a0, int a1, int a2, int a3);

    const l3d_point &operator = (const l3d_point &right);

    void print(void)
    {
      printf("%f %f %f %f",
             l3d_real_to_float(a[0]),
             l3d_real_to_float(a[1]),
             l3d_real_to_float(a[2]),
             l3d_real_to_float(a[3]));
    }

    l3d_real a[4];
};

//- useful defines for accessing matrix elements occurring in standard
//- positions for l3d_point:
#define X_ a[0]
#define Y_ a[1]
#define Z_ a[2]
#define W_ a[3]

//- function for grabbing a temporary point object from a global
//- pre-allocated pool of temporary objects.
extern l3d_point &l3d_get_point_temp(void);

inline l3d_point::l3d_point(void) {
  a[0] = a[1] = a[2] = a[3] = 0;
}

inline l3d_point::l3d_point(l3d_real a0, l3d_real a1, l3d_real a2, l3d_real a3) {
  a[0] = a0;
  a[1] = a1;
  a[2] = a2;
  a[3] = a3;
}

inline l3d_point::l3d_point(int a0, int a1, int a2, int a3) {
  a[0] = int_to_l3d_real(a0);
  a[1] = int_to_l3d_real(a1);
  a[2] = int_to_l3d_real(a2);
  a[3] = int_to_l3d_real(a3);
}

inline l3d_point::l3d_point(const l3d_point &right) {
  a[0] = right.a[0];
  a[1] = right.a[1];
  a[2] = right.a[2];
  a[3] = right.a[3];
}

inline const l3d_point &l3d_point::operator = (const l3d_point &right) {
  a[0] = right.a[0];
  a[1] = right.a[1];
```

```
   a[2] = right.a[2];
   a[3] = right.a[3];

   return *this;
}

inline const l3d_point &l3d_point::set(l3d_real a0, l3d_real a1, l3d_real a2, l3d_real a3) {
   a[0] = a0;
   a[1] = a1;
   a[2] = a2;
   a[3] = a3;

   return *this;
}

inline const l3d_point &l3d_point::set(int a0, int a1, int a2, int a3) {
   a[0] = int_to_l3d_real(a0);
   a[1] = int_to_l3d_real(a1);
   a[2] = int_to_l3d_real(a2);
   a[3] = int_to_l3d_real(a3);

   return *this;
}

inline const l3d_point &operator * (const l3d_point& l,
                                    const l3d_real aScalar)
{
   l3d_point &res = l3d_get_point_temp();
   res.set(
      l3d_mulrr(l.a[0], /* TIMES */ aScalar),
      l3d_mulrr(l.a[1], /* TIMES */ aScalar),
      l3d_mulrr(l.a[2], /* TIMES */ aScalar),
      l3d_mulrr(l.a[3], /* TIMES */ aScalar));

   return res;
}

#endif
```

Listing 3-3: `point.cc`

```
#include "point.h"
#include "../../tool_os/memman.h"

//- Global pool of temporary variables for point operations.

const int l3d_max_point_temp = 15;
l3d_point &l3d_get_point_temp(void) {
   static int nbuf=0;
   static l3d_point buf[l3d_max_point_temp];

   if(nbuf>=l3d_max_point_temp) nbuf=0;
   return buf[nbuf++];
}
```

Listing 3-4: `coord.h`

```
#ifndef _COORD_H
#define _COORD_H
#include "../../tool_os/memman.h"

#include "../../geom/point/point.h"
```

```
const int max_transformed_intermediates = 2;
class l3d_coordinate {
  public:
  l3d_coordinate(void) {transform_stage = 0; }

    l3d_point original;
    l3d_point transformed;
    char transform_stage;

    l3d_point transformed_intermediates[max_transformed_intermediates];

    void reset(void) {transform_stage = 0; transformed = original; }
    void transform(const l3d_matrix &m, int count) {
      if (transform_stage != count) {
        transform_stage = count;
        transformed = m | transformed;
      }
    }
};

#endif
```

The class `l3d_point` represents a set of four numbers, of the form (x, y, z, w). These numbers represent a location in space, in terms of displacements along coordinate axes. Since `l3d_point` contains four numbers, it can represent locations in 1D, 2D, 3D, or 4D space. As odd as it might sound at this point, we do in fact later need to deal with four-dimensional space, although only briefly. In this chapter, we only use the first two numbers, since we only need to specify 2D locations; the last two coordinates, z and w, are simply ignored.

The class `l3d_coordinate` represents a transformable coordinate location in space. It stores two variables of type `l3d_point`, named `original` and `transformed`. The idea is that the `original` member should store the original, never-to-be-modified location, while the `transformed` member should store some transformed version of the original location: perhaps moved slightly, rotated, scaled, or even (as we see in Chapter 5) projected from 3D into 2D. In 3D graphics, the particular transformations applied to a particular coordinate can change if the object containing the coordinate moves, or if the virtual "camera" observing the object moves. See Chapter 6 for a detailed discussion of transformations. Saving the original coordinate thus becomes necessary, since we repeatedly apply different transformations to the original coordinate. We call a coordinate that is used to define a polygon a *vertex*.

NOTE You can liken the need to save the original coordinate to the need to save an original paper document when making copies. If you repeatedly make copies of copies, the image quality eventually degrades. Similarly, if we continue to apply mathematical transformations to already transformed coordinates, the coordinates slowly drift away from their "true" positions due to numerical computational inaccuracy. Saving the original coordinate in the `original` member variable means that we always start applying transformations to the original, 100% accurate coordinate location.

The `transform_stage` member is a counter indicating at which "stage" of transformation this coordinate is during the processing for a particular frame. For instance, let us say we have an object defined by 1,000 vertices. Assume that we need to perform three transformations on all of these vertices for a particular frame. Again, for now, simply think of a transformation as a change in position. (Chapter 6 covers transformations in detail.) Assume further that our traversal of the vertices is not in any particular order and might visit a vertex more than once. (The following paragraph explores this assumption in more detail.) The `transform_stage` variable is like a "flag" allowing us to know if a particular vertex has already been transformed during this frame or not. For instance, before any transformations for this frame are done, we call the `reset` routine for all vertices, which sets `transform_stage` to 0 and `transformed` to `original`. To perform the first transformation, which we will call transformation number 1, we look for all vertices whose `transform_stage` is not 1. Initially, this will be all vertices. As soon as we transform a vertex, we set its `transform_stage` to be the current transformation number. Since our vertex traversal might visit a vertex more than once, we compare each visited vertex's `transform_stage` with the current transformation number; if it is the same, we know that we have already visited this vertex for this frame and do not need to do the (time-consuming) vertex transformation again. After the first transformation, all transformed vertices will have a `transform_stage` of 1. The next transformation is number 2, and the process repeats, this time transforming only vertices which are not yet at transformation stage 2. This entire process is repeated for each frame. The actual transformation of the coordinate is done via a matrix. Chapter 6 covers transformations and matrices in detail.

In case you are wondering why the vertex traversal might visit a vertex more than once, the reason is that many polygons might share one vertex list. For a given viewpoint, only some of these polygons will be visible. The vertex traversal algorithm is: for all visible polygons, transform each of the polygon's vertices if the vertex is not already transformed. The fact that vertices are shared means that some or even all of a polygon's vertices might have already been transformed if the neighboring polygon has already been transformed. This strategy requires us to check if a vertex has already been transformed by using the `transform_stage` variable, but it also allows us to completely avoid transforming vertices which are not visible (i.e., which do not belong to any visible polygon). Doing the extra check is typically cheaper than blindly transforming all vertices, especially if there are many vertices, many of which may be invisible. We therefore transform only visible vertices. However, it's also important to mention that for physical simulation purposes, where objects physically interact, we might still need to transform invisible vertices if these vertices represent some physical part of an object which can affect the virtual world even if this action is taking place in a currently invisible location. On the other hand, with such physical simulation, we often use a simplified version of the geometry (e.g., spherical or box-like) for the simulation to simplify physics computations, meaning that the original vertices used for drawing might not actually be used at all for the simulation purposes. An example of this would be using a sphere for physical collision detection purposes (as discussed in the companion book *Advanced Linux 3D Graphics Programming*).

The next member of `l3d_coordinate` that is of interest is the `transformed_intermediates` array. As we mentioned above, typical processing of coordinates involves an original location, a series of one or more transformations, and a final transformed location. The purpose of the `transformed_intermediates` array is to provide a temporary storage location, within the coordinate itself, which can be used to save the location at a particular transformation stage. For instance, let us say we perform three transformations one after another on a coordinate, then at some point later we need to know where the coordinate was after the second transformation was applied. We can store this information in an element of the `transformed_intermediates` array, immediately after we perform the second transformation. Then, later, even after more transformations have been applied, we can look up the old location in the coordinate to determine its earlier position. Therefore, we are storing older, "intermediate" transformed locations within the `transformed_intermediates` array. The alternative to storing the transformed intermediates within the coordinate itself would be for the application code to declare a separate list of coordinates for saving intermediate locations. The size and order of this list would need to be maintained in parallel with the original list of polygon coordinates—a rather tedious task, since the list of polygon coordinates may change due to a 2D clipping operation (covered in detail later in this chapter). The need for storing intermediate locations can be seen in Chapter 6, where we must "remember" the position of coordinates after the camera transformation, although another transformation (the perspective projection) has already been applied to the coordinate.

The method `transform` actually effects a transformation: it changes the position of the point, updating the `transform_stage` counter and storing the new transformed point in the `transformed` member variable. First, though, we check to see if the point has already been transformed by comparing the current transformation stage (parameter `count`) with the transformation stage of the vertex (member `l3d_coordinate::transform_stage`); if `count` equals `transform_stage`, then the point has already been transformed earlier. The actual transformation of the point is performed by means of a matrix multiplication, so an explanation of this method must wait until Chapter 6, on matrices and transformations. We do not yet use the `transform` method in this chapter.

To summarize, `l3d_point` represents a single location in 1D, 2D, 3D, or 4D space. Class `l3d_coordinate` has two main `l3d_point` objects, an original and a transformed one, as well as a sort of "history list" of points for storing any arbitrary intermediate transformed locations. The transformed coordinate is always initialized to equal the original coordinate at the beginning of each frame (method `reset`), after which it may be transformed by zero or more transformations (method `transform`). After any number of transformations, the application may choose to save the current location in one of the intermediate storage locations (member `transformed_intermediates`), so that the old location may be referenced later. In the end, the transformed coordinate must represent a point in 2D pixel space, since ultimately the points must be used to plot images on-screen. The whole idea is that a `l3d_coordinate` is more than just a single location in space: it is an original location, a number of optional intermediate locations, and a final location.

For now, the most important thing to remember about the `original` and `transformed` members is that the transformed coordinate is the one which is finally used to display the pixels on the screen. An application must at some point put the final pixel coordinates in the `transformed` member variable. For the examples in this chapter, we will place the pixel coordinates directly in the `original` member, and call `reset` to copy `original` into `transformed`. In other words, we do not yet apply any transformation between `original` and `transformed`.

NOTE In Chapter 5, we perform the 3D to 2D projection, which transforms 3D space into 2D pixel space. In this case, the `original` member variable contains the 3D space coordinate, which is transformed through projection into 2D pixel space. The final 2D pixel coordinate ends up in the `transformed` member.

Two-Part Vertex Lists

Using the `l3d_coordinate` class, we can represent locations in space. The topic of this section is rasterization of polygons, so we are interested in using `l3d_coordinate` objects to specify the vertices (i.e., corner points) of a polygon.

The strategy we will follow is this: we define a vertex list separate from the polygon object, and store a pointer to a pointer to this list within a polygon object. The polygon's vertices are then defined by a list of indices into the external vertex list. Figure 3-4 illustrates this concept.

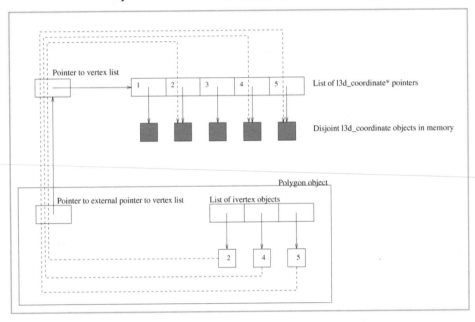

Figure 3-4: Polygons are defined by a list of indices into an external list accessed through a pointer to a pointer. By changing the external list elements or by changing the external pointer to the list, the polygon's definition is also changed without needing to manipulate the internals of the polygon itself. This technique can be used for animation.

This strategy may seem quite roundabout. It might seem more appropriate to store a list of `l3d_coordinate` objects within each polygon. This, however, fails to take into account the fact that polygons rarely exist in isolation; more often, they are grouped with other polygons to form objects—especially when we move to 3D polygons. Grouping polygons means that many polygons might be able to share vertices, which eliminates duplicate processing of vertices at the same location in two different polygons. Furthermore, storing vertices in an external list allows us to change the polygon's appearance very easily by changing the external list—a technique invaluable for vertex animation or *morphing*, of which we see an example later in this chapter.

Specifically, the external vertex list strategy has the following concrete benefits:

- By allowing the list to be external to the polygon, we enable multiple polygons to share vertices within the same list. Each shared vertex must be transformed only once, instead of multiple times (as would be the case if each polygon had its own copy of the vertex).

- By changing the contents of the external vertex list, we can change the appearance of the polygon by changing individual vertices.

- By changing the external pointer to point to a different vertex list altogether, we can change the appearance of the polygon by swapping out the entire vertex list.

We use a combination of two data structures to store a list of vertices: l3d_list and l3d_two_part_list. Class l3d_list is a dynamically growable list which is like an array, but which automatically expands and allocates more space as necessary. The elements are accessed as normal through the array index operator []. Class l3d_two_part_list is an extension of l3d_list and partitions the list of items into two parts: a fixed part and a varying part. The fixed part is fixed in size and never changes; the varying part is based on some dynamic calculation and changes often in size. However—and this is the whole point of the l3d_two_part_list—both the fixed and the varying parts are accessed identically. If we stored the fixed and varying parts in two separate lists, any references to list items would need to specify if the item comes out of the fixed or the varying list, which makes for rather inconvenient code. With the l3d_two_part_list, external users don't need to worry about whether the referenced item is fixed or varying. This uniformity of access is primarily of use in clipping, which we cover later in this chapter; clipping can create temporary (varying) vertices which must be accessible exactly like normal (fixed) vertices, but which may vary wildly in number from frame to frame.

Listing 3-5 is the source code for the list classes. At this point it is not necessarily important to know exactly how the classes work (though their code is quite straightforward); more important is understanding how to use the classes, which we cover next.

Listing 3-5: `list.h`

```
#ifndef __LIST_H
#define __LIST_H
#include "../tool_os/memman.h"

template<class Item> class l3d_list_item_factory {
  public:
  virtual Item *create(void) {return new Item ; }
    virtual ~l3d_list_item_factory() {}
};

template<class Item> class l3d_list
{
  protected:
    bool is_my_factory;
  public:
    int max_items;
    l3d_list_item_factory<Item> *factory;

    Item **items;
    int num_items;
```

```
l3d_list(int initial_size) {
  factory = new l3d_list_item_factory<Item>;
  is_my_factory = true;
  num_items = 0;
  max_items = initial_size;

  items = new Item* [max_items];
  for(int i=0; i<max_items; i++) {
    items[i] = factory->create();
  }
};

l3d_list(void) {
  factory = new l3d_list_item_factory<Item>;
  is_my_factory = true;
  num_items = 0;
  max_items = 10;

  items = new Item* [max_items];
  for(int i=0; i<max_items; i++) {
    items[i] = factory->create();
  }
};

l3d_list(int initial_size, l3d_list_item_factory<Item> *factory) {
  this->factory = factory;
  is_my_factory = false;
  num_items = 0;
  max_items = initial_size;

  items = new Item* [max_items];
  for(int i=0; i<max_items; i++) {
    items[i] = factory->create();
  }
}

~l3d_list(void) {
  for(int i=0; i<max_items; i++) {
    delete items[i];
  }
  delete [] items;
  if(is_my_factory) {delete factory; }
};

int next_index(void) {
  if ( num_items < max_items ) {

    return num_items ++;
  }else {

    int oldsize = max_items;
    max_items += 20;

    Item **bigger_items = new Item* [max_items];
    int i;
    for(i=0; i<oldsize; i++) {
      bigger_items[i] = items[i];
    }
    for(; i < max_items; i++) {
      bigger_items[i] = factory->create();
```

```
          }
          delete [] items;
          items = bigger_items;

          return num_items++;
        }
    }

    Item & operator [] (int idx) const {return *items[idx]; }

    l3d_list<Item> & operator = ( const l3d_list<Item> &r ) {
      while(num_items < r.num_items) {
        next_index();
      }

      for(int i=0; i<r.num_items; i++) {
        *items[i] = *(r.items[i]);
      }

      num_items = r.num_items;

      return *this;

    }

};

template<class Item> class l3d_two_part_list {
  protected:
    l3d_list_item_factory<Item> *factory;
  public:
    l3d_list<Item> *list;
    int num_fixed_items;
    int num_varying_items;
    int max_varying_items;

    l3d_two_part_list<Item> & operator= (const l3d_two_part_list<Item> &r) {
      *list = *r.list;
      num_fixed_items = r.num_fixed_items;
      num_varying_items = r.num_varying_items;
      factory = r.factory;
      max_varying_items = r.max_varying_items;
      return *this;
    }

    l3d_two_part_list(int fixed_size) {
      num_fixed_items = fixed_size;
      max_varying_items = fixed_size > 1;
      list = new l3d_list<Item> (fixed_size + max_varying_items);
      for(register int i=0; i<fixed_size+max_varying_items; i++) {
        list->next_index();
      }
      num_varying_items = 0;
    };

    l3d_two_part_list(int fixed_size, l3d_list_item_factory<Item> *factory) {
      this->factory = factory;
      num_fixed_items = fixed_size;
      max_varying_items = fixed_size > 1;
      list = new l3d_list<Item> (fixed_size + max_varying_items, factory);
```

```
      for(register int i=0; i<fixed_size+max_varying_items; i++) {
        list->next_index();
      }
      num_varying_items = 0;
    };

    ~l3d_two_part_list(void) {
      delete list;
    };

    int next_varying_index(void) {
      if ( num_varying_items < max_varying_items) {
        return num_fixed_items + num_varying_items++;
      }else {
        list->next_index();
        max_varying_items++;
        return num_fixed_items + num_varying_items++;
      }
    };

    Item & operator[] (int index) const {return *(list->items[index]); }
};

#endif
```

Using these list classes is easy. They are declared as template classes so that they work with any data type. Let's first begin with the `l3d_list` class.

To use `l3d_list`, do the following:

1. Declare an instance of the list, providing the data type as the template parameter and passing the initial size of the list to the constructor. The initial size must be greater than zero.

2. Call `next_index` before storing any new element into the list, to obtain the next free index within the list. This also causes the list to grow if you exceed the current size of the list.

3. Store and access elements into the list using the array index operator []. Never attempt to access an element which you have not already allocated by having called `next_index`.

4. Query the number of items via the `num_items` member. Valid indices range from 0 to `num_items` - 1.

5. Effectively empty or reduce the size of the list by setting `num_items` to zero or a smaller number. Never set `num_items` to a larger number; use `next_index` to increase the size of the list.

6. Copy the list by assigning it to another `l3d_list` object. This makes a full copy of the list and its contents; the two copies are completely independent of one another and contain no pointers to common objects (unless the contents of the list themselves are pointers, in which case the two lists contain separate copies of pointer objects, which point to the same locations in memory).

 NOTE The creation of the list elements occurs through an abstract factory; the copying of list elements, through a possibly virtual assignment operator; and the access of list elements, through an abstract class pointer in the overloaded array index operator [ ]. This means that by providing a new factory (via the `l3d_list` constructor) and overriding a virtual assignment operator =, an existing `l3d_list` in already existing code can be extended after the fact to work with new subclasses, and the original code is still guaranteed to work because the internal access to the list elements is done through an abstract class pointer. A detailed example of this technique appears in the companion book, *Advanced Linux 3D Graphics Programming*, when we extend the existing polygon class to store texture coordinate information with each vertex, without needing to change any of the already existing code. By default, an abstract factory is automatically created and destroyed if you do not provide one; the flexibility is there if you need it, but does not burden you if you do not.

The other list class is the l3d_two_part_list. Again, a two-part list consists of a fixed part, whose size never changes, and a varying part, whose size may change greatly over time. The list elements in both the fixed part and the varying part are accessed identically (with the array operator [ ]). To use an l3d_two_part_list, do the following:

1. Declare an instance of the list, providing the data type as the template parameter and passing the initial fixed size of the list to the constructor. The initial size must be greater than zero.

2. Store and access fixed items in the list by using the array index operator []. Valid indices for fixed items range from 0 to num_fixed_items – 1. Do not store fixed items outside of this range. Do not change the num_fixed_items variable.

3. Call next_varying_index before storing any element in the varying part of the list, to obtain the next free index within the varying part. This also causes the varying part of the list to grow if you exceed the current size of the list.

4. Store and access elements in the varying part of the list using the array index operator [ ]. Never attempt to access an element in the varying part which you have not already allocated by having called next_varying_index.

5. Query the number of varying items via the num_varying_items member. Valid indices for varying items range from num_fixed_items to num_fixed_items + num_varying_items – 1.

6. Effectively empty or reduce the size of the varying part of the list by setting num_varying_items to zero or a smaller number. Never set num_varying_items to a larger number; use next_varying_index to increase the size of the varying part of the list.

7. Copy the list by assigning it to another l3d_two_part_list object. This makes a full copy of the fixed and varying parts of the list and its contents; the two copies are completely independent of one another and contain no pointers to common objects (unless, again, the contents are themselves pointers).

Notice that access to both fixed and varying items is done uniformly through the array access operator [ ].

 NOTE The earlier comments about factory creation, virtual assignment, and polymorphic access all apply to l3d_two_part_list as well. This is because l3d_two_part_list internally uses an l3d_list to store the items.

We use two-part lists for storing vertices (i.e., objects of type l3d_coordinate) which are later used to define polygons. A typical creation of a vertex list looks as follows:

```
vlist = new l3d_two_part_list<l3d_coordinate> ( 4 );
(*vlist)[0].original.X_ = float_to_l3d_real(100.0);
(*vlist)[0].original.Y_ = float_to_l3d_real(100.0);

(*vlist)[1].original.X_ = float_to_l3d_real(200.0);
(*vlist)[1].original.Y_ = float_to_l3d_real(150.0);

(*vlist)[2].original.X_ = float_to_l3d_real(150.0);
(*vlist)[2].original.Y_ = float_to_l3d_real(200.0);

(*vlist)[3].original.X_ = float_to_l3d_real( 50.0);
(*vlist)[3].original.Y_ = float_to_l3d_real(120.0);
```

First we create an object of type l3d_two_part_list with a data type of l3d_coordi-nate. The constructor parameter 4 indicates the size of the fixed part of the two-part list. We then initialize the first four elements, with indices 0 through 3, simply by using the array access operator [ ]. Each element of the list is an object of type l3d_coordinate, which we can manipulate directly. In the code snippet above, we initialize the original member of the l3d_coordi-nate, which is what an application program does to initially define a vertex list. The varying part of the two-part list is not used above, and is first used during the clipping operation covered later.

Defining Polygons: Indices into a Vertex List

As we just saw, a two-part vertex list is declared in order to specify vertices to be used by one or more polygons. Inside of the polygon itself, we store indices into this external vertex list by using a l3d_list. Since we now understand the general use of the l3d_list and l3d_two_part_list data structures, we are in a position to look at the definition of the polygon class itself. See Listings 3-6 and 3-7.

Listing 3-6: polygon.h

```
#ifndef __POLYGON_H
#define __POLYGON_H
#include "../../tool_os/memman.h"

#include "../../system/sys_dep.h"
#include "../../math/matrix.h"
#include "../vertex/coord.h"
#include "../../datastr/list.h"

#define MAX_VERTICES 150
#define MAX_CLIP_VERTICES 20
#define MAX_FACETS 300
#define MAX_XFORMS 7
#define PTS_PER_FACET 20
#define TEX_WIDTH 64
#define TEX_HEIGHT 64

#define DEFAULT_IVERTICES_PER_POLY 10

class l3d_rasterizer_2d;

class l3d_polygon_ivertex {
  public:
    int ivertex;

    virtual l3d_polygon_ivertex& operator= (const l3d_polygon_ivertex &r) {
```

```
        ivertex = r.ivertex;
        return *this;
    }

    virtual ~l3d_polygon_ivertex(void) {
    }
};

class l3d_polygon_ivertex_items_factory :
      public l3d_list_item_factory<l3d_polygon_ivertex>
{
  public:
    virtual l3d_polygon_ivertex_items_factory *clone(void);
};

class l3d_polygon_2d {
  protected:

  public:
    l3d_polygon_ivertex_items_factory *iv_items_factory;
    l3d_polygon_2d(void) {iv_items_factory = NULL; };

    l3d_polygon_2d(int num_pts);

    l3d_polygon_2d(const l3d_polygon_2d &r);

    void init(int num_pts);
    virtual ~l3d_polygon_2d(void);

    l3d_two_part_list<l3d_coordinate> **vlist;

    l3d_list<l3d_polygon_ivertex>
    *ivertices,
    *clip_ivertices,
    *temp_clip_ivertices;

    void init_clip_ivertices(void);

    void swap_temp_and_main_clip_lists(void);

    virtual void clip_segment_to_edge_2d
    (l3d_polygon_ivertex *ivertex,
     const l3d_point *pC0, const l3d_point *pC1,
     int crossedge_idx0,int crossedge_idx1);
    virtual int clip_to_edge_2d
    (const l3d_point *pPoint1, const l3d_point *pPoint2);
    int clip_to_polygon_2d(const l3d_polygon_2d *p_poly);
    int side_of_point(const l3d_point *p,
                      const l3d_point *p1,
                      const l3d_point *p2);

    int next_clipidx_left(int idx, int count) const;
    int next_clipidx_right(int idx, int count) const;

  virtual void draw(l3d_rasterizer_2d *r) {}
    virtual l3d_polygon_2d *clone(void);
};

inline int l3d_polygon_2d::next_clipidx_left(int idx, int count) const {
  idx = idx - 1;
```

```
    if(idx<0) idx = count-1;
    return idx;
}

inline int l3d_polygon_2d::next_clipidx_right(int idx, int count) const {
    idx = idx + 1;
    if(idx>=count) idx = 0;
    return idx;
}

inline int l3d_polygon_2d::side_of_point(const l3d_point *p,
        const l3d_point *p1, const l3d_point *p2)
{
    l3d_real s;

    const l3d_real EPSILON=float_to_l3d_real(0.05);

    #ifdef FIXED_POINT_MATH

#undef FX_PRECIS
#undef FX_PRECIS_QUOT
#undef FX_PRECIS_MASK
#undef FX_PRECIS_MAX
#undef FX_CVT
#undef FX_CVT_BACK

    #define FX_PRECIS 8
    #define FX_PRECIS_QUOT 8

    #define FX_SIGN_MASK    0x80000000L
    #define FX_ALLBITS_MASK 0xFFFFFFFFL

    #define FX_PRECIS_MASK 0x000000FFL
    #define FX_PRECIS_MAX 256.0

    #define FX_CONVERT > FX_PRECIS_DEFAULT-FX_PRECIS
    #define FX_CONVERT_BACK < FX_PRECIS_DEFAULT-FX_PRECIS

    #else

    #define FX_CONVERT
    #define FX_CONVERT_BACK

    #endif

    l3d_vector normal_vector_pointing_inside_segment
    (p1->Y_ - p2->Y_,
     p2->X_ - p1->X_,
     int_to_l3d_real(0),
     int_to_l3d_real(0));

#ifndef FIXED_POINT_MATH
    s = dot(normal_vector_pointing_inside_segment, *p - *p1);
#else

    //- explicitly formulate dot product for fixed point to avoid overflow
      s =
        l3d_mulrr(normal_vector_pointing_inside_segment.X_ FX_CONVERT,
                (p->X_ - p1->X_) FX_CONVERT)
```

```
              + l3d_mulrr((normal_vector_pointing_inside_segment.Y_) FX_CONVERT,
                       (p->Y_ - p1->Y_) FX_CONVERT ) ;

#endif

  if(s<-EPSILON) return -1;
  else if(s>-EPSILON) return 1;
  else return 0;

#include "../../math/fix_prec.h"

}

#include "../../raster/rasteriz.h"

#endif
```

Listing 3-7: `polygon.cc`

```
#include "polygon.h"
#include <string.h>
#include "../../tool_os/memman.h"

l3d_polygon_ivertex_items_factory *
l3d_polygon_ivertex_items_factory::clone(void) {
  return new l3d_polygon_ivertex_items_factory;
}

l3d_polygon_2d::l3d_polygon_2d(int num_pts) {
  iv_items_factory = new l3d_polygon_ivertex_items_factory;
  init(num_pts);
}

void l3d_polygon_2d::init(int num_pts) {
  ivertices = new l3d_list<l3d_polygon_ivertex>
              (num_pts, iv_items_factory);
  clip_ivertices = new l3d_list<l3d_polygon_ivertex>
                   (num_pts, iv_items_factory);
  temp_clip_ivertices = new l3d_list<l3d_polygon_ivertex>
                        (num_pts, iv_items_factory);
}

l3d_polygon_2d::~l3d_polygon_2d(void) {
  delete ivertices;
  delete clip_ivertices;
  delete temp_clip_ivertices;

  delete iv_items_factory;
}

inline void l3d_polygon_2d::init_clip_ivertices(void) {

  *clip_ivertices = *ivertices ;
}

inline void l3d_polygon_2d::swap_temp_and_main_clip_lists(void) {

  l3d_list<l3d_polygon_ivertex> *temp;
  temp = clip_ivertices;
  clip_ivertices = temp_clip_ivertices;
  temp_clip_ivertices = temp;
```

```
}

void l3d_polygon_2d::clip_segment_to_edge_2d
(l3d_polygon_ivertex *ivertex,
 const l3d_point *pC0, const l3d_point *pC1,
 int crossedge_idx0,int crossedge_idx1)
{

#ifdef FIXED_POINT_MATH

#undef FX_PRECIS
#undef FX_PRECIS_QUOT
#undef FX_SIGN_MASK
#undef FX_ALLBITS_MASK
#undef FX_PRECIS_MASK
#undef FX_PRECIS_MAX
#undef l3d_fix_new_prec
#undef l3d_fix_norm_prec

#define FX_PRECIS 8
#define FX_PRECIS_QUOT 8

#define FX_SIGN_MASK      0x80000000L
#define FX_ALLBITS_MASK 0xFFFFFFFFL

#define FX_PRECIS_MASK 0x000000FFL
#define FX_PRECIS_MAX 256.0

#define l3d_fix_new_prec(x) ((x) > (FX_PRECIS_DEFAULT-FX_PRECIS))
#define l3d_fix_norm_prec(x) ((x) < (FX_PRECIS_DEFAULT-FX_PRECIS))

#else

#define l3d_fix_new_prec(x) (x)
#define l3d_fix_norm_prec(x) (x)

#endif

  l3d_real t,x_intersect,y_intersect,denom;

  denom =
    l3d_mulrr(l3d_fix_new_prec
              ((**vlist)[ (*clip_ivertices)[crossedge_idx1].ivertex ].transformed.X_ -
               (**vlist)[ (*clip_ivertices)[crossedge_idx0].ivertex ].transformed.X_ )
              ,
              l3d_fix_new_prec(pC1->Y_ - pC0->Y_) )
    -
    l3d_mulrr(l3d_fix_new_prec
              ((**vlist)[ (*clip_ivertices)[crossedge_idx1].ivertex ].transformed.Y_ -
               (**vlist)[ (*clip_ivertices)[crossedge_idx0].ivertex ].transformed.Y_)
              ,
              l3d_fix_new_prec(pC1->X_ - pC0->X_ ) );

  if (denom == 0) {
    printf("shouldnt be here: cannot clip segment to edge");
    ivertex->ivertex= -1;
    return;
  }

  t=
```

```
        l3d_divrr(l3d_mulrr(l3d_fix_new_prec(pC1->X_ - pC0->X_)
                        ,
                        l3d_fix_new_prec
                        ((**vlist)[(*clip_ivertices)[crossedge_idx0].ivertex].transformed.Y_
                         -pC0->Y_)
                        )
            +
            l3d_mulrr(l3d_fix_new_prec(pC1->Y_ - pC0->Y_)
                        ,
                        l3d_fix_new_prec(pC0->X_ -
                                    (**vlist)[(*clip_ivertices)[crossedge_idx0].ivertex]
                                        .transformed.X_)
                        )

            ,
            denom);

  x_intersect =
    (l3d_fix_new_prec
      ((**vlist)[(*clip_ivertices)[crossedge_idx0].ivertex].transformed.X_) )
    +
    l3d_mulrr(t,
            l3d_fix_new_prec
              ((**vlist)[(*clip_ivertices)[crossedge_idx1].ivertex].transformed.X_ -
               (**vlist)[(*clip_ivertices)[crossedge_idx0].ivertex].transformed.X_)
            );
  y_intersect =
    (l3d_fix_new_prec
      ((**vlist)[(*clip_ivertices)[crossedge_idx0].ivertex].transformed.Y_) )
    +
    l3d_mulrr(t,
            l3d_fix_new_prec
              ((**vlist)[(*clip_ivertices)[crossedge_idx1].ivertex].transformed.Y_ -
               (**vlist)[(*clip_ivertices)[crossedge_idx0].ivertex].transformed.Y_ )
            );

  int new_idx = (*vlist)->next_varying_index();
  (**vlist)[new_idx].original.X_ =
    (**vlist)[new_idx].transformed.X_ =
      l3d_fix_norm_prec(x_intersect);
  (**vlist)[new_idx].original.Y_ =
    (**vlist)[new_idx].transformed.Y_ =
      l3d_fix_norm_prec(y_intersect);

#include "../../math/fix_prec.h"

  ivertex->ivertex = new_idx;
  return;
}

int l3d_polygon_2d::clip_to_edge_2d
(const l3d_point *pPoint1, const l3d_point *pPoint2)
{
  int idx0,idx1;
  int crossedge0_idx0,crossedge0_idx1,crossedge1_idx0,crossedge1_idx1;
  int newedge_ivertex0, newedge_ivertex1;
  int i;
  l3d_polygon_ivertex new_ivertex0, new_ivertex1;

  int extends_outside_edge=0;
```

```
idx0 = 0;
idx1 = next_clipidx_right(idx0, clip_ivertices->num_items);
//-  search for 1st crossing edge FROM outside idx0 TO inside idx1
while( ! (side_of_point(&((**vlist)[(*clip_ivertices)[idx0].ivertex].transformed),
                        pPoint1, pPoint2) < 1
          &&
          side_of_point(&((**vlist)[(*clip_ivertices)[idx1].ivertex].transformed),
                        pPoint1, pPoint2) == 1 )
     )
{
  idx0=idx1;

  if(side_of_point
     (&((**vlist)[(*clip_ivertices)[idx0].ivertex].transformed),
      pPoint1,pPoint2) == -1 ) {extends_outside_edge = 1; }

  //- did we loop through all vertices without finding an edge cross?
  if(idx0 == 0) {
    //- all points (and thus the current point) are "outside"...

    if(extends_outside_edge)
    {
      return 0;
    }

    //- all points (and thus the current point) are "inside"...
    else
    {
      return 1;
    }
  }

  //- still looking for the crossing edge
  idx1=next_clipidx_right(idx0, clip_ivertices->num_items);
}

crossedge0_idx0 = idx0;
crossedge0_idx1 = idx1;

idx0=idx1;
idx1=next_clipidx_right(idx0, clip_ivertices->num_items);

//- search for next crossing edge, FROM inside idx0 TO outside idx1
while( !

       (
         side_of_point(&((**vlist)[(*clip_ivertices)[idx1].ivertex].transformed),
                       pPoint1,pPoint2) < 1 )
     )
{
  idx0=idx1;
  //- did we loop through all vertices without finding 2nd z-plane cross?
  if(idx0==crossedge0_idx0) {
    fprintf(stderr,"shouldn't be here! can't find 2nd crossing edge");
    return 0;
  }

  //- continue looking for 2nd cross
  idx1=next_clipidx_right(idx0, clip_ivertices->num_items);
```

```
    }

    crossedge1_idx0 = idx0;
    crossedge1_idx1 = idx1;

    clip_segment_to_edge_2d(&new_ivertex0,
                            pPoint1, pPoint2,
                            crossedge0_idx0,crossedge0_idx1);
    if ( (newedge_ivertex0 = new_ivertex0.ivertex) == -1)
    {
      return 0;
    }

    clip_segment_to_edge_2d(&new_ivertex1,
                            pPoint1, pPoint2,
                            crossedge1_idx0,crossedge1_idx1);
    if ( (newedge_ivertex1 = new_ivertex1.ivertex) == -1 )
    {
      return 0;
    }

    temp_clip_ivertices->num_items = 0;
    (*temp_clip_ivertices)[temp_clip_ivertices->next_index()].ivertex =
      newedge_ivertex0;

    for(i=crossedge0_idx1;
        i!=crossedge1_idx0;
        i=next_clipidx_right(i,clip_ivertices->num_items))
    {
      (*temp_clip_ivertices)[temp_clip_ivertices->next_index()].ivertex =
        (*clip_ivertices)[i].ivertex;
    }

    (*temp_clip_ivertices)[temp_clip_ivertices->next_index()].ivertex =
      (*clip_ivertices)[crossedge1_idx0].ivertex;
    (*temp_clip_ivertices)[temp_clip_ivertices->next_index()].ivertex =
      newedge_ivertex1;

    swap_temp_and_main_clip_lists();

    return 1;
}

int l3d_polygon_2d::clip_to_polygon_2d(const l3d_polygon_2d *pClipPoly)
{
  int idx0,idx1;

  if (   (clip_ivertices->num_items == 0)
      || (pClipPoly->clip_ivertices->num_items == 0)
     )
  {
    return 0;
  }

  idx0 = pClipPoly->clip_ivertices->num_items-1;
  idx1 = 0;
  while(1) {
    if(!clip_to_edge_2d(&((**(pClipPoly->vlist)) [
                         (*pClipPoly->clip_ivertices)[idx0].ivertex
                       ].transformed),
```

```
                                 &((**(pClipPoly->vlist)) [
                                    (*pClipPoly->clip_ivertices)[idx1].ivertex
                                 ].transformed)) )
        {
          clip_ivertices->num_items=0;
          return 0;
        }

        idx0 = idx1;
        if(idx0==pClipPoly->clip_ivertices->num_items-1) break;
        idx1++;
      }

      return 1;
    }

    l3d_polygon_2d::l3d_polygon_2d(const l3d_polygon_2d &r) {

      iv_items_factory = r.iv_items_factory->clone();
      init(DEFAULT_IVERTICES_PER_POLY);

      vlist = r.vlist;
      *ivertices = *r.ivertices;
      *clip_ivertices = *r.clip_ivertices;
      *temp_clip_ivertices = *r.temp_clip_ivertices;
    }

    l3d_polygon_2d* l3d_polygon_2d::clone(void) {
      return new l3d_polygon_2d(*this);
    }
```

The majority of the polygon.cc file deals with code for analytical clipping of the 2D polygon, which we cover in the next section. For now, we are more interested in the data structures used within the l3d_polygon_2d class for specifying polygon geometry.

The l3d_polygon_2d class declares a pointer to a pointer to a vertex list, for the animation and efficiency reasons we explained earlier:

```
        l3d_two_part_list<l3d_coordinate> **vlist;
```

File polygon.cc also declares a class of type l3d_polygon_ivertex, which represents an index into a vertex list. For now, such a vertex index is just an integer value, which is interpreted as an index into the external vertex list pointed to indirectly by the variable above. We could subclass l3d_polygon_ivertex to store additional information with each vertex index, such as a color value or a texture coordinate (as is done in the companion book *Advanced Linux 3D Graphics Programming*). Notice that we declare the assignment operator = to be virtual, so that when l3d_list copies elements, it does so through the virtual assignment operator. This leaves the door open for later adding new subtypes of l3d_polygon_ivertex.

```
    class l3d_polygon_ivertex {
      public:
        int ivertex;

        virtual l3d_polygon_ivertex& operator= (const l3d_polygon_ivertex &r) {
          ivertex = r.ivertex;
          return *this;
        }

        virtual ~l3d_polygon_ivertex(void) {
```

```
   }
};
```

Again, to allow for future flexibility with new vertex index types, we declare an abstract factory to create the l3d_polygon_ivertex objects:

```
class l3d_polygon_ivertex_items_factory :
    public l3d_list_item_factory<l3d_polygon_ivertex>
{
  public:
    virtual l3d_polygon_ivertex_items_factory *clone(void);
};
```

The factory provides a virtual clone method to create a new factory of the same type; when copying a polygon, we also should copy the vertex index factory so that the copied polygon can produce the same kind of vertex indices as the original polygon. (In the companion book *Advanced Linux 3D Graphics Programming*, we override this clone method because we need textured vertex indices; also, see the upcoming discussion in a few paragraphs on the polygon's clone method.) We create this factory during creation of the polygon object, in the polygon constructor:

```
l3d_polygon_2d::l3d_polygon_2d(int num_pts) {
  iv_items_factory = new l3d_polygon_ivertex_items_factory;
  init(num_pts);
}
```

Finally, when initializing the polygon object, we create three l3d_list objects to hold our l3d_polygon_ivertex objects. These are the lists of indices into the external vertex list. Notice in the following code that we pass the factory object to the constructor so that the list will use the factory when filling, expanding, or copying the elements in the list. Later on, we can swap out the factory with a subtype-compatible one, without "breaking" our old code.

```
void l3d_polygon_2d::init(int num_pts) {
  ivertices = new l3d_list<l3d_polygon_ivertex>
                 (num_pts, iv_items_factory);
  clip_ivertices = new l3d_list<l3d_polygon_ivertex>
                    (num_pts, iv_items_factory);
  temp_clip_ivertices = new l3d_list<l3d_polygon_ivertex>
                          (num_pts, iv_items_factory);
}
```

An application program will typically create and initialize an l3d_polygon_2d object as follows:

```
facet = new l3d_polygon_2d_flatshaded ( 4 );
facet->vlist = & vlist;
facet->final_color = xcolor;
(*(facet->ivertices))[facet->ivertices->next_index()].ivertex = 0;
(*(facet->ivertices))[facet->ivertices->next_index()].ivertex = 1;
(*(facet->ivertices))[facet->ivertices->next_index()].ivertex = 2;
(*(facet->ivertices))[facet->ivertices->next_index()].ivertex = 3;
```

Assuming the external variable vlist is a pointer to an already created l3d_two_part_list object, then the above code snippet works as follows. First, we create a new l3d_polygon_2d object, passing a parameter of 4 to the constructor, indicating that the polygon initially consists of four vertices (this number can grow if the polygon is clipped, as we see later). Next, we initialize the polygon's vlist member to be the address of the external pointer vlist. After setting the polygon's color, we initialize each of the polygon's vertex indices. The polygon's vertex indices are accessible through the `ivertices` member (which stands for index to vertices). As we saw above, the `ivertices` member is a list (more precisely, a pointer to a list) of type `l3d_list`, containing elements of type `l3d_polygon_ivertex`. We access the list's elements via the array access operator [ ], each time calling the `next_index` method on the list to obtain the next free array index. After specifying the next free list element inside of the operator [ ], we have access to the `l3d_polygon_ivertex` object stored at this location in the list. We finally set the `ivertex` member of this object, which represents the index into the external vertex list pointed to indirectly by `vlist`. For instance, the first `ivertex` assignment in the above code snippet effectively says, "the first vertex of this polygon is the vertex with index number 0 in the external vertex list." Notice, again, that the polygon's vertices are not explicitly defined, but rather indirectly, which allows for flexibility in changing the polygon's appearance without needing access to the polygon's internals; we just change the external list.

The three constructors of `l3d_polygon_2d` warrant a brief discussion. The first constructor with the `num_pts` parameter creates and initializes a 2D polygon. The second constructor with no parameters creates but does not initialize a 2D polygon. The reason we might need an uninitialized polygon is if we subclass from `l3d_polygon_2d` but take care of the polygon initialization in the new subclass, either by calling another base class constructor from a different base class (in the case of multiple inheritance possibly with virtual base classes), or by performing the initialization in the constructor of the new subclass. An example of this appears in the companion book *Advanced Linux 3D Graphics Programming*, with class `l3d_polygon_3d_textured`.

The third and last constructor is a custom copy constructor. Due to the complexity of the `l3d_polygon_2d` class, involving pointers to lists and contained objects, the semantics for the C++ default copy constructor (member-by-member copy) are not sufficient. Of particular note is that the custom copy constructor copies the lists of vertices and the contents of the lists. This is accomplished by copying the lists themselves (through an assignment such as `*ivertices=*r.ivertices`), and not just the pointers to the lists (which, with a statement such as `ivertices=r.ivertices`, would result in two pointers to the same list, not two separate copies of the list). Copying entire lists and their contents is possible because of the overloaded = operator in template class `l3d_list`, which then asks each object in the list to copy itself via another possibly overloaded = operator belonging to the object. Thus, a copy of a polygon has the same structure as the original, but can be freely altered without affecting the original: the copy of the list has no pointers to objects also pointed to by the original. This complete separation between original and copy is the desired copy semantic, and is therefore defined in a custom copy constructor.

The `clone` method of `l3d_polygon_2d` is a virtual method which creates a new polygon object of the same type (`l3d_polygon_2d`) and returns a pointer to this newly created polygon object. Creation of the new object is done with the copy constructor, meaning that a fully separate copy of the polygon is created. This method provides a convenient way of duplicating a polygon. We need this virtual method `clone` because later subclasses of `l3d_polygon_2d` can still be accessed through an abstract pointer of type `l3d_polygon_2d*`. This means we might need to clone a polygon, accessed through an abstract pointer, without knowing its exact subtype.

Therefore, subclasses of l3d_polygon_2d simply override the virtual clone method to create a new polygon of the correct concrete subtype, returning an abstract pointer, of type l3d_polygon_2d*, to the new cloned polygon. The need for cloning polygons arises when we want to split a polygon into two halves. To do this, we clone the polygon, creating two identical copies. Then for one polygon we clip away one particular half of the polygon, and for the other polygon we clip away exactly the other half of the polygon. The result is two polygons which together have the same shape as the original polygon, but which are two separate polygons which can be manipulated separately. See Chapter 7 for an implementation of the polygon split algorithm, and see the companion book *Advanced Linux 3D Graphics Programming* for a discussion of visible surface algorithms requiring polygon splits.

 NOTE All polygon subclasses which might need to be cloned (and split) must override the method clone.

The l3d_polygon_2d class only represents the geometry (shape) of a polygon, not its color or any other visible attributes. In other words, l3d_polygon_2d is a purely mathematical description of polygon geometry. The class l3d_polygon_2d_flatshaded is subclassed from l3d_polygon_2d, and represents a polygon with a single color. The member variable final_color represents the color with which the polygon will be drawn; this color is specified in "native" format, using the ext_to_native function discussed earlier. The overridden method draw, which by default did nothing in parent class l3d_polygon_2d, asks the rasterizer to draw the polygon, which, in turn, asks its rasterizer implementation to draw the polygon, using an algorithm we cover in the next section. Also, notice that l3d_polygon_2d_flatshaded overrides the clone method, creating and returning a flat-shaded polygon object.

Listing 3-8: p_flat.h

```
#ifndef __P_FLAT_H
#define __P_FLAT_H
#include "../../tool_os/memman.h"

#include "polygon.h"

class l3d_polygon_2d_flatshaded :
    virtual public l3d_polygon_2d
{
  public:
    unsigned long final_color;

    l3d_polygon_2d_flatshaded(void) {};

    l3d_polygon_2d_flatshaded(int num_pts) :
    l3d_polygon_2d(num_pts) {};

    void draw(l3d_rasterizer_2d *r) {
      r->draw_polygon_flatshaded(this);
    }

    l3d_polygon_2d_flatshaded(const l3d_polygon_2d_flatshaded &r);
    virtual l3d_polygon_2d *clone(void);
```

```
};

#endif
```

Listing 3-9: `p_flat.cc`

```
#include "p_flat.h"
#include "../../math/matrix.h"
#include "../../tool_os/memman.h"

l3d_polygon_2d* l3d_polygon_2d_flatshaded::clone(void) {
  return new l3d_polygon_2d_flatshaded(*this);
}

l3d_polygon_2d_flatshaded::l3d_polygon_2d_flatshaded
(const l3d_polygon_2d_flatshaded &r)
    : l3d_polygon_2d(r)
{
  final_color = r.final_color;
}
```

Figure 3-5 illustrates the class diagram for the polygon-related classes.

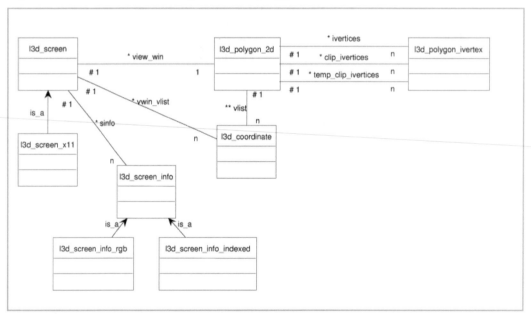

Figure 3-5: Class diagram for polygon-related classes.

Drawing the Polygon

Now that we have a flexible set of classes for specifying vertex lists and polygons, we can discuss the actual rasterization of polygons. For the time being, we are interested in drawing polygons filled with one color, which is also called flat-shading. The flat-shading polygon rasterization function in l3d is `l3d_rasterizer_2d_sw_imp::draw _polygon_flatshaded`. This function takes as a parameter a pointer to an `l3d_polygon_2d_flatshaded` object as described in the previous section.

The approach we will take to drawing a polygon is to draw a series of horizontal spans of pixels, one on top of another. Recall that a span is simply a continuous sequence of pixels. You can imagine this process as being similar to stacking wooden planks of various length, one on top of another. Figure 3-6 illustrates this process. By drawing a series of horizontal spans on top of each other, we can approximate the appearance of any convex polygon.

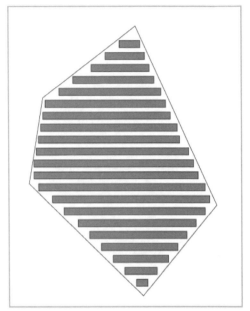

Figure 3-6: Any convex polygon can be rasterized as a series of horizontal spans.

Notice that only convex polygons can be rasterized in this fashion. A concave polygon might have holes in it or curving sections which might require multiple spans to be drawn for each row of the polygon (Figure 3-7). Since any concave polygon can be decomposed into a set of convex polygons, it is not a great limitation that our rasterization routines only work for convex polygons.

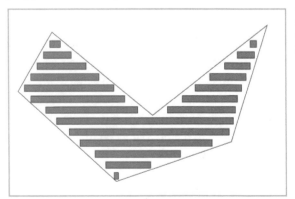

Figure 3-7: Concave polygons cannot as easily be rasterized as spans, because multiple spans might be required per row.

The algorithm for rasterizing convex polygons is based upon the line rasterization algorithm we discussed earlier. The idea is to start at the top vertex of the polygon, and find the edge immediately to the left and immediately to the right of the top vertex. We then step in the positive *y*-direction (downward) along the left edge and the right edge simultaneously, calculating the *x* coordinate for the left edge and the right edge incrementally by adding the inverse slope, exactly as we did when rasterizing lines. But instead of drawing the edges themselves, we draw a horizontal span between the edges; specifically, for each *y* coordinate, we draw a span between the left *x* coordinate and the right *x* coordinate. While stepping vertically along the left and right edges, we need to notice when we have finished processing one edge (i.e., when the current *y* coordinate is greater than the edge's largest *y* coordinate), because then we must search for the next adjacent edge so that the vertical stepping can continue with the next edge. When we have processed all edges (which is also when we reach the bottommost vertex of the polygon), we are finished.

NOTE The polygon rasterization algorithm we describe can therefore rasterize any convex polygon. Many simple 3D engines can only rasterize triangles or quads (four-sided polygons), because of the belief that rasterizing these simpler primitives is easier than rasterizing arbitrary convex polygons, and because any polygon can be decomposed into triangles. Although, in theory, any polygon can in fact be decomposed into triangles, in practice it is often a great hinderance if a 3D engine can only fundamentally draw triangles or quads. This is because for applications such as portal rendering (described in the companion book *Advanced Linux 3D Graphics Programming*), we need to draw and clip to arbitrary convex polygons. Furthermore, clipping (covered in the next section) can add new vertices to any polygon. If an arbitrary convex polygon must first be decomposed into triangles before we can do anything with it, this opens up a Pandora's box of practical problems. Conceptually we want to deal with a convex polygon as a whole, but in practice we are forced to juggle a set of disjointed and possibly changing triangles which are all accessed and stored separately, and on top of that, have also lost the delineating border of the original polygon. It's always a sign of trouble if the implementation of an idea radically differs from the conceptual framework used to think about the idea. Supporting arbitrary convex polygons early on eliminates many headaches later. And, as we just saw in the previous paragraph, rasterizing an arbitrary convex polygon is not more difficult than rasterizing a triangle; we simply need to keep track of current edges on the left and right sides of the polygon during rasterization.

The steps for the algorithm are as follows:

1. Find the topmost and bottommost vertices of the polygon (i.e., those with the smallest and largest *y* coordinate) by sequentially searching through the vertices. We will draw the polygon starting from the top (smallest *y*) and proceeding towards the bottom (largest *y*).

2. Create a zero-height left edge as an initialization step. This left edge consists of two vertices: a left-start vertex and a left-end vertex. Initialize both of these to be the top vertex.

3. Create a zero-height right edge as an initialization step. This right edge consists of two vertices: a right-start vertex and a right-end vertex. Initialize both of these to be the top vertex.

4. Start a loop to go from the top *y* coordinate to the bottom *y* coordinate (or the bottom of the screen, whichever comes first). We will draw one horizontal span of pixels for each *y* coordinate.

5. Check if the left edge has any remaining height with respect to the current *y* coordinate. This is the distance between the *y* coordinate of left-end and the current *y* coordinate. If this is zero, then this left edge has no height with respect to the current *y* coordinate, either because the edge itself is of zero height (because its starting and ending *y* coordinates are the same) or

because the current y coordinate, which we increase in each loop iteration, has passed the end of this edge. In either case, search for a new left edge of non-zero height in the counterclockwise direction. If we loop through all edges and find no new edge of non-zero height, the polygon has been completely drawn.

5a. After finding a left edge of non-zero height, initialize the current left x coordinate to be the x coordinate of left-start (the topmost vertex of the left edge).

6. Check to see if the right edge has any remaining height with respect to the current y coordinate. This is the distance between the y coordinate of right-end and the current y coordinate. If this is zero, then this right edge has no height with respect to the current y coordinate, either because the edge itself is of zero height or because the current y coordinate, which we increase in each loop iteration, has passed the end of this edge. In either case, search for a new right edge of non-zero height in the clockwise direction. If we loop through all edges and find no new edge of non-zero height, then the polygon has been completely drawn.

6a. After finding a right edge of non-zero height, initialize the current right x coordinate to be the x coordinate of right-start (the topmost vertex of the right edge).

7. Begin a loop which goes from the current y coordinate until the end of the y coordinate of the left edge or the right edge, whichever is reached first.

8. Draw a span of pixels between the left and right edges at the current y coordinate.

9. Increase the y coordinate by one, and "step" the left-x and right-x coordinates by adding the inverse edge slopes to them. This is the same strategy we used for rasterizing lines. Continue the loop begun in Step 7.

10. After exiting the loop, we have now stepped the y coordinate past the bottom of one or both of the edges. Continue the loop begun in step 4 to look for the next left and/or right edge (if any).

Referring back to Listing 2-41, you can see that the `draw_polygon_flatshaded` method of class `l3d_rasterizer_2d_sw_imp` is commented with each of the steps listed above. Also, notice the macro `VTX(i)` in the listing from Chapter 2. As we have seen, the polygon's vertices are defined by indices into a list which is accessed through a pointer to a pointer. While this allows for the most flexible polygon definition, it makes accessing the vertices from within the polygon a bit awkward at times. The `VTX(i)` macro allows for a more convenient access to the actual `l3d_coordinate` object associated with a particular vertex in the polygon's vertex index list.

 NOTE Notice also that the `VTX(i)` macro accesses the transformed (not the original) member of the vertex list pointed to by a vertex index in the clipped vertex index list (list `clip_ivertices` and not list `ivertices`). This means that we only ever draw transformed, clipped polygons, or more accurately, that the definition for the polygon to be drawn is taken out of the storage area reserved for the transformed, clipped data. Whether the data stored in this storage area has actually been transformed and clipped or not is irrelevant; the point is to understand where the rasterizer implementation looks for the final, to-be-rasterized definition of the polygon data. It looks in the polygon's clipped vertex index list, and takes the associated transformed coordinates out of the external vertex list. This is the most general and most common case.

There is, however, one slightly tricky part about the polygon rasterization code. It stems from the fact that pixel coordinates are integer coordinates; however, the polygon coordinates are ultimately from type `l3d_real`. We therefore need to convert real to integer coordinates. When we drew lines, we treated this issue somewhat casually, since we don't use the line drawing function very often. With polygons, however, the situation looks a bit different; it is important to define a consistent real-to-integer rounding convention to eliminate cracks between adjacent polygons and to determine which pixels are "inside" the polygon and which are not. Collectively, we can call these issues *sub-pixel rasterization* issues, which we now look at in more detail.

Sub-Pixel Correct Rasterization

Polygon coordinates, as we have seen, are stored as type `l3d_real`, not as integers. There are two reasons for this. First, 2D polygon coordinates, in the context of 3D graphics, arise out of a 3D-to-2D projection operation, which takes place in a continuous real-valued 3D space. Therefore, the 2D coordinates that come from a projection operation will be real-valued and not integer values. (See Chapter 5.) Second, allowing 2D polygon coordinates to be real values allows for so-called *sub-pixel correct rasterization*, which creates a smooth "flowing" effect for polygon edges as the polygon moves across the screen at a rate of less than one pixel per frame. This is important, for instance, when the virtual camera or player is moving slowly through a scene.

The fundamental problem is that we need to convert real values into integer values. Until now, we have dealt with pixel coordinates in an integer coordinate system. The coordinate (0,0), for instance, represents the pixel at an offset of 0 rows and 0 columns from the upper-leftmost pixel in the image. An integer pixel coordinate therefore specifies the region of space occupied by a pixel. When dealing with real-valued coordinates, however, the situation is completely different: a real-valued coordinate does not specify an occupied space, unlike integer pixel coordinates; a real-valued coordinate specifies an infinitely small point, with no size, at a particular location. Therefore, if we want to work with pixels in a real-valued coordinate system, we have to decide what space a pixel occupies in the real-valued coordinate system. For instance, if we say that a pixel is located at an integer location of "0" horizontally, does the pixel occupy the space starting at real-valued x coordinate 0 and ending at 1, or the space ending at real-valued x coordinate 0 and starting at –1, or the space extending halfway to the left and halfway to the right of real-valued x coordinate 0, starting at –0.5 and ending at 0.5? The same questions apply to the vertical coordinate. The choice is arbitrary, but I find it is most intuitive to take the "starting at" approach. This means that the pixel (x,y), specified in integer pixel-space coordinates, occupies in a real-valued coordinate system the space from x up to but not including $x+1$ in the horizontal direction, and the space from y up to but not including $y+1$ in the vertical direction. Another way of saying this is that the integer coordinates of a pixel in an integer reversed-y coordinate system correspond to the position of the pixel's upper-left corner in a real-valued reversed-y coordinate system. This system ensures that every part of all visible pixels lies within the non-negative quadrant of the real-valued coordinate system. Any other approach would mean that parts of the pixels in row 0 and column 0 would "hang off the edge" of the coordinate system, extending partially into the negative region. This would mathematically cause no problems but seems conceptually a bit odd.

There are fundamentally two goals we would like to achieve:

1. Only pixels whose upper-left corner is "inside" of the polygon should be drawn.
2. For adjacent polygons sharing an edge, the pixels on the shared edge should be drawn by one and only one polygon. No pixel should be drawn twice; no pixel should be left undrawn.

The first requirement is not an absolute must, but is very useful to understand what we are trying to accomplish and follows naturally from a consistent coordinate definition. The second requirement is much more important, because otherwise we can have quite ugly black gaps where polygons meet at the edges, a condition which could be called polygonal periodontitis. A consistent real-to-integer conversion makes sure that the edges of polygons line up perfectly.

To achieve these goals, we follow these simple rules when rasterizing a polygon:

1. In the vertical direction, for an edge whose real-valued y coordinates range from start_y to end_y, we define the edge to extend starting from ceil(start_y) and extending up to and including ceil(end_y) -1.
2. In the horizontal direction, for a span whose real-valued x coordinates range from left_x to right_x, we define the span to extend starting from the pixel at ceil(left_x) and extending up to and including the pixel at ceil(right_x) -1.

The `ceil(x)` function, where x is a real value, is the mathematical ceiling function. It returns the smallest integer larger than x. In other words, it rounds upward in the positive direction.

These rules have two effects. The first effect comes about through the use of the ceiling function, and effectively associates the upper-left corner of each pixel with the corresponding real-valued coordinate. The second effect comes from the "-1" term, which, in combination with the ceiling function, effectively guarantees that shared edges, both horizontal and vertical, will only be drawn by one polygon. Let's look at this a bit more closely.

By taking the ceil(start_y) coordinate, we initialize y to be the first row of pixels whose upper edge lies on or below the start_y coordinate. By stepping horizontally starting from ceil(left_x), we find the first pixel whose left edge lies on or to the right of the left_x coordinate. Taken together, this means that the upper-left corner of all pixels found in this way lie on or below the top edge and on or to the right of the left edge—in other words, "inside" the left and top edges.

The ceil(end_y) coordinate is the first row of pixels whose upper edge lies on or below the end_y coordinate. Reasoning backwards, then, ceil(end_y) -1 is the last row of pixels whose upper edge lies strictly above the end_y coordinate. The ceil(right_x) coordinate is the first pixel whose left edge lies on or to the right of the right_x coordinate. Reasoning backwards, ceil(right_x) -1 is the last pixel whose left edge lies strictly to the left of the right_x coordinate. Taken together, this means that the upper-left corner of all pixels found in this way lies strictly above the bottom edge and strictly to the left of the right edge—in other words, "inside" the bottom and right edges.

The results of the two previous paragraphs together mean that all pixels lie inside the polygon, and that the last pixel not drawn horizontally or vertically is the first pixel drawn in an adjacent polygon. For instance, the point with x coordinate 7.32718 is rounded down to 7 if it is used as a right_x coordinate (ceil(right_x) -1 = ceil(7.32718) -1 = $8 - 1 = 7$), but is rounded up to 8 if it is used as a left_x coordinate (ceil(left_x) = ceil(7.32718) = 8). The same logic applies for vertical edges. This consistently ensures that each pixel belongs to one and only one polygon.

NOTE As mentioned in the discussion of rasterizing lines, the DDA algorithm presented here is not necessarily always 100 percent accurate. The fact that the next value of x is dependent on the previous value can conceivably lead to numerical drift for extremely long lines or edges, since a small inaccuracy in the initial computation of x cumulatively increases as we step along the edge. This could, conceivably, cause a pixel whose upper-left corner is not strictly within the polygon to occasionally be drawn. In practice, this is rarely a problem (typically only with texture mapping, and even then there are workarounds). In any event, we still never have gaps between polygons with the approach presented above, since a pixel is always drawn by one and only one edge.

The only additional thing we need to do is to realize that the mathematically "true" edge always goes from the real-valued start_y and end_y y coordinates, and that the "true" span extends horizontally from left_x to right_x. However, we draw the edge vertically starting at ceil(start_y), and horizontally starting at ceil(left_x). This means that when we initialize our x and y variables to step along the edge, we must make an initial *sub-pixel correction*. Since we start vertically drawing at y coordinate ceil(y_start), we have skipped over the top, sub-pixel part of the edge, whose size is ceil(y_start) – y_start. This means that the first x coordinate we draw along the edge should be initialized not to the starting x coordinate of the edge, but rather to the starting x coordinate plus (ceil(y_start) – y_start) * inverse_slope.

Similarly, when drawing a horizontal span, we start drawing the span not at left_x, but at ceil(left_x); we have thus skipped over the left, sub-pixel part of the span, whose size is ceil(left_x) – start_x. However, for flat-shaded polygons, we have no variable which depends on the x coordinate, and thus do not need any sub-pixel correction. Note that some texture mapping or lighting schemes (described in the companion book *Advanced Linux 3D Graphics Programming*) require a sub-pixel correction in both the horizontal and vertical directions, since in this case the texture or other coordinates do indeed depend on both x and y, and any sub-pixel portions that are "skipped over" must be accounted for.

Figure 3-8 illustrates the rasterization and sub-pixel correction process for a triangle. We have two edges on the left, and one edge on the right. For the first left edge and the first right edge, we skip the sub-pixel top part of the triangle, and actually start drawing at ceil(start_y). Thus the vertical portion of the triangle labeled "sub-pixel correction" is the vertical amount we skip, which we must compensate for in the horizontal edge variables. Also notice that we skip the very last sub-pixel part of an edge, since we draw up to ceil(end_y) – 1 and not up to ceil(end_y). This skipped portion, however, belongs exactly to the pixel which will be drawn by an edge underneath the current one, thereby ensuring that, vertically, each pixel is only drawn by one edge or polygon.

Horizontally, the process works similarly in Figure 3-8. The dark dots represent the true x coordinate of the edge for the given y coordinate. The circles represent the ceiling of the true x coordinate. We thus start drawing the edge a bit to the right of the true left edge; specifically, we begin drawing with the first pixel whose upper-left corner lies on or to the right of the true edge. We continue horizontally up but not including ceil(right_x), which is the first pixel whose upper-left corner is strictly to the right of the right edge. We thus stop drawing the edge a bit to the left of the true right edge. The difference between ceil(x) and the true x is the sub-pixel "jump" in x which would need to be accounted for if any variables depend on x, but as noted above, nothing depends on x for flat-shaded polygons.

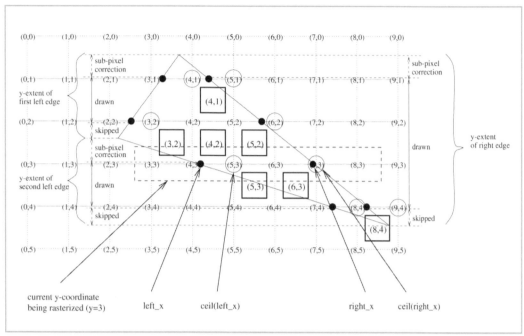

Figure 3-8: Rasterization and sub-pixel correction. Notice that only pixels whose upper-left corners are inside of the polygon are drawn.

In the C++ source code for `draw_polygon_flatshaded`, the sub-pixel correction due to the skipped *y* part takes place in the code for Steps 5a and 6a, and is commented with the phrase "sub-pixel correction."

Polygon Clipping in 2D

Until this point, we have implicitly assumed that the polygons we draw all have coordinates which lie within the boundaries of the screen. In general, this is not the case. In the 2D domain, we often want to model 2D figures which are larger than the pixel dimensions of the screen. In this case we can only display part of our figures on the screen at a time. This means that very often, parts of our polygons will lie outside of the screen coordinates. And in the 3D world, we generate 2D polygons by projecting polygons from 3D space into 2D space. Polygons generated in this way are also very often partially (or totally, but this is a culling and not a clipping issue) invisible.

Any polygon which is partially off-screen must be clipped. Recall, our polygon rasterization code draws into an off-screen buffer by directly setting bytes in memory, bytes whose address is calculated via the formula $(x + width * y) * bytes\_per\_pixel$. If our screen is 800×600 pixels with a depth of 2 bytes per pixel, this means we have 1,920,000 bytes in the off-screen buffer. Without clipping, if we try to plot a point at coordinate (77281, 33892), the rasterization formula would blindly comply, yielding an address 54,381,762 bytes from the beginning of the buffer, which is 52,461,763 bytes too far into no-man's land (also known as crash-your-program land). To keep our memory accesses within safe bounds, we need to clip our polygons so that all vertices lie within valid screen coordinates.

There are several approaches to clipping polygons. Clipping lines is similar, and clipping points is trivial (discard the point if it lies outside of the screen coordinates).

 NOTE We present the clipping strategies below in the context of clipping 2D polygons, but the ideas extend readily to 3D as well. Chapter 7 covers this in more detail.

Discard the Polygon Completely

The easiest and most visually disturbing means of "clipping" polygons is to refrain from drawing the polygon completely if any of its vertices lie outside of the screen. This method can work if most of the polygons are small, so that discarding one polygon does not cause significantly large parts of the image to disappear. This method fails if there are many large polygons, because we then completely discard very large portions of geometry as soon as one single part (in this case, vertex) of that geometry is invisible.

Discard Invalid Vertices Only

The next approach to polygon clipping is to discard vertices which lie outside of the screen, thereby reducing the number of vertices in the polygon. Figure 3-9 illustrates this idea. The problem with this approach is that discarding vertices causes the invisible part of the polygon to disappear. In the top half of Figure 3-9, the rightmost vertex lies outside of the screen boundaries and is discarded. This yields the result in the bottom half of Figure 3-9, where only three vertices remain. The section marked "Incorrectly omitted area" should ideally still be visible, but is incorrectly clipped away by discarding the offending vertex.

This approach can work if the geometry consists of smaller polygons with many vertices each, so that discarding one vertex has a less disruptive effect on the rest of the geometry. If many large polygons with few vertices each are used, this approach is visually unpleasing.

Scissoring or Scanline Clipping

The next approach to polygon clipping is to perform clipping during the rasterization process, in the rasterizer implementation itself. As we mentioned, a software rasterizer implementation draws polygons as a series of horizontal spans. If we "clamp" the left and right edges of each span to the left and right screen boundaries, we can ensure that the polygon gets correctly clipped to the screen. A similar clamping must take place in the vertical direction, but we must be careful that the initialization of the rasterization algorithm also takes place correctly. We originally assumed that the polygon is rasterized from the top vertex to the bottom vertex; however, if the top vertex is beyond the top edge of the screen, the initialization steps in the polygon rasterization algorithm must search for the first left edge and right edge which are at least partially visible, and start the algorithm at the first visible part of each edge. It is a bit complicated, but it can be done. This approach to polygon clipping is called *scanline clipping* or *scissoring*.

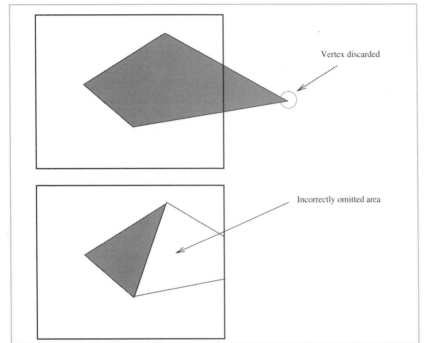

Figure 3-9:
Clipping by
discarding
vertices

Vertex discarded

Incorrectly omitted area

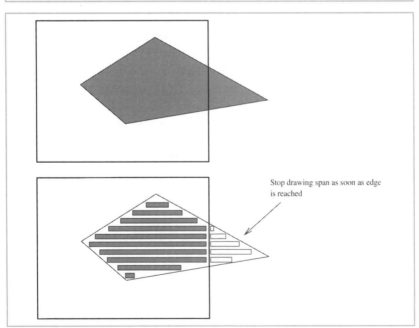

Figure 3-10:
Scanline clipping,
also called
scissoring.

Stop drawing span as soon as edge
is reached

This clipping algorithm is relatively easy to understand and implement. It also allows clipping to non-polygonal regions; this requires storing an array of left-clamp values and right-clamp values for each row in the frame buffer. We then clip each span to the left-clamp and right-clamp values appropriate for the current row.

There are three serious drawbacks to this method of clipping. First of all, it requires two extra comparisons for each and every span to be drawn to the screen, which slows down as the screen size increases. Second, although it can be fairly easily implemented for flat-shaded polygons, as soon as we associate more information with each polygon vertex (lighting or texture coordinates), a scanline clipping algorithm becomes a headache to manage because the discarded portion of the span must be accounted for in the computation of lighting or texture coordinates for the span, similar to the way that we needed to account for a discarded sub-pixel portion of an edge or a span. Such extra accounting clutters the code with extra comparisons and calculations during initialization and for each span. Finally, this method of clipping assumes a software rasterizer implementation which has direct control over the spans to be drawn. This algorithm cannot be effectively accelerated with hardware, since accessing spans at the hardware level, even if it were possible, would require so many function calls that the overhead would outweigh any performance gain from the hardware.

Analytical 2D Clipping

The most flexible method for polygon clipping is to perform so-called "analytical 2D clipping." In this approach, we clip one polygon to the boundaries of another polygon. Both polygons must be convex, a limitation which by now should come as no surprise to you. In the case of clipping to the screen, we define a rectangular polygon which encompasses the screen, and clip all polygons to be drawn against this rectangular polygon. This is the clipping method implemented in l3d. Specifically, this rectangular clip polygon for the screen is stored in the l3d_screen class, in member variables view_win and vwin_vlist, which we previously promised would be explained later. Having now encountered polygons, we now can understand what exactly these variables are. The view_win variable is of type l3d_polygon_2d, and is the polygon data structure itself for the screen's clip window. The vwin_vlist variable is an l3d_two_part_list containing objects of type l3d_coordinate defining the corners of the clip window. This is a completely typical polygon configuration as we saw earlier—a polygon object with an external two-part vertex list.

 NOTE Notice that the view_win variable is of type l3d_polygon_2d and not of l3d_polygon_2d_flatshaded, since the clip window never needs to be drawn and thus does not need the color attribute and drawing functions provided by l3d_polygon_2d_flatshaded.

Let's now discuss the polygon-to-polygon clipping algorithm itself. Let us call the polygon to be clipped the target polygon, and the polygon being clipped against the clip polygon. The goal is to redefine the target polygon so that all of its vertices lie "inside of" the clip polygon, ensuring that the shape of the final, clipped polygon corresponds exactly to the shape of that part of the original target polygon which lies inside the clip polygon. In other words, we want to avoid the distortion which occurs with the "discard invalid vertices" algorithm.

The first thing to define is what we mean by "inside of the clip polygon." We previously mentioned, in the original discussion of polygons, that this book uses the clockwise vertex ordering convention for specifying polygons. Then, we can say that a point is "inside" of a clip polygon if, for all edges in the clip polygon, the point lies on the right side of the edge when looking along the edge in a clockwise direction with respect to the clip polygon. We can also call the right side of an edge the "inside side" of an edge. This means that testing for containment within a polygon reduces to a series of simple tests. If the point lies on the inside side of each and every edge, then the point must lie inside of the entire polygon.

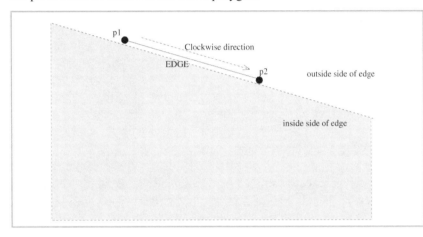

Figure 3-11: A point is on the "inside side" of a polygon's edge if it is on the right side when looking clockwise along the edge.

The clipping algorithm itself takes a similar "divide-and-conquer" approach. For each edge of the target polygon, we clip it against each edge of the clip polygon. To avoid confusion in the following discussion, let us call the edges in the target polygon "segments." To clip a segment to an edge of the clip polygon means to calculate an intersection between the segment and the infinitely long line containing the edge of the clip polygon. (The fact that we clip the target polygon's segments against infinitely long edges—as opposed to just the finitely long edge—is not a problem, because we clip the target polygon against all infinitely long edges making up the clip polygon.) To do this, we search for the first segment of the target polygon that has one endpoint outside the clip edge and one endpoint inside the clip edge. If no such segment can be found, then either the target polygon is completely inside or completely outside of the clip polygon, and no clipping needs to be done.

If we do find such a segment, then we have found the point where the target polygon is crossing either from inside the clip polygon to the outside, or from the outside to the inside. We call this situation an *edge cross*, because the segment has crossed an edge. Since the target polygon is convex, for a given edge there are either zero or two edge crosses. We see the benefit of convexity here: all convex polygons are "simple," loop-like, somewhat O-shaped figures. If an O-shaped figure crosses an edge at one point, then there must also be a second crossing point where the "O" loops back on itself, thereby crossing the edge a second time. (Note that if the "O" touches the edge at one point, this does not count as a "crossing.") Therefore, if we find one edge cross, we know there must be a second edge cross, and we must search for it.

With the two crossing segments thus found, we then calculate the exact intersection points between the crossing segments and the edge which was crossed. This creates two new vertices, both lying exactly on the clip edge and both also lying on the crossing segments.

These newly calculated intersection points are used as new vertices in the polygon. We use these two new vertices to redefine two segments and to add a new segment to the target polygon. We redefine the two crossing segments so that they no longer extend outside of the polygon, but only extend up to the newly calculated clip vertices. We then "close up" the polygon by adding a new segment joining the newly calculated clip vertices.

Figure 3-12 illustrates this process for clipping against the rightmost edge of the screen. One vertex lies outside of the clip polygon. The two edges attached to this vertex are found as being crossing segments, because one vertex for each edge lies inside and one outside of the clip polygon. We compute the intersection points between the crossing segments and the clip edge, yielding the new clip vertices indicated by the shaded circles in the bottom half of the figure. The two crossing segments are changed so that they only extend up to the newly calculated clip vertices, and a new segment is created between the new clip vertices.

The example in Figure 3-12 only shows clipping against the right edge of the clip polygon, but the exact same procedure is followed for all edges of the clip polygon. Also, there may be more than just one vertex outside of the clip edge; there could be many. Even if there are many vertices outside of the clip polygon, we are still only interested in finding the two crossing segments. We then discard not just one but all vertices outside of the clip polygon.

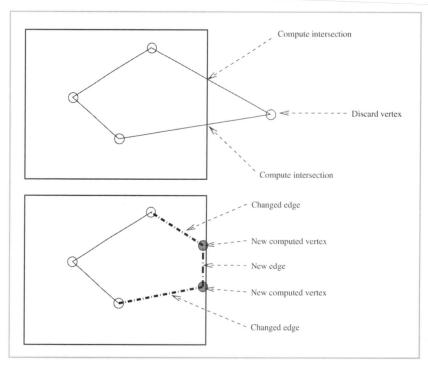

Compute intersection

Discard vertex

Compute intersection

Changed edge

New computed vertex

New edge

New computed vertex

Changed edge

Figure 3-12: Analytical 2D clipping.

NOTE Although I independently reasoned out and implemented this clipping algorithm for l3d, the algorithm turns out to be a variant of the famous Sutherland-Hodgman polygon clipping algorithm [SUTH74]. The algorithm presented here, however, limits itself to clipping convex polygons against other convex polygons, whereas the Sutherland-Hodgman algorithm clips either concave or convex polygons against another convex polygon. I believe that the convexity restrictions placed on the algorithm presented here allow it to be faster than the general Sutherland-Hodgman algorithm, because we know that there are either exactly zero or two crossing segments.

Notice that during this process, new vertices are created. Also notice that the polygon's definition changes, since the edges and therefore the contents of the vertex index list change in number and size. If the polygon is clipped against a clip polygon with many edges, then it is conceivable that none of the original edges or vertices remain after a clipping operation. Furthermore, if the polygon is moving, then some vertices which did not need to be clipped in the previous frame might now need to be clipped, and vice versa.

Now we can understand fully the purpose of the two-part list data structure introduced earlier. The fixed part defines the original vertices of the polygon. The varying part is the storage for the clip vertices which are generated during clipping. There might be no vertices generated during clipping, or there might be dozens; it all depends on the shapes and positions of the target and clip polygons. Furthermore, if multiple polygons share the same vertex list, the vertex list will contain clip-generated vertices for all polygons using the list. With moving polygons, the clipping vertices and indices to these can change every frame. It is clear that a dynamically growable, dynamically clearable data structure is needed here. This is exactly the role of the two-part list. Before every new clipping operation, we reset the varying part of the vertex list by setting num_varying_items to 0; this essentially "deletes" all clip-generated vertices and allows the clipping operation to begin again with the original polygon definition.

Inside of the polygon itself, we have three lists of indices to vertices: ivertices, clip_ivertices, and temp_clip_ivertices. These lists define the polygon by listing the vertices in clockwise order. Variable ivertices contains the original, never-to-be-changed definition of which vertices in the external list define this polygon. Variable clip_ivertices initially contains exactly the same contents as ivertices, and is initialized with the function init_clip_ivertices. During a clipping operation, we build the new definition of the polygon (i.e., the new list of indices to vertices, since we need to add indices to any clip vertices and discard indices of any vertices outside of the clip polygon) inside of the temp_clip_ivertices list. This is because to build the new list, we need to reference the old list; we cannot easily update the clip_ivertices list "in-place." After creating the new vertex-index list in temp_clip_ivertices, we call swap_temp_and_main_clip_lists to swap the temporary and the main clip_ivertices lists. At this point the clip operation for one edge is done, any new vertices have been placed in the varying part of the external two-part vertex list, and any new indices to these new vertices have been placed in the clip_ivertices list. Notice that any newly created vertices in the external two-part vertex list are accessible via their index exactly as the original vertices are—this is the advantage of the two-part list. The ivertices lists (more importantly, the users of these lists, such as the rasterizer implementation) don't know or care if the referenced vertices are original vertices or clip-generated vertices; during rasterization, for instance, this is completely irrelevant.

Note that the `ivertices` lists are from type `l3d_list`, not `l3d_two_part_list`. This is because these vertex-index lists can change completely based upon a clipping operation; we might need to discard all indices to original vertices and replace them with indices to clip-generated vertices. This is also why we have a temporary and a main clipping vertex-index list; we create a possibly entirely new list based on the old list. This is in contrast to the external vertex list, where the original vertices themselves always remain accessible, but clip-generated vertices might be inserted in addition to, but not instead of, the originals.

TIP Remember that the rasterizer uses the `clip_ivertices` list, not the `ivertices` list, to determine the vertices that make up the polygon, and that the transformed coordinate for these vertices, not the original coordinate, is used to draw the polygon to the screen.

The actual polygon clipping is done in class `l3d_polygon_2d` in function `clip_to_polygon_2d`, which takes a pointer to the clip polygon as a parameter. This function returns 1 if the polygon still is visible after clipping to the clip polygon, or 0 if the polygon has been completely clipped away. The function simply loops through all edges of the clip polygon, clipping the target polygon against each clip edge via the function `clip_to_edge_2d`. Function `clip_to_edge_2d` searches for the two crossing segments as outlined above, using the helper function `side_of_point` to determine if a point is on the inside side or the outside side of a clip edge. Function `clip_to_edge_2d` then calls `clip_segment_to_edge_2d` to calculate the exact intersection points between the crossing segments and the clip edge. Functions `next_clipidx_left` and `next_clipidx_right` return the next index in a counterclockwise and clockwise direction, respectively. These functions "wrap around" if they go past the last or first index; in other words, the index to the left of the first index is the last index, and the index to the right of the last index is the first index.

NOTE Notice that the polygon clipping is implemented in the `l3d_polygon_2d` class, not in the `l3d_polygon_2d_flatshaded` class. This is because polygon clipping is a mathematical operation independent of any display attributes.

It's worth commenting briefly on the functions `side_of_point` and `clip_segment_to_edge_2d`. These functions use a bit of geometry to calculate the position of a point relative to an edge and to intersect a polygon segment with a clip edge. Let's cover each function separately.

The `side_of_point` function uses the concept of point subtraction as well as the as-of-yet undefined function `dot` to compute a vector dot product. The sign of the vector dot product (positive or negative) then determines which side of the line segment the point is on (inside or outside). See Chapter 5 for details.

The `clip_segment_to_edge_2d` function uses simple geometry to compute an intersection between two lines. The idea is to derive the line equation for both the segment to be clipped and for the clipping edge against which the segment is clipped. We then solve the equations simultaneously for the intersection point. Let's go through the details of the derivation so that you can understand the solution technique and apply it elsewhere.

The slope-intercept equation of a line, as we saw earlier during the discussion of line rasterization, is $y = mx + B$. This equation, however, fails if the line is completely vertical (since the slope m would be infinite). There is a more flexible line equation which is valid for lines of any orientation. The line passing through points (x_0, y_0) and (x_1, y_1) is:

Equation 3-5 $(y_1 - y_0)x - (x_1 - x_0)y + (x_1 y_0 - y_1 x_0) = 0$

You can derive this equation from the slope-intercept form by realizing that m is $(y_1-y_0)/(x_1-x_0)$, solving for B in terms of x_0, y_0, x_1, and y_1, replacing the explicit forms of m and B in the slope-intercept equation, collecting all terms on one side of the equation so that zero is on the other side, and finally simplifying to eliminate the division by (x_1-x_0), which is the reason that the slope-intercept form fails for vertical lines. We thereby arrive at the above line equation which holds for all line orientations.

Next, let us say that the segment which is being clipped goes from coordinates (x_{0seg}, y_{0seg}) to (x_{1seg}, y_{1seg}). The equation for this line is then:

Equation 3-6 $(y_{1_{seg}} - y_{0_{seg}})x - (x_{1_{seg}} - x_{0_{seg}})y + (x_{1_{seg}} y_{0_{seg}} - y_{1_{seg}} x_{0_{seg}}) = 0$

Now, let us augment this formula with information from the second line, namely, the line containing the edge against which it is being clipped. For this, we use the parametric form of the line, expressing position based upon a time variable t. (We could use the same previous implicit line equation, but this complicates the math needlessly.) Assuming the edge being clipped against goes from (x_{0edge}, y_{0edge}) to (x_{1edge}, y_{1edge}), then the parametric form of the line going between these two points is:

Equation 3-7 $x = x_{0_{edge}} + t(x_{1_{edge}} - x_{0_{edge}})$

Equation 3-8 $y = y_{0_{edge}} + t(y_{1_{edge}} - y_{0_{edge}})$

Notable is that when $t=0$, the (x,y) coordinates are at (x_{0edge}, y_{0edge})—the starting point. When $t=1$, the (x,y) coordinates are at (x_{1edge}, y_{1edge})—the ending point. If $t=0.5$, the (x,y) coordinates are exactly halfway between the starting and ending points. This is the idea behind the parametric form of an equation: to parameterize the function in terms of a "time variable" t. A more mathematically rigorous way of thinking about the parameter t is a percentage of distance; $t=0.1$ means that the point is 10% of the distance between the starting and ending points.

Using the parametric form of the line equation for the clipping edge, and plugging these results into the implicit line equation for segment to be clipped, we obtain:

Equation 3-9 $(y_{1_{seg}} - y_{0_{seg}})(x_{0_{edge}} + t(x_{1_{edge}} - x_{0_{edge}}))$
$- (x_{1_{seg}} - x_{0_{seg}})(y_{0_{edge}} + t(y_{1_{edge}} - y_{0_{edge}}))$
$\qquad + (x_{1_{seg}} y_{0_{seg}} - y_{1_{seg}} x_{0_{seg}}) \quad = \quad 0$

Solving for t gives us:

Equation 3-10

$$t = \frac{(x_{1_{seg}} - x_{0_{seg}})(y_{0_{edge}} - y_{0_{seg}}) + (y_{1_{seg}} - y_{0_{seg}})(x_{0_{seg}} - x_{0_{edge}})}{(x_{1_{edge}} - x_{0_{edge}})(y_{1_{seg}} - y_{0_{seg}}) - (y_{1_{edge}} - y_{0_{edge}})(x_{1_{seg}} - x_{0_{seg}})}$$

This gives us the "intersection time" (as a percentage of distance) between the segment and the edge. If the denominator in the above calculation is zero, then the segment and edge are parallel and do not intersect; this corresponds to an intersection time of infinity (i.e., never). This should, however, never happen, since before we call this routine at all we first check if the segment does indeed cross the edge, via `side_of_point`. In the normal event that t is not zero, we can then use the value of t to determine the actual coordinates of intersection by substituting the determined value of t back into the original parametric line in Equations 3-7 and 3-8.

In this way we obtain the exact (x,y) coordinates of the intersection between the segment and the edge. Having obtained the intersection point, we then insert a new vertex into the polygon's two-part vertex list, and we return an index to this vertex so that the calling function can redefine the clipped segment to extend only up to the intersection point with the edge.

TIP Emacs has a freely available symbolic math module (Calc, current version 2.02f, included on the CD-ROM) which can do very powerful symbolic algebra manipulations, allowing for highly automated symbolic (as opposed to purely numeric) solutions to equations such as the ones above. A symbolic algebra package can be a 3D programmer's best friend, as it eliminates the tedious, error-prone, and above all time-consuming manual solution of the myriad of equations which form the very basis of 3D graphics. The companion book *Advanced Linux 3D Graphics Programming* provides a detailed example of using Calc to derive the equations needed for texture mapping.

The X11 SHM Extension: l3d_screen_x11_shm

Although this topic does not strictly belong under the heading "Software Rasterization," it is nevertheless very important to software rasterization. The X11 MIT shared-memory extension (MIT-SHM) is a mechanism for copying an XImage faster to the display. Image copying speed is an important issue with software rasterization, and is often a bottleneck. Since X is a client-server system, normally every request to copy an XImage to the screen must go through the X server and some local communications protocol, causing the XImage data to be copied around in memory needlessly. If the X server and client are on the same machine, the shared memory extension allows the XImage to store its off-screen buffer in an area of memory accessible both to your application and to the X server. This means that the exact bytes you write in memory will be read at the same location by the X server, which eliminates the client-server overhead of copying the XImage. (Although at some level the image is still "copied" from main memory to video memory, using shared memory eliminates as much overhead as possible at the X level.)

Thanks to l3d's modular structure, adding support for shared memory XImages is no more difficult than creating a new screen subclass, creating a new factory returning objects of this new screen type, and updating the factory manager to allow choosing the new factory. The application program remains unchanged.

The following two listings illustrate the additions necessary, in a new class `l3d_screen_x11_shm`, subclassed from `l3d_screen_x11`.

Listing 3-10: sc_x11sh.h

```
#ifndef __SC_X11SH_H
#define __SC_X11SH_H
#include "../tool_os/memman.h"

#include "sc_x11.h"
#include <X11/extensions/XShm.h>
#include <sys/shm.h>
#include <sys/ipc.h>

class l3d_screen_x11_shm : public l3d_screen_x11 {
  protected:
    XShmSegmentInfo shminfo;

  public:
    l3d_screen_x11_shm(int xsize, int ysize)
    : l3d_screen_x11(xsize,ysize) {}
    virtual ~l3d_screen_x11_shm(void);
    XImage *create_ximage(void);
    void create_buffer(void);
    void blit_screen(void);
};

class l3d_screen_factory_x11_shm : public l3d_screen_factory {
  public:
    l3d_screen *create(int xsize, int ysize) {
      l3d_screen_x11_shm *s;
      s = new l3d_screen_x11_shm(xsize,ysize);

      /* create offscreen buffer and ximage */

      s->ximg = s->create_ximage();
      s->create_buffer();

      return s;
    }
};

#endif
```

Listing 3-11: sc_x11sh.cc

```
#include "sc_x11.h"
#include <stdlib.h>
#include "../tool_os/memman.h"

l3d_screen_x11::l3d_screen_x11(int xsize, int ysize) :
    l3d_screen(xsize,ysize)
{

  XPixmapFormatValues *pixmap_formats;
  int i, count;

  dpy = XopenDisplay(NULL);

  pixmap_formats = XListPixmapFormats(dpy, &count);
  for(i=0, depth=0; i<count; i++) {
```

```
   if(pixmap_formats[i].depth > depth) {
     depth        = pixmap_formats[i].depth;
     bytespp      = pixmap_formats[i].bits_per_pixel / BITS_PER_BYTE;
     scanline_pad = pixmap_formats[i].scanline_pad;
   }
}
Xfree(pixmap_formats);
printf("max depth of display %d", depth);
printf("bytes per pixel: %d", bytespp);

bufsize = xsize * ysize * bytespp;

vis = DefaultVisual(dpy,0);
w = XcreateWindow(dpy,
                    DefaultRootWindow(dpy),
                    100, 100,
                    xsize, ysize,
                    0,
                    depth,
                    CopyFromParent,
                    vis,
                    0, NULL);
XStoreName(dpy, w, "l3d application");
XMapWindow(dpy, w);

switch(vis->c_class) {

    XVisualInfo vi;
    int result;

  case PseudoColor:
    result=
      XMatchVisualInfo(dpy, DefaultScreen(dpy), depth, PseudoColor, &vi);
    if(result) {
      printf("visual is PseudoColor (indexed),");
      printf("colormapsize %d,", vi.colormap_size);
      printf("bits per rgb %d",vis->bits_per_rgb);

      col_cells = new unsigned long[vi.colormap_size];
      sinfo = new l3d_screen_info_indexed(vi.colormap_size,
                                          (1<vis->bits_per_rgb)-1,
                                          (1<vis->bits_per_rgb)-1,
                                          (1<vis->bits_per_rgb)-1);
      printf("is indexed");
    }else {
      printf("no information for PseudoColor visual");
    }

    break;

  case TrueColor:
    result=
      XMatchVisualInfo(dpy, DefaultScreen(dpy), depth, TrueColor, &vi);
    if(result) {
      printf("visual is TrueColor, %d bytes per pix, %d bytes per rgb",
             bytespp,
             vi.depth / BITS_PER_BYTE);
      col_cells = NULL;
      sinfo = new l3d_screen_info_rgb(vis->red_mask,
                                      vis->green_mask,
```

```
                                    vis->blue_mask,
                                    bytespp,
                                    vi.depth / BITS_PER_BYTE);
    }else {
      printf("Couldn't get visual information, XmatchVisualInfo");
      exit(-1);
    }
    break;

  case StaticColor: printf("unsupported visual StaticColor");break;
  case GrayScale:   printf("unsupported visual GrayScale");break;
  case StaticGray:  printf("unsupported visual StaticGray");break;
  case DirectColor: printf("unsupported visual DirectColor");break;
  }

  XSelectInput(dpy, w, KeyPressMask);
  gc = DefaultGC(dpy, DefaultScreen(dpy));

}

l3d_screen_x11::~l3d_screen_x11(void) {
  delete sinfo;
  XdestroyImage(ximg);
  if(col_cells) delete [] col_cells;
  XcloseDisplay(dpy);
}

inline void l3d_screen_x11::blit_screen(void) {
  XPutImage(dpy, w, gc, ximg,
            0,0,0,0,  /* source x,y; destination x,y */
            xsize, ysize);
}

void l3d_screen_x11::open_screen(void) {
}

void l3d_screen_x11::close_screen(void) {

}

void l3d_screen_x11::refresh_palette(void) {

  l3d_screen_info_indexed *si;
  if ((si = dynamic_cast<l3d_screen_info_indexed *>(sinfo))) {

    int idx;

    cmap = XCreateColormap(dpy, w, vis, AllocNone);

    XAllocColorCells(dpy, cmap, TRUE, NULL, 0, col_cells,
                     (int)pow(2.0, (double)depth));

    for(idx=0; idx<si->palette_size; idx++) {
      XColor xcolor;

      xcolor.pixel = idx;
      xcolor.red = (int) (( (float)si->palette[idx].red /
                            si->palette_max_red ) * 65535);
      xcolor.green = (int) (( (float)si->palette[idx].green /
                              si->palette_max_green ) * 65535);
```

```
        xcolor.blue = (int)( ( (float)si->palette[idx].blue /
                            si->palette_max_blue ) * 65535);
        xcolor.flags = DoRed | DoGreen | DoBlue;
        XAllocColor(dpy, cmap, &xcolor);
        XStoreColor(dpy, cmap, &xcolor);
      }
      XSetWindowColormap(dpy, w, cmap);
    }

  }

  XImage *l3d_screen_x11::create_ximage(void) {
    return XCreateImage(dpy, vis, depth,
                        Zpixmap,
                        0,
                        (char *)buffer,
                        xsize, ysize,
                        scanline_pad,
                        0);

  }

  void l3d_screen_x11::create_buffer(void) {
    buffer = new unsigned char [xsize*ysize*bytespp];
    sinfo->p_screenbuf = buffer;
  }
```

The variable shminfo is a storage area for the XImage to obtain the location of the shared memory segment used to store the image data.

The overridden create_ximage method creates a shared-memory XImage instead of a normal one. It first calls XShmCreateImage with the address of the shminfo variable as a new parameter. Next, we call shmget to allocate a shared memory segment, and shmat to attach this shared memory to the current process. Finally we call XShmAttach to attach the shared memory segment to the XImage.

The overridden blit_screen method calls XShmPutImage (instead of XPutImage) to copy the image to the server's screen, using shared memory.

The overridden create_buffer method sets the internal screen buffer pointer, in the screen and in the screen information object, to be the shared memory segment allocated earlier.

The overridden virtual destructor calls XShmDetach to detach the shared memory segment from the X server, destroys the XImage, and finally releases the shared memory segment back to the system with shmdt.

The X11 DGA Extension

The Direct Graphics Access or XFree86-DGA extension to X allows a client application to have direct access to the video frame buffer. This is theoretically the fastest access that a client program can have to the video memory. However, we have seen that XImages assume a linear storage of image data, which is (relatively) easy to understand. With XFree86-DGA, the arrangement of the video buffer memory depends on the video card itself. In many cases this may be a non-linear arrangement. Non-linear arrangements of video memory can sometimes defy human comprehension and efficient processing, since the byte-to-pixel mapping might be based on a planar or other arbitrary arrangement of memory. The intuitive formula *offset* = (*x* + (*width* * *y*)) * *bytes_per_pixel* would then be invalid for direct access of non-linear video memory.

For this reason, we do not cover DGA further; in my opinion, it is not worth the extra trouble it incurs. SHM is fast and flexible enough for software rendering; real 3D hardware acceleration can go through Mesa (covered in the last section in this chapter).

Sample Programs

We have now covered the most important 2D graphics topics and their implementation as reusable C++ classes in l3d. The following sample programs serve to reinforce the concepts presented earlier and illustrate use of the polygon structures and the clipping and rasterization routines.

Sample Program XForm

Listing 3-12 draws and clips a number of polygon objects and lines at random locations on the screen. Its main purpose is to demonstrate the storage, rasterization, and clipping of polygons.

Listing 3-12: main.cc for sample program xform

```cpp
#include "../lib/geom/polygon/p_flat.h"
#include "../lib/tool_2d/screen.h"
#include "../lib/tool_os/dispatch.h"
#include "../lib/raster/rasteriz.h"
#include "../lib/tool_2d/si_idx.h"
#include "../lib/tool_2d/si_rgb.h"
#include "../lib/system/factorys.h"

#include <stdlib.h>
#include <string.h>
#include <stdio.h>
#include <math.h>
#include <stdarg.h>

class my_pipeline : public l3d_pipeline {
  public:
    l3d_screen *screen;
    l3d_rasterizer_2d *rasterizer;
    l3d_rasterizer_2d_imp *ras_imp;

    l3d_two_part_list<l3d_coordinate> *vlist;

    int c;

    my_pipeline(void);
    virtual ~my_pipeline(void);
    void key_event(int ch);
    void update_event(void);
    void draw_event(void);

    void init(void);
    virtual void pixel(char **p,int a,int b,int c, int d){};
};

my_pipeline::my_pipeline(void) {
  screen = factory_manager_v_0_1.screen_factory->create(640,480);
  ras_imp = factory_manager_v_0_1.
```

```
                ras_2d_imp_factory->create(640,480,screen->sinfo);
    rasterizer = new l3d_rasterizer_2d(ras_imp);

    vlist = new l3d_two_part_list<l3d_coordinate> ( 3 );

}

my_pipeline::~my_pipeline(void) {
  delete screen;
  delete ras_imp;
  delete rasterizer;
  delete vlist;
}

void my_pipeline::key_event(int c) {
  switch(c) {
    case 'q': exit(0);
  }
}

void my_pipeline::update_event() {
  int i;
  int x,y;

  for(i=0; i<7 ; i++) {

    int px=rand()%1200-640, py=rand()%800-400;

    (*vlist)[0].transformed.X_ = int_to_l3d_real(100+px);
    (*vlist)[0].transformed.Y_ = int_to_l3d_real(100+py);
    (*vlist)[1].transformed.X_ = int_to_l3d_real(300+px);
    (*vlist)[1].transformed.Y_ = int_to_l3d_real(150+py);
    (*vlist)[2].transformed.X_ = int_to_l3d_real(70+px);
    (*vlist)[2].transformed.Y_ = int_to_l3d_real(120+py);

    l3d_polygon_2d_flatshaded p(3);

    p.vlist = &vlist;
    (*(p.ivertices))[p.ivertices->next_index()].ivertex = 0;
    (*(p.ivertices))[p.ivertices->next_index()].ivertex = 1;
    (*(p.ivertices))[p.ivertices->next_index()].ivertex = 2;

    int r,g,b;

    unsigned long col;
    l3d_screen_info_indexed *si_idx;
    l3d_screen_info_rgb *si_rgb;
    if (si_idx = dynamic_cast<l3d_screen_info_indexed *>( screen->sinfo )) {
      col = rand() % si_idx->get_palette_size();
    }else if (si_rgb = dynamic_cast<l3d_screen_info_rgb *>(screen->sinfo)) {

      r = rand() % ((si_rgb->red_mask) > (si_rgb->red_shift));
      g = rand() % ((si_rgb->green_mask) > (si_rgb->green_shift));
      b = rand() % ((si_rgb->blue_mask) > (si_rgb->blue_shift));

      col =  r<si_rgb->red_shift |
             g<si_rgb->green_shift |
             b<si_rgb->blue_shift;
    }
```

```
        p.final_color = col;

        vlist->num_varying_items = 0;
        p.init_clip_ivertices();

        if (p.clip_to_polygon_2d(screen->view_win)) {
          rasterizer->draw_polygon_flatshaded(&p);
        }

        x = rand() % 540;
        y = rand() % 380;
        rasterizer->draw_line(0,0,x,y,col);

    }
}

void my_pipeline::draw_event(void) {
  screen->blit_screen();
}

main() {
  l3d_dispatcher *d;
  my_pipeline *p;

  factory_manager_v_0_1.choose_factories();
  d = factory_manager_v_0_1.dispatcher_factory->create();

  p  = new my_pipeline();
  d->pipeline = p;
  d->event_source = p->screen;

  d->start();

  delete p;
  delete d;
}
```

The program follows the usual five-step structure typical of l3d programs. The main action occurs
in `update_event`. First, we define a vertex list with vertices at random locations:

```
int px=rand()%1200-640, py=rand()%800-400;

(*vlist)[0].transformed.X_ = int_to_l3d_real(100+px);
(*vlist)[0].transformed.Y_ = int_to_l3d_real(100+py);
(*vlist)[1].transformed.X_ = int_to_l3d_real(300+px);
(*vlist)[1].transformed.Y_ = int_to_l3d_real(150+py);
(*vlist)[2].transformed.X_ = int_to_l3d_real(70+px);
(*vlist)[2].transformed.Y_ = int_to_l3d_real(120+py);
```

Notice that we work directly with the transformed coordinate, since this is the one which is used
during rasterization. Normally we would put our coordinates in the original coordinate and perform some calculations to transform the original into the transformed coordinate, but this program
is so simple that we work directly with the transformed coordinates.

Next we define a polygon based upon this vertex list. Remember, we could define many more
vertices in the vertex list and share the list among several polygons. In this example the vertex list
is only used by one polygon.

```
l3d_polygon_2d_flatshaded p(3);
```

```
p.vlist = &list;
(*(p.ivertices))[p.ivertices->next_index()].ivertex = 0;
(*(p.ivertices))[p.ivertices->next_index()].ivertex = 1;
(*(p.ivertices))[p.ivertices->next_index()].ivertex = 2;
```

After defining the polygon we assign it a random color, with different code being executed based on whether the screen is based on an indexed or a RGB color model.

```
int r,g,b;

unsigned long col;
l3d_screen_info_indexed *si_idx;
l3d_screen_info_rgb *si_rgb;
if (si_idx = dynamic_cast<l3d_screen_info_indexed *>( screen->sinfo )) {
  col = rand() % si_idx->get_palette_size();
}else if (si_rgb = dynamic_cast<l3d_screen_info_rgb *>(screen->sinfo)) {

  r = rand() % ((si_rgb->red_mask) > (si_rgb->red_shift));
  g = rand() % ((si_rgb->green_mask) > (si_rgb->green_shift));
  b = rand() % ((si_rgb->blue_mask) > (si_rgb->blue_shift));

  col =  r<si_rgb->red_shift |
         g<si_rgb->green_shift |
         b<si_rgb->blue_shift;

}
p.final_color = col;
```

The final thing we do with the polygon is clip it. First, we set num_varying_items of the vertex list to be 0, to effectively erase all clip vertices. (The clip vertices are not really erased; the space allocated for them is simply marked as free.) Next, we call init_clip_ivertices to initialize the polygon for the clip operation (copying the ivertices list into the clip_ivertices list). Then we call the actual clipping routine, passing the screen's clip window as the clip polygon. This clips the polygon to the screen, possibly adding new vertices into the vertex list and adding new indices to these vertices in the polygon's clip_ivertices list. If the clip function returns a non-zero value, the polygon is still partially visible after the clip operation and should be drawn, a task which we execute through the rasterizer.

```
vlist->num_varying_items = 0;
p.init_clip_ivertices();

if (p.clip_to_polygon_2d(screen->view_win)) {
  rasterizer->draw_polygon_flatshaded(&p);
}
```

Finally, we also draw a line from (0,0) to a random location.

```
x = rand() % 540;
y = rand() % 380;
rasterizer->draw_line(0,0,x,y,col);
```

Press **q** to exit this sample program.

Figure 3-13: The output from program *xform,* which draws random lines and clipped polygons using the classes and algorithms discussed earlier.

Sample Program Morph2d

The next program illustrates the technique of vertex animation for dynamically changing or morphing a polygon. We have four different polygon shapes, all with the same number of vertices. By changing the external vertex list, we can change the polygon's shape to be any one of our four defined shapes, without needing to alter the polygon itself.

In this program, we define a new class, l3d_vertex_interpolator, which is used to interpolate the positions between two different vertex lists. The idea is that instead of defining every single vertex list for each shape we want to animate, we only define a small number of important frames of animation (also called *key frames*). We then interpolate (step along) the vertices between these key frames. This allows us to easily and smoothly convert one vertex list into another by moving each point in the first vertex list closer and closer to the point in the second vertex list. For each frame of animation, we "step" the position of the source point a certain distance towards the destination point. The amount by which we move each point is determined by the total number of steps and the distance between the points. Note that not all points in the vertex list move at the same speed. For instance, if the original x coordinate of a point is 0, and the final x coordinate is 100, and we want to interpolate in 10 steps, each step moves the point 10 pixels closer to the final x coordinate. However, we might also have a second point in the vertex list, whose original x coordinate is 0 and whose final x coordinate is 500. We still must interpolate in 10 steps, since all points in the vertex list should reach their final positions at the same time, but for this new point each step must move the point by 50 pixels in order to reach its target coordinate of 500 within 10 steps. In general, each vertex in a vertex list during an interpolation process will move with its own individual speed toward its own destination.

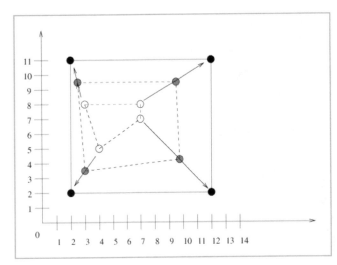

Figure 3-14: The idea behind vertex interpolation. Each vertex in the original polygon (shown hollow) moves towards a vertex in the new polygon (shown in black). All vertices should end up at their respective destinations at the same time. Since each vertex has a different distance to travel, and since the amount of time to travel is fixed, each vertex travels with a different speed towards its destination. The gray dots indicate the vertices interpolated halfway between the starting and ending positions.

Listing 3-13: `verint.h`

```
#include "system/sys_dep.h"
#include "datastr/list.h"
#include "geom/vertex/coord.h"
#include "../../tool_os/memman.h"

class l3d_vertex_interpolator {
  public:
    int steps;
    int pos;
    int dimension;

    l3d_two_part_list<l3d_coordinate> *list;

    l3d_list<l3d_vector> *deltas;

    l3d_vertex_interpolator(void) {
      list = new l3d_two_part_list<l3d_coordinate> ( 1 );
      deltas = new l3d_list<l3d_vector> ( 1 );
    }

    ~l3d_vertex_interpolator(void) {
      delete list;
      delete deltas;
    }

    void start(const l3d_two_part_list<l3d_coordinate> & source,
               const l3d_two_part_list<l3d_coordinate> & dest,
               int steps, int dimension)
    {
      this->steps = steps;
      this->dimension = dimension;

      *list = source;

      deltas->num_items = 0;

      int i,j;
```

```
      for(i=0; i<list->num_fixed_items; i++) {
        for(j=0; j<dimension; j++) {
          deltas->next_index();
          (*deltas)[i].a[j] =
            l3d_divri(dest[i].original.a[j] - source[i].original.a[j],
                      steps);
        }
      }

      pos = 0;
    }

    bool step(void) {
      int i,j;
      for(i=0; i<list->num_fixed_items; i++) {
        for(j=0; j<dimension; j++) {
          (*list)[i].original.a[j] += (*deltas)[i].a[j];
        }
      }

      pos++;
      return pos < steps;
    }

};
```

Listing 3-14: morph2d.cc

```
#include <stdio.h>
#include <stdlib.h>

#include "tool_2d/screen.h"
#include "geom/polygon/polygon.h"
#include "raster/rasteriz.h"
#include "datastr/list.h"
#include "geom/vertex/verint.h"

#include "../lib/tool_2d/screen.h"
#include "../lib/tool_os/dispatch.h"
#include "../lib/raster/rasteriz.h"
#include "../lib/tool_2d/scrinfo.h"
#include "../lib/system/factorys.h"

class my_pipeline : public l3d_pipeline {
  protected:
    static const int num_frames = 4;
    l3d_rasterizer_2d_imp *ri;
    l3d_rasterizer_2d *r;
    l3d_vertex_interpolator interp;
    l3d_two_part_list<l3d_coordinate> *vlist, *vlist_frames[num_frames];
    l3d_polygon_2d_flatshaded *facet;

    int frame_no;
    bool currently_interpolating;

  public:
    l3d_screen *s;
    my_pipeline(void);
    virtual ~my_pipeline(void);
    void update_event(void);
    void key_event(int ch);
```

```
        void draw_event(void);
};

my_pipeline::my_pipeline(void) {
  s = factory_manager_v_0_1.screen_factory->create(320,200);
  ri = factory_manager_v_0_1.ras_2d_imp_factory->create(320,200,s->sinfo);
  r = new l3d_rasterizer_2d(ri);

  s->sinfo->ext_max_red = 255;
  s->sinfo->ext_max_green = 255;
  s->sinfo->ext_max_blue = 255;
  s->sinfo->ext_to_native(0,0,0); //- allocate black background color
  unsigned long color = s->sinfo->ext_to_native(0, 128, 255);
  s->refresh_palette();

  s->open_screen();

  vlist_frames[0] = new l3d_two_part_list<l3d_coordinate> ( 4 );
  (*vlist_frames[0])[0].original.X_ = float_to_l3d_real(100.0);
  (*vlist_frames[0])[0].original.Y_ = float_to_l3d_real(100.0);

  (*vlist_frames[0])[1].original.X_ = float_to_l3d_real(200.0);
  (*vlist_frames[0])[1].original.Y_ = float_to_l3d_real(150.0);

  (*vlist_frames[0])[2].original.X_ = float_to_l3d_real(150.0);
  (*vlist_frames[0])[2].original.Y_ = float_to_l3d_real(200.0);

  (*vlist_frames[0])[3].original.X_ = float_to_l3d_real( 50.0);
  (*vlist_frames[0])[3].original.Y_ = float_to_l3d_real(120.0);

  vlist_frames[1] = new l3d_two_part_list<l3d_coordinate> ( 4 );
  (*vlist_frames[1])[0].original.X_ = float_to_l3d_real(100.0);
  (*vlist_frames[1])[0].original.Y_ = float_to_l3d_real(100.0);

  (*vlist_frames[1])[1].original.X_ = float_to_l3d_real(200.0);
  (*vlist_frames[1])[1].original.Y_ = float_to_l3d_real(100.0);

  (*vlist_frames[1])[2].original.X_ = float_to_l3d_real(150.0);
  (*vlist_frames[1])[2].original.Y_ = float_to_l3d_real(200.0);

  (*vlist_frames[1])[3].original.X_ = float_to_l3d_real(140.0);
  (*vlist_frames[1])[3].original.Y_ = float_to_l3d_real(200.0);

  vlist_frames[2] = new l3d_two_part_list<l3d_coordinate> ( 4 );
  (*vlist_frames[2])[0].original.X_ = float_to_l3d_real(-100.0);
  (*vlist_frames[2])[0].original.Y_ = float_to_l3d_real(100.0);

  (*vlist_frames[2])[1].original.X_ = float_to_l3d_real(200.0);
  (*vlist_frames[2])[1].original.Y_ = float_to_l3d_real(100.0);

  (*vlist_frames[2])[2].original.X_ = float_to_l3d_real(950.0);
  (*vlist_frames[2])[2].original.Y_ = float_to_l3d_real(200.0);

  (*vlist_frames[2])[3].original.X_ = float_to_l3d_real(940.0);
  (*vlist_frames[2])[3].original.Y_ = float_to_l3d_real(200.0);

  vlist_frames[3] = new l3d_two_part_list<l3d_coordinate> ( 4 );
  (*vlist_frames[3])[0].original.X_ = float_to_l3d_real(100.0);
  (*vlist_frames[3])[0].original.Y_ = float_to_l3d_real(150.0);
```

```
    (*vlist_frames[3])[1].original.X_ = float_to_l3d_real(100.0);
    (*vlist_frames[3])[1].original.Y_ = float_to_l3d_real(100.0);

    (*vlist_frames[3])[2].original.X_ = float_to_l3d_real(250.0);
    (*vlist_frames[3])[2].original.Y_ = float_to_l3d_real(200.0);

    (*vlist_frames[3])[3].original.X_ = float_to_l3d_real(100.0);
    (*vlist_frames[3])[3].original.Y_ = float_to_l3d_real(200.0);

    frame_no = 0;
    currently_interpolating = false;
    vlist = vlist_frames[frame_no];

    facet = new l3d_polygon_2d_flatshaded ( 4 );
    facet->vlist = & vlist;
    facet->final_color = color;
    (*(facet->ivertices))[facet->ivertices->next_index()].ivertex = 0;
    (*(facet->ivertices))[facet->ivertices->next_index()].ivertex = 1;
    (*(facet->ivertices))[facet->ivertices->next_index()].ivertex = 2;
    (*(facet->ivertices))[facet->ivertices->next_index()].ivertex = 3;

}

my_pipeline::~my_pipeline(void) {
  delete vlist_frames[0];
  delete vlist_frames[1];
  delete vlist_frames[2];
  delete vlist_frames[3];
  delete s;
  delete ri;
  delete r;
  delete facet;
}

void my_pipeline::update_event(void) {
  if(currently_interpolating) {
    vlist = interp.list;
    if(! interp.step()) {
      currently_interpolating = false;
    }
  }else {
    frame_no++;
    if(frame_no >= num_frames) {frame_no = 0; }
    int next_frame = frame_no + 1;
    if(next_frame >= num_frames) {next_frame = 0; }

    vlist = vlist_frames[frame_no];
    interp.start( *vlist_frames[frame_no], *vlist_frames[next_frame],
                  50, 2);

    currently_interpolating = true;
  }
}

void my_pipeline::draw_event(void) {
  vlist->num_varying_items = 0;
  for(int i=0; i<vlist->num_fixed_items; i++) {(*vlist)[i].reset(); }
  facet->init_clip_ivertices();

  facet->clip_to_polygon_2d(s->view_win);
```

```
          r->clear_buffer();
          r->draw_polygon_flatshaded(facet);
          s->blit_screen();
        }

        void my_pipeline::key_event(int ch) {
          switch(ch) {
            case 'q': done = 1;
          }
        }

        main() {
          factory_manager_v_0_1.choose_factories();

          l3d_dispatcher *d;
          my_pipeline *p;

          d = factory_manager_v_0_1.dispatcher_factory->create();

          p = new my_pipeline();
          d->pipeline = p;
          d->event_source = p->s;

          d->start();

          delete d;
          delete p;

        }
```

The constructor creates four different vertex lists in an array. The program then interpolates the vertex positions of the polygon from vertex list 0 to vertex list 1, then from list 1 to 2, then from 2 to 3, then finally back from 3 to 0 again.

The two functions in this program which control the morphing are update_event and draw_event. In update_event, we either start the interpolator by calling start, or we step the interpolator by calling step. Calling start initializes an internal vertex list and computes the speed necessary for each point in the source list to reach the final point in the destination list, in a given number of steps. Calling step moves each point by its previously calculated speed, inexorably towards its final destination. When step returns 0, the interpolation has finished. While interpolation is taking place, we set the polygon's vertex list to be the vertex list which is being calculated within the interpolator.

Function draw_event clips the shape-shifting polygon to the screen. First, it effectively deletes any clip-generated vertices by setting num_varying_items in the vertex list to 0. Then, it calls reset on each vertex in the vertex list; this sets the transformed member of each coordinate to equal the original member and resets the transform_stage variable to 0. The last initialization step is to call init_clip_ivertices to copy the original vertex-index list into the clipped vertex-index list. Then we clip and draw the polygon, using the clipped, transformed polygon vertices during the final rasterization.

The vertex animation technique illustrated by this program can be used, with much greater visual impact, in 3D. The companion book *Advanced Linux 3D Graphics Programming* discusses this.

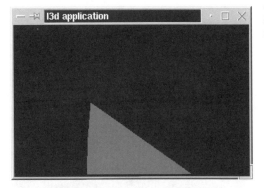

Figure 3-15: One frame from program `morph2d`, illustrating a changing shape.

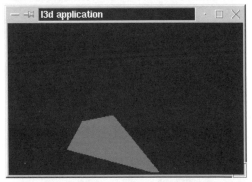

Figure 3-16: The shape from the previous figure changes slowly into another.

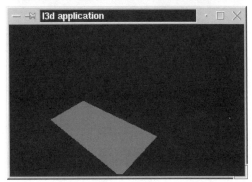

Figure 3-17: Another stage in polygonal metamorphosis.

Hardware-Accelerated Rasterization

The sample programs so far have all used a software rasterization implementation to draw points, lines, and polygons into the frame buffer. As discussed in Chapter 1, support for 3D hardware acceleration under Linux is becoming widespread, and the interface we can use to take advantage of hardware acceleration is Mesa. Let's take a closer look at Mesa, OpenGL, and the OpenGL Utility Toolkit GLUT, then see how we can incorporate Mesa subclasses, and thereby hardware acceleration, into our l3d classes.

Mesa and OpenGL

OpenGL is a standard software interface to graphics hardware. It is a procedural rather than descriptive system, meaning that the programmer tells OpenGL what to draw and how to draw it, rather than describing what the final result must look like. OpenGL is a state machine; various commands are issued to set a certain mode of operation, then commands are issued which react based upon the current state settings.

Mesa is a freely available library, written by Brian Paul, implementing the OpenGL syntax. Since official OpenGL certification costs time and money, and since Mesa is freely available, it is quite understandable that Mesa is not and probably will not be an officially certified "OpenGL implementation." Nevertheless, in practice, programs written for OpenGL will work with Mesa, and under Linux, they will work with hardware acceleration.

We will use the terms "Mesa" and "OpenGL" somewhat interchangeably. Whenever we are talking about concepts that are generally applicable to any OpenGL implementation, we will usually say "OpenGL." If we are specifically talking about concepts particular to the Linux Mesa library (such as hardware acceleration), we will say "Mesa."

The OpenGL Utility Toolkit (GLUT)

The OpenGL Utility Toolkit or GLUT, written by Mark Kilgard, is a window system-independent toolkit designed to make writing complete OpenGL programs easier, with windowed output and user input. "Pure" OpenGL commands are independent of any windowing or operating system (very much like the `l3d_rasterizer_2d_sw_imp` class) and therefore provide no direct means of creating windowed output or reading user input. GLUT forms an additional layer on top of OpenGL to enable easier creation of complete OpenGL programs.

We will treat OpenGL and GLUT (or more specifically, Mesa and GLUT) as one logical system, not distinguishing whether a function comes from OpenGL or from GLUT. For our purposes, Mesa and GLUT are like one library, which allows us to access accelerated 3D hardware in a standardized way.

A Sample Program with Mesa and GLUT

The following program, `mesaflat`, demonstrates basic use of Mesa and GLUT to draw a series of random triangles to the screen.

 NOTE To compile this program, you must have the Mesa library installed, as described in the Appendix. After compilation, the executable file for this program is placed in the same directory as the source file (since this program does not use l3d and therefore does not follow the l3d directory structure of separate source and binary directory trees).

Listing 3-15: `mesaflat.cc`

```
#include <stdio.h>
#include <stdlib.h>
#include <GL/glut.h>

void display(void) {
```

```
    int i;
    int x,y;

    for(i=0; i<7 ; i++) {
      x = rand() % 540;
      y = rand() % 380;

      glBegin(GL_POLYGON);
      glColor3i(rand(), rand(), rand());
      glVertex2i(x,y);
      glVertex2i(x+100,y+10);
      glVertex2i(x+70,y+100);
      glEnd();
    }
    glutSwapBuffers();

    glFlush();
}

void init(void) {
  glClearColor(0.0,0.0,0.0,0.0);
  glMatrixMode(GL_PROJECTION);
  glLoadIdentity();
  gluOrtho2D(0, 640, 480, 0);
  glMatrixMode(GL_MODELVIEW);
  glLoadIdentity();
  glTranslatef(0.375, 0.375, 0.0);
  glViewport(0,0,640,480);
}

void update(void) {
  glutPostRedisplay();
}

void key(unsigned char c, int x, int y) {
  switch(c) {
    case 'q': exit(0);
  }
}

main(int argc, char *argv[]) {
  glutInit(&argc, argv);
  glutInitDisplayMode(GLUT_DOUBLE|GLUT_RGB);
  glutInitWindowSize(640,480);
  glutInitWindowPosition(100,100);
  glutCreateWindow("hello");
  init();
  glutDisplayFunc(display);
  glutIdleFunc(update);
  glutKeyboardFunc(key);
  glutMainLoop();
  return 0;
}
```

The first thing we do is to include the GLUT header file, GL/glut.h. This also automatically includes other standard OpenGL header files such as GL/gl.h and GL/glu.h.

The program's execution begins in main. We call glutInit to initialize GLUT. This should be called before any other GLUT routine. Next, we call glutInitDisplayMode and specify the options GLUT_DOUBLE and GLUT_RGB. This means that we want an RGB color model (as opposed to an indexed color model, GLUT_INDEX), and a double-buffered window so that we can perform smooth animation. We then call `glutInitWindowSize` and `glutInitWindowPosition` to set the parameters for window size and position, and call `glutCreateWindow` to create the window. The function `init` (covered in the next paragraph) initializes the OpenGL drawing parameters by calling OpenGL (not GLUT) functions directly. The next step in `main` is to register callback functions with GLUT. GLUT is an event-driven system, and we call specific GLUT functions to plug in our own event-handling functions which GLUT will automatically call when certain events occur. In this program, we call `glutDisplayFunc` to register a callback function whenever the application should display itself; `glutIdleFunc` to register a callback function which updates the application; and `glutKeyboardFunc` to register a callback function for responding to keyboard input. Finally, we call `glutMainLoop`, which enters the GLUT main event-handling loop. This loop never exits; GLUT takes control of the application and calls any callback functions which you have previously registered. This is the typical event-driven approach: your program is not "in control," but instead "is controlled by" (or influenced by) outside events.

The `init` function directly calls pure OpenGL functions to set drawing parameters. Remember, OpenGL is a state machine. Therefore, we typically call functions to "set the state" of the machine, then call action functions to perform graphics drawing based on the current machine state (which can determine color, line width, fill pattern, and so forth). In the case of `init`, we first call `glClearColor` to set the background color which will be used to clear the buffer. Clearing the buffer is done through a call to `glClear`, similar to the way that the `clear_buffer` routine in `l3d_rasterizer_2d_sw_imp` class called `memset` to set the bytes in the XImage data to zero. The remaining lines in the function `init` call the appropriate OpenGL functions to allow us to use OpenGL as a 2D rasterization layer, by effectively disabling the so-called "projection transformation" and "model-view transformation." These transformations are first selected by calling `glMatrixMode`, and are disabled by calling `glLoadIdentity`, which loads a so-called "identity matrix" for the projection and model-view transformations. Chapter 6 discusses matrices and transformations in more detail. The important thing for now is to understand that these lines in the `init` function simply set the OpenGL state such that we can treat OpenGL as a 2D rasterizer (with hardware acceleration).

The `display` function is the most important function in a GLUT program. It should contain all GLUT or OpenGL commands necessary to draw the image you wish to display. In this sample program, `display` draws a series of polygons at random locations. First, we call `glBegin(GL_POLYGON)` to set the OpenGL state to be "polygon-drawing mode." Then we call `glColor3i` to set the current color to some random combination of red, green, and blue. With the state now set to polygon mode and the color set to a random value, we call `glVertex2i` to specify vertices for the geometric primitive currently being specified, in this case a polygon. After specifying three vertices, we call `glEnd` to tell OpenGL that we have finished specifying the polygon.

NOTE OpenGL supports primitives other than polygons: the valid primitive types which can be passed to glBegin are GL_POINTS, GL_LINES, GL_LINE_STRIP, GL_LINE_LOOP, GL_TRIANGLES, GL_TRIANGLE_STRIP, GL_TRIANGLE_FAN, GL_QUADS, GL_QUAD_STRIP, and GL_POLYGON. We will concentrate on GL_POINTS, GL_LINES, and GL_POLYGON. The other primitives are special cases of these three, and can sometimes be faster if the underlying hardware directly supports these other primitives.

The last two lines in the function `display` call the GLUT function `glutSwapBuffers`, which copies the now completely-drawn off-screen buffer into the on-screen buffer, and the function `glFlush`, which tells OpenGL to in any event immediately begin execution of the commands we just specified. In a client-server OpenGL setup, the client might, for instance, wait for more commands to fill up a network buffer before it actually sends the OpenGL commands to the server to begin drawing. Calling `glFlush` makes sure that the process starts right away.

The function `update` calls the GLUT function `glutPostRedisplay`, which tells GLUT to call the display function again at the next opportunity.

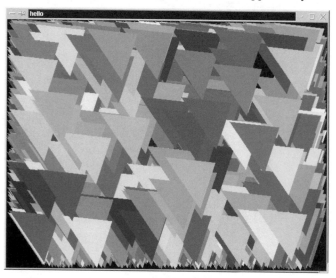

Figure 3-18: Output from sample program `mesaflat`, which draws 2D polygons using OpenGL and GLUT as a 2D rasterization layer.

To summarize, an OpenGL program using GLUT begins by initializing GLUT and OpenGL, then registers event callback functions, the most important of which is the display callback, and finally calls `glutMainLoop` to enter GLUT's main loop.

Mesa and 3DFX Hardware Acceleration

The Mesa library for Linux offers support for hardware acceleration for 3Dfx cards. Specifically, the OpenGL functions are then translated through a Mesa device driver into calls to the Glide library, which is the direct interface to the 3Dfx hardware. In this way, we can use normal OpenGL commands and still take advantage of hardware acceleration.

In order to use 3Dfx hardware acceleration with Mesa, you must have the Glide library for Linux installed on your system, as described in the Appendix. Of course, you also need a 3Dfx video card.

As mentioned in Chapter 1, a lot of active development is currently underway to support more 3D hardware under Linux and X, all of which revolves around using OpenGL/Mesa as the common interface to the different hardware-accelerated cards. Check the WWW sites listed in the Appendix for the latest information.

Let's now take a look at the l3d classes necessary for supporting Mesa, then see how we can run our previous sample programs with Mesa and hardware acceleration.

Classes for Using Mesa

We can easily extend l3d to use Mesa as a rasterization layer. By doing so, existing l3d programs remain unchanged but can now take advantage of new screen and rasterizer implementation classes which interface to Mesa and hardware acceleration. Through new abstract factories which create and return Mesa-specific objects, existing code simply receives a Mesa screen instead of an X11 screen or a Mesa rasterizer implementation instead of a software rasterizer implementation. Since existing code goes through the abstract screen and rasterizer implementation interfaces, no change or even recompilation of the original code is necessary to support Mesa. This is the real meaning of code extensibility—adding new features in the future, without touching old code.

Figure 3-19 shows the new Mesa-specific classes, which the following sections describe in more detail.

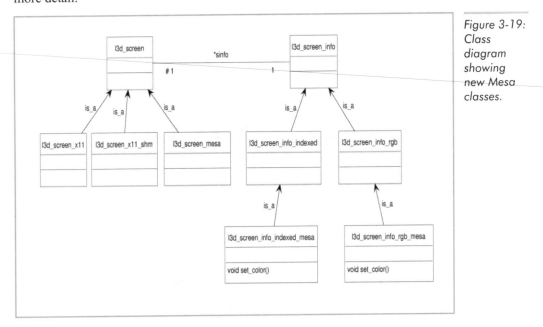

Figure 3-19: Class diagram showing new Mesa classes.

l3d_screen_mesa

Class l3d_screen_mesa, subclassed from l3d_screen, represents a display device using the Mesa library under the X Window System on a Linux machine.

Listing 3-16: `sc_mesa.h`

```
#ifndef __SC_MESA_H
#define __SC_MESA_H
#include "../tool_os/memman.h"

#include "screen.h"
#include "si_imes.h"
#include "si_rmes.h"
#include <GL/glut.h>
#include <X11/Intrinsic.h>
#include <X11/Xlib.h>

class l3d_screen_mesa : public l3d_screen {
  public:
    l3d_screen_mesa(int xsize, int ysize);
    void open_screen(void);
    void blit_screen(void);
};

class l3d_screen_factory_mesa : public l3d_screen_factory {
  public:
    l3d_screen *create(int xsize, int ysize) {
      return new l3d_screen_mesa(xsize,ysize);
    }
};

#endif
```

Listing 3-17: `sc_mesa.cc`

```
#include "sc_mesa.h"
#include <stdlib.h>
#include "../tool_os/memman.h"

l3d_screen_mesa::l3d_screen_mesa(int xsize, int ysize) :
    l3d_screen(xsize,ysize)
{
  int argc=1;
  char *argv[1];
  argv[0] = "a";

  Visual *vis;
  int depth=0, bytespp=0, scanline_pad=0;
  Display *dpy;
  XPixmapFormatValues *pixmap_formats;
  int i, count;

  //- establish connection to X server

  dpy = XopenDisplay(NULL);

  //- find out the supported depths of this server and take the max depth

  pixmap_formats = XListPixmapFormats(dpy, &count);
  for(i=0, depth=0; i<count; i++) {
    if(pixmap_formats[i].depth > depth) {
      depth        = pixmap_formats[i].depth;
      bytespp      = pixmap_formats[i].bits_per_pixel / BITS_PER_BYTE;
      scanline_pad = pixmap_formats[i].scanline_pad;
    }
  }
```

```
            Xfree(pixmap_formats);
            printf("max depth of display %d", depth);
            printf("bytes per pixel: %d", bytespp);

            bufsize = xsize * ysize * bytespp;

            vis = DefaultVisual(dpy,0);

            switch(vis->c_class) {

              case PseudoColor:
                sinfo = new l3d_screen_info_indexed_mesa(255, 65535, 65535, 65535);
                glutInit(&argc, argv);
                glutInitDisplayMode(GLUT_DOUBLE|GLUT_INDEX);
                glutInitWindowSize(xsize,ysize);
                glutInitWindowPosition(100,100);
                glutCreateWindow("l3d");

                glClearColor(0.0,0.0,0.0,0.0);
                glMatrixMode(GL_PROJECTION);
                glLoadIdentity();
                gluOrtho2D(0, xsize, ysize, 0);
                glMatrixMode(GL_MODELVIEW);
                glLoadIdentity();
                glTranslatef(0.375, 0.375, 0.0);
                glViewport(0,0,xsize,ysize);

                break;
              case TrueColor:
                sinfo = new l3d_screen_info_rgb_mesa(vis->red_mask, vis->green_mask,
                                                     vis->blue_mask, bytespp);
                glutInit(&argc, argv);
                glutInitDisplayMode(GLUT_DOUBLE|GLUT_RGB);
                glutInitWindowSize(xsize,ysize);
                glutInitWindowPosition(100,100);
                glutCreateWindow("l3d");

                glClearColor(0.0,0.0,0.0,0.0);
                glMatrixMode(GL_PROJECTION);
                glLoadIdentity();
                gluOrtho2D(0, xsize, ysize, 0);
                glMatrixMode(GL_MODELVIEW);
                glLoadIdentity();
                glTranslatef(0.375, 0.375, 0.0);
                glViewport(0,0,xsize,ysize);

                break;
              case StaticColor: printf("unsupported visual StaticColor");break;
              case GrayScale:   printf("unsupported visual GrayScale");break;
              case StaticGray:  printf("unsupported visual StaticGray");break;
              case DirectColor: printf("unsupported visual DirectColor");break;
            }

          }

          inline void l3d_screen_mesa::blit_screen(void) {
            glutSwapBuffers();
            glFlush();
          }
```

```
void l3d_screen_mesa::open_screen(void) {
}
```

The constructor first queries the X server for the color model (indexed or RGB) and color depth. Depending on the color model, we create an `l3d_screen_info_mesa` screen-information object (covered in the next section) to store the color information about the screen. We then initialize GLUT, calling `glutInitDisplayMode` with either GLUT_INDEX or GLUT_RGB, depending on the color model. Finally we create the window and initialize OpenGL for use as a 2D rasterizer, exactly as we saw in the sample program `mesaflat`.

The overridden method `blit_screen` calls `glutSwapBuffers` and `glFlush` to copy the off-screen buffer into the on-screen buffer, exactly as we saw in the sample program `mesaflat`.

l3d_screen_info_rgb_mesa, l3d_screen_info_indexed_mesa

Class `l3d_screen_info_rgb_mesa`, subclassed from class `l3d_screen_info_rgb`, represents screen information for a Mesa screen using an RGB color model. Class `l3d_screen_info_indexed_mesa`, subclassed from class `l3d_screen_info`, represents screen information for a Mesa screen using an indexed color model.

Listing 3-18: `si_rmes.h`

```
#ifndef _SI_RMES_H
#define _SI_RMES_H
#include "../tool_os/memman.h"

#include <GL/glut.h>
#include "si_rgb.h"

class l3d_screen_info_rgb_mesa : public l3d_screen_info_rgb {
  public:
    l3d_screen_info_rgb_mesa(unsigned long red_mask, unsigned long green_mask,
                             unsigned long blue_mask, char bytes_per_pixel):
    l3d_screen_info_rgb(red_mask, green_mask, blue_mask, bytes_per_pixel,
                        3)
    {

      this->red_mask =   0x000000FF;
      this->green_mask = 0x0000FF00;
      this->blue_mask =  0x00FF0000;
      this->bytes_per_pixel = 4;
      this->bytes_per_rgb = 3;

      compute_color_resolution();
    };

    void set_color(unsigned long col) {
      glColor4f( (float)(col & red_mask)   / red_mask,
                 (float)(col & green_mask) / green_mask,
                 (float)(col & blue_mask)  / blue_mask,
                 1.0 );
    }

    void compute_light_table(void) {};
    void compute_fog_table(void) {};
    void light_native(unsigned char *pcolor, int intensity) {};
    void fog_native(unsigned char *pcolor, int intensity)  {};
```

```
        };

        #endif
```

Listing 3-19: `si_imes.h`

```
#ifndef _SI_IMES_H
#define _SI_IMES_H
#include "../tool_os/memman.h"

#include <GL/glut.h>
#include "si_idx.h"

class l3d_screen_info_indexed_mesa : public l3d_screen_info_indexed {
  public:
    l3d_screen_info_indexed_mesa(int palette_size,
                                 int max_red, int max_green, int max_blue) :
    l3d_screen_info_indexed(palette_size, max_red, max_green, max_blue) {};

    void set_color(unsigned long col) {glIndexi(col); }
};

#endif
```

Overridden method `set_color` in `l3d_screen_info_rgb_mesa` calls `glColor4f` to set the OpenGL color. The function takes as parameters floating-point values in the range from 0.0 to 1.0 representing red, green, and blue intensities. We scale the specified RGB values to lie within this range. The fourth parameter is an *alpha* parameter, specifying transparency; we specify 1.0, meaning no transparency.

Overridden method `set_color` in `l3d_screen_info_indexed_mesa` calls `glIndexi` to select the current color index in the color palette.

l3d_dispatcher_mesa

Class `l3d_dispatcher_mesa`, subclassed from class `l3d_dispatcher`, represents an event dispatcher within the context of a GLUT program.

Listing 3-20: `dis_mesa.h`

```
#ifndef _DIS_MESA_H
#define _DIS_MESA_H
#include "../tool_os/memman.h"

#include "dispatch.h"
#include <GL/glut.h>

class l3d_dispatcher_mesa : public l3d_dispatcher {
  private:
    static l3d_dispatcher *last_dispatcher;
    static void glut_display_func(void);
    static void glut_idle_func(void);
    static void glut_keyboard_func(unsigned char key, int x, int y);

  public:
    l3d_dispatcher_mesa(void);
    void start(void);
};

class l3d_dispatcher_factory_mesa : public l3d_dispatcher_factory {
```

```
    public:
      l3d_dispatcher *create(void) {
        return new l3d_dispatcher_mesa;
      }
  };

  #endif
```

Listing 3-21: `dis_mesa.cc`

```
#include "dis_mesa.h"
#include "../tool_os/memman.h"

l3d_dispatcher *l3d_dispatcher_mesa::last_dispatcher;

l3d_dispatcher_mesa::l3d_dispatcher_mesa(void) {
  l3d_dispatcher_mesa::last_dispatcher = this;
}

void l3d_dispatcher_mesa::glut_display_func(void) {
  l3d_dispatcher_mesa::last_dispatcher->pipeline->draw_event();
  glutPostRedisplay();
}

void l3d_dispatcher_mesa::glut_idle_func(void) {
  l3d_dispatcher_mesa::last_dispatcher->pipeline->update_event();
}

void l3d_dispatcher_mesa::glut_keyboard_func(unsigned char key, int x, int y) {
  l3d_dispatcher_mesa::last_dispatcher->pipeline->key_event(key);

  //- unfortunately GLUT doesnt provide a clean way of exiting, so
  //- we have to jump out of the program here if the pipeline says
  //- it is done
  if(l3d_dispatcher_mesa::last_dispatcher->pipeline->done) exit(0);
}

void l3d_dispatcher_mesa::start(void) {
  glutDisplayFunc(l3d_dispatcher_mesa::glut_display_func);
  glutIdleFunc(l3d_dispatcher_mesa::glut_idle_func);
  glutKeyboardFunc(l3d_dispatcher_mesa::glut_keyboard_func);
  glutMainLoop();
}
```

Static member `last_dispatcher` points to the last-created instance of a `l3d_dispatcher_mesa` object. There will normally only be one dispatcher in a program, but if more are created, `last_dispatcher` points to the last one.

Static member function `glut_display_func` is the callback routine passed to `glutDisplayFunc`, and is called by GLUT whenever the program is allowed to display itself. This function calls `draw_event` of the associated pipeline object, allowing the pipeline to respond, then calls `glutPostRedisplay` to cause GLUT to redraw the screen at the next opportunity. This is a static member function because GLUT cannot accept a normal C++ member function as a callback (due to the hidden "this" pointer parameter present in normal member functions). Since this is a static member function, we cannot access any member variables, and thus must access the pipeline through the static `last_dispatcher` member.

Static member function `glut_idle_func` is the callback routine passed to `glutIdleFunc`, and is called by GLUT whenever the program is allowed to update itself. This function calls `update_event` of the associated pipeline object, allowing the pipeline to respond.

Static member function `glut_keyboard_func` is the callback routine passed to `glutKeyboardFunc`, and is called by GLUT whenever the program has received keyboard input. This function calls `key_event` of the associated pipeline object, allowing the pipeline to respond.

Overridden method `start` registers the static member functions with GLUT by calling `glutDisplayFunc`, `glutIdleFunc`, and `glutKeyboardFunc`. It then enters the `glutMainLoop`, which then assumes responsibility for event dispatching and calling the registered callback routines.

l3d_rasterizer_2d_mesa_imp

Class `l3d_rasterizer_2d_mesa_imp`, subclassed from class `l3d_rasterizer_2d_imp`, represents a rasterizer implementation using Mesa function calls.

Listing 3-22: `ras_mesa.h`

```
#ifndef __RAS_MESA_H
#define __RAS_MESA_H
#include "../tool_os/memman.h"

#include <GL/glut.h>
#include "rasteriz.h"

class l3d_rasterizer_2d_mesa_imp :
      virtual public l3d_rasterizer_2d_imp
{
  public:
    l3d_rasterizer_2d_mesa_imp(int xs, int ys, l3d_screen_info *si);

    void clear_buffer(void);
    void draw_point(int x, int y, unsigned long col);
    void draw_line(int x0, int y0, int x1, int y1, unsigned long col);
    void draw_polygon_flatshaded(const l3d_polygon_2d_flatshaded *p_poly);
};

class l3d_rasterizer_2d_mesa_imp_factory :
  public l3d_rasterizer_2d_imp_factory {
  public:
    l3d_rasterizer_2d_imp *create(int xs, int ys, l3d_screen_info *si);
};

#endif
```

Listing 3-23: `ras_mesa.cc`

```
#include "ras_mesa.h"
#include <math.h>
#include "../tool_os/memman.h"

l3d_rasterizer_2d_imp * l3d_rasterizer_2d_mesa_imp_factory::create
(int xs, int ys, l3d_screen_info *si)
{
  return new l3d_rasterizer_2d_mesa_imp(xs,ys,si);
}
```

```
l3d_rasterizer_2d_mesa_imp::l3d_rasterizer_2d_mesa_imp
(int xs, int ys, l3d_screen_info *si)
    : l3d_rasterizer_2d_imp(xs,ys,si)
{}

void l3d_rasterizer_2d_mesa_imp::clear_buffer(void) {
  glClear(GL_COLOR_BUFFER_BIT);
}

void l3d_rasterizer_2d_mesa_imp::draw_point(int x, int y, unsigned long col) {
  glBegin(GL_POINTS);
  sinfo->set_color(col);
  glVertex2i(x,y);
  glEnd();
}

void l3d_rasterizer_2d_mesa_imp::draw_line(int x0, int y0, int x1, int y1,
    unsigned long col)
{
  glBegin(GL_LINES);
  sinfo->set_color(col);
  glVertex2i(x0,y0);
  glVertex2i(x1,y1);
  glEnd();
}

void l3d_rasterizer_2d_mesa_imp::draw_polygon_flatshaded
(const l3d_polygon_2d_flatshaded *p_poly)
{
  int i;

  glBegin(GL_POLYGON);
  sinfo->set_color(p_poly->final_color);
  for(i=0; i<p_poly->clip_ivertices->num_items; i++) {
    glVertex2i(iceil((**(p_poly->vlist))
                      [(*p_poly->clip_ivertices)[i].ivertex].transformed.X_),
               iceil((**(p_poly->vlist))
                      [(*p_poly->clip_ivertices)[i].ivertex].transformed.Y_));
  }
  glEnd();
}
```

The overridden method `clear_buffer` calls OpenGL function `glClear`, which we briefly mentioned earlier, with a parameter of `GL_COLOR_BUFFER_BIT`. This clears the off-screen buffer containing the visible pixels (colors) for the image, meaning that the image in the off-screen buffer is erased. OpenGL can keep track of a number of buffers in addition to the color buffer; valid parameters to `glClear` are `GL_COLOR_BUFFER_BIT`, `GL_DEPTH_BUFFER_BIT`, `GL_STENCIL_BUFFER_BIT`, and `GL_ACCUM_BUFFER_BIT`. We only use the color buffer in this book. Overridden method `draw_point` draws a point using OpenGL calls as follows. First, we set the state to be "point-drawing mode" by calling `glBegin(GL_POINTS)`. Next, we set the color of the point to be drawn by calling the `set_color` method of the screen-information object. This calls the appropriate OpenGL color-setting routine, depending on whether the color model is RGB or indexed. Next, we call `glVertex2i` to set the coordinates of the point to be drawn. Finally, we call `glEnd` to finish drawing the point.

Overridden method `draw_line` draws a line using OpenGL calls as follows. First, we set the state to be "line-drawing mode" by calling `glBegin(GL_LINES)`. Next, we set the color of the line to be drawn by calling the `set_color` method of the screen-information object. This calls the appropriate OpenGL color-setting routine, depending on whether the color model is RGB or indexed. Next, we call `glVertex2i` twice, to specify the starting and ending coordinates of the line. In line-drawing mode, the first call to `glVertex2i` specifies the start coordinate; the second, the end coordinate. Finally, we call `glEnd` to finish drawing the line.

Overridden method `draw_polygon_flatshaded` draws a polygon using OpenGL calls as follows. First, we set the state to be "polygon-drawing mode" by calling `glBegin(GL_POLYGON)`. Next, we set the color of the polygon to be drawn by calling the `set_color` method of the screen-information object. This calls the appropriate OpenGL color-setting routine, depending on whether the color model is RGB or indexed. Next, we loop through all of the clipped vertex indices referenced in the `clip_ivertices` member of the polygon. For each vertex index, we access the actual vertex and take its transformed member. We specify this transformed, clipped vertex to OpenGL with `glVertex2i`. After looping through all clipped vertex indices for the polygon, we call `glEnd` to finish drawing the polygon.

Running the Sample Programs with Mesa

All of the l3d sample programs up to this point will work unchanged with Mesa. The factory manager allows choosing the Mesa factories at program start, after which point everything in the program then transparently accesses Mesa. We saw in the very first l3d program `drawdot` that the first thing you see from an l3d program is the following question:

```
which configuration?
1. Software X11
2. Software X11 with SHM extension
3. Mesa (with 3DFX h/w accel if installed with Mesa)
```

Although you might not have guessed it, choosing 3 configures the program to use the Mesa factories.

If you run a sample l3d program and choose 3 expecting immediately to see full-screen hardware-accelerated graphics, you might be disappointed at first. This is because by default, Mesa uses its own accurate but sometimes slow software rendering routines. Mesa can be dynamically configured to use hardware-accelerated or software rendering.

To tell Mesa to use full-screen hardware acceleration, follow these steps:

1. Become the root user on your machine. Type **su**, enter the password for the user "root," and press **Enter**. To access the 3Dfx video hardware, you need the special privileges of the root user.

2. Type **export MESA_GLX_FX = f** and press **Enter**. This tells Mesa to use full-screen hardware-accelerated rendering ("f").

3. Ensure that the `LD_LIBRARY_PATH` environment variable points to the directories where you installed Mesa and Glide. See the Appendix for more details.

After performing the above three steps, and still as the root user, you can run any Mesa program with full-screen hardware acceleration. Often, the current directory will not be in the search path for the root user (for security reasons), so you may need to type **./program_name** (with a preceding dot and slash character) to execute programs in the current directory. With an l3d program, as soon as you choose the Mesa configuration, the 3D video hardware switches into full-screen mode, your multi-window X environment disappears, and you see your graphics program full-screen and accelerated. You will immediately notice the speed difference when running with hardware acceleration.

NOTE   Notice that the fact that you must become the root user to access 3Dfx hardware acceleration is a sign of the lack of integration between this method of 3D hardware acceleration and the X Window system, which is why the efforts to incorporate hardware acceleration into X are so important. More recent versions of the 3Dfx Linux driver do, however, allow for non-root access to the 3D hardware.

One problem with full-screen 3Dfx graphics is that if your program crashes or enters an infinite loop, the video hardware still remains "connected" to the 3D graphics card, meaning you see a frozen or a black image. By default, you do not return to the X environment. You can try to press **Alt+Tab** to change the focus back to the shell window from which you started the program, then try pressing **Ctrl+C** to terminate the offending program, in which case you can sometimes recover from a frozen or crashed program. However, this is no guarantee.

One way around this problem is to use the 3Dfx "window hack," introduced in Chapter 1. This uses the 3Dfx hardware to render the image off-screen at the full accelerated speed of the hardware, but then uses a "hack" to copy the image back into video memory to display it in an X window. Follow these steps to enable the "window hack":

1. Shut down the X server. If your window manager provides a convenient means of doing so (for instance, via the K-menu in KDE), then end X through the window manager. If your window manager provides no such function, you can press **Ctrl+Alt+Backspace**, which forcefully kills the X server.

2. Restart the X server in 16-bpp mode: type **startx -- -bpp 16** and press **Enter**. Shutting down and restarting the X server in 16-bpp mode is not strictly necessary, but leads to the best performance.

3. Become the root user. Type **su**, press **Enter**, enter the root password, and press **Enter**.

4. Type **export MESA_GLX_FX="window"** and press **Enter** to enable window rendering.

5. Type **export SST_VGA_PASS=1** and press **Enter**. This "stops video signal switching," according to the Mesa documentation on the 3Dfx driver.

6. Type **export SST_NOSHUTDOWN=1** and press **Enter**. This also is to stop video signal switching.

7. Ensure that the LD_LIBRARY_PATH environment variable points to the libraries where you installed Mesa and Glide (see the Appendix).

After performing the above steps, and still as the root user, you can run any Mesa program with windowed hardware acceleration. Remember, this will not be nearly as fast as full-screen hardware acceleration, but is still usually faster than pure Mesa software rendering. As noted above, as the root user you might not be able to execute programs in the current directory without typing a dot and a slash before the program name.

The newly released XFree86 4.0 incorporates the Direct Rendering Infrastructure, mentioned in Chapter 1. This means that accelerated 3D graphics under X has become a reality for Linux. A number of popular 3D cards are supported, but exactly how to enable this acceleration depends on your specific graphic card. You might need to load a special operating system module before starting the X server, and you might need to update your dynamic library search path to use the hardware-accelerated OpenGL libraries provided by XFree86 4.0. You also might need to start your X server with a particular color depth. See the XFree86 4.0 documentation for details, or consult their web page at `http://www.xfree86.org`. Also, if your 3D card is not yet supported by XFree86 4.0, you might have luck with the drivers from the Utah-GLX project at `http://utah-glx.sourceforge.net`.

Summary

In this chapter, we looked at ways of drawing specific geometric primitives onto the 2D raster display. We looked at all of the following topics:

- Rasterization and clipping of points, lines, and polygons in 2D
- Storage structures for 2D polygons
- Polygon morphing in 2D by interpolating between vertex lists and changing a vertex list pointer
- Accelerated 2D graphics through MIT-SHM
- Basic OpenGL programming with Mesa and GLUT
- 3DFX hardware acceleration through Mesa

We now know how to access the screen, and how to use rasterization algorithms to draw dots, lines, and polygons on the screen. In other words, we now can write programs to draw simple 2D graphics under Linux. The next chapter begins our journey into the next dimension—into the world of 3D.

Chapter 4

3D Vision and Perception

Overview

This chapter explains the fundamental concepts enabling the apparent display of 3D graphics on a 2D screen. We say "apparent display" because, essentially, 3D graphics is the creation of 2D images which appear to be 3D. Achieving this appearance requires an understanding of the perceptual, physical, and geometrical factors involved in 3D viewing. Human vision results from the mind's three-dimensional perception of physical light rays; studying vision, then, allows us to understand geometrically how 3D graphics works.

In this chapter, we define what we want to accomplish with 3D graphics, examine the physics and geometry of vision, and present our first 3D program. We cover the following topics:

- The visual goal of 3D graphics
- Human visual perception of 3D objects, and why 2D images can appear 3D
- The concept of parallax
- Using qualitative knowledge about 3D perception to produce simple 3D graphics
- The problems with a simple qualitative approach to 3D graphics.

The Goal of 3D Graphics

We often hear that a program has great 3D graphics, or that a particular animation sequence looks amazingly 3D. But what exactly is meant by "3D graphics" anyway? For the purposes of this chapter, we define 3D graphics as follows.

3D graphics is the creation of a two-dimensional image or series of images on a flat computer screen such that the visual interpretation of the image or series of images is that of a three-dimensional image or series of images.

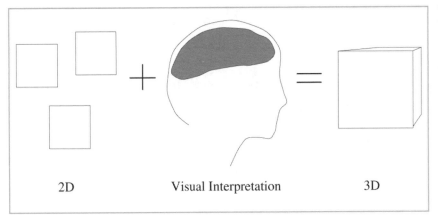

Figure 4-1: Definition of 3D graphics.

Let's examine each part of this definition in more detail.

- Two-dimensional image: As detailed in the previous chapter, the computer screen is divided into a two-dimensional grid of individually controllable pixels. By activating or deactivating pixels at selected (x,y) positions, we specify a 2D image.

- Series of images: By displaying a rapid succession of similar but slightly differing 2D images, the illusion of 2D motion can be produced. By displaying a rapid succession of 2D images, each of whose visual interpretation is that of a 3D image, the illusion of 3D motion can be produced.

- Flat computer screen: The computer screen (or monitor) is the computer's main visual output device. The pixellated two-dimensional images described in the first item are displayed physically as luminous phosphors or dots on the computer monitor. Physically, the display surface of the monitor is flat or very close to flat. Thus, all of the (x,y) pixel coordinates which the computer can plot will physically lie in a two-dimensional plane in space. (This fact allows us to understand and mathematically compute the equations necessary for the so-called "planar perspective projections"; see Chapter 5.)

NOTE Not all screens are flat. For instance, some large, immersive, 3D movie theaters project images on a huge cylindrical or spherical screen encompassing the entire field of vision. If we want to use 3D computer graphics to compute images for projection onto such non-flat display surfaces, we would need to use slightly more complicated projection formulas than the ones presented in this chapter. Fortunately, typical displays for personal computers are indeed flat, and we therefore assume for this book that the target display is also flat. Furthermore, we also assume that we only have one screen on which we generate images; however, larger virtual reality environments such as CAVEs often use multiple screens to surround the viewer, all calculated and updated simultaneously, with a corresponding increase in required computing power. Again, the typical personal computer will only have one screen.

■ Visual interpretation: The human eye receives the light rays from the image on the computer screen and sends signals to the brain for visual interpretation. We must understand how the eye and mind receive and interpret light rays from real-world, three-dimensional objects, if we are to "fool" the eye/mind into interpreting the light rays coming from a two-dimensional image as the light rays coming from a three-dimensional object.

Notice that our current definition of 3D graphics only concerns itself with the visual component—and indeed, strictly speaking, graphics does deal only with that which is "graphic" or visual. In the field of 3D graphics, however, we often wish to imitate not only the way the 3D world looks, but also how it behaves. In particular, 3D games, virtual reality environments, and other interactive 3D programs require some resemblance to the real world in order to create a convincing illusion of a virtual environment. Objects should not be able to pass through one another (collision detection), should accelerate and decelerate realistically (physics), and generally should behave according to rules similar to or at least reminiscent of the physical laws governing our ordinary, observable, physical reality. We can use the term "simulation" to describe any program code which deals with modeling the behavior of 3D objects. A sample program later in this chapter implements simulation code in order to control the movement of dots in a variety of physically realistic ways. Later chapters also implement various types of simulation code such as collision detection, sound, and acceleration. This allows us to create believable and entertaining 3D worlds.

For now, though, let's return to the visual part of 3D graphics.

Moving from 2D to 3D

The 2D graphics concepts presented in Chapter 2 are fundamentally easy and intuitive to understand and visualize. While a robust, flexible, extendable Linux implementation of the 2D concepts raises many practical issues, the actual geometric 2D graphics concepts themselves are not difficult to understand. However, while the geometry of 2D graphics is easy, it is not clear how to start making the move to 3D. Perhaps the most natural question, one which you might have at this moment, is the following:

"My screen is 2D, and I know how to plot 2D points. But how do I plot 3D points on a 2D screen?"

Or, put in somewhat more mathematical terms:

"I want to plot a 3D point of the form (x,y,z) on my 2D (x,y) screen. I know what to do with the x and y coordinates, but what do I do with the z coordinate?"

This question is a bit deeper than it might appear at first. To answer it, we first consider how humans see objects at all. With this understanding, it will then be possible to understand how a 2D image may be made to appear like the physical 3D objects in our world. The next chapter then examines the mathematical answer to the question, which involves 3D linear perspective.

Vision and Optics: 3D in the Physical World

The following sections discuss the geometry of visual perception and optics. We develop a geometrical model of the way humans perceive light, and use this model to understand how visual ambiguities can occur. In particular, we see how 2D images may appear to be 3D. We then use this basic knowledge to write a program displaying a crude but passable 3D animation.

The Retina: Biochemical Vision

The retina forms the biochemical basis for vision in humans. It is a small patch of photosensitive tissue located near the back of the eyeball. Light striking the retina causes certain cells (called rods and cones) to send a message to the brain indicating that light has been perceived.

Therefore, the physical basis for vision is light striking the retina. The particular patterns of light striking the retina determine which particular rods and cones in the retina fire off a signal to the brain. The mind then interprets all the signals from the retina and gives us what we call the sensation of vision. Regardless of whether we are looking at a flat, depthless picture or the tremendous three-dimensional expanse of the Grand Canyon, our visual perception all comes down to light striking the retina.

 NOTE We stated that light striking the retina forms the physical basis for vision. Of course, we have two eyes and therefore two retinas. The brain's synthesis of the two slightly different images received by both eyes provides a very strong sensation of 3D perception, called *binocular vision* or *stereopsis*. However, in this book, we ignore this effect, assuming effectively that we are looking at the world through only one eye (*monocular vision*). This is a reasonable limitation, because most computers have only one display monitor, at which both eyes look. Thus, binocular depth cues cannot currently be implemented on the average personal computer. Of course, devices exist which actually do present slightly differing views to each eye separately and thus do provide for true binocular depth perception. These devices typically take the form of some sort of a visor, helmet, or glasses. Although prices have come down for such devices, they are still by no means standard equipment, and thus we assume monocular vision.

But how, exactly, does light "strike the retina"? By what mechanism and in what manner does light travel? What is light?

These questions may seem peripheral to a text dealing with 3D graphics, but I feel it is vital for a 3D programmer to understand how the eye perceives objects in order to be able to "fool" the eye into seeing 3D images on a 2D screen. Many 3D texts simply draw "rays" or "projectors" from objects to the eye, without ever explaining what these rays represent, where they come from, or what happens to them when they enter the eye. As we are about to see, these rays form the very basis of vision.

The Geometry of Light

For the purposes of this book, it is convenient to concentrate on the particulate properties of light, from which we know that light energy radiates in straight lines outward from all points in all directions. We call these lines of light energy *light rays*. Light rays travel in straight lines unless bent by some agent or device. The only light-bending device we will need to consider in this book—and then only briefly—is the lens within the human eye. When a light ray passes through the eye's lens and strikes the retina, the light ray causes a biochemical reaction to take place in the retina, which then causes a signal to be sent to the brain; this is interpreted as the sensation of sight.

The following series of diagrams illustrate visually the path of light rays for a variety of viewing situations. We trace the light rays from their point of origin (points on the perceived object) to the point of perception (points where the light rays strike the retina). Along the way, we establish several diagrammatical conventions used throughout the book. Recall, again, the purpose of this discussion on human vision is to understand perception of real-world 3D objects as well as perception of 2D images. We will see at the end how the perception of one can seem like a perception of the other, thus allowing a 2D image (or series of images) to be perceived as 3D.

Single Point

Figure 4-2 illustrates the visual situation with the simplest object possible, a single point source of light. This point, located at the right of the figure, radiates an infinite number of light rays in all directions. Of all the light rays emanating from this point, only a small fraction (those rays drawn with a solid line in the figure) actually are perceived from the particular position of the eye, called the *viewpoint*. We will call these light rays the *seen light rays*. Seen rays are therefore the particular subset of all light rays emanating from a point or a set of points, which pass through the eye's lens, strike the retina, and are perceived. This particular subset depends on the position of the eye. Due to the optical properties of the eye's convex lens, all of the seen light rays coming from one point focus to exactly one point on the retina, due to the refractive (light-bending) properties of the focusing lens. Thus, the seen light rays emanating from the single point in space are focused to a single point on the retina, and are therefore perceived by the mind as a single point.

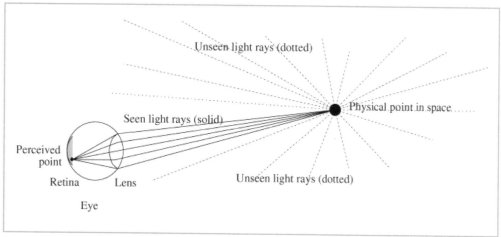

Figure 4-2: Perception of a point.

Two Points

Figure 4-3 illustrates the same situation, but with two points. To reduce diagram clutter, only the seen light rays are drawn; the unseen light rays are omitted. This convention will be used throughout the book. Notice in Figure 4-3 that for the light rays falling on the retina, the up/down orientation of points 1 and 2 is actually reversed from the actual physical up/down orientation. That is, the image falling on the retina is inverted with respect to the physical up/down orientation of the object. However, the mind internally "inverts" the image back so it is perceived right-side-up.

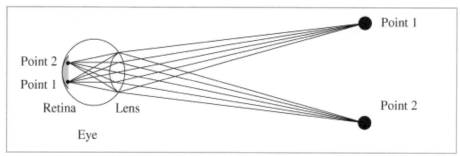

Figure 4-3: Perception of two points.

Figure 4-3 illustrates only two points, but already the diagram is cluttered with light rays. As a further diagrammatical convention, future diagrams will only draw one light ray per point per eye. (Usually only one eye will be illustrated per diagram since, recall, we are ignoring the effects of binocular vision.) Since all the light rays from one physical point focus to one point on the retina, we are not losing any information by making this diagrammatical simplification. Figure 4-4 is the same as Figure 4-3, but with this convention applied.

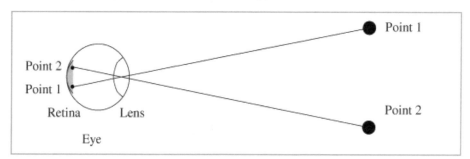

Figure 4-4: Perception of two points, one seen ray per point.

Let us establish one more diagrammatical convention before continuing. Only "significant" points within the objects of interest will be considered. Since each object theoretically consists of an infinite number of points, we cannot illustrate the behavior of light rays for all of these infinite points. Instead, we concentrate on the points which most naturally are significant to the object under observation. Some examples are:

Object	Significant points
Line	Two endpoints
Triangle	Three vertices
Cube	Eight vertices
Arbitrary 2D polygon	Polygon's vertices in 2D
Arbitrary 3D polygonal object	Shared vertices of all comprising polygons in 3D

We will see later that a convenient representation of 3D objects is 3D polygonal modeling. Furthermore, the most natural method of representing 3D polygonal objects in a data structure is to store the 3D coordinates of the object's vertices, just as in Chapter 2 we stored the 2D coordinates of polygons' vertices in an `l3d_two_part_list`.

The following list summarizes the diagrammatical conventions which will be used throughout the rest of the book:

- Only seen rays are drawn.
- Only one seen ray per point per eye is drawn; monocular vision is assumed.
- Only "significant" points within objects of interest are considered.
- Usually, for space reasons, light rays will be drawn as terminating when they reach the eye, though actually the light rays pass through the eye's lens and only stop once they reach the retina.

Lines

Figure 4-5 illustrates the light rays for a series of identically sized line segments placed at different distances from the eye. For diagrammatical reasons we will only consider the endpoints of each line segment, though recall that, in reality, light is radiated from all points on each line segment. There are three line segments in this figure, which will be referred to by their endpoints: segment 1a-1b, segment 2a-2b, and segment 3a-3b. Segment 1a-1b is nearest to the eye; segment 3a-3b is farthest from the eye. The perceived image of the real-world segment 1a-1b is the segment 1a-1b on the retina; similarly for segments 2a-2b and 3a-3b. Notice that segment 1a-1b, closest to the eye, has the largest perceived image; segment 3a-3b, farthest from the eye, has the smallest perceived image. This fits with common sense; farther objects appear smaller.

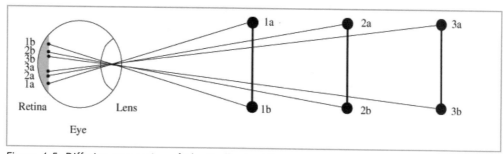

Figure 4-5: Differing perception of identically sized lines.

Now observe Figure 4-6, which presents line segments of differing sizes. Here, segment 1a-1b is the smallest but also the nearest segment to the eye. Segment 2a-2b is slightly larger but farther from the eye; segment 3a-3b is the largest segment but is also the farthest from the eye. Notice that the light rays from all of these segments end up striking the same points on the retina. That is, the perception of size of segments 1a-1b, 2a-2b, and 3a-3b is identical, though physically they are of differing sizes. Why is this? The answer is that the seen light rays which emanate from segment 1a-1b are exactly the same as (i.e., follow the same paths as) the seen light rays from segments 2a-2b and 3a-3b. Since the physical basis of perception is seen light rays striking the retina, all three line segments are perceived identically. This also fits with common experience, since a small but close-up object is indistinguishable from an identical but larger object located farther from the eye. This is why the special effects crews for movies can use miniature models for spectacular explosions and other movie magic; if filmed from a close enough viewpoint, miniature models look just like their real-life counterparts as seen from a greater distance.

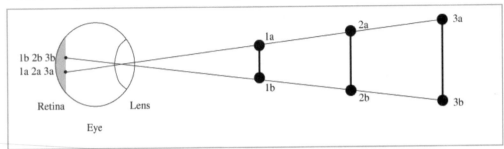

Figure 4-6: Identical perception of differently sized lines.

Figure 4-6 implies a number of interesting properties about visual perception. First of all, monocular vision is inherently ambiguous. Given an image on the retina, we can uniquely determine the light rays which cause that image to be formed. We cannot, however, uniquely determine the physical location of points in space which are emitting those light rays. In Figure 4-6, the image on the retina (retina segment 1a-1b, which is identical to retina segments 2a-2b and 3a-3b) implies that the two illustrated light rays are striking the eye, but we do not know if these rays originate from segment 1a-1b, segment 2a-2b, segment 3a-3b, or even from some entirely different object which, by virtue of its position relative to the eye, happens to radiate light rays along the same paths.

NOTE Binocular vision provides additional depth information unobtainable from just one eye; three eyes would provide even more. Such techniques are often used in image processing applications, using multiple cameras to capture multiple simultaneous views of a scene. Even with multiple cameras, however, ambiguity still remains.

Since vision is ambiguous, we can make one object look like another object if the same light rays strike the eye from each object. In particular, if we can create a 2D image such that the seen light rays radiated from this 2D image match the seen light rays for some 3D object, then the eye will perceive the 2D image just as it would perceive the 3D object! This was the miraculous "linear perspective" discovery made during the Renaissance.

Note well, however, that this does not mean that the 2D image will look like the 3D object from all viewpoints. If the viewpoint changes, then the set of seen rays—the subset of all rays radiated from the 2D image—will change. However, the set of seen rays will not change in the same manner as the set of seen rays from the 3D object would change for the same viewpoint change. An example is a photograph of the front face of a cube. If we look at the cube and the photograph straight on, they appear identical. But if we move our head up a bit and look down, then with the physical cube we can see a bit of its top face. With the photograph of the cube, however, our viewpoint change only causes foreshortening of the photograph itself, but we do not see the top of the cube in the photograph. This is what is meant when we say that for a change in viewpoint, the seen rays for a 3D object do not change in the same manner as the seen rays for a 2D image of that 3D object. This is why a photograph, while it can look 3D from one viewpoint, cannot look 3D from all viewpoints and therefore is quickly recognizable by the brain as being a flat projection of a 3D image.

NOTE   As an interesting aside, a few novelty "3D cameras" attempt to create a 3D image by integrating several 2D images from different viewpoints into one image, and coating the surface of the photograph with a special optical screen which allows a different image to be seen depending on the viewpoint. Most such cameras, however, only compensate for left-right viewpoint changes, not up-down viewpoint changes. In a similar vein, immersive virtual reality environments such as CAVEs attempt to track the movements of the viewer's head (or even eyes, in some cases) and re-create the 2D image to correspond to the new viewpoint, thereby contributing to the illusion that the viewer is looking at and moving in relation to a real 3D object. But update latency (delay) is always a problem with such systems.

A Cube

Until now, the light ray diagrams have been essentially 2D. Figure 4-7 illustrates a 3D cube and the seen light rays which are radiated from the cube's corners and strike the eye. For simplicity we only consider the corners of the cube, rather than all the infinite points lying along each edge and face of the cube. We also omit the diagrammatical details of the light rays entering the eye, being focused by the lens, and striking the retina; instead, the rays are drawn as terminating at the eye.

A 2D plane cuts through the light rays in the middle of Figure 4-7. In this diagram, we have traced the light rays from the cube and have intersected them with the 2D plane. The resulting image on the plane radiates light rays in such a way that the seen rays from this image are identical to the seen rays from the actual 3D cube, for the given viewpoint. Given the rays that strike the eye, we cannot tell if we are looking at the actual 3D cube or if we are looking at the 2D image of the 3D cube. Or, put another way, if we are looking at the 2D image, it may be interpreted by the mind as a 3D object—which is exactly the goal of 3D graphics we defined earlier.

Later in this chapter, we deal with the precise mathematical question of projection: given a viewpoint and a 3D object, how do we obtain a 2D image for which the seen light rays from the given viewpoint are identical to the seen light rays from the 3D object? But before tackling that question, let's address one other important 3D concept, *parallax*, and then put some of this theory into practice with our first 3D graphics program, "runway lights."

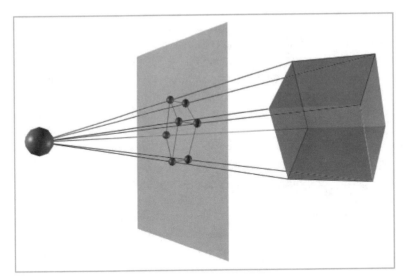

Figure 4-7: Identical perception of a 3D cube and a flat 2D image of a cube. The eye is at the left of the figure.

Parallax

In this section, we look at the concept of parallax—a strong cue which can help trick the mind into seeing 3D images from a dynamic 2D scene. By understanding and implementing a parallax effect, we can create a simple yet convincing 3D display.

Definition of Parallax

Parallax is the phenomenon that an object a given distance from a viewer moving with a given velocity across the field of vision appears to move more quickly than a more distant object moving with the same velocity. An example from everyday life will make this clear. Let's say you're driving along the highway. The road is clear, so you turn your head to look out the passenger side window. You notice that the trees along the side of the road appear to be zipping by at a great speed, but the mountains in the distance hardly appear to move at all. This difference in perceived speed is the parallax effect.

How Parallax Comes About

The geometrical analysis in Figure 4-8 illustrates why this is so. In the left half of Figure 4-8 we have two dots: one nearer to the eye (hollow) and one farther from the eye (solid). Let us say that both dots move the same physical distance from left to right. The perceived movement is the movement of the focused points on the retina, which is determined by the geometry of the seen light rays. As you can intuitively see from Figure 4-8, the nearer the point is to the eye, the greater the perceived movement, and the farther the point, the smaller the perceived movement. In other words, the perceived movement varies inversely with the distance from the eye.

A somewhat more mathematical justification may be seen in the right half of Figure 4-8. For a given fixed physical distance from point *a* to point *b*, we wish to determine the perceived distance (point *d* to point *e*) as a function of the distance of the point from the eye (point *c* to point *f*). The distance *de* (perceived distance) depends on the size of the angle *dce*. If we simplify the situation

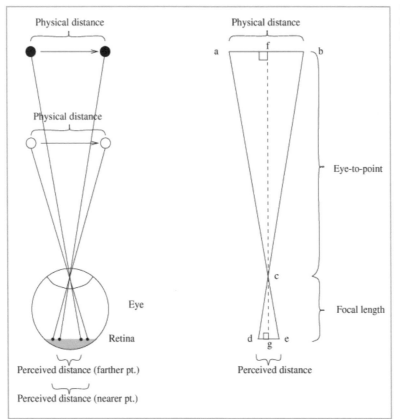

Figure 4-8: Analysis of parallax.

and consider the half-perceived-distance *dg*, as part of the half-triangle *dcg*, then we can say that the distance *dg* depends on the size of the angle *dcg*. Distance *cg* (focal length of the eye) is fixed. As angle *dcg* grows larger, so does its tangent (tan(*dcg*) = *dg*/*cg*); since *cg* is fixed, *dg* must grow larger as angle *dcg* grows larger, and *dg* must grow smaller as angle *dcg* grows smaller. Extending this to the whole distance *de* and the whole triangle *dce*, we may then conclude that perceived distance *de* varies directly with the size of the angle *dce*.

Angle *dce* and angle *acb* are equal, since they are opposite angles; therefore, perceived distance *de* varies directly with the size of angle *acb*. Let us again simplify and consider only the half-triangle *acf* and the half-physical-distance *af*. The physical distance *af* is fixed. As distance from the eye (length *cf*) increases, the tangent of angle *acf* decreases (tan(*acf*) = *af*/*cf*), since *cf* is fixed. As tan(*acf*) decreases, so does *acf*. Extending this result to the whole triangle *acb*, we may conclude that as distance from the eye (length *cf*) increases, angle *acb* decreases—in other words, the size of angle *acb* varies inversely with the distance from the eye *cf*. Combining this with the previous result that perceived distance *de* varies directly with the size of angle *acb*, we may finally conclude that for a fixed distance *ab*, the perceived distance *de* varies inversely with the distance from the eye *cf*, which is the same result we obtained from our earlier informal observation.

> **NOTE** The preceding two explanations of parallax—geometric and mathematic—illustrate an important way of understanding and discovering new 3D graphics concepts. First, we observe a behavior or a property of a system under consideration. Then, we attempt to understand and explain it geometrically. Finally, to verify and crystallize our understanding, we analyze the situation mathematically.

Why Parallax is Important

Parallax is important because it provides a cue or a visual suggestion to the viewer that one object is closer than another, thereby producing the illusion of 3D depth. We are so used to seeing and experiencing parallax in our ordinary visual perception that any parallax-like movement will likely be interpreted as parallax. If two on-screen objects move in a parallax-like manner, then this movement will very likely be interpreted by the viewer as parallax, creating the illusion of depth.

Later in this chapter we investigate the mathematics necessary to create a 2D image for which the seen light rays duplicate those of a 3D image. As it turns out, by solving this problem we also automatically generate the parallax effect. That is, the process of projection, as described later, "correctly" or "realistically" transforms 3D images into 2D images, including the effects of parallax.

"Runway Lights"—A Simple 3D Program

We've now made a number of qualitative observations about human perception of 3D objects:

1. Perceived size, that is, perceived distance between points, decreases with distance from viewer.

2. Perceived speed decreases with distance from viewer—the parallax effect.

3. If seen light rays for a 2D image correspond to seen light rays for a 3D object, the 2D image may be interpreted by the mind as a 3D image.

Let us now apply this qualitative knowledge by writing a program to simulate the 3D appearance of runway lights at night. First, we translate our qualitative knowledge into C++ code, then discuss the shortcomings of this purely qualitative approach. This paves the way for the following discussion of mathematically correct perspective projection, which is the only way to realistically display arbitrary 3D objects from an arbitrary 3D viewpoint on a 2D screen.

Runway Lights: Physical Situation

Physically, runway lights are arranged on airport grounds in a more or less grid-like fashion: there are evenly spaced rows of lights, each row with a number of evenly spaced lights. As the airplane taxis down the runway, parallel to the rows of runway lights, a viewer looking out the airplane window will see the runway lights moving horizontally across the field of vision.

Figure 4-9 illustrates the situation; the airplane is moving down the page, with the runway lights located to the right of the page. The viewer, sitting in the airplane, is looking out of the airplane window and is observing the relative motion of the runway lights. The viewer cannot see all of the runway lights at once; his field of view is limited by, among other things, the physical boundaries of the airplane window. There are therefore definite leftmost and rightmost "boundaries" beyond which radiated light rays cannot be perceived. These boundaries are shown by the dashed lines in the figure, and represent the field of view, a topic that we cover in more detail in Chapter 5.

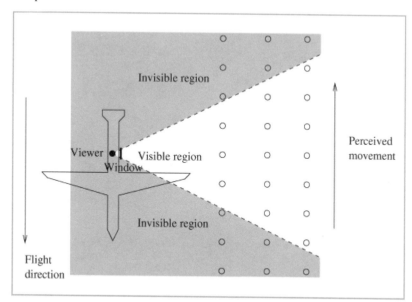

Figure 4-9: Physical viewing situation for runway lights.

What the viewer sees, therefore, is the region of lights in the figure labeled "visible region." Notice that the visible region grows in size with the distance from the viewer. This means that the viewer sees more lights in the furthest row and fewer lights in the nearest row. Furthermore, we "know" from common experience that the nearest row will appear vertically lowest in the window; the farthest row, highest. Distant things appear higher because we look down on the ground. If we could put our head below ground and look up at the ground, then distant objects would appear lower on-screen; if we put our head exactly at ground level, then both near and distant objects appear at the same level on-screen, namely eye level.

If you are somewhat unsettled by the imprecise nature of the previous assumptions, don't worry—remember, this is our first attempt at a 3D program, and the goal for now is to see if an informal, qualitatively justified implementation of 3D graphics can yield acceptable results.

Code Listing

To implement all of this, we plot a series of dots on the screen as shown in Figure 4-10. We have three rows of dots, representing the three rows of runway lights we would see out the window of the airplane.

Listing 4-1: `runway.cc`: runway lights

```
#include <stdlib.h>
#include <stdio.h>

#include "../lib/tool_2d/screen.h"
#include "../lib/tool_os/dispatch.h"
#include "../lib/raster/rasteriz.h"
#include "../lib/tool_2d/scrinfo.h"
```

```
#include "../lib/system/factorys.h"

#define MAXDOTS 500
#define NEARDOTS_INTERVAL 1
#define MEDDOTS_INTERVAL 2
#define FARDOTS_INTERVAL 4

//- STEP 1: CHOOSE THE FACTORIES

void choose_factories(void) {
  factory_manager_v_0_1.choose_factories();
}

//- STEP 2: DECLARE A PIPELINE SUBCLASS

class my_pipeline : public l3d_pipeline {
  protected:
    l3d_rasterizer_2d_imp *ri;
    l3d_rasterizer_2d *r;

    unsigned long color;

    int neardots_x[MAXDOTS], neardots_y, neardot_x_spacing, neardots_ctr,
    meddots_x[MAXDOTS], meddots_y, meddot_x_spacing, meddots_ctr,
    fardots_x[MAXDOTS], fardots_y, fardot_x_spacing, fardots_ctr,
    num_neardots, num_meddots, num_fardots;

  public:
    l3d_screen *s;
    my_pipeline(void);
    virtual ~my_pipeline(void);

    void key_event(int ch);  //- from dispatcher
    void update_event(void); //- from dispatcher
    void draw_event(void);   //- from dispatcher
};

my_pipeline::my_pipeline(void) {
  s = factory_manager_v_0_1.screen_factory->create(320,200);
  ri = factory_manager_v_0_1.ras_2d_imp_factory->create(320,200,s->sinfo);
  r = new l3d_rasterizer_2d(ri);

  s->sinfo->ext_max_red =
    s->sinfo->ext_max_green =
      s->sinfo->ext_max_blue = 255;
  s->sinfo->ext_to_native(0, 0, 0); //- allocate black background color
  color = s->sinfo->ext_to_native(255, 255, 255);
  s->refresh_palette();

  int i,x;
  neardots_y = 180;
  neardot_x_spacing=20;
  neardots_ctr = NEARDOTS_INTERVAL;
  for(i=0, x=0; x<320 && i < MAXDOTS; i++) {
    neardots_x[i] = x;
    x+=neardot_x_spacing;
  }
  num_neardots=i;

  /* Middle row of runway lights */
```

```
    meddots_y = 140;                    /* middle row: higher on screen */
    meddot_x_spacing=10;                /* middle row: medium spacing */
    meddots_ctr = MEDDOTS_INTERVAL;     /* middle row: medium speed */
    /* squeeze as many lights as possible into a row, with the given spacing */
    for(i=0, x=0; x<320 && i < MAXDOTS; i++) {
      meddots_x[i] = x;
      x+=meddot_x_spacing;
    }
    num_meddots=i;

    /* Farthest row of runway lights */
    fardots_y = 120;                    /* farthest row: highest up on screen */
    fardot_x_spacing=7;                 /* farthest row: tightly spaced */
    fardots_ctr = FARDOTS_INTERVAL;     /* farthest row: slow movement */
    /* squeeze as many lights as possible into a row, with the given spacing */
    for(i=0, x=0; x<320 && i < MAXDOTS; i++) {
      fardots_x[i] = x;
      x+=fardot_x_spacing;
    }
    num_fardots=i;
}

my_pipeline::~my_pipeline(void) {
  delete s;
  delete ri;
  delete r;
}

void my_pipeline::key_event(int ch) {
  switch(ch) {
    case 'q': {
        exit(0);
      }
  }
}

void my_pipeline::update_event() {
  int i;

  /* move all dots */
  neardots_ctr--;
  if (neardots_ctr == 0) {/* neardots move once every NEARDOTS_INTERVAL */
    neardots_ctr = NEARDOTS_INTERVAL;
    for(i=0;i<num_neardots;i++) {
      neardots_x[i] --;
      if(neardots_x[i]<0) neardots_x[i] += 320;
    }
  }
  meddots_ctr--;
  if (meddots_ctr == 0) {/* meddots move once every MEDDOTS_INTERVAL */
    meddots_ctr = MEDDOTS_INTERVAL;
    for(i=0;i<num_meddots;i++) {
      meddots_x[i] --;
      if(meddots_x[i]<0) meddots_x[i] += 320;
    }
  }
  fardots_ctr--;
  if (fardots_ctr == 0) {/* fardots move once every FARDOTS_INTERVAL */
    fardots_ctr = FARDOTS_INTERVAL;
    for(i=0;i<num_fardots;i++) {
```

```
        fardots_x[i] -;
        if(fardots_x[i]<0) fardots_x[i] += 320;
      }
    }
  }

void my_pipeline::draw_event(void) {
  int i;
  r->clear_buffer();
  /* plot all dots */

  for(i=0; i<num_neardots; i++) {
    r->draw_point(neardots_x[i],neardots_y,color);
  }
  for(i=0; i<num_meddots; i++) {
    r->draw_point(meddots_x[i],meddots_y,color);
  }
  for(i=0; i<num_fardots; i++) {
    r->draw_point(fardots_x[i],fardots_y,color);
  }

  s->blit_screen();
}

main() {
  choose_factories();

  l3d_dispatcher *d;
  my_pipeline *p;

  //- STEP 3: CREATE A DISPATCHER

  d = factory_manager_v_0_1.dispatcher_factory->create();

  //- STEP 4: CREATE A PIPELINE

  //- plug our custom behavior pipeline into the dispatcher
  p  = new my_pipeline();

  //- STEP 5: START DISPATCHER

  d->pipeline = p; //- polymorphic assignment
  d->event_source = p->s;
  d->start();

  delete d;
  delete p;
}
```

The following paragraphs describe the characteristics of the program which reflect the observations we have made thus far.

Size Decreases with Distance

The size of the horizontal spacing between lights in the nearest row is large; in the farthest row, small. The program variables with names ending in _spacing control the horizontal dot spacing. In a similar manner, the vertical spacing between the rows themselves, controlled by the variables ending in _y, also decreases with greater distance. The middle row of dots is closer to the top, distant row than to the bottom, near row. In the vertical direction, this apparent size shrinkage is called *foreshortening*.

Field of View

The farthest row has the most dots; the nearest row, the fewest. Dependent on the spacing between lights, we squeeze the maximum number of lights into the on-screen space available in the row of pixels. Tight spacing yields many dots; wide spacing, few.

Parallax

The speed of movement in the nearest row is fast; in the farthest row, slow. We store and initialize a countdown counter for each row. Each time the countdown counter for a row hits zero, all dots in that row are moved left and the counter is reset. The countdown counter for the nearest row is set to a low value (yielding fast movement); for the farthest row, it is set to a high value (yielding slower movement).

2D Seen Rays = 3D Seen Rays

The set of seen light rays radiating from the 2D on-screen image may be interpreted by the mind in one of two ways: as the seen light rays coming from a flat 2D picture of dots, or as the seen light rays coming from a 3D field of runway lights. See Figure 4-11. Due to the combination of visual cues, in particular the parallax cue, the animation appears convincingly 3D.

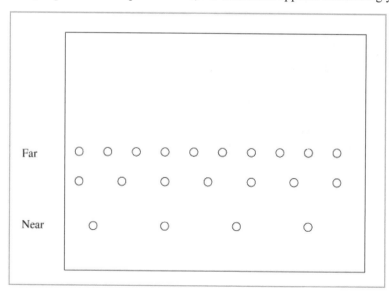

Figure 4-10: Plotting runway lights on the screen.

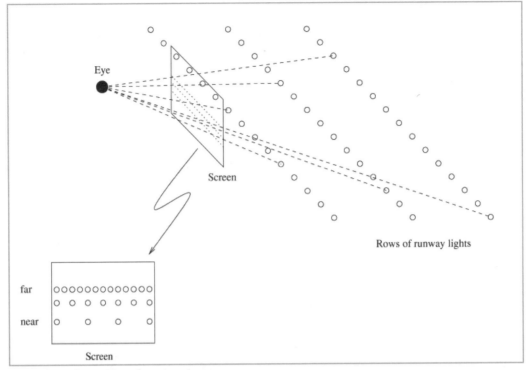

Figure 4-11: Perception of moving dots on-screen.

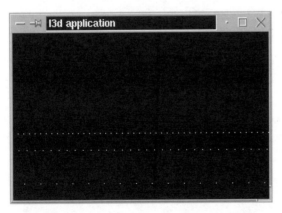

Figure 4-12: Output from the program
`runway`.

Evaluation of "Runway Lights" Program

If you run the runway lights program, you will probably agree that the effect is at least a passable simulation of 3D runway lights moving horizontally across the field of vision. We have therefore succeeded in transforming our qualitative knowledge about 3D perception into a qualitatively passable 3D graphics program.

But why do we say "qualitative?" Let's look at all the factors we control in the program:

■ Dot spacing for near, medium, and far rows (the `_spacing` terms in the code)

- Dot speed for near, medium, and far rows (the _INTERVAL terms in the code)
- Vertical position on-screen of near, medium, and far rows (the _y terms in the code)

You might be wondering how we decided on the values for these terms in the code. The answer is, these terms were assigned by trial and error. We observed and qualitatively reasoned that near dots are more widely spaced than far dots, that near dots appear to move faster than far dots, and that near dots appear vertically lower than far dots. However, the quantitative, hard, cold numbers in the code were determined by trial and error, within the qualitative guidelines we observed, until the results appeared satisfactory.

We might like to think that if the results look fine, then a qualitative approach suffices. And indeed, some of the earliest video games used exactly such qualitative techniques to simulate 3D effects in, for instance, left-to-right scrolling games. There might have been cars in the foreground, trees in the middle, and mountains in the background, all scrolling by in a very similar fashion to the runway lights we just programmed.

If we look more closely, however, we will start to realize some difficult to insurmountable problems with the qualitative approach we just took:

- How can we make the dots move toward the user or in any direction other than horizontal?
- How can we display more complicated objects than dots?
- How can we allow the user to independently move around in a 3D world?
- How can we allow the user to point the eye in a different direction (to look up, down, or diagonally, for instance)?

If we try to use this qualitative approach to 3D graphics in more general 3D situations, we quickly realize that such an approach is not useful for much more than an optical attention-getter. As soon as you need to display, manipulate, and move around in 3D data, the qualitative observations we made and implemented are simply not enough.

The problem is that we are still fundamentally working with 2D data and not with 3D data. We were able to cheat because we qualitatively happened to notice that the 3D motion of horizontal rows of runway lights is simple 2D horizontal motion (although we did make some interesting and correct observations about the relationships between distance from the viewer and perceived size and speed). So we programmed some simple horizontal 2D lines of dots on-screen and moved these dots horizontally in accordance with the qualitative observations we had made earlier. But we are moving 2D dots in a 3D fashion; we are not truly modeling and moving 3D data. It is a special case and a lucky coincidence that horizontal 3D motion translates into simple horizontal 2D motion. This is not the case in general, and leads to the inability of this approach to handle the other situations described above (arbitrary movement, display of more complicated objects, and so forth).

In order to correctly and flexibly implement 3D graphics, we must make the commitment to model our data in 3D, then determine a way to convert or project the 3D data onto our 2D display. This process is called *planar perspective projection* and is the topic of the next chapter.

Summary

In this chapter we defined 3D graphics and took a close look at the physics and geometry of vision. We observed that when the seen light rays from a 2D image duplicate the seen light rays from a 3D object, the 2D image will "look 3D."

We also made several qualitative observations about perception of 3D objects, and implemented these observations in an ad-hoc way in the demonstration program "runway lights." The program generated a believable 3D effect, yet was not flexible enough to allow for interactive display and manipulation of arbitrary 3D data.

We realized that the problem with the approach of the "runway lights" program is that it is a 2D simulation of 3D phenomena. The program is actually modeling the movement of the runway lights in 2D, not in 3D. It is this shortcoming which does not allow this approach or similar approaches to be applied to arbitrary viewing of arbitrary 3D data. The next chapter tackles this subject head on. How do we model 3D data, and exactly how do we display this 3D data on a 2D screen?

Chapter 5

Perspective Projection

Overview

This chapter explains the concepts, equations, and implementation details for displaying arbitrary 3D graphics on a 2D screen. Creating a general-purpose 3D graphics program requires a mathematical approach to generating 2D images from 3D data. This chapter is an introduction to the mathematics of 3D graphics. In particular, we look at the process of planar perspective projection.

This chapter formalizes the qualitative observations made in Chapter 4, which result in a set of equations—the *perspective projection* equations—which mathematically convert 3D data into a 2D form suitable for display. Using this knowledge, we then develop a better, mathematically correct version of the sample 3D program from the previous chapter, and see how much more flexible this approach is. We also look at a 3D program which uses the polygon drawing routines from Chapter 3 to display 3D polygonal graphics.

This chapter covers the following topics:

- 3D coordinate systems and vectors
- Modeling 3D data with 3D points
- The perspective projection equation for a single point
- Field of view
- Projecting lines, polygons, and polyhedra from 3D into 2D
- The general structure of a 3D engine

Projection from 3D to 2D

In computer graphics, *projection* refers to the transformation of points in a coordinate system of n dimensions into points in a coordinate system of less than n dimensions. For the purposes of 3D graphics, this means transforming 3D points into 2D points. The 3D points represent physical points modeling a 3D object, and the projected 2D points are the 2D representation of the object which we display on-screen by using the 2D graphics classes we developed in Chapters 2 and 3.

We are interested in a very specific kind of 3D-to-2D projection. In particular, we would like the results of the projection to be such that a viewer regarding the 2D projected points is "fooled" into seeing the original set of 3D points. As we mentioned earlier in Chapter 4, this is our main goal in 3D graphics and is achieved when the seen light rays from the 2D image correspond to the seen light rays from the 3D object. This is called a *planar geometric perspective projection*. We focus exclusively on this form of projection, because it produces 2D images which look realistic, simulating the light rays we would see if we were actually looking at the 3D objects being modeled. Farther objects appear smaller, parallel lines converge on the horizon, parallax is produced, and perspective foreshortening is precisely handled with this type of projection. Perspective projection produces images very similar to those which would be produced by a physical camera viewing a 3D scene, capturing the seen light rays through a lens and recording them on a flat 2D film surface.

Another type of projection which is commonly seen is the *parallel* or *orthographic projection*, which can be useful in situations where the exact measurements of a 3D object must be conveyed in a 2D diagram—in architecture or engineering diagrams, for instance. Other projections include non-planar projections and non-geometric projections, such as the projections onto a curved screen which we mentioned earlier. Again, in this book we focus only on perspective projection, which is all we need to produce realistic 3D images on a flat 2D screen.

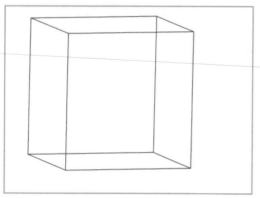

Figure 5-1: Parallel projection of a cube.

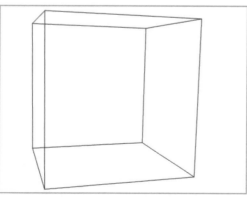

Figure 5-2: Perspective projection of the same cube.

The Inputs and Outputs to the Projection Process

As mentioned above, we may view projection as a conversion process from points in 3D into points in 2D. The 3D points being projected represent the real world being modeled and must be stored in the application program in some sort of data structure—in particular, an l3d_two_part_list containing l3d_coordinate objects, as we saw in Chapter 3 for 2D polygons.

The 3D points form part of the "inputs" to the projection process. A complete list of necessary inputs follows; we discuss each input in detail in the coming sections.

■ 3D points to be transformed

■ Desired horizontal and vertical field of view

■ Pixel width and pixel height of the screen

As "output" come the transformed or projected points in 2D pixel coordinates, ready for plotting on a 2D raster display using the routines of Chapter 3. The projection is done in such a way that the resulting 2D points generate the same seen light rays as if we were actually looking at the original set of 3D points.

Points Form Objects

Until now, we have only talked about projecting 3D points into 2D points. What about more complicated objects such as lines or polygons? For instance, a line in 3D mathematically consists of an infinite number of points. Do we need to project all of these points from 3D into 2D in order to display the line in 2D? Fortunately, the answer is no. The projection of a 3D line into 2D is also a line. Therefore, in order to project a 3D line into 2D, we only need to project the line's 3D endpoints into 2D, then draw a 2D line between the projected endpoints. The proof is shown in Figure 5-3. If we consider the seen light rays for all points lying on the line (using the simplification that only one seen light ray per point is drawn), we notice that all the seen light rays lie within the triangle defined by the three points p_1, p_2, and Eye. Projection, as we will see in the following section, is the mathematical process of calculating intersections between seen light rays and the screen plane. The projection of a line is therefore the intersection between the triangle p_1-p_2-Eye and the screen plane. This intersection is a line, since the triangle lies within a plane, and the intersection of a plane and another plane—the screen in our case—is in general a line. Therefore, the projection of a 3D line into 2D is also a line, and we need only project the endpoints into 2D.

 NOTE The fact that we only project the endpoints of the line from 3D into 2D has a subtle implication—namely, that we only know the real 3D location of the projected endpoints of the line. For each of the 2D pixels lying between the two endpoints, we do not immediately know exactly which point on the original 3D line projects to this 2D pixel, even though we do know that some point on the 3D line must project to the 2D pixel, due to the above proof. The trickiness comes from the fact that the perspective projection is a non-linear mapping from 3D into 2D, meaning that the midpoint of the projected 2D line does not correspond to (i.e., is not the 2D point resulting from the projection of) the midpoint of the original 3D line. More generally, the issue is to non-linearly compute the original pre-projection 3D coordinates for each drawn 2D pixel which does not directly result from a projection operation. The z buffer and texture mapping algorithms require exactly this computation. See the companion book, *Advanced Linux 3D Graphics Programming*, for a detailed discussion of the "reverse projection" issue and its solution in relation to these advanced polygon drawing algorithms.

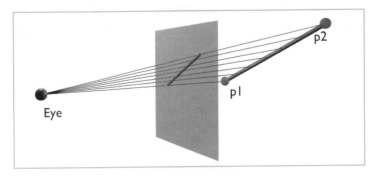

Figure 5-3: Proof that projection of a 3D line is a 2D line. Thin lines indicate seen light rays.

We can use lines to define polygons, and furthermore, we can use polygons to define 3D polyhedra. Therefore, knowing how to project points means knowing how to project lines (by projecting the two corresponding endpoints), how to project polygons (by projecting all the constituent lines), and how to project polyhedra (by projecting all the constituent polygons). This means that point projection is all we need in order to project the entire geometry of an object from 3D into 2D. The last sample program in this chapter illustrates precisely how to use projected points to draw a 3D polygonal object.

3D Coordinate Systems and Vectors

In order to specify 3D points to be projected, we must define a *3D world coordinate system*. A 3D world coordinate system (also called 3D WC) is a means of specifying points belonging to objects in a 3D virtual world. For instance, we might define a wall in our virtual world as being a square polygon. To specify this wall, we would specify its four corner points or vertices as 3D coordinates: for instance, these vertices might be located at the four points (0,0,50), (0,100,50), (100,100,50), and (100,0,50). Specifying these points is the way that 3D programs define the virtual world which is then projected onto the 2D screen for display. Through the projection process, we see the objects we have modeled in the 3D world coordinate system. Note that the units in 3D WC are irrelevant to the projection process itself; you can use any units which are convenient for the virtual world being modeled. If you are modeling microscopic objects, microns might be a good choice; if you are modeling houses and cars, meters or feet might be good choices. As long as your 3D WC units are consistent throughout your program, it is unimportant what these units actually are—at least for the projection process.

NOTE Although the 3D WC units are irrelevant for the projection process itself, they may very well be relevant for a realistic physical simulation. An object moving 3 mm/second should have quite a different impact upon collision than an object moving 3 km/second. In this case you simply need to convert whatever units you are using for 3D WC into the appropriate units for the physics equation being used to simulate the physical behavior.

Points in 3D are conceptually specified by an ordered triple of the form (x,y,z), where x represents displacement along the x axis, y represents displacement along the y axis, and the new coordinate z represents displacement along the (as-of-yet undefined) z axis. We define a fixed point, the 3D origin, which has coordinates $(0,0,0)$, the intersection point of all three axes. The point (x,y,z) is located by starting at the origin, moving x units along the x axis, y units along the y axis, and z units along the z axis. It is useful to think of the x axis as corresponding to length, the y axis as height, and the z axis as depth.

Similar to the different approaches seen in Chapter 2 for specifying 2D coordinates, where we had to decide in which direction the axes pointed relative to one another, there are also different approaches for specifying 3D coordinates. These are known as *right-handed 3D Cartesian coordinates* and *left-handed 3D Cartesian coordinates*, illustrated in Figures 5-4 and 5-5, respectively. In this book we use left-handed coordinates.

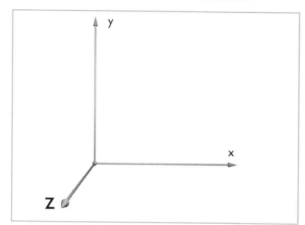

Figure 5-4: Right-handed 3D coordinate system. The z axis comes out of the page.

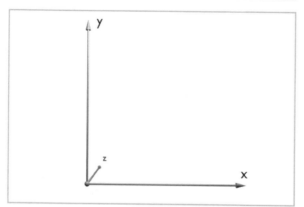

Figure 5-5: Left-handed 3D coordinate system. The z axis goes into the page.

The difference between left-handed and right-handed coordinate systems lies in how we choose to define the orientation of the z axis in relation to the orientation of the x and y axes. The relationship is mathematically expressed by using a concept called the *vector cross product*. Interpreting the cross product geometrically can be done by observing the physical relationship between fingers on your left or your right hand, which leads to the terms left-handed and right-handed. We return to this topic of "handedness" after discussing the cross product.

Let us, therefore, now take a brief detour to discuss vectors and mathematical operations defined on vectors. Vectors play an important role in all parts of 3D graphics, so an understanding of their definition and use is vital. Then, by using vectors, we can mathematically define the difference between left-handed and right-handed coordinate systems.

Definition of Vectors

Mathematically, a vector in n-dimensional space is simply a list of n numbers, also called an n-tuple. In 2D space a vector is a 2-tuple of the form (v_1, v_2). In 3D space a vector is a 3-tuple, or triple, of the form (v_1, v_2, v_3). In 4D space, a vector is a 4-tuple (v_1, v_2, v_3, v_4). The components of the vector, in contrast to the components of a point, do not represent a location in space, but rather a displacement in space.

Conceptually, a vector is a directed displacement in space, such as "3 kilometers southwest." A vector has a magnitude (length) and a direction. In this example, the magnitude of the vector is 3 kilometers; the direction is southwest. Informally, we may think of a vector as an "arrow" with a particular length and which points a particular direction. The position of the arrow in space is irrelevant; only the magnitude and the direction define the vector.

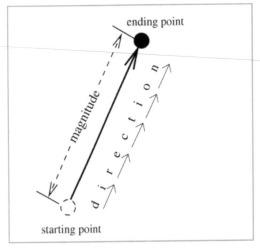

Figure 5-6: A vector represents magnitude and displacement in a particular direction.

Even though a vector itself has no location, it may be defined by two locations, or points, in 3D space. In fact, this is very often the case in 3D graphics, for reasons having to do with transforming vectors (Chapter 6). When using two points, we then define the vector as the directed distance from the first point to the second point. The first point may be thought of as the "starting point" for the vector; the second, the "ending point." These would correspond to the base and tip of the arrow. Given a starting and an ending point, we obtain the vector between them by subtracting the starting point from the ending point (the next section describes the exact meaning of "subtracting two points"). Equivalently, given a starting point and a vector, we arrive at the ending point by adding the vector to the starting point. This reinforces the idea that a vector is a directed displacement; by adding a displacement of the proper magnitude and direction to the starting point, we arrive exactly at the ending point. See Figure 5-7.

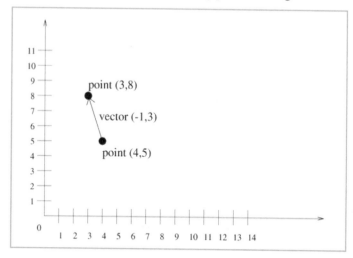

Figure 5-7: The vector (–1,3) as defined by the starting point (4,5) and ending point (3,8). Adding the vector (–1,3) to the starting point (4,5) gives us the ending point (–1+4, 5+3) or (3,8). Equivalently, subtracting the starting point from the ending point gives us the vector.

Two vectors are said to be equal if their magnitude and direction are identical. In Figure 5-8, the two thicker vectors are equal, since their magnitudes and directions are identical. Even though the starting and ending points for each of the two thick vectors are different, the magnitude and direction are identical, meaning that the vectors are identical. The other vectors are not equal to the thicker vectors, because their direction or size are different.

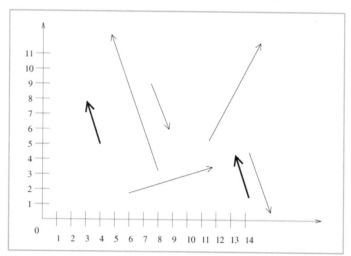

Figure 5-8: Various vectors in 2D space. The two thick vectors are equal, since their magnitudes and directions are equal. All other vectors are not equal to the thick vectors or each other.

We use vectors in mathematical formulas to represent simultaneously magnitude (length of the arrow, or distance between the two points) and direction (the path from the arrow's base or first point to its tip or second point). For instance, in 3D graphics, vectors may be used to indicate the direction in 3D space that the eye is pointing (see Chapter 6), the direction and intensity of light falling on a surface (see the companion book *Advanced Linux 3D Graphics Programming*), or the velocity (speed and direction) of a particular moving object.

Adding and Subtracting Vectors and Points

Points define location in 3D space. Vectors define directed displacement of a particular size. Points and vectors may be added or subtracted in a number of ways, but not all ways make sense.

First, let's discuss those combinations that do make sense. Adding two vectors gives a combined displacement vector which would result if we applied each vector separately to a point. For instance, a vector moving 2 kilometers west may be added to a vector moving 2 kilometers south to yield a vector moving 2 kilometers southwest. Mathematically, given vector $v=(v_1,v_2,v_3)$ and $w=(w_1,w_2,w_3)$, we define the new vector $v+w$ as follows:

Equation 5-1 $$vector\ v + vector\ w = (v_1, v_2, v_3) + (w_1, w_2, w_3) = (v_1 + w_1, v_2 + w_2, v_3 + w_3)$$

In other words, we simply add the components of each vector to one another. You can think of vector addition as the application of the first vector's displacement followed by the application of the second vector's displacement. Geometrically, if you place the base of vector v at the tip of vector w, you arrive at the tip of the vector $v+w$.

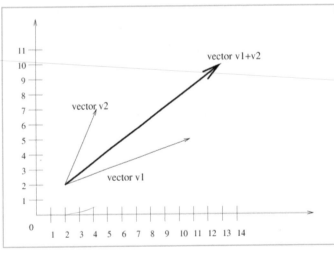

Figure 5-9: Addition of two vectors yields a combined vector. The two thin vectors combine to yield the thick vector.

Subtracting a vector from another vector can be thought of as adding its negative. So, given vector $v=(v_1,v_2,v_3)$ and $w=(w_1,w_2,w_3)$, then the new vector $v-w$ is:

Equation 5-2 $$vector\ v - vector\ w = (v_1, v_2, v_3) - (w_1, w_2, w_3) = (v_1 - w_1, v_2 - w_2, v_3 - w_3)$$

Adding a vector to a point gives a new point which is offset in the direction and magnitude specified by the vector. Mathematically, given point $p=(x_1,y_1,z_1)$ and vector $v=(v_1,v_2,v_3)$, then the new point $p+v$ is located at absolute position defined by:

Equation 5-3 $$point\ p + vector\ v = (x_1, y_1, z_1) + (v_1, v_2, v_3) = (x_1 + v_1, y_1 + v_2, z_1 + v_3)$$

Adding a vector to a point is the same thing as adding a point to a vector.

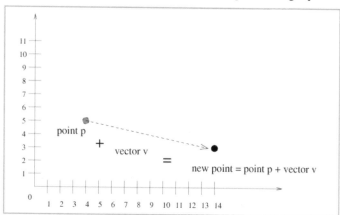

Figure 5-10: Addition of a vector and a point yields a new point.

Subtracting a vector from a point can again be thought of as adding the negative vector to the point. So, given point $p=(x_1,y_1,z_1)$ and vector $v=(v_1,v_2,v_3)$, then new point $p-v$ is located at absolute position given by:

Equation 5-4 $point \; p - vector \; v = (x_1, y_1, z_1) - (v_1, v_2, v_3) = (x_1 - v_1, y_1 - v_2, z_1 - v_3)$

Subtracting one point from another point gives the directed distance between the points—in other words, it gives us the *vector* from the first point to the second point. Mathematically, given point

Equation 5-5 $\begin{aligned} point \; p_2 - point \; p_1 &= (x_2, y_2, z_2) - (x_1, y_1, z_1) \\ &= (x_2 - x_1, y_2 - y_1, z_2 - z_1) \end{aligned}$

$p_1=(x_1,y_1,z_1)$ and point $p_2=(x_2,y_2,z_2)$, then the vector p_2-p_1 is given by:

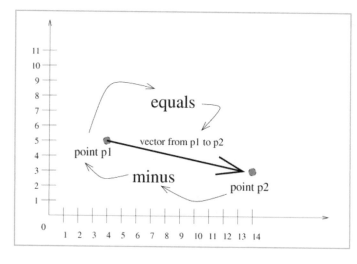

Figure 5-11: Subtracting point p_2 from point p_1 gives the vector from p_1 to p_2.

This is the vector from p_1 to p_2. Notice that we subtract the starting point from the ending point to get the vector from the starting point to the ending point.

Combinations that do not make sense are: adding two points, or subtracting a point from a vector. Neither one of these operations has any physical meaning, and so these operations are undefined.

Notice that both vectors and points are represented as (x,y,z) triples. However, it is very important to distinguish between points and vectors! Just by looking, there is no way to tell if a particular triple (x,y,z) represents a point (an absolute location) or a vector (a relative displacement). It all depends on the context. (Chapter 6 discusses the concept of homogeneous coordinates, where we introduce a fourth coordinate to 3D points and 3D vectors, which then does indeed allow a mathematical distinction between points and vectors.) If, for instance, a formula or a piece of program code is computing vector cross products (a topic covered later in this chapter), it will (or had better) be manipulating the (x,y,z) triples as vectors, meaning that all values are relative displacements. If in another context points are being computed to determine the location of an object, then the (x,y,z) triples must be interpreted as absolute locations. We attempt to avoid this confusion in C++ code by declaring separate classes for points and vectors, with carefully defined point-vector operations as described above. But in mathematical notation, both points and vectors are just tuples of numbers whose interpretation depends on the context. If you are ever confused as to whether you are or should be dealing with a vector or a point, then the relevant question to ask is, "Is this value a relative displacement or an absolute location?"

The Relationship Between Points and Vectors

Although points and vectors are separate concepts, we should, however, note the following relationship between points and vectors: for a given point location (x,y,z), the vector displacement (x,y,z) will arrive at exactly this point location, assuming we start at the origin $(0,0,0)$. In other words, we can reach point (x,y,z) by starting at point $(0,0,0)$ and moving along the vector (x,y,z). This vector displacement, like all vectors, can be defined by a starting point and an ending point: the starting point of the vector is $(0,0,0)$; the ending point is (x,y,z). The vector between any two points is, as we saw earlier, simply the difference between the ending and the starting points: in this case, $(x-0,y-0,z-0)=(x,y,z)$.

In fact, our very definition of the location of a point relies on vector math. What is the meaning of point (x,y,z)? It means we start at the origin of our coordinate system $(0,0,0)$, move x units along the x axis, y units along the y axis, and z units along the z axis. This movement is a vector displacement of (x,y,z) from the origin! In this sense, points and vectors are closely related yet distinct concepts.

Some 3D texts might appear to refer interchangeably to a tuple (x,y,z) as both a point and a vector. This can be slightly confusing, but it is important to understand whether a point or a vector is required within the context of the immediate problem. Again, a point is a location; a vector is a displacement; the relationship is that the point can define the tip of a vector whose starting point is the origin $(0,0,0)$. In this book, I have done my best to avoid indiscriminately interchanging points and vectors and to explicitly state whenever the focus of the discussion changes from a point to a vector or vice versa.

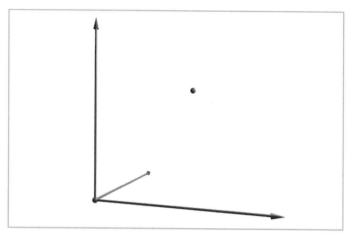

Figure 5-12: The 3D point (6,8,6). It is located at absolute position x=6, y=8, z=6.

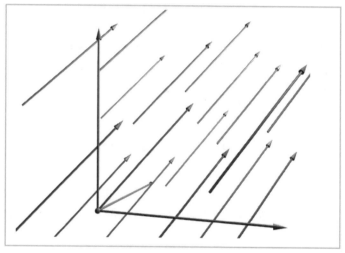

Figure 5-13: The 3D vector (6,8,6). It is a displacement of 6 units in the x direction, 8 units in the y direction, and 6 units in the z direction. The vector has a direction and a magnitude, but no location. Therefore, all of the vectors shown in this figure are examples of the vector (6,8,6), since they all have equal magnitude and direction.

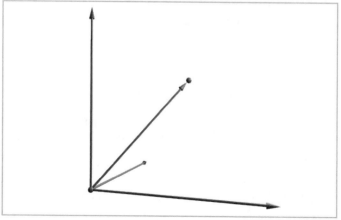

Figure 5-14: One particular instance of the vector (6,8,6), which is defined by two points: the point (0,0,0) and the point (6,8,6). This vector starts at the origin and ends at the point whose coordinates are equal to the vector displacement.

Multiplying a Vector by a Scalar

We have just seen how the concepts of addition and subtraction apply to vectors and points. Vectors also may be multiplied in a number of different ways. The first way is to multiply a vector by a *scalar*. A scalar is simply a single number, as opposed to a tuple of numbers. The product of a vector and a scalar is again a vector. Specifically, given vector $v=(v_1,v_2,v_3)$ and scalar s, the equation is:

Equation 5-6 $vector\ v\cdot scalar\ s = (v_1, v_2, v_3)\cdot s = (s\cdot v_1, s\cdot v_2, s\cdot v_3)$

In other words, we simply multiply each component of the vector by the scalar. For instance:

Equation 5-7 $vector\ (3,7,5)\cdot scalar\ 2 = (6,14,10)$

The vector is thus "scaled" by the scalar amount. If, for instance, the vector represents a velocity, we can use vector-scalar multiplication to increase or decrease the velocity.

Multiplying a Vector by a Vector: the Dot Product

Another way of multiplying vectors is the *vector dot product*. The dot product is a binary operation taking two vectors and giving a scalar as a result. The dot product between vector v and vector w is written $v{\bullet}w$ and is read "v dot w." If $v=(v_1,v_2,v_3)$ and $w=(w_1,w_2,w_3)$, then the dot product $v{\bullet}w$ is:

Equation 5-8 $vector\ v\cdot vector\ w = (v_1, v_2, v_3)\cdot(w_1, w_2, w_3) = (v_1 w_1 + v_2 w_2 + v_3 w_3)$

In other words, we simply multiply each component of the first vector by the corresponding component of the second vector, and add all such products together. Again, notice that the final result is not a vector, but rather a scalar. The dot product is symmetric; in other words, $v{\bullet}w$ is the same as $w{\bullet}v$.

 NOTE Unfortunately, standard mathematical notation allows the dot symbol to represent both regular multiplication of two scalars with one another, as well as the vector dot product. Therefore, if you see the dot symbol, you should not immediately assume that the vector dot product is intended. As with points and vectors, it depends on the context: if vectors are being multiplied with the dot operator, then the vector dot product is indeed meant. But, if any of the quantities involved are scalars, then a scalar multiplication is meant. Incidentally, the other obvious choices for a symbol to represent scalar multiplication would be the cross symbol ×, used in grade-school texts, or the star symbol *, often used in computer texts. But both of these symbols also have other mathematical meanings (cross product and convolution), so there really is no completely context-independent way of uniquely writing scalar multiplication. Often, when the context allows it, a scalar multiplication of two quantities a and b is simply written ab, with no symbol. This is also standard mathematical convention, but has the disadvantage—especially in computer texts, where multi-character variables are the norm—that it might look like the single quantity named "ab" is meant, rather than the product of the quantities "a" and "b."

The dot product has several useful properties: it can define distance between two points as well as the angle between two vectors. Let's explore these properties a bit more closely, as we use them extensively later.

The Dot Product and the Concept of Length

In 2D, we can use the Pythagorean theorem to determine the length of a line segment going from point (x_0, y_0) to (x_1, y_1). The Pythagorean theorem states that for a right triangle with sides of length a and b and a hypotenuse of length c, the following equation holds:

Equation 5-9 $c^2 = a^2 + b^2$

Or equivalently:

Equation 5-10 $c = \sqrt{a^2 + b^2}$

In other words, the length of the hypotenuse, c, is the square root of the sum of the squares of the lengths of the sides. If we consider the line segment from (x_0, y_0) to (x_1, y_1) to be the hypotenuse of a right triangle, then applying the Pythagorean theorem yields:

Equation 5-11 $dist\ between\ (x_0, y_0)\ and\ (x_1, y_1) = \sqrt{(x_1 - x_0)^2 + (y_1 - y_0)^2}$

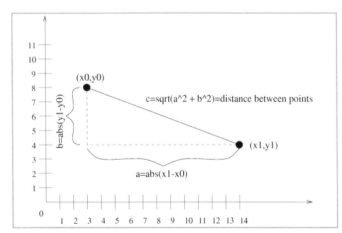

Figure 5-15: Using the Pythagorean theorem to compute distance. The distance to be computed is viewed as the hypotenuse of a right triangle, of which the lengths of the sides are known.

Now, consider the vector from (x_0, y_0) to (x_1, y_1). This vector is, according to the point subtraction rule defined earlier, (x_1-x_0, y_1-y_0). Furthermore, consider the dot product of this vector with itself:

Equation 5-12 $(x_1 - x_0, y_1 - y_0) \cdot (x_1 - x_0, y_1 - y_0)$
$$= (x_1 - x_0)(x_1 - x_0) + (y_1 - y_0)(y_1 - y_0)$$
$$= (x_1 - x_0)^2 + (y_1 - y_0)^2$$

Interestingly, this is the square of the distance. In other words, the distance between two points is the square root of the dot product of the vector v, where v is the vector from the first point to the second point.

Equation 5-13 $dist\ between\ points\ p_1\ and\ p_2 = \sqrt{(p_2 - p_1) \cdot (p_2 - p_1)}$

Remember that subtracting two points yields a vector; it is for this reason that we can use the dot product operation on the vector (p_2-p_1).

We can also use these results to find the result of an arbitrary vector, independently of any points which might have been used to define the vector. The length of an arbitrary vector is the square root of the vector dotted with itself. A vector's length is also called its *magnitude* and is written $|v|$.

Equation 5-14 $$length\ of\ vector\ \ v = |v| = \sqrt{v \cdot v}$$

These formulas hold not only in 2D, but also in 3D. We compute the length of a vector in 3D by taking the 3D dot product of the vector with itself and taking the square root. Similarly, the distance between two known points in 3D is computed by finding the 3D vector between the two points, taking the dot product of this vector with itself, and taking the square root.

A common operation in 3D graphics is to compare two distances, to see which is greater. To do this, we could compute the distances by using the formula above, taking the square root of the dot product for each displacement vector, then comparing the resulting distances. While this works perfectly, it is more work than is necessary; we can actually skip the square root operation and save some computation time if we are only interested in the relative comparison of the distances. In this case, we can simply compute the dot of the first vector with itself, and compare this with the dot of the second vector with itself. This means we are comparing squared distances instead of actual distances. But the relationship between the two distances (first longer than second, or second longer than first) remains the same even if we do not perform the square root operation; often, all we are interested in is the relationship between distances, and not the actual distances.

The Dot Product and Unit Vectors

A *unit vector* is a vector whose length is exactly one. Unit vectors simplify some formulas involving vectors; if we know that the length is one, we can sometimes omit certain calculations. Given a vector of arbitrary length, we can scale it to become a unit vector by dividing all of its elements by the length of the vector. This process is called *normalizing a vector*. The length of the vector is, of course, computed by using the dot product. Mathematically, given vector $v=(v_1,v_2,v_3)$, the normalized vector is:

Equation 5-15 $$\left(\frac{v_1}{|v|}, \frac{v_2}{|v|}, \frac{v_3}{|v|}\right)$$

The normalized vector points in the same direction as the original vector; only its length is changed.

The Dot Product and the Concept of Angle

An alternate definition of the dot product involves the angle between the vectors. Given vectors v and w, we can also define the dot product to be:

Equation 5-16 $$v \cdot w = |v|\,|w| \cos \theta$$

where θ is the angle between the two vectors. Recall from trigonometry the important points along the curve of the cosine function:

Equation 5-17
$$\begin{aligned}
\cos(0°) &= 1.0 \\
\cos(90°) &= 0.0 \\
\cos(180°) &= -1.0 \\
\cos(270°) &= 0.0 \\
\cos(360°) &= 1.0
\end{aligned}$$

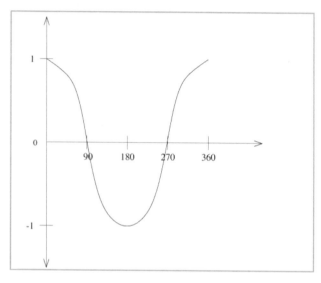

Figure 5-16: The cosine function.

Rearranging the formula allows us to solve for θ, the angle between the vectors:

Equation 5-18 $\theta = \cos^{-1}(\dfrac{v \cdot w}{|v| \, |w|})$

Recall that $\cos^{-1}(x)$ is the inverse cosine function, and should be read "the angle whose cosine is x." Notice that if v and w are normalized, then the division is unnecessary since both vector lengths are one.

Often, we don't need to perform the inverse cosine operation. For instance, to determine if two vectors are perpendicular, we simply need to check if the dot product is zero. Furthermore, for some operations it is enough to know just the sign and not the value of the dot product. The sign by itself allows us to classify whether the angle θ is between 90-270 degrees (negative dot product) or if the angle is between 0-90 or 270-360 degrees (positive dot product), without going through the trouble of computing the actual angle with an inverse cosine. For instance, the 3D operation of back-face culling uses the sign of the dot product (see the companion book *Advanced Linux 3D Graphics Programming* for details). Furthermore, the side_of_point function from Chapter 3 also uses the sign of the dot product as an angle test. In Chapter 3, we postponed the explanation of the workings of the function. Now let's look at it again in detail.

The Dot Product and the side_of_point Function

Recall in Chapter 3 that the class `l3d_polygon_2d` introduced a function `side_of_point` used in 2D polygon clipping. This function takes as input a point to be tested and two endpoints of a line segment. The function returns a positive value if the point is on the inside side of the edge and a negative value of the point is outside. (Refer to Chapter 3 for precise definitions of the "inside side" and "outside side" of a polygon edge.)

With the dot product, we can now understand exactly how the function `side_of_point` works. First, we compute a vector which is perpendicular to the segment and which points inside the segment. This can be done starting at the segment's starting point and by swapping the x and y displacements to arrive at a new ending point. For instance, in Figure 5-17, the edge goes from point p_1 to point p_2, moving a distance of dx horizontally and dy vertically. To compute the inward-pointing vector perpendicular to this edge, we again start at p_1, but move a distance of $-dy$ *horizontally* and a distance of dx *vertically*, thereby swapping the x and y displacements. The vector from point p_1 to this new point is the inward-pointing vector perpendicular to the edge. To verify that the new vector is indeed perpendicular, notice that the dot product of the perpendicular vector with the vector from p_1 to p_2 is zero.

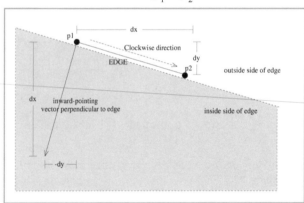

Figure 5-17: Computing an inward-pointing 2D vector perpendicular to an edge, by swapping the x and y displacements. Note that the coordinates are 2D pixel coordinates; x increases to the right, and y increases downward.

Next, we compute the vector from the first point of the edge p_1 to the point being tested.

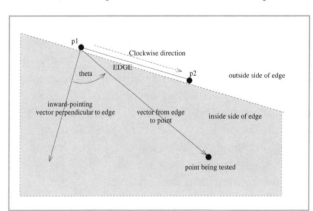

Figure 5-18: Computing the vector from the first point of the edge to the point being tested.

The angle θ is the angle between the perpendicular vector and the edge-point vector. Observe that θ will be between 0-90 degrees or 270-360 degrees if the point is on the inside side of the edge; conversely, θ will be between 90-270 degrees if the point is on the outside side of the edge. Using our knowledge of where the cosine function is positive and negative, we can further observe that the cosine of θ will be positive if the point is inside of the edge, and negative if the point is outside of the edge. Finally, using the definition of the dot product in terms of the cosine (Equation 5-16), we see that the sign of the dot product (positive or negative) is always the same as the sign of the cosine term (since the first two terms, being vector lengths, will always be positive).

In other words, if the sign of the dot product is positive, the point is inside the edge. If the sign of the dot product is negative, the point is outside the edge. This is why the `side_of_point` function works.

The important thing to notice here is how we managed to specify the problem "on which side of an edge is the point located?" in terms of carefully constructed vectors and a dot product. Chapter 7 extends this same concept to 3D; polygon clipping in 3D requires us to ask on which side of a plane a 3D point is located.

The Dot Product and the Concept of Vector Projection

From the preceding sections, we know that the dot product of two vectors can be expressed as the product of their magnitudes and the cosine of the angle between them. If one of the vectors is a unit vector, the dot product represents the length of the projection of the non-unit vector onto the unit vector.

Figure 5-19 illustrates the concept of vector projection. To project vector w onto vector v, we "drop" a line from the tip of w down to v, so that the dropped line intersects v at a right angle. Then, the portion of v up until the intersection is the projection of w into v.

More abstractly, the projection of vector w onto vector v answers the question, "how much of the direction represented by vector w is in the direction represented by vector v?" You can also think of the projection as the "shadow" cast by w onto v, assuming the light source is infinitely far

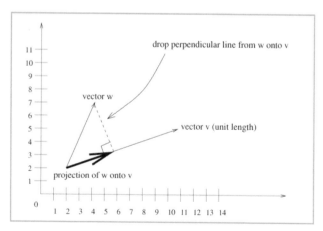

Figure 5-19: The projection of one vector onto another.

away and emitting light rays exactly perpendicular to v.

From trigonometry we can deduce that the projection of w onto v in Figure 5-19 is the cosine of the angle between w and v, multiplied by the original length of w. (Trigonometrically, the cosine is defined as length of the adjacent edge divided by the length of the hypotenuse, so the length of the adjacent edge (the projection) is the length of the hypotenuse (w) times the cosine.) And if vector v has length one, then this is the same as the dot product between v and w.

Therefore: if v is a unit vector and w is any vector, then $v \cdot w$ is the length of the projection of w onto v.

Multiplying a Vector by a Vector: the Cross Product

A final way to multiply two vectors is the vector *cross product*. The cross product multiplies two vectors and returns another vector as a result. This is in contrast to the dot product, which yields a scalar. Mathematically the cross product of vector $v=(v_1,v_2,v_3)$ and $w=(w_1,w_2,w_3)$ is the vector defined as follows:

Equation 5-19 $\quad v \times w = (v_2 w_3 - v_3 w_2, \, v_3 w_1 - v_1 w_3, \, v_1 w_2 - v_2 w_1)$

The symbol $\times$ represents the cross product and is read "cross," as in "v cross w." (The derivation of the cross product, since it involves matrices and determinants, is covered in Chapter 6.) The magnitude of the resulting vector is:

Equation 5-20 $\quad |v \times w| = |v| \, |w| \sin \theta$

θ is the angle between the two vectors. Compare this with the dot product, which returned a scalar equal to $|v||w|\cos\theta$. Remember, though, that the cross product returns a vector; the dot product is simply a scalar.

The cross product has an important geometrical interpretation. Given two vectors v and w in 3D space, these two vectors will, in general, lie within a unique plane. (If the two vectors lie on top of one another, then they lie within a line, which is then contained by an infinite number of planes.) For now, we define a *plane* as an infinite, thin, flat surface with arbitrary orientation in 3D space; Chapter 7 presents the mathematical definition, which relies upon the dot product. The cross product of v and w has the property that it defines a vector in 3D space which is perpendicular to the plane containing v and w. We also use the term normal to refer to the concept of 3D perpendicularity, as in, "the normal vector to a plane."

 NOTE Do not confuse a normalized vector, whose length is one, with a normal vector, which is perpendicular to a particular surface. A normal vector, like any other vector, is normalized if its length is one. And any vector, regardless of whether it is a normal vector or not, can be normalized by scaling it to a length of one. Thus, vector normalization, which deals with the length of a vector, has nothing to do with normal vectors, which deal with the relationship of a vector to a surface.

As an example, imagine two vectors, one horizontal and one vertical, lying on the sheet of paper you are now reading. Such vectors could lie along the x and y axes in Figures 5-5 and 5-4. Call the horizontal vector x, call the vertical vector y, and call the cross product of x and y the vector z. Vector z will be normal to the plane of the sheet of paper in which x and y lie. But z can have two possible orientations. z can point out of the paper, as in Figure 5-4, in which case we name the coordinate system xyz a *right-handed* coordinate system. Or, vector z can point into the paper, as in Figure 5-5, in which case we call the coordinate system xyz a *left-handed* coordinate system.

Left-handed and Right-handed Coordinate Systems

We use the terms left-handed coordinate system and right-handed coordinate system because we may use either our left hand or our right hand to determine the orientation of the vector cross product. Consider a left-handed coordinate system as an example. If we have a vector x and a vector y, the direction of the cross product is determined as follows. Lay your left hand along the x vector such that the base of your left hand is at the base of the vector x, and the fingertips of your left hand point towards the tip of the vector x. The open palm of your left hand must face in the same direction that vector y points, so that if you curl your fingers towards your palm, the fingers curl towards vector y. Then, the direction in which your left thumb points is the direction of the cross product. For right-handed coordinates, you use your right hand in the above procedure. Notice that for two given vectors, the cross product in left-handed coordinates points in the opposite direction as compared with right-handed coordinates. Also, unlike the dot product, the cross product is not symmetric: $x \times y$ is not the same as $y \times x$; in particular, $x \times y = -(y \times x)$.

We choose to use left-handed coordinates for the following reason. In order to develop the mathematics of perspective projection in the following sections, we begin with a simplified "standard" eye location and orientation—namely, with the eye located at the 3D origin, looking straight down the z axis, and perfectly right-side-up. As we see later, this corresponds to aligning the 3D x and y axes with the screen's horizontal and vertical directions. The positive z axis then points into the screen, moving away from the viewer. This is a natural interpretation, since increasing values of z correspond to increasing distance from the viewer. In a right-handed system, increasing z would represent decreasing distance from the viewer. Thus we have chosen a left-handed 3D coordinate system.

 NOTE Literature in the field of mathematics typically uses a right-handed coordinate system. Also, 3D modeling packages or libraries vary as to the preferred coordinate system—some left-handed, some right-handed. Furthermore, some 3D libraries (such as SGI's Performer, or the CAVELib for programming CAVE applications) have the z axis pointing vertically upward, with the y axis pointing forward away from the viewer. The choice of which coordinate system to use is arbitrary, but should be consistent within a program. In Chapter 6, we see how to use matrices to convert between arbitrary coordinate systems, should the need arise.

The l3d_vector Class

With all this talk of vectors, let's now look at the C++ class which implements vectors. We also look at a simple program which adds and subtracts vectors and points. This program doesn't display any graphics; it merely serves to reinforce the fundamental vector concepts and the relationship between vectors and points. The next sample program, called `dots`, uses vectors to control the movement of dots in various ways.

The class `l3d_vector` defines a vector having four components, just as the class `l3d_point` from Chapter 3 defined a point having four components. This means that our vectors can represent displacements in 1D, 2D, 3D, or 4D space, depending on how many components of the vector we choose to use. The operators defined in class `l3d_vector` implement quite straightforwardly the mathematical operations on vectors and points described in the previous sections.

Listing 5-1: `vector.h`

```
#ifndef __VECTOR_H
#define __VECTOR_H
#include "../tool_os/memman.h"

#include <math.h>
#include <stdio.h>
#include "../system/sys_dep.h"
#include "math_fix.h"
#include "sincos.h"
#include "../geom/point/point.h"

class l3d_vector {
  public:

    l3d_vector(void);
    l3d_vector(l3d_real a0, l3d_real a1, l3d_real a2, l3d_real a3);
    l3d_vector(int a0, int a1, int a2, int a3);
    const l3d_vector &set(l3d_real a0, l3d_real a1, l3d_real a2, l3d_real a3);
    const l3d_vector &set(int a0, int a1, int a2, int a3);

    void print(void)
    {
      printf("%f %f %f %f",
             l3d_real_to_float(a[0]),
             l3d_real_to_float(a[1]),
             l3d_real_to_float(a[2]),
             l3d_real_to_float(a[3]));
    }
    l3d_real a[4];
};

//- useful defines for accessing matrix elements occurring in standard
//- positions for l3d_vector:
#define X_ a[0]
#define Y_ a[1]
#define Z_ a[2]
#define W_ a[3]

#define U_ a[0]
#define V_ a[1]
#define N_ a[2]

//- function for grabbing a temporary vector object from a global
//- pre-allocated pool of temporary objects.
extern l3d_vector &l3d_get_vector_temp(void);

inline l3d_vector::l3d_vector(void) {
  a[0] = a[1] = a[2] = a[3] = 0;
}
```

```
inline l3d_vector::l3d_vector(l3d_real a0, l3d_real a1, l3d_real a2, l3d_real a3) {
  a[0] = a0;
  a[1] = a1;
  a[2] = a2;
  a[3] = a3;
}

inline l3d_vector::l3d_vector(int a0, int a1, int a2, int a3) {
  a[0] = int_to_l3d_real(a0);
  a[1] = int_to_l3d_real(a1);
  a[2] = int_to_l3d_real(a2);
  a[3] = int_to_l3d_real(a3);
}

inline const l3d_vector &l3d_vector::set(l3d_real a0, l3d_real a1, l3d_real a2, l3d_real a3) {
  a[0] = a0;
  a[1] = a1;
  a[2] = a2;
  a[3] = a3;

  return *this;
}

inline const l3d_vector &l3d_vector::set(int a0, int a1, int a2, int a3) {
  a[0] = int_to_l3d_real(a0);
  a[1] = int_to_l3d_real(a1);
  a[2] = int_to_l3d_real(a2);
  a[3] = int_to_l3d_real(a3);

  return *this;
}

inline const l3d_vector &operator * (const l3d_vector& l,
                                     const l3d_real aScalar)
{
  l3d_vector &res = l3d_get_vector_temp();
  res.set(
    l3d_mulrr(l.a[0], /* TIMES */ aScalar),
    l3d_mulrr(l.a[1], /* TIMES */ aScalar),
    l3d_mulrr(l.a[2], /* TIMES */ aScalar),
    l3d_mulrr(l.a[3], /* TIMES */ aScalar));

  return res;
}

inline const l3d_vector& cross(const l3d_vector &l, const l3d_vector &r) {
  l3d_vector &res = l3d_get_vector_temp();

  #define V(q) l.a[(q-1)]
  #define W(q) r.a[(q-1)]

  res.set(
    l3d_mulrr(V(2),W(3)) - l3d_mulrr(V(3),W(2)),
    l3d_mulrr(V(3),W(1)) - l3d_mulrr(V(1),W(3)),
    l3d_mulrr(V(1),W(2)) - l3d_mulrr(V(2),W(1)),
    int_to_l3d_real(0) );

  #undef V
  #undef W
```

```
    return res;
}

inline const l3d_real dot(const l3d_vector &l, const l3d_vector &r) {
  return l3d_mulrr(l.a[0],r.a[0])
       + l3d_mulrr(l.a[1],r.a[1])
       + l3d_mulrr(l.a[2],r.a[2])
       + l3d_mulrr(l.a[3],r.a[3]) ;


}

inline const l3d_vector& normalized(const l3d_vector &l) {
  l3d_vector &res = l3d_get_vector_temp();
  l3d_real    mm_vec_magnitude;

  mm_vec_magnitude = l3d_sqrt( dot(l,l) );

  if ((mm_vec_magnitude > float_to_l3d_real(0.01))
      || (mm_vec_magnitude < float_to_l3d_real(-0.01)))
  {

    res.set(
      l3d_divrr(l.a[0],mm_vec_magnitude),
      l3d_divrr(l.a[1],mm_vec_magnitude),
      l3d_divrr(l.a[2],mm_vec_magnitude),
      l3d_divrr(l.a[3],mm_vec_magnitude));
  }

  return res;
}

inline const l3d_vector& operator + (const l3d_vector &l,
                                     const l3d_vector &right)
{
  l3d_vector& res = l3d_get_vector_temp();
  res.set(
    l.X_ + right.X_,
    l.Y_ + right.Y_,
    l.Z_ + right.Z_,
    l.W_ + right.W_);
  return res;
}

inline const l3d_vector& operator - (const l3d_vector &l,
                                     const l3d_vector &right)
{
  l3d_vector& res = l3d_get_vector_temp();
  res.set(
    l.X_ - right.X_,
    l.Y_ - right.Y_,
    l.Z_ - right.Z_,
    l.W_ - right.W_);

  return res;
}

inline const l3d_point& operator + (const l3d_point &l,
                                    const l3d_vector &right)
{
  l3d_point& res = l3d_get_point_temp();
```

```
        res.set(
          l.X_ + right.X_,
          l.Y_ + right.Y_,
          l.Z_ + right.Z_,
          l.W_ + right.W_);

        return res;
      }

      inline const l3d_point& operator + (const l3d_vector &l,
                                          const l3d_point &right)
      {
        l3d_point& res = l3d_get_point_temp();
        res.set(
          l.X_ + right.X_,
          l.Y_ + right.Y_,
          l.Z_ + right.Z_,
          l.W_ + right.W_);

        return res;
      }

      inline const l3d_vector& operator - (const l3d_point &l,
                                           const l3d_point &right)
      {
        l3d_vector& res = l3d_get_vector_temp();
        res.set(
          l.X_ - right.X_,
          l.Y_ - right.Y_,
          l.Z_ - right.Z_,
          l.W_ - right.W_);

        return res;
      }

      inline const l3d_point& operator - (const l3d_point &l,
                                          const l3d_vector &right)
      {
        l3d_point& res = l3d_get_point_temp();
        res.set(
          l.X_ - right.X_,
          l.Y_ - right.Y_,
          l.Z_ - right.Z_,
          l.W_ - right.W_);

        return res;
      }

      #endif
```

Listing 5-2: `vector.cc`

```
      #include "vector.h"
      #include "../tool_os/memman.h"

      //- Global pool of temporary variables for vector operations.

      const int l3d_max_vector_temp = 15;
      l3d_vector &l3d_get_vector_temp(void) {
        static int nbuf=0;
```

```
      static l3d_vector buf[l3d_max_vector_temp];

      if(nbuf>=l3d_max_vector_temp) nbuf=0;
      return buf[nbuf++];
    }
```

One interesting feature of the overloaded operators for the `l3d_vector` (and `l3d_point`) class is the way that they allocate new intermediate objects to return. In general, an overloaded binary operator operating on a particular class needs to return a new object reflecting the result of the operation. For instance, the expression `(a+b)*c` requires two intermediates: one to hold the result of `a+b` and one to hold the final result of `(a+b)*c`.

One way to return new objects from overloaded binary operators is to declare the return type of the operator to be of the desired class and having the final `return` statement in the function body return an object of the desired type, which then automatically gets duplicated via the copy constructor and returned as a new intermediate object to the calling function. The compiler automatically generates code to allocate, copy, and destroy such intermediate objects, making use of overloaded operators quite natural. The problem with this is that complicated expressions such as `a+(b+(c-d*3-(e+f)))` cause several intermediate objects to be created, copied, and destroyed, which, although it all happens automatically and correctly behind the scenes, can be inefficient.

An alternative approach, suggested by creator of the C++ language Bjarne Stroustrup [STRO97] and implemented for the `l3d_vector` and `l3d_point` classes, is to declare a fixed pool of pre-allocated intermediate objects. The operators themselves simply grab one of these pre-allocated objects any time they need to return an intermediate object, thus sparing the object creation overhead during operator invocation. Furthermore, the operators return references to the intermediate objects rather than the objects themselves, thus sparing the copy constructor overhead. Since only references are being passed around, we also avoid the overhead of destruction of the intermediate objects after expression evaluation. The only disadvantage to this approach is that if any one single expression is so long that it requires more intermediate objects than have been allocated in the fixed pool, an overflow and incorrect result will occur (unless we explicitly check for this condition, but this would slow down every operator invocation with an additional overflow check).

Sample Program Using Vectors

The following program, `vecmath`, simply declares two point and vector objects and performs various operations on them. Trace through the program and make sure you can calculate the results manually, and then check your results by running the program.

Listing 5-3: `vecmath.cc`

```
#include <stdio.h>
#include "../lib/geom/point/point.h"
#include "../lib/math/vector.h"

int main(int argc, char **argv) {
  l3d_point p1(int_to_l3d_real(5),
               int_to_l3d_real(5),
               int_to_l3d_real(4),
```

```
                int_to_l3d_real(1)),
p2(int_to_l3d_real(2),
   int_to_l3d_real(7),
   int_to_l3d_real(3),
   int_to_l3d_real(1));
l3d_vector v1,v2,v3;
l3d_real scalar;

printf("Point P1 = (%f,%f,%f,%f)",
       l3d_real_to_float(p1.X_),
       l3d_real_to_float(p1.Y_),
       l3d_real_to_float(p1.Z_),
       l3d_real_to_float(p1.W_));
printf("Point P2 = (%f,%f,%f,%f)",
       l3d_real_to_float(p2.X_),
       l3d_real_to_float(p2.Y_),
       l3d_real_to_float(p2.Z_),
       l3d_real_to_float(p2.W_));

v1 = p2 - p1;
printf("The vector V1 from P1 to P2 = P2 - P1 = (%f,%f,%f,%f)",
       l3d_real_to_float(v1.X_),
       l3d_real_to_float(v1.Y_),
       l3d_real_to_float(v1.Z_),
       l3d_real_to_float(v1.W_));

v2.set(int_to_l3d_real(10),
       int_to_l3d_real(10),
       int_to_l3d_real(10),
       int_to_l3d_real(0));
printf("A different vector V2 = (%f,%f,%f,%f)",
       l3d_real_to_float(v2.X_),
       l3d_real_to_float(v2.Y_),
       l3d_real_to_float(v2.Z_),
       l3d_real_to_float(v2.W_));

p1 = p1 + v2;
printf("Moving from P1 in the direction of V2 = P1 + V2 = (%f,%f,%f,%f)",
       l3d_real_to_float(p1.X_),
       l3d_real_to_float(p1.Y_),
       l3d_real_to_float(p1.Z_),
       l3d_real_to_float(p1.W_));

v1 = v1 + v2;
printf("The combined displacement of V1 and V2 = V1 + V2 = (%f,%f,%f,%f)",
       l3d_real_to_float(v1.X_),
       l3d_real_to_float(v1.Y_),
       l3d_real_to_float(v1.Z_),
       l3d_real_to_float(v1.W_));

v1.set(int_to_l3d_real(1),
       int_to_l3d_real(0),
       int_to_l3d_real(0),
       int_to_l3d_real(0));
v2.set(int_to_l3d_real(0),
       int_to_l3d_real(1),
       int_to_l3d_real(0),
       int_to_l3d_real(0));
v3 = cross(v1,v2);
printf("The cross product of (%f,%f,%f,%f) and (%f,%f,%f,%f) "
```

```
                        "is (%f,%f,%f,%f)",
                        l3d_real_to_float(v1.X_),
                        l3d_real_to_float(v1.Y_),
                        l3d_real_to_float(v1.Z_),
                        l3d_real_to_float(v1.W_),
                        l3d_real_to_float(v2.X_),
                        l3d_real_to_float(v2.Y_),
                        l3d_real_to_float(v2.Z_),
                        l3d_real_to_float(v2.W_),
                        l3d_real_to_float(v3.X_),
                        l3d_real_to_float(v3.Y_),
                        l3d_real_to_float(v3.Z_),
                        l3d_real_to_float(v3.W_));

            v1.set(int_to_l3d_real(1),
                   int_to_l3d_real(0),
                   int_to_l3d_real(0),
                   int_to_l3d_real(0));
            v2.set(int_to_l3d_real(0),
                   int_to_l3d_real(1),
                   int_to_l3d_real(0),
                   int_to_l3d_real(0));
            v3 = cross(v2,v1);
            printf("The cross product of (%f,%f,%f,%f) and (%f,%f,%f,%f) "
                   "is (%f,%f,%f,%f)",
                        l3d_real_to_float(v2.X_),
                        l3d_real_to_float(v2.Y_),
                        l3d_real_to_float(v2.Z_),
                        l3d_real_to_float(v2.W_),
                        l3d_real_to_float(v1.X_),
                        l3d_real_to_float(v1.Y_),
                        l3d_real_to_float(v1.Z_),
                        l3d_real_to_float(v1.W_),
                        l3d_real_to_float(v3.X_),
                        l3d_real_to_float(v3.Y_),
                        l3d_real_to_float(v3.Z_),
                        l3d_real_to_float(v3.W_));
            v1.set(int_to_l3d_real(1),
                   int_to_l3d_real(0),
                   int_to_l3d_real(0),
                   int_to_l3d_real(0));
            v2.set(int_to_l3d_real(1),
                   int_to_l3d_real(1),
                   int_to_l3d_real(0),
                   int_to_l3d_real(0));
            scalar = dot(v1,v2);
            printf("The dot product of (%f,%f,%f,%f) and (%f,%f,%f,%f) "
                   "is %f",
                        l3d_real_to_float(v1.X_),
                        l3d_real_to_float(v1.Y_),
                        l3d_real_to_float(v1.Z_),
                        l3d_real_to_float(v1.W_),
                        l3d_real_to_float(v2.X_),
                        l3d_real_to_float(v2.Y_),
                        l3d_real_to_float(v2.Z_),
                        l3d_real_to_float(v2.W_),
                        scalar);
          }
```

NOTE This program uses the fourth component of the vector and point objects, which is the homogeneous w coordinate. Chapter 6 explains the purpose and significance of this component. For now, simply observe that the w coordinate is 1 for 3D points, and is 0 for 3D vectors.

The Mathematics of Projection

With the previous material on 3D coordinate systems and vectors, we now have a basis for specifying locations and orientations in 3D space. Our goal is now to develop an equation for converting from 3D world coordinates, which specify the locations of objects in our virtual world, to 2D pixel coordinates, which we use to plot the projected images on-screen. We develop this equation through a strongly geometrical approach, in effect modeling the physical viewing situation (you sitting in front of your computer screen) in 3D WC.

The Physical Viewing Situation

Let's first consider the physical viewing situation. As depicted in Figure 5-20, you physically sit in front of a computer screen with a physical distance of $d_{Physical}$ between the eye and the screen. The screen has a physical width of $w_{Physical}$ and a physical height of $h_{Physical}$. Some typical values might be $d_{Physical}$=40cm, $w_{Physical}$=40cm, and $h_{Physical}$=30cm.

We assume that your eye is horizontally and vertically positioned at the center of the screen, and is furthermore focused on the center of the screen. That is, you are looking straight at the screen, the vertical screen center is at eye level, and the horizontal screen center is aligned with the horizontal eye position. Your gaze is focused on the center of the screen as opposed to, for instance, looking at the corner of the screen. Your eye is furthermore oriented perfectly right-side-up so that a vertical line on your computer screen appears vertical to you; that is, your head is not tilted sideways or upside-down.

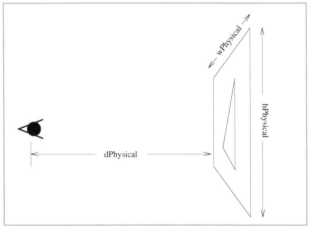

Figure 5-20: The physical viewing situation.

The situation we are simulating with 3D graphics is shown in Figure 5-21. We treat the screen as if it were a window on the world. You are sitting on one side of the window and we pretend that the world is on the other side of the window. Your eye would then perceive light rays traveling from the objects in the world, through the window, to your eye, and finally through the eye's lens to the retina. We want to generate on this window, our screen, a series of points such that the seen light rays are the same as the seen light rays would be for objects lying on the other side of the window. For a given 3D point, this is mathematically accomplished by calculating the intersection between the seen light ray and the screen, and lighting the pixel at the point of intersection. The intersection points are illustrated in Figure 5-21 as the dark dots on the 2D window.

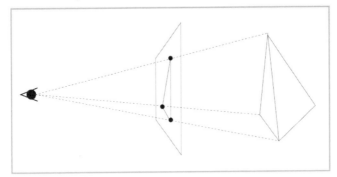

Figure 5-21: The screen as a window on the world.

As previously mentioned, we model our world in the computer by defining points in a 3D world coordinate system. Therefore, in order to calculate intersections between light rays and the screen, we must also model the physical screen and the viewer's eye in 3D world coordinates. Figure 5-22 illustrates this situation. We have a left-handed 3D WC system, with the eye being placed at the origin of this system. The physical screen is modeled as a 2D window lying in the plane defined by $z = d_{WC}$.

We call the 2D plane the *projection plane*, and the window the *projection plane window*. The projection plane is infinite in width and height, but our screen is not—hence the need to define a window or subset of the infinite projection plane. The contents of the projection plane window are then mapped to the 2D screen for display. The projection plane window has a width, expressed in 3D WC units, of w_{WC} and a height of h_{WC}. We calculate the intersections between the seen light rays and the projection plane, and map those intersection points lying within the projection plane window to the physical screen. The mapping from the projection plane window to the physical screen coordinates is nothing more than a simple scaling operation, as we see a little later.

A few moments of thought about the above formulation bring some questions to mind:

- Calculating WC window size: How do we calculate d_{WC}, w_{WC}, and h_{WC} from the known values of $d_{Physical}$, $w_{Physical}$, and $h_{Physical}$?
- Eye location: If the eye is fixed at the origin, how can we move the eye to see other parts of the virtual world?
- Eye orientation: The eye is always oriented such that the direction "up" for the eye is also "up" in 3D WC. We name this situation "perfectly right-side-up." Furthermore, the eye is always looking straight ahead along the z axis. What if we want the eye to look at a point which does not lie along the z axis? Or, what if we want to tilt the eye such that vertical lines appear diagonal or such that the eye is "upside-down"?

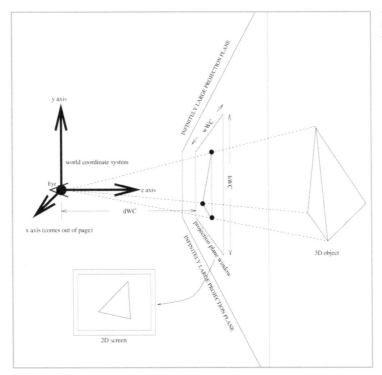

Figure 5-22: The entire 3D viewing process.

With regard to the first question, calculation of WC window size, we will see soon that it is the ratios among d_{WC}, w_{WC}, and h_{WC} which are more important, not their actual values. We can therefore choose any values for these terms as long as their ratios correspond in a certain way. With regard to the last two questions, Chapter 6 illustrates that these situations can all be transformed into the simplified situation developed above (eye at the origin, perfectly right-side-up, and looking straight ahead).

With all of this in mind, we now develop the mathematics necessary for the simplified viewing situation, examining later how other more general viewing situations can all be transformed to this formulation.

Calculating Intersections

Let us now consider a single point in 3D space whose coordinates in 3D WC are (x,y,z). As a 3D application programmer you would specify this point as part of some 3D object you are modeling. This point could represent the tip of a spaceship, the corner of a wall, or the peak of a mountain. In addition to knowing the coordinates of the point (x,y,z), we also know that the eye is located at the origin $(0,0,0)$, based on our assumption earlier of a simplified viewing situation. We want to compute the intersection between the seen light ray, traveling from (x,y,z) to the eye at $(0,0,0)$, and the 2D plane located at $z = d_{WC}$, which is the 2D plane in which our projection plane window lies.

This intersection point will have coordinates (x_p, y_p, d_{WC}), where x_p and y_p are the unknowns. The subscript p indicates that we are solving for projected coordinates; later, these projected coordinates will be mapped (scaled) to the 2D pixel coordinates of Chapter 2. Recall that we assume for the time being that we know d_{WC}; this term will, when we later combine the intersection formula with a screen mapping formula, be simplified to a ratio, called field of view, which we can then compute.

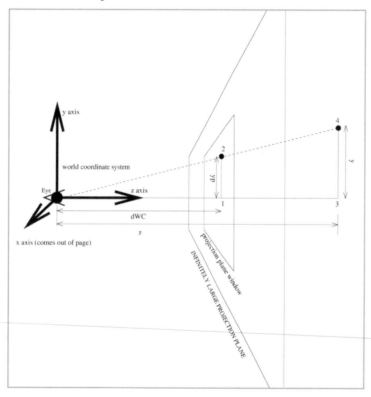

Figure 5-23: Calculating intersection (x_p, y_p) of seen light ray from 3D point (x,y,z) with 2D plane at $z=d_{WC}$. Side view of the situation, looking along the x axis toward the origin.

Figures 5-23 and 5-24 illustrate this situation. Figure 5-23 depicts a side view of the viewing situation, looking across the x axis towards the origin. Figure 5-24 depicts a bird's-eye view, looking down along the y axis towards the origin. Our strategy is to use a "divide-and-conquer" approach to calculate the intersection point. In particular, we compute the x intersection point and the y intersection point independently of one another, using the top and side views, respectively.

Let us use Figure 5-23, the side view, to help us calculate the y coordinate y_p of the projected point. All points of interest in the figure are numbered for notational convenience. Observe that the smaller triangle formed by Eye-1-2 is geometrically similar to the larger triangle Eye-3-4. When we say "similar" we mean this in the mathematical sense—namely, the ratios of the sides of one triangle will be the same as the ratios of the corresponding sides of any similar triangle. With this knowledge, we can state that the height:width ratio of the smaller triangle is the same as the height:width ratio of the larger.

Equation 5-21 shows equating similar triangles using the y and z coordinates. Note that the quantity d_{WC} is not the total distance from the eye to point 1 (which would require considering

Equation 5-21
$$\frac{y_p}{d_{WC}} = \frac{y}{z}$$

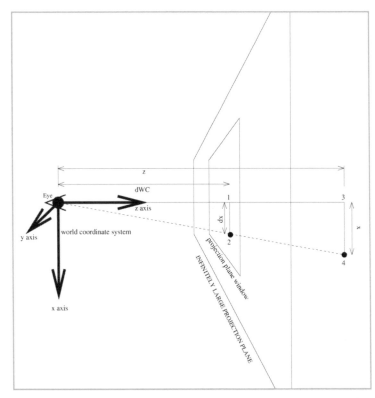

Figure 5-24: Calculating intersection (x_p, y_p) of seen light ray from 3D point (x, y, z) with 2D plane at $z = d_{WC}$. Birds-eye view of the situation, looking down the y axis toward the origin.

both x and z components of point 1), but instead represents only the displacement in the z direction (ignoring any displacement in the x direction). Similarly, the quantity z is not the distance from the eye to point 3, but is instead simply the displacement in the z direction. A development using distance instead of single-axis displacement is also possible but needlessly complicates the derivation.

A similar development for Figure 5-24 gives the result:

Equation 5-22
$$\frac{x_p}{d_{WC}} = \frac{x}{z}$$

If we multiply both sides of each of these equations by d_{WC}, we obtain the following mathematical formulas for perspective projection.

Equation 5-23
$$x_p = d_{WC}\frac{x}{z}$$
$$y_p = d_{WC}\frac{y}{z}$$

So, at least from a mathematical standpoint, this is the answer to the question raised at the beginning of Chapter 4, "What do I do with the z coordinate?" With the simplified viewing situation (eye at origin, perfectly right-side-up, looking along z axis), you simply divide by z and multiply by the distance between the eye and the screen.

The question remains as to what value to use for this screen distance d_{WC}. Let us answer this question indirectly by combining the above perspective projection equations with a screen mapping equation which maps the projected coordinates (which are still in WC) to pixel coordinates (which we can then plot directly on the screen). In the process, the term d_{WC} then occurs in a ratio, which we call the field of view. We then discuss how we compute this field of view term.

Mapping to 2D Pixel Coordinates

The projected intersection coordinates (x_p, y_p) tell us, in 3D world coordinates, where the seen light ray from a particular point intersects the projection plane. We cannot, however, use these coordinates directly for plotting pixels; we first need to convert these projected world coordinates into pixel coordinates. This is essentially a scaling operation, with the one additional complication that the scaling to the pixel coordinates should preserve the width/height ratio on the projection plane.

Figure 5-25 illustrates the scaling operation and the necessity of preserving the width/height ratio. On the top, we have the projection plane window, which in this case is a square. On the bottom, we have the screen, which, for illustrative purposes, is much wider than it is high. We have three options for mapping the projection plane window onto the screen. First, we can simply scale the x and y coordinates of the projection plane window to fit within the screen, but this results in distortion if the physical screen width/height ratio size differs from the projection plane window's width/height ratio. Second, we can scale the projection plane window such that its height maps exactly to the screen's height, and its width maps to a proportionally large area of the screen width. Third, we can scale the projection plane window such that its width maps exactly to the screen's

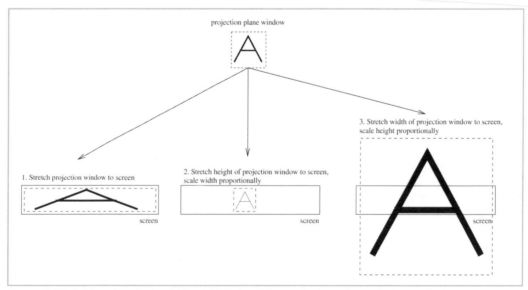

Figure 5-25. Left: scaling both width and height of the projection plane window to fit the screen. Middle: scaling just the height to fit the screen, and scaling the width proportionally. Right: scaling just the width to fit the screen, and scaling the height proportionally.

width, and its height maps to a proportionally large area of the screen's height. The term "proportionally" here means, "such that the physical width/height ratio on-screen matches the width/height ratio of the projection plane window."

We should choose the second or third options if we wish to avoid stretching or squashing distortions when mapping from the projection plane window to the screen. Both the second and third options preserve the width/height ratio, so it does not matter which we choose. Here, we choose to map the width of the projection plane window to the full width of the screen, and accordingly scale the height to be proportionally large enough so that the physical width/height ratio on-screen matches the width/height ratio of the projection plane window.

 NOTE Fortunately, for most monitors and display modes offered by graphic cards, pixels are square-shaped, with equal width and height. This means that the physical width and height of the display screen can be specified in pixels. If the pixels were not physically square, being wider than they were high, for instance, then you would have to pick some other uniformly sized physical unit of measurement, such as centimeters, and calculate the pixels/cm in the vertical direction and the pixels/cm in the horizontal direction in order to be able to compute the physical size of the screen given its pixel dimensions. Again, since most modern displays have square pixels, you can just use the pixels themselves as a physical unit of measurement.

Under the assumption that we map the projection plane window's width to the full width of the screen, and given world-space intersection coordinates (x_p, y_p), we arrive at screen-space (i.e., pixel) coordinates (x_s, y_s) via the following formulas:

Equation 5-24

$$x_s = \frac{xoffset_{WC}}{w_{WC}} \cdot w_s$$

$$y_s = \frac{yoffset_{WC}}{h_{WC}} \cdot \frac{h_{WC}/w_{WC}}{h_{Phys}/w_{Phys}} \cdot h_s$$

$$= \frac{yoffset_{WC}}{w_{WC}} \cdot \frac{w_{Phys}}{h_{Phys}} \cdot h_s$$

The terms w_s and h_s represent the pixel width and height of the output screen. The terms w_{WC} and h_{WC} represent the width and height of the projection plane window, in world coordinates—these terms are currently unknown. The terms $xoffset_{WC}$ and $yoffset_{WC}$ represent the distance (still in world coordinate units) between the intersection coordinate and the left or top sides of the projection plane window, respectively. These offset terms are calculated as follows:

Equation 5-25

$$xoffset_{WC} = x_p - winleft_{WC}$$
$$yoffset_{WC} = wintop_{WC} - y_p$$

$winleft_{WC}$ and $wintop_{WC}$ are the WC coordinates of the left and top edges of the projection plane window. Notice that the $yoffset_{WC}$ term is computed as $wintop_{WC} - y_p$ and not $y_p - wintop_{WC}$. This is because our 3D world coordinate system has x increasing to the right and y increasing towards the top. However, pixel coordinates have y increasing towards the bottom. Thus, we need to reverse the sense of "top" and "bottom" for (x_p, y_p), in 3D WC, in order to arrive at the 2D pixel coordinates (x_s, y_s).

We take these offsets and divide them by the WC width and height of the projection plane window in order to get a unit-less relative position of the intersection point with respect to the width and height of the projection plane window. Then, we multiply these relative positions by the pixel width and pixel height of the screen, effectively scaling the displacements to the screen size, to obtain the actual pixel coordinates which we then draw.

Remember, though, we cannot in general scale both the x and y displacements to the full screen size if we wish to avoid stretching or squashing. Since we have chosen to scale the x displacement to the full screen size, the y displacement needs to be scaled proportionally. Thus, in Equation 5-24, the term $(h_{WC}/w_{WC})/(h_{Phys}/w_{Phys})$ is the scaling factor which ensures that the physical size of the coordinates in the y direction maintain their width/height ratio with the physical size of the coordinates in the x direction. Notice that if we multiply this term with the y displacement, we end up dividing $yoffset_{WC}$ by w_{WC} and not by h_{WC}. This makes sense: we compute the percentage displacement for both x and y with respect to the chosen, fixed x size, then scale the y displacement by the physical screen's width/height ratio (w_{Phys}/h_{Phys}) to obtain a proportionally large y coordinate whose physical height on-screen has the same percentage displacement as the original y coordinate's displacement in WC with respect to the projection plane window. With square pixels, as we said earlier, we can use the pixel dimensions of the window, such as 400 pixels by 300 pixels, to obtain the values for h_{Phys} and w_{Phys}. With non-square pixels (a situation which is nowadays more unlikely), we must choose a square (i.e., uniform) unit of measurement and scale the pixel dimensions differently in the horizontal and vertical directions to arrive at the physical sizes h_{Phys} and w_{Phys}.

Substituting the above equations for $xoffset_{WC}$ and $yoffset_{WC}$ into the original equations for (x_s, y_s) gives the following formula for going from the 3D projected intersection point (x_p, y_p) to 2D pixel coordinates (x_s, y_s):

Equation 5-26
$$x_s = \frac{x_p - winleft_{WC}}{w_{WC}} w_s$$
$$y_s = \frac{wintop_{WC} - y_p}{w_{WC}} \cdot \frac{w_{Phys}}{h_{Phys}} \cdot h_s$$

Substituting the original formulas for x_p and y_p yields:

Equation 5-27
$$x_s = \frac{d_{WC}\frac{x}{z} - winleft_{WC}}{w_{WC}} w_s$$
$$y_s = \frac{wintop_{WC} - d_{WC}\frac{y}{z}}{w_{WC}} \cdot \frac{w_{Phys}}{h_{Phys}} \cdot h_s$$

We can express $wintop_{WC}$ and $winleft_{WC}$ in terms of h_{WC} and w_{WC} by using the assumptions we made earlier that the eye is horizontally and vertically centered on the screen, and that the eye is at the origin (0,0,0). Equation 5-28 shows computing the top and left of the projection plane window in terms of its height and width.

Equation 5-28
$$winleft_{WC} = -0.5w_{WC}$$
$$wintop_{WC} = 0.5h_{WC}$$

Substituting these terms into the WC-to-pixel mapping equations above:

Equation 5-29
$$x_s = \frac{d_{WC}\frac{x}{z} - (-0.5w_{WC})}{w_{WC}} w_s$$
$$y_s = \frac{0.5h_{WC} - d_{WC}\frac{y}{z}}{w_{WC}} \cdot \frac{w_{Phys}}{h_{Phys}} \cdot h_s$$

We can rearrange the equations slightly to obtain:

Equation 5-30
$$x_s = \left(\frac{d_{WC}}{w_{WC}}\frac{x}{z} + 0.5\right)w_s$$
$$y_s = \left(-\frac{d_{WC}}{w_{WC}}\frac{y}{z} + 0.5\frac{h_{WC}}{w_{WC}}\right)\cdot\frac{w_{Phys}}{h_{Phys}}\cdot h_s$$

We can also distribute the multiplication by w_{Phys}/h_{Phys} in the y_s term to give:

Equation 5-31
$$y_s = \left(-\frac{d_{WC}}{w_{WC}}\frac{w_{Phys}}{h_{Phys}}\frac{y}{z} + 0.5\frac{h_{WC}}{w_{WC}}\frac{w_{Phys}}{h_{Phys}}\right)h_s$$

Notice that d_{WC} and w_{WC} now only appear in a ratio, d_{WC}/w_{WC}. Furthermore, this ratio occurs both in the equation for x_s and also in the equation for y_s, though in the equation for y_s this ratio is multiplied by w_{Phys}/h_{Phys}. Let us use the term fov_x to denote the ratio appearing in the x_s equation, and let us use the term fov_y to denote the multiplied ratio appearing in the equation for y_s. Finally, let us use the term $scale_y$ to denote the term $(h_{WC}/w_{WC})*(w_{Phys}/h_{Phys})$ appearing in the equation for y_s. This $scale_y$ term is responsible for ensuring that the width/height ratio is the same between the projection plane window and the physical screen. Applying these notational conventions, we obtain:

Equation 5-32
$$fov_x = \frac{d_{WC}}{w_{WC}}$$
$$fov_y = fov_x\frac{w_{Phys}}{h_{Phys}}$$
$$scale_y = \frac{h_{WC}}{w_{WC}}\frac{w_{Phys}}{h_{Phys}}$$
$$x_s = \left(fov_x\frac{x}{z} + 0.5\right)w_s$$
$$y_s = \left(-fov_y\frac{y}{z} + 0.5 scale_y\right)h_s$$

Equation 5-32 shows perspective projection from WC to screen coordinates. As is evident from this equation, and as we claimed earlier, the actual values of d_{WC}, w_{WC}, and h_{WC} are not as important as their ratios. In particular, only two ratios remain: the fov_x ratio d_{WC}/w_{WC}, and the ratio h_{WC}/w_{WC} appearing in the $scale_y$ term.

We can eliminate the h_{WC}/w_{WC} term—indeed, the entire $scale_y$ term—if we assume that the width/height ratio of the projection plane window, expressed by w_{WC}/h_{WC}, is identical to the physical width/height ratio of the screen, expressed by w_{Phys}/h_{Phys}. If these two ratios are the same, then the $scale_y$ term multiplies the reciprocal of this ratio with itself, which gives a result of 1. Thus, the $scale_y$ term vanishes under this assumption.

Then, the only remaining terms involving the WC window size are d_{WC} and w_{WC}. What values should we use for these terms? One possibility would be simply to use the physical screen's distance from the viewer and its width. This would be the most "realistic" approach, but as we will see shortly, it can be useful to exaggerate the physical parameters in order to allow more flexible viewing possibilities.

Let's first see what, physically, the fraction d_{WC}/w_{WC} represents. After understanding what this fraction physically represents, we can then make an informed decision about how to choose the actual values.

Field of View: the Connection Between Window Size and Distance

Figure 5-26 illustrates the physical meaning of the term d_{WC}/w_{WC}. In the figure, we are looking down along the y axis. The projection plane window (which represents the screen) is the quadrilateral to the right of the figure.

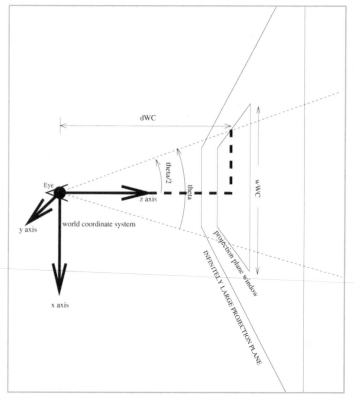

Figure 5-26: Relationship between horizontal field of view θ ("theta" in the diagram), w_{WC}, and d_{WC}.

Recall that the projection plane window is a conceptual representation of a physical window on a physical 3D world whose objects radiate physical light rays. Imagine a small window in an otherwise opaque wall. We can only see a small part of the world through the window; the window limits the amount of the world we can see. We cannot see light rays which do not pass through the window. In Figure 5-26 we have drawn two dotted lines representing the horizontal limits of vision; any light rays which do not fall between the two dotted lines do not pass through the window and therefore cannot be seen. (Note that the use of a dotted line is actually a diagrammatical simplification; in actuality, the horizontal visibility is bounded by two planes.) The amount of the world which we can see horizontally is called the horizontal field of view, which we represent by the angle θ between the two dotted lines.

Let us now determine the relationship between the horizontal field of view angle θ and the viewing parameters d_{WC} and w_{WC}. Instead of considering the entire angle θ, it is easier if we consider the angle $\theta/2$. We draw a line which bisects θ; this line goes through the eye and intersects the projection plane window at a right angle, exactly dividing the window into two horizontally equal halves (this is because of the assumption that the eye is horizontally and vertically centered on the screen). We can now observe a right triangle denoted by the bold lines in Figure 5-26, whose width and height are known quantities. From trigonometry, we know that the cotangent function (denoted cot) can relate the width and height of our right triangle. Specifically,

Equation 5-33
$$\frac{d_{WC}}{0.5 w_{WC}} = \cot(0.5\theta)$$
$$2\frac{d_{WC}}{w_{WC}} = \cot(0.5\theta)$$
$$\frac{d_{WC}}{w_{WC}} = 0.5\cot(0.5\theta)$$

We see now that the ratio d_{WC}/w_{WC} is half of the cotangent of half of the horizontal field of view angle. We therefore call this ratio the horizontal field of view term. We multiply this field of view term by a constant, the ratio of physical screen width to height, to arrive at the corresponding vertical field of view term.

Determining the Horizontal Field of View Term

By the above definitions of the horizontal field of view term, we can either choose to define this term as a ratio of viewing width/distance or as a cotangent of a field of view angle. Let's look at both approaches.

Determining Field of View Term as Ratio of Width/Distance

As mentioned earlier, one approach to determining the field of view term d_{WC}/w_{WC} is simply to use the physical values of w_{Phys} and d_{Phys} in place of w_{WC} and d_{WC}. This yields the most physically "correct" results, displaying on the screen what we would actually see if our screen were really a physical window through which we were looking at a 3D world. For instance, if we have a sample physical screen width of 40 cm, a height of 30 cm, and a viewing distance of 40 cm, then substituting these values for w_{WC} and d_{WC} yields a ratio of 40cm/40cm = 1.0 for the horizontal field of view term. We multiply this by the physical width/height ratio of the screen, which is 40cm/30cm, or 1.333333, to arrive at the vertical field of view term. Here, the vertical field of view term would be 1.0*1.333333, or 1.333333.

If this result is the most physically correct, why should we consider any other approach to determining the field of view terms? The answer is that we often would like to exaggerate the size of our screen, to pretend that we have a larger screen so that we may see more of the world. For instance, imagine that your screen is actually 40 cm wide by 30 cm high and that you are actually sitting 40 cm from the screen. Now imagine using a physical window of exactly this size and distance as the windshield of your car. If you can accurately imagine this situation, it should become clear to you that you would see only a small portion of the world through such a window, in comparison to the amount of the world you normally see through a car's windshield. If we are programming a race car simulator, we would like the amount of the world we see on-screen to correspond to the amount of the world we would see sitting in a real car, and not necessarily the amount of the world we would see if we had a window of the physical size and distance of our computer screen.

The above discussion implies that we are "stretching reality," so to speak. That is, we have a computer screen of a certain size and distance. In order for the physical sizes of the images displayed on-screen (and consequently, the physical sizes of the images projected on the eye's retina) to accurately reflect the world we are modeling, we would have to use the physical viewing parameters to calculate the field of view term. However, accuracy of the physical sizes of on-screen images is not necessarily the most important factor. More important to the reality of a simulation is the amount of the world we see. If we give up the accuracy of the physical image size, we can gain accuracy in the amount of the world we see.

NOTE For immersive virtual reality environments, such as a CAVE in which the viewer is surrounded by multiple life-size projections of 3D images, both physical image size and the amount of the world the user sees should be accurate in order to create the most realistic experience possible.

If we want to model the amount of the world we see, it is easiest to use the second approach to calculating the field of view term—namely, using the cotangent of the field of view angle.

Determining Field of View Term as the Cotangent of the Field of View Angle

As we just mentioned, it is better not to concentrate on the accuracy of the physical sizes of our on-screen images, but instead to concentrate on the amount of the world we see through our screen. The "amount" of the world we see on-screen is most easily and intuitively represented by the horizontal field of view angle q. Taking half of the cotangent of half of this angle gives the horizontal field of view term, which we then use in our 3D WC to pixel coordinate mapping formula.

The human eye is physically able to see approximately a 100 degree field of vision horizontally. Therefore, to create a natural-looking perspective projection, as the human eye would see it, we should use 0.5*cot(0.5*100 degrees) as the horizontal field of view term. This works out to be 0.41955. For the vertical field of view term, we multiply this by the physical screen's width/height ratio, which for this example is 40cm/30cm, or 1.333333. Multiplying this by the horizontal field of view term yields a vertical field of view term of 0.54555. These field of view terms assume, however, that the physical screen physically encompasses the viewer's entire field of vision. This may be the case with extremely large screens (the CAVE, for instance, uses a series of screens each sized 3 meters by 3 meters) or with 3D glasses, but for a normal computer screen which only encompasses a small part of the viewer's field of view, a smaller field of view angle might be better, such as 60 degrees. This would yield a horizontal field of view term of 0.5*cot(0.5*60)=0.86603, and a vertical field of view term of 1.333333*0.86603=1.1547.

We can adjust these values if we wish to create some visually interesting effects. In particular, if we use unusually large values for q, we get an uncanny fish-eye type of effect, since we see more of the scene than our eyes would normally allow us to see. With the sample programs in Chapter 7 (and with all programs which use the `l3d_pipeline_world` class), you can interactively manipulate the field of view by pressing x, Shift+x, y, or Shift+y to decrease or increase the horizontal or vertical field of view terms, respectively.

Changing the field of view terms can be thought of as being the computer graphics equivalent of a photographer changing the focal length of a camera lens.

Summary of Perspective Projection

The final equations we have for perspective projection are the following:

Equation 5-34
$$
\begin{aligned}
x_s &= \left(\tfrac{x}{z}(0.5\cot(0.5\theta)) + 0.5\right)w_s \\
&= \tfrac{x}{z}(0.5\cot(0.5\theta)w_s) + 0.5w_s \\
y_s &= \left(-\tfrac{y}{z}(0.5\cot(0.5\theta)) \cdot \tfrac{w_{Phys}}{h_{Phys}} + 0.5\,scale_y\right)h_s \\
&= -\tfrac{y}{z}(0.5\cot(0.5\theta)) \cdot \tfrac{w_{Phys}}{h_{Phys}} \cdot h_s) + 0.5\,scale_y h_s
\end{aligned}
$$

Equation 5-34 shows perspective projection from WC to screen coordinates using field of view angle. Notice that apart from x, y, and z, all other quantities are constants. These equations map from 3D WC to 2D pixel coordinates, under the following assumptions: that we have a left-handed 3D WC system, that the eye in 3D WC is located at the origin looking straight along the positive z axis and is perfectly right-side-up, that you as a viewer of the computer screen have your eye centered horizontally and vertically on the physical screen, and that θ represents the horizontal field of view angle. The division by z effects the perspective foreshortening which occurs due to the geometric laws governing light rays. The field of view angle controls the amount of foreshortening. The h_s, w_s, and 0.5 terms map from projected world coordinates into 2D screen coordinates with a given screen width, height, and centered eye position. The w_{Phys}/h_{Phys} term converts from the horizontal to the vertical field of view term. The $scale_y$ term ensures that the width/height ratio of the physical screen is the same as that of the projection plane window, and is 1 if the physical screen and projection plane window have the same relative proportions.

Sample Program: Dots

This sample program serves to solidify the concepts presented in this chapter. It contains three 3D demonstrations in one—runway lights, star field, and snow. Specify a command-line parameter of 0, 1, or 2 to choose which demonstration to run, for instance, dots 0. With no parameter, the program executes the runway lights demo.

Listing 5-4: `dots.cc`

```
#include <stdlib.h>
#include <stdio.h>

#include "../lib/tool_2d/screen.h"
#include "../lib/tool_os/dispatch.h"
#include "../lib/raster/rasteriz.h"
#include "../lib/tool_2d/scrinfo.h"
#include "../lib/system/factorys.h"

#include "../lib/geom/point/point.h"
#include "../lib/math/vector.h"
```

```
#include "../lib/math/matrix.h"

#define MAXDOTS 150

#define PI 3.14159265

enum progtypes {RUNWAY, STARS, SNOW };

progtypes progtype;

//- STEP 1: CHOOSE THE FACTORIES

void choose_factories(void) {
  factory_manager_v_0_1.choose_factories();
}

//- STEP 2: DECLARE A PIPELINE SUBCLASS

l3d_real fovx, fovy;
int xsize, ysize;
//- in a real program these projection parameters, which are set by the main
//- program but used by the dot's projection routines, would not be global
//- but rather in a "projection parameters" class, used by both the dot
//- class and the main program class

class mydot {
  public:
    l3d_coordinate position;
    l3d_vector displacement;
    l3d_vector velocity;
    mydot(void) {position.original.set(int_to_l3d_real(0),
                                       int_to_l3d_real(0),
                                       int_to_l3d_real(0),
                                       int_to_l3d_real(1)); }
    virtual void place_dot(void) = 0;
    virtual void move_dot(void) = 0;
    virtual void project_dot(void) {
      position.transformed.X_ =
        l3d_mulri(l3d_mulrr(l3d_divrr( position.transformed.X_,
                                       position.transformed.Z_),
                            fovx),
                  xsize)
        +
        int_to_l3d_real(xsize > 1);

      position.transformed.Y_ =
        l3d_mulri(l3d_mulrr(l3d_divrr(-position.transformed.Y_,
                                       position.transformed.Z_),
                            fovy),
                  ysize)
        +
        int_to_l3d_real(ysize > 1);

    }
};

class my_pipeline : public l3d_pipeline {
  protected:
    l3d_rasterizer_2d_imp *ri;
```

```
        l3d_rasterizer_2d *r;

        unsigned long color;

        mydot *dots[MAXDOTS];
        int numdots;

        long i, j;
        long wc_win_width, wc_win_height, wc_win_dist, fov;
        long wc_win_left, wc_win_top;

        virtual int out_of_wc_bounds(l3d_point const &p)=0;
    public:
        l3d_screen *s;
        my_pipeline(void);
        virtual ~my_pipeline(void);

        void key_event(int ch);  //- from dispatcher
        void update_event(void); //- from dispatcher
        void draw_event(void);   //- from dispatcher
};

my_pipeline::my_pipeline(void) {
    s = factory_manager_v_0_1.screen_factory->create(320,240);
    ri = factory_manager_v_0_1.ras_2d_imp_factory->create(320,240,s->sinfo);
    r = new l3d_rasterizer_2d(ri);

    s->sinfo->ext_to_native(0,0,0); //- allocate black background color
    s->sinfo->ext_max_red =
        s->sinfo->ext_max_green =
            s->sinfo->ext_max_blue =  255;
    color = s->sinfo->ext_to_native(255, 255, 255);
    s->refresh_palette();

    xsize = s->xsize;
    ysize = s->ysize;
    fovx = float_to_l3d_real(1.0/tan(50./180. * PI));
    fovy = l3d_mulrr(fovx,float_to_l3d_real(320.0/240.0));
      //- 320/240 is the physical screen size ratio, which is 4/3 or 1.3333
}

my_pipeline::~my_pipeline(void) {

    int dot_i = 0;
    for(dot_i=0; dot_i<numdots; dot_i++) {
        delete dots[dot_i];
    }

    delete s;
    delete ri;
    delete r;
}

void my_pipeline::key_event(int ch) {
    switch(ch) {
        case 'q': {
            exit(0);
        }
    }
```

```
  }

void my_pipeline::update_event() {
  int i;

  /* move and display all dots */
  for(i=0;i<numdots;i++) {
    //- dynamics / simulation
    dots[i]->position.reset();
    dots[i]->move_dot();
    if(out_of_wc_bounds(dots[i]->position.transformed)) {
      dots[i]->place_dot();
    }

    //- perspective projection
    dots[i]->project_dot();
  }
}

void my_pipeline::draw_event(void) {
  int i;
  r->clear_buffer();

  for(i=0;i<numdots;i++) {
    //- culling
    if(dots[i]->position.transformed.X_>=0 &&
       dots[i]->position.transformed.X_ <= int_to_l3d_real(s->xsize) &&
       dots[i]->position.transformed.Y_ >= 0 &&
       dots[i]->position.transformed.Y_ <= int_to_l3d_real(s->ysize))
    {
      //- rasterization
      r->draw_point(ifloor(dots[i]->position.transformed.X_),
                    ifloor(dots[i]->position.transformed.Y_),
                    color);
    }
  }

  s->blit_screen();
}

//-
//- runway pipeline subclass
//-

class dot_runway_light : public mydot {
  public:
    void place_dot(void); //- virtual
    void move_dot(void); //- virtual
};

void dot_runway_light::place_dot(void) {
  position.reset();

  displacement.X_ = int_to_l3d_real(xsize);
  velocity.set(int_to_l3d_real(-5),
               int_to_l3d_real(0),
               int_to_l3d_real(0),
               int_to_l3d_real(0));
}
```

```
void dot_runway_light::move_dot(void) {
  displacement = displacement + velocity;
  position.reset();
  position.transformed = position.transformed + displacement;
}

class my_pipeline_runway : public my_pipeline {
  public:
    my_pipeline_runway(void) {
      int dot_i = 0;
      for(dot_i=0; dot_i<MAXDOTS; dot_i++) {
        dots[dot_i] = new dot_runway_light;
      }

      dot_i = 0;
      for(i=-200; i<200; i+=40) {
        for(j=100; j<500; j+=40) {
          dots[dot_i]->position.reset();
          dots[dot_i]->displacement.set(int_to_l3d_real(i),
                                        int_to_l3d_real(-70),
                                        int_to_l3d_real(j),
                                        int_to_l3d_real(0));
          dots[dot_i]->velocity.set(int_to_l3d_real(-5),
                                    int_to_l3d_real(0),
                                    int_to_l3d_real(0),
                                    int_to_l3d_real(0));
          dot_i++;
        }
      }
      numdots = dot_i;
    }

    int out_of_wc_bounds(l3d_point const &p);
};

int my_pipeline_runway::out_of_wc_bounds(l3d_point const &p) {
  return(p.X_<int_to_l3d_real(-200));
}

//-
//- snow pipeline subclass
//-

class dot_snowflake : public mydot {
  public:
    void place_dot(void); //- virtual
    void move_dot(void); //- virtual
};

void dot_snowflake::place_dot(void) {
  displacement.set(int_to_l3d_real( - (rand() % xsize)),
                   int_to_l3d_real(100 + (rand()%100)),
                   int_to_l3d_real(64 + (rand()%ysize)),
                   int_to_l3d_real(0));
  position.reset();
  velocity.set(int_to_l3d_real(rand()%2),
               int_to_l3d_real(-1),
               int_to_l3d_real(0),
               int_to_l3d_real(0));
```

```
    }

    void dot_snowflake::move_dot(void) {
      displacement = displacement + velocity;
      position.reset();
      position.transformed = position.transformed + displacement;
      velocity.set(int_to_l3d_real(rand()%2),
                   int_to_l3d_real(-1),
                   int_to_l3d_real(0),
                   int_to_l3d_real(0));
    }

    class my_pipeline_snow : public my_pipeline {
      public:
        my_pipeline_snow(void) {
          int i;

          for(i=0; i<MAXDOTS; i++) {
            dots[i] = new dot_snowflake();
            dots[i]->place_dot();
          }
          numdots = MAXDOTS;
        }
        int out_of_wc_bounds(l3d_point const &p);
    };

    int my_pipeline_snow::out_of_wc_bounds(l3d_point const &p) {
      return(p.Y_<int_to_l3d_real(-70));
    }

    //-
    //- star field pipeline subclass
    //-

    class dot_star : public mydot {
      public:
        void place_dot(void); //- virtual
        void move_dot(void); //- virtual
    };

    void dot_star::place_dot(void) {
      displacement.set(int_to_l3d_real(1000 - (rand() % 2000)),
                       int_to_l3d_real(1000 - (rand() % 2000)),
                       int_to_l3d_real(200 + (rand()%1000)),
                       int_to_l3d_real(0));
      position.reset();
      velocity.set(int_to_l3d_real(0),
                   int_to_l3d_real(0),
                   int_to_l3d_real(-10),
                   int_to_l3d_real(0));
    }

    void dot_star::move_dot(void) {
      displacement = displacement + velocity;
      position.reset();
      position.transformed = position.transformed + displacement;
    }

    class my_pipeline_stars : public my_pipeline {
      public:
```

```
    my_pipeline_stars(void) {

      int i;

      for(i=0; i<MAXDOTS; i++) {
        dots[i] = new dot_star();
        dots[i]->place_dot();
      }
      numdots = MAXDOTS;
    }
    int out_of_wc_bounds(l3d_point const &p);
};

int my_pipeline_stars::out_of_wc_bounds(l3d_point const &p) {
  return(p.Z_<int_to_l3d_real(20));
}

int main(int argc, char **argv) {
  if(argc==2) {
    sscanf(argv[1], "%d", &progtype);
  }
  else {
    progtype = RUNWAY;
  }

  choose_factories();

  l3d_dispatcher *d;
  my_pipeline *p;

  //- STEP 3: CREATE A DISPATCHER

  d = factory_manager_v_0_1.dispatcher_factory->create();

  //- STEP 4: CREATE A PIPELINE

  //- plug our custom behavior pipeline into the dispatcher
  switch(progtype) {
    case RUNWAY: p = new my_pipeline_runway(); break;
    case STARS: p = new my_pipeline_stars(); break;
    case SNOW: p = new my_pipeline_snow(); break;
  }

  //- STEP 5: START DISPATCHER

  d->pipeline = p; //- polymorphic assignment
  d->event_source = p->s;
  d->start();

  delete d;
  delete p;
}
```

The following code implements the perspective projection:

```
class mydot {

    virtual void project_dot(void) {
      position.transformed.X_ =
        l3d_mulri(l3d_mulrr(l3d_divrr( position.transformed.X_,
                                       position.transformed.Z_),
```

```
                          fovx),
                xsize)
        +
        int_to_l3d_real(xsize > 1);

        position.transformed.Y_ =
            l3d_mulri(l3d_mulrr(l3d_divrr(-position.transformed.Y_,
                                          position.transformed.Z_),
                            fovy),
                ysize)
        +
        int_to_l3d_real(ysize > 1);

}
```

These few lines therefore embody the essence of this chapter. Once you understand the idea behind this formula, its implementation is extremely simple.

The rest of the program concerns itself with the placement and movement of dots in a particular manner, depending on whether we are modeling runway lights (which move constantly in the *x* direction), stars (which move constantly towards the viewer in the *z* direction), or snow (which falls constantly downward in the *y* direction). This code is a simple example of the type of "simulation code" we mentioned earlier, which causes objects to move in a physically realistic way. Notice that we use vectors to move the points; adding a vector to a point gives us a new, displaced point.

Regardless of the type of object and movement being modeled, the process of perspective projection is the same for all cases. This shows that once we understand and implement a mathematically correct perspective projection, we can use it to display any type of 3D data. This is in contrast to the "pseudo-3D" approach taken in the original runway lights program.

Figure 5-27: Output from the program `dots`, operating in "runway lights" mode.

The Parts of a 3D Engine

Let us take a moment to study the structure of this program, since it contains many important features of a complete rendering engine. We will see this same general structure as we add more routines to the l3d library.

The Rendering Pipeline

The program exhibits the typical five-step structure of event-driven l3d programs, covered in detail in Chapter 2. As usual, a custom pipeline subclass forms the heart of our application. We declare an abstract pipeline subclass my_pipeline, with the main methods of interest being update_event and draw_event.

```
void my_pipeline::update_event() {
  int i;

  /* move and display all dots */
  for(i=0;i<numdots;i++) {
    //- dynamics / simulation
    dots[i]->position.reset();
    dots[i]->move_dot();
    if(out_of_wc_bounds(dots[i]->position.transformed)) {
      dots[i]->place_dot();
    }

    //- perspective projection
    dots[i]->project_dot();
  }
}

void my_pipeline::draw_event(void) {
  int i;
  r->clear_buffer();

  for(i=0;i<numdots;i++) {
    //- culling
    if(dots[i]->position.transformed.X_ >=0 &&
       dots[i]->position.transformed.X_ <= int_to_l3d_real(s->xsize) &&
       dots[i]->position.transformed.Y_ >= 0 &&
       dots[i]->position.transformed.Y_ <= int_to_l3d_real(s->ysize))
    {
      //- rasterization
      r->draw_point(ifloor(dots[i]->position.transformed.X_),
                    ifloor(dots[i]->position.transformed.Y_),
                    color);
    }
  }

  s->blit_screen();
}
```

Taken together, the update_event and draw_event methods loop through and process all points—moving, projecting, and displaying them. When speaking of 3D engines, we refer to such a loop as the *3D pipeline*. We can see that all points pass through a series of steps before they are actually displayed on screen. First they are moved, then they are projected, then they are tested to see if they are within the screen bounds, then they are finally displayed. We can think of this series of steps as being a "pipeline" through which the 3D data points are "pumped."

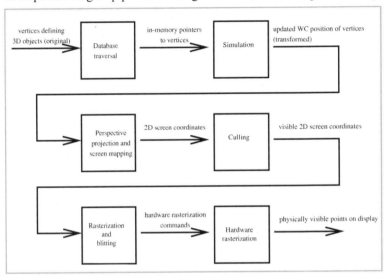

Figure 5-28: One example of a 3D pipeline.

Database and Database Traversal

This program deals with displaying dots; dots are the 3D objects of interest in this application. The my_pipeline class, since it represents the main application (Chapter 2), declares the program's main database of dot objects as shown below. Notice that we declare pointers to abstract dot objects instead of creating the objects automatically; this is so that we can insert objects of different concrete dot subclasses into the object database.

```
class my_pipeline : public l3d_pipeline {

    mydot *dots[MAXDOTS];
    int numdots;
```

In general, a 3D engine contains an in-memory database of the 3D objects which are being modeled. This "database" may be no more than a simple linear list of objects; in other words, the database in memory does not necessarily need to offer advanced storage features of full-fledged database management systems (index and key management, concurrent access, transaction logging, etc.). The 3D objects in the database are usually 3D polyhedra, but again, in this simple example they are simply dots.

The mydot class is an abstract parent class representing a dot in 3D space which can place, move, and project itself. Our object database in this program consists of abstract pointers to dot objects.

The position member of the dot class stores the dot's position, and is a variable of type l3d_coordinate. Recall from Chapter 2 that an l3d_coordinate consists of two points: an original and a transformed point. The original point contains the original definition of the geometry; the transformed point is the temporary storage area for all movement and projection operations and, after all frame processing is done, contains the final pixel coordinates to be plotted on screen. The `position.original` member of every dot object in this sample program is always (0,0,0); in other words, we choose to define all points as initially being located at the origin.

The `displacement` member variable reflects the displacement from `position.original` (which, for this program, is always (0,0,0)) to the current position. The current position, unlike the original position, changes every frame since the dots are moving. The current position is therefore given by `position.original + displacement`, which is a point plus a vector.

The `velocity` member represents the speed and direction with which the dot is moving. We add the current position, computed as described above, and the velocity vector to obtain the new position. This is again a point plus vector addition, yielding a new point.

The abstract `place_dot` method places the dot in an initial, valid location, by setting the `displacement` member. We override this method in dot subclasses.

The abstract `move_dot` method moves the dot to a new location. Again, we override this method in dot subclasses, since each dot subclass moves differently.

We derive subclasses from `mydot` to define special types of dots which have specialized movement behaviors (see next section).

We must examine all objects in the database to update their positions and to see if they need to be displayed. This occurs in the `update_event` method of the `my_pipeline` class, where we loop through all dots in a `for` loop. We use the term *database traversal* for the process of going through the objects in the database. With increasing database size, it becomes important to limit the portion of the database we have to update or display for each frame of animation. See the companion book *Advanced Linux 3D Graphics Programming* for details.

Simulation

We declare a dot subclass for each type of dot we want to simulate: runway lights (class `dot_runway_light`), snowflakes (class `dot_snowflake`), or stars (class `dot_star`). Each dot subclass knows how to move itself; the main pipeline code simply asks each dot to update its own position. We can think of updating the dots' positions as updating the object database, since the dots define the object database. The following code segments initialize (method `place_dot`) and dynamically modify (method `move_dot`) the positions of the various kinds of dots. This is an example of simulation code, which physically simulates movement according to some rules.

```
class dot_runway_light : public mydot {
  public:
    void place_dot(void); //- virtual
    void move_dot(void); //- virtual
};

void dot_runway_light::place_dot(void) {
  position.reset();

  displacement.X_ = int_to_l3d_real(xsize);
  velocity.set(int_to_l3d_real(-5),
               int_to_l3d_real(0),
               int_to_l3d_real(0),
               int_to_l3d_real(0));
```

```
    }

    void dot_runway_light::move_dot(void) {
      displacement = displacement + velocity;
      position.reset();
      position.transformed = position.transformed + displacement;
    }


    class dot_snowflake : public mydot {
      public:
        void place_dot(void); //- virtual
        void move_dot(void); //- virtual
    };

    void dot_snowflake::place_dot(void) {
      displacement.set(int_to_l3d_real( - (rand() % xsize)),
                       int_to_l3d_real(100 + (rand()%100)),
                       int_to_l3d_real(64 + (rand()%ysize)),
                       int_to_l3d_real(0));
      position.reset();
      velocity.set(int_to_l3d_real(rand()%2),
                   int_to_l3d_real(-1),
                   int_to_l3d_real(0),
                   int_to_l3d_real(0));
    }

    void dot_snowflake::move_dot(void) {
      displacement = displacement + velocity;
      position.reset();
      position.transformed = position.transformed + displacement;
      velocity.set(int_to_l3d_real(rand()%2),
                   int_to_l3d_real(-1),
                   int_to_l3d_real(0),
                   int_to_l3d_real(0));
    }


    class dot_star : public mydot {
      public:
        void place_dot(void); //- virtual
        void move_dot(void); //- virtual
    };

    void dot_star::place_dot(void) {
      displacement.set(int_to_l3d_real(1000 - (rand() % 2000)),
                       int_to_l3d_real(1000 - (rand() % 2000)),
                       int_to_l3d_real(200 + (rand()%1000)),
                       int_to_l3d_real(0));
      position.reset();
      velocity.set(int_to_l3d_real(0),
                   int_to_l3d_real(0),
                   int_to_l3d_real(-10),
                   int_to_l3d_real(0));
    }

    void dot_star::move_dot(void) {
      displacement = displacement + velocity;
      position.reset();
      position.transformed = position.transformed + displacement;
    }
```

By changing coordinates in 3D WC we are modeling movement of the objects in the 3D virtual world. This movement is modeled in the most natural way possible. For instance, in the class `dot_star`, we update the dot position for a star by decreasing its z coordinate (via a velocity vector with a negative z component). Based on the definition of the left-handed 3D WC system we are using, decreasing the z coordinate means moving toward the viewer—precisely the motion we wish to model. In the case of `dot_runway_light`, we model the horizontal movement for runway lights by decreasing the x coordinate. Finally, in the case of `dot_snowflake`, the movement is modeled as a drift downward (decreasing the y coordinate) and also a possible random drift right (increasing the x coordinate by a random amount). We implement all movements by using velocity vectors, adding a vector to the current position to give a new position.

So to model movement in the 3D world, we manipulate the points or objects in the 3D world database. Since for now our eye is at a fixed location in 3D space, we can't keep moving points forever in the same direction: they will become invisible sooner or later. Each subclass of `my_pipeline` overrides the virtual function `out_of_wc_bounds` to define when a dot has passed outside of some application-specific boundary. When this occurs, the dot needs to be repositioned so that it is visible again.

```
int my_pipeline_runway::out_of_wc_bounds(l3d_point const &p) {
  return(p.X_<int_to_l3d_real(-200));
}
```

```
int my_pipeline_snow::out_of_wc_bounds(l3d_point const &p) {
  return(p.Y_<int_to_l3d_real(-70));
}
```

```
int my_pipeline_stars::out_of_wc_bounds(l3d_point const &p) {
  return(p.Z_<int_to_l3d_real(20));
}
```

For instance, we model snowflakes as falling downwards. When a snowflake passes down beyond a certain y level it hits the ground and melts, effectively disappearing. In our program, whenever a snowflake disappears or passes out of bounds, we reinitialize its position with new values (via `place_dot`), effectively creating a new snowflake to replace the old one. In computer memory, of course, it is the same snowflake repositioned somewhere else, but this fact is hidden from the viewer.

Notice again that we never change a dot's original coordinate. (Recall that we mentioned this in Chapter 2, in the introductory discussion on the purpose of the `original` and `transformed` members of the `l3d_coordinate` class.) Instead, to change its position, we update a separate displacement vector. This displacement vector displaces the original coordinate to the current location via a vector-point addition, storing the results in the transformed coordinate. Then we update this current location with the current velocity vector, again storing the new results in the transformed coordinate. Finally, we project this updated current location from 3D into 2D, again storing the results in the transformed coordinate. The transformed coordinate then finally contains the pixel coordinates to be plotted on-screen.

The necessity of using such an original-transformed scheme becomes more apparent when we group points into objects, as we do in the next sample program. In this case, it is essential that we save the original points defining an object and always perform any movement by starting with the original points and storing the results in a separate transformed storage area. The alternative, constantly updating the original points "in-place" to reflect the new position, will eventually, due to inevitable numerical inaccuracies during repeated computations, lead to the points drifting apart from one another until the relative positions of the points no longer correspond to the original shape of the object. If an object just consists of one point, as in this sample program, you would probably never notice the problem, but when an object consists of many points, you eventually would.

Perspective Projection and Screen Mapping

The `update_event` method of the `my_pipeline` subclass asks each dot to project itself by calling `project_dot`, which implements the perspective projection and screen mapping developed earlier in this chapter.

In general, we should avoid projecting any points which have z values less than or equal to 0. Points with $z=0$ are problematic because the perspective projection works by dividing by z. Dividing by 0 is, of course, impossible. Points with $z<0$ are physically points located behind the viewer. We should also avoid projecting these points since our eyes can only see objects in front of us. Mathematically, projection of a point behind the eye is possible; it will however be vertically inverted with respect to the original point and has no physical significance.

In this program, we handle these z value issues by ensuring that z values are always positive. For the demonstrations runway lights and snow, we always explicitly assign a positive z value; for the star field, we reset z if it falls below 20 (via routine `out_of_wc_bounds`). In general, we solve this problem by using 3D polygons for modeling, and by clipping these 3D polygons against a near z clip plane so that only positive z values remain (Chapter 7).

Culling

In the `draw_event` method, which draws the projected points, the code for actually plotting a point is enclosed within a simple `if` statement which prevents off-screen points from being drawn. Off-screen points are points whose projected values fall outside of the screen boundaries; for the given eye location and field of view, they are not visible. These unseen points should not be drawn.

```
//- culling
if(dots[i]->position.transformed.X_>=0 &&
    dots[i]->position.transformed.X_ <= int_to_l3d_real(s->xsize) &&
    dots[i]->position.transformed.Y_ >= 0 &&
    dots[i]->position.transformed.Y_ <= int_to_l3d_real(s->ysize))
{
```

This step may seem obvious, but the more generally applicable idea is quite important. More advanced culling schemes can determine much earlier that a particular point or polygon cannot possibly be seen. The earlier we determine that a point or polygon cannot be seen, the more processing time we can save and the faster our program will run. (Recall the discussion on hardware acceleration in Chapter 1—"cull what you can, accelerate what you can't.") For instance, in the `dots` program, we only cull points after projecting them, which is quite late in the pipeline. What if we had 50 million points? For a given viewpoint, only a tiny fraction, say 5%, of these points are visible. Would we have to project all 50 million points—meaning 50 million divide operations—only to determine that 95% are invisible? Culling schemes attempt to eliminate a point from further consideration as early as possible.

Rasterization

Once the point has made it this far through the 3D pipeline, it has been projected, mapped to the screen, and is visible. We only need to plot it, which is done in line by calling the 2D graphics routine to plot a pixel from Chapter 2.

```
r->draw_point(ifloor(dots[i]->position.transformed.X_),
              ifloor(dots[i]->position.transformed.Y_),
              color);
```

With more complicated polyhedral 3D objects, as in the next sample program, we use the projected points to draw a polygon instead of just a dot.

Blitting

Due to the double-buffering scheme introduced in Chapter 2, we rasterize all graphics off-screen, then make the off-screen graphics buffer visible all at once. This is the `blit_screen` method called as the last line of the `draw_event` method.

```
s->blit_screen();
```

3D Polygonal Graphics

We claimed earlier that projecting points from 3D to 2D is enough to project any object from 3D into 2D. To project a line from 3D into 2D, we simply project the endpoints and draw a line in 2D between the projected endpoints. To project a polygon, we project the vertices of the polygon and draw a 2D polygon using the projected vertices. This is conceptually equivalent to projecting the endpoints of each edge from 3D to 2D, and drawing each edge as a line in 2D; drawing a filled polygon then simply means drawing 2D horizontal lines between the 2D projected edges.

Since we developed code in Chapter 3 for drawing 2D polygons, projecting polygons from 3D into 2D is therefore as simple as combining the perspective projection equation with the 2D polygon drawing routines. This is what the next sample program, spikes, does.

Listing 5-5: `spikes.cc`

```
#include <stdlib.h>
#include <stdio.h>

#include "../lib/tool_2d/screen.h"
#include "../lib/tool_os/dispatch.h"
#include "../lib/raster/rasteriz.h"
#include "../lib/tool_2d/scrinfo.h"
#include "../lib/system/factorys.h"

#include "../lib/geom/point/point.h"
#include "../lib/math/vector.h"
```

```
#include "../lib/math/matrix.h"

#define MAXSPIKES 150
#define PI 3.14159265

unsigned long red_color;
unsigned long green_color;
unsigned long blue_color;

//- STEP 1: CHOOSE THE FACTORIES

void choose_factories(void) {
  factory_manager_v_0_1.choose_factories();
}

//- STEP 2: DECLARE A PIPELINE SUBCLASS

l3d_real fovx, fovy;
int xsize, ysize;

class spike {
  public:

    l3d_two_part_list<l3d_coordinate> *vlist;
    l3d_polygon_2d_flatshaded *faces[3];
    l3d_vector displacement;
    l3d_vector velocity;

    spike(void) {
      //- declare common shared vertex list for all polygons
      vlist = new l3d_two_part_list<l3d_coordinate> (4);
      int i=0;
      (*vlist)[i++].original.set(int_to_l3d_real(0),
                                 int_to_l3d_real(0),
                                 int_to_l3d_real(100),
                                 int_to_l3d_real(1));
      (*vlist)[i++].original.set(int_to_l3d_real(10),
                                 int_to_l3d_real(10),
                                 int_to_l3d_real(100),
                                 int_to_l3d_real(1));
      (*vlist)[i++].original.set(int_to_l3d_real(10),
                                 int_to_l3d_real(0),
                                 int_to_l3d_real(100),
                                 int_to_l3d_real(1));
      (*vlist)[i++].original.set(int_to_l3d_real(0),
                                 int_to_l3d_real(0),
                                 int_to_l3d_real(0),
                                 int_to_l3d_real(1));

      //- define polygons in terms of indices into shared vertex list
      faces[0] = new l3d_polygon_2d_flatshaded(3);
      faces[0]->vlist = & vlist; //- shared vertex list
      (*(faces[0]->ivertices))[faces[0]->ivertices->next_index()].ivertex = 3;
      (*(faces[0]->ivertices))[faces[0]->ivertices->next_index()].ivertex = 0;
      (*(faces[0]->ivertices))[faces[0]->ivertices->next_index()].ivertex = 1;

      faces[1] = new l3d_polygon_2d_flatshaded(3);
      faces[1]->vlist = & vlist; //- shared vertex list
      (*(faces[1]->ivertices))[faces[1]->ivertices->next_index()].ivertex = 3;
      (*(faces[1]->ivertices))[faces[1]->ivertices->next_index()].ivertex = 1;
```

```
    (*(faces[1]->ivertices))[faces[1]->ivertices->next_index()].ivertex = 2;

    faces[2] = new l3d_polygon_2d_flatshaded(3);
    faces[2]->vlist = & vlist; //- shared vertex list
    (*(faces[2]->ivertices))[faces[2]->ivertices->next_index()].ivertex = 3;
    (*(faces[2]->ivertices))[faces[2]->ivertices->next_index()].ivertex = 2;
    (*(faces[2]->ivertices))[faces[2]->ivertices->next_index()].ivertex = 0;
  }

  ~spike(void) {
    delete faces[0];
    delete faces[1];
    delete faces[2];
    delete vlist;
  }

  void place_spike(void) {
    displacement.set(int_to_l3d_real(1000 - (rand() % 2000)),
                     int_to_l3d_real(1000 - (rand() % 2000)),
                     int_to_l3d_real(100 + (rand()%1000)),
                     int_to_l3d_real(1));
    velocity.set(int_to_l3d_real(0),
                 int_to_l3d_real(0),
                 int_to_l3d_real(-(rand()%75 + 5)),
                 int_to_l3d_real(0));

    int q;
    for(q=0; q<vlist->num_fixed_items; q++) {
      (*vlist)[q].reset();
      (*vlist)[q].transformed =         (*vlist)[q].transformed + displacement;
    }
  }

  void move_spike(void) {
    displacement = displacement + velocity;

    int q;
    for(q=0; q<vlist->num_fixed_items; q++) {
      (*vlist)[q].reset();
      (*vlist)[q].transformed =         (*vlist)[q].transformed + displacement;
    }
  }

  void project_spike() {
    int v;

    for(v=0; v<vlist->num_fixed_items; v++) {
      (*vlist)[v].transformed.X_ =
        l3d_mulri(l3d_mulrr(l3d_divrr( (*vlist)[v].transformed.X_,
                                       (*vlist)[v].transformed.Z_),
                            fovx),
                  xsize)
        +
        int_to_l3d_real(xsize > 1);

      (*vlist)[v].transformed.Y_ =
        l3d_mulri(l3d_mulrr(l3d_divrr(-(*vlist)[v].transformed.Y_,
                                       (*vlist)[v].transformed.Z_),
                            fovy),
                  ysize)
```

```
                   +
               int_to_l3d_real(ysize > 1);
          }
      }

};

class my_pipeline : public l3d_pipeline {
  protected:
    l3d_rasterizer_2d_imp *ri;
    l3d_rasterizer_2d *r;

    spike spikes[MAXSPIKES];
    long i, j;
    long wc_win_width, wc_win_height, wc_win_dist, fov;
    long wc_win_left, wc_win_top;
    int numspikes;

    virtual int out_of_wc_bounds(l3d_point const &p);

  public:
    l3d_screen *s;
    my_pipeline(void);
    virtual ~my_pipeline(void);

    void key_event(int ch);  //- from dispatcher
    void update_event(void); //- from dispatcher
    void draw_event(void);   //- from dispatcher
};

my_pipeline::my_pipeline(void) {
  s = factory_manager_v_0_1.screen_factory->create(320,200);
  ri = factory_manager_v_0_1.ras_2d_imp_factory->create(320,200,s->sinfo);
  r = new l3d_rasterizer_2d(ri);

  s->sinfo->ext_max_red =
    s->sinfo->ext_max_green =
      s->sinfo->ext_max_blue = 255;
  s->sinfo->ext_to_native(0,0,0); //- allocate black background color
  red_color = s->sinfo->ext_to_native(255, 0, 0);
  green_color = s->sinfo->ext_to_native(0, 255, 0);
  blue_color = s->sinfo->ext_to_native(0,0, 255);
  s->refresh_palette();

  fovx = float_to_l3d_real(0.5*1.0/tan(50./180. * PI));
  fovy = float_to_l3d_real(0.5*1.0/tan(30./180. * PI));
  xsize = s->xsize;
  ysize = s->ysize;

  numspikes = MAXSPIKES;
  for(i=0; i<MAXSPIKES; i++) {
    spikes[i].place_spike();

    spikes[i].faces[0]->final_color = red_color;
    spikes[i].faces[1]->final_color = green_color;
    spikes[i].faces[2]->final_color = blue_color;
  }
}
```

```
my_pipeline::~my_pipeline(void) {
  delete s;
  delete ri;
  delete r;
}

void my_pipeline::key_event(int ch) {
  switch(ch) {
    case 'q': {
        exit(0);
      }
  }
}

void my_pipeline::update_event() {
  int i;

  for(i=0;i<numspikes;i++) {
    spikes[i].move_spike();
    if(out_of_wc_bounds( (*spikes[i].vlist)[3].transformed))
      //- we use the vertex with index 3 because we know that this is the
      //- vertex which has the smallest z-component of all vertices.
      //- in general we don't know which vertex is foremost (since
      //- the object might be rotated or morphed, for instance),
      //- so in general we either need to check all vertices or
      //- we need to clip all vertices to make sure they are valid.
    {
      spikes[i].place_spike();
    }

    spikes[i].project_spike();
  }
}

void my_pipeline::draw_event(void) {
  int i;
  r->clear_buffer();

  for(i=0;i<numspikes;i++) {
    for(int f=0; f<3; f++) {
      spikes[i].faces[f]->init_clip_ivertices();
      spikes[i].faces[f]->clip_to_polygon_2d(s->view_win);
      r->draw_polygon_flatshaded(spikes[i].faces[f]);
    }
  }
  s->blit_screen();
}

int my_pipeline::out_of_wc_bounds(l3d_point const &p) {
  return(p.Z <int_to_l3d_real(1));
}

int main(int argc, char **argv) {
  choose_factories();

  l3d_dispatcher *d;
  my_pipeline *p;

  //- STEP 3: CREATE A DISPATCHER
```

```
    d = factory_manager_v_0_1.dispatcher_factory->create();

    //- STEP 4: CREATE A PIPELINE

    //- plug our custom behavior pipeline into the dispatcher
    p  = new my_pipeline();

    //- STEP 5: START DISPATCHER

    d->pipeline = p; //- polymorphic assignment
    d->event_source = p->s;
    d->start();

    delete d;
    delete p;
}
```

Overview of Program "Spikes"

This program is essentially the same as the star field simulation from the previous program. However, instead of projecting and animating just dots, we project sets of dots, defined in the spike class. Each set of dots defines three polygons in 3D which geometrically form the sides of a pyramid pointing towards the viewer—a spike.

The spike class declares a common vertex list vlist, containing four vertices defined in 3D. Furthermore, the faces array holds three polygons, each of which is defined in terms of indices into this common, external vertex list.

Does the structure of this code look familiar? It should, because all of the polygon examples from the previous chapter used this same structure: each polygon contains a pointer to an external vertex list and is defined in terms of indices into this external vertex list. The only difference from Chapter 3 is that we are treating the points in the vertex list as 3D points (x,y,z) instead of 2D points (x,y). Since our existing l3d_point class already can handle up to 4D points, no new point class is required.

Each polygon in the spike references the same vertex list. For instance, the point with index 3 appears in all three polygons; the other points all appear in two polygons. If each polygon had stored its own vertex list, this would mean a wasteful and dangerous duplication of data: wasteful because identical points are being subjected to the same computations, and dangerous because any redundant data duplication leads to the danger of inconsistencies among the various copies.

These spikes appear to fly towards the viewer as did the stars from the previous star field simulation. As with the previous program, notice the use of vectors for movement and the fact that the original coordinates of a spike object are never changed, only the transformed coordinates.

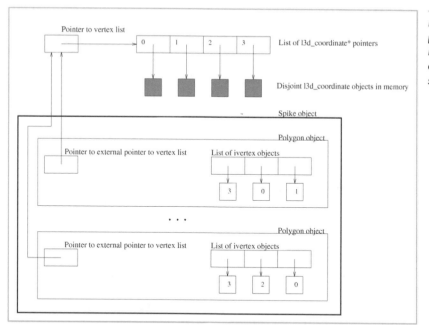

Figure 5-29: Each polygon in a spike is defined in terms of the same shared vertex list.

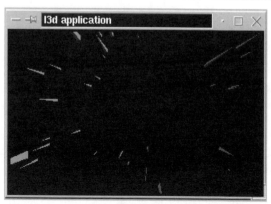

Figure 5-30: Polygonal 3D graphics from the sample program *spikes*.

From Dots to Polygons

The following list summarizes the important changes from the previous dots program.

- We define a spike in terms of several points, not just one point as in the dots program. These several points are stored in a vertex list, which is an l3d_two_part_list of l3d_coordinate objects. After the initial assignment, we never change the original member of these l3d_coordinate objects, only the transformed member. The original members represent the "pure" geometric definition of the spike object.

- The spike object defines several polygons in terms of the vertex list.

- Initialization and movement of the spike's location (methods place_spike and move_spike) must initialize and move all of the points in the vertex list. We therefore have several loops going from 0 to `vlist->num_fixed_items`, to loop through the vertices in the fixed part of the vertex list. (Recall that we have a fixed part, consisting of the original vertices, and a temporary varying part, reserved for clipping purposes.)

- Projection of the spike (method `project_spike`) must also project all of the points in the vertex list and not just one point as in the `dots` program.
- Drawing the spike (method `draw_event` in `my_pipeline`) requires us to draw each polygon in the spike. For this, we simply loop through all polygons for each spike and draw each polygon exactly as we did in the previous chapter (first clipping, then drawing).

Importantly, notice that we can use exactly the same 2D polygon drawing routines from the previous chapter to draw projected 3D polygons. We define the spike's vertices in 3D in a vertex list, and then define 3D polygons referencing these 3D vertices. By projecting the spike's vertices from 3D into 2D, all 3D polygons then automatically become 2D polygons, since they now all reference 2D vertices. Conveniently, and not at all accidentally, we can then draw these 2D polygons exactly as discussed in Chapter 3, even though the now 2D polygons' vertices actually arose out of a 3D-to-2D projection operation. The flattened, projected vertices get stored into the `transformed` members of the vertices, which (as mentioned in Chapter 2) are the points used for drawing and which are separate from the original, in this case three-dimensional definition of the spike geometry.

 NOTE We clip the polygon in 2D after the 3D to 2D projection. This can produce new 2D vertices. These new vertices, unlike the original projected 3D vertices, do not result directly from a 3D-to-2D projection operation. As mentioned earlier in this chapter, this is an issue for algorithms which need to know the original, pre-projection 3D location of each 2D point on-screen. The companion book *Advanced Linux 3D Graphics Programming* discusses such algorithms (e.g., texture mapping and z buffering).

The pipeline for the `spikes` program is the same as that of the `dots` program, except that the points are grouped into objects. The group of `original` coordinate values belonging to a spike define the original geometry of a spike, but not its location. We only obtain location after adding a displacement or positional vector to the original geometry. If you like, you can loosely think of this as a class-object relationship: the original geometry (the class) is a template defining how the object must look but not where specifically it is; the transformed geometry (the object) is a particular instance of the original geometry located at a particular offset from the origin and possibly having undergone further transformations.

Because the `original` coordinates define the geometry of an object but not its location, we can also refer to them as *object coordinates*. Object coordinates allow us to define an object's geometry relative to itself (i.e., "the first button is always 2 cm left of the second button") rather than always having to specify coordinates with respect to a containing world coordinate system. In other words, object coordinates represent the innate geometry of the object, independently of where the object is located. These object coordinates get transformed into world coordinates, representing the actual location of one instance of the object. World coordinates change whenever the object changes position; object coordinates only change if the object changes shape. Chapter 6 discusses the concept of multiple coordinate systems, and the transformations among them, in more detail.

Summary

In this chapter we defined 3D graphics, examined the physics of vision, and derived the mathematics of projection. We discussed:

- 3D coordinate systems and vectors
- 3D-to-2D projection through division by the z coordinate
- Projecting dots and polygons
- Modeling 3D objects as a set of 3D polygons
- The general structure of a 3D engine

Let's take a moment and reflect on the material we have covered up to this point in the book. We have learned about Linux programming and debugging, Linux tools, the X Window System, plotting pixels in arbitrary colors in arbitrary bit depths, double buffering, animation, drawing 2D lines and polygons, vertex morphing using a vertex interpolator, the physics and geometry of vision, 3D coordinate systems, 3D vectors, projecting from 3D into 2D, modeling 3D polygonal objects, and the general structure of a 3D engine.

The knowledge summarized above provides a very solid basis for Linux 3D graphics programming. 3D games have been written with little more than this. I encourage you to expand on the sample programs in this chapter and create some simple 3D demonstration programs of your own. For instance, try to use the vertex interpolator class introduced in Chapter 3 to do 3D polygon morphing in the `spikes` program. (The companion book *Advanced Linux 3D Graphics Programming* implements 3D polygon morphing.) Try to define and draw more complex polygonal objects than spikes—for instance, a six-sided cube or a desk. Do you ever notice any drawing anomalies when displaying more complicated polygonal objects? (Chapter 7 touches upon these problems, collectively called *hidden surface removal*, and presents one solution, the so-called "painter's algorithm.") There's nothing like learning by doing.

The preceding chapters have provided enough information to produce simple 3D demos, screen savers, or even games under Linux. The remainder of the book presents more generally applicable techniques for creating larger and more flexible 3D applications—techniques with which every 3D programmer should be familiar. The techniques presented in the rest of the book provide a solid basis for dealing with real problems in real 3D programs, ranging from technical issues, such as arbitrary camera orientation, to practical issues, such as creating interesting 3D models using the free Blender 3D modeling package for Linux (included on the CD-ROM).

Specifically, the next chapter deals with 3D transformations and the mathematical tool we use for manipulating them, the matrix. We have already encountered a simple form of transformation: movement of an object in 3D by adding a velocity vector. More generally, 3D transformations also allow rotation and scaling of objects in 3D (in addition to many other effects). Furthermore, combining transformations allows us to move and orient the eye, or any other object, arbitrarily in 3D, which is a major step in creating believable, interactive 3D applications.

Chapter 6

Matrices and Transformations

Overview

In the previous chapter, we saw how to project 3D points into 2D points for display on-screen. We assumed a simple and fixed-eye location and orientation, and animation of the 3D points was fairly rudimentary: runway lights moving right to left, snow falling downward, spikes flying directly forward.

In this chapter, we look at how transformations can be used to model movement of 3D points in more complicated ways—for instance, an asteroid tumbling through space while rotating about all three axes in 3D. We also see how transformations can transform an arbitrary eye location and orientation into the standard location and orientation assumed in the last chapter. This accomplishes two important goals: objects can move more flexibly in 3D, and the camera can look at these objects from any angle. These contribute greatly to the realism of a 3D program, enabling a completely 3D walk-through or "fly-through" of the virtual world. At the end of this chapter we develop a 3D simulation program which allows you to fly through a virtual world and look at the objects from any position and orientation.

This chapter is a bit heavy on the math, but this is unavoidable; true 3D graphics involves a lot of linear algebra and trigonometry. But rest assured: with only a bit of clear thinking and a good geometric visualization capacity, none of the math presented in this chapter is very difficult, and you always see the results of your efforts as a more realistic or visually pleasing 3D program. The math for 3D graphics is a very broad and fascinating field, so enjoy it!

This chapter covers the following topics:

- Definition of transformations
- Non-matrix form of translation, rotation, and scaling transformations
- Definition of matrices and matrix-vector math
- Matrix form of translation, rotation, and scaling transformations
- Combining transformations via matrix-matrix multiplication
- Arbitrary camera and object orientation and rotation
- Matrices and coordinate systems
- Perspective projection as a non-linear warping transformation of 3D space

Introduction to Transformations

A *transformation* in 3D graphics defines a precise way of altering the position of a 3D point in the 3D world coordinate system. We can apply a transformation to one, several, or all points in a 3D space.

If we apply a transformation only to selected points within the 3D space, we can think of the transformation as being a tool to move particular objects around. An example of this would be transforming the individual vertices of a single spaceship object in order to move it within the 3D world coordinate system. On the other hand, if we apply a transformation to all points in a 3D space, then we can think of the transformation as transforming the entire 3D space and all objects in it. An example of this would be the perspective projection itself, covered in the previous chapter, which applies to all points uniformly, dividing each point's x and y coordinate by its z coordinate. Another example is the camera transformation, covered later in this chapter, which converts an arbitrary camera location and orientation into the standard camera location and orientation required by the perspective projection of the previous chapter.

NOTE In Chapter 4, which focused on the human perceptual mechanisms which play a role in 3D graphics, we used the term "eye" to refer to the location of the viewer in the virtual 3D space. Starting with this chapter, we also use the term "camera" to denote the location of the virtual viewer. Both terms are common in the 3D literature.

Two points can define the base and tip of a vector, as we saw in Chapter 5. Thus, transformations can also change vectors, by altering the vector's starting and/or ending point. Remember that the vector itself, though, is the directed displacement between the two points.

The three most important geometric transformations we need to understand for 3D graphics are translation, rotation, and scaling. The main thrust of this chapter, therefore, is on developing, understanding, using, and combining these transformations. Let's start by geometrically defining these transformations. For each transformation, we will look at:

- A description of the transformation
- An illustration of the transformation in 2D space, applied to multiple points
- A simplified illustration of the transformation in 3D space, applied to a single point. Since a book is a 2D medium, the illustrations of the 3D transformations are applied only to a single point to reduce diagram clutter.

Translation

Translation is moving a point by a given offset in the x, y, and/or z axis directions. You can think of a translation as "pushing" a point in a given direction by a given amount. The following are all examples of translations.

- Move a point 5 units (in 3D world coordinates) to the left.
- Move a point 3 units vertically along the y axis and -2 units horizontally to the left along the x axis.
- Move a point 1 unit along the x axis, 32 units along the y axis, and -5 units along the z axis.

A translation can be implemented as a component-wise vector addition, as done in Chapter 5. But, as we see later in this chapter, a matrix is actually the preferred form for representing transformations, including translation.

NOTE   In the discrete world of digital computers, a translation—or any transformation, for that matter—occurs instantaneously. That is to say, at one particular point in time a coordinate has a particular value, such as 0. After transformation, at a later point in time, the coordinate might have a value of 5. This raises some issues if the transformation models a real-world physical movement. In the real world, an object cannot move from position 0 to position 5 without also passing through all points in between. In the computer world, however, the position "jumps" or "teleports" instantaneously from 0 to 5, without ever having been located at any of the points in between. This can cause problems for collision detection or other physically based simulation, since an object jumping from position 0 to position 5 never collides or interacts with objects located between these two positions. The solution to this problem requires that physically based simulation routines do more than merely compare the instantaneous "snapshot" positions of interacting objects; they must also account for objects' movement (velocity). Mathematically, this means not only considering the instantaneous location, but also the higher-order derivatives of location—velocity, the first derivative, and for more realism, acceleration, the second derivative. Recall from calculus that the derivative of a variable with respect to another variable is nothing more than the limit approaching zero of the change in the first divided by the change in the second. Velocity is thus the instantaneous change in location with respect to time; acceleration is the instantaneous change in velocity with respect to time. This topic is covered in the companion book *Advanced Linux 3D Graphics Programming*, where we discuss collision detection.

Figure 6-1 illustrates the translation of four points, defining a box, in 2D space. The box—or, more precisely, each of the four vertices defining the box—is translated by 2 units in the x direction and −1 units in the y direction.

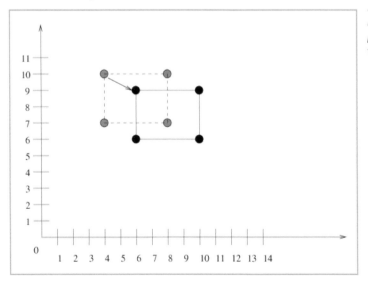

Figure 6-1: Translation of points in 2D space. The box is translated by (2,−1).

Figure 6-2 illustrates translation of a single point in 3D space.

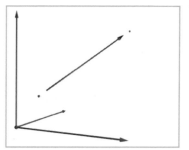

Figure 6-2: Translation of a point in 3D space.

Rotation

Rotation is the movement of a point in a circle. In 2D, we specify a rotation with an angle θ (written "theta"). Rotation of the point by an angle θ means moving the point θ degrees in the counterclockwise direction along a circle, with the center of the circle at the origin.

Figure 6-3 illustrates the rotation of a box in 2D space. The box is rotated by an angle θ (in this case, 27 degrees) counterclockwise around the origin. Rotation of the entire box is equivalent to rotating each of its defining vertices. Each vertex in the figure has been rotated by θ degrees about the origin counterclockwise. This has been illustrated in the figure only for the lower-left vertex of the box, but all vertices are rotated by the same amount; otherwise, the shape of the box would change after rotation.

Notice that in addition to rotating, the box also changes position (assuming, for instance, that we define the box's "position" to be at its center). Later in this chapter we take another look at this phenomenon and a way around it; often we wish to rotate an object about its own center.

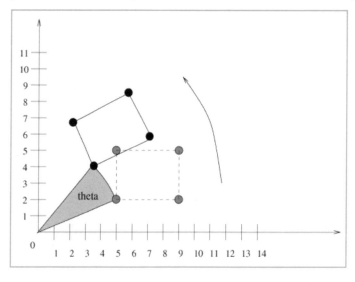

Figure 6-3: Rotation of points in 2D space.

For 3D rotation, in addition to θ, we must also specify an axis around which we wish to rotate the point (x, y, or z axis). A positive rotation angle θ specifies a clockwise rotation around the given axis, when looking along the positive axis toward the origin. This is consistent with a left-handed coordinate system; if you point your thumb in the positive direction of the axis of rotation, your fingers curl in the direction of rotation for a positive angle—clockwise. A negative rotation angle rotates in the counterclockwise direction with respect to the axis of rotation.

Figures 6-4, 6-5, and 6-6 illustrate positive rotations around the x, y, and z axes for a given 3D point. In each case the arrow in the diagram represents the direction of positive rotation.

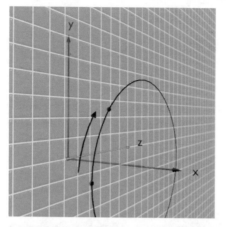

Figure 6-4: 3D rotation of a point in a circle about the x axis.

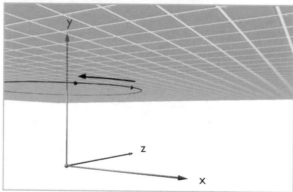

Figure 6-5: 3D rotation of a point in a circle about the y axis.

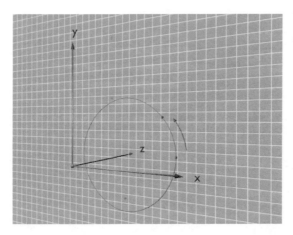

Figure 6-6: 3D rotation of a point in a circle about the z axis.

Notice carefully the convention we just defined for the concept of "clockwise" in 3D space. A 3D rotation takes place in a clockwise direction around an axis when looking along the positive axis toward the origin. More generally, we can say that rotation around a vector is in a clockwise direction around the vector when looking along the vector from its tip to its base. If we look along the axis or vector in the opposite direction (from base to tip), the rotation appears to take place in the opposite direction (counterclockwise instead of clockwise). This is why a positive 2D rotation was defined counterclockwise (with respect to the page), but a positive 3D rotation is defined clockwise (with respect to the axis of rotation). In reality, the 2D and 3D rotations take place in exactly the same direction; it is merely our point of view which is different. By taking the 2D coordinate system and adding a left-handed z axis, which points into the page, we are looking from the base to the tip of the z axis. From this point of view, a positive rotation appears to be counterclockwise. But if we imagine changing our point of view so that we are looking from the tip to the base of the z axis, the positive rotation appears to take place in the clockwise direction, which is consistent with the left-hand rule we defined above.

If you are having trouble visualizing this, the following series of diagrams should help. They show how a counterclockwise rotation viewed from the base of the vector is the same as a clockwise rotation viewed from the tip of the vector. To keep clockwise and counterclockwise straight, simply ask yourself, "in which direction is the axis of rotation pointing?" Then, imagine viewing the situation from the tip of this vector looking towards its base. From this point of view, a positive rotation angle is clockwise. Alternatively, you can completely forget about clockwise and counterclockwise and simply point the thumb of your left hand along the positive direction of the axis of rotation. The direction in which your fingers curl is the positive direction of rotation.

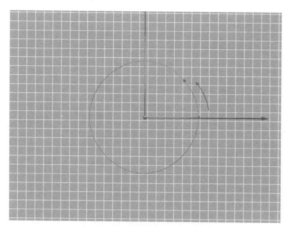

Figure 6-7: An apparently counterclockwise rotation in the positive direction of rotation. This corresponds to the 2D rotation illustrated in Figure 6-3.

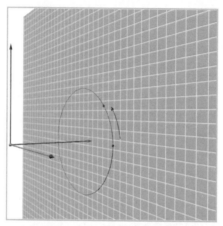

Figure 6-8: If we change our point of view...

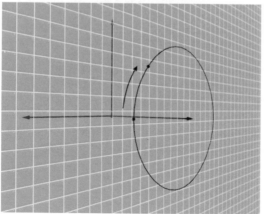

Figure 6-9: ...so that we are looking from the tip to the base of the vector...

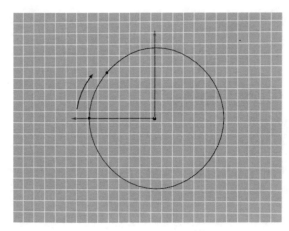

Figure 6-10: ...then the same rotation appears to take place in the clockwise direction. The rotation is the same and is still in the positive direction; only our point of view has changed. The point of view in this figure (looking from the tip to the base of the rotation vector) is the point of view we need in order to apply the rule that a positive rotation takes place in the "clockwise" direction. Alternatively, use your left hand to determine the direction of positive rotation.

Scaling

Scaling is stretching the distance of a point from the origin. A 3D point with coordinates (x,y,z) may be thought of as the point obtained by starting at the origin and moving a distance of x units along the x axis, y units along the y axis, and z units along the z axis. If we scale the point (x,y,z), we multiply x, y, and z by scaling factors s_x, s_y, and s_z to define a new point. This has the effect of increasing or decreasing the displacements in the x, y, and z directions. Scaling factors greater than one move a point farther from the origin (expansive movement); scaling factors smaller than one move a point closer to the origin (contractive movement).

If s_x, s_y, and s_z are all equal, we call the scaling a *uniform scaling*; otherwise, we call it a *non-uniform scaling*. We use uniform scaling to change the size of an object uniformly in all directions. Non-uniform scaling stretches an object by varying amounts along the different coordinate axes.

NOTE Non-uniform scaling is a bit tricky to handle, since a non-uniform scaling of a polygon changes its shape: it is stretched unequally in different directions. This change in shape also causes a change in length of the polygon's surface normal vector (Chapter 7). If the surface normal vector was normalized before, it will no longer be normalized after non-uniform scaling, which could be a problem if any code assumes that the vectors are normalized.

Figure 6-11 illustrates uniform scaling of a box in 2D space. The box is scaled by a factor of 0.5. Notice that the box is not only smaller, but also closer to the origin. Sometimes this is desirable, but usually not. Later in this chapter we see how to scale an object while leaving its (center) location the same.

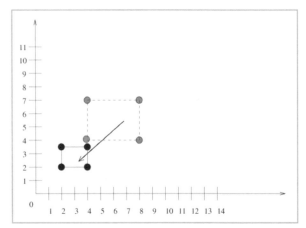

Figure 6-11: Uniform scaling by 0.5 of a box in 2D space. The box is not only smaller, but also closer to the origin.

Figure 6-12 illustrates a 3D point (*2,2,2*) and the 3D points resulting from uniform scale operations of 0.5 and 1.5.

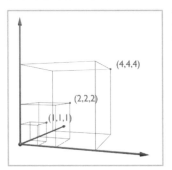

Figure 6-12: Uniform scale operations (0.5 and 1.5 scale factors) of a point at (2,2,2).

What is... the *Matrix?*

We have now developed an intuitive, geometric feeling for the transformations of translation, rotation, and scaling. How do we represent these transformations mathematically? The standard of representing transformations relies upon a mathematical construct called the *matrix*, which comes with its own set of mathematical rules. Therefore, to further understand transformations, we must first answer the fundamental question:

What is the *Matrix?*

If you want to find out, read on. (Otherwise, take the blue pill.)

Definitions: Matrices and Vectors

A *matrix* (plural matrices) is a rectangular, two-dimensional grid of numbers. The size of a matrix is expressed as *m×n*, where *m* is the number of rows in the matrix and *n* is the number of columns. Note the reversal of terms in comparison to conventional expressions of width times height. If *m* is 1, the matrix has only one row, and is called a *row matrix* or, equivalently, a *row vector*. If *n* is 1, the matrix has only one column, and is called a *column matrix* or a *column vector*. We can therefore think of a vector as a single column or row of numbers, whereas a matrix consists of multiple columns and rows of numbers. In fact, we can view a matrix as being a collection of row vectors or a collection of column vectors.

$$\begin{bmatrix} 17 & 2 & 89 & 12 \\ -3 & 8 & 1.75 & 0 \\ 1 & 18 & -2.5 & 1 \\ 11 & 1 & 16 & 32 \end{bmatrix} \quad \begin{bmatrix} 1 \\ 64 \\ 88 \\ 5 \end{bmatrix} \quad \begin{bmatrix} 7 & 11 & 9 & 1 \end{bmatrix}$$

Figure 6-13: Matrices. Left to right: a 4×4 matrix, a 4×1 matrix or column vector, and a 1×4 matrix or row vector.

A column vector is normally written vertically as a column of numbers. This vertical notation, however, does not integrate well into the horizontal flow of running text. Therefore, within running text, we can write column vectors horizontally but with a superscripted T. This means that the horizontal (row) vector has been written "transposed," and is actually a vertical column vector. The following figure shows two different ways of writing a column vector.

$$\begin{bmatrix} x \\ y \\ z \\ w \end{bmatrix} = \begin{bmatrix} x & y & z & w \end{bmatrix}^T$$

Figure 6-14: Two equivalent notations for writing a column vector.

It might appear that a row vector and a column vector are essentially identical, since they are both simply tuples of numbers. However, we must distinguish between row vectors and column vectors because the orientation (horizontal or vertical) plays an important role in the rules governing matrix arithmetic, covered later in this chapter.

A Note on the Term "Vector"

In the context of matrix operations, we are using the term "vector" in a new way. In Chapter 5, a vector was a displacement in space. Here, the term "row vector" or "column vector" refers to a notational convention used to describe an *n*-tuple. A row vector or a column vector is a tuple of numbers written within square brackets and subject to the mathematical rules governing matrix arithmetic, presented later. A row vector or a column vector can be used as a notation for specifying the 3D points or 3D vectors covered in Chapter 5.

In other words, a column vector (the notation) can be used to describe a 3D vector (a spatial displacement) or a 3D point (a spatial location). If the meaning of the term "vector" is clear from the context, we will simply say "vector." Otherwise, we will explicitly say "row vector" or "column vector" to refer to the notational convention, and say "2D vector" or "3D vector" to refer to a spatial displacement.

Writing 3D Points and 3D Vectors in Matrix Notation

In Chapter 5, we wrote points and vectors as ordered lists in parentheses, such as point (x,y,z) or vector (v_1,v_2,v_3). Now, we introduce a new notation using 4×1 column vectors to represent 3D points and 3D vectors. The reason for this change in notation is to allow a consistent notation—namely, the matrix notation—for expressing and combining points, vectors, and transformations.

The notation is as follows:

- A 3D vector (v_1, v_2, v_3) is written in matrix notation as the 4×1 column vector $[v_1, v_2, v_3, 0]^T$.
- A 3D point (x, y, z) is written in matrix notation as the 4×1 column vector $[x, y, z, 1]^T$. (This is usually the case, but see below for cases when the fourth coordinate is not 1.)

Notice that we use an additional fourth coordinate in this notation. This fourth coordinate is the homogeneous coordinate, which has an important significance in 3D graphics and is discussed below.

The Homogeneous W Coordinate

We mentioned in Chapter 5 that it is important to distinguish between points and vectors: points are locations; vectors are displacements. (Here we are talking about 3D vectors, not column vectors.) Using matrix notation, we can distinguish between points and vectors by introducing an extra coordinate, the so-called *homogeneous coordinate*. Points and vectors in three dimensions can be naturally expressed with three numbers, as we saw in Chapter 5. The homogeneous coordinate is therefore a fourth coordinate in addition to the x, y, and z values. We call this fourth coordinate w.

For points, we normally set the homogeneous coordinate to 1. (But see below for an explanation of when w is not 1.) For vectors, we set the homogeneous coordinate to 0.

Notice what happens when we subtract a point from another point using this convention. Given point $p_1 = [x_1, y_1, z_1, 1]^T$ and $p_2 = [x_1, y_1, z_1, 1]^T$, the difference $p_2 - p_1$ should be a vector, since a point minus a point yields a vector displacement between the two points, as we saw in Chapter 5. Performing the component-wise subtraction, we see that $p_2 - p_1 = [x_2 - x_1, y_2 - y_1, z_2 - z_1, 1 - 1]^T = [x_2 - x_1, y_2 - y_1, z_2 - z_1, 0]^T$. Notice that after subtraction, the homogeneous coordinate is zero. According to our convention, this indicates a vector, not a point—exactly the expected result from a point-point subtraction. Similarly, we can also verify the other point-vector rules presented in Chapter 5. Adding two vectors yields a vector, since the homogeneous coordinate is 0 for both vectors and is thus 0 after addition. Adding a point and a vector yields a point, since the vector has a w of 0 and the point has a w of 1, yielding a w after addition of 1—a point.

The Meaning of W

The homogeneous coordinate w is, however, more than just a "flag" signaling if a column vector $[x, y, z, w]^T$ represents a 3D point or a 3D vector. Specifically, the mathematical significance of the w coordinate is as follows:

- The homogeneous point $[x, y, z, w]^T$ corresponds to the 3D point $(x/w, y/w, z/w)$. The term "homogeneous point" simply refers to the four-coordinate notation for a 3D point or 3D vector.

That is, given a homogeneous point with an arbitrary value of w (not just 0 or 1), we divide the other components by w to arrive at the corresponding point in "normal" 3D space. Notice that several homogeneous points map to the same 3D point. $[3, 4, 5, 1]^T$, $[6, 8, 10, 2]^T$, or $[1.5, 2, 2.5, 0.5]^T$ all correspond to the 3D point $(3, 4, 5)$, since $(3/1, 4/1, 5/1) = (6/2, 8/2, 10/2) = (1.5/0.5, 2/0.5, 2.5/0.5)$.

This is the reason for the term "homogeneous coordinates": several points in 4D space correspond to one point in 3D space; therefore, by dividing by w, we are homogenizing the 4D space, mapping several 4D points onto the same 3D point.

In other words, w is simply a divisor. It provides a convenient notation for expressing a built-in dividing factor into our notation for describing a 3D point. Let us assume for now that $w \geq 0$. (This will always be the case for all transformations in this book.) Notice that for values of $w > 1$, the corresponding 3D (x,y,z) coordinates are smaller than the homogeneous x, y, and z, because they get divided by a large w value. For $0 < w < 1$, the corresponding 3D (x,y,z) coordinates are larger than the homogeneous x, y, and z, because they get divided by a fractional w value, which is effectively a multiplication. (For instance, dividing by 0.25 is the same as multiplying by 4.) For $w=1$, the corresponding 3D (x,y,z) coordinates are the same as the homogeneous x, y, and z.

TIP Think of the homogeneous coordinate w as the weight of a point.

It is helpful to think of w as the "weight" of a point with respect to a gravitational center at the origin $(0,0,0)$. For a given homogeneous point $[x,y,z,w]^T$, the larger the weight ($w>1$), the more the homogeneous point gets pulled in towards the origin before arriving at the corresponding 3D coordinates. The smaller the weight ($0<w<1$), the more the homogeneous point gets pushed away from the origin. For a normal weight ($w=1$), the homogeneous point is neither pushed nor pulled.

Therefore, a homogeneous point with $w=1$, such as $[x,y,z,1]^T$, corresponds to the 3D point at the same coordinates (x,y,z). This is why we said earlier that a 3D point (x,y,z) can be written in matrix notation as $[x,y,z,1]^T$; dividing by a w of 1 leaves the x, y, and z coordinates unchanged. We now can see, though, that in actuality any homogeneous point of the form $[kx,ky,kz,k]^T$, for all non-zero k, would correspond to 3D point (x,y,z).

But what about vectors? We said that a 3D vector (v_1,v_2,v_3) is written in matrix notation as $[v_1,v_2,v_3,0]^T$. This would correspond to the location in 3D at $(v_1/0,v_2/0,v_3/0)$. We can't divide by zero. Is this a contradiction?

Not at all. A 3D vector is not a 3D point, and therefore the homogeneous representation of a 3D vector corresponds to no point in 3D space. A 3D vector represents displacement in 3D space. Homogeneous points with $w=0$ are also called "points at infinity," since a division by zero can be thought of as a multiplication by infinity. Therefore, a 3D vector represents a particular 3D displacement with a magnitude and direction, and is "located," if you will, infinitely beyond the outermost edges of the 3D space. The 3D space itself holds locations; infinitely beyond the 3D space, where $w=0$, is where vectors are "located."

Admittedly, homogeneous coordinates take a while to get used to. If you get confused, remember just two rules. If you like to think mathematically, w is simply a divisor. If you like to think geometrically, w is a weight.

Why Homogeneous Coordinates

We use homogeneous coordinates in 3D graphics for several reasons, but three are of primary importance in this book and in particular in this chapter:

1. Homogeneous coordinates allow a consistent matrix representation of the three important geometric transformations—rotation, scaling, and translation. Without homogeneous coordinates, translation cannot be expressed as a matrix.

2. Homogeneous coordinates allow the perspective transformation, which is a division, to be expressed as a matrix, since w is a divisor and allows each point to encode its perspective division within its w coordinate. Other non-linear transformations, involving divisions, can also be expressed in matrix form through use of homogeneous coordinates.

3. Homogeneous coordinates are often used by 3D graphics hardware, requiring us to provide the w coordinate in some cases.

Combining Matrices and Column Vectors

We now have an application for 4×1 column vectors: they can be used to represent 3D points or vectors. But what about a larger matrix of numbers, which consists of many rows and columns? What is the purpose, in 3D graphics, of using such matrices?

We use matrices to represent transformations on 3D points represented as column vectors. Translation, rotation, and scaling may all be represented by a specially structured matrix. In order to understand this, we must first examine the mathematical operations we can perform with matrices and column vectors. We then can see how matrices can transform one column vector into another through the use of matrix arithmetic.

Mathematical Operations on Matrices

A number of operations may be defined for manipulating matrices, but two operations are particularly important for 3D graphics: the operation of multiplying a matrix by a scalar, and the operation of multiplying a matrix by another matrix. The former is referred to as scalar multiplication; the latter, matrix multiplication or composition. When there is no confusion, we use the general term "multiplication" to refer to either operation, though the term "composition" refers solely to the operation of matrix-matrix multiplication.

Scalar-Matrix Multiplication

A scalar, as we saw in Chapter 5, is simply a number—3.5, –87.88153, or the square root of 479 are all examples of scalars. You can think of a scalar as a single value used to scale another value or set of values. In the case of scalar-matrix multiplication, a scalar is used to uniformly scale all values in the matrix. Specifically, the result of multiplying a matrix by a scalar is a new matrix, of the same row-column dimension, whose individual elements are the elements of the original matrix times the scalar. The following equation illustrates the process for a 4×4 matrix, but the process is the same for any size matrix (including row vectors and column vectors).

Equation 6-1 shows an example of scalar-matrix multiplication. The scalar 3 is applied to the 4×4 matrix. The resulting matrix is the same size (also 4×4) and its elements are obtained by multiplying the corresponding element in the original matrix by the scalar.

Equation 6-1

$$3 \cdot \begin{bmatrix} 1.1 & 2.2 & 3.3 & 4.4 \\ 5.5 & 6.6 & 7.7 & 8.8 \\ 9.9 & 10.1 & 11.2 & 12.3 \\ 13.4 & 14.5 & 15.6 & 16.7 \end{bmatrix} = \begin{bmatrix} 3 \cdot 1.1 & 3 \cdot 2.2 & 3 \cdot 3.3 & 3 \cdot 4.4 \\ 3 \cdot 5.5 & 3 \cdot 6.6 & 3 \cdot 7.7 & 3 \cdot 8.8 \\ 3 \cdot 9.9 & 3 \cdot 10.1 & 3 \cdot 11.2 & 3 \cdot 12.3 \\ 3 \cdot 13.4 & 3 \cdot 14.5 & 3 \cdot 15.6 & 3 \cdot 16.7 \end{bmatrix}$$

$$= \begin{bmatrix} 3.3 & 6.6 & 9.9 & 13.2 \\ 16.5 & 19.8 & 23.1 & 26.4 \\ 29.7 & 30.3 & 33.6 & 36.9 \\ 40.2 & 45.5 & 46.8 & 50.1 \end{bmatrix}$$

Matrix-Matrix Multiplication, or Composition

A matrix may also be multiplied by another matrix, though this process is slightly more complicated than that of scalar multiplication. Scalar multiplication was simply defined; we could multiply any matrix by any scalar. However, with matrix-matrix multiplication, we cannot multiply just any matrix by any other matrix. The following rules govern matrix-matrix multiplication:

- Size is important. We may multiply a matrix A with a matrix B (denoted as AB) only if the number of columns in A equals the number of rows in B. We can say this mathematically, that matrix A with an arbitrary size $m \times n$ (rows×columns) may be multiplied with another matrix B only if matrix B has dimension $n \times r$. n, the number of rows in B, is the same n, the number of columns in A, and r is any size.

- If matrix A is $m \times n$, and matrix B is $n \times r$, the dimension of the resulting matrix AB is $m \times r$.

- Order is important. Matrix AB, the result of multiplying A with B, is generally not the same as matrix BA, the result of multiplying B with A. In fact, BA might not even be defined if the dimensions of B and A do not allow multiplying B by A.

- In the resultant matrix AB, the scalar entry located at row i and column j is determined by taking the vector dot product of row i from A and column j from B. Since, by the definition of matrix multiplication, the number of columns in A is the same as the number of rows in B, row i from A and column j from B will have the same number of elements, thereby facilitating the dot product operation.

Example: 4×4 Matrix Times 4×4 Matrix

Let's look at an example to make the process of matrix-matrix multiplication somewhat more concrete. We want to multiply two 4×4 matrices, A and B. We call the resulting matrix C: $C=AB$.

The size of the resulting matrix will also be 4×4. Recall that if matrix A is of size $m \times n$, and matrix B is of size $n \times r$, the result of multiplying A times B is a matrix of size $m \times r$.

Let us denote the contents of our matrices with subscripted variables: the variable name denotes the corresponding matrix, the first subscript denotes the column of the entry, and the second subscript denotes the row of the entry.

Equation 6-2

$$\begin{bmatrix} c_{11} & c_{12} & c_{13} & c_{14} \\ c_{21} & c_{22} & c_{23} & c_{24} \\ c_{31} & c_{32} & c_{33} & c_{34} \\ c_{41} & c_{42} & c_{43} & c_{44} \end{bmatrix} = \begin{bmatrix} a_{11} & a_{12} & a_{13} & a_{14} \\ a_{21} & a_{22} & a_{23} & a_{24} \\ a_{31} & a_{32} & a_{33} & a_{34} \\ a_{41} & a_{42} & a_{43} & a_{44} \end{bmatrix} \begin{bmatrix} b_{11} & b_{12} & b_{13} & b_{14} \\ b_{21} & b_{22} & b_{23} & b_{24} \\ b_{31} & b_{32} & b_{33} & b_{34} \\ b_{41} & b_{42} & b_{43} & b_{44} \end{bmatrix}$$

We know the values a_{11} through a_{44} and b_{11} through b_{44}; they are the "input" matrices we are multiplying. We wish to determine the values c_{11} through c_{44}. As a representative example, let us determine the value for one entry in C, c_{32}; all other values are determined similarly.

c_{32} is in row 3 and column 2. As we defined earlier, this element in the resultant matrix is defined by taking the dot product of row 3 in matrix A and column 2 in matrix B:

Equation 6-3

$$\begin{bmatrix} c_{11} & c_{12} & c_{13} & c_{14} \\ c_{21} & c_{22} & c_{23} & c_{24} \\ c_{31} & \boxed{c_{32}} & c_{33} & c_{34} \\ c_{41} & c_{42} & c_{43} & c_{44} \end{bmatrix} = \begin{bmatrix} a_{11} & a_{12} & a_{13} & a_{14} \\ a_{21} & a_{22} & a_{23} & a_{24} \\ \boxed{a_{31} \quad a_{32} \quad a_{33} \quad a_{34}} \\ a_{41} & a_{42} & a_{43} & a_{44} \end{bmatrix} \begin{bmatrix} b_{11} & \boxed{b_{12}} & b_{13} & b_{14} \\ b_{21} & b_{22} & b_{23} & b_{24} \\ b_{31} & b_{32} & b_{33} & b_{34} \\ b_{41} & b_{42} & b_{43} & b_{44} \end{bmatrix}$$

We compute the dot product of row 3 from A and column 2 from B as defined in Chapter 5: multiply all corresponding elements in the two vectors and add them.

Equation 6-4

$$c_{32} = a_{31}b_{12} + a_{32}b_{22} + a_{33}b_{32} + a_{34}b_{42}$$

The same process is repeated for all elements of C. Just to make sure it's all clear, let's calculate the value for one other element in C, c_{11}, which is at row 1, column 1. We therefore take the dot product of row 1 from A and column 1 from B:

Equation 6-5

$$\begin{bmatrix} \boxed{c_{11}} & c_{12} & c_{13} & c_{14} \\ c_{21} & c_{22} & c_{23} & c_{24} \\ c_{31} & c_{32} & c_{33} & c_{34} \\ c_{41} & c_{42} & c_{43} & c_{44} \end{bmatrix} = \begin{bmatrix} \boxed{a_{11} \quad a_{12} \quad a_{13} \quad a_{14}} \\ a_{21} & a_{22} & a_{23} & a_{24} \\ a_{31} & a_{32} & a_{33} & a_{34} \\ a_{41} & a_{42} & a_{43} & a_{44} \end{bmatrix} \begin{bmatrix} \boxed{b_{11}} & b_{12} & b_{13} & b_{14} \\ b_{21} & b_{22} & b_{23} & b_{24} \\ b_{31} & b_{32} & b_{33} & b_{34} \\ b_{41} & b_{42} & b_{43} & b_{44} \end{bmatrix}$$

The dot product of row 1 from A and column 1 from B is the value at c_{11}:

Equation 6-6

$$c_{11} = a_{11}b_{11} + a_{12}b_{21} + a_{13}b_{31} + a_{14}b_{41}$$

Example: 4×4 Matrix Times 4×1 Column Vector

We can also multiply a matrix A by a column vector P, since a column vector is after all simply a one-column matrix. The exact same restrictions and rules apply to the dimensions of the two matrices A and P; A must have the same number of columns as P has rows. For instance, we could multiply a 4×4 matrix by a 4×1 column vector. The resulting matrix, let us call it Q, is a 4×1 matrix—the same size as P.

NOTE Notice that we cannot multiply a 4×4 matrix with a 1×4 row vector, because the dimensions of the two matrices are incorrect for matrix multiplication. This is why we stated earlier that it is important to distinguish between row vectors and column vectors. Although conceptually each is simply a list of numbers, the orientation determines which matrix operations we can carry out. Also notice that we could multiply a 1×4 row vector by a 4×4 matrix—that is, the multiplication with a row vector is possible if we reverse the order of the multiplication. To avoid confusion, though, we should choose just one convention and use it consistently. As stated earlier, we have chosen the column vector notation for this book.

Equation 6-7

$$\begin{bmatrix} q_{11} \\ q_{21} \\ q_{31} \\ q_{41} \end{bmatrix} = \begin{bmatrix} a_{11} & a_{12} & a_{13} & a_{14} \\ a_{21} & a_{22} & a_{23} & a_{24} \\ a_{31} & a_{32} & a_{33} & a_{34} \\ a_{41} & a_{42} & a_{43} & a_{44} \end{bmatrix} \begin{bmatrix} p_{11} \\ p_{21} \\ p_{31} \\ p_{41} \end{bmatrix}$$

For example, to calculate element q_{21} of the resultant matrix, we take the dot product of row 2 from the first matrix A and column 1, which happens to be the only column, of the second matrix P:

Equation 6-8

$$\begin{bmatrix} q_{11} \\ \boxed{q_{21}} \\ q_{31} \\ q_{41} \end{bmatrix} = \begin{bmatrix} a_{11} & a_{12} & a_{13} & a_{14} \\ a_{21} & a_{22} & a_{23} & a_{24} \\ a_{31} & a_{32} & a_{33} & a_{34} \\ a_{41} & a_{42} & a_{43} & a_{44} \end{bmatrix} \begin{bmatrix} p_{11} \\ p_{21} \\ p_{31} \\ p_{41} \end{bmatrix}$$

Taking the dot product of row 2 from A and column 1 from P gives q_{21}.

Equation 6-9 $q_{21} = a_{21}p_{11} + a_{22}p_{21} + a_{23}p_{31} + a_{24}p_{41}$

Other elements of Q are determined similarly.

Multiple Matrix Multiplications

We may multiply a series of more than two matrices, yielding one final resultant matrix. For instance, we might have $Z=ABCDEFG$.

We evaluate such a series of multiplications by performing the multiplications from right to left, always using the newly resulting matrix as the right-hand term of the next leftmost matrix. For instance, we would evaluate the above expression first by multiplying F and G: $Z=ABCDE(FG)$ After computing this matrix, we then multiply E by the newly obtained result FG: $Z=ABCD(E(FG))$ We continue in this manner, yielding a final order of operations of $Z=A(B(C(D(E(FG)))))$.

NOTE Mathematically, matrix multiplication is commutative, meaning that $(AB)C = A(BC)$. However, the above right-to-left style of thinking about matrix multiplications makes it easier to understand the geometrical meaning of multiple transformations expressed by matrices, as we see later in this chapter.

In general, we must ensure with such a chained multiplication that sizes of all the matrices, including the intermediate result matrices, allow for matrix-matrix multiplication. That is to say, the size of matrix FG must be matrix-multiplication compatible with the size of matrix E. Similarly, the size of EFG must be compatible with D; the size of $DEFG$ must be compatible with C, and so forth. In the special case of 3D graphics, we are usually dealing with square matrices of all the same size—4×4. Multiplying a 4×4 matrix with a 4×4 matrix always yields another 4×4 matrix as a result. We therefore do not need to worry about compatibility of matrix sizes for multiple matrix multiplications.

The Identity Matrix

A special matrix is the *identity matrix*. The identity matrix, denoted *I*, has the property that for a given matrix *A*, *IA=A*. In other words, multiplying a matrix *A* with the identity matrix results in the same matrix *A*.

The identity matrix is a square matrix; that is, its number of rows is equal to the number of columns. Furthermore, the elements along the main diagonal of the matrix (from upper left to lower right) are all 1; all other elements in the matrix are 0. The 4×4 identity matrix appears below.

Equation 6-10
$$\begin{bmatrix} 1 & 0 & 0 & 0 \\ 0 & 1 & 0 & 0 \\ 0 & 0 & 1 & 0 \\ 0 & 0 & 0 & 1 \end{bmatrix}$$

Try multiplying the identity matrix with another 4×4 matrix or with a 4×1 column vector to verify that the matrix remains unchanged.

Matrix Inverse

The *inverse* of a matrix *M* is denoted M^{-1}, and is the matrix such that $MM^{-1}=I$ and $M^{-1}M=I$. In other words, multiplying a matrix with its inverse yields the identity matrix. For real-valued matrices (the only kind we deal with in this book), if $MM^{-1}=I$ is true, then $M^{-1}M=I$ is also true, and vice versa. In other words, when finding an inverse, we do not need to verify that the multiplication of the inverse on both the left and the right yields *I*; it is enough to verify one or the other.

In general, computing the inverse of a matrix is not necessarily easy; it essentially amounts to solving a system of simultaneous linear equations. It is also possible that the inverse might not exist. If the inverse exists, the matrix is said to be *invertible*.

For some special matrices, the inverse is extremely easy to compute. In particular, a 4×4 matrix representing a 3D rotation (which we haven't seen yet, but will develop shortly) can be inverted simply by taking its *transpose*, which amounts to swapping the rows and columns of the matrix. Furthermore, the inverse of a rotation matrix represents the opposite rotation; indeed, the inverse of any transformation matrix represents the opposite effect of the original transformation. This is the reason that the matrix inverse is of interest.

 TIP The inverse of any transformation matrix represents the opposite transformation.

If the inverse of a transformation matrix does not exist, then this means that the transformation expressed by the matrix is not reversible. For instance, a matrix consisting of all zeros reduces every point to the point (0,0,0). Such a matrix is not reversible. As a more realistic example, the 3D-to-2D perspective projection as described in Chapter 5 is also not reversible because the third dimension (the *z* coordinate) gets completely flattened into a flat plane; afterwards, it is impossible to recover the original depth information destroyed by the perspective projection. As we see later in this chapter, however, there is an alternative formulation of the perspective projection, called the *perspective transformation*, which does allow recovery of depth information, and which is therefore expressed as an invertible matrix.

NOTE The *determinant* of a matrix, covered later in this chapter, is a tool for determining whether a matrix is invertible or not.

Matrix Transpose

The transpose of a matrix M, denoted M^T, is obtained by making each row of the original matrix into a column in a new matrix. The transpose of a 4×4 matrix is again a 4×4 matrix. However, the transpose of a 4×1 matrix is a 1×4 matrix, and the transpose of a 1×4 matrix is a 4×1 matrix. This is why we can use the transpose notation to write vertical column vectors using a horizontal notation within running text: $[x,y,z,w]^T$ is the transpose of a horizontal 1×4 row vector, yielding a vertical 4×1 column vector. The following equation shows the transpose of a 4×4 matrix.

Equation 6-11
$$\begin{bmatrix} a_{11} & a_{12} & a_{13} & a_{14} \\ a_{21} & a_{22} & a_{23} & a_{24} \\ a_{31} & a_{32} & a_{33} & a_{34} \\ a_{41} & a_{42} & a_{43} & a_{44} \end{bmatrix}^T = \begin{bmatrix} a_{11} & a_{21} & a_{31} & a_{41} \\ a_{12} & a_{22} & a_{32} & a_{42} \\ a_{13} & a_{23} & a_{33} & a_{43} \\ a_{14} & a_{24} & a_{34} & a_{44} \end{bmatrix}$$

As mentioned earlier, the main reason the matrix transpose is interesting is because in certain cases the transpose of a matrix—which is easy to compute—is also the inverse of the matrix.

The l3d_matrix Class

The following listings present the l3d class for 4×4 matrices, `l3d_matrix`. The class contains a 4×4 array of `l3d_real` values for storing the matrix elements, and defines a series of operators conforming to the rules of matrix arithmetic. We use the vertical bar (or *pipe*, in Linux terminology) "|" as the operator for matrix-matrix multiplication.

The entries in the matrix are from type `l3d_real`. As discussed in Chapter 3, we use the `float_to_l3d_real` macro to convert from floating-point values to the real values in the matrix. To set the values in the matrix, we can either call a constructor with 16 `l3d_real` values or with 16 integer values (but we cannot mix the two within one constructor call). Alternatively, after creation of the matrix, you can use the `set` method, taking either 16 `l3d_real` or integer values, to set all values in the matrix at once. The 16 values are in row-major order; that is, first you specify the four values left to right in the first row, then the four values from the second row, then the four values from the third row, and finally the four values form the fourth row.

Note that the matrix-vector multiplication as implemented here omits some computations based on the structure of typical matrices used in 3D graphics. In particular, when using matrices to represent translation, rotation, and scaling transformations (which we discuss shortly), then the bottom row of the matrix will always be [0,0,0,1]. Also, the fourth component of vectors is always zero. With this knowledge, we can simply omit those terms involving the multiplication by zero, since their result is zero. It would also be possible to optimize the matrix-matrix multiplication in this manner. The danger with this sort of optimization is that matrices not conforming to this special structure would be incorrectly multiplied.

To access a particular element in the matrix, use the variable a of the matrix object, which is a 4×4 array of `l3d_real` values. The first index of the array references the column; the second index, the row.

Listing 6-3 is a sample program illustrating the use of the matrix classes by declaring and multiplying some random matrices. Run the program and verify the math by hand to test your understanding of matrix math.

All functions beginning with the prefix `l3d_mat_` represent matrix forms of important geometric transformations. We'll cover these functions and their derivation shortly.

Listing 6-1: `matrix.h`

```
#ifndef __MATRIX_H
#define __MATRIX_H
#include "../tool_os/memman.h"

#include <stdio.h>
#include <math.h>
#include "../system/sys_dep.h"
#include "math_fix.h"
#include "sincos.h"
#include "vector.h"
#include "../geom/point/point.h"

class l3d_matrix {
  public:
    l3d_matrix(void);
    l3d_matrix(l3d_real a00,l3d_real a01,l3d_real a02,l3d_real a03,
               l3d_real a10,l3d_real a11,l3d_real a12,l3d_real a13,
               l3d_real a20,l3d_real a21,l3d_real a22,l3d_real a23,
               l3d_real a30,l3d_real a31,l3d_real a32,l3d_real a33);
    l3d_matrix(int a00,int a01,int a02,int a03,
               int a10,int a11,int a12,int a13,
               int a20,int a21,int a22,int a23,
               int a30,int a31,int a32,int a33);
    l3d_matrix(const l3d_matrix &right);
    const l3d_matrix &set(l3d_real a00,l3d_real a01,l3d_real a02,l3d_real a03,
                          l3d_real a10,l3d_real a11,l3d_real a12,l3d_real a13,
                          l3d_real a20,l3d_real a21,l3d_real a22,l3d_real a23,
                          l3d_real a30,l3d_real a31,l3d_real a32,l3d_real a33);
    const l3d_matrix &set(int a00,int a01,int a02,int a03,
                          int a10,int a11,int a12,int a13,
                          int a20,int a21,int a22,int a23,
                          int a30,int a31,int a32,int a33);

    l3d_matrix &operator = (const l3d_matrix &right);

    void print(void)
    {
      int i,j;
      for(j=0;j<4;j++) {
        for(i=0;i<4;i++) {
          printf("%f ", l3d_real_to_float(a[j][i]));
        }
        printf("");
      }
    }
};

    l3d_real a[4][4];
};

extern l3d_matrix &l3d_get_matrix_temp(void);
```

```
//- useful defines for accessing matrix elements occurring in standard
//- positions for l3d_vector:

#define X_ a[0]
#define Y_ a[1]
#define Z_ a[2]
#define W_ a[3]

#define U_ a[0]
#define V_ a[1]
#define N_ a[2]

inline l3d_matrix::l3d_matrix() {

  a[0][0]=0; a[0][1]=0; a[0][2]=0; a[0][3]=0;
  a[1][0]=0; a[1][1]=0; a[1][2]=0; a[1][3]=0;
  a[2][0]=0; a[2][1]=0; a[2][2]=0; a[2][3]=0;
  a[3][0]=0; a[3][1]=0; a[3][2]=0; a[3][3]=0;
}

inline l3d_matrix::l3d_matrix(l3d_real a00,l3d_real a01,l3d_real a02,l3d_real a03,
                              l3d_real a10,l3d_real a11,l3d_real a12,l3d_real a13,
                              l3d_real a20,l3d_real a21,l3d_real a22,l3d_real a23,
                              l3d_real a30,l3d_real a31,l3d_real a32,l3d_real a33)
{
  a[0][0]=a00; a[0][1]=a01; a[0][2]=a02; a[0][3]=a03;
  a[1][0]=a10; a[1][1]=a11; a[1][2]=a12; a[1][3]=a13;
  a[2][0]=a20; a[2][1]=a21; a[2][2]=a22; a[2][3]=a23;
  a[3][0]=a30; a[3][1]=a31; a[3][2]=a32; a[3][3]=a33;


}

inline l3d_matrix::l3d_matrix(int a00,int a01,int a02,int a03,
                              int a10,int a11,int a12,int a13,
                              int a20,int a21,int a22,int a23,
                              int a30,int a31,int a32,int a33)
{
  a[0][0]=int_to_l3d_real(a00); a[0][1]=int_to_l3d_real(a01);
  a[0][2]=int_to_l3d_real(a02); a[0][3]=int_to_l3d_real(a03);

  a[1][0]=int_to_l3d_real(a10); a[1][1]=int_to_l3d_real(a11);
  a[1][2]=int_to_l3d_real(a12); a[1][3]=int_to_l3d_real(a13);

  a[2][0]=int_to_l3d_real(a20); a[2][1]=int_to_l3d_real(a21);
  a[2][2]=int_to_l3d_real(a22); a[2][3]=int_to_l3d_real(a23);

  a[3][0]=int_to_l3d_real(a30); a[3][1]=int_to_l3d_real(a31);
  a[3][2]=int_to_l3d_real(a32); a[3][3]=int_to_l3d_real(a33);
}

inline l3d_matrix::l3d_matrix(const l3d_matrix &right) {
  a[0][0]=right.a[0][0]; a[0][1]=right.a[0][1];
  a[0][2]=right.a[0][2]; a[0][3]=right.a[0][3];

  a[1][0]=right.a[1][0]; a[1][1]=right.a[1][1];
  a[1][2]=right.a[1][2]; a[1][3]=right.a[1][3];

  a[2][0]=right.a[2][0]; a[2][1]=right.a[2][1];
  a[2][2]=right.a[2][2]; a[2][3]=right.a[2][3];
```

```
     a[3][0]=right.a[3][0]; a[3][1]=right.a[3][1];
     a[3][2]=right.a[3][2]; a[3][3]=right.a[3][3];
}

inline l3d_matrix &l3d_matrix::operator = (const l3d_matrix &right) {
   a[0][0]=right.a[0][0]; a[0][1]=right.a[0][1];
   a[0][2]=right.a[0][2]; a[0][3]=right.a[0][3];

   a[1][0]=right.a[1][0]; a[1][1]=right.a[1][1];
   a[1][2]=right.a[1][2]; a[1][3]=right.a[1][3];

   a[2][0]=right.a[2][0]; a[2][1]=right.a[2][1];
   a[2][2]=right.a[2][2]; a[2][3]=right.a[2][3];

   a[3][0]=right.a[3][0]; a[3][1]=right.a[3][1];
   a[3][2]=right.a[3][2]; a[3][3]=right.a[3][3];

   return *this;
}

inline const l3d_matrix &l3d_matrix::set(l3d_real a00,l3d_real a01,l3d_real a02,l3d_real a03,
      l3d_real a10,l3d_real a11,l3d_real a12,l3d_real a13,
      l3d_real a20,l3d_real a21,l3d_real a22,l3d_real a23,
      l3d_real a30,l3d_real a31,l3d_real a32,l3d_real a33)
{
   a[0][0]=a00; a[0][1]=a01; a[0][2]=a02; a[0][3]=a03;
   a[1][0]=a10; a[1][1]=a11; a[1][2]=a12; a[1][3]=a13;
   a[2][0]=a20; a[2][1]=a21; a[2][2]=a22; a[2][3]=a23;
   a[3][0]=a30; a[3][1]=a31; a[3][2]=a32; a[3][3]=a33;

   return *this;
}

inline const l3d_matrix &l3d_matrix::set(int a00,int a01,int a02,int a03,
      int a10,int a11,int a12,int a13,
      int a20,int a21,int a22,int a23,
      int a30,int a31,int a32,int a33)
{
   a[0][0]=int_to_l3d_real(a00); a[0][1]=int_to_l3d_real(a01);
   a[0][2]=int_to_l3d_real(a02); a[0][3]=int_to_l3d_real(a03);

   a[1][0]=int_to_l3d_real(a10); a[1][1]=int_to_l3d_real(a11);
   a[1][2]=int_to_l3d_real(a12); a[1][3]=int_to_l3d_real(a13);

   a[2][0]=int_to_l3d_real(a20); a[2][1]=int_to_l3d_real(a21);
   a[2][2]=int_to_l3d_real(a22); a[2][3]=int_to_l3d_real(a23);

   a[3][0]=int_to_l3d_real(a30); a[3][1]=int_to_l3d_real(a31);
   a[3][2]=int_to_l3d_real(a32); a[3][3]=int_to_l3d_real(a33);

   return *this;
}

inline l3d_matrix& operator |(const l3d_matrix &l, const l3d_matrix &r) {
   l3d_matrix &res = l3d_get_matrix_temp();

   res.set(l3d_mulrr(l.a[0][0],r.a[0][0])
          +l3d_mulrr(l.a[0][1],r.a[1][0])
          +l3d_mulrr(l.a[0][2],r.a[2][0])
          +l3d_mulrr(l.a[0][3],r.a[3][0]),
```

```
l3d_mulrr(l.a[0][0],r.a[0][1])
+l3d_mulrr(l.a[0][1],r.a[1][1])
+l3d_mulrr(l.a[0][2],r.a[2][1])
+l3d_mulrr(l.a[0][3],r.a[3][1]),
l3d_mulrr(l.a[0][0],r.a[0][2])
+l3d_mulrr(l.a[0][1],r.a[1][2])
+l3d_mulrr(l.a[0][2],r.a[2][2])
+l3d_mulrr(l.a[0][3],r.a[3][2]),
l3d_mulrr(l.a[0][0],r.a[0][3])
+l3d_mulrr(l.a[0][1],r.a[1][3])
+l3d_mulrr(l.a[0][2],r.a[2][3])
+l3d_mulrr(l.a[0][3],r.a[3][3]),
l3d_mulrr(l.a[1][0],r.a[0][0])
+l3d_mulrr(l.a[1][1],r.a[1][0])
+l3d_mulrr(l.a[1][2],r.a[2][0])
+l3d_mulrr(l.a[1][3],r.a[3][0]),
l3d_mulrr(l.a[1][0],r.a[0][1])
+l3d_mulrr(l.a[1][1],r.a[1][1])
+l3d_mulrr(l.a[1][2],r.a[2][1])
+l3d_mulrr(l.a[1][3],r.a[3][1]),
l3d_mulrr(l.a[1][0],r.a[0][2])
+l3d_mulrr(l.a[1][1],r.a[1][2])
+l3d_mulrr(l.a[1][2],r.a[2][2])
+l3d_mulrr(l.a[1][3],r.a[3][2]),
l3d_mulrr(l.a[1][0],r.a[0][3])
+l3d_mulrr(l.a[1][1],r.a[1][3])
+l3d_mulrr(l.a[1][2],r.a[2][3])
+l3d_mulrr(l.a[1][3],r.a[3][3]),
l3d_mulrr(l.a[2][0],r.a[0][0])
+l3d_mulrr(l.a[2][1],r.a[1][0])
+l3d_mulrr(l.a[2][2],r.a[2][0])
+l3d_mulrr(l.a[2][3],r.a[3][0]),
l3d_mulrr(l.a[2][0],r.a[0][1])
+l3d_mulrr(l.a[2][1],r.a[1][1])
+l3d_mulrr(l.a[2][2],r.a[2][1])
+l3d_mulrr(l.a[2][3],r.a[3][1]),
l3d_mulrr(l.a[2][0],r.a[0][2])
+l3d_mulrr(l.a[2][1],r.a[1][2])
+l3d_mulrr(l.a[2][2],r.a[2][2])
+l3d_mulrr(l.a[2][3],r.a[3][2]),
l3d_mulrr(l.a[2][0],r.a[0][3])
+l3d_mulrr(l.a[2][1],r.a[1][3])
+l3d_mulrr(l.a[2][2],r.a[2][3])
+l3d_mulrr(l.a[2][3],r.a[3][3]),
l3d_mulrr(l.a[3][0],r.a[0][0])
+l3d_mulrr(l.a[3][1],r.a[1][0])
+l3d_mulrr(l.a[3][2],r.a[2][0])
+l3d_mulrr(l.a[3][3],r.a[3][0]),
l3d_mulrr(l.a[3][0],r.a[0][1])
+l3d_mulrr(l.a[3][1],r.a[1][1])
+l3d_mulrr(l.a[3][2],r.a[2][1])
+l3d_mulrr(l.a[3][3],r.a[3][1]),
l3d_mulrr(l.a[3][0],r.a[0][2])
+l3d_mulrr(l.a[3][1],r.a[1][2])
+l3d_mulrr(l.a[3][2],r.a[2][2])
+l3d_mulrr(l.a[3][3],r.a[3][2]),
l3d_mulrr(l.a[3][0],r.a[0][3])
+l3d_mulrr(l.a[3][1],r.a[1][3])
+l3d_mulrr(l.a[3][2],r.a[2][3])
+l3d_mulrr(l.a[3][3],r.a[3][3]));
```

```
      return res;
}

inline l3d_vector &operator |(const l3d_matrix &l, const  l3d_vector &r) {
   l3d_vector &res = l3d_get_vector_temp();

   res.set(
      l3d_mulrr(  l.a[0][0],r.a[0]) +
      l3d_mulrr(     l.a[0][1],r.a[1]) +
      l3d_mulrr(     l.a[0][2],r.a[2]) ,
      //- r.a[3] is 0 for our vectors: +l3d_mulrr(     l.a[0][3],r.a[3]),
      l3d_mulrr(  l.a[1][0],r.a[0]) +
      l3d_mulrr(     l.a[1][1],r.a[1]) +
      l3d_mulrr(     l.a[1][2],r.a[2]) ,
      //- r.a[3] is 0 for our vectors:     l3d_mulrr(     l.a[1][3],r.a[3]),
      l3d_mulrr(  l.a[2][0],r.a[0]) +
      l3d_mulrr(     l.a[2][1],r.a[1]) +
      l3d_mulrr(     l.a[2][2],r.a[2]) ,
      //- r.a[3] is 0 for our vectors:     l3d_mulrr(     l.a[2][3],r.a[3]),

      //- l.a[3][0] is 0 for our matrices:    l3d_mulrr( l.a[3][0],r.a[0]) +
      //- l.a[3][1] is 0 for our matrices:    l3d_mulrr(   l.a[3][1],r.a[1]) +
      //- l.a[3][2] is 0 for our matrices:    l3d_mulrr(   l.a[3][2],r.a[2]) +
      l3d_mulrr(     l.a[3][3],r.a[3]) ) ;

   return res;
}

inline l3d_matrix& operator * (const l3d_matrix &l,
                               const l3d_real aScalar)
{
   l3d_matrix &res = l3d_get_matrix_temp();
   res.set (
      l3d_mulrr(      l.a[0][0] , aScalar),
      l3d_mulrr(      l.a[0][1] , aScalar),
      l3d_mulrr(      l.a[0][2] , aScalar),
      l3d_mulrr(      l.a[0][3] , aScalar),

      l3d_mulrr(       l.a[1][0] , aScalar),
      l3d_mulrr(       l.a[1][1] , aScalar),
      l3d_mulrr(       l.a[1][2] , aScalar),
      l3d_mulrr(       l.a[1][3] , aScalar),

      l3d_mulrr(       l.a[2][0] , aScalar),
      l3d_mulrr(       l.a[2][1] , aScalar),
      l3d_mulrr(       l.a[2][2] , aScalar),
      l3d_mulrr(       l.a[2][3] , aScalar),

      l3d_mulrr(       l.a[3][0] , aScalar),
      l3d_mulrr(       l.a[3][1] , aScalar),
      l3d_mulrr(       l.a[3][2] , aScalar),
      l3d_mulrr(       l.a[3][3] , aScalar)) ;

   return res;
}

inline  l3d_matrix &l3d_mat_translate(l3d_real x, l3d_real y, l3d_real z) {
   l3d_matrix &res = l3d_get_matrix_temp();

   res.set(int_to_l3d_real(1),int_to_l3d_real(0),int_to_l3d_real(0),x,
```

```
                  int_to_l3d_real(0),int_to_l3d_real(1),int_to_l3d_real(0),y,
                  int_to_l3d_real(0),int_to_l3d_real(0),int_to_l3d_real(1),z,
                  int_to_l3d_real(0),int_to_l3d_real(0),int_to_l3d_real(0),int_to_l3d_real(1) );
    return res;
}

inline  l3d_matrix &l3d_mat_scale(l3d_real x, l3d_real y, l3d_real z) {
    l3d_matrix &res = l3d_get_matrix_temp();

    res.set(int_to_l3d_real(x),int_to_l3d_real(0),int_to_l3d_real(0),int_to_l3d_real(0),
            int_to_l3d_real(0),int_to_l3d_real(y),int_to_l3d_real(0),int_to_l3d_real(0),
            int_to_l3d_real(0),int_to_l3d_real(0),int_to_l3d_real(z),int_to_l3d_real(0),
            int_to_l3d_real(0),int_to_l3d_real(0),int_to_l3d_real(0),int_to_l3d_real(1) );
    return res;
}

inline  l3d_matrix &l3d_mat_rotx(int theta) {
    l3d_matrix &res = l3d_get_matrix_temp();

    res.set ( int_to_l3d_real(1),int_to_l3d_real(0),int_to_l3d_real(0),int_to_l3d_real(0),
              int_to_l3d_real(0),cos_lu[theta],-sin_lu[theta],int_to_l3d_real(0),
              int_to_l3d_real(0),sin_lu[theta],cos_lu[theta],int_to_l3d_real(0),
              int_to_l3d_real(0),int_to_l3d_real(0),int_to_l3d_real(0),int_to_l3d_real(1) );
    return res;
}

inline l3d_matrix &l3d_mat_roty(int theta) {
    l3d_matrix &res = l3d_get_matrix_temp();

    res.set(cos_lu[theta],int_to_l3d_real(0),sin_lu[theta],int_to_l3d_real(0),
            int_to_l3d_real(0),int_to_l3d_real(1),int_to_l3d_real(0),int_to_l3d_real(0),
            -sin_lu[theta],int_to_l3d_real(0),cos_lu[theta],int_to_l3d_real(0),
            int_to_l3d_real(0),int_to_l3d_real(0),int_to_l3d_real(0),int_to_l3d_real(1) );
    return res;
}

inline  l3d_matrix &l3d_mat_rotz(int theta) {
    l3d_matrix &res = l3d_get_matrix_temp();

    res.set(cos_lu[theta],-sin_lu[theta],int_to_l3d_real(0),int_to_l3d_real(0),
            sin_lu[theta],cos_lu[theta],int_to_l3d_real(0),int_to_l3d_real(0),
            int_to_l3d_real(0),int_to_l3d_real(0),int_to_l3d_real(1),int_to_l3d_real(0),
            int_to_l3d_real(0),int_to_l3d_real(0),int_to_l3d_real(0),int_to_l3d_real(1));
    return res;
}

inline  l3d_matrix &l3d_mat_rotu(const l3d_vector &u, int theta) {
    l3d_matrix &res = l3d_get_matrix_temp();

    res.set
    (l3d_mulrr(u.X_,u.X_) + l3d_mulrr(cos_lu[theta], int_to_l3d_real(1)-l3d_mulrr(u.X_,u.X_)),
     l3d_mulrr(l3d_mulrr(u.X_,u.Y_) , int_to_l3d_real(1)-cos_lu[theta])-l3d_mulrr(u.Z_,sin_lu[theta]),
     l3d_mulrr(l3d_mulrr(u.Z_,u.X_) , int_to_l3d_real(1)-cos_lu[theta])+l3d_mulrr(u.Y_,sin_lu[theta]),
     int_to_l3d_real(0),

     l3d_mulrr(l3d_mulrr(u.X_,u.Y_) , int_to_l3d_real(1)-cos_lu[theta])+l3d_mulrr(u.Z_,sin_lu[theta]),
     l3d_mulrr(u.Y_,u.Y_) + l3d_mulrr(cos_lu[theta], int_to_l3d_real(1)-l3d_mulrr(u.Y_,u.Y_)),
     l3d_mulrr(l3d_mulrr(u.Y_,u.Z_), int_to_l3d_real(1)-cos_lu[theta]) - l3d_mulrr(u.X_,sin_lu[theta]),
     int_to_l3d_real(0),

     l3d_mulrr(l3d_mulrr(u.Z_,u.X_), int_to_l3d_real(1)-cos_lu[theta]) - l3d_mulrr(u.Y_,sin_lu[theta]),
     l3d_mulrr(l3d_mulrr(u.Y_,u.Z_), int_to_l3d_real(1)-cos_lu[theta]) + l3d_mulrr(u.X_,sin_lu[theta]),
```

```
        l3d_mulrr(u.Z_,u.Z_) + l3d_mulrr(cos_lu[theta], int_to_l3d_real(1)-l3d_mulrr(u.Z_,u.Z_)),
        int_to_l3d_real(0),

        int_to_l3d_real(0),
        int_to_l3d_real(0),
        int_to_l3d_real(0),
        int_to_l3d_real(1) );

    return res;
}

inline l3d_point &operator |(const l3d_matrix &l, const  l3d_point &r) {
    l3d_point &res = l3d_get_point_temp();

    res.set(
        l3d_mulrr(  l.a[0][0],r.a[0]) +
        l3d_mulrr(     l.a[0][1],r.a[1]) +
        l3d_mulrr(     l.a[0][2],r.a[2]) +
        //- r.a[3] is normally 1 for points:    l3d_mulrr(     l.a[0][3],r.a[3]),
        l.a[0][3]              ,
        l3d_mulrr(  l.a[1][0],r.a[0]) +
        l3d_mulrr(     l.a[1][1],r.a[1]) +
        l3d_mulrr(     l.a[1][2],r.a[2]) +
        //- r.a[3] is normally 1 for points:    l3d_mulrr(     l.a[1][3],r.a[3]),
        l.a[1][3],
        l3d_mulrr(  l.a[2][0],r.a[0]) +
        l3d_mulrr(     l.a[2][1],r.a[1]) +
        l3d_mulrr(     l.a[2][2],r.a[2]) +
        //- r.a[3] is normally 1 for points:    l3d_mulrr(     l.a[2][3],r.a[3]),
        l.a[2][3],
        //- l.a[3][0] is 0 for our matrices:    l3d_mulrr(  l.a[3][0],r.a[0]) +
        //- l.a[3][1] is 0 for our matrices:    l3d_mulrr(     l.a[3][1],r.a[1]) +
        //- l.a[3][2] is 0 for our matrices:    l3d_mulrr(     l.a[3][2],r.a[2]) +
        l3d_mulrr(     l.a[3][3],r.a[3]) ) ;

    return res;
}

#endif
```

Listing 6-2: `matrix.cc`

```
#include "matrix.h"
#include "../tool_os/memman.h"

const int l3d_max_matrix_temp = 15;
l3d_matrix &l3d_get_matrix_temp(void) {
    static int nbuf=0;
    static l3d_matrix buf[l3d_max_matrix_temp];

    if(nbuf>=l3d_max_matrix_temp) nbuf=0;
    return buf[nbuf++];
}
```

Listing 6-3: Sample program demonstrating matrix multiplication, `matmul.cc`

```
#include <stdio.h>

#include "math/matrix.h"

int main(int argc, char *argv[]) {
    l3d_matrix a, b, c;
    l3d_point p;
```

```
        a.set(2,0,0,0,
              0,2,0,0,
              0,0,2,0,
              0,0,0,1);

        b.set(float_to_l3d_real(1.1),
              float_to_l3d_real(2.2),
              float_to_l3d_real(3.3),
              float_to_l3d_real(4.4),
              float_to_l3d_real(5.5),
              float_to_l3d_real(6.6),
              float_to_l3d_real(7.7),
              float_to_l3d_real(8.8),
              float_to_l3d_real(9.9),
              float_to_l3d_real(10.10),
              float_to_l3d_real(11.11),
              float_to_l3d_real(12.12),
              float_to_l3d_real(13.13),
              float_to_l3d_real(14.14),
              float_to_l3d_real(15.15),
              float_to_l3d_real(16.16)) ;

        p.set(5,6,7,1);

        printf("matrix a is:");
        a.print();

        printf("b is:");
        b.print();

        printf("a|b is:");
        (a|b).print();

        printf("c=a|b is:");
        c = a | b;
        c.print();

        printf("b|a is:");
        (b|a).print();

        printf("p is:");
        p.print();

        printf("|p is:");
        (a|p).print();

        printf("|b|p is:");
        (a|b|p).print();

        printf("|p is:");
        (c|p).print();

        printf("|a|p is:");
        (b|a|p).print();

        printf("c*2 is:");
        (c * int_to_l3d_real(2)).print();

        printf("c*2|p is:");
        (c*int_to_l3d_real(2)|p).print();
    }
```

What's All This Got to Do with 3D Graphics?

It's time to build some practical examples in 3D graphics upon the preceding mathematical foundation.

We mentioned earlier that we can use column vectors of dimension 4×1 to represent 3D points. We also saw that if we multiply a 4×4 matrix A with a 4×1 column vector P, we obtain a new 4×1 column vector Q, the same size as the original column vector P. From a functional point of view, we can therefore view the column vector Q as a transformed copy of the original column vector P. The individual numbers within the 4×4 matrix A combined with the rules for matrix multiplication define exactly how the elements of P get transformed into the elements of Q.

Furthermore, we also saw that we can multiply several matrices together by recursively applying the multiplication rule for two matrices. If we multiply an arbitrary sequence of 4×4 matrices together, we always obtain a 4×4 matrix as a result. We can therefore construct a long chain of matrices to be multiplied as follows.

Equation 6-12
$$\underset{Q}{\underbrace{4 \times 1}} = \underset{ABCDEF}{\underbrace{4 \times 4}}\ \underset{P}{\underbrace{4 \times 1}}$$

Each of the matrices A, B, C, D, E, and F is 4×4; multiplying them all gives a 4×4 matrix; and multiplying this by the 4×1 column vector P, representing a point, yields a transformed 4×1 column vector Q, representing the location of the transformed point. The transformation going from P to Q is defined by the combined effect of all of the matrices A through F, applied in the order F, E, D, C, B, A (because of the multiplication order we defined for matrices).

Importantly, notice that the combined effect of several transformation matrix multiplications can be achieved by first multiplying all transformation matrices together to obtain one composite transformation matrix, then using this one composite matrix to transform one or several points. If we have to apply five transformations to 1000 points, we don't need to do 5000 matrix multiplications (5*1000), but instead only 1005 (5+1000): first we combine all five transformations into one composite matrix, then multiply this composite matrix with each of the 1000 points. One matrix can therefore embody several transformations: for instance, a scale, a rotation, a translation, another scale, and finally a perspective projection can all be represented with one single transformation matrix, obtained by multiplying the individual transformation matrices together. We see examples of such combined transformation matrices later in this chapter.

You can think of a 4×4 transformation matrix A as the mathematical equivalent of a subroutine. This subroutine takes point P as its input, performs some transformation specified entirely with the contents of A (which might consist of several individual transformations strung together into one), and returns a new point Q as output.

Consider again the multiplication between a matrix and a column vector illustrated in Equation 6-7. The vector $[p_{11}, p_{21}, p_{31}, p_{41}]^T$ can be interpreted as the original or old location of a 3D homogeneous point $[x, y, z, w]^T$. The elements $[q_{11}, q_{21}, q_{31}, q_{41}]^T$ can be interpreted as the new location of the point. Then, if you perform the matrix multiplication, notice that you can interpret the elements of the matrix as follows:

- a_{11} controls how much of the old x appears in the new x.
- a_{12} controls how much of the old y appears in the new x.
- a_{13} controls how much of the old z appears in the new x.
- a_{14} controls how much of the old w appears in the new x; if $w=1$, then proper translation occurs (see next section).
- a_{21} controls how much of the old x appears in the new y.
- a_{22} controls how much of the old y appears in the new y.
- a_{23} controls how much of the old z appears in the new y.
- a_{24} controls how much of the old w appears in the new y.

The rest of the elements of the matrix are interpreted in the same manner.

To summarize, we use 4×1 column vectors to represent 3D points and vectors, and we use 4×4 matrices to represent transformations. We use the operation of matrix-matrix multiplication to multiply a 4×4 matrix or a series of 4×4 matrices by a 4×1 column vector P. The result of such a matrix-matrix multiplication is a new transformed 4×1 column vector Q.

With this understanding of matrices and transformations, we can now understand the `l3d_coordinate::transform` method which was left unexplained in Chapter 2. This method simply takes the current position of an `l3d_coordinate`, as stored in the `transformed` member variable, and applies a given transformation (passed as parameter m) to the point by performing a matrix multiplication of m with `transformed`, again storing the new result in member variable `transformed`.

Mathematical Equations for Translation, Rotation, and Scaling

We now have a framework within which we can represent 3D points, 3D vectors, and transformations as matrices. We also know that a 4×4 matrix can transform a 3D point. Let us now develop some specific 4×4 transformation matrices which have a physical significance: the transformations to translate, rotate, and scale a 3D point. In the following sections we will first develop each individual transformation without matrices, to understand the underlying physical and geometrical idea. We then develop a matrix version of the transformation which we can apply to a 3D point through the use of a matrix-matrix multiplication.

Translation

Translating a point means moving a point from its current position to a new position which is specified in terms of offsets in the x, y, and z axis directions.

Expressed without Matrices

Mathematically, we say that for a given 3D point (x,y,z), and for given 3D offsets t_x, t_y, and t_z, the translated point is obtained by adding the offsets to the point's coordinates. Therefore the translated point in 3D is located at $(x+t_x, y+t_y, z+t_z)$. We may mathematically denote this translation as $T(t_x, t_y, t_z)$.

Expressed in Matrix Form

To write translation in matrix form, we first represent the point (x,y,z) as a 4×1 column vector.

Equation 6-13
$$\begin{bmatrix} x \\ y \\ z \\ 1 \end{bmatrix}$$

Then, the translation $T(t_x,t_y,t_z)$ is the following 4×4 matrix.

Equation 6-14
$$T(t_x, t_y, t_z) = \begin{bmatrix} 1 & 0 & 0 & t_x \\ 0 & 1 & 0 & t_y \\ 0 & 0 & 1 & t_z \\ 0 & 0 & 0 & 1 \end{bmatrix}$$

If we multiply the translation matrix by the point $[x,y,z,1]^T$, we obtain the new translated point $[x+t_x,y+t_y,z+t_z,1]^T$.

Equation 6-15
$$\begin{bmatrix} 1 & 0 & 0 & t_x \\ 0 & 1 & 0 & t_y \\ 0 & 0 & 1 & t_z \\ 0 & 0 & 0 & 1 \end{bmatrix} \begin{bmatrix} x \\ y \\ z \\ 1 \end{bmatrix} = \begin{bmatrix} x+t_x \\ y+t_y \\ z+t_z \\ 1 \end{bmatrix}$$

Try this matrix-vector multiplication for yourself and verify that the resulting point is in fact as stated above. Notice that if you try the same multiplication with the homogeneous coordinate set to 0, i.e., using $[x,y,z,0]^T$, you will see that the result is the same: $[x,y,z,0]^T$. Therefore, we see that the homogeneous coordinate needs to be present, and needs to be 1 in order for translation expressed as a matrix to work.

 NOTE We stated earlier that a homogeneous coordinate of 0 corresponds to a vector. A vector, as we saw in the last chapter, has a magnitude and direction, but no position. Therefore, trying to translate a vector—that is, trying to change its position—yields the same vector.

The l3d_mat_translate Function

The function `l3d_mat_translate`, which we saw earlier in Listing 6-1, constructs a translation matrix. As input, the function takes three parameters representing the translational offsets in the x, y, and z directions. As output, the function returns a translation matrix having the form described in the previous section, so that multiplication of a column vector with this matrix translates the point represented by the column vector.

Rotation

Rotation of a 3D point is moving it in a circle perpendicular to and with center on the x, y, or z axis. (Later we see how to rotate about an arbitrary axis, which is more complicated.)

Expressed without Matrices

For a 3D point (x_0, y_0, z_0), we geometrically define the rotations about the x, y, and z axes as follows:

- Rotation about x axis: Moving a point along the circle which lies in the 2D plane $x=x_0$ and whose center is $(x_0,0,0)$.

- Rotation about y axis: Moving a point along the circle which lies in the 2D plane $y=y_0$ and whose center is $(0,y_0,0)$.

- Rotation about z axis: Moving a point along the circle which lies in the 2D plane $z=z_0$ and whose center is $(0,0,z_0)$.

From geometry, we know that a circle is defined as the set of all points in a plane a fixed distance r from a given center point. Let us consider the case of rotation of a point (x,y,z) around the z axis, as shown in Figure 6-15. The center point of the circle is $(0,0,z)$; the plane within which the circle lies is $z=z_0$. The radius of the circle is the distance from the circle's center point $(0,0,z)$ to any and every point on the circle. The given point to be rotated (x,y,z) must lie on the circle, and thus we define the radius of the circle as the distance from center $(0,0,z)$ to point (x,y,z). Let us call the circle's radius r. We do not calculate r because, as we will see shortly, the actual value of r does not appear in the final rotation equations and matrices. (The radius can be computed with the distance formula from Chapter 5.)

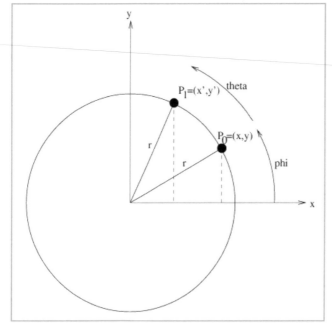

Figure 6-15: Rotation of a point in 3D space around the z axis. The z axis is not shown and is pointing straight into the paper. Notice that the z coordinate for both the old point and the new point are the same.

The z axis has been eliminated from the diagram for simplicity; illustrated is the circle of rotation in the plane $z=2$. The original point is p_0 with coordinates (x,y,z). We wish to rotate this point by an angle θ around the z axis to find the new point p_1 at (x',y',z'). With respect to the axis of rotation, the z axis, the rotation is in the clockwise direction, which corresponds to the left-hand rule.

However, in this diagram, we are looking along the opposite direction along the axis of rotation (looking outward away from the origin instead of toward the origin), which is why the rotation appears to be counterclockwise in the diagram.

Let us call the angle between the original point p_0 and the x axis ϕ (written "phi"). If we form two right triangles as shown in Figure 6-15, then we can define the cosine and sine of angle ϕ in terms of the coordinates of p_0 and r, the radius of the circle of rotation:

Equation 6-16
$$\cos \phi = \tfrac{x}{r}$$
$$\sin \phi = \tfrac{y}{r}$$

We can furthermore express the coordinates x' and y' of the new point in terms of the angle $\phi+\theta$, which is the combined angle of rotation starting at zero degrees. (Recall, we do not need to compute a new z coordinate for p_1 since rotation is about the z axis and therefore the z coordinate is identical for p_0 and p_1.) By doing this and utilizing the previous expressions for $\cos\phi$ and $\sin\phi$, we obtain the following equations for the new coordinates after rotation.

Equation 6-17
$$
\begin{aligned}
x' &= r\cos(\phi + \theta) \\
&= r\cos\phi\,\cos\theta - r\sin\phi\,\sin\theta \\
&= r\tfrac{x}{r}\cos\theta - r\tfrac{y}{r}\sin\theta \\
&= x\cos\theta - y\sin\theta \\
y' &= r\sin(\phi + \theta) \\
&= r\cos\phi\,\sin\theta + r\sin\phi\,\cos\theta \\
&= r\tfrac{x}{r}\sin\theta + r\tfrac{y}{r}\cos\theta \\
&= x\sin\theta + y\cos\theta \\
z' &= z
\end{aligned}
$$

NOTE Notice that for the development of these equations we use the trigonometric expansions for the terms $\cos(\phi+\theta)=\cos\phi\,\cos\theta - \sin\phi\,\sin\theta$, and $\sin(\phi+\theta)=\sin\phi\,\cos\theta + \cos\phi\,\sin\theta$.

A similar development for rotations around the y and z axes yields the following results.

Equation 6-18
$$
\begin{aligned}
x' &= x\cos\theta + z\sin\theta \\
y' &= y \\
z' &= -x\sin\theta + z\cos\theta
\end{aligned}
$$

Equation 6-18 shows rotation around the y axis, where y stays the same and we calculate new values for x and z.

Equation 6-19
$$
\begin{aligned}
x' &= x \\
y' &= y\cos\theta - z\sin\theta \\
z' &= y\sin\theta + z\cos\theta
\end{aligned}
$$

Equation 6-19 shows rotation around the x axis, where x stays the same and we calculate new values for y and z.

TIP You can interpret the rotation equation $y'=x*sin\phi + y*cos\phi$ as meaning: how much of the old x would you like in the new y, and how much of the old y would you like in the new y? Since the sine and cosine functions are 90 degrees displaced from one another, one goes up while the other goes down. Similar logic applies for all of the other rotation equations.

Expressed in Matrix Form

The above equations for rotation treat each coordinate of the new point separately; that is, a formula is provided for the new x, y, and/or z coordinate. If we express the rotation as a matrix, we can think of the operation as a whole—"rotation" (expressed as a matrix) of a "point" (expressed as a column vector).

Let us use the term $R_x(\theta)$ to denote the matrix which rotates a point by an angle θ around the x axis, similarly for $R_y(\theta)$ and $R_z(\theta)$. Assuming we express the 3D point to be rotated as a 4×1 column vector, we obtain the following rotation matrices from the separate rotation formulas developed in the previous section.

Equation 6-20
$$R_x(\theta) = \begin{bmatrix} 1 & 0 & 0 & 0 \\ 0 & cos\theta & -sin\theta & 0 \\ 0 & sin\theta & cos\theta & 0 \\ 0 & 0 & 0 & 1 \end{bmatrix}$$

Equation 6-21
$$R_y(\theta) = \begin{bmatrix} cos\theta & 0 & sin\theta & 0 \\ 0 & 1 & 0 & 0 \\ -sin\theta & 0 & cos\theta & 0 \\ 0 & 0 & 0 & 1 \end{bmatrix}$$

Equation 6-22
$$R_z(\theta) = \begin{bmatrix} cos\theta & -sin\theta & 0 & 0 \\ sin\theta & cos\theta & 0 & 0 \\ 0 & 0 & 1 & 0 \\ 0 & 0 & 0 & 1 \end{bmatrix}$$

As verification of the above, if we multiply the matrix $R_x(\theta)$ by the point $[x,y,z,1]^T$, we obtain the new rotated point exactly as derived above:

Equation 6-23
$$\begin{bmatrix} 1 & 0 & 0 & 0 \\ 0 & cos\theta & -sin\theta & 0 \\ 0 & sin\theta & cos\theta & 0 \\ 0 & 0 & 0 & 1 \end{bmatrix} \begin{bmatrix} x \\ y \\ z \\ 1 \end{bmatrix} = \begin{bmatrix} x \\ y\,cos\theta - z\,sin\theta \\ y\,sin\theta + z\,cos\theta \\ 1 \end{bmatrix}$$

Similarly, multiplication with matrices $R_y(\theta)$ and $R_z(\theta)$ yields exactly the results of the non-matrix forms of the rotation equations developed earlier.

As a final verification that the above rotation formulas really work, you can try multiplying the rotation matrix $R_z(90°)$ by the point $[1,0,0,1]^T$, which is one unit along the positive x axis. You should obtain the new point $[0,1,0,1]^T$, which is one unit along the positive y axis. This is the result of rotating the original point 90° in the positive direction (for a left-handed system, clockwise) around the z axis.

The l3d_mat_rotx, l3d_mat_roty, and l3d_mat_rotz Functions

The functions l3d_mat_rotx, l3d_mat_roty, and l3d_mat_rotz, which we saw earlier in Listing 6-1, construct rotation matrices for rotating around the x, y, and z axes, respectively. As input, the functions take a single parameter θ representing the number of degrees by which the point should be rotated. As we discussed earlier in this chapter when we introduced rotation, a positive angle θ represents a clockwise rotation when looking along the axis of rotation from its tip towards its base. As output, the functions return a rotation matrix which, when multiplied with a column vector, rotate the column vector by θ degrees around the appropriate axis.

Scaling

To scale a 3D point is to multiply by a factor s the point's distance from the origin along the x, y, and z axes. For a uniform scaling, we scale x, y, and z by the same amounts; for a non-uniform scaling, we scale them by different amounts.

Expressed without Matrices

Remembering the relationship between points and vectors (Chapter 5), we know that the coordinates of a point represent its displacement from the origin. Since scaling a point means scaling the displacement from the origin, we simply multiply x, y, and z by scaling factors, which might be all the same for a uniform scaling, but which may all be different in the case of a non-uniform scaling.

   Let us call the coordinates of the scaled point (x',y',z'). Given scaling factors of s_x, s_y, and s_z for the three coordinate axes, the following formulas perform scaling about the origin:

Equation 6-24
$$x' = s_x x$$
$$y' = s_y y$$
$$z' = s_z z$$

We use the term $S(s_x, s_y, s_z)$ to denote the scaling operation.

Expressed in Matrix Form

Scaling expressed in matrix form is as follows:

Equation 6-25
$$S(s_x, s_y, s_z) = \begin{bmatrix} s_x & 0 & 0 & 0 \\ 0 & s_y & 0 & 0 \\ 0 & 0 & s_z & 0 \\ 0 & 0 & 0 & 1 \end{bmatrix}$$

Multiplying this matrix by a column vector, you can see that the x component gets multiplied by s_x, the y component by s_y, and the z component by s_z.

The l3d_mat_scale Function

The function l3d_mat_scale, which we saw earlier in Listing 6-1, constructs a scaling matrix for scaling about the origin. As input, the function takes three parameters for the scaling factor in the x, y, and z directions. As output, the function returns a scaling matrix which, when multiplied with a column vector, scales the column vector by the given amounts in the x, y, and z directions.

Sample Program: Rotspikes

The following sample program, rotspikes, illustrates the use of rotation matrices. It is similar to the program spikes from Chapter 5, in that spike-shaped objects fly towards the viewer. Here, however, the spikes also have a random rotational velocity in the *x*, *y*, and *z* directions. The spikes thus appear to be tumbling toward the viewer instead of flying straight ahead. This effect could be used, for instance, to simulate flying debris coming from an explosion.

Listing 6-4: rotspikes.cc

```
#include <stdlib.h>
#include <stdio.h>

#include "../lib/tool_2d/screen.h"
#include "../lib/tool_os/dispatch.h"
#include "../lib/raster/rasteriz.h"
#include "../lib/tool_2d/scrinfo.h"
#include "../lib/system/factorys.h"

#include "../lib/geom/point/point.h"
#include "../lib/math/vector.h"
#include "../lib/math/matrix.h"

#define MAXSPIKES 150
#define PI 3.14159265

unsigned long red_color;
unsigned long green_color;
unsigned long blue_color;

//- STEP 1: CHOOSE THE FACTORIES

void choose_factories(void) {
  factory_manager_v_0_1.choose_factories();
}

//- STEP 2: DECLARE A PIPELINE SUBCLASS

l3d_real fovx, fovy;
int xsize, ysize;

class spike {
  public:

    l3d_two_part_list<l3d_coordinate> *vlist;
    l3d_polygon_2d_flatshaded *faces[3];
    l3d_vector displacement;

    int rx, ry, rz, drx, dry, drz;
    l3d_vector velocity;

    spike(void) {
      //- declare common shared vertex list for all polygons
      vlist = new l3d_two_part_list<l3d_coordinate> (4);
      int i=0;
      (*vlist)[i++].original.set(int_to_l3d_real(0),
                                 int_to_l3d_real(0),
                                 int_to_l3d_real(100),
                                 int_to_l3d_real(1));
```

```
    (*vlist)[i++].original.set(int_to_l3d_real(10),
                               int_to_l3d_real(10),
                               int_to_l3d_real(100),
                               int_to_l3d_real(1)));
    (*vlist)[i++].original.set(int_to_l3d_real(10),
                               int_to_l3d_real(0),
                               int_to_l3d_real(100),
                               int_to_l3d_real(1)));
    (*vlist)[i++].original.set(int_to_l3d_real(0),
                               int_to_l3d_real(0),
                               int_to_l3d_real(0),
                               int_to_l3d_real(1)));

    //- define polygons in terms of indices into shared vertex list
    faces[0] = new l3d_polygon_2d_flatshaded(3);
    faces[0]->vlist = & vlist; //- shared vertex list
    (*(faces[0]->ivertices))[faces[0]->ivertices->next_index()].ivertex = 3;
    (*(faces[0]->ivertices))[faces[0]->ivertices->next_index()].ivertex = 0;
    (*(faces[0]->ivertices))[faces[0]->ivertices->next_index()].ivertex = 1;

    faces[1] = new l3d_polygon_2d_flatshaded(3);
    faces[1]->vlist = & vlist; //- shared vertex list
    (*(faces[1]->ivertices))[faces[1]->ivertices->next_index()].ivertex = 3;
    (*(faces[1]->ivertices))[faces[1]->ivertices->next_index()].ivertex = 1;
    (*(faces[1]->ivertices))[faces[1]->ivertices->next_index()].ivertex = 2;

    faces[2] = new l3d_polygon_2d_flatshaded(3);
    faces[2]->vlist = & vlist; //- shared vertex list
    (*(faces[2]->ivertices))[faces[2]->ivertices->next_index()].ivertex = 3;
    (*(faces[2]->ivertices))[faces[2]->ivertices->next_index()].ivertex = 2;
    (*(faces[2]->ivertices))[faces[2]->ivertices->next_index()].ivertex = 0;
  }

  ~spike(void) {
    delete faces[0];
    delete faces[1];
    delete faces[2];
    delete vlist;
  }

  void place_spike(void) {
    displacement.set(int_to_l3d_real(1000 - (rand() % 2000)),
                     int_to_l3d_real(1000 - (rand() % 2000)),
                     int_to_l3d_real(100 + (rand()%1000)),
                     int_to_l3d_real(1));
    velocity.set(int_to_l3d_real(0),
                 int_to_l3d_real(0),
                 int_to_l3d_real(-(rand()%75 + 5)),
                 int_to_l3d_real(0));
    rx = ry = rz = 0;
    drx = (rand() % 16 - 8);
    dry = (rand() % 16 - 8);
    drz = (rand() % 16 - 8);

    l3d_matrix transform;

    transform =
      l3d_mat_translate(displacement.a[0],
                        displacement.a[1],
```

```
                                    displacement.a[2]);

        l3d_mat_rotz(rz) | l3d_mat_roty(ry) | l3d_mat_rotx(rx) ;

        int q;
        for(q=0; q<vlist->num_fixed_items; q++) {
          (*vlist)[q].reset();
          (*vlist)[q].transformed =      transform | (*vlist)[q].transformed;
        }
      }

  void move_spike(void) {
    displacement = displacement + velocity;
    rx = rx + drx;
    if(rx<0) {rx += 360; }
    if(rx>=360) {rx -= 360; }
    ry = ry + dry;
    if(ry<0) {ry += 360; }
    if(ry>=360) {ry -= 360; }
    rz = rz + drz;
    if(rz<0) {rz += 360; }
    if(rz>=360) {rz -= 360; }
    l3d_matrix transform;

    transform =
      l3d_mat_translate(displacement.a[0],
                        displacement.a[1],
                        displacement.a[2]) |

      l3d_mat_rotz(rz) | l3d_mat_roty(ry) | l3d_mat_rotx(rx) ;
    int q;
    for(q=0; q<vlist->num_fixed_items; q++) {
      (*vlist)[q].reset();
      (*vlist)[q].transformed =      transform | (*vlist)[q].transformed;
    }
  }

  void project_spike() {
    int v;

    for(v=0; v<vlist->num_fixed_items; v++) {
      (*vlist)[v].transformed.X_ =
        l3d_mulri(l3d_mulrr(l3d_divrr( (*vlist)[v].transformed.X_,
                                       (*vlist)[v].transformed.Z_),
                            fovx),
                  xsize)
        +
        int_to_l3d_real(xsize > 1);

      (*vlist)[v].transformed.Y_ =
        l3d_mulri(l3d_mulrr(l3d_divrr(-(*vlist)[v].transformed.Y_,
                                       (*vlist)[v].transformed.Z_),
                            fovy),
                  ysize)
        +
        int_to_l3d_real(ysize > 1);
    }
  }
```

```
    };

    class my_pipeline : public l3d_pipeline {
      protected:
        l3d_rasterizer_2d_imp *ri;
        l3d_rasterizer_2d *r;

        spike spikes[MAXSPIKES];
        long i, j;
        long wc_win_width, wc_win_height, wc_win_dist, fov;
        long wc_win_left, wc_win_top;
        int numspikes;

        virtual int out_of_wc_bounds(l3d_point const &p);

      public:
        l3d_screen *s;
        my_pipeline(void);
        virtual ~my_pipeline(void);

        void key_event(int ch);   //- from dispatcher
        void update_event(void); //- from dispatcher
        void draw_event(void);    //- from dispatcher
    };

    my_pipeline::my_pipeline(void) {
      s = factory_manager_v_0_1.screen_factory->create(320,200);
      ri = factory_manager_v_0_1.ras_2d_imp_factory->create(320,200,s->sinfo);
      r = new l3d_rasterizer_2d(ri);

      s->sinfo->ext_max_red =
        s->sinfo->ext_max_green =
          s->sinfo->ext_max_blue =   255;
      s->sinfo->ext_to_native(0,0,0); //- allocate black background color
      red_color = s->sinfo->ext_to_native(255, 0, 0);
      green_color = s->sinfo->ext_to_native(0, 255, 0);
      blue_color = s->sinfo->ext_to_native(0,0, 255);
      s->refresh_palette();

      fovx = float_to_l3d_real(0.5*1.0/tan(50./180. * PI));
      fovy = float_to_l3d_real(0.5*1.0/tan(30./180. * PI));
      xsize = s->xsize;
      ysize = s->ysize;

      numspikes = MAXSPIKES;
      for(i=0; i<MAXSPIKES; i++) {
        spikes[i].place_spike();

        spikes[i].faces[0]->final_color = red_color;
        spikes[i].faces[1]->final_color = green_color;
        spikes[i].faces[2]->final_color = blue_color;
      }
    }

    my_pipeline::~my_pipeline(void) {
      delete s;
      delete ri;
      delete r;
    }
```

```
void my_pipeline::key_event(int ch) {
  switch(ch) {
    case 'q': {
        exit(0);
      }
  }
}

void my_pipeline::update_event() {
  int i;

  for(i=0;i<numspikes;i++) {
    spikes[i].move_spike();
    if(out_of_wc_bounds( (*spikes[i].vlist)[0].transformed)
        || out_of_wc_bounds( (*spikes[i].vlist)[1].transformed)
        || out_of_wc_bounds( (*spikes[i].vlist)[2].transformed)
        || out_of_wc_bounds( (*spikes[i].vlist)[3].transformed))
      //- we must check all vertices of the spike since its orientation
      //- is now arbitrary, and any point might be the foremost point
      //- which has now moved out of bounds
    {
      spikes[i].place_spike();
    }

    spikes[i].project_spike();
  }
}

void my_pipeline::draw_event(void) {
  int i;
  r->clear_buffer();

  for(i=0;i<numspikes;i++) {
    for(int f=0; f<3; f++) {
      spikes[i].faces[f]->init_clip_ivertices();
      spikes[i].faces[f]->clip_to_polygon_2d(s->view_win);
      r->draw_polygon_flatshaded(spikes[i].faces[f]);
    }
  }
  s->blit_screen();
}

int my_pipeline::out_of_wc_bounds(l3d_point const &p) {
  return(p.Z_<int_to_l3d_real(1));
}

int main(int argc, char **argv) {
  choose_factories();

  l3d_dispatcher *d;
  my_pipeline *p;

  //- STEP 3: CREATE A DISPATCHER

  d = factory_manager_v_0_1.dispatcher_factory->create();

  //- STEP 4: CREATE A PIPELINE
```

```
//- plug our custom behavior pipeline into the dispatcher
p   = new my_pipeline();

//- STEP 5: START DISPATCHER

d->pipeline = p; //- polymorphic assignment
d->event_source = p->s;
d->start();

delete d;
delete p;
}
```

Figure 6-16: Output from sample program `rotspikes`.

Let's look at the changes from the original `spikes` program of Chapter 5. First of all, we declare some variables to hold the rotation angles as well as the rotational velocities in each spike.

```
int rx, ry, rz, drx, dry, drz;
```

Next, in the functions `place_spike` and `move_spike`, we initialize and update the rotational variables, respectively. Then, we use both the rotation angles, representing the rotation, and the displacement vector, representing the translation, to form appropriate transformation matrices using the `l3d_mat_` functions. We multiply all of these rotation matrices together, using the matrix multiplication operator |, and store the result in the composite matrix variable `transform`.

```
transform =
  l3d_mat_translate(displacement.a[0],
                    displacement.a[1],
                    displacement.a[2]) |

l3d_mat_rotz(rz) | l3d_mat_roty(ry) | l3d_mat_rotx(rx) ;
```

After computing the combined transformation matrix consisting of the translation and all three rotations, we apply the transformation matrix to each point in the spike, by multiplying the matrix with the point. In the original `spikes` program of Chapter 5, we simply added a displacement vector to the spike's position. Here, we multiply a general transformation matrix with the spike's position, thereby applying several transformations at once.

```
for(q=0; q<vlist->num_fixed_items; q++) {
  (*vlist)[q].reset();
  (*vlist)[q].transformed =      transform | (*vlist)[q].transformed;
}
```

Finally, we also have to change the out-of-bounds check for the spike. In Chapter 5, we simply checked vertex number three to see if it was out of bounds or not. This is because the vertex had a fixed orientation, and we knew that vertex three would always be the foremost vertex nearest to the camera (located, recall, at the origin). Furthermore, since the spikes only move forward, we knew in Chapter 5 that the foremost vertex would be the first one to move out of bounds. However, with the new `rotspikes` program, these assumptions no longer hold. The spike may have an arbitrary orientation; any one of the four vertices of the spike might be foremost, and therefore any of the four vertices might be out of bounds at any given time. Therefore, the out-of-bounds check needs to be augmented to check all vertices of a spike to determine if the spike needs to be repositioned.

```
spikes[i].move_spike();
if(out_of_wc_bounds( (*spikes[i].vlist)[0].transformed)
   || out_of_wc_bounds( (*spikes[i].vlist)[1].transformed)
   || out_of_wc_bounds( (*spikes[i].vlist)[2].transformed)
   || out_of_wc_bounds( (*spikes[i].vlist)[3].transformed))
  //- we must check all vertices of the spike since its orientation
  //- is now arbitrary, and any point might be the foremost point
  //- which has now moved out of bounds
{
  spikes[i].place_spike();
}
```

With this sample program, we have now seen how to use the rotation matrix functions. Furthermore, we have also seen how to combine several transformations into one composite transformation matrix. Let's now look more closely at this concept of combining transformations.

Combining Transformations

We mentioned earlier in this chapter that we can combine a series of 4×4 transformation matrices to apply several transformations to a point. In the following sections, we see concrete applications of this powerful and flexible technique. The unifying idea is that we break up a complicated 3D transformation into a series of simple 3D transformations. We combine the simple 3D transformation matrices by multiplying them together, and finally multiply the composite transformation matrix with the 3D point to be transformed.

Simple Sequential Transformations

The simplest example of a combined transformation is the case where we naturally geometrically think of sequentially applying one transformation, then another. An example of such simple sequential transformations is the spike movement in the example program `rotspikes`. First, we want to rotate the spike according to its random rotational velocities. Then, we want to translate the spike to its current position. See Figure 6-17.

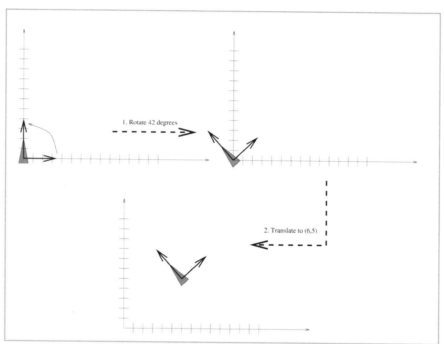

Figure 6-17: Rotational, then translational movement in `rotspikes`. *The spike undergoes a local rotational movement around the origin, which happens also to be the spike's local origin. This is similar to the earth spinning around its own axis. Then, the spike is translated to its final position.*

Mathematically, recall that we defined that a series of matrix multiplications *ABCD* is performed in the order *D*, *C*, *B*, *A*. Assume we are given a rotation matrix *R*, a translation matrix *T*, and a point *P*. Then, in order to apply the rotation first and the translation next, we should take the product of *TRP*. You can see in the source code for `rotspikes` that we do exactly this when we compute the total transformation matrix `transform`: the leftmost matrix is the translation matrix, followed by three rotation matrices, followed finally by the original point. This means that the order of application of the transformations is right to left, even though they are written left to right.

Notice that if we reverse the order of the transformations, we arrive at an entirely different end result. Consider again the example with *T*, *R*, and *P*. Assume that instead of computing *TRP*, we compute *RTP*. This has the effect of first applying the translation matrix *T* (since it is rightmost), followed by the rotation matrix *R*. The effect is as seen in Figure 6-18. First, we displace the object away from the origin. Then we perform a rotation—but rotation, as we defined earlier, takes place around the origin. Since the object has already been displaced away from the origin but the rotation still takes place around the origin, the object gets rotated in a large arc with the origin as the center. This is similar to the earth revolving around the sun.

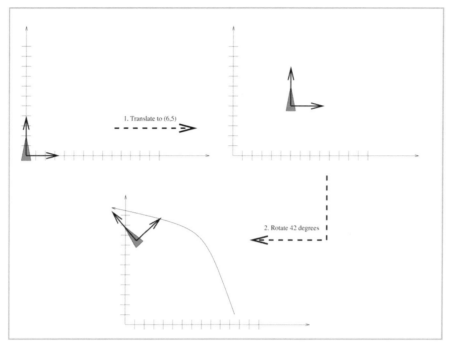

1. Translate to (6,5)

2. Rotate 42 degrees

Figure 6-18: Applying the translation before the rotation (RTP) results in an "orbital" revolution instead of a local rotation, similar to the earth orbiting around the sun. This is because the rotation around the origin takes place after the object has already been displaced away from the origin.

What we learn from this, then, is that the order of application transformations is very important. The parallel with matrix multiplication is clear. Matrices, which represent transformations, also must be multiplied in a particular order; changing the order of multiplication, in general, changes the result, just as changing the order of transformations changes the result.

Rotation or Scaling About an Arbitrary Point

The rotation and scaling formulas developed earlier were defined with respect to the origin. This means that if we rotate a series of points (defining an object), the object is not only rotated but is also given a new position. Similarly, if we scale down an object, it is not only smaller, but also closer to the origin; if we scale it up, it is farther from the origin.

NOTE   For the time being, assume that the "position" of an object defined by several points is the center among all of the points. The precise meaning of the "position" of an object requires us to define a so-called *object coordinate system*, the origin of which is then the "position" of the object. We cover this topic later in this chapter in the discussion about matrices and coordinate systems.

Often, we would like to rotate or scale an object about its own center. This way, the center point of an object stays in the same position in space, with the rest of the object changing its orientation or size. Figures 6-19 and 6-20 illustrate these ideas of *local rotation* and *local scaling*.

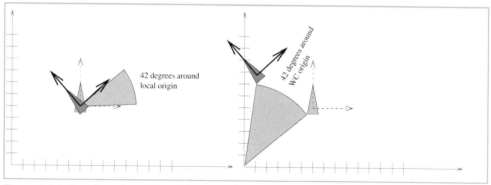

Figure 6-19: Rotation about the origin versus local rotation in 2D space.

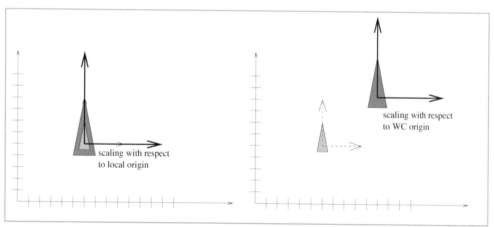

Figure 6-20: Scaling about the origin versus local scaling in 2D space.

The solution to this problem is simple: we first translate all points of the object such that the desired center of rotation or scaling is moved to the origin in world coordinates. Then, we use the normal rotation or scaling matrix to perform rotation or scaling about the origin. Finally, we translate all points of the object back by an amount exactly opposite to that of the initial translation.

Remembering that a series of matrix multiplications represents geometric operations performed right to left, we can write the equation for local rotation as follows:

Equation 6-26 $T(x, y, z) \, R \, T(-x, -y, -z)$

Consider what happens when we multiply this matrix with a series of points belonging to an object. Assume the center location of the object is at (x,y,z). The rightmost matrix $T(-x,-y,-z)$, which is geometrically applied first, translates all points of the object such that the object's center is exactly at the origin. The next matrix, in right-to-left order, is the desired rotation matrix, or series of rotation matrices. Since the translation matrix has already been applied, all points of the object are centered about the origin in world coordinates. Therefore, we can use the normal rotation matrices we derived earlier for rotation about the origin. Finally, after the rotation is complete, we translate the object back to its original location by applying the opposite translation, $T(x,y,z)$. See Figure 6-21.

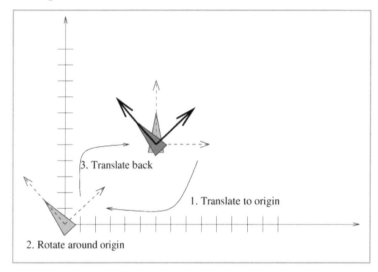

Figure 6-21: Local rotation as a series of transformations.

3. Translate back

1. Translate to origin

2. Rotate around origin

Similarly, we can express local scaling as a series of transformations which translate the object's points to the origin, scale the points with respect to the origin, and translate the points back. Mathematically:

Equation 6-27 $$T(x, y, z) \, S(s_x, s_y, s_z) \, T(-x, -y, -z)$$

Arbitrary Camera Position and Orientation

One of the most important applications of transformation matrices is the transformation of an arbitrary camera position and orientation into the standard camera position and orientation discussed earlier (camera at origin, looking straight down z axis, perfectly right-side-up). We need to do this because the perspective projection equations developed in Chapter 5 all assume that the camera is in the standard position and orientation, but we would like to allow our virtual camera to be arbitrarily positioned and oriented.

We solve this problem by application of a series of matrices. First, we need to state the problem more precisely. To allow the camera to be arbitrarily located and oriented in space, we first need a convention for specifying the camera's position and orientation in 3D space.

How to Specify an Arbitrary Camera Position and Orientation

We specify the camera's 3D position by a point, which we call the VRP, for View Reference Point. We specify the camera's orientation with three normalized and orthogonal vectors, which we call the up vector VUP, the forward vector VFW, and the right vector VRI. (The terms VRP and VUP are from the book *Computer Graphics: Principles and Practices* [FOLE92].) The VUP points in the direction that the camera perceives as an "up" direction; the VFW, in the "forward" direction; and the VRI, in the "right" direction. Notice that these vectors form a left-handed coordinate system; VRI×VUP=VFW.

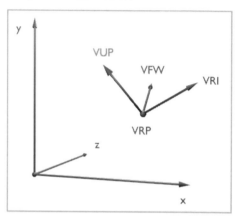

Figure 6-22: Specifying an arbitrary camera location orientation with one point and three vectors.

Given this convention for specifying the camera's location and orientation, we want to find a transformation matrix that translates the VRP to the origin and rotates the VRI, VUP, and VFW vectors to align with the x, y, and z axes, respectively. After this transformation, the camera has the standard position and orientation required for the perspective projection equation of Chapter 5.

Deriving the Matrix

With the precise problem formulation given above, the problem's solution is straightforward. We use two steps. First, we translate the camera's position to the origin. Second, we rotate the camera's orientation so that the camera is perfectly right-side-up and is looking straight down the z axis.

The first transformation, translating the VRP to the origin, is simply a translation by the negative of each component of VRP:

Equation 6-28
$$\begin{bmatrix} 1 & 0 & 0 & -VRP_x \\ 0 & 1 & 0 & -VRP_y \\ 0 & 0 & 1 & -VRP_z \\ 0 & 0 & 0 & 1 \end{bmatrix}$$

After this transformation, the VRP is at the origin, as shown in Figure 6-23. The vectors VRI, VUP, and VFW all now have a starting point located at the origin (0,0,0).

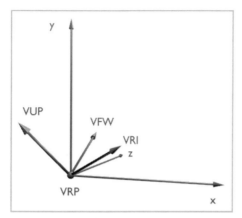

The second transformation, the rotation, is a bit trickier. Given three origin-based vectors, VRI, VUP, and VFW, how can we rotate these into the x, y, and z axes? We solve this problem by approaching it in reverse. First, we determine how we can rotate the x, y, and z axes into the VRI, VUP, and VFW vectors. Then, we take the inverse of this matrix to find the opposite transformation which rotates VRI, VUP, and VFW into the x, y, and z axes.

We can represent each axis x, y, and z with a vector of length one along the corresponding axis. The x axis vector is therefore $[1,0,0,0]^T$; the y axis, $[0,1,0,0]^T$; and the z axis, $[0,0,1,0]^T$. Let us name these vectors i, j, and k, respectively.

Now, let us assume we have a matrix Q of the following form:

Equation 6-29

$$\begin{bmatrix} A & B & C & 0 \\ D & E & F & 0 \\ G & H & I & 0 \\ 0 & 0 & 0 & 1 \end{bmatrix}$$

This matrix transforms the i vector into the first column of Q, namely $[A,D,G,0]^T$, the j vector into the second column $[B,E,H,0]^T$, and the k vector into the third column $[C,F,I,0]^T$. (Try performing the matrix multiplication between Q and $[1,0,0,0]^T$ to verify this.) This is an important observation; the first three columns of the matrix represent the vectors to which the i, j, and k vectors get transformed after multiplication with the matrix.

This means that the following matrix rotates the vectors i, j, and k into VRI, VUP, and VFW:

Equation 6-30

$$\begin{bmatrix} VRI_x & VUP_x & VFW_x & 0 \\ VRI_y & VUP_y & VFW_y & 0 \\ VRI_z & VUP_z & VFW_z & 0 \\ 0 & 0 & 0 & 1 \end{bmatrix}$$

If we invert this matrix, we obtain the matrix which performs the opposite rotation, rotating VRI, VUP, and VFW into i, j, and k. Fortunately, in this particular case, this matrix is easy to invert. (Although, as noted earlier, computing a matrix inverse is not always easy.) For this matrix, we simply take its transpose to find the inverse. Therefore, the desired rotation matrix is:

Equation 6-31
$$\begin{bmatrix} VRI_x & VRI_y & VRI_z & 0 \\ VUP_x & VUP_y & VUP_z & 0 \\ VFW_x & VFW_y & VFW_z & 0 \\ 0 & 0 & 0 & 1 \end{bmatrix}$$

To verify that this really is the inverse, recall the definition of the matrix inverse: $M^{-1}M=I$. If we perform this multiplication, we see why the inverse in this case works:

Equation 6-32
$$\begin{bmatrix} VRI_x & VRI_y & VRI_z & 0 \\ VUP_x & VUP_y & VUP_z & 0 \\ VFW_x & VFW_y & VFW_z & 0 \\ 0 & 0 & 0 & 1 \end{bmatrix} \begin{bmatrix} VRI_x & VUP_x & VFW_x & 0 \\ VRI_y & VUP_y & VFW_y & 0 \\ VRI_z & VUP_z & VFW_z & 0 \\ 0 & 0 & 0 & 1 \end{bmatrix} = \begin{bmatrix} 1 & 0 & 0 & 0 \\ 0 & 1 & 0 & 0 \\ 0 & 0 & 1 & 0 \\ 0 & 0 & 0 & 1 \end{bmatrix}$$

Notice that if you perform this matrix multiplication, it is a series of dot products between mutually orthogonal, unit size vectors. This is the reason that the matrix inverse is the matrix transpose. The dot of a unit vector with itself gives one, explaining the 1 entries in the result. The dot of a unit vector with an orthogonal vector gives zero, explaining the 0 entries in the result. The final result is the identity matrix, verifying that the transpose is indeed the inverse in this special case.

In general, any series of rotation matrices multiplied together yields a matrix of the form shown in Equation 6-29. Therefore, any such matrix may be inverted by taking its transpose. But, if a series of rotation matrices is multiplied with any other matrix (scaling or translation, for instance), then the inverse may no longer be computed as the transpose.

 TIP A 4×4 rotation matrix or composition of rotation matrices may be inverted by taking its transpose.

 CAUTION If a rotation matrix is concatenated with any matrix other than a rotation matrix, the inverse can no longer always be computed as the transpose.

The Final Camera Transformation Matrix

Combining the VRP translation matrix with the VRI, VUP, and VFW rotation matrix yields the following equation for converting from camera to world coordinates:

Equation 6-33
$$M_{world \leftarrow camera} = \begin{bmatrix} VRI_x & VRI_y & VRI_z & 0 \\ VUP_x & VUP_y & VUP_z & 0 \\ VFW_x & VFW_y & VFW_z & 0 \\ 0 & 0 & 0 & 1 \end{bmatrix} \begin{bmatrix} 1 & 0 & 0 & -VRP_x \\ 0 & 1 & 0 & -VRP_y \\ 0 & 0 & 1 & -VRP_z \\ 0 & 0 & 0 & 1 \end{bmatrix}$$

Notice that the resulting matrix, since it consists of both a rotation matrix and a translation matrix, cannot be inverted simply by taking its transpose. We can, however, easily compute the inverse matrix, by multiplying the inverse transformation matrices in the opposite order; we do know how to compute the inverses of the individual component matrices. We start with the inverse rotation matrix, which is merely the transpose of the camera rotation matrix. This undoes the rotation of the camera. We then multiply this with the inverse translation matrix. The inverse translation matrix is merely the identical translation matrix with negated translation terms in the last column. This matrix undoes the camera translation, moving the camera back to its original position. If we call the inverse rotation matrix R^{-1} and the inverse translation matrix T^{-1}, then the combined matrix $T^{-1}R^{-1}$ is the inverse of the complete camera transformation matrix.

After application of the final camera transformation matrix, the camera is at the origin and is perfectly right-side-up, looking straight down the positive z axis. See Figure 6-24. This is the camera location and orientation needed for the perspective projection.

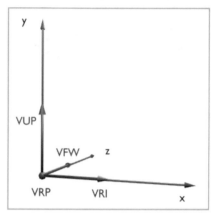

Figure 6-24: The camera position and orientation after application of the final camera transformation matrix.

We apply this matrix to all points specified in world coordinates to obtain the points' coordinates with respect to the camera. Then, these transformed points may be projected with the perspective projection equation of Chapter 5.

The l3d_moveable Class

The l3d class which allows specification of an arbitrary location and orientation for a camera is the l3d_moveable class, given in Listings 6-5 and 6-6.

Listing 6-5: moveable.h

```
#ifndef __MOVEABLE_H
#define __MOVEABLE_H
#include "../tool_os/memman.h"

#include "../system/sys_dep.h"
#include "../math/matrix.h"
#include "../geom/point/point.h"

class l3d_moveable {
  public:
    l3d_moveable(void);

    l3d_point VRP, VFW_tip, VUP_tip, VRI_tip;
    l3d_vector VFW, VUP, VRI;

    l3d_matrix viewing_xform;
    l3d_matrix inverse_viewing_xform;

    void calculate_viewing_xform(void);

    virtual int update(void);      //- update position of camera
    l3d_real
    rot_VUP_velocity,
```

```
            rot_VRI_velocity,
            rot_VFW_velocity,
            VUP_velocity,
            VRI_velocity,
            VFW_velocity,
            VUP_thrust,
            VRI_thrust,
            VFW_thrust;
        void rotateVFW(void);
        void rotateVUP(void);
        void rotateVRI(void);
        void translateVFW(void);
        void translateVUP(void);
        void translateVRI(void);

        virtual void transform(const l3d_matrix &m);
    };
    #endif
```

Listing 6-6: moveable.cc

```
    #include <stdio.h>
    #include <math.h>
    #include "moveable.h"
    #include "../tool_os/memman.h"

    l3d_moveable::l3d_moveable(void) {

      VRP.set(int_to_l3d_real(50),int_to_l3d_real(5),int_to_l3d_real(50),int_to_l3d_real(0));

      VUP.set(float_to_l3d_real(0.0),float_to_l3d_real(1.0),float_to_l3d_real(0.0),
              float_to_l3d_real(0.0));
      VFW.set(float_to_l3d_real(0.0), float_to_l3d_real(0.0), float_to_l3d_real(1.0),
              float_to_l3d_real(0.0));
      VRI = cross(VUP,VFW);

      VUP_tip=VRP+VUP;
      VFW_tip=VRP+VFW;
      VRI_tip=VRP+VRI;

      VFW_velocity = int_to_l3d_real(0);
      VUP_velocity = int_to_l3d_real(0);
      VRI_velocity = int_to_l3d_real(0);
      VFW_thrust = int_to_l3d_real(0.2);
      VUP_thrust = int_to_l3d_real(0.2);
      VRI_thrust = int_to_l3d_real(0.2);

      rot_VUP_velocity = int_to_l3d_real(0);
      rot_VRI_velocity = int_to_l3d_real(0);
      rot_VFW_velocity = int_to_l3d_real(0);

      calculate_viewing_xform();
    }

    void l3d_moveable::translateVFW() {
      VRP.X_ = VRP.X_ + l3d_mulrr(VFW.X_, VFW_velocity);
      VUP_tip.X_ = VUP_tip.X_ + l3d_mulrr(VFW.X_, VFW_velocity);
      VFW_tip.X_ = VFW_tip.X_ + l3d_mulrr(VFW.X_, VFW_velocity);
      VRI_tip.X_ = VRI_tip.X_ + l3d_mulrr(VFW.X_, VFW_velocity);

      VRP.Y_ = VRP.Y_ + l3d_mulrr(VFW.Y_, VFW_velocity);
```

```
    VUP_tip.Y_ = VUP_tip.Y_ + l3d_mulrr(VFW.Y_, VFW_velocity);
    VFW_tip.Y_ = VFW_tip.Y_ + l3d_mulrr(VFW.Y_, VFW_velocity);
    VRI_tip.Y_ = VRI_tip.Y_ + l3d_mulrr(VFW.Y_, VFW_velocity);

    VRP.Z_ = VRP.Z_ + l3d_mulrr(VFW.Z_, VFW_velocity);
    VUP_tip.Z_ = VUP_tip.Z_ + l3d_mulrr(VFW.Z_, VFW_velocity);
    VFW_tip.Z_ = VFW_tip.Z_ + l3d_mulrr(VFW.Z_, VFW_velocity);
    VRI_tip.Z_ = VRI_tip.Z_ + l3d_mulrr(VFW.Z_, VFW_velocity);

  }

  void l3d_moveable::translateVRI() {
    VRP.X_ = VRP.X_ + l3d_mulrr(VRI.X_, VRI_velocity);
    VUP_tip.X_ = VUP_tip.X_ + l3d_mulrr(VRI.X_, VRI_velocity);
    VFW_tip.X_ = VFW_tip.X_ + l3d_mulrr(VRI.X_, VRI_velocity);
    VRI_tip.X_ = VRI_tip.X_ + l3d_mulrr(VRI.X_, VRI_velocity);

    VRP.Y_ = VRP.Y_ + l3d_mulrr(VRI.Y_, VRI_velocity);
    VUP_tip.Y_ = VUP_tip.Y_ + l3d_mulrr(VRI.Y_, VRI_velocity);
    VFW_tip.Y_ = VFW_tip.Y_ + l3d_mulrr(VRI.Y_, VRI_velocity);
    VRI_tip.Y_ = VRI_tip.Y_ + l3d_mulrr(VRI.Y_, VRI_velocity);

    VRP.Z_ = VRP.Z_ + l3d_mulrr(VRI.Z_, VRI_velocity);
    VUP_tip.Z_ = VUP_tip.Z_ + l3d_mulrr(VRI.Z_, VRI_velocity);
    VFW_tip.Z_ = VFW_tip.Z_ + l3d_mulrr(VRI.Z_, VRI_velocity);
    VRI_tip.Z_ = VRI_tip.Z_ + l3d_mulrr(VRI.Z_, VRI_velocity);

  }

  void l3d_moveable::translateVUP() {
    VRP.X_ = VRP.X_ + l3d_mulrr(VUP.X_, VUP_velocity);
    VUP_tip.X_ = VUP_tip.X_ + l3d_mulrr(VUP.X_, VUP_velocity);
    VFW_tip.X_ = VFW_tip.X_ + l3d_mulrr(VUP.X_, VUP_velocity);
    VRI_tip.X_ = VRI_tip.X_ + l3d_mulrr(VUP.X_, VUP_velocity);

    VRP.Y_ = VRP.Y_ + l3d_mulrr(VUP.Y_, VUP_velocity);
    VUP_tip.Y_ = VUP_tip.Y_ + l3d_mulrr(VUP.Y_, VUP_velocity);
    VFW_tip.Y_ = VFW_tip.Y_ + l3d_mulrr(VUP.Y_, VUP_velocity);
    VRI_tip.Y_ = VRI_tip.Y_ + l3d_mulrr(VUP.Y_, VUP_velocity);

    VRP.Z_ = VRP.Z_ + l3d_mulrr(VUP.Z_, VUP_velocity);
    VUP_tip.Z_ = VUP_tip.Z_ + l3d_mulrr(VUP.Z_, VUP_velocity);
    VFW_tip.Z_ = VFW_tip.Z_ + l3d_mulrr(VUP.Z_, VUP_velocity);
    VRI_tip.Z_ = VRI_tip.Z_ + l3d_mulrr(VUP.Z_, VUP_velocity);

  }

  void l3d_moveable::rotateVUP() {
    int angle=l3d_real_to_int(rot_VUP_velocity);
    l3d_matrix a;

    if(angle<0) angle+=360;  //- convert negative angle into 360-angle

    VFW = l3d_mat_rotu(VUP, angle) | VFW;
    VRI = cross(VUP,VFW);   //- calculate VRI based on VUP and new VFW

  }

  void l3d_moveable::rotateVRI() {
```

```
  int angle=l3d_real_to_int(rot_VRI_velocity);

  if(angle<0) angle+=360;  //- convert negative angle into 360-angle

 VFW = l3d_mat_rotu(VRI,angle) | VFW;
 VUP = cross(VFW,VRI);  //- calculate VUP based on VRI and new VFW

}

void l3d_moveable::rotateVFW() {
  int angle=l3d_real_to_int(rot_VFW_velocity);
  if(angle<0) angle+=360;
  VUP = l3d_mat_rotu(VFW,angle) | VUP;
  VRI = cross(VUP,VFW);  //- calculate VRI based on VFW and new VUP

}

int l3d_moveable::update(void) {

  if(VFW_velocity != int_to_l3d_real(0)) {
    VFW_velocity = l3d_mulrr(VFW_velocity,float_to_l3d_real(0.95));
  }
  if(VRI_velocity != int_to_l3d_real(0)) {
    VRI_velocity = l3d_mulrr(VRI_velocity,float_to_l3d_real(0.95));
  }
  if(VUP_velocity != int_to_l3d_real(0)) {
    VUP_velocity = l3d_mulrr(VUP_velocity,float_to_l3d_real(0.95));
  }
  if(rot_VUP_velocity != int_to_l3d_real(0)) {
    rot_VUP_velocity = l3d_mulrr(rot_VUP_velocity,float_to_l3d_real(0.85));
  }
  if(rot_VRI_velocity != int_to_l3d_real(0)) {
    rot_VRI_velocity = l3d_mulrr(rot_VRI_velocity,float_to_l3d_real(0.85));
  }
  if(rot_VFW_velocity != int_to_l3d_real(0)) {
    rot_VFW_velocity = l3d_mulrr(rot_VFW_velocity,float_to_l3d_real(0.85));
  }

  if(rot_VUP_velocity) rotateVUP();
  if(rot_VRI_velocity) rotateVRI();
  if(rot_VFW_velocity) rotateVFW();

  if(VFW_velocity) translateVFW();
  if(VUP_velocity) translateVUP();
  if(VRI_velocity) translateVRI();

  //- It is important to normalize our camera vectors now, since repeated
  //- application of relative rotational transformations will eventually,
  //- due to numerical round off error, cause the length of these vectors
  //- to no longer be one. This subsequently causes problems in the calculation
  //- of the camera rotation matrix, which assumes that the vectors VFW,
  //- VRI, and VUP are all unit vectors (i.e. length 1). It would also be
  //- possible to do the normalization during computation of the camera
  //- rotation matrix, but this is not the approach chosen here.

  VFW = normalized(VFW);
  VRI = normalized(VRI);
  VUP = normalized(VUP);
```

```
   calculate_viewing_xform();

   return 0;
}

void l3d_moveable::calculate_viewing_xform(void) {

   l3d_matrix R, TnVRP;
   l3d_matrix inverse_R, inverse_TnVRP;

   //- Translate VRP to origin

   TnVRP.set
   (int_to_l3d_real(1),int_to_l3d_real(0),int_to_l3d_real(0),-VRP.X_,
    int_to_l3d_real(0),int_to_l3d_real(1),int_to_l3d_real(0),-VRP.Y_,
    int_to_l3d_real(0),int_to_l3d_real(0),int_to_l3d_real(1),-VRP.Z_,
    int_to_l3d_real(0),int_to_l3d_real(0),int_to_l3d_real(0),
    int_to_l3d_real(1) );

   //-  Rotate VRI (View RIght vector)    into positive X-axis,
   //-         VUP (View UP vector)       into positive Y-axis,
   //-         VFW (View ForWard vector) into positive Z-axis.

   R.set
   ( VRI.X_,  VRI.Y_,  VRI.Z_,  int_to_l3d_real(0),
     VUP.X_,  VUP.Y_,  VUP.Z_,  int_to_l3d_real(0),
     VFW.X_,  VFW.Y_,  VFW.Z_,  int_to_l3d_real(0),
     int_to_l3d_real(0),
     int_to_l3d_real(0),
     int_to_l3d_real(0),
     int_to_l3d_real(1) );

   viewing_xform = R | TnVRP;

   //- calculate the inverse matrix by applying the inverse transformations
   //- in the reverse order.

   //- First, undo the rotation: the inverse is the transpose of the original
   //- rotation matrix.

   inverse_R.set
   ( VRI.X_,  VUP.X_,  VFW.X_,  int_to_l3d_real(0),
     VRI.Y_,  VUP.Y_,  VFW.Y_,  int_to_l3d_real(0),
     VRI.Z_,  VUP.Z_,  VFW.Z_,  int_to_l3d_real(0),
     int_to_l3d_real(0),
     int_to_l3d_real(0),
     int_to_l3d_real(0),
     int_to_l3d_real(1) );

   //- next, undo the translation: simply translate by the opposite amount

   inverse_TnVRP.set
   (int_to_l3d_real(1),int_to_l3d_real(0),int_to_l3d_real(0),VRP.X_,
    int_to_l3d_real(0),int_to_l3d_real(1),int_to_l3d_real(0),VRP.Y_,
    int_to_l3d_real(0),int_to_l3d_real(0),int_to_l3d_real(1),VRP.Z_,
    int_to_l3d_real(0),int_to_l3d_real(0),int_to_l3d_real(0),
    int_to_l3d_real(1) );

   //- concatenate the inverse matrices: first undo the rotation, then undo the
   //- translation
```

```
    inverse_viewing_xform = inverse_TnVRP | inverse_R;
}

void l3d_moveable::transform(const l3d_matrix &m) {

}
```

The class `l3d_moveable` represents a moveable object with arbitrary orientation.

The member VRP stores the location of the moveable object. The members VFW, VUP, and VRI are unit vectors representing the orientation of the moveable object. The members `VFW_tip`, `VUP_tip`, and `VRI_tip` store the locations of the tips of the vectors VFW, VUP, and VRI, relative to the VRP.

The member `viewing_xform` stores the composite matrix that effects the viewing transformation, which moves the VRP to the origin and rotates such that the VRI, VUP, and VFW vectors align with the x, y, and z axes. The method `calculate_viewing_xform` calculates the composite viewing transformation matrix, as described above, and stores it in the `viewing_xform` variable. Also, we compute the inverse viewing transformation matrix, using a concatenation of the individual inverse matrices as described earlier. This inverse viewing matrix comes in handy if we need to compute a so-called "viewing frustum" in world space, which is often done as part of a culling scheme and which is covered in the companion book *Advanced Linux 3D Graphics Programming*.

The above members and methods deal with representing position and orientation. The remaining members and methods allow for movement of the object. For instance, in the `spikes` and `rotspikes` programs, the spike class updated its position and orientation. The `l3d_moveable` class is a generalization of the concept of an object, such as the spike, which can update its own position. The `l3d_moveable` class offers support for linear movement in a particular direction, and for rotation about the VRI, VUP, and VFW axes, which, importantly, may be oriented arbitrarily in space.

NOTE   Other types of movement would include movement along predefined or mathematically specified paths, such as a spiral or a helix. Of course, all types of movement can be simulated by a series of short linear movements, which are supported by `l3d_moveable`.

Specifically, the member variables `VUP_velocity`, `VRI_velocity`, and `VFW_velocity` represent the linear velocity (in world coordinate units per time interval) of the object in the directions of the VUP, VRI, and VFW vectors, respectively. For instance, if, with respect to its own orientation, the object is moving "forward", then its `VFW_velocity` would be greater than zero. Notice that all velocities are therefore specified in relation to the object's own orientation, instead of in relation to the fixed world coordinate axes. Using the local VUP, VRI, and VFW vectors for specifying velocities tends to be the most natural way of specifying object movement in an arbitrary 3D environment.

The member variables `VUP_thrust`, `VRI_thrust`, and `VFW_thrust` represent the increase to the VUP, VRI, or VFW velocity when a "thrust" is applied. We can think of the object as a spaceship, with rocket thrusters for propelling the vehicle in the VUP, VRI, or VFW directions. The thrust variables represent the amount of change for each application of thrust in a particular direction.

The methods `translateVFW`, `translateVUP`, and `translateVRI` change the position (in other words, the VRP) of the object by using the velocity in the VFW, VUP, and VRI directions. This is done by using simple vector addition. VRI, VUP, and VFW are all unit vectors—that is, they all have length 1. Therefore, to move 1 unit in the VFW direction, we simply compute VRP+VFW (point+vector, yielding a point). To move 2 units in the VRI direction, we simply compute VRP+2*VRI (point+scalar*vector, yielding a point).

The member variables `rot_VUP_velocity`, `rot_VRI_velocity`, and `rot_VFW_velocity` represent the rotational velocity (in degrees per time interval) of the object around the VUP, VRI, and VFW axes, respectively. This means that the object can rotate around its own VUP, VRI, or VFW axes. The methods `rotateVUP`, `rotateVRI`, and `rotateVFW` apply the rotation determined from the rotational velocities. Rotating an object about its own orientation axes is a naturally occurring operation, but a bit of a tricky one—the coming section titled "Rotation About an Arbitrary Axis" covers this in detail.

NOTE The movement mechanisms illustrated so far are overly simplistic because they are not based on time. For instance, `VFW_velocity` represents the change in VRP in the direction of VFW, per time unit. However, the method `translateVFW`, which adds `VFW_velocity` to VRP, does not take physically elapsed time into account, instead simply adding `VFW_velocity` to VRP. This would only be accurate if `translateVFW` were called at a regularly physically occurring time interval. But due to varying scene complexity and the varying amount of time it takes to draw each different frame, `translateVFW` is not called regularly, as we noted in Chapter 2 during the discussion of the pipeline event mechanisms. Therefore, for a more realistic, so-called *frame-rate-independent* or *real-time*, simulation, `translateVFW` would need to keep track of the elapsed physical time (by calling a system timer routine) since the last call of the routine, and multiply the elapsed physical time with the `VFW_velocity` to scale it accordingly. In this way, longer elapsed time yields greater change in position; shorter elapsed time yields smaller change in position. (The companion book *Advanced Linux 3D Graphics Programming* has examples of this sort of code.) For now, the examples use this simplistic movement mechanism because it requires less code, but with the side effect that the faster or slower your computer is, the faster or slower the apparent motion on-screen will be.

The method `transform` applies a particular transformation matrix to the object, by multiplying the matrix with the orientation vectors.

The method `update` slowly decreases all velocities to simulate a deceleration. It also applies the current velocities to change the current position and orientation, by calling the rotate and translate methods. Finally, after changing the position and orientation, it recalculates the viewing transformation matrix.

The l3d_camera Class

The class `l3d_camera` derives from `l3d_moveable`. It merely adds the following member variables: `fovx`, the horizontal field of view term from Chapter 5; `fovy`, the vertical field of view term; `near_z`, the near z clipping plane; and `far_z`, the far z clipping plane. The field of view terms require no further explanation here; Chapter 7 covers the clipping planes in more detail.

Briefly, the clipping planes clip away parts of polygons which are either too close to or too far from the eye.

Rotation About an Arbitrary Axis

So far, we have seen how to rotate points around the x, y, and z axes, with respect to either a local or global origin. However, it is often difficult to express a desired rotation purely in terms of rotations around the x, y, and z axes. In such cases, it is more natural to view the rotation in terms of a locally defined *rotation axis*. For instance, let's say we are programming a flight simulator. The airplane being simulated can have an arbitrary orientation expressed in terms of forward, up, and right vectors, as we saw in the class `l3d_moveable`. When the player rotates the plane to the left, it should rotate with respect to its own local orientation and not with respect to the global coordinate axes. In Figure 6-25, this means that we wish to rotate the plane around the vector v instead of around the x, y, or z axis. (We store and transform the starting and ending points of vector v along with the coordinates of the airplane geometry, so that the vector v always has the same position relative to the airplane geometry.)

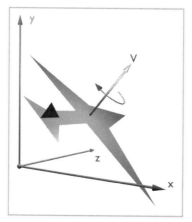

Figure 6-25: We want to rotate the airplane around the vector v.

The rotation matrices we have seen so far only deal with rotations around the principal coordinate axes. But now, we need to develop a rotation matrix for rotating a point about an arbitrary vector $v=[v_1,v_2,v_3,0]^T$.

Our strategy, based on Chris Hecker's four-part series of articles "Physics" [HECK97], is as follows. First, we consider the rotation equations we derived earlier for rotation around the z axis; then, we rewrite this rotation equation in vector form; finally, for an arbitrary axis of rotation, we find the correct vectors to plug into the vector rotation equation.

We begin with the equations for rotation around the z axis.

Equation 6-34
$$\begin{aligned} x' &= x\cos\theta - y\sin\theta \\ y' &= x\sin\theta + y\cos\theta \\ z' &= z \end{aligned}$$

Assume that the starting y coordinate is zero. In other words, the starting point before rotation lies upon the x axis. Then, the rotation equations become:

Equation 6-35
$$x' = x\cos\theta$$
$$y' = x\sin\theta$$
$$z' = z$$

Since the y coordinate is zero, the x coordinate is also the radius of rotation. Call this radius of rotation r. We can then write the rotation equation in vector form as follows. p' is the new point after rotation.

Equation 6-36
$$p' = [r\cos\theta, r\sin\theta, z, 1]^T$$

We can view this equation as a point plus a vector: the center of rotation at point $(0,0,z)$ plus the vector effecting the rotation.

Equation 6-37
$$p' = [0, 0, z, 1]^T + [r\cos\theta, r\sin\theta, 0, 0]^T$$

Furthermore, we can split up the vector effecting the rotation into two vectors: one acting in the horizontal direction, and one acting in the vertical direction. These vectors have a length equal to the radius of rotation.

Equation 6-38
$$p' = [0, 0, z, 1]^T + [r, 0, 0, 0]^T\cos\theta + [0, r, 0, 0]^T\sin\theta$$

Replacing the horizontal vector with i and the vertical vector with j yields:

Equation 6-39
$$p' = o + i\cos\theta + j\sin\theta$$

Let us consider this equation for a moment. It says that if we are given a horizontal vector i and a vertical vector j, both of which have a length equal to the radius of rotation, and given an original point which lies on the tip of the vector i, then rotating the point about the center o and within the plane defined by i and j yields a new point as defined by the equation.

Notice that this vector form of the rotation equation is free of all absolute references to x, y, or z locations. Instead, the equation consists entirely of relative references defined in terms of a center of rotation o and orientation vectors i and j. This is the key to generalizing the rotation equation to rotation about an arbitrary axis. The next task, therefore, is to analyze the geometrical situation for rotation around an arbitrary axis, and to compute the vectors o, i, and j.

If you have been particularly attentive, you might have raised an eyebrow upon having seen the above phrase "vectors o, i, and j." Indeed, o is not a vector, but is a point! (If you noticed this yourself, you should also pat yourself on the back—it's exactly this kind of attention to detail that is required to solve those late-night bugs which crop up in your 3D engine.) Why have we suddenly referred to o as a vector? Recall from Chapter 5 the relationship between points and vectors: starting at the origin $(0,0,0)$, the vector (x,y,z) extends exactly to reach point (x,y,z). In the derivation which follows, it is more convenient to consider the vector from the origin point $(0,0,0)$ to point o, rather than the point itself. We could perform the derivation based on the point o by constantly writing $[0,0,0,1]^T + vector$ to refer to the point, and $point - [0,0,0,1]^T$ to refer to the vector, but this notational clumsiness distracts from the main focus of the equations, which are difficult enough already. Focusing exclusively on the vectors makes the equations more straightforward.

Therefore, we perform the following derivation using the vector from the origin to point o, which we simply refer to henceforth as o. Also, instead of point p, we consider the vector v from the origin to point p; similarly for point p' and vector v'.

Figure 6-26 illustrates the geometric situation for rotation about an arbitrary axis. Let's consider the diagram one step at a time.

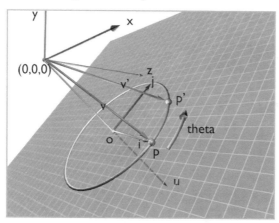

Figure 6-26: Rotation about an arbitrary axis.

First of all, we have the axis of rotation, which is the vector u in the diagram. Let us assume without loss of generality that u is of unit length and has its starting point at the origin. If u is not of unit length we can always normalize it before the rotation; if u does not start at point $(0,0,0)$ we can use the "translate-rotate-translate back" strategy discussed earlier for local rotation.

The point to be rotated is point p. The vector from the origin to point p is v. The plane of rotation is the plane perpendicular to the axis of rotation and containing point p. The center of rotation o is a point lying on the axis of rotation and contained within the plane of rotation. The new point after rotation is p'; the vector from the origin to this point is v'. We wish to solve for vector v' (and by doing so also find point p').

We know vectors v and u. To solve for v', we need to compute the vectors o, i, and j in terms of v and u, and plug these vectors into the vector version of the rotation equation.

Vector o points in the same direction as vector u, but has a different length. We compute the length vector o by projecting v onto u with the dot product, as described in Chapter 5. We can do this because vector u is a unit vector. We then multiply this vector length by the vector u to get the vector o.

Equation 6-40 $o = (v \cdot u)u$

We can rewrite the dot product as a matrix multiplication:

Equation 6-41 $o = u^T v u$

Since u is ordinarily a column vector, u^T is a row vector; multiplying this row vector with the column vector v is exactly the same as a dot product operation.

Next, to be consistent with the vector rotation equation developed earlier, we need to define a vector i which goes from the center of rotation o to the point being rotated p. This is simply the difference point p – point o, or equivalently vector v – vector o.

Equation 6-42 $$i = v - o$$

Substituting the earlier expression for o yields:

Equation 6-43 $$i = v - u^T v u$$

Finally, the "vertical" vector j is the cross product $u{\times}v$. Using the left-hand rule for cross products, this yields the vector pointing in the direction shown in the diagram. The magnitude of this cross product vector is $|u||v|\sin\theta$. $|u|$ is 1 and $\sin\theta$ is $|i|/|v|$, so the magnitude of j is the same as the magnitude of i.

Equation 6-44 $$j = n \times u$$

We can now substitute these equations for o, u, and v into the vector version of the rotation equation.

Equation 6-45 $$v' = o + i\,\cos\theta + j\,\sin\theta$$

yields the following result:

Equation 6-46 $$v' = u^T v u + (v - u^T v u)\cos\theta + (u \times v)\sin\theta$$

We're almost there. This equation indeed rotates any vector v about the vector u. But we want to find a single rotation matrix which does this rotation. This means we must isolate the vector v in the above equation so that we have an equation of the form $v'{=}Mv$. M is the matrix which, when applied to a column vector, rotates this column vector about the vector u.

To isolate v, we need to move it to the rightmost side of every expression in which it occurs. This requires a bit of cleverness. We use the following two rules:

Equation 6-47 $$u^T v u = u u^T v$$

Equation 6-48

$$u \times v = \begin{bmatrix} 0 & -u_3 & u_2 & 0 \\ u_3 & 0 & -u_1 & 0 \\ -u_2 & u_1 & 0 & 0 \\ 0 & 0 & 0 & 1 \end{bmatrix} \begin{bmatrix} v_1 \\ v_2 \\ v_3 \\ v_4 \end{bmatrix} = \tilde{u}v$$

Verifying these two rules is a simple but useful exercise in vector-matrix arithmetic, left to the reader (that means you). With the first rule, you will notice that after performing the matrix multiplication on the left-hand side, the elements of the resulting matrix are all coefficients to the elements of v, meaning that v can be "pulled out" to yield the right-hand side of the equation. With the second rule, we see that we can express a cross product operation as a matrix multiplication.

We simply need to construct a special matrix using the elements of the left-hand vector arranged in the particular order shown. We write this special matrix in shorthand by using the tilde operator. If you perform the matrix multiplication, you can see that the result is identical to the definition of the cross product from Chapter 5, but writing the cross product as a matrix multiplication allows us to isolate v.

Using these two rules allows us to rewrite the vector rotation equation as follows:

Equation 6-49 $$v' = uu^T v + cos\theta(v - uu^T v) + sin\theta\ \tilde{u}v$$

Rearranging to isolate v gives:

Equation 6-50 $$v' = (uu^T + (cos\theta)(I - uu^T) + (sin\theta)\ \tilde{u})v$$

We now have an expression involving only v', a rotation matrix, and v.

Equation 6-51
$$v' = Mv$$
$$M = uu^T + (cos\theta)(I - uu^T) + (sin\theta)\ \tilde{u}$$

The matrix M, computed solely from elements of the vector of rotation u, rotates any point about the vector u, assuming that u is a unit vector and starts at the origin.

Performing this matrix multiplication yields a final rotation matrix of:

Equation 6-52

$$\begin{bmatrix} u_1^2 + cos\theta(1 - u_1^2) & u_1u_2(1 - cos\theta) - u_3 sin\theta & u_3u_1(1 - cos\theta) + u_2 sin\theta & 0 \\ u_1u_2(1 - cos\theta) + u_3 sin\theta & u_2^2 + cos\theta(1 - u_2^2) & u_2u_3(1 - cos\theta) - u_1 sin\theta & 0 \\ u_3u_1(1 - cos\theta) - u_2 sin\theta & u_2u_3(1 - cos\theta) + u_1 sin\theta & u_3^2 + cos\theta(1 - u_3^2) & 0 \\ 0 & 0 & 0 & 1 \end{bmatrix}$$

The l3d_mat_rotu Function

The library function l3d_mat_rotu, which we saw earlier in Listing 6-1, computes the rotation matrix to rotate a point about a given unit vector. It simply implements the final rotation matrix derived above.

Sample Program: Camspikes

The sample program camspikes is a fully 3D simulation allowing arbitrary positioning of the camera within the virtual world. It allows you to interactively fly through a landscape of moving spikes. You can also turn off the spike movement if you want to practice flying through a static scene. The keyboard controls are as follows:

0:	Stop spike animation
1 (number):	Start spike animation
j:	Rotate left (rotates around the VUP axis)
l (letter):	Rotate right (rotates around the VUP axis)
i:	Thrust forward (translates along the VFW axis)
k:	Thrust backward (translates along the VFW axis)
J:	Roll left (rotates around the VFW axis)

L:	Roll right (rotates around the VFW axis)
I:	Pitch forward (rotates around the VRI axis)
K:	Pitch backward (rotates around the VRI axis)
s:	Thrust left (translates along the VRI axis)
f:	Thrust right (translates along the VRI axis)
e:	Thrust up (translates along the VUP axis)
d:	Thrust down (translates along the VUP axis)
v:	Cycle through to the next thrust level

Notice that the camera navigation is done with respect to the camera's own local orientation axes, which is a natural means of movement for an arbitrary environment. If the environment were not arbitrary, but instead, for instance, contained a fixed "floor" area, then it might make sense to restrict movement to be on and rotation to be relative to the floor. However, for this program, there is no fixed environment or orientation, so a completely free, locally defined movement system is preferable. The movement keys allow for rotation and translation along all of the three local orientation axes VRI, VUP, and VFW.

Immediately after starting the program, the spikes will be rotating and flying towards you. You can press **0** immediately to stop the spikes' movement, then use the navigation keys described above to navigate through the now "frozen" spikes. After you get a sense for the movement, press **1** (number one) to see the moving spikes from a different viewpoint. Press **q** to exit the program.

Listing 6-7: `camspikes.cc`

```
#include <stdlib.h>
#include <stdio.h>

#include "../lib/tool_2d/screen.h"
#include "../lib/tool_os/dispatch.h"
#include "../lib/raster/rasteriz.h"
#include "../lib/tool_2d/scrinfo.h"
#include "../lib/system/factorys.h"

#include "../lib/geom/point/point.h"
#include "../lib/math/vector.h"
#include "../lib/math/matrix.h"
#include "../lib/view/camera.h"

#define MAXSPIKES 150
#define PI 3.14159265

unsigned long red_color;
unsigned long green_color;
unsigned long blue_color;

//- STEP 1: CHOOSE THE FACTORIES

void choose_factories(void) {
  factory_manager_v_0_1.choose_factories();
}

//- STEP 2: DECLARE A PIPELINE SUBCLASS

l3d_real fovx, fovy;
```

```
int xsize, ysize;

class spike {
  public:

    l3d_two_part_list<l3d_coordinate> *vlist;
    l3d_polygon_2d_flatshaded *faces[3];
    l3d_vector displacement;

    l3d_vector velocity;

    spike(void) {
      //- declare common shared vertex list for all polygons
      vlist = new l3d_two_part_list<l3d_coordinate> (4);
      int i=0;
      (*vlist)[i++].original.set(int_to_l3d_real(0),
                                 int_to_l3d_real(0),
                                 int_to_l3d_real(100),
                                 int_to_l3d_real(1));
      (*vlist)[i++].original.set(int_to_l3d_real(10),
                                 int_to_l3d_real(10),
                                 int_to_l3d_real(100),
                                 int_to_l3d_real(1));
      (*vlist)[i++].original.set(int_to_l3d_real(10),
                                 int_to_l3d_real(0),
                                 int_to_l3d_real(100),
                                 int_to_l3d_real(1));
      (*vlist)[i++].original.set(int_to_l3d_real(0),
                                 int_to_l3d_real(0),
                                 int_to_l3d_real(0),
                                 int_to_l3d_real(1));

      //- define polygons in terms of indices into shared vertex list
      faces[0] = new l3d_polygon_2d_flatshaded(3);
      faces[0]->vlist = & vlist; //- shared vertex list
      (*(faces[0]->ivertices))[faces[0]->ivertices->next_index()].ivertex = 3;
      (*(faces[0]->ivertices))[faces[0]->ivertices->next_index()].ivertex = 0;
      (*(faces[0]->ivertices))[faces[0]->ivertices->next_index()].ivertex = 1;

      faces[1] = new l3d_polygon_2d_flatshaded(3);
      faces[1]->vlist = & vlist; //- shared vertex list
      (*(faces[1]->ivertices))[faces[1]->ivertices->next_index()].ivertex = 3;
      (*(faces[1]->ivertices))[faces[1]->ivertices->next_index()].ivertex = 1;
      (*(faces[1]->ivertices))[faces[1]->ivertices->next_index()].ivertex = 2;

      faces[2] = new l3d_polygon_2d_flatshaded(3);
      faces[2]->vlist = & vlist; //- shared vertex list
      (*(faces[2]->ivertices))[faces[2]->ivertices->next_index()].ivertex = 3;
      (*(faces[2]->ivertices))[faces[2]->ivertices->next_index()].ivertex = 2;
      (*(faces[2]->ivertices))[faces[2]->ivertices->next_index()].ivertex = 0;
    }

    ~spike(void) {
      delete faces[0];
      delete faces[1];
      delete faces[2];
      delete vlist;
    }

    void place_spike(void) {
```

```
      displacement.set(int_to_l3d_real(1000 - (rand() % 2000)),
                       int_to_l3d_real(1000 - (rand() % 2000)),
                       int_to_l3d_real(200),
                       int_to_l3d_real(1));
      velocity.set(int_to_l3d_real(0),
                   int_to_l3d_real(0),
                   int_to_l3d_real(-10-rand()%40),
                   int_to_l3d_real(0));

    l3d_matrix transform;

    transform =
      l3d_mat_translate(displacement.a[0],
                        displacement.a[1],
                        displacement.a[2]);

    int q;
    for(q=0; q<vlist->num_fixed_items; q++) {
      (*vlist)[q].reset();
      (*vlist)[q].transformed =  transform | (*vlist)[q].transformed;
    }
  }

  void move_spike(void) {
    displacement = displacement + velocity;
  }

  void reset(void) {
    int q;
    for(q=0; q<vlist->num_fixed_items; q++) {
      (*vlist)[q].reset();
    }
  }

  void apply_xform(const l3d_matrix & m) {
    int q;
    for(q=0; q<vlist->num_fixed_items; q++) {
      (*vlist)[q].transformed =  m | (*vlist)[q].transformed;
    }
  }

  void project_spike() {
    int v;

    for(v=0; v<vlist->num_fixed_items; v++) {
      (*vlist)[v].transformed.X_ =
        l3d_mulri(l3d_mulrr(l3d_divrr( (*vlist)[v].transformed.X_,
                                       (*vlist)[v].transformed.Z_),
                            fovx),
                  xsize)
        +
        int_to_l3d_real(xsize > 1);

      (*vlist)[v].transformed.Y_ =
        l3d_mulri(l3d_mulrr(l3d_divrr(-(*vlist)[v].transformed.Y_,
                                      (*vlist)[v].transformed.Z_),
                            fovy),
                  ysize)
        +
        int_to_l3d_real(ysize > 1);
```

```
        }
      }
};

class my_pipeline : public l3d_pipeline {
  protected:
     l3d_rasterizer_2d_imp *ri;
     l3d_rasterizer_2d *r;

     spike spikes[MAXSPIKES];
     long i, j;
     long wc_win_width, wc_win_height, wc_win_dist, fov;
     long wc_win_left, wc_win_top;
     int numspikes;

     virtual int out_of_wc_bounds(l3d_point const &p);

     l3d_camera *camera;

  public:
     l3d_screen *s;
     int animation;
     my_pipeline(void);
     virtual ~my_pipeline(void);

     void key_event(int ch);  //- from dispatcher
     void update_event(void); //- from dispatcher
     void draw_event(void);   //- from dispatcher
};

my_pipeline::my_pipeline(void) {
  s = factory_manager_v_0_1.screen_factory->create(320,200);
  ri = factory_manager_v_0_1.ras_2d_imp_factory->create(320,200,s->sinfo);
  r = new l3d_rasterizer_2d(ri);

  s->sinfo->ext_max_red =
    s->sinfo->ext_max_green =
      s->sinfo->ext_max_blue = 255;
  s->sinfo->ext_to_native(0,0,0); //- allocate black background color
  red_color = s->sinfo->ext_to_native(255, 0, 0);
  green_color = s->sinfo->ext_to_native(0, 255, 0);
  blue_color = s->sinfo->ext_to_native(0,0, 255);
  s->refresh_palette();

  fovx = float_to_l3d_real(0.5*1.0/tan(50./180. * PI));
  fovy = float_to_l3d_real(0.5*1.0/tan(30./180. * PI));
  xsize = s->xsize;
  ysize = s->ysize;

  numspikes = MAXSPIKES;
  for(i=0; i<MAXSPIKES; i++) {
    spikes[i].place_spike();

    spikes[i].faces[0]->final_color = red_color;
    spikes[i].faces[1]->final_color = green_color;
    spikes[i].faces[2]->final_color = blue_color;
  }

  camera = new l3d_camera;
```

```
      camera->fovx = 0.41955;
      camera->near_z = 0.01;
      camera->far_z = 100;

      animation = 1;
    }

    my_pipeline::~my_pipeline(void) {
      delete s;
      delete ri;
      delete r;
      delete camera;
    }

    void my_pipeline::key_event(int ch) {
      switch(ch) {
        case 'q': {
            exit(0);
          }
        case 'j':
          if(camera->rot_VUP_velocity>int_to_l3d_real(-95))
            camera->rot_VUP_velocity -= int_to_l3d_real(5);
          break;
        case 'l':
          if(camera->rot_VUP_velocity<int_to_l3d_real( 95))
            camera->rot_VUP_velocity += int_to_l3d_real(5);
          break;
        case 'J':
          if(camera->rot_VFW_velocity<int_to_l3d_real( 95))
            camera->rot_VFW_velocity += int_to_l3d_real(5);
          break;
        case 'L':
          if(camera->rot_VFW_velocity>int_to_l3d_real(-95))
            camera->rot_VFW_velocity -= int_to_l3d_real(5);
          break;
        case 'I':
          if(camera->rot_VRI_velocity<int_to_l3d_real( 95))
            camera->rot_VRI_velocity += int_to_l3d_real(5);
          break;
        case 'K':
          if(camera->rot_VRI_velocity>int_to_l3d_real(-95))
            camera->rot_VRI_velocity -= int_to_l3d_real(5);
          break;
        case 'k':
          if(camera->VFW_velocity    >int_to_l3d_real(-90))
            camera->VFW_velocity -= camera->VFW_thrust;
          break;
        case 'i':
          if(camera->VFW_velocity     <int_to_l3d_real( 90))
            camera->VFW_velocity += camera->VFW_thrust;
          break;
        case 's':
          if(camera->VRI_velocity    >int_to_l3d_real(-90))
            camera->VRI_velocity -= camera->VRI_thrust;
          break;
        case 'f':
          if(camera->VRI_velocity     <int_to_l3d_real( 90))
            camera->VRI_velocity += camera->VRI_thrust;
          break;
        case 'd':
```

```
        if(camera->VUP_velocity    >int_to_l3d_real(-90))
          camera->VUP_velocity -= camera->VUP_thrust;
        break;
      case 'e':
        if(camera->VUP_velocity    <int_to_l3d_real( 90))
          camera->VUP_velocity += camera->VUP_thrust;
        break;

        //- field-of-view modification
      case 'X':
        camera->fovx = camera->fovx + float_to_l3d_real(0.1);
        break;
      case 'x':
        camera->fovx = camera->fovx - float_to_l3d_real(0.1);
        break;
      case 'Y':
        camera->fovy = camera->fovy + float_to_l3d_real(0.1);
        break;
      case 'y':
        camera->fovy = camera->fovy - float_to_l3d_real(0.1);
        break;

        //- speed
    case 'v': case 'V':
        camera->VUP_thrust += int_to_l3d_real(1.0);
        if(camera->VUP_thrust  > 3.0) {
          camera->VUP_thrust  -= int_to_l3d_real(3.0);
        }
        camera->VFW_thrust = camera->VUP_thrust;
        camera->VRI_thrust = camera->VUP_thrust;
        break;

      case '1':
        animation = 1;
        break;
      case '0':
        animation = 0;
        break;
    }
}

void my_pipeline::update_event() {
  int i;

  camera->update();

  for(i=0;i<numspikes;i++) {

    if(animation) {
      spikes[i].move_spike();
    }
    spikes[i].reset();

    spikes[i].apply_xform(
      l3d_mat_translate(spikes[i].displacement.a[0],
                        spikes[i].displacement.a[1],
                        spikes[i].displacement.a[2])
    );

    //- "transformed" now contains MODEL COORDINATES
```

```
            if(out_of_wc_bounds( (*spikes[i].vlist)[0].transformed)
                || out_of_wc_bounds( (*spikes[i].vlist)[1].transformed)
                || out_of_wc_bounds( (*spikes[i].vlist)[2].transformed)
                || out_of_wc_bounds( (*spikes[i].vlist)[3].transformed))
               //- we must check all vertices of the spike since its orientation
               //- is now arbitrary, and any point might be the foremost point
               //- which has now moved out of bounds
            {
               spikes[i].place_spike();
            }

            spikes[i].apply_xform(camera->viewing_xform);
            //- "transformed" now contains VIEW (or CAMERA) COORDINATES

    }
}

void my_pipeline::draw_event(void) {
  int i;
  r->clear_buffer();

  for(i=0;i<numspikes;i++) {
    int v;
    int infront = 1;
    for(v=0;v<spikes[i].vlist->num_fixed_items;v++) {

      //- at this point, "transformed" is in view coordinates
      if( (*spikes[i].vlist)[v].transformed.a[2] < camera->near_z ) {
        infront = 0;
        break;
      }
    }

    if(infront) {
      spikes[i].project_spike();

      for(int f=0; f<3; f++) {
        spikes[i].faces[f]->init_clip_ivertices();
        spikes[i].faces[f]->clip_to_polygon_2d(s->view_win);
        r->draw_polygon_flatshaded(spikes[i].faces[f]);
      }
    }
  }
  s->blit_screen();
}

int my_pipeline::out_of_wc_bounds(l3d_point const &p) {
  return(p.Z_<int_to_l3d_real(1)));
}

int main(int argc, char **argv) {
  choose_factories();

  l3d_dispatcher *d;
  my_pipeline *p;

  //- STEP 3: CREATE A DISPATCHER

  d = factory_manager_v_0_1.dispatcher_factory->create();
```

```
//- STEP 4: CREATE A PIPELINE

//- plug our custom behavior pipeline into the dispatcher
p  = new my_pipeline();

//- STEP 5: START DISPATCHER

d->pipeline = p; //- polymorphic assignment
d->event_source = p->s;
d->start();

delete d;
delete p;
}
```

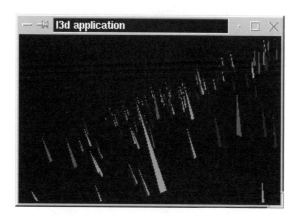

Figure 6-27: Output from sample program `camspikes`. *Notice that the viewpoint is slightly above the spikescape, looking diagonally down, with a tilted horizon.*

The code is similar to that of the `rotspikes` program, so we'll only cover the important differences here.

First of all, there are a few nominal changes which do not need much description:

- The new member `my_pipeline::camera` is a pointer to an `l3d_camera` object that contains the location and orientation of the eye or camera in the virtual world. In method `spike::move_spike`, we now only compute the new position variables, but do not yet compute and multiply a transformation matrix, as we did in `rotspikes`.

- The new method `spike::reset` resets all points of a spike by copying the original coordinate into the transformed coordinate, for reasons discussed at length in Chapter 2 and 5. After an invocation of `reset`, the spike is back at its original location in object coordinates, with no transformations applied.

- The new method `spike::apply_xform` multiplies all points in the spike by the supplied transformation matrix.

- The constructor for `my_pipeline` creates and initializes an `l3d_camera` object, and the destructor frees it.

- The `my_pipeline::key_event` method checks for input of any of the navigational keys described above, and updates the camera's rotational or translational velocity accordingly. These velocities are used to update the camera's position in the method `l3d_moveable::update`, which also computes the viewing transformation matrix.

Now, let's look at the more significant changes.

The `my_pipeline::update_event` routine calls the camera's `update` method, which applies the velocities to change the camera's position, and which computes the viewing transformation matrix. Next, it calls `move_spike` to update the variables containing the spike's position, if the animation is enabled. Then, the spike's coordinates are reset, and we apply the translational and rotational matrices to the spike's points. After this, the vertices of the spike are now in world coordinates. We must now check to see if the spike is out of bounds (`out_of_wc_bounds`) and needs to be repositioned to be within the world coordinate boundaries. Finally, after ensuring that the spike is validly positioned, we apply the new camera transformation matrix in `camera->viewing_xform`. This matrix has the effect of transforming the entire world such that the camera, however it is positioned or oriented in the world, has the standard camera position and orientation described in Chapter 5. This way, we fulfill the requirements for the perspective projection equation of Chapter 5. Notice that we did not need to change the `project_spike` routine to accommodate the arbitrary camera position and orientation; the perspective projection remains exactly the same.

The `my_pipeline::draw_event` performs a new check before projecting, clipping, and drawing the spike—namely, that the spike is in front of the camera. Previously, with the `rotspikes` program, the camera was fixed at the origin and only the spikes moved. In `rotspikes`, then, the `out_of_wc_bounds` method made sure that no spikes moved behind the camera. However, with a moveable camera as in `camspikes`, it's not so easy: we can move the camera anywhere, so any spike might potentially be behind the camera. As mentioned previously, we should not project any points which lie behind the camera, since these points are not physically visible. In `draw_event`, we check if any points of the spike are behind the camera—in other words, if any points have a $z<0$ (after the camera transformation has been applied). If any points of the spike are behind the camera, we refrain from drawing the spike entirely, and proceed to try to draw the next spike.

NOTE Not drawing a spike if any single one of its points is behind the camera is similar to the 2D clipping strategy of discarding a polygon if any of its points lies outside of the clip edge. Just as the 2D all-or-nothing strategy is somewhat limiting, so is the 3D all-or-nothing approach of `camspikes`. A better approach is to clip away only the parts of the 3D object which are behind the camera (or more specifically, the parts which are in front of the near clipping plane). Chapter 7 covers this topic, called 3D clipping, in detail.

With this sample program, we now have a flight-simulator style arbitrary camera movement. We achieved this by specifying a camera location and orientation via the point VRP and the vectors VRI, VUP, and VFW. Then, we used the rotation matrix for rotation about an arbitrary axis to allow for rotation of the camera around its own axes VRI, VUP, or VFW. Translation of the camera along its own axes is comparatively simple, since it merely requires vector addition. Finally, we developed a matrix to move and orient the entire world (and the camera) such that the camera is at the origin with the standard orientation. After application of this camera transformation matrix, we can use the standard perspective projection of Chapter 5 to project the world from 3D into 2D.

Additional Notes on Matrices

We've already seen a few interesting tricks with vector and matrix math. We know how to use matrices to effect simple geometric transformations (the so-called *affine* transformations, which preserve parallelism of lines but not necessarily distance and angle), how to combine these transformations, and how to write dot and cross products as matrix multiplications. Now, let's take a brief look at some other important matrix concepts which often arise in 3D graphics. You may not need these concepts immediately, and we touch on them only indirectly in the rest of this book, but this section is useful for a broader understanding of matrices.

Inverting a Matrix

The inverse of a matrix is useful because it represents the opposite transformation of the transformation of the original matrix.

We have already seen that for rotation matrices, the inverse is the transpose, which is easy to compute.

In other cases, we may know the individual transformations which were multiplied together to arrive at a final matrix M. In such a case, we can compute the inverse of M by applying the opposite transformations in the opposite order. For instance, if we have a matrix $M=R_x(20)T(1,1,1)$, this matrix M first translates by $(1,1,1)$, then rotates around the x axis by 20 degrees. Therefore, we can compute the inverse of this matrix by applying the opposite transformations in the opposite order: $M^{-1}=T(-1,-1,-1)R_x(-20)$. By the definition of inverse, MM^{-1} must equal I, and so must $M^{-1}M$. If we then look at MM^{-1}, we see that this first applies a rotation, then a translation, then an opposite translation, then an opposite rotation—giving in effect, no transformation equivalent to the identity matrix ($MM^{-1}=I$). Looking further at $M^{-1}M$, we see that this first applies a translation, then a rotation, then an opposite rotation, then an opposite translation—again yielding in effect no transformation, or the identity matrix. Thus, $M^{-1}M=I$. So, by applying the opposite transformations in the opposite order, we can undo the effect of the original transformation, and can in this manner compute the inverse.

In some cases, we might know nothing about the matrix we need to invert. For general matrices, there may or may not be an inverse. We can use the determinant of a matrix (covered in the next section) to determine if there is an inverse or not. Assuming there is an inverse, there are a number of ways to actually compute the inverse. The simplest to understand is to write the matrix equation as $MM^{-1}=I$. All elements of M and I are known; all elements of M^{-1} are unknown. Assuming M is a 4×4 matrix, then so is M^{-1}. Treating the 16 elements of M^{-1} as unknown variables and performing the matrix multiplication gives 16 equations with 16 unknowns. This system of linear equations may be solved to find the 16 unknown variables, which are then the elements of the inverse matrix M^{-1}. The technique of Gaussian elimination, covered in any linear algebra textbook, can be used to solve the system of equations. Under Linux, you can use the Calc package, which can be installed as part of Emacs, to automatically solve such systems of equations. The companion book *Advanced Linux 3D Graphics Programming* provides a detailed example of using Calc to invert matrices needed for texture mapping.

Alternatively, we can use a method called *Cramer's rule* to determine a matrix inverse by computing a large number of determinants [FOLE92]. To compute the inverse of M, we first compute an intermediate matrix M', which we will then use to compute the actual inverse. Let each entry of M' be called M_{ij}. The value of entry M_{ij} in matrix M' is the determinant of the sub-matrix of the original matrix M with row i and column j deleted, then multiplied by the value $(-1)^{i+j}$. After computing all of these determinants to find the intermediate matrix M', the actual inverse of M is $(1/\det(M))(M')^T$. The notation $\det(M)$ denotes the determinant of the matrix M, which we now describe.

Determinant of a Matrix

The *determinant* of a matrix is a single number which can be used to determine whether the matrix has an inverse or not. If the determinant is zero, the matrix does not have an inverse. If the determinant is non-zero, the matrix has an inverse. More generally, since any $n \times n$ matrix represents a transformation of n-dimensional space, the determinant's value tells us the volume change effected by the transformation [FOLE92]. A determinant of zero means that the n-dimensional volume has been reduced to zero because of the complete loss of one or more dimensions; such a transformation is non-reversible, and such a matrix is also non-invertible. A determinant of one means that no volume change is effected by the transformation; greater than one, that a volumetric expansion has taken place; less than one, that a contraction has taken place.

Computing a determinant is a recursive process. As a starting point, we define the determinant of the following 2×2 matrix:

Equation 6-53
$$\begin{bmatrix} A & B \\ C & D \end{bmatrix}$$

The determinant in this case, which we write as $\det(M)$, is defined to be AD–BC.

For larger matrices, the determinant is defined recursively in terms of the determinants of the sub-matrices. The equation for the determinant of an arbitrary matrix is as follows.

Equation 6-54
$$det(M) = \sum_{i=1}^{n} (-1)^{i+1} a_{1i} det(submat_{1i})$$

The term a_{1i} indicates the single value at matrix row 1 and column i. The term $submat_{1i}$ denotes the sub-matrix obtained by deleting row 1 and column i from the matrix M. The sub-matrix, thus, is one row and one column smaller than the original matrix M. The -1 term, which is raised to the power $(i+1)$, causes every second determinant to be evaluated negatively.

In other words, the determinant of a matrix is defined in terms of a weighted sum of the determinants of the smaller sub-matrices (where every second determinant is evaluated negatively). These determinants of the sub-matrices, in turn, are also defined recursively, until the sub-matrices are finally of size 2×2, at which point we use the AD-BC determinant definition for a 2×2 matrix.

For example, say we wish to compute the determinant of the following 3×3 matrix:

Equation 6-55
$$\begin{bmatrix} a_{11} & a_{12} & a_{13} \\ a_{21} & a_{22} & a_{23} \\ a_{31} & a_{32} & a_{33} \end{bmatrix}$$

Using the recursive definition for determinants, this expands to:

Equation 6-56
$$(-1)^2 a_{11} det \left(\begin{bmatrix} a_{22} & a_{23} \\ a_{32} & a_{33} \end{bmatrix} \right) + (-1)^3 a_{12} det \left(\begin{bmatrix} a_{21} & a_{23} \\ a_{31} & a_{33} \end{bmatrix} \right) + (-1)^4 a_{13} det \left(\begin{bmatrix} a_{21} & a_{22} \\ a_{31} & a_{32} \end{bmatrix} \right)$$

Computing the 2×2 determinants and evaluating the (−1) terms yields:

Equation 6-57 $a_{11}a_{22}a_{33} - a_{11}a_{23}a_{32} - a_{12}a_{21}a_{33} + a_{12}a_{23}a_{31} + a_{13}a_{21}a_{32} - a_{13}a_{22}a_{31}$

This is therefore the determinant of a 3×3 matrix.

Now, consider the following matrix:

Equation 6-58
$$\begin{bmatrix} i & j & k \\ v_1 & v_2 & v_3 \\ w_1 & w_2 & w_3 \end{bmatrix}$$

Let vector $v=[v_1,v_2,v_3]^T$, and vector $w=[w_1,w_2,w_3]^T$. Furthermore, let vector $i=[1,0,0]^T$, vector $j=[0,1,0]^T$, and vector $k=[0,0,1]^T$.

Taking the determinant of this matrix yields:

Equation 6-59 $iv_2w_3 - iv_3w_2 - jv_1w_3 + jv_3w_1 + kv_1w_2 - kv_2w_1$

Collecting the terms for i, j, and k yields:

Equation 6-60 $i(v_2w_3 - v_3w_2) + j(v_3w_1 - v_1w_3) + k(v_1w_2 - v_2w_1)$

Finally, remembering that i, j, and k are vectors, and performing the vector addition on these vectors yields a final single vector of:

Equation 6-61 $[v_2w_3 - v_3w_2, v_3w_1 - v_1w_3, v_1w_2 - v_2w_1]^T$

This vector is the cross product of the vectors v and w as defined in Chapter 5. Thus, by using the matrix determinant in this manner, we arrive at the cross product.

Perspective Projection as a Transformation Matrix

The homogeneous w coordinate allows us to associate a division with a point. One consequence of this is that we can represent the perspective projection as a matrix.

In its simplest form, the perspective projection can be expressed as $x_s=x/z, y_s=y/z$. (Recall, the actual final perspective projection developed in Chapter 5 also multiplies these terms with a field of view term, adds x and y offsets to compensate for the fact that the screen coordinates start at the upper-left corner and not in the center of the screen, and finally reverses the orientation of the y

axis to increase downward instead of upward.) The matrix which effects this perspective projection is:

Equation 6-62

$$\begin{bmatrix} 1 & 0 & 0 & 0 \\ 0 & 1 & 0 & 0 \\ 0 & 0 & d & 0 \\ 0 & 0 & 1 & 0 \end{bmatrix}$$

Notice what happens if we multiply this projection matrix with a point. The point $[x,y,z,1]^T$ becomes $[x,y,dz,z]^T$ after projection. Importantly, the w coordinate is a variable dependent on the input point—a situation which we have not yet encountered. We said earlier in this chapter that to return from homogeneous coordinates to normal 3D space, we divide by w. This means that the projected point becomes $[x/z,y/z,d,1]^T$ in 3D space. We divide x and y by z, and z becomes a constant equal to the projection plane's distance from the eye. This is exactly the expected result from a perspective projection.

The complete perspective projection as developed in Chapter 5, including the reversed y axis and the upper-left origin of the screen coordinate system, can be expressed as the following matrix:

Equation 6-63

$$\begin{bmatrix} \frac{w_{screen}}{2}\cot\frac{\theta}{2} & 0 & \frac{w_{screen}}{2} & 0 \\ 0 & -\frac{h_{screen}}{2}\frac{w_{Phys}}{h_{Phys}}\cot\frac{\theta}{2} & scale_y\frac{h_{screen}}{2} & 0 \\ 0 & 0 & d & 0 \\ 0 & 0 & 1 & 0 \end{bmatrix}$$

Multiplying this matrix with the point $[x,y,z,1]^T$, and dividing x, y, and z by the fourth coordinate w yields:

Equation 6-64

$$\left[\frac{x}{z}(0.5\cot(0.5\theta)w_{screen}) + 0.5w_{screen}, -\frac{y}{z}(0.5\cot(0.5\theta)\frac{w_{Phys}}{h_{Phys}}h_{screen}) + 0.5scale_yh_{screen}, d, 1\right]^T$$

This result is identical to that derived in Chapter 5, except for addition of the z component, which is equal to the distance d between the eye and the projection plane.

Notice that this matrix reduces the entire z dimension to a plane. In other words, for any input z, the output z will be the constant d. This is an example of a non-reversible transformation and a non-invertible matrix. After projecting the coordinates from 3D into 2D, we irrecoverably lose the original depth information stored in the z coordinate. We only have a flat picture—a projection.

There are cases where we would like to have perspective foreshortening, but also still retain the original depth information stored in the z coordinate. In this way, we can recover the original 3D point after perspective transformation, in case we need to go from the projected screen coordinate back to the original 3D coordinate. This procedure forms the basis for texture mapping, covered in the companion book *Advanced Linux 3D Graphics Programming*.

The following matrix performs perspective foreshortening, while retaining depth information. We call this a *perspective transformation matrix*, in contrast to the dimension-reducing perspective projection of Chapter 5. The matrix is identical to the normal perspective projection matrix, but with an additional entry of 1 in row 3 and column 4. This element of the matrix is the key to preserving the depth information.

Equation 6-65
$$\begin{bmatrix} \frac{w_{screen}}{2}\cot\frac{\theta}{2} & 0 & \frac{w_{screen}}{2} & 0 \\ 0 & -\frac{h_{screen}}{2}\frac{w_{Phys}}{h_{Phys}}\cot\frac{\theta}{2} & scale_y\frac{h_{screen}}{2} & 0 \\ 0 & 0 & d & 1 \\ 0 & 0 & 1 & 0 \end{bmatrix}$$

Multiplying this matrix with a point $[x,y,z,1]^T$ yields:

Equation 6-66
$$\left[\frac{x}{z}(0.5\cot(0.5\theta)w_{screen})+0.5w_{screen}, -\frac{y}{z}(0.5\cot(0.5\theta)\frac{w_{Phys}}{h_{Phys}}h_{screen})+0.5scale_y h_{screen}, d+\frac{1}{z}, 1\right]^T$$

The x and y terms after application of this matrix are the same as with the normal perspective projection matrix. But notice that the z term after multiplying with the perspective matrix (let us call this the "screen-z term") is now no longer a flat plane d as it was previously, but is instead the value of $d+1/z$. The entry of 1 in row 3 and column 4 of the projection transformation matrix causes a "+1" to appear in the screen-z term after perspective, and after the homogeneous division by w (which has a value of z because of the entry of 1 at row 4 and column 3), this term becomes $1/z$. In other words, after transformation into screen space, the screen-x and screen-y values have been properly projected and can be plotted on-screen, and the screen-z value is a constant plus this new $1/z$ term (where z is the original 3D z coordinate). In other words, after the perspective transformation, we have a ready-to-plot (x,y) location, as well as a screen-z coordinate which is related to the reciprocal of the original 3D z coordinate. Therefore, the original 3D z coordinate is no longer smashed flat into a plane, causing the loss of an entire dimension; instead, the z coordinate is transformed into a "screen-z" or $1/z$ term.

The $1/z$ term has some interesting properties and uses. Notice that the $1/z$ term arises from an augmented projection matrix and enables us to associate depth information, which is related to the original 3D depth of z, with each projected (x,y) point. These properties come in handy for z-buffering and texture mapping, both of which are described and implemented in the companion book *Advanced Linux 3D Graphics Programming*.

OpenGL, Matrices, and Hardware-Accelerated Geometry

The OpenGL library has some functions which deal with matrices. Some functions require a matrix as a parameter; some functions compute a matrix based on input parameters. First, let's look at the OpenGL matrix system; then we'll see how OpenGL matrices are specified via program code; and finally, we'll take a look at some of the functions which OpenGL offers for manipulating and computing matrices.

The OpenGL transformation system is based upon a *matrix stack*, which is nothing more than a last-in-first-out list of matrices. OpenGL offers a few functions to manipulate the top matrix on the stack; most importantly, you can replace it with another matrix or multiply it with another matrix. You can also "push" or "pop" the matrix stack: pushing creates a new copy of the top matrix on the stack and makes the new copy the current matrix; popping discards the top matrix on the stack, so that the matrix underneath becomes current. Pushing and popping are useful for hierarchically built objects, to "remember" a certain location (pushing) and to return to it later (popping).

There are three matrix stacks in OpenGL: the GL_MODELVIEW matrix stack, the GL_PROJECTION matrix stack, and the GL_TEXTURE matrix stack.

As we saw in Chapter 3, we can use the OpenGL glVertex2i command to specify vertices of a polygon to be drawn. There are also corresponding functions glVertex3f and glVertex4f which allow the specification of vertices in 3D space; glVertex3f uses normal 3D coordinates, while glVertex4f uses homogeneous 3D coordinates with an extra w parameter. All glVertex* commands to specify geometry in OpenGL transform the geometry by the matrix currently at the top of the GL_MODELVIEW stack. It is very important to know which matrix is currently at the top of the GL_MODELVIEW stack in order to correctly specify geometry. Effecting transformations in OpenGL is therefore done by loading or appropriately modifying the top matrix of the GL_MODELVIEW matrix stack, then issuing a glVertex* command to specify a location which is transformed by the current GL_MODELVIEW matrix. The points we specify using glVertex* eventually get projected from 3D into 2D using the projection matrix at the top of the GL_PROJECTION matrix stack, after which the points and their associated polygons (after additional scaling and clipping) can be drawn on-screen.

NOTE   Recall that in Chapter 3, in the mesaflat program and in the l3d_screen_mesa class, we set the projection and model-view matrices to the identity matrix, effectively disabling all OpenGL transformations. It is exactly in this way, by disabling OpenGL transformations, that we can use OpenGL as a 2D rasterization layer.

Following is a list of OpenGL functions which manipulate the matrices and the matrix stacks. Some of these functions take a matrix as a parameter. In OpenGL, we specify matrices as a linear array of 16 float values m_1, m_2, ... , m_{16}, where the values form a matrix as follows:

Equation 6-67
$$\begin{bmatrix} m_1 & m_5 & m_9 & m_{13} \\ m_2 & m_6 & m_{10} & m_{14} \\ m_3 & m_7 & m_{11} & m_{15} \\ m_4 & m_8 & m_{12} & m_{16} \end{bmatrix}$$

CAUTION   Notice carefully the exact positions of the values m_1 to m_{16}. If you declare a 4×4 of float values in C++, then element [i][j] of the array refers to the element in row i and column j. However, the element [i][j] of this matrix refers to the element which will be interpreted by OpenGL as being at row j and column i. In other words, OpenGL has a column-major storage convention, whereas C++ (and most post-1977 languages) have a row-major storage convention. According to *OpenGL Programming Guide, Second Edition*, matrices to be passed to OpenGL should be declared float[16] to "avoid confusion" (or at least, to draw attention to it) [WOO97].

NOTE For those OpenGL functions requiring floating-point values, the function name typically ends with the letter f. There is typically an equivalent routine, ending with the letter d, which takes integer values instead.

- `glMatrixMode(GLenum mode)` chooses the currently active matrix stack: either `GL_MODELVIEW`, `GL_PROJECTION`, or `GL_TEXTURE`. The currently active matrix is the top matrix of the currently active matrix stack. Only one matrix stack and one matrix can be active at any given time, and only the active matrix can be modified.
- `glLoadIdentity(void)` sets the active matrix to the 4×4 identity matrix.
- `glLoadMatrix(const float *m)` sets the active matrix to the 4×4 matrix specified by m.
- `glMultMatrixf(const float *m)` multiplies the active matrix by the 4×4 matrix specified by m, and stores the result in the active matrix, overwriting the previous matrix.
- `glTranslatef(float x, float y, float z)` internally computes a translation matrix which moves a point by the given x, y, and z offsets, multiplies the active matrix by the translation matrix, and stores the resulting matrix in the active matrix, overwriting the previous matrix.
- `glRotatef(float angle, float x, float y, float z)` internally computes a rotation matrix which rotates a point about by the given `angle` in degrees around the vector (x,y,z), multiplies the active matrix by the rotation matrix, and stores the resulting matrix in the active matrix, overwriting the previous matrix. When looking from point (x,y,z) toward the origin, a positive angle is in the clockwise direction. Alternatively, when looking from the origin towards point (x,y,z), a positive angle is in the counterclockwise direction.
- `glScalef(float x, float y, float z)` internally computes a scaling matrix for the given scaling factors x, y, and z, multiplies the active matrix by the scaling matrix, and stores the resulting matrix in the active matrix, overwriting the previous matrix.

You might wonder why you would want to use OpenGL's functions for specifying and multiplying matrices. After all, l3d also has a matrix class, and it is absolutely essential to understand exactly how matrix operations work, which is the reason that l3d—primarily intended to teach 3D concepts—implements these operations explicitly in code instead of handing them off to OpenGL. Is there any advantage to using OpenGL functions to manipulate matrices? As you might have expected, the answer is, "maybe." First of all, using OpenGL functions to compute matrices ties you to using OpenGL as the underlying graphics library; although since OpenGL is a standard, this is not necessarily important. If you are committed to OpenGL, then using OpenGL matrix functions can lead to improved performance, if dedicated transformation-capable hardware is available. In this case, OpenGL sends the matrix data to the 3D hardware to be computed, which lessens the burden on the application processor, leading to better performance. If no dedicated transformation-capable 3D hardware is available, there is no performance benefit to using OpenGL matrix functions.

But as with all things, there is a catch to this possible acceleration. Notice that the entire stack-based model is best viewed as a write-only system. You choose which matrix stack you wish to modify, you multiply or directly assign the top matrix, the results of which then get stored on the stack. You can then issue additional commands to change the matrix further. But nowhere have we said that you can easily read the contents of the currently active matrix. Using OpenGL's matrix functions instructs the hardware to change or multiply the current matrix in a certain way. Obtaining the intermediate results of these computations, for use within the application program, may result in performance degradation. The reason for this is that the hardware is likely optimized for performing the matrix operations quickly, but not necessarily for reading the intermediate results of matrix computations. Asking the 3D hardware to return the results of intermediate calculations can be viewed as an "interruption" in the streamlined operation of the 3D pipeline, which might negate the performance gains obtained in the first place by using hardware-accelerated transformations through the OpenGL matrix functions.

NOTE You can call `glGetFloatv(GL_MODELVIEW_MATRIX, m)` to return the contents of the OpenGL model-view matrix, where `m` is an array of 16 elements of type `GLfloat`. Similarly, the parameters `GL_PROJECTION_MATRIX` and `GL_TEXTURE_MATRIX` return the values for these matrices. Remember to be careful about the column-major order of the returned elements!

An example will hopefully make it clearer when this situation might arise. Let's say you wanted to rewrite the `camspikes` program to exclusively use OpenGL matrix functions. The program first positions a spike in world coordinates, then transforms it via the viewing transformation, then checks to see if it is in front of the camera, and finally it projects and draws the spike. The part which would be questionable in OpenGL is immediately after application of the viewing transformation matrix: the check to see if the transformed coordinates are in front of the camera. This check takes place after a transformation matrix has been applied, but before the point has been completely transformed for display on-screen. In other words, we need intermediate results from a matrix calculation taking place somewhere in the middle of the graphics pipeline. Getting these intermediate results may be slow enough to negate the gains afforded by the accelerated transformation hardware.

One solution to this problem, in order to take advantage of both hardware-accelerated transformations and to allow the program to access intermediate results, is to have two computation pathways within the application code. One computation pathway operates on a simplified version of the geometry with fewer vertices (so there is less computation to be done). These matrix computations are done on the main CPU, so that access to all of the intermediate results is possible. Typically, the computations in this stage should reduce the work to be done in the next stage by eliminating large numbers of objects (such as those behind the camera, or which are otherwise invisible). In the second computation pathway, after the preliminary calculations have been performed on the main CPU and have hopefully reduced the number of objects to be considered in the second stage, the complete object geometry and transformations can be sent with OpenGL matrix commands to the 3D hardware accelerator. The hardware then uses its specialized circuitry to compute the matrix transformations quickly and to display the appropriate pixels on-screen, without needing to send any intermediate computation results back to the main CPU.

Matrices and Coordinate Systems

The camera transformation matrix developed earlier, when applied to a 3D point expressed in 3D world coordinates, tells us where the point is with respect to the camera. The camera transformation moves and rotates the entire world, including all geometry and the camera, such that the camera is in the standard viewing position at the origin, looking along the positive z axis, and perfectly right-side-up.

The camera transformation is one example of a so-called "change in coordinate system." A coordinate system, as we defined in Chapter 2, provides a way of uniquely identifying the location of points in space. However, multiple coordinate systems may refer to the same points. This means that the concept of "location" in space is always with respect to a particular coordinate system. If we wish to refer to the same point but with respect to a different coordinate system, we must change the coordinate system.

The following series of figures illustrates this concept of a change in coordinate system. In Figure 6-28, we have two points. What are the (x,y) coordinates of these two points?

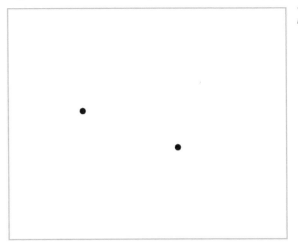

Figure 6-28: Two points.

Of course, without any coordinate system, we have no way of referring to the locations of the points. If we add a coordinate system C, as in Figure 6-29, then we identify the locations with respect to the coordinate axes: the points are at (3,8) and (11,5).

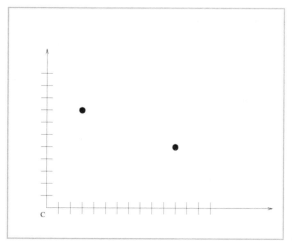

Figure 6-29: A coordinate system.

We can, however, also refer to the point with respect to any other coordinate system. For instance, with respect to the second coordinate system D in Figure 6-30, with a translated origin and scaled axes, the points are located at (0,4.2) and (11.75,0).

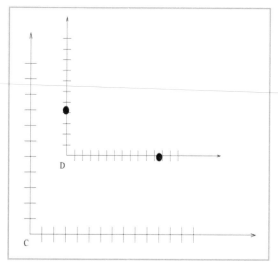

Figure 6-30: A second coordinate system.

The third coordinate system E in Figure 6-31 is translated, scaled, and rotated. With respect to this coordinate system, the points are located at (13,10.5) and (0,4.75).

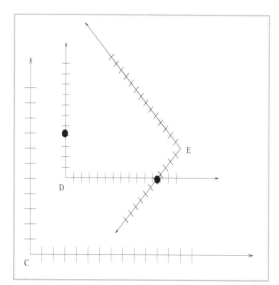

Figure 6-31: A third coordinate system.

The question is, if we have the coordinates of the point in one coordinate system, how do we find the coordinates of the point in another coordinate system? For the camera transformation, we can state the problem as follows. For a given point (x,y,z) in the world coordinate system, what are the new coordinates of this point with respect to the camera coordinate system? More generally, given

- a first coordinate system C,
- a second coordinate system D, and
- the coordinates (x,y,z) of a point in the C coordinate system,

how can we find the new coordinates (x',y',z') of the point in the second coordinate system D?

We can specify a coordinate system in n dimensions with an origin point and a list of n orthogonal vectors, called the *basis vectors*. In normal 3D world coordinates, the origin is point $[0,0,0,1]^T$, and the three basis vectors are the $[1,0,0,0]^T$, $[0,1,0,0]^T$, and $[0,0,1,0]^T$. These vectors represent a displacement of magnitude one along the x, y, and z axes, respectively. Indeed, these vectors define the directions and the unit size along the three coordinate axes.

It follows that we can specify an arbitrary coordinate system by specifying any origin and three orthogonal basis vectors. (Theoretically the vectors don't even have to be orthogonal, but allowing the vectors to be non-orthogonal does not bring any practical benefit.) Therefore, our earlier specification of camera location and orientation (via VRP, VRI, VUP, and VFW) is actually a specification of a coordinate system.

Recall how we derived the camera transformation matrix. We observed that the first three columns of a matrix represent the three new vectors to which the vectors $i=[1,0,0,0]^T$, $j=[0,1,0,0]^T$, and $k=[0,0,1,0]^T$ are transformed after multiplication with the matrix. Also, the last column of a matrix, since it is the part of the matrix which encodes a translation, represents the new point to which the origin $[0,0,0,1]^T$ is translated after multiplication with the matrix.

Therefore, we can interpret any matrix as a set of three vectors (the first three columns) and an origin point (the last column). Since three vectors and an origin point define a coordinate system in

3D, we can therefore interpret any 4×4 matrix as a coordinate system, and can specify any coordinate system as a 4×4 matrix. By multiplying a point with this matrix, we obtain the world coordinates of the point as seen relative to the coordinate system of the matrix. In other words, if we have a matrix M and a point P, then in the matrix product MP, the matrix M represents the coordinate system in which P is specified. The product MP yields the location of P in the world coordinate system.

By inverting a matrix representing a coordinate system, we obtain the reverse transformation. Therefore, the matrix product $M^{-1}P$ yields the coordinates relative to P of the point as seen relative to the world coordinate system. Notice that this is exactly the opposite formulation from the previous paragraph. In other words, if we have a matrix M and a point P, in the matrix product $M^{-1}P$, the original matrix M represents the coordinate system with respect to which we want to find the location of P; P itself has been specified with respect to the world coordinate system. (Contrast with the previous paragraph.) The product $M^{-1}P$ yields the location of P in the coordinate system of M.

TIP When you see the matrix product MP, think of this as answering the question, "P, which has been specified relative to M, is at what location in world coordinates?" When you see M^{-1}P, think of this as answering the question, "P, which has been specified in world coordinates, is at what location relative to M?"

The above explains how we can convert between world coordinates and an arbitrary coordinate system C. We can also convert between arbitrary coordinate systems. Given two arbitrary coordinate systems represented by matrices C and D, and given a point P specified in the coordinate system of C, we wish to find the coordinates of the point specified in the coordinate system of D. We can name this conversion as a change in coordinate system from C coordinates to D coordinates. The matrix that converts from C coordinates to D coordinates is $D^{-1}C$. Recall from the discussion of matrix multiplication that this expression has the effect of first applying C, then applying D^{-1}. The multiplication with matrix C converts a point specified in C coordinates into a point specified in world coordinates. Then, the multiplication with matrix D^{-1} converts a point specified in world coordinates to a point specified in D coordinates. Thus, with this matrix, we effect a change from C coordinates to D coordinates.

Notice that if the C coordinates are world coordinates, then the matrix C is the identity matrix, and the transform simply becomes D^{-1}. Furthermore, if D coordinates are camera coordinates, then D^{-1} converts a point specified in world coordinates into a point specified in camera coordinates—which is exactly the result we developed earlier.

Typical Coordinate Systems in 3D Graphics

A natural question to ask at this point is, "which coordinate systems arise in 3D graphics?" In general, any time we need to look at 3D points from a particular point of view in 3D space, we define a coordinate system. This is a general problem-solving technique in 3D graphics; many interesting questions in 3D can be answered by viewing the problem as a change in coordinate system.

We have already seen world coordinates, which we can think of as the grand, universal coordinate system in which we ultimately specify all locations. All points must eventually be expressed in world coordinates because the perspective projection, which is the only tool we use to visualize the virtual world, transforms world coordinates into screen coordinates.

Screen coordinates, as we have used them so far, are a 2D coordinate system for plotting pixels on-screen. Therefore, the perspective projection can be thought of as a non-reversible change in coordinate system, from world coordinates to screen coordinates. The projection is non-reversible because data gets irrevocably lost when we discard the third dimension to come into the two dimensions of the screen. However, as we saw above in the discussion of perspective projection as a matrix, it is also possible to perform perspective projection (and its associated foreshortening effects) while still preserving the third dimension in a screen-z or $1/z$ term; with the addition of the $1/z$ term, the projection process is then indeed reversible.

The reversibility of the projection process plays an important role in the process of texture mapping, which needs to convert from screen coordinates back into world coordinates and then finally into texture coordinates. See the companion book *Advanced Linux 3D Graphics Programming* for details on the math and concepts behind texture mapping and for an explanation of texture coordinates.

Camera coordinates allow us to view points in terms of their location with respect to a camera's location and orientation. Generalizing the idea, so-called *object coordinates* (also sometimes called *local coordinates*) allow us to view or define points with respect to an object's position and orientation. For instance, if we are defining the coordinates for the corners of a triangle, it is convenient to define only one point in world coordinates as a reference point. This point is the origin of the object coordinate system and also conveniently is a single location which represents "the position" of the object in world coordinates. We can then define the corners or vertices of the object in terms of their locations with respect to the object coordinate system, instead of with respect to the world coordinate system.

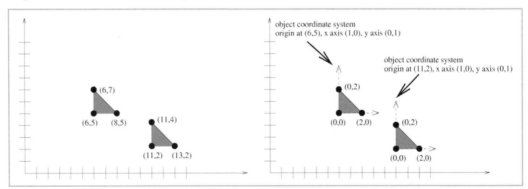

Figure 6-32: World coordinates versus object coordinates.

Figure 6-32 compares world coordinates with object coordinates. On the left, the coordinates of two triangles are specified in world coordinates. Based on the world coordinates, it is difficult to ascertain that the two sets of coordinates actually describe the same triangle. Furthermore, we have no concept of the "location"—a single point describing the position—of a triangle. We only have a set of "raw" vertices in world coordinates. On the right, the coordinates of the same two triangles are given, each time using a local coordinate system with its origin at the lower-left corner of the triangle. Using local or object coordinates, it is clear that we are dealing with the same object; only the placement of the object's coordinate system within the world coordinate system has changed. (Here, only the placement has changed via a translation, but we could also rotate or scale the local coordinate system.) Also, the origin of each local coordinate system can be thought of as a single point conveniently describing the "location" of each triangle. Through a change in coordinate system, the coordinates in the object coordinate systems may be converted into world coordinates.

Using object coordinates leads to a style of thinking where each object defines its own geometry in terms of its own local and isolated coordinate system. Placing the object within a world coordinate system may then be viewed as a change in coordinate system from object to world coordinates. Through this transformation, we transform points with respect to a local origin and orientation into points with respect to a global origin and orientation.

Notice that whereas we typically use the camera coordinate system to transform from world coordinates into camera coordinates for projection, we typically use an object coordinate system in the opposite direction: we transform from object coordinates into world coordinates, to place all of the points of an object into the world coordinate system.

Remember, this list of coordinate systems is meant to be illustrative, not exhaustive. Coordinate systems and changes among them are important and valuable concepts which arise again and again in 3D graphics.

Right-to-left vs. Left-to-right Interpretation

Until now, we have said that the order of operations for transformations expressed as matrices is right to left: the transformation of the rightmost matrix is applied first; that of the leftmost matrix, last. This is a perfectly valid and self-consistent definition. It is noteworthy, however, that another way of thinking allows a left-to-right interpretation of matrix transformations. It is vital to understand that this second way of thinking is just that—a way of thinking. It does not affect in any way whatsoever the order of matrices in the code you write; this remains the same. What changes is the way you interpret the meaning of a left-to-right sequence of matrices.

Let us assume we have a translation matrix T, a rotation matrix R, and a point P. If we consider the matrix multiplication TRP, as in the rotspikes program, we have until now interpreted this as applying a rotation about the WC origin first, then a translation in the WC system. This means we always consider the effect of a transformation with respect to the outermost world coordinate system which contains all objects. Indeed, we defined all transformations with respect to WC.

The alternative interpretation for the matrix multiplication TRP is to imagine that all transformations take place within a local coordinate system, and that all transformations affect this same local coordinate system. Under this interpretation, we must then consider the effect of the matrices left to right. We begin with a local coordinate system which corresponds with the world coordinate system. Then, we first transform the local coordinate system by translating it to some position (the leftmost matrix T). Next, with respect to the transformed coordinate system, we perform a rotation about the origin of the transformed coordinate system. Further transformations, such as scalings, further translations, or further rotations, are all interpreted, left to right, as changing the size, location, or orientation of the local coordinate system. After each transformation of the local coordinate system, the next transformation operates within this transformed coordinate system. Interpreting transformations as affecting a local coordinate system permits (indeed, mandates) a left-to-right interpretation of the matrices.

A left-to-right interpretation of matrix operations, where transformations affect and take place within a local coordinate system, can be useful for thinking about *hierarchical transformations*, such as the movement of an arm hierarchy. Consider a model of an arm where we have an upper arm, a forearm, a hand, and fingers. At the top of the hierarchy is the upper arm. Any translation or rotation of the upper arm should translate everything attached to the arm—that is, everything beneath it in the hierarchy. This means the forearm, hand, and fingers should be affected when the upper arm moves. Similarly, any transformation of the forearm should transform the hand and fingers; any transformation of the hand should transform the fingers. The hierarchy is thus upper arm-forearm-hand-fingers. With respect to a world coordinate system, transformations should take place from the lowest level to the highest level of the hierarchy. For instance, to move a finger, we should first apply all finger rotations and translations with the finger still at the origin. Call this matrix M_f. Then, having positioned the finger properly, we proceed to position the finger with respect to the hand transformations (M_h), with respect to the forearm transformations (M_a), and finally with respect to the upper arm transformations (M_u). With respect to a world coordinate system, we interpret matrices right to left and would thus write the transformation of a finger as $M_u M_a M_h M_f$. But, with respect to a local coordinate system, we can interpret the same transformation sequence left to right. First, the frame of reference is world coordinates. Then, we use M_u to define a new frame of reference with respect to the upper arm. With respect to the new frame of reference, we then specify, left to right, the frame of reference with respect to the forearm (M_a) and the hand (M_h). Finally, with the frame of reference being the hand, we specify the new position of the finger in this frame of reference by using M_f.

TIP   To interpret a series of matrices *ABCD* right to left, think of all transformations as occurring within world coordinates. Each subsequent matrix from right to left causes a new transformation of the point with respect to world coordinates: first move to the location specified by *D* within world coordinates, then move further to *C*, then move further to *B*, then move further to *A*. To interpret left to right, think of all transforms as occurring within an incrementally changing frame of reference. First, look at the world from the frame of reference of world coordinates. Then, apply *A* to your frame of reference, to look at the world from *A*. From within this changed frame of reference, apply *B* to look at the world from *B*, then apply *C* to look at the world from *C*, then finally *D* to look at the world from *D*. Finally, coordinates are specified with respect to this accumulated frame of reference.

To summarize: a right-to-left interpretation converts a coordinate specified in a local coordinate system to a coordinate in a world coordinate system. A left-to-right interpretation converts an entire world coordinate system to a local coordinate system in which points are then specified.

If this confuses you, I suggest that you stick with the right-to-left interpretation of matrix operations, where all transformations take place with respect to a global world coordinate system which contains all objects. This tends to be easier to understand at first. But again, the order of matrices is identical for both ways of thinking, and the end result is the same. It is only a question of how you interpret the meaning of the chain of transformations.

Summary

In this chapter, we looked at transformations and matrices. We saw how to mathematically manipulate matrices, and how to geometrically apply matrices to effect translation, rotation, and scaling. We also saw how to combine transformations to achieve more complicated motion, such as rotation about an arbitrary axis or arbitrary camera movement. Sample programs illustrated complex object movement and a camera which could be freely positioned within the virtual world. We developed l3d library classes to handle matrices, transformations, arbitrary orientations, and a camera. Finally, we looked at some more abstract matrix concepts, including inverses, determinants, projection, and the relationship between matrices and coordinate systems.

The knowledge in this chapter may take a while to digest, but it all definitely belongs in the 3D programmer's bag of tricks. Understanding matrices and transformations allows you to model any sort of orientation or movement in 3D space.

Having now gotten a grip on transformations, it is now time to turn some more serious attention to the things to which we apply the transformations: polygonal 3D objects. In Chapter 7, we look at the whys and hows of polygonal 3D objects, including practical and geometrical issues.

Chapter 7

Polygonal Modeling and Rendering in 3D

Overview

This chapter takes a closer look at 3D polygons, which form the foundation of contemporary interactive 3D graphics. Chapter 3 already covered 2D polygonal graphics, and Chapters 5 and 6 used ad hoc structures to store 3D polygonal data. In this chapter, we take a more detailed look at storing, manipulating, and drawing 3D polygons. We cover the following topics:

- Reasons for using 3D polygons
- Geometry of 3D polygons, including normal vectors, 3D clipping, and planes
- Grouping polygons into 3D objects, and grouping objects into a world

This chapter represents a change in style from the previous chapters. While Chapters 5 and 6 were heavy on the theory and relatively light on the code, the first part of this chapter is fairly heavy on the code whereas the theory is comparatively easy to understand. The statement "group polygons to form 3D objects" is easy enough in theory, but a number of important practical issues must be addressed to create working C++ code for 3D polygonal objects. The focus of the first part of the chapter is therefore to understand the structural and geometrical properties of 3D polygons, and to devise appropriate and reusable C++ classes in the l3d library for manipulating and grouping 3D polygons. It is admittedly somewhat tedious work to devise and implement the classes needed for 3D polygonal objects. The problems are largely structural in nature: deciding when a separate temporary list is needed, providing means to reset lists at the beginning of a frame, avoiding erroneous double-transformation of vertices, using linked lists to save sequential search time, and so forth. But this work pays off by providing a flexible object structure.

This chapter presents the following sample programs: clipz illustrating near z clipping, fltsim illustrating creation of polygonal 3D objects with subclassed and plug-in behavior, and objcopy illustrating the use of object copy constructors and planar clipping to split an object into two separate pieces.

Reasons for 3D Polygonal Modeling

We've been using polygons since Chapter 3, where we defined the meaning of a 2D polygon and developed routines for drawing polygons. In Chapters 5 and 6 we projected the vertices of polygons from 3D into 2D, allowing us to store and view 3D polygonal data by projecting the 3D polygons into 2D polygons, which we then drew using the routines of Chapter 3. Now, it's time to focus on the specifics of 3D polygonal modeling and rendering.

A *3D polygon* is a 2D polygon oriented and positioned arbitrarily in 3D space. This means that a 3D polygon is a flat, bounded area in 3D space. By *flat* we mean that all of the points belonging to the polygon must lie on a plane; we mathematically define the meaning of a plane later in this chapter. The area of a 3D polygon, as with 2D polygons, is bounded by a series of straight, connected edges.

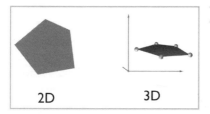

2D   3D

Figure 7-1: 2D polygons and 3D polygons.

By using a series of small and adjacently positioned flat polygons, we can describe or at least approximate any surface in 3D. For curved surfaces, the larger the number of polygons, the better the approximation. See Figure 7-2.

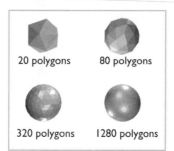

20 polygons   80 polygons

320 polygons   1280 polygons

Figure 7-2: Polygons in 3D can approximate any 3D surface.

In interactive 3D graphics, we typically only model the surface of an object, since the outer surface is usually all we see of any opaque object. This means that when using 3D polygonal techniques, the interior of an object is generally not modeled. Instead, we only describe the infinitely thin outer surface of an object. Surface modeling shows its limitations when we wish to break open or cut away parts of an object to see its interior. In such cases, if we only use polygons to model the surface of an object, we would see a hollow cutaway view of the object, as if the object were constructed of cardboard but empty inside. See Figure 7-3.

Figure 7-3: If a 3D polygonal object is cut open, it becomes obvious that only the surface is modeled and that the interior is hollow.

In spite of this limitation, 3D polygons offer a fairly versatile, straightforward, and fast means of describing 3D surfaces. Assuming we only wish to model surfaces—which is most often the case for the kinds of interactive 3D graphics applications this book is about—polygons are typically the best choice. They are mathematically simple to describe and conceptually easy to understand, which makes writing and understanding algorithms for manipulating and rendering polygons comparatively easy. The simplicity of 3D polygons has also led to widespread hardware acceleration of common operations on 3D polygons. Modern 3D acceleration hardware is capable of drawing staggering numbers of polygons to the screen per second, meaning that high visual complexity can be achieved with acceptable run-time performance.

Alternatives to 3D polygons include modeling curved surfaces, or using a volumetric representation of data (*voxels*, short for volume pixels) instead of merely a surface representation. See Figure 7-4. Using mathematical descriptions of curved surfaces instead of flat polygonal surfaces allows for a more accurate representation of real-world curved surfaces, which continues to appear round at all magnifications. With polygons, if the viewer is close enough to the object, the inherent flatness of the polygons can become apparent, though by using large numbers of polygons, this problem can be alleviated. Voxels are a volumetric means of data representation which can be likened to building an object, including the interior, from a huge number of tiny cubes. Just as a 2D image can be approximated by a large number of tiny squares (pixels) within a 2D grid, so can any 3D object be approximated by a large number of tiny cubes within a 3D grid. A special case of voxel graphics is the *height field*, which records the height of a large number of small points on a finely spaced 2D grid. This can be useful for modeling landscapes consisting of hills and mountains. Voxel representations require much more storage space than a polygonal representation, because they model the entire volume and not just the surface.

Figure 7-4: Curved surface, voxels, and height field.

The main problem with non-polygonal representations of 3D graphics is that they are not as simple as polygons. Simplicity is important, because in interactive 3D graphics we indeed interact with the 3D model, requiring us to test objects for collision or intersection, to classify the positions of objects relative to one another, and so forth. All of these are mathematical operations which, for polygons, are straightforward, easily understood, and can be accelerated through hardware. For voxels and curved surfaces, the math for manipulating or testing the geometry is more complicated, typically not supported well in hardware, and in the case of voxels requires dealing with much larger amounts of data. Nevertheless, there are applications which do use non-polygonal representation of their data, either because they must (for instance, if the interior of an object must be accurately modeled, such as in medical imaging), or to experiment with finding efficient and innovative non-polygonal storage and rendering methods.

The rest of the chapter focuses exclusively on polygons. The next several sections deal with the *geometry* of 3D polygons. By this, we mean the essential geometrical and mathematical properties of a 3D polygon, operations which we can perform on 3D polygons using these properties, and the C++ classes necessary for storing and manipulating these properties. This information allows us to model and manipulate 3D polygonal objects or environments in a more general way than we have done so far. Let's start by taking a brief look at the C++ class for storing and manipulating 3D polygons. Then we discuss the concepts in the class one by one.

Extending Polygons from 2D into 3D

The example programs of Chapter 5 and Chapter 6 used the l3d_polygon_2d class to store polygons in 3D, projecting the coordinates of the polygon into 2D and then rasterizing the polygon with a 2D rasterizer class. While this works, it is not the best solution because, as we are about to see, more general operations on polygons in 3D require storing additional 3D information with the polygon as well as performing geometrical computations in 3D. To accommodate these new features of 3D polygons, we define a new class l3d_polygon_3d, shown in Listings 7-1 and 7-2. Notice that l3d_polygon_3d inherits from l3d_polygon_2d. Therefore, a 3D polygon is a 2D polygon with additional features. This means that all of the features of 2D polygons, such as 2D clipping or vertex animation, are also available in 3D polygons. Also, any existing routines expecting a 2D polygon can also work with a 3D polygon.

Listing 7-1: poly3.h

```
#ifndef __POLY3_H
#define __POLY3_H
#include "../../tool_os/memman.h"

#include "polygon.h"

class l3d_rasterizer_3d;

class l3d_polygon_3d :
     virtual public l3d_polygon_2d
{
  public:
  l3d_polygon_3d(void) : l3d_polygon_2d() {};

    l3d_polygon_3d(int num_pts) : l3d_polygon_2d(num_pts) {};

    virtual ~l3d_polygon_3d(void) {};

    l3d_coordinate sfcnormal;
    l3d_coordinate center;
    void compute_sfcnormal();
    void compute_center();
    l3d_real zvisible;
```

```
      virtual void init_transformed(void);
      virtual void transform(const l3d_matrix &m, int count);
      virtual void set_transform_stage(int count);
      virtual void after_camera_transform(void);
      void camera_transform(const l3d_matrix &m, int count) {
        transform(m, count);
        after_camera_transform();
      }
      virtual void clip_segment_to_near_z
      (l3d_polygon_ivertex *ivertex,
       l3d_real zclip, int idx0, int idx1);
      virtual int clip_near_z(l3d_real zclip);
      virtual void draw(l3d_rasterizer_3d *r) {}
      l3d_polygon_3d(const l3d_polygon_3d &r);
      l3d_polygon_2d *clone(void);
    };

    struct l3d_polygon_3d_node {
      l3d_polygon_3d *polygon;
      l3d_polygon_3d_node *prev,*next;
    };


    #include "../../raster/rast3.h"

    #endif
```

Listing 7-2: poly3.cc

```
    #include "poly3.h"
    #include <string.h>
    #include "../../tool_os/memman.h"

    void l3d_polygon_3d::init_transformed(void) {
      sfcnormal.reset();
      center.reset();
    }

    void l3d_polygon_3d::compute_sfcnormal() {
      const l3d_real collinear_epsilon = float_to_l3d_real(0.999);
      int found_noncollinear_points = 0;
      int p0,p1,p2;
      for(p0=0; p0<ivertices->num_items; p0++) {
        p1 = p0 + 1;
        if(p1 >= ivertices->num_items) {p1 = 0; }
        p2 = p1 + 1;
        if(p2 >= ivertices->num_items) {p2 = 0; }

        l3d_vector v1 =
          (**vlist)[(*ivertices)[p1].ivertex].original -
          (**vlist)[(*ivertices)[p0].ivertex].original;

        l3d_vector v2 =
          (**vlist)[(*ivertices)[p2].ivertex].original -
          (**vlist)[(*ivertices)[p0].ivertex].original;

        //- if angle between vectors is too close to 0 or 180 deg, they are
        //- almost in a straight line, so we choose the next 3 points
        if(l3d_abs(dot(normalized(v1),normalized(v2)))
           < int_to_l3d_real(collinear_epsilon))
        {
          sfcnormal.original = center.original + normalized(cross(v1,v2));
```

```
          found_noncollinear_points = 1;
      }
   }

}

void l3d_polygon_3d::compute_center() {

  l3d_real xsum=0, ysum=0, zsum=0;
  register int i;

  for (i=0; i<ivertices->num_items; i++) {
    xsum += (**vlist)[(*ivertices)[i].ivertex].original.X_;
    ysum += (**vlist)[(*ivertices)[i].ivertex].original.Y_;
    zsum += (**vlist)[(*ivertices)[i].ivertex].original.Z_;
  }

  center.original.set(
    l3d_divri(xsum, i),
    l3d_divri(ysum, i),
    l3d_divri(zsum, i),
    int_to_l3d_real(1) );
}

void l3d_polygon_3d::clip_segment_to_near_z
(l3d_polygon_ivertex *ivertex, l3d_real zclip, int idx0, int idx1)
{
  l3d_real x0,y0,z0,  x1,y1,z1,  t,  clip_x, clip_y, clip_z;

  if((**vlist)[ (*ivertices)[idx0].ivertex ].transformed.Z_ > zclip) {
    x0 = (**vlist)[ (*ivertices)[idx1].ivertex ].transformed.X_;
    y0 = (**vlist)[ (*ivertices)[idx1].ivertex ].transformed.Y_;
    z0 = (**vlist)[ (*ivertices)[idx1].ivertex ].transformed.Z_;

    x1 = (**vlist)[ (*ivertices)[idx0].ivertex ].transformed.X_;
    y1 = (**vlist)[ (*ivertices)[idx0].ivertex ].transformed.Y_;
    z1 = (**vlist)[ (*ivertices)[idx0].ivertex ].transformed.Z_;
  }
  else {
    x0 = (**vlist)[ (*ivertices)[idx0].ivertex ].transformed.X_;
    y0 = (**vlist)[ (*ivertices)[idx0].ivertex ].transformed.Y_;
    z0 = (**vlist)[ (*ivertices)[idx0].ivertex ].transformed.Z_;

    x1 = (**vlist)[ (*ivertices)[idx1].ivertex ].transformed.X_;
    y1 = (**vlist)[ (*ivertices)[idx1].ivertex ].transformed.Y_;
    z1 = (**vlist)[ (*ivertices)[idx1].ivertex ].transformed.Z_;
  }

  t = l3d_divrr( zclip-z0, z1-z0);

  clip_x = x0 + l3d_mulrr( x1-x0 , t );
  clip_y = y0 + l3d_mulrr( y1-y0 , t );
  clip_z = zclip;

  int new_idx = (*vlist)->next_varying_index();

  (**vlist)[ new_idx ].transform_stage = 0;
  (**vlist)[ new_idx ].original.X_ =
    (**vlist)[ new_idx ].transformed.X_ = clip_x;
  (**vlist)[ new_idx ].original.Y_ =
```

```
    (**vlist)[ new_idx ].transformed.Y_ = clip_y;
  (**vlist)[ new_idx ].original.Z_ =
    (**vlist)[ new_idx ].transformed.Z_ = clip_z;
  (**vlist)[ new_idx ].original.W_ =
    (**vlist)[ new_idx ].transformed.W_ = int_to_l3d_real(1);

  ivertex->ivertex = new_idx;
}

int l3d_polygon_3d::clip_near_z(l3d_real zclip) {
  int idx0,idx1;
  int crossedge0_idx0,crossedge0_idx1,crossedge1_idx0,crossedge1_idx1;
  int newedge_ivertex0, newedge_ivertex1;
  int i;
  int dir;
#define FIRST_CROSS_FRONT_TO_BACK 0
#define FIRST_CROSS_BACK_TO_FRONT 1

  l3d_polygon_ivertex new_ivertex0, new_ivertex1;

  idx0=0;
  idx1=next_clipidx_right(idx0, clip_ivertices->num_items);

  temp_clip_ivertices->num_items = 0;

  while(
    !( ((**vlist)[ (*clip_ivertices)[idx0].ivertex ].transformed.Z_ > zclip
       && (**vlist)[ (*clip_ivertices)[idx1].ivertex ].transformed.Z_ <=zclip)
       ||
       ((**vlist)[ (*clip_ivertices)[idx0].ivertex ].transformed.Z_ <=zclip
       && (**vlist)[ (*clip_ivertices)[idx1].ivertex ].transformed.Z_ > zclip)))
  {
    (*temp_clip_ivertices)[temp_clip_ivertices->next_index()].ivertex =
      (*clip_ivertices)[idx0].ivertex;
    idx0=idx1;

    if(idx0==0) {

      if ((**vlist)[ (*clip_ivertices)[idx0].ivertex ].transformed.Z_ <=zclip)
        return 0;

      else
      {
        return 1;
      }

    }

    idx1=next_clipidx_right(idx0, clip_ivertices->num_items);
  }
  if ((**vlist)[ (*clip_ivertices)[idx0].ivertex ].transformed.Z_ > zclip
     && (**vlist)[ (*clip_ivertices)[idx1].ivertex ].transformed.Z_ <=zclip)
  {dir = FIRST_CROSS_FRONT_TO_BACK; }else {dir = FIRST_CROSS_BACK_TO_FRONT; }

  crossedge0_idx0 = idx0;
  crossedge0_idx1 = idx1;

  idx0=idx1;
  idx1=next_clipidx_right(idx0, clip_ivertices->num_items);
```

```
while(
  !( ((**vlist)[ (*clip_ivertices)[idx0].ivertex ].transformed.Z_ > zclip
     && (**vlist)[ (*clip_ivertices)[idx1].ivertex ].transformed.Z_ <=zclip)
     ||
     ((**vlist)[ (*clip_ivertices)[idx0].ivertex ].transformed.Z_ <=zclip
     && (**vlist)[ (*clip_ivertices)[idx1].ivertex ].transformed.Z_ > zclip)))
{
  idx0=idx1;
  if(idx0==crossedge0_idx0) {
    fprintf(stderr,"shouldn't be here! can't find 2nd crossing edge");
    return 0;
  }

  idx1=next_clipidx_right(idx0, clip_ivertices->num_items);
}

crossedge1_idx0 = idx0;
crossedge1_idx1 = idx1;

clip_segment_to_near_z(&new_ivertex0, zclip,
                       crossedge0_idx0,crossedge0_idx1);
newedge_ivertex0 = new_ivertex0.ivertex;

clip_segment_to_near_z(&new_ivertex1, zclip,
                       crossedge1_idx0,crossedge1_idx1);
newedge_ivertex1 = new_ivertex1.ivertex;

{
  idx0=idx1; idx1=next_clipidx_right(idx0, clip_ivertices->num_items);
}

temp_clip_ivertices->num_items = 0;

if(dir==FIRST_CROSS_FRONT_TO_BACK) {
  (*temp_clip_ivertices)[temp_clip_ivertices->next_index()].ivertex =
    newedge_ivertex1;

  for(i=crossedge1_idx1;
      i!=crossedge0_idx0;
      i=next_clipidx_right(i,clip_ivertices->num_items))
  {
    (*temp_clip_ivertices)[temp_clip_ivertices->next_index()].ivertex =
      (*clip_ivertices)[i].ivertex;

  }
  (*temp_clip_ivertices)[temp_clip_ivertices->next_index()].ivertex =
    (*clip_ivertices)[crossedge0_idx0].ivertex;

  (*temp_clip_ivertices)[temp_clip_ivertices->next_index()].ivertex =
    newedge_ivertex0;

  swap_temp_and_main_clip_lists();
}else {
  (*temp_clip_ivertices)[temp_clip_ivertices->next_index()].ivertex =
    newedge_ivertex0;

  for(i=crossedge0_idx1;
      i!=crossedge1_idx0;
      i=next_clipidx_right(i, clip_ivertices->num_items))
  {
```

```
       (*temp_clip_ivertices)[temp_clip_ivertices->next_index()].ivertex =
         (*clip_ivertices)[i].ivertex;

    }
    (*temp_clip_ivertices)[temp_clip_ivertices->next_index()].ivertex =
      (*clip_ivertices)[crossedge1_idx0].ivertex;

    (*temp_clip_ivertices)[temp_clip_ivertices->next_index()].ivertex =
      newedge_ivertex1;

    swap_temp_and_main_clip_lists();
  }

  return 1;
}

void l3d_polygon_3d::transform(const l3d_matrix &m, int count) {
  register int i;
  for(i=0; i<clip_ivertices->num_items; i++) {
    (**vlist)[ (*clip_ivertices)[i].ivertex ].transform(m, count);
  }

  sfcnormal.transform(m, count);
  center.transform(m, count);

}

void l3d_polygon_3d::set_transform_stage(int count) {
  register int i;
  for(i=0; i<clip_ivertices->num_items; i++) {
    (**vlist)[ (*clip_ivertices)[i].ivertex ].transform_stage = count;
  }

  sfcnormal.transform_stage = count;
  center.transform_stage = count;

}

l3d_polygon_2d* l3d_polygon_3d::clone(void) {
  return new l3d_polygon_3d(*this);
}

l3d_polygon_3d::l3d_polygon_3d(const l3d_polygon_3d &r) {

  iv_items_factory = r.iv_items_factory->clone();
  init(DEFAULT_IVERTICES_PER_POLY);

  vlist = r.vlist;
  *ivertices = *r.ivertices;
  *clip_ivertices = *r.clip_ivertices;
  *temp_clip_ivertices = *r.temp_clip_ivertices;

  sfcnormal = r.sfcnormal;
  center = r.center;
  zvisible = r.zvisible;
}

void l3d_polygon_3d::after_camera_transform(void) {
}
```

l3d_polygon_3d, like l3d_polygon_2d, has three constructors: one to create and initialize, one to create but not initialize for use by subclasses, and a copy constructor. It also overrides the clone method, as we saw in Chapter 3.

Let's begin our examination of l3d_polygon_3d by looking at the member variable sfcnormal, which represents the *surface normal vector* to the polygon.

Surface Normal Vectors

We mentioned earlier in this chapter that most modeling in interactive 3D graphics deals only with the surface of the objects being modeled. If we pick any point on an arbitrary surface in 3D, an important property of the surface is the normal vector to the surface at the chosen point. The *normal vector* to a surface at a given point is a vector that is perpendicular to the surface at the point. The normal vector therefore defines the orientation of a surface at a particular point.

The reason we are interested in the normal vector to a surface is that the orientation of the surface is important for several geometrical computations. For instance, to compute the amount of light falling on a surface, we need to compute the angle between the direction of the incident light and the normal vector to the surface. Another example requiring normal vectors is back-face culling, where polygons facing away from the viewer (as determined by the direction of the normal vector) are not drawn to save time. Finally, the process of collision detection also requires the use of normal vectors to determine the distance between a point and a polygon. All of these topics are covered in the companion book *Advanced Linux 3D Graphics Programming*.

For convenience, normal vectors in 3D are typically scaled so that they have a length of one; in other words, we typically *normalize* (Chapter 5) normal vectors in 3D. This is because some operations on 3D normal vectors, which we see later in this chapter, are easier to compute if the normal vectors are normalized.

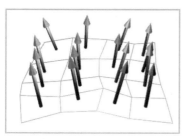

Figure 7-5: Normal vectors.

 NOTE Normal vectors are also called *surface normals*, or simply *normals*.

For a flat surface, such as a polygon, calculating the normal vector is quite easy. Recall from Chapter 5 that the cross product of two vectors yields a new vector which is perpendicular to the plane defined by the first two vectors. Also, subtracting two points yields a vector between the two points. Since by definition all points of a polygon must lie in a plane, we can simply take any three consecutive points of the polygon in order (for our left-handed convention, this means clockwise), which we can call $p_1, p_2,$ and p_3. Since the three points are consecutive, p_2 lies after p_1, and p_3

lies after p_2. The surface normal is the vector given by the cross product $(p_2-p_1) \times (p_3-p_1)$. After computing the cross product, we usually normalize the vector, by dividing by its magnitude.

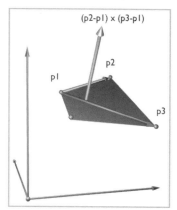

Figure 7-6: Calculating the normal vector of a polygon.

The points p_1, p_2, and p_3 chosen to compute the normal vector must not lie in a straight line. If they do, the cross product computation will return the vector (0,0,0). Furthermore, if the points lie "almost" in a straight line, the cross product will be "close to" the vector (0,0,0), which might cause problems with numerical accuracy due to the extremely small values involved. (The normalization process divides a vector by its magnitude; if the vector is very small, dividing by its magnitude means dividing by a very small number, which can be numerically inaccurate.) Thus, if the cross product is too small, you can choose the next three points p_2, p_3, and p_4 to compute a better (i.e., more reasonably sized) cross product vector.

Although we can easily compute surface normals from polygonal data, this is not always done. This is because often polygons are used as an approximation of a real surface, but do not represent the real surface. For instance, a curved surface cannot be completely accurately represented by a series of polygons—the fewer the polygons, the worse the approximation. This means that the surface normal calculated using the polygon's vertices might not always be exactly equal to the true surface normal of the actual surface approximated by polygons, simply because the polygon in this case is not the surface: it is an approximation to the surface. The surface normal calculated by using the polygon's vertices will be close to the true surface normal, but we may be able to use an analytical (mathematical) description of the surface to compute a more representative surface normal for the area of the surface approximated by the polygon. In this book, however, we will always use surface normals computed from the polygonal data itself.

Storing Normal Vectors as Base and Tip Points

In class `l3d_polygon_3d`, we use two member variables to store the surface normal vector. Specifically, we use one variable, `center`, to store the base point of the normal vector, which we define to be the geometric center of the polygon (hence the name "center"). We use a second variable, `sfcnormal`, to store the tip point of the normal vector. Both of these variables are of type `l3d_coordinate`. Recall from Chapter 5 that we can subtract the tip point from the base point to obtain the corresponding vector, and that we can add the vector to the base point to obtain the tip point. Therefore, internally we store the vector as two points, and whenever we need to know the actual vector, we subtract the base point from the tip point.

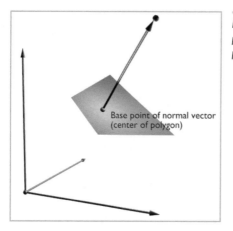

Figure 7-7: We store a surface normal vector as a base point (located at the center of the polygon) and a tip point.

Base point of normal vector (center of polygon)

You might wonder why we use two `l3d_coordinate` objects to store a normal vector instead of using one `l3d_vector` object. The reason is for uniformity of the transformation code. Recall that we use matrices to effect transformations, and that an `l3d_coordinate` object stores several `l3d_point` objects: an original point, zero or more optional transformed intermediate points, and a final transformed point. By storing vectors as two `l3d_coordinate` objects, one for the base and one for the tip, we can transform vectors just as we transform points, via method `l3d_coordinate::transform`. Indeed, when we transform the points of an object from object space into world space and into camera space, we must also transform the normal vectors along with the geometry, so that after transformation the vector still has the same orientation relative to the transformed geometry. (However, transforming normal vectors is in general even more complicated; see the section titled "Transforming Normal Vectors.")

Furthermore, we can access the original or transformed intermediate positions of the vector by retrieving the corresponding entries out of the `l3d_coordinate` objects, one for the base and one for the tip, and subtracting base from tip. This gives us the orientation of the vector at a previous point in time, which corresponds exactly to retrieving the old positions of geometry from an `l3d_coordinate`. In other words, storing vectors as pairs of `l3d_coordinate` objects leads to a uniformity of code for transforming points and vectors, including the retrieval of older entries out of the `l3d_coordinate` object. (Storing vectors as `l3d_vector` objects would require creating a similar system of original, intermediate, and final vector orientations for `l3d_vector` objects, resulting in another class similar to `l3d_coordinate`, but just for vectors.)

In general, whenever we need to store a vector which needs to be transformed with other points, we store the vector as two points: a base and a tip. These two points are stored in two `l3d_coordinate` objects, in the `original` member variables. We can then transform the base and tip `l3d_coordinate` objects via `l3d_coordinate::transform`. To retrieve the actual vector (the directed displacement) from the base and tip points, we subtract the base point from the tip point, accessed through `l3d_coordinate::transformed` (or `trans-formed_intermediates`, if we need to determine the vector at a previous intermediate point in time).

 CAUTION   Be very attentive when implementing mathematical formulas requiring vectors as inputs. Always pay attention to whether the formula needs the vector or the tip point of the vector. Typical formulas in 3D graphics require the vector and not the tip point, so always be sure in such cases to subtract the base point from the tip point to obtain the vector.

In class `l3d_polygon_3d`, the method `compute_center` computes the geometric centroid of the polygon simply by averaging the x, y, and z coordinates of all vertices in the polygon. This computation is done in object coordinates, i.e., with the `original` member of the `l3d_coordinate` objects forming the polygon. We then use this center point as the base point of the surface normal vector.

The method `compute_sfcnormal` computes the surface normal vector by taking a cross product as described above, searching through the points for any consecutive series of three points which do not lie in a straight line (measured by using the dot product). After computing the vector, we normalize it, then add it to the base point (member variable `center`) to obtain the tip point of the vector, which, like the base point, is in object coordinates. We then store this tip point in the member `sfcnormal`.

Orientation of Normal Vectors

For a given surface, there are two vectors, not just one, which are perpendicular to the surface. These two normal vectors point in exactly opposite directions: one points inward, the other points outward. We define the outward pointing normal vector to be the one computed as described in the previous section by taking a cross product of vectors using three points taken from the polygon in clockwise order. This is consistent with a left-handed coordinate system. Take your left hand, and hold it such that the direction of your hand from palm to finger points in the same direction as the order of the polygon vertices. The direction your thumb points is the direction of the outward-pointing normal vector.

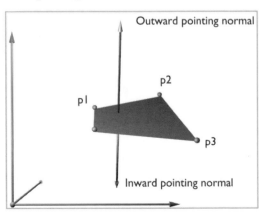

Figure 7-8: Inward- and outward-pointing normal vectors. The outward-pointing normal vector is the one pointing in the direction of your thumb when the fingers of your left hand curl in the direction of the polygon's vertices.

In this book, the normal vector that we compute and store with each polygon is the outward-pointing normal vector.

Given an outward-pointing surface normal vector to a polygon and a camera located in 3D space, an interesting question of orientation is whether the normal is pointing towards the camera or away from the camera. If the normal points towards the camera, we can say that the normal (and the polygon) are *forward-facing*. If the normal points away from the camera, we can say that the normal (and the polygon) are *backward-facing*.

Assuming all points have been transformed into the left-handed camera coordinate system introduced in Chapter 5, the orientation of the normal vector can be determined quite easily by examining the sign of the z coordinate of the normal vector: if it is negative, the normal vector is pointing towards the origin and therefore towards the camera; if it is positive, the normal vector is pointing away from the origin and therefore away from the camera. Figure 7-9 illustrates this computation.

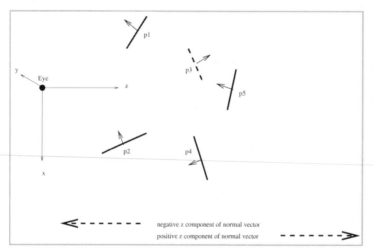

Figure 7-9: Back-face determination in camera coordinates. We simply examine the sign of the z coordinate of the surface normal. Here, polygon p3 faces away from the camera.

In the more general case, we might want to determine whether a face is backward- or forward-facing in world coordinates. This can save on processing time because it eliminates the need to perform an additional matrix multiplication to convert to camera coordinates before performing back-face determination. In world coordinates, we take the dot product of the surface normal vector with the vector from the polygon's center (or actually from any point on the polygon) to the camera's location. If the dot product is positive, the polygon is front-facing (facing towards the camera); if the dot product is negative, the polygon is back-facing (facing away from the camera); if the dot product is zero, the polygon is being viewed exactly on its edge. This dot product can be interpreted as the cosine of the angle between the surface normal vector and the polygon-to-camera vector. If the angle is 0 to 90 degrees or 270 to 360 degrees, then the polygon is pointing toward the camera, and the cosine and therefore the dot product are positive. If the angle is 90 to 270 degrees, the polygon is pointing away from the camera, and the cosine and dot product are negative.

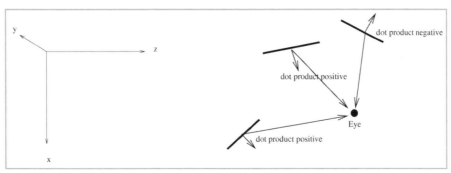

Figure 7-10: Back-face determination in world coordinates using dot products.

 NOTE OpenGL uses a different method for performing back-face determination: it defines a vertex order for each polygon, and checks after perspective projection in screen coordinates to see if the vertex order has been reversed. If it has been reversed, this means that the polygon is being viewed from its back side.

The classification of polygons into backward-facing or forward-facing polygons plays an important role in the operation of back-face culling, which is covered in the companion book *Advanced Linux 3D Graphics Programming*.

Vertex Normal Vectors

The surface normal vector that we just described is a single vector representing the orientation of the surface. If we have several polygons sharing several vertices, then it is also possible to specify normal vectors for the vertices shared by polygons. Such normal vectors are called *vertex normals*. We might want to specify vertex normals in order to provide additional information about the orientation of the surface at the points between polygons. This additional orientation information can then, for instance, lead to improved lighting calculations, simply because more surface orientation information, in the form of more normal vectors, is available upon which to compute light intensities. The vertex normal for a particular vertex can be computed either by averaging the surface normals from all polygons sharing the vertex (possibly a weighted average based on the angle the polygon forms with the vertex) or by using some formula based on the mathematical description of the surface at the vertex point, assuming a mathematical description of the surface is known.

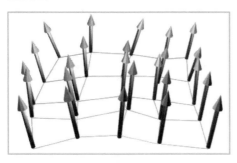

Figure 7-11: Vertex normals are specified at the vertices shared by polygons.

Transforming Normal Vectors

In general, transforming normal vectors is tricky. This is because a normal vector is not just any vector, but is instead a special vector with a constraint on its orientation. By definition, this vector must always be normal (perpendicular) to a given surface. We use matrices to effect transformations. If we transform the points of a surface by a matrix M, and use the same matrix to transform the normal vector to the surface, the normal vector still might not be perpendicular to the surface, as it was before the transformation. In particular, if the transformation matrix M only involves translation, rotation, and uniform scaling matrices, we can use the same matrix for transforming points and normal vectors. But, if the transformation matrix M involves any other angle- or length-changing operations, such as non-uniform scaling or shearing, then transforming the normal vector with the same transformation matrix M yields an incorrect result: the normal vector will no longer be perpendicular to the surface as it was before. Figure 7-12 illustrates this phenomenon.

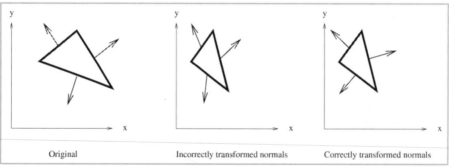

Original   Incorrectly transformed normals   Correctly transformed normals

Figure 7-12: Transforming normals by the same matrix used to transform points might yield incorrect results if the transformation changes lengths or angles. Here, the transformation is a non-uniform scaling of 0.5 in the x direction.

For the program code in this book, we restrict ourselves to transformations which do not change the angles or lengths of the original data. Therefore, in our program code, we use the same matrix M for transforming points and normal vectors—indeed, we store normal vectors as base and tip points (not vectors), subtracting base from tip to retrieve the vector. This leads to code which is simpler to understand, but which is not correct in all cases. For completeness, though, let us consider exactly how to transform normal vectors in the general case. The mathematical derivation presented here is taken from *Open GL Programming Guide, Second Edition* [WOO97].

As mentioned above, a normal vector is a special entity; it must be perpendicular to a particular surface. Generally, we can say that a normal vector n must always be perpendicular to another vector v, where the vector v lies within the surface to which n is perpendicular. This is the constraint which must be maintained in order for the normal vector to be "normal" to the surface. Mathematically, we can express this constraint as the vector dot product $nv=0$. Remember, the dot product represents the cosine of the angle between two vectors; this means that the cosine of the angle between the two vectors must remain zero for the two vectors to be defined as being "normal" to one another. Expressed in matrix form, we can rewrite this dot product as a matrix-matrix multiplication: $n^{\mathrm{T}}v=0$. This means that the transpose of the normal vector dotted with the vector to which the normal is perpendicular yields a result of zero.

Now, consider an arbitrary transformation matrix M which transforms v. The result after transformation is Mv. Therefore, the normal to this transformed vector must satisfy the constraint that the dot product of the normal and the transformed vector is still zero. If we call the transformed vector n', the mathematical constraint that must be satisfied is $n'^{\mathrm{T}}Mv=0$.

The equation $n^{\mathrm{T}}M^{-1}Mv=0$ satisfies the constraint. You can verify this by recognizing that the matrix product $M^{-1}M$ reduces to the identity matrix, yielding the original constraint $n^{\mathrm{T}}v=0$. Now, recall that the term Mv in this equation represents the transformed vector, to which the transformed normal must be perpendicular. Remembering our original interpretation of the constraint, this means that term $n^{\mathrm{T}}M^{-1}$ in the above equation must be the transpose of the transformed normal vector, because we said earlier that the transpose of the normal vector $(n^{\mathrm{T}}M^{-1})$ dotted with the vector to which the normal is perpendicular (Mv) yields a result of zero.

We therefore know that the transpose of the transformed normal vector is $n^{\mathrm{T}}M^{-1}$. Therefore, the transformed normal vector itself is the transpose of the transpose of the transformed normal vector—in other words, $(n^{\mathrm{T}}M^{-1})^{\mathrm{T}}$. A general rule of matrix multiplication is that the transpose of a matrix product AB, represented as $(AB)^{\mathrm{T}}$, is equal to $B^{\mathrm{T}}A^{\mathrm{T}}$—we transpose each matrix, and reverse the order of multiplication. (Verify this by realizing that taking the transpose of each matrix reverses the row-column sense of each matrix, and reversing the order of multiplication again reverses the row-column sense of the multiplication, yielding the same result as the original multiplication.) Using this rule, this means that the transformed normal vector is $(M^{-1})^{\mathrm{T}}(n^{\mathrm{T}})^{\mathrm{T}}$, or equivalently, $(M^{-1})^{\mathrm{T}}n$.

Finally, we can recognize that this last equation expresses the transformed normal vector in terms of a matrix multiplication with the original normal vector. Therefore, the matrix which transforms normal vectors is $(M^{-1})^{\mathrm{T}}$—the transpose of the inverse of the matrix M used to transform the original vector or point.

Again, for the code in this book, we make the simplification that we only use translation, rotation, and uniform scaling matrices, thereby allowing us to use the same matrices for transforming points and normals. It is important, however, to realize that this is a simplification, and that, in general, we must compute a matrix inverse and transpose in order to transform normal vectors correctly in all cases.

 NOTE Instead of transforming a normal vector as described above, we could recompute the normal after transforming the geometry.

Transforming 3D Polygons

Transforming a 3D polygon allows us to change its location and orientation in space. Chapter 6 showed how to use matrices and the `l3d_matrix` class to effect transformations on points. We also saw in Chapter 3 the class `l3d_coordinate`, which stores an original location, zero or more intermediate transformed locations, and a final transformed location.

Transforming a 3D polygon, however, requires us to transform more than just the `l3d_coordinate` objects forming the vertices of the polygon. In general, when we say "transforming a polygon," we actually mean "transforming the `l3d_coordinate` objects of the polygon, and transforming any other relevant geometrical attributes of the polygon." Specifically, for now, this means additionally transforming the surface normal. Just as class `l3d_coordinate` provides methods to allow transforming a point by a matrix, the class `l3d_polygon_3d` similarly provides such transformation methods to allow transforming a 3D polygon (including geometry and normal) by a matrix.

Methods for Transforming a Polygon

Let's now look at the methods in `l3d_polygon_3d` dealing with transforming a polygon. Most of these methods are virtual. The reason for this is that to transform a polygon, we must transform all "relevant geometric attributes" of the polygon. For now, as we said, the relevant geometric attributes, other than the vertices, are the base and tip points of the surface normal vector. Later, subclasses of `l3d_polygon_3d` will introduce extra geometrical attributes which also need to be transformed. Overriding these virtual transformation methods allows subclasses to transform any extra geometrical attributes.

The virtual method `init_transformed` resets the positions of all transformable members of the polygon, excluding the vertex list, back to their original (as opposed to transformed) locations. Here, we call `sfcnormal.reset` and `center.reset` to reset the tip and base of the surface normal vector to be at their original positions. We do not reset the vertex list of the polygon, because the vertex list is probably a vertex list shared among several polygons, as discussed in Chapter 3. It would be inefficient for each polygon to reset the entire external vertex list, since each polygon only uses a small part of the list; however, we could use the `transform_stage` member of the vertices to ensure that each vertex gets reset only once, at the cost of executing several `if` statements. Instead, we require that the entire vertex list be reset externally. This means that `init_transformed` is responsible for resetting all polygon attributes, excluding the vertices, to their original positions.

The virtual method `transform` transforms all vertices and additional attributes of the polygon by the given matrix m. It does so by calling `l3d_coordinate::transform` for each vertex. Furthermore, we also transform the base and tip of the surface normal vector. This method uses the clipped list of vertex indices (`clip_ivertices`) instead of the original list (`ivertices`), as do all methods which might temporarily change the polygon. Chapter 3 discusses the `clip_ivertices` member. This means that before calling `transform`, the `clip_ivertices` member of the polygon must have already been initialized (`l3d_polygon_2d::init_clip_ivertices`).

The virtual method `set_transform_stage` resets the `transform_stage` counter for all vertices and for all additional polygon attributes to a particular value. Here, we assign `transform_stage` for each vertex (in the clipped vertex index list), for the surface normal base, and for the surface normal tip. Remember that the `transform_stage` variable is checked within `l3d_coordinate` to see if a coordinate has already been transformed or not; if so, we do not transform the coordinate a second time. We use the method `set_transform_stage` to reset this counter. If some polygons have undergone more or fewer transformations than others, but we want to make sure that all following transformations are applied equally to all polygons, we would call `set_transform_stage` on all polygons to ensure that all polygons are at the same transformation stage. Then, all subsequent transformations will definitely be applied to all polygons. This sort of situation can arise when we have a child object contained within another parent object; the child object in this case might have undergone more transformations than the parent object due to its own local movement within the parent object. This means that the child object's polygons would have a higher transformation stage than those in the parent object. But we may still at some later point in time wish to apply some global transformations equally to all polygons in the child and parent objects. In such a case we should call `set_transform_stage` before applying the global transformations, to ensure that all polygons are transformed and none are incorrectly skipped over because they already coincidentally had a higher `transform_stage` from a previous extra transformation. See the companion book *Advanced Linux 3D Graphics Programming* for an example of this, where an object contained within a sector in a portal environment may have undergone more transformations than the containing sector itself.

The virtual method `after_camera_transform` allows the polygon to perform any additional processing after application of the camera transformation as described in Chapter 6. In `l3d_polygon_3d` this method is empty, but subclasses can override this method. This method is called immediately after the camera transformation has been applied to the polygon's vertices (also see next method `camera_transform`). The reason for having this method is that some computations in 3D require the camera space coordinates of the vertices of a polygon. By overriding `after_camera_transform`, the polygon can access the camera space coordinates, because all of its vertices at the time of the invocation of this routine are in camera space. The polygon can then save the camera space coordinates in one of the `transformed_intermediates`. Later access to the camera space coordinates is then possible, even after the polygon's vertices have undergone additional transformations (such as perspective projection), by accessing the previously saved `transformed_intermediates` item.

The method `camera_transform` works closely with the method `after_camera_transform`. Method `camera_transform` simply calls method `transform`, then method `after_camera_transform`. The idea is that this method `camera_transform` should be called instead of the method `transform` whenever the transformation matrix being applied is the camera transformation matrix. As mentioned before, many interesting computations in 3D require the coordinates right after application of the camera transformation matrix. But the `transform` method itself has no way of knowing whether an arbitrary matrix is indeed being used as a camera transformation matrix or not. Therefore, the application program itself must explicitly call `camera_transform` instead of `transform` whenever the matrix being applied is the camera transformation matrix. By adhering to this convention, we notify the polygon that the camera space coordinates are now available, and allow the polygon to perform any camera space processing or to save the camera space coordinates for later use.

Step-by-Step Guide to Transforming 3D Polygons

The following list summarizes the typical operations needed in order to correctly transform a 3D polygon. To begin transforming a polygon from its original position to a new position, follow the steps below.

1. Reset the external vertex list for the polygon by calling `reset` for each vertex in the list. Eliminate any varying items in the external vertex list by setting `num_varying_items` to zero. Note that if this vertex list is shared among polygons, then the vertex list will be reset for all polygons (which is the desired effect).

2. Call `init_transformed` to allow the polygon to reset any additional geometric attributes back to their original, untransformed positions.

3. Call `init_clip_ivertices` (described in Chapter 3) to initialize the clip vertex index list from the original vertex index list.

4. The polygon and all of its attributes are now in their original, untransformed, non-clipped state. Call `transform`, possibly multiple times, to effect transformations on the polygon. Maintain an external `transform_stage` counter, increasing it with every call to `transform`. Pass the current `transform_stage` counter to every call of `transform`. Reset `transform_stage` to zero whenever you reset the polygon's vertex list (step 1).

5. Call `camera_transform` instead of `transform` if the matrix being applied is the camera transformation matrix and if the polygon needs to do any camera-space processing. Declare a polygon subclass and override the virtual method `after_camera_transform` to perform camera-space processing within the polygon.

6. Call `set_transform_stage` to manually set the transformation stage to a particular value, for all vertices and for all additional geometric attributes of the polygon.

The upcoming sample program, `clipz`, provides functions which automate much of the "house-keeping" work involved with transforming a 3D polygon. The l3d class `l3d_object` also builds on this idea, yielding an easy-to-use framework for transforming groups of 3D polygons.

Now that we know how to transform a 3D polygon and its relevant geometrical attributes, let's turn to another important geometrical concern with 3D polygons: near z clipping.

Near Z Clipping

Due to the physical properties of light, we can only see objects in front of our eyes. The perspective projection equation developed in Chapter 5 divides the camera space x and y coordinates by z, and assumes that z is positive—in other words, in front of the camera. Applying perspective projection to a point whose camera space z is negative is mathematically possible but physically unrealistic, resulting in a reversal of up and down orientation. Attempting to apply perspective projection to a point with $z=0$ results in a division by zero and a run-time error. Finally, even if z is positive, very small values of z (for instance, $z=0.000000000001$) result in extremely large projected coordinates, which can cause numerical instability or overflows when attempting to rasterize or otherwise manipulate the projected coordinates.

All of this implies that for a robust perspective projection, the z values should not be smaller than a certain small, positive z value. Until now, we have dealt with this problem in a fairly loose manner. The sample programs of Chapters 5 and 6 simply refrained from drawing an entire polygon if any vertex of the polygon had a z value less than a certain lower bound. This treatment is similar to the 2D clipping strategy, covered in Chapter 3, of "discard the polygon completely": if any vertices are invalid, refrain from drawing the entire polygon. This strategy has the same problem in 3D as it does in 2D: entire polygons or groups of polygons suddenly disappear as soon as any one of their vertices has a z value which is too small.

In 2D, we turned to analytical clipping to mathematically compute which parts of the polygon should be clipped away and which parts should be retained, finally drawing the retained part of the polygon. We can use the same strategy in 3D to ensure that the z values of our polygons never drop below a certain value. Specifically, we define a *near z clipping plane*, analogous to the 2D clipping edge we defined in Chapter 3 for clipping 2D polygons. Just like a 2D clipping edge, a 3D clipping plane has an "inside side" and an "outside side." We clip 3D polygons to the near z plane by checking all vertices of the polygon to see if they are on the inside side or the outside side of the clipping plane. If they are all on the outside side, we discard the entire polygon. If they are all on the inside side, we accept the entire polygon. If some are on the inside and some are on the outside side, we find each *crossing segment* of the polygon, where one vertex lies on the inside side and the next vertex lies on the outside side. Just as in 2D, there will always be either zero or two crossing segments for convex polygons, due to the O-shaped nature of convex polygons. We then clip each crossing segment to the near z plane, creating new temporary clip vertices and indices to these clip vertices. The process is entirely analogous to the process of analytical 2D polygon clipping: we have merely extended the process to 3D.

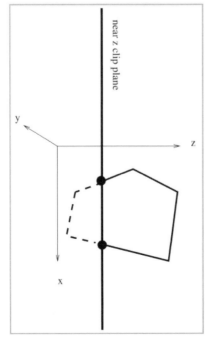

Figure 7-13: Analytical clipping of 3D polygons against the near z plane. Dotted lines indicate the portion of the polygon that is clipped away.

This entire procedure is called *near z clipping* and ensures that all z values of vertices passed on to the perspective projection have a minimum positive value, thereby avoiding any mirroring, division by zero, or numerical instability effects caused by negative, zero, or extremely small positive z values.

Implementing near z clipping is a simple extension of the 2D clipping idea. From 2D clipping, we already have the structures in place for dealing with the creation of temporary clipped vertices, temporarily redefining the polygon's geometry to reference the new clipped vertices, and resetting the polygon back to its original non-clipped state. Therefore, implementing near z plane clipping requires only a few new steps. Specifically, we need to do the following:

1. Define the near z plane mathematically.
2. Define the inside side and the outside side of the near z plane.
3. Classify a 3D point as being on the inside side or the outside side of the near z plane.
4. Calculate the intersection between a crossing segment (a line segment with one vertex inside and outside the near z plane) and the near z plane.

With these four operations, we can then use exactly the same logic we used for 2D clipping: classify points with respect to the clipping plane, find crossing segments, clip crossing segments to the inside side, and rebuild the polygon definition to use the new clipped edges and vertices.

Let's now discuss each of the four new operations needed for near z plane clipping.

Define the Near Z Plane Mathematically

In camera coordinates (in other words, after we have applied the camera transformation to all points) the near z clipping plane is a plane stretching infinitely in the x and y directions, with a fixed z value. You can think of the near z clipping plane as an infinitely wide and high flat surface positioned vertically at some distance in front of the camera.

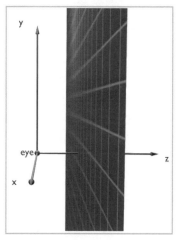

Figure 7-14: The near z clipping plane.

Fortunately, the mathematical definition of a near z clipping plane is very simple: it is simply an equation of the form $z=z_{clip}$, where z_{clip} is the desired z coordinate of the clipping plane, below which points will be clipped. z_{clip} is therefore the minimum allowable z value.

In C++, this means that we only need a single number to represent the near z clipping plane. The method `l3d_polygon_3d::clip_near_z` clips a 3D polygon to a near z plane, and takes as input a single parameter `zclip`, which represents the near z clipping plane against which the polygon should be clipped. Furthermore, the class `l3d_camera`, which we saw in Chapter 6, contains a member variable `near_z`, which is the near z clipping plane for the camera. This clipping plane is then passed to the `clip_near_z` method.

Define the Inside and Outside Sides of the Near Z Plane

Having defined the near z clipping plane, we next need to define the inside and outside sides of the clipping plane. As with clipping edges in 2D, we define the inside side of a clipping plane to be the side on which vertices are allowed to be located. We define the outside side to be the side of the plane on which vertices must not be located. We must clip polygon edges which cross from the inside side to the outside side, so that they stop before crossing over to the outside side.

 CAUTION   The definition of the inside side as being the side which remains after clipping is not necessarily universal among all graphics texts; when reading other literature, the sides of a plane may be defined differently.

The purpose of the near z clipping plane is to eliminate points with z coordinates that are too small, i.e., too close to the camera. Therefore, the outside side of the near z clipping plane, where points must be clipped, is the side nearer to the camera than z_{clip}. Mathematically, this means that the outside side is defined by the equation $z < z_{clip}$. The inside side is therefore the opposite: all points on or beyond the near clipping plane or, mathematically, $z \geq z_{clip}$.

Classify a Point as being Inside or Outside

For all polygon vertices, we must test to see if the vertex is on the inside side or the outside side of the clipping plane. If we find any pair of two consecutive vertices where one is on the inside side and one is on the outside side, then we have found a crossing segment and must clip this segment to the plane.

To classify a point as being inside or outside the near z clipping plane, we simply use the formulas we defined above for the inside and outside sides. If the z coordinate of a particular point is less than the z_{clip} value, the point is outside. If the z coordinate is greater than or equal to z_{clip}, the point is inside.

Calculate the Intersection Between a Crossing Segment and the Near Z Plane

The last operation we need in order to perform near z plane clipping is the calculation of the intersection between a crossing segment and the near z plane. Fortunately, this computation is somewhat easier than in the 2D case, where we computed the intersection between an arbitrary crossing segment and an arbitrary clipping edge.

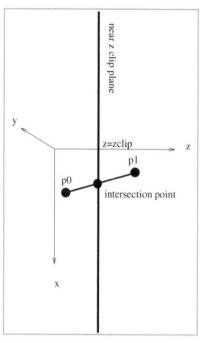

Figure 7-15: Computing the intersection between a crossing segment and the near z clipping plane.

Assume that the crossing segment crosses from the outside side to the inside side. Call the invalid z value z_0 and the valid z value z_1. This means that the z component of the edge starts out invalid on the outside, but becomes valid by the time it reaches the end of the segment. We use a parameter t to represent the fractional percentage of the invalid z distance divided by the total z distance: $t=(z_{clip}-z_0)/(z_1-z_0)$.

This t parameter tells us, then, how much of the total segment is invalid from the first invalid point to the second valid point. Call the first point (x_0,y_0,z_0) and the second point (x_1,y_1,z_1). Then, the intersection of the crossing segment with the near z clip plane is given by $(x_0+t(x_1-x_0)$, $y_0+t(y_1-y_0)$, $z_{clip})$. For both the x and y displacements, we simply take the entire displacement, multiply it by t to get the invalid part of the displacement, and add this to the invalid starting point to arrive exactly at the first valid point on the displacement—in other words, at the intersection point between the crossing segment and the near z plane.

The method `l3d_polygon_3d::clip_segment_to_near_z` performs exactly this computation. Given as input a near z clipping plane and two indices to vertices forming a crossing segment, the routine first orders the vertices to go from outside the plane to inside the plane. Then, it computes the t value, computes the corresponding intersection point based on t, creates a new vertex, sets the position of this vertex to be the just-computed intersection point, and finally returns an index to the newly created vertex. The calling routine is then responsible for taking this newly created vertex and redefining the polygon geometry.

Putting It All Together

The method `l3d_polygon_3d::clip_near_z` performs the entire near z clipping operation. Its operation is very straightforward if you recall the logic behind the 2D analytical clipping process from Chapter 3. First, we loop through all of the `clip_ivertices`, checking each vertex to see if it is inside or outside. If it is inside, we add the vertex to the temporary list of vertices, `temp_clip_ivertices`. But if the vertex is outside, then we clip the current segment to the near z plane, add the clipped vertex to `temp_clip_ivertices`, and look for the next segment crossing back inside the z plane. Once we find the second crossing segment, we again clip it to the near z plane, add the clipped vertex to `temp_clip_ivertices`, then add the rest of the vertices from `clip_ivertices` to the `temp_clip_ivertices`. The code also has to account for the reverse case, where the first crossing is outside to inside and the second crossing is inside to outside, as well as cases where the polygon is either completely outside or completely inside.

At this point, `temp_clip_ivertices` contains some or all of the vertices from the original `clip_ivertices` list, and also possibly two new vertices if any part of the original polygon was clipped away. Then, we simply call `swap_temp_and_main_clip_lists` to make the current definition of the polygon correspond to the results of our clipping operation. Finally, we return a value of 0 to the caller if the polygon was completely clipped away, or 1 if some part of the polygon remained after the clipping operation.

Linked Lists of Polygons

We have just seen how to clip polygons to the near z plane. After such a clipping operation, it is possible that the polygon has been completely clipped away if all of its vertices were outside the near z clipping plane. We should refrain from doing further processing (such as additional transformations, projection, or rasterization) on any polygons which have been completely clipped away: any further processing of such a polygon is a waste of time since it has been clipped away and therefore does not contribute to the final image for the current frame. (The viewpoint might change for the next frame, however, meaning that a polygon completely clipped away in the last frame might still become visible in the next frame.)

At the beginning of each new frame, since the viewpoint might have changed from the previous frame, we initially consider all polygons as being potentially visible. Then, we perform various clipping operations, which might result in some polygons being completely clipped away. So for each frame, for all polygons in a scene, we need to keep track of which polygons should be further processed, and which ones should not be further processed because they have already been completely clipped away in this frame.

One way of doing this is to keep the flag `is_valid` with each polygon. If the polygon has not been clipped away, `is_valid` is 1; as soon as it is clipped away, `is_valid` is set to 0. By checking the value of this flag, we could determine whether or not to continue processing the polygon.

The problem with a flag variable is that we still need to check each and every polygon to see if it is still valid. If we have clipped away several polygons, this would imply many redundant checks on polygons which have already been clipped away. A more attractive option is to use a linked list of polygons. At the beginning of each frame, all polygons are potentially visible, and are inserted into the list. If a polygon is clipped away, we simply remove it from the list, and relink the surrounding elements together to skip the clipped away polygon. Then, after all clipping operations are done, we simply need to traverse the linked list and draw all polygons in the list; we do not need to perform a test on every single polygon to see if it is still valid or not.

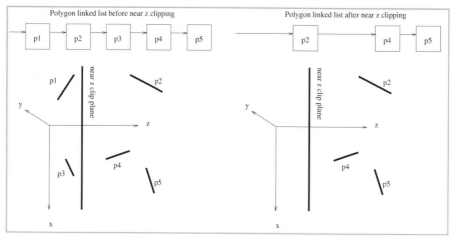

Figure 7-16: Using a linked list to keep track of polygons.

 NOTE We've said that at the beginning of each frame, since the viewpoint may have changed from the last frame, all polygons are considered potentially visible and are thus inserted into the linked list at the beginning of the frame. In a typical application, though, the viewpoint does not tend to change drastically from one frame to another. This implies that the polygons that were visible in the last frame will probably remain visible for a few frames to come; those that were invisible will probably remain invisible. If we are clever, we can try to reuse the contents of the previous visible polygon list to more quickly build up the visible polygon list for the new frame. Such an approach is said to "exploit frame coherence," because it tries to reuse the results from the previous frame to save work in the current frame.

The upcoming sample program, `clipz`, uses a linked list of polygons to keep track of all polygons which have not been completely clipped away. The C++ structure we use to create the linked list is `l3d_polygon_3d_node`.

```
struct l3d_polygon_3d_node {
    l3d_polygon_3d *polygon;
    l3d_polygon_3d_node *prev,*next;
};
```

The member variable `polygon` is a pointer to a 3D polygon. The member variables `next` and `prev` point to the next and previous nodes in the linked list. We set `prev` or `next` to NULL at the beginning or end of the list, respectively. Since we are keeping track of previous and next nodes, this is a doubly linked list.

Drawing 3D Polygons: Flat Shading

The class `l3d_polygon_3d`, similar to its ancestor `l3d_polygon_2d`, represents the geometry of a 3D polygon and not its appearance. Therefore, we cannot rasterize an l3d_polygon_3d to the screen. Since this is a book on computer graphics and not computational geometry, it would be a shame if we couldn't see our 3D polygons on screen. Therefore, let's now look at a simple 3D polygon subclass which we can rasterize to the screen: l3d_polygon_3d_flatshaded. As we saw in Chapter 3, a flat-shaded polygon is one which we rasterize with a single color. In the companion book *Advanced Linux 3D Graphics Programming*, we encounter other descendants of l3d_polygon_3d which store and use additional 3D information such as texture or light map coordinates for more advanced rasterization and a more impressive visual appearance. For now, though, we start with a single-colored, flat-shaded 3D polygon. Listings 7-3 and 7-4 contain the code for class l3d_polygon_3d_flatshaded.

Listing 7-3: p3_flat.h

```
#include "p_flat.h"
#include "poly3.h"

#ifndef __P3_FLAT_H
#define __P3_FLAT_H
#include "../../tool_os/memman.h"

class l3d_rasterizer_3d;

class l3d_polygon_3d_flatshaded :
     virtual public l3d_polygon_2d_flatshaded,
     virtual public l3d_polygon_3d
{
  public:

    l3d_polygon_3d_flatshaded(int num_faces) :
    l3d_polygon_3d(num_faces),
    l3d_polygon_2d_flatshaded(num_faces),
    l3d_polygon_2d(num_faces)
  {}

    unsigned long color;
    int light_intensity;

    void draw(l3d_rasterizer_3d *r );
    l3d_polygon_3d_flatshaded(const l3d_polygon_3d_flatshaded &r);
    l3d_polygon_2d *clone(void);
};

#include "../../raster/rast3.h"

#endif
```

Listing 7-4: p3_flat.cc

```
#include "p3_flat.h"
#include "../../math/matrix.h"
#include "../../tool_os/memman.h"

void l3d_polygon_3d_flatshaded::draw(l3d_rasterizer_3d *r ) {
  r->draw_polygon_flatshaded(this);
}

l3d_polygon_2d* l3d_polygon_3d_flatshaded::clone(void) {
  return new l3d_polygon_3d_flatshaded(*this);
}
```

```
l3d_polygon_3d_flatshaded::l3d_polygon_3d_flatshaded
(const l3d_polygon_3d_flatshaded &r)
    : l3d_polygon_3d(r),
    l3d_polygon_2d_flatshaded(r),
    l3d_polygon_2d(r)
{
  color = r.color;
  light_intensity = r.light_intensity;
}
```

The class `l3d_polygon_3d_flatshaded` inherits from class `l3d_polygon_2d_flatshaded` and from class `l3d_polygon_3d`. (Notice that the base classes are virtual, which ensures that the common ancestral components are only created once.) This means it has the 3D surface normal and the clipping capabilities of a 3D polygon, and the single-colored drawing capabilities of a 2D flat-shaded polygon. We can therefore clip a 3D flat-shaded polygon in 3D by using the routines inherited from `l3d_polygon_3d`, and can also pass the 3D polygon to a rasterizer to be rasterized as a 2D flat-shaded polygon.

The constructors for `l3d_polygon_3d_flatshaded` are a normal initializing constructor and a copy constructor. The overridden `clone` method uses the copy constructor, as we have seen before.

The new member variables `color` and `light_intensity` provide a means of separating the color of the polygon from the intensity of the light falling on the polygon. Recall that for the 2D flat-shaded polygon, we only stored one color value, in a member variable named `final_color`. The name `final_color` implies that the color used in the 2D flat-shaded case is exactly the color which we pass to the rasterizer layer, and which will appear on-screen. With 3D flat-shaded polygons, however, we can do better than this. We can define a certain color and store it in the `color` member variable. Then, separately from the color, we can compute a light intensity falling on the surface, by means of one of the formulas covered below in the section on computing light. We can then store this light intensity in member variable `light_intensity`. Then, by combining the color and the light intensity (through a light table as described in Chapter 2), we arrive at a final color to be displayed on screen, and store this in the `final_color` member variable inherited from `l3d_polygon_2d`. The separation of color and intensity makes it easy to recompute a new final color value if the light intensity changes.

The overridden `draw` method draws a flat-shaded 3D polygon by passing it on to a rasterizer of type `l3d_rasterizer_3d`, which then forwards the request to a rasterizer implementation of type `l3d_rasterizer_3d_imp`. The 3D rasterizer and implementation classes inherit from their 2D counterparts, and drawing flat-shaded polygons is done by forwarding the request to the 2D rasterizer. Later, other polygon types (such as texture-mapped or light-mapped polygons) will make use of new features of the 3D rasterizer class not available in the 2D rasterizer.

NOTE The preceding statement, that the 3D rasterizer forwards the flat-shaded drawing request to the 2D rasterizer, is not entirely accurate. In the case of the software rasterizer, the 3D rasterizer does indeed simply forward the request to the 2D rasterizer, which is the reason we don't cover the 3D rasterizer class in more detail in this book. However, in the case of the Mesa/OpenGL rasterizer, the 3D rasterizer changes the screen coordinate system so that the (0,0) point is in the center of the screen and not in the upper-left corner as usual. This change in coordinate system means that the 2D Mesa rasterizer routines, which assumed that the

(0,0) point was in the upper-left corner, cannot be used; the 3D Mesa rasterizer must reimplement the exact same OpenGL calls as the 2D Mesa rasterizer, but based on a screen-centered coordinate system and not an upper-left coordinate system. The reason that the 3D rasterizer must make such a change in coordinate system has to do with texture mapping, a topic covered in the companion book *Advanced Linux 3D Graphics Programming*.

Sample Program: clipz

The previous sections discussed several concepts dealing with the geometrical definition and manipulation of 3D polygons: the definition of a surface normal, storing a surface normal as a base and tip point, transforming the geometry and the normal together, clipping against the near z plane, and using a linked list to keep track of which polygons deserve further processing. We also declared a flat-shaded 3D polygon subclass which we can rasterize and see on-screen. Now, let's look at a sample program which illustrates the use of the 3D polygons in practice.

The sample program `clipz` is similar in structure and function to the `camspikes` program of Chapter 6: a number of pointed objects fly toward you, and you can stop the motion and navigate freely through the scene. The main difference between this program and `camspikes` is that we clip the spike objects to the near z plane. See this for yourself as follows:

1. Compile the program and change to the binary output directory. Type **clipz** and press **Enter**. Notice the menu of possible factories; type **1**, and press **Enter** to choose the standard X11 factories. The program opens a new window and begins execution.

2. Notice the spikes flying towards you. Press **0** to stop the movement of the spikes. Use the navigation keys (as described in Chapter 6 for the `camspikes` program) to fly towards one of the spikes.

3. Use the navigation keys to position yourself close to the tip of a spike. Rotate the viewpoint so that you are looking directly forward at the tip of a spike.

4. Briefly press **i** to fly forward slowly. Continue to press **i** until the tip of the spike disappears.

5. Notice that the entire spike does not suddenly disappear as you slowly get closer, but instead that the portion of the spike that is too close is clipped away. As you approach closer by pressing the **i** key, more and more of the spike gets clipped away. As you retreat further by pressing the **k** key, more and more of the spike becomes visible again, until the entire spike is again visible. Press **q** to end the program.

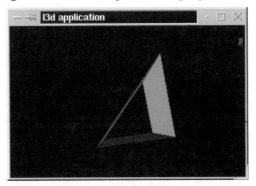

Figure 7-17: Using a linked list to keep track of polygons.

Listing 7-5: `clipz.cc`

```cpp
#include <stdlib.h>
#include <stdio.h>

#include "../lib/geom/polygon/poly3.h"
#include "../lib/tool_2d/screen.h"
#include "../lib/tool_os/dispatch.h"
#include "../lib/raster/rasteriz.h"
#include "../lib/tool_2d/scrinfo.h"
#include "../lib/system/factorys.h"

#include "../lib/geom/point/point.h"
#include "../lib/math/vector.h"
#include "../lib/math/matrix.h"
#include "../lib/view/camera.h"

#define MAXSPIKES 50
#define PI 3.14159265

unsigned long red_color;
unsigned long green_color;
unsigned long blue_color;

//- STEP 1: CHOOSE THE FACTORIES

void choose_factories(void) {
  factory_manager_v_0_1.choose_factories();
}

//- STEP 2: DECLARE A PIPELINE SUBCLASS

l3d_real fovx, fovy;
int xsize, ysize;

class spike {
  public:

    l3d_two_part_list<l3d_coordinate> *vlist;
    l3d_polygon_3d_flatshaded *faces[3];

    l3d_polygon_3d_node *nonculled_polygon_nodes;
    l3d_list<l3d_polygon_3d_node> polygon_node_pool;

    l3d_vector displacement;
    l3d_vector velocity;

    int transform_stage;

    spike(void) {
      //- declare common shared vertex list for all polygons
      vlist = new l3d_two_part_list<l3d_coordinate> (4);
      int i=0;
      (*vlist)[i++].original.set(int_to_l3d_real(0),
                                 int_to_l3d_real(0),
                                 int_to_l3d_real(50),
                                 int_to_l3d_real(1));
      (*vlist)[i++].original.set(int_to_l3d_real(50),
                                 int_to_l3d_real(50),
                                 int_to_l3d_real(50),
                                 int_to_l3d_real(1));
```

```
    (*vlist)[i++].original.set(int_to_l3d_real(50),
                               int_to_l3d_real(0),
                               int_to_l3d_real(50),
                               int_to_l3d_real(1));
    (*vlist)[i++].original.set(int_to_l3d_real(0),
                               int_to_l3d_real(0),
                               int_to_l3d_real(0),
                               int_to_l3d_real(1));

    //- define polygons in terms of indices into shared vertex list
    faces[0] = new l3d_polygon_3d_flatshaded(3);
    faces[0]->vlist = & vlist; //- shared vertex list
    (*(faces[0]->ivertices))[faces[0]->ivertices->next_index()].ivertex = 3;
    (*(faces[0]->ivertices))[faces[0]->ivertices->next_index()].ivertex = 0;
    (*(faces[0]->ivertices))[faces[0]->ivertices->next_index()].ivertex = 1;

    faces[1] = new l3d_polygon_3d_flatshaded(3);
    faces[1]->vlist = & vlist; //- shared vertex list
    (*(faces[1]->ivertices))[faces[1]->ivertices->next_index()].ivertex = 3;
    (*(faces[1]->ivertices))[faces[1]->ivertices->next_index()].ivertex = 1;
    (*(faces[1]->ivertices))[faces[1]->ivertices->next_index()].ivertex = 2;

    faces[2] = new l3d_polygon_3d_flatshaded(3);
    faces[2]->vlist = & vlist; //- shared vertex list
    (*(faces[2]->ivertices))[faces[2]->ivertices->next_index()].ivertex = 3;
    (*(faces[2]->ivertices))[faces[2]->ivertices->next_index()].ivertex = 2;
    (*(faces[2]->ivertices))[faces[2]->ivertices->next_index()].ivertex = 0;

    nonculled_polygon_nodes = NULL;
  }

  ~spike(void) {
    delete faces[0];
    delete faces[1];
    delete faces[2];
    delete vlist;
  }

  void init_nonculled_list(void) {
    l3d_polygon_3d_node *prev=NULL;

    polygon_node_pool.num_items = 0;
    for (int i=0; i<3; i++) {
      if(faces[i]) {
        int next_pool_idx = polygon_node_pool.next_index();
        polygon_node_pool[next_pool_idx].polygon = faces[i];
      }else {
      }
    }

    for(int i=0;i<polygon_node_pool.num_items; i++) {
      polygon_node_pool[i].prev = prev;
      polygon_node_pool[i].next = NULL;
      if (prev) {
        prev->next = &polygon_node_pool[i];
      }
      prev = &polygon_node_pool[i];
    }

    nonculled_polygon_nodes = &polygon_node_pool[0];
```

```
    }

    void place_spike(void) {
      displacement.set(int_to_l3d_real(1000 - (rand() % 2000)),
                       int_to_l3d_real(1000 - (rand() % 2000)),
                       int_to_l3d_real(200),
                       int_to_l3d_real(1));
      velocity.set(int_to_l3d_real(0),
                   int_to_l3d_real(0),
                   int_to_l3d_real(-10-rand()%40),
                   int_to_l3d_real(0));

      l3d_matrix transform;

      transform =
        l3d_mat_translate(displacement.a[0],
                          displacement.a[1],
                          displacement.a[2]);

      transform_stage = 0;
      reset();
      apply_xform(transform);
    }

    void move_spike(void) {
      displacement = displacement + velocity;
    }

    void reset(void) {
      init_nonculled_list();

      vlist->num_varying_items = 0;

      for(register int ivtx=0;
          ivtx<vlist->num_fixed_items;
          ivtx++)
      {
        (*vlist)[ivtx].reset();
      }

      l3d_polygon_3d_node *n;
      n = nonculled_polygon_nodes;
      while(n) {
        n->polygon->init_clip_ivertices();
        n->polygon->init_transformed();
        n=n->next;
      }

      transform_stage = 0;
    }

    void apply_xform(const l3d_matrix & m) {

      transform_stage++;

      l3d_polygon_3d_node *n;
      n = nonculled_polygon_nodes;
      while(n) {
        n->polygon->transform(m, transform_stage);
        n = n->next;
```

```
        }
    }

    void project_spike(void) {

      transform_stage++;

      l3d_polygon_3d_node *n;
      n = nonculled_polygon_nodes;
      while(n) {
        int iv;

        for(iv=0; iv<n->polygon->clip_ivertices->num_items; iv++) {
          if ( (**n->polygon->vlist)[ (*n->polygon->clip_ivertices)[iv].ivertex ].transform_stage !=
transform_stage) {
            (**n->polygon->vlist)[ (*n->polygon->clip_ivertices)[iv].ivertex ].transform_stage =
transform_stage;

            (**n->polygon->vlist)[ (*n->polygon->clip_ivertices)[iv].ivertex ].transformed.X_ =
              l3d_mulri(l3d_mulrr(l3d_divrr( (**n->polygon->vlist)[
(*n->polygon->clip_ivertices)[iv].ivertex ].transformed.X_,
                                            (**n->polygon->vlist)[
(*n->polygon->clip_ivertices)[iv].ivertex ].transformed.Z_),
                                  fovx),
                        xsize)
              +
              int_to_l3d_real(xsize > 1);

            (**n->polygon->vlist)[ (*n->polygon->clip_ivertices)[iv].ivertex ].transformed.Y_ =
              l3d_mulri(l3d_mulrr(l3d_divrr(-(**n->polygon->vlist)[
(*n->polygon->clip_ivertices)[iv].ivertex ].transformed.Y_,
                                             (**n->polygon->vlist)[
(*n->polygon->clip_ivertices)[iv].ivertex ].transformed.Z_),
                                  fovy),
                        ysize)
              +
              int_to_l3d_real(ysize > 1);
          }
        }
        n = n->next;
      }
    }

};

class my_pipeline : public l3d_pipeline {
  protected:
    l3d_rasterizer_2d_imp *ri;
    l3d_rasterizer_2d *r;

    spike spikes[MAXSPIKES];
    long i, j;
    long wc_win_width, wc_win_height, wc_win_dist, fov;
    long wc_win_left, wc_win_top;
    int numspikes;

    virtual int out_of_wc_bounds(l3d_point const &p);

    l3d_camera *camera;
```

```
    public:
      l3d_screen *s;
      int animation;
      my_pipeline(void);
      virtual ~my_pipeline(void);

      void key_event(int ch);  //- from dispatcher
      void update_event(void); //- from dispatcher
      void draw_event(void);   //- from dispatcher
};

my_pipeline::my_pipeline(void) {
  s = factory_manager_v_0_1.screen_factory->create(320,200);
  ri = factory_manager_v_0_1.ras_2d_imp_factory->create(320,200,s->sinfo);
  r = new l3d_rasterizer_2d(ri);

  s->sinfo->ext_max_red =
    s->sinfo->ext_max_green =
      s->sinfo->ext_max_blue =  255;
  s->sinfo->ext_to_native(0,0,0); //- allocate black background color
  red_color = s->sinfo->ext_to_native(255, 0, 0);
  green_color = s->sinfo->ext_to_native(0, 255, 0);
  blue_color = s->sinfo->ext_to_native(0,0, 255);
  s->refresh_palette();

  fovx = float_to_l3d_real(0.5*1.0/tan(50./180. * PI));
  fovy = float_to_l3d_real(0.5*1.0/tan(30./180. * PI));
  xsize = s->xsize;
  ysize = s->ysize;

  numspikes = MAXSPIKES;
  for(i=0; i<MAXSPIKES; i++) {
    spikes[i].place_spike();

    spikes[i].faces[0]->final_color = red_color;
    spikes[i].faces[1]->final_color = green_color;
    spikes[i].faces[2]->final_color = blue_color;
  }

  camera = new l3d_camera;
  camera->fovx = 0.41955;
  camera->near_z = 0.01;
  camera->far_z = 100;

  animation = 1;
}

my_pipeline::~my_pipeline(void) {
  delete s;
  delete ri;
  delete r;
  delete camera;
}

void my_pipeline::key_event(int ch) {
  switch(ch) {
    case 'q': {
        exit(0);
      }
    case 'j':
```

```
    if(camera->rot_VUP_velocity>int_to_l3d_real(-95))
      camera->rot_VUP_velocity -= int_to_l3d_real(5);
    break;
case 'l':
    if(camera->rot_VUP_velocity<int_to_l3d_real( 95))
      camera->rot_VUP_velocity += int_to_l3d_real(5);
    break;
case 'J':
    if(camera->rot_VFW_velocity<int_to_l3d_real( 95))
      camera->rot_VFW_velocity += int_to_l3d_real(5);
    break;
case 'L':
    if(camera->rot_VFW_velocity>int_to_l3d_real(-95))
      camera->rot_VFW_velocity -= int_to_l3d_real(5);
    break;
case 'I':
    if(camera->rot_VRI_velocity<int_to_l3d_real( 95))
      camera->rot_VRI_velocity += int_to_l3d_real(5);
    break;
case 'K':
    if(camera->rot_VRI_velocity>int_to_l3d_real(-95))
      camera->rot_VRI_velocity -= int_to_l3d_real(5);
    break;
case 'k':
    if(camera->VFW_velocity    >int_to_l3d_real(-90))
      camera->VFW_velocity -= camera->VFW_thrust;
    break;
case 'i':
    if(camera->VFW_velocity    <int_to_l3d_real( 90))
      camera->VFW_velocity += camera->VFW_thrust;
    break;
case 's':
    if(camera->VRI_velocity    >int_to_l3d_real(-90))
      camera->VRI_velocity -= camera->VRI_thrust;
    break;
case 'f':
    if(camera->VRI_velocity    <int_to_l3d_real( 90))
      camera->VRI_velocity += camera->VRI_thrust;
    break;
case 'd':
    if(camera->VUP_velocity    >int_to_l3d_real(-90))
      camera->VUP_velocity -= camera->VUP_thrust;
    break;
case 'e':
    if(camera->VUP_velocity    <int_to_l3d_real( 90))
      camera->VUP_velocity += camera->VUP_thrust;
    break;

    //- field-of-view modification
case 'X':
    camera->fovx = camera->fovx + float_to_l3d_real(0.1);
    break;
case 'x':
    camera->fovx = camera->fovx - float_to_l3d_real(0.1);
    break;
case 'Y':
    camera->fovy = camera->fovy + float_to_l3d_real(0.1);
    break;
case 'y':
    camera->fovy = camera->fovy - float_to_l3d_real(0.1);
```

```
      break;

      //- speed
   case 'v': case 'V':
      camera->VUP_thrust += int_to_l3d_real(1.0);
      if(camera->VUP_thrust  > 3.0) {
        camera->VUP_thrust  -= int_to_l3d_real(3.0);
      }
      camera->VFW_thrust = camera->VUP_thrust;
      camera->VRI_thrust = camera->VUP_thrust;
      break;

    case '1':
      animation = 1;
      break;
    case '0':
      animation = 0;
      break;
  }
}

void my_pipeline::update_event() {
  int i;

  camera->update();

  for(i=0;i<numspikes;i++) {

    if(animation) {
      spikes[i].move_spike();
    }
    spikes[i].reset();

    spikes[i].apply_xform(
      l3d_mat_translate(spikes[i].displacement.a[0],
                        spikes[i].displacement.a[1],
                        spikes[i].displacement.a[2])
    );

    //- "transformed" now contains WORLD COORDINATES
    if(out_of_wc_bounds( (*spikes[i].vlist)[0].transformed)
       || out_of_wc_bounds( (*spikes[i].vlist)[1].transformed)
       || out_of_wc_bounds( (*spikes[i].vlist)[2].transformed)
       || out_of_wc_bounds( (*spikes[i].vlist)[3].transformed))
      //- we must check all vertices of the spike since its orientation
      //- is now arbitrary, and any point might be the foremost point
      //- which has now moved out of bounds
    {
      spikes[i].place_spike();
    }

    spikes[i].apply_xform(camera->viewing_xform);
    //- "transformed" now contains VIEW (or CAMERA) COORDINATES

    l3d_polygon_3d_node *n;
    n = spikes[i].nonculled_polygon_nodes;
    while(n) {
      if(n->polygon->clip_near_z(int_to_l3d_real(10)))
      {
```

```
      }else {

        if(n->prev) {
          n->prev->next = n->next;
        }else {
          spikes[i].nonculled_polygon_nodes = n->next;
        }

        if(n->next) {
          n->next->prev = n->prev;
        }
      }
      n = n->next;
    }

  }
}

void my_pipeline::draw_event(void) {
  int i;
  r->clear_buffer();

  for(i=0;i<numspikes;i++) {
    spikes[i].project_spike();

    l3d_polygon_3d_node *n;
    n = spikes[i].nonculled_polygon_nodes;
    while(n) {
      n->polygon->clip_to_polygon_2d(s->view_win);
      l3d_polygon_3d_flatshaded *pflat;
      pflat = dynamic_cast<l3d_polygon_3d_flatshaded *>(n->polygon);
      if(pflat) {
        r->draw_polygon_flatshaded(pflat);
      }
      n = n->next;
    }
  }
  s->blit_screen();
}

int my_pipeline::out_of_wc_bounds(l3d_point const &p) {
  return(p.Z<int_to_l3d_real(1));
}

int main(int argc, char **argv) {
  choose_factories();

  l3d_dispatcher *d;
  my_pipeline *p;

  //- STEP 3: CREATE A DISPATCHER

  d = factory_manager_v_0_1.dispatcher_factory->create();

  //- STEP 4: CREATE A PIPELINE

  //- plug our custom behavior pipeline into the dispatcher
  p = new my_pipeline();
```

```
//- STEP 5: START DISPATCHER

d->pipeline = p; //- polymorphic assignment
d->event_source = p->s;
d->start();

delete d;
delete p;
}
```

Fundamentally, this program works very similarly to its predecessor from Chapter 6, program camspikes. Therefore, let's just focus on the differences between the two programs. The changes all deal with using the new features of 3D polygons we discussed earlier: transformation, surface normals, linked lists of polygons, and near z clipping.

First of all, we have made some small and easy changes. All references to l3d_polygon_2d_flatshaded objects have been replaced with references to l3d_polygon_3d_flatshaded objects; since l3d_polygon_3d_flatshaded inherits from l3d_polygon_2d_flatshaded, this replacement is rather easy. In the spike constructor, we also have changed the spike's geometry to be shorter, so that the effect of near z clipping—the whole point of this program—can be seen more easily.

Changes to the Spike Class

The spike class has undergone some important changes. We have added a linked list pointer nonculled_polygon_nodes and a growable l3d_list of l3d_polygon_nodes.

```
class spike {
public:

    l3d_polygon_3d_node *nonculled_polygon_nodes;
    l3d_list<l3d_polygon_3d_node> polygon_node_pool;
```

The idea is the following. A spike object consists of polygons, but any number of these polygons might be completely clipped away due to a near z clip operation. As we mentioned earlier in the discussion of linked lists of polygons, an efficient way to keep track of which polygons require further processing and which do not is to use a linked list of polygon nodes, simply removing a node from the list as soon as its corresponding polygon has been completely clipped away. We allocate a pool of polygon nodes, one for each polygon in the spike, and at the beginning of a frame, we insert all of these nodes from the pool into a linked list. As we perform successive clipping operations, some polygons might disappear completely. If they do, we simply remove them from the linked list, for this frame. After the frame is drawn and when processing begins for the next frame, we again copy all polygons from the pool into the linked list, and remove them from the list as necessary.

Specifically, the polygon_node_pool is the pool of polygon nodes described above. It is a standard growable l3d_list of l3d_polygon_node objects. Each polygon in the spike requires one corresponding l3d_polygon_node in the pool. The routine init_nonculled_list ensures this simply by accessing one element in the pool for each polygon; the list grows automatically if necessary to accommodate all accessed entries. If the list is already large enough, it does not grow, and the existing node entries are reused.

```
polygon_node_pool.num_items = 0;
```

```
for (int i=0; i<3; i++) {
  if(faces[i]) {
    int next_pool_idx = polygon_node_pool.next_index();
    polygon_node_pool[next_pool_idx].polygon = faces[i];
  }else {
  }
}
```

After ensuring that each polygon has a node in the pool, we then create a linked list of polygon nodes by linking all the nodes together: we assign the `prev` and `next` members of each node to point to the previous or next member in the pool. Finally, we assign the linked list pointer `nonculled_polygon_nodes` to point to the first node in the linked list.

```
for(int i=0;i<polygon_node_pool.num_items; i++) {
  polygon_node_pool[i].prev = prev;
  polygon_node_pool[i].next = NULL;
  if (prev) {
    prev->next = &polygon_node_pool[i];
  }
  prev = &polygon_node_pool[i];
}

nonculled_polygon_nodes = &polygon_node_pool[0];
```

At this point, `nonculled_polygon_nodes` points to the head element of a linked list of polygon nodes, with one node for each polygon in the spike object. During clipping operations, we might discard a polygon completely, in which case we simply remove the polygon from the linked list by assigning the `next` and `prev` members of the surrounding nodes to point around the removed polygon node. After drawing the current frame and before beginning to process the next frame, we call `init_nonculled_list` again, to reset the linked list to once again contain all polygon nodes.

NOTE The names of the linked list variables refer to non-culled polygons instead of non-clipped polygons. This is because in general, a polygon might be discarded (culled) for reasons other than just near z plane clipping. The companion book *Advanced Linux 3D Graphics Programming* discusses culling schemes in more detail. Using the term "culled" for the linked list of polygons points out that the linked list structure is useful for removing polygons, for whatever culling reason, from further consideration.

We have also added a new variable `transform_stage` to the `spike` class. Just as a polygon can have a transformation stage, we now allow a spike (a collection of polygons) to have a transformation stage. This transformation stage for the entire spike represents the transformation stage to which all non-culled polygons belonging to the spike should be brought. In turn, the polygons should ensure that all of their vertices are brought to the transformation stage of the polygon. Ultimately, as we saw in Chapters 2 and 6, the `l3d_coordinate::transform` method checks the `transform_stage` variable of the `l3d_coordinate`, and applies the given transformation m to the coordinate if the coordinate is not already at the proper transformation stage.

Accordingly, the `apply_xform` method of the spike has also been changed to make use of the transformation stage variable. Previously, `apply_xform` simply blindly applied the given transformation matrix m to all points of the spike. Now, however, `apply_xform` increases the spike's `transform_stage` counter, because a new transformation is being applied, then forwards the transformation request along with the transformation stage on to all of the polygon objects in the `nonculled_polygon_list`. This implies that already culled polygons, which have been taken out of the list, are not transformed at all, which is exactly what we want. Each non-culled polygon is then asked to transform itself by using the transformation matrix m and the current transformation stage passed in parameter `count`. In this program, each polygon is a 3D polygon, which transforms itself by transforming all of its vertices and also the base and tip points of the surface normal vector. Already transformed points, as determined by comparing the point's `transform_stage` with the `count` parameter, are not transformed a second time.

The `project_spike` routine has undergone similar changes. Instead of blindly projecting all vertices as we did earlier, we now increase the transformation stage of the spike, loop through all non-culled polygons (not all vertices), and for all vertices of each non-culled polygon, we transform the vertex by calling `l3d_coordinate::transform`, which takes care of checking the vertex to see if it has already been transformed, and transforming it if necessary.

The `reset` method, which as we saw in Chapter 6 resets the spike's vertices to the original untransformed positions, has been extended to reset the additional 3D attributes we have added to the spike class. First of all, we call `init_nonculled_list` to copy all polygon nodes belonging to the spike back into the linked list `nonculled_polygon_list`; due to clipping operations, we might have removed some polygons from this list. Next, we set `num_varying_items` of the vertex list back to zero; this effectively deletes any clipping vertices which might have been generated from a previous clip operation. Next, we reset each vertex, which copies the original location into the transformed location. Then, for each polygon, we call `init_clip_ivertices` to copy the original, permanent vertex index list into the clip vertex index list, where it may be freely modified by clipping operations. We also call `init_transformed` for each polygon, to allow the polygon to reset any information it needs to reset—in this case, the 3D polygon must reset the base and tip points of the surface normal vector (method `l3d_polygon_3d::init_transformed`). Finally, we set the `transform_stage` for the entire spike to be 0. After all of these operations, the spike, all of its vertices, and all of its polygons have been reset to their initial, untransformed position and orientation in object coordinates, and we may begin transformation and clipping operations as usual.

 TIP Notice that the `transform_stage` variable, the `apply_xform` method, and the `reset` method taken together all follow the steps outlined in the section titled "Step-by-Step Guide to Transforming 3D Polygons." These new variables and methods encapsulate the functionality needed to transform 3D polygons as described earlier. We use the same basic framework for transforming 3D polygons when we develop the general l3d class for 3D polygonal objects, `l3d_object`.

Changes to the Pipeline Class

The pipeline class in the `clipz` program has also undergone some changes from the `camspikes` program. The most significant change is in the `update` method, which now performs the near z clipping operation. The following code performs the near z clip.

```
l3d_polygon_3d_node *n;
n = spikes[i].nonculled_polygon_nodes;
```

```
while(n) {
  if(n->polygon->clip_near_z(int_to_l3d_real(10)))
  {
  }else {

    if(n->prev) {
      n->prev->next = n->next;
    }else {
      spikes[i].nonculled_polygon_nodes = n->next;
    }

    if(n->next) {
      n->next->prev = n->prev;
    }
  }
  n = n->next;
}
```

We begin with a pointer to the non-culled polygon list of the spike object. For each polygon in this linked list, we try to clip it against the near *z* plane using the `clip_near_z` method of the polygon. If this routine returns 0, the polygon was completely clipped away, and we simply remove it from the list by redirecting the previous and next nodes around the removed node.

The `my_pipeline::draw_event` method is simpler than its counterpart in the previous program `camspikes`. In particular, we no longer need to do a camera space test to see if the spike is in front of the camera. Because we have performed near *z* plane clipping, we know that polygons that are still in the non-culled list must be in front of the camera; otherwise, they would have been clipped away completely by the near *z* plane and thus removed from the non-culled list. So, for each spike, we perform perspective projection of all vertices belonging to all polygons in the non-culled list, then we loop through the non-culled polygon list, clip the projected polygon against the 2D view window, and finally draw the polygon.

Summary

With this program we have seen a simple example of using the `l3d_polygon_3d` class. This sample program illustrated the use of linked lists of polygons, transformation stages, and near *z* clipping. It did not yet, however, illustrate use of the surface normal; applications of the surface normal (such as back-face culling and lighting) appear in the companion book *Advanced Linux 3D Graphics Programming*.

Grouping Polygons into Objects

Since Chapter 5, some sample programs have declared ad hoc classes for storing groups of polygons to form objects. Since this book deals primarily with polygonal 3D graphics, it makes sense to try to abstract the common ideas from these classes into a general, reusable class for storing polygonal objects.

We call a group of 3D polygons a *3D object*, or just *object* for short. Do not confuse this term with the object-oriented meaning of the word "object" (an instance of a class).

Creating a generally reusable 3D object class allows us to collect the common attributes and operations on 3D objects into one convenient package. We can then subclass a 3D object to add special attributes or behaviors. The idea is that we create, position, and communicate with a number of autonomous, self-updating 3D objects in order to define and interact with a virtual 3D world. In a space combat simulator, for instance, the spaceships and the photon torpedoes would be modeled as instances of a 3D object class, with different geometry and behaviors defined. The spaceship objects would know how to rotate, move, and fire torpedoes; the torpedo objects would know how to move along a particular trajectory and how to explode upon impact. As we see later, we can redefine the geometry and behavior of a 3D object either by declaring a subclass or by writing a plug-in.

The class for 3D objects, then, is an important building block for our interactive 3D applications, at a level of abstraction higher than the level of raw, ungrouped polygons. Let's now look at this class in detail: class l3d_object.

The l3d_object Class

The class l3d_object is a group of 3D polygons forming a logical whole. Listings 7-6 and 7-7 present the class l3d_object.

Listing 7-6: object3d.h

```
#ifndef __OBJECT3D_H
#define __OBJECT3D_H
#include "../../tool_os/memman.h"

#include "../../system/sys_dep.h"
#include "../../view/camera.h"
#include "../../math/matrix.h"
#include "../texture/texture.h"
#include "../polygon/poly3.h"
#include "../../datastr/list.h"
#include "../point/point.h"
#include "../../dynamics/plugins/plugload.h"

#define MAX_XFORMS 7

class l3d_object
{

  public:

    l3d_object(int num_fixed_vertices);
    char name[80];
    virtual ~l3d_object(void);
    l3d_object& operator= (const l3d_object &r);

    l3d_object *parent;

    virtual int update(void);

    l3d_matrix modeling_xform;
    l3d_matrix modeling_xforms[MAX_XFORMS];
    int num_xforms;
```

```
    l3d_two_part_list<l3d_coordinate> *vertices;

    l3d_list<l3d_polygon_3d *> polygons;
    l3d_list<l3d_polygon_3d_node> polygon_node_pool;
    l3d_polygon_3d_node *nonculled_polygon_nodes;

    void init_nonculled_list(void);

    int transform_stage;

    virtual void reset(void);
    virtual void transform(const l3d_matrix &m);
    void after_camera_transform(void)
    {

      l3d_polygon_3d_node *n = nonculled_polygon_nodes;
      while(n) {
        for(register int i=0; i<n->polygon->clip_ivertices->num_items; i++) {
          {
            (**n->polygon->vlist)[ (*n->polygon->clip_ivertices)[i].ivertex ]
            .transformed_intermediates[1] =
              (**n->polygon->vlist)[ (*n->polygon->clip_ivertices)[i].ivertex ]
              .transformed;
          }
        }

        n = n->next;
      }

      n = nonculled_polygon_nodes;
      while(n) {
        n->polygon->after_camera_transform();

        n = n->next;
      }

    }

    void camera_transform(l3d_matrix const &m) {

      transform(m);
      after_camera_transform();
    }

    void apply_perspective_projection
    (const l3d_camera &aCamera, int xsize, int ysize);

    char plugin_name[1024];
    l3d_plugin_loader *plugin_loader;
    void (*plugin_constructor)(l3d_object *target, void *data);
    void (*plugin_update)(l3d_object *target);
    void (*plugin_destructor)(l3d_object *target);
    void (*plugin_copy_data)(const l3d_object *target,l3d_object *copy_target);
    void *plugin_data;
};

inline void l3d_object::apply_perspective_projection(const l3d_camera &aCamera,
    int xsize, int ysize)
{
```

```
        transform_stage++;

        l3d_polygon_3d_node *n = nonculled_polygon_nodes;
        while(n) {
          for(register int i=0; i<n->polygon->clip_ivertices->num_items; i++) {

            if ((**(n->polygon->vlist))[(*n->polygon->clip_ivertices)[i].ivertex].
                transform_stage != transform_stage )
            {
              l3d_point *v;
              v = & ( (**(n->polygon->vlist))
                      [(*n->polygon->clip_ivertices)[i].ivertex ].transformed );

#define COORD ( (**(n->polygon->vlist)) [(*n->polygon->clip_ivertices)[i].ivertex ] )

              (**(n->polygon->vlist))[(*n->polygon->clip_ivertices)[i].ivertex ].
              transform_stage = transform_stage;

              v->X_  = l3d_mulri(l3d_divrr(l3d_mulrr(v->X_,
                                                    /* TIMES */ aCamera.fovx),
                                          /* DIVBY */ v->Z_),
                              /* TIMES */ xsize) + int_to_l3d_real(xsize>1);
              v->Y_ = int_to_l3d_real(ysize>1) -
                      l3d_mulrr(l3d_divrr(l3d_mulrr(v->Y_,
                                                    aCamera.fovy),
                                        v->Z_)  ,
                              ysize) ;

            }
          }
          n = n->next;
        }
      }

      #endif
```

Listing 7-7: `object3d.cc`

```
      #include <stdio.h>
      #include <stdlib.h>
      #include "object3d.h"
      #include "../../view/camera.h"
      #include "../../tool_os/memman.h"

      l3d_object::l3d_object(int num_fixed_vertices) {

        vertices = new l3d_two_part_list<l3d_coordinate> ( num_fixed_vertices );

        nonculled_polygon_nodes = NULL;

        transform_stage = 0;
        num_xforms = 0;

        parent = NULL;

        plugin_constructor = NULL;
        plugin_update = NULL;
        plugin_destructor = NULL;
      }


      l3d_object & l3d_object::operator= (const l3d_object &r) {
```

```
      strcpy(name, r.name);
      parent = r.parent;

      num_xforms = r.num_xforms;
      modeling_xform = r.modeling_xform;
      for(int i=0; i<r.num_xforms; i++) {
        modeling_xforms[i] = r.modeling_xforms[i];
      }


      *vertices = *r.vertices; //- copy list and contents, not just pointer to list

      polygons = r.polygons;
      for(int i=0; i<r.polygons.num_items; i++) {
        l3d_polygon_3d *p = dynamic_cast<l3d_polygon_3d *>(r.polygons[i]->clone());
        if(p) {
          p->vlist = &vertices;
          polygons[i] = p;
        }else {
          printf("error during cloning: somehow a non-3d polygon is in an object!");
        }
      }

      polygon_node_pool = r.polygon_node_pool;

      //- nonculled_polygon_nodes points to a polygon node in the polygon
      //- node pool. since we are making a copy, we have to point to the
      //- *corresponding* entry in the *new* node pool, which means we have to
      //- find the INDEX of the entry in the original list.

      nonculled_polygon_nodes = NULL;
      for(int i=0; i<r.polygon_node_pool.num_items; i++) {
        if(r.nonculled_polygon_nodes == &r.polygon_node_pool[i]) {
          nonculled_polygon_nodes = &polygon_node_pool[i];
        }
      }

      transform_stage = r.transform_stage;
      strcpy(plugin_name, r.plugin_name);
      if(r.plugin_loader) {
        plugin_loader = r.plugin_loader->clone();
      }else {
        plugin_loader = NULL;
      }
      plugin_constructor = r.plugin_constructor;
      plugin_update = r.plugin_update;
      plugin_destructor = r.plugin_destructor;
      plugin_copy_data = r.plugin_copy_data;
      if(r.plugin_copy_data) {
        (*r.plugin_copy_data)(&r, this);
      }else {
        plugin_data = NULL;
      }

      return *this;
    }

    void l3d_object::init_nonculled_list(void) {
      l3d_polygon_3d_node *prev=NULL;

      polygon_node_pool.num_items = 0;
```

```
    for (int i=0; i<polygons.num_items; i++) {
      if(polygons[i]) {
        int next_pool_idx = polygon_node_pool.next_index();
        polygon_node_pool[next_pool_idx].polygon = polygons[i];
      }else {
      }
    }

    for(int i=0;i<polygon_node_pool.num_items; i++) {
      polygon_node_pool[i].prev = prev;
      polygon_node_pool[i].next = NULL;
      if (prev) {
        prev->next = &polygon_node_pool[i];
      }
      prev = &polygon_node_pool[i];
    }

    if(polygon_node_pool.num_items > 0) {
      nonculled_polygon_nodes = &polygon_node_pool[0];
    }else {
      nonculled_polygon_nodes = NULL;
    }
}

l3d_object::~l3d_object() {

  for(int i=0; i<polygons.num_items;i++) {
    delete polygons[i];
  }

  if(vertices) delete vertices;

  if(plugin_destructor) {
    (*plugin_destructor)(this);
  }

  if(plugin_loader) {
    plugin_loader->close();
  }

  if(plugin_loader) delete plugin_loader;
}

int l3d_object::update(void) {
  if(plugin_update) {
    (*plugin_update)(this);
  }

  return 1;
}

void l3d_object::transform(const l3d_matrix &m) {

  transform_stage++;

  l3d_polygon_3d_node *n = nonculled_polygon_nodes;

  while(n) {

    n->polygon->transform(m, transform_stage);
```

```
      n = n->next;
    }
  }

void l3d_object::reset(void) {
  init_nonculled_list();
  transform_stage = 0;

  vertices->num_varying_items = 0;

  for(register int ivtx=0;
      ivtx<vertices->num_fixed_items;
      ivtx++)
  {
    (*vertices)[ivtx].reset();
  }

  l3d_polygon_3d_node *n;
  n = nonculled_polygon_nodes;
  while(n) {
    n->polygon->init_clip_ivertices();
    n->polygon->init_transformed();
    n=n->next;
  }
}
```

Most of the class l3d_object is a generalization of the concepts we have already seen from the spike class in the previous sample program clipz. Let's now look at the members and methods of an l3d_object.

Creating and Copying 3D Objects

The l3d_object constructor takes a single integer parameter representing the number of fixed vertices belonging to the object. The vertices of the object are defined in an l3d_two_part_list, which needs to know how much space to allocate for the fixed and varying parts of the list, hence the need for a parameter in the constructor.

The member variable name allows us to save a character string with this object which lets us later search for an object by name in a larger list of many objects.

The overridden operator= allows us to completely copy the contents of one l3d_object into another. The idea is that if we wish to split an object into two halves, we can easily do so by copying the object, cutting away one half of one object, and cutting away the other half of the other object. The result is two objects which, together, have the same shape as the original object, but which are completely separate. Recall that the reason for the existence of the l3d_polygon_2d::clone method (Chapter 3) is the same: to allow for splitting a polygon into two pieces. Since an object is a collection of polygons, it should come as no surprise that the l3d_object::operator= calls the virtual method l3d_polygon_2d::clone to clone all of the object's polygons. Later in this chapter we see how to split a polygon or an entire polygonal object into two (or more) pieces.

Defining the Geometry of a 3D Object

Seen purely geometrically, a 3D object is a collection of 3D polygons. (3D objects also have behavior, but we cover that later.) After creating an l3d_object with the constructor, the object initially has no geometry defined. The purpose of the following member variables and methods is to allow the definition of polygonal geometry in a 3D object.

Defining Vertices

The first step in defining the geometry of a 3D object is to define a list of vertices in 3D. The variable vertices is a pointer to a two-part list of l3d_coordinate objects. The l3d_object constructor creates the two-part list at object creation time, with the fixed part of the list having the number of vertices specified by the constructor parameter. Recall that the fixed part of the list stores the permanent definition of the vertices; the varying part of the vertex list is temporary storage for new vertices created during an analytical clipping operation. The l3d_object destructor deletes the list. Because the size of the fixed part of the vertex list depends on the parameter passed to the constructor, it is not possible to allocate the vertex list statically; a static allocation would most likely have either too few or too many fixed vertices. Too many fixed vertices would only waste space, but too few would be a disaster, as clipping operations would then overwrite the original vertices with new clip vertices, irrevocably destroying the original geometry after a clip operation. For this reason, we allocate the vertex list vertices dynamically, and the variable vertices is a pointer to the list and not the list itself.

Therefore, when an l3d_object is created, the vertex list is also automatically created. We should then fill this vertex list with all vertices needed by all polygons forming the object. This is the same approach we have been taking with the sample programs in Chapter 5 and 6: the spike object declares one list of vertices, which are then referenced by all polygons belonging to the spike. File formats for saving 3D models also often use such an approach. First the file presents one list of vertices, followed by many polygons defined in terms of the same vertex list. As we see in Chapter 8, the Videoscape file format used by the 3D modeling program Blender has exactly such a format.

We fill in the vertex list by assigning values to the original member of the l3d_coordinate objects. The original member, recall, defines a permanent, never-to-be-changed part of the object geometry, which is exactly what we need to define when initializing a 3D object.

Here is an excerpt from the upcoming sample program, fltsim, which defines the vertex list for a l3d_object descendant. Notice that the constructor calls the base class l3d_object constructor with a parameter of 4, meaning that four fixed vertices will be made available in the vertex list. The derived class constructor then accesses the first four elements of the vertex list, setting the original member of each vertex to be the desired location of the vertex in object coordinates. Notice that since the variable vertices is a pointer to the list, to access the list itself (and the elements within the list), we must reference *vertices and not vertices.

```
pyramid::pyramid(void) :
    l3d_object(4)
{
  (*vertices)[0].original.set
  (float_to_l3d_real(0.),
```

```
float_to_l3d_real(0.),
float_to_l3d_real(0.),
float_to_l3d_real(1.));
(*vertices)[1].original.set
(float_to_l3d_real(10.0),
float_to_l3d_real(0.),
float_to_l3d_real(0.),
float_to_l3d_real(1.));
(*vertices)[2].original.set
(float_to_l3d_real(0.),
float_to_l3d_real(10.),
float_to_l3d_real(0.),
float_to_l3d_real(1.));
(*vertices)[3].original.set
(float_to_l3d_real(0.),
float_to_l3d_real(0.),
float_to_l3d_real(10.),
float_to_l3d_real(1.));
```

Graphically, you can picture the object at this point as in Figure 7-18. We have defined a number of vertices in 3D space and have associated a number with each vertex, representing its position in the list *vertices. However, the vertices are all unconnected at this point. Thus comes the next step: connecting the vertices to form polygons.

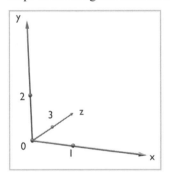

Figure 7-18: After defining the vertex list, the object may be seen as a set of unconnected points in 3D space.

Defining Polygons

After filling in the vertex list as described above, we can then create an arbitrary number of 3D polygons defined in terms of these vertices. The variable polygons is a list of pointers to the 3D polygons making up the 3D object. This list is a normal growable l3d_list object, meaning that the rules for accessing the list, described in Chapter 3, still apply. In particular, we should remember to call next_index on the list to get the next free index in the list, since this also allows the list to grow automatically if necessary.

To insert a polygon into the list, we carry out the following steps.

1. Retrieve the next free index in the polygon list by calling polygons.next_index. Let us call this new free index pi.

2. Create a new polygon object with new, and assign a pointer to this new polygon object to polygons[pi], the next element of the list. Let us call a pointer to the new polygon p.

3.   Assign the polygon's pointer to a pointer to a vertex list to point to the `vertices` member of the 3D object. The statement `p->vlist=&vertices` accomplishes this. See Chapter 3 for an explanation of why the `vlist` member of the polygon is a pointer to a pointer to a vertex list.

4.   Define the polygon in terms of indices into the vertex list. Do this by fetching the next free index from the vertex index list with `p->ivertices->next_index`. Let us call this next free index `i`. Then, assign an integer value to the `(*p->ivertices)[i].ivertex`. The integer value is the integer index of the desired vertex in the vertex array accessed through `p->vlist`. Continue assigning entries in the `ivertices` list until all vertices of the polygon have been defined. The order of the entries in the `ivertices` list is very important! According to our left-handed rule, the order of the entries in `ivertices` must correspond to a clockwise list of the polygon's vertices when looking at the front face of the polygon (the front face of a polygon, recall, is the face on the side of the polygon in the direction which the normal vector points).

5.   Call `p->compute_center` and `p->compute_sfcnormal` to compute the base and tip points of the surface normal vector.

NOTE   In the companion book *Advanced Linux 3D Graphics Programming*, where we deal with texture mapped and light mapped polygons, we will perform additional initialization steps to initialize the texture space of each polygon.

Step 4 above, the definition of the polygon in terms of a vertex index list, warrants a bit more attention. In particular, as noted, we should make sure to specify the vertex indices in the correct order when defining our polygons. If we specify the vertices in the incorrect order, then our polygon might face in the wrong direction. See Figures 7-19 and 7-20 for an illustration of this problem. In Figure 7-19, we have a polygon whose surface normal and front side are pointing upwards. Therefore, in the figure, we are looking at the front side of the polygon. As we said, the correct order in the vertex index list is clockwise when looking at the front face of the polygon. So this upward-facing polygon can be defined as any of the following vertex index lists: [0,3,1], [3,1,0], or [1,0,3]. All of these orderings of the vertex indices are clockwise when looking at the front side of the polygon.

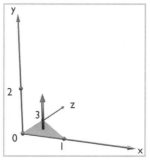

Figure 7-19: Defining a polygon. This upward-facing polygon may be defined as the vertex index list [0,3,1], [3,1,0], or [1,0,3].

On the other hand, let us say we want to define the polygon to face downwards, as in Figure 7-20. In this figure, the vertex normal and therefore the front face of the polygon are facing downwards. Thus, in the figure we are looking at the back side of the polygon, not the front side! But the polygon definition relies upon us looking at the front side of the polygon. Therefore, it is helpful to imagine seeing the polygon from its front side, as depicted in Figure 7-21. In this figure, we are looking at the same downward-facing polygon, but from its front side. Now, it is clear what the order of the vertex indices must be: any clockwise ordering, when looking at the polygon's front face, is valid. The valid definitions of this polygon are [3,0,1], [0,1,3], or [1,3,0].

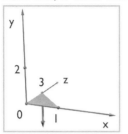

Figure 7-20: This downward-facing polygon may be defined as the vertex index list [3,0,1], [0,1,3], or [1,3,0].

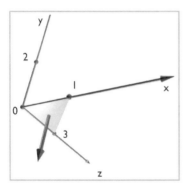

Figure 7-21: Looking at the downward-facing polygon from the bottom side makes it easier to understand the vertex ordering.

Now that we're clear on vertex ordering, let's look at some other members of the class `l3d_object` which also deal with polygons.

Class `l3d_object` defines a linked list of polygons in order to eliminate completely clipped away polygons from further processing in a particular frame. The member variables `polygon_node_pool` and `nonculled_polygon_nodes` form this linked list, just as we saw in the `spike` class of the `clipz` program. The function `init_nonculled_list`, called at the beginning of each frame, ensures that each polygon in the `polygons` list has a node in the pool, then links all nodes together into a complete linked list and points the pointer `nonculled_polygon_nodes` to the first element of the list.

 TIP The `polygons` list, of type `l3d_list`, always contains all polygons for the object, and is the "permanent" list of polygons forming the 3D object. The linked list `nonculled_poly-gon_nodes`, on the other hand, is a temporary list of polygons which have not been culled away for the current frame. `nonculled_polygon_nodes` initially contains all polygons for the object (at the beginning of each frame), but after clipping operations may contain fewer polygons if any were clipped away completely. The relationship between the two polygon lists `polygons` and `nonculled_polygon_nodes` can be likened to the relationship between the two vertex index lists `ivertices` and `clip_ivertices`, which we saw in Chapter 3.

The member variable `parent` is a pointer to another `l3d_object`. This allows for hierarchical modeling of 3D objects, where objects "belong to" or are contained within other objects. The companion book *Advanced Linux 3D Graphics Programming* presents an example of this, where we assign 3D objects to rooms in a portal engine. In this case, the parent of each contained object is the room object.

Specifying Transformations

Just as we can transform individual polygons in 3D, we also want to be able to transform entire polygonal objects. Transforming a 3D object transforms all of its polygons and any additional 3D attributes belonging to the entire object. Class `l3d_object` contains a number of member variables and functions to specify transformations for the 3D object.

As we saw earlier, transforming 3D polygons is complicated due to a number of factors: original and transformed positions, transformation stages, shared vertex lists, vertex index lists in both original and clipped form, surface normal data, and the special significance of the camera transformation. The goal of the `l3d_object` transformation functions is to try to encapsulate the complicated transformation process into an easy-to-use interface.

The `l3d_object` transformation methods follow the same structure for transformations presented in the sample program `clipz`. Specifically, we introduce a transformation counter `transform_stage` to keep track of the transformation stage for the entire object. The method `reset` resets the entire object back into a non-clipped and untransformed state: it sets transformation stage to 0, copies all polygons into the non-culled linked list, deletes all temporary clip vertices from the vertex list, resets all vertices to their original positions, and resets all polygons (including surface normal or other information) to their original positions.

The method `transform` increases `transform_stage` and applies the supplied transformation matrix to all non-culled polygons in the object, by traversing the `nonculled_polygon_nodes` list. The method `apply_perspective_projection` similarly increases the transformation stage, then transforms all vertices of all surviving polygons by applying the perspective projection of Chapter 5.

NOTE It is also possible to implement the perspective projection via a matrix multiplication with the perspective transformation matrix presented in Chapter 6. In this case, you can forget about the method `apply_perspective_projection`. But, if you use the perspective transformation matrix, the w component of the resulting point after multiplication with the matrix will not be 1. This means that after the transformation with the perspective matrix, you must homogenize the point by dividing all of its components (x, y, z, and w) by the w component. With a perspective projection matrix, the value of w is equal to the value of the original z coordinate (or some constant multiple thereof), meaning that a division by w effectively divides by the 3D z coordinate, thereby effecting the perspective projection. At the end you should have a point of the form $[x,y,z,1]^T$, where x and y are the screen coordinates of the projected point, and z is either a constant or a 1/z "screen-z" value, depending on whether you used a non-invertible flattening perspective matrix or the depth-preserving version.

We noted earlier the importance of the camera transformation, and that 3D polygons provide the methods `camera_transform` and `after_camera_transform` to enable any special processing immediately after application of the camera transform. Similarly, class `l3d_object` offers the methods `camera_transform` and `after_camera_transform`. We call `l3d_object::camera_transform` instead of `l3d_object::transform` if the transformation matrix being passed is the camera transform. This simply calls `l3d_object::transform` followed by a call to `l3d_object::after_camera_transform`, which then saves the camera space coordinates of all polygons in transformed intermediate number 1. Furthermore, `l3d_object::after_camera_transform` calls `l3d_polygon_3d::after_camera_transform` for each non-culled polygon in the object, thereby allowing the non-culled polygons also to perform any polygon-specific processing with the camera space coordinates.

Finally, a 3D object provides storage space for a number of transformation matrices (the exact number is controlled by the `#define MAX_XFORMS`). By storing a number of separate transformation matrices with a 3D object, we can support the idea of successive or hierarchical transformations, as explained in Chapter 6. The matrix array `modeling_xforms` contains the separate modeling transformations to be applied to the object, and the counter `num_xforms` is the number of transformations.

The single matrix `modeling_xform` represents a concatenation (i.e., multiplication) of all matrices in the `modeling_xforms` array. By convention, we define that the single matrix `modeling_xform` must always be kept up to date; if any code changes the contents of the `modeling_xforms` array, it must also immediately update the single `modeling_xform` array by re-multiplying all matrices in the array. This convention allows us always to transform the object from object coordinates into world coordinates via a single matrix multiplication with matrix `modeling_xform`. The alternative would have been to always require calling code to concatenate all matrices in the object's matrix array, which would likely be more inefficient because we would then always be multiplying all matrices in the matrix array even if no entries had changed. By requiring that any change to the matrix array immediately update the single composite transformation matrix, we only remultiply the matrices when we need to and always have a single matrix representing the entire transformation.

 NOTE By appropriately defining accessor functions on the matrix, we could also store a "dirty" flag with the matrix, indicating whether the individual component matrices are newer than the composite matrix. Then, when accessing the composite matrix, if the dirty flag is set, we recompute the matrix and reset the dirty flag to be false. This recomputes the composite matrix at the last possible moment.

Implicit Position and Orientation

Class `l3d_object` does not explicitly store position and orientation as in the class `l3d_moveable`, but instead takes a different approach and uses the composite transformation matrix as a coordinate system. The first three columns of the composite transformation matrix therefore represent the VRI, VUP, and VFW vectors; the last column represents the point VRP. We could store this information explicitly in class `l3d_object`, but this would be redundant because, as we saw at the end of Chapter 6, the matrix itself implicitly contains the position and orientation of the object. The companion book *Advanced Linux 3D Graphics Programming* presents an example of a plug-in object (the "seeker" object) which extracts its position and orientation from the composite transformation matrix.

Inheritable Behavior

The `l3d_object` member variables and methods we have looked at so far all deal with an essentially static view of the 3D object. But, an object which doesn't move or change in any way isn't very interesting. The virtual method `update`, therefore, provides a means for an object to change itself autonomously. By declaring subclasses of `l3d_object`, we can override the virtual `update` method to perform any sort of update appropriate to the object class. For instance, a car class might update itself by changing its position to move along its forward vector; a balloon class might update itself by moving upward along the world's y axis. Such changes are typically done by changing one or more of the transformation matrices in the `modeling_xforms` array. Remember, if you make any changes to this array, you must also immediately update the composite `modeling_xform` array by multiplying all of the `modeling_xforms` together.

The main program loop should periodically call `update` on all objects which are allowed to change themselves at a particular point in time. This function call is virtual, and is bound at run time to the appropriate `update` method of the actual object being accessed. Each object then updates itself—perhaps by changing its position, orientation, velocity, or shape. This leads to a natural modeling of our virtual world: we populate the world with objects, and the objects know how to update themselves. This also leads to a maintainable code structure: instead of having one humongous, global update function sticking its fingers into every object and manipulating everyone's vertices, vectors, and velocities, we have a clean division of labor where each object type is responsible for its own behavior and no one else's.

By default the `l3d_object::update` method effectively does nothing. We say "effectively" because what it actually does is try to call a plug-in, if one is attached to the object. By default, no plug-in is attached to the object, and thus the `l3d_object::update` method does nothing. To associate some interesting behavior with an object, we can create a new subclass of `l3d_object` and override `update` to do something more interesting.

While extending behavior through subclassing is a key object-oriented technique, it is not without disadvantages. If we create a new subclass, we must then modify our program to create an instance of the new subclass and must recompile the program. An interesting alternative to this, which we just alluded to, is a plug-in system. This allows the introduction of new object types and behaviors into a program without recompiling the original program. Let's look at this technique in more detail.

Plug-in Behavior

In general, a *plug-in* is a program module which is developed separately from and usually long after the existence of a separate host program. The plug-in program module extends the functionality of the host program in new ways which might not have been foreseen by the original creators of the host program. The interesting requirement for a host program supporting plug-ins is that it must be able to run with program modules whose existence and type are specified completely dynamically at run time.

What we'd like to do now is develop a plug-in system for 3D objects. By this we mean that we would like to compile a program which is then able to dynamically load an arbitrary plug-in at run time, and to associate the program code in the plug-in with an `l3d_object`. In this way, the `l3d_object` is defined completely in terms of the plug-in, meaning essentially that we have "plugged in" a new object into our application program. The attraction of this approach is that it truly requires no change to the host program; new object types can be developed separately as plug-ins and can be imported into our virtual world at run time.

 NOTE An alternative to plug-in systems is offered by *scripting* systems. With a scripting system, we control a 3D object by writing a small program in a custom scripting language. The script, which is evaluated at run time by a script interpreter within the host program, then controls the appearance and behavior of the 3D object. You can think of a scripting system as a plug-in system where the plug-in data is the source code of the script.

Thankfully, the Linux operating system offers support for dynamic libraries, meaning that an object file can be loaded at run time, and the symbols in the object file can then be accessed exactly as if they were part of the original program. This is the key to creating a plug-in system. We define a plug-in interface as a small set of function signatures (function names and parameter lists). Writing a plug-in then amounts to writing a small C file, with no main function, which implements exactly the functions in the plug-in interface. The plug-in source file is compiled not into an executable file, but instead into a special dynamic library or shared object file, with the file extension of `.so`.

Then, at run time, we can load a plug-in (through the operating system routine `dlopen`, covered later in this section) by specifying the filename of its shared object file. We load the object file and dynamically bind the functions in the object file into the address space of the program—actually a rather impressive feat, if you stop and think about it. At this point, the host program can call the functions defined in the shared object file exactly as if they had been defined in the host program itself.

Therefore, we can (and will) create a plug-in system for 3D objects according to the following plan.

1. Define a series of functions through which a host program can create, update, copy, and destroy plug-in 3D objects.
2. Declare pointers to these functions, and to any data required by these functions, in the `l3d_object` class.
3. Write a plug-in and compile it into a dynamic library file.
4. Provide a plug-in loader which calls the operating system routines to load the shared object file from disk and which binds the functions in the shared object file to the function pointers in the `l3d_object` class.

The 3D Object Plug-in Interface

For plug-in 3D objects, we essentially need to perform four operations on the plug-in: create, update, copy, and destroy it. Therefore, we define our plug-in interface in terms of the following four functions.

- `void constructor(l3d_object *target, void *data)`
- `void update(l3d_object *target)`
- `void copy_data(const l3d_object *target, l3d_object *copy_target)`
- `void destructor(l3d_object *target)`

Notice that these are plain C functions, not C++ member functions. The reason for this is that the Linux dynamic library mechanism (as well as most other dynamic library mechanisms on other operating systems) has much better support for C functions than C++ member functions. All sorts of ugly issues, such as name mangling, crop up when trying to export C++ member functions. Since we are restricting ourselves to plain C functions, and since the plug-in functions are meant to alter the appearance and behavior of an instance of type `l3d_object`, the plug-in functions somehow need to access the memory of the `l3d_object` object which they are supposed to modify. This is the purpose of the parameter `target` in each of the plug-in functions; `target` points to the `l3d_object` which the plug-in function should modify. This is incidentally the same reason that C++ member functions all have a hidden `this` parameter.

We use the plug-in system by creating an empty `l3d_object`, and then calling the plug-in functions to let the plug-in initialize and change the object. Therefore, the first step before calling any plug-in functions is to create an empty `l3d_object` and save a pointer to it. Then, we pass this pointer to all plug-in functions.

The plug-in function `constructor` should be called with an empty `l3d_object`. This function should initialize the data in the `l3d_object`, typically by defining vertices and polygons. The `data` parameter is a void pointer to any data that the plug-in needs from an external source in order to initialize the object properly, similar to the way that we pass parameters to a normal C++ constructor in order to tell the constructor any information necessary to create the object. In C++ we can declare any number of different constructors to initialize an object based on different input parameters, but with a plug-in interface we cannot dynamically declare new constructor functions. Therefore we must make do with exactly one function, but add a void parameter to allow the calling program to pass any data, cast to a void pointer, to the plug-in constructor. The plug-in constructor must then cast the void pointer back into a pointer to the data type it is expecting, and can then use the data to initialize the object properly. This is, of course, not a type-safe mechanism; if the calling program passes data which is in a different format than is expected by the plug-in constructor, then the program will most likely crash. This is the price of a truly dynamic plug-in system.

The plug-in function `update` is called from `l3d_object::update`, which in turn is called from the main application processing loop. The plug-in function `update` has the same role as the member function `l3d_object::update`; it should update the object in some plug-in specific manner. The plug-in function has a pointer to the object, and so is free to change the object in any way it wishes.

NOTE It is easiest to understand the plug-in system if we restrict the plug-in function to accessing only the public data of the `l3d_object`. So anything that the plug-in needs to change must be declared public. Ways around this would require using friend functions and/or static member functions.

The plug-in function `copy_data` is called from within the `l3d_object` assignment operator. This asks the plug-in to copy its plug-in data from itself into the plug-in object referenced by parameter `copy_target`. In this way, the target of the assignment operation contains an identical copy of the contents of the source. The reason that we ask the plug-in itself to copy the plug-in data is that the plug-in data is only known to the plug-in; externally, it is merely a void pointer to some unknown data. The plug-in itself must cast the void pointer into a meaningful pointer, at which point the plug-in can create another copy of this data to be stored separately in another object.

Finally, the plug-in function `destructor` is called from the `l3d_object` destructor. This allows the plug-in to free any memory it has allocated or to perform any last operations just before the object to which the plug-in functions belong is destroyed.

These four functions define the interface between a program and the functionality stored in an external plug-in. The next step is to declare pointers to the plug-in functions in the `l3d_object` class.

Pointers to the Plug-in Functions and Data

A plug-in is nothing more than a set of functions which are bound at run time to a particular 3D object. Therefore, the 3D object class `l3d_object` must provide function pointers that will point to the functions dynamically loaded out of the plug-in.

The following excerpt from `object3d.h` declares the plug-in function pointers in class `l3d_object`. After loading and binding the plug-in (covered in the next section), we can then call the plug-in routines through these function pointers.

```
void (*plugin_constructor)(l3d_object *target, void *data);
void (*plugin_update)(l3d_object *target);
void (*plugin_destructor)(l3d_object *target);
void (*plugin_copy_data)(const l3d_object *target,l3d_object *copy_target);
void *plugin_data;
```

Notice also the member variable `plugin_data`, which is a void pointer. This pointer is designed to be accessed by the plug-in functions in order to point to any dynamically allocated data which the plug-in might need to use. For instance, say that a plug-in, in its constructor, needs to allocate some memory which will then be used by the plug-in's `update` function. The plug-in function `constructor` can allocate memory with `new` as normal, but the question is, where should the constructor save a pointer to this newly allocated memory, so that later on the `update` function can access it? The answer is to save a pointer to any allocated memory in the `l3d_object` itself, in the member variable `plugin_data`. The plug-in function `copy_data` creates a duplicate of this data; function `destructor` is responsible for deleting any memory allocated in this manner.

Now let's see how we can write a plug-in.

Writing a Plug-in

Writing a plug-in essentially amounts to implementing the main plug-in functions `constructor`, `update`, `copy_data`, and `destructor`. But, there are a few issues which need special attention.

First, we must enclose all of the above plug-in functions within an `extern "C"` block. In other words, before the declaration of these functions we need the line:

```
extern "C" {
```

After the declaration of the three main plug-in functions, we close the `extern "C"` block with a closing brace (}).

The purpose of this `extern "C"` block is to allow exporting of the plug-in function names so that they may be referenced and loaded later. Without `extern C`, the names would be mangled according to the compiler-specific name mangling convention for encoding C++ function arguments within the name, and it would be difficult if not impossible to reference and load the plug-in functions according to their now mangled names.

NOTE You can verify this for yourself by writing a simple one-line C++ program consisting of one empty function. Save the program in `file.cc`. Compile the program to an object file: type **gcc -c file.cc**. This creates the object file `file.o`. Dump all symbols from the object file: type **nm file.o**. Notice that the function name appears, but has been "mangled" to encode the parameters and return type of the function. Now, re-edit `file.cc` and enclose the function within an `extern "C"` block. Recompile the program and re-run nm. Notice that the function name now appears it its original, unmangled form in the object file.

Implementing the plug-in functions is straightforward; you simply program the required functionality in each plug-in function in standard C++. As mentioned earlier, the `constructor` function should initialize the `l3d_object` passed in the `target` parameter, by declaring vertices and polygons and performing any other necessary initialization. The `update` function updates the `target` by changing any attributes of `target` it needs to (shape, location, orientation, speed), and the `destructor` function performs any necessary cleanup. Remember, if the `constructor` needs to allocate any data needed by the `update` function, store a pointer to this data in `target->plugin_data`, so that you can access the data again later.

Compiling a plug-in requires a bit of a change to the compilation process. If we have written a `.cc` file containing the code for the plug-in functions as described above, we first compile this `.cc` file into an `.o` file (a normal object file) as usual. Then, we need to make a dynamic library from this object file. To do this, we invoke the linker g++ on the object file with a command line option of `-shared` and specify the output file with `-o name.so`, where "name" is the desired output filename. This creates a dynamic library from the object file. This dynamic library can then be loaded into a running program with the function call `dlopen`—our next topic.

NOTE See the Makefiles in the directory `$L3D/binaries/linux_x/float/app/lib/dynamics/plugins` to see concrete examples of how plug-ins are compiled.

Classes for Loading Plug-ins

Loading a plug-in means making its symbols (i.e., functions) available for use within the current program. To load plug-ins, we declare an abstract class l3d_plugin_loader, shown in Listing 7-8. We require one plug-in loader object per plug-in. This is because the plug-in loader maintains a handle on the dynamic library file, and separate plug-ins in separate dynamic libraries require separate handles.

This class l3d_plugin_loader contains four pure virtual methods. The method load takes a filename as a parameter and loads the file as a dynamic library, maintaining a handle on the library. The find_symbol method looks for a particular symbol in the dynamic library and returns a pointer to it. In our case, the symbol is a function name, and the returned pointer is a function pointer. The close method releases the handle on the dynamic library. The clone method causes the plug-in loader object to create another copy of itself, which is needed when copying plug-in objects (the new plug-in object should also have its own plug-in loader).

The way we use 3D object plug-ins is to ask the plug-in loader to load the dynamic library file containing the plug-in. Then, we ask the plug-in loader to look for the symbols with the names "constructor," "update," "copy_data," and "destructor." The plug-in loader finds these symbols within the dynamic library and returns pointers to these functions. We assign these pointers to the function pointers we declared in l3d_object: plugin_constructor, plugin_update, plugin_copy_data, and plugin_destructor. After assigning values to the function pointers, we can then call the plug-in functions through the function pointers to invoke the plug-in functionality.

Listing 7-8: plugload.h

```
#ifndef __PLUGLOAD_H
#define __PLUGLOAD_H
#include "../../tool_os/memman.h"

class l3d_plugin_loader {
  public:
    virtual void load(const char *filename)=0;
    virtual void *find_symbol(char *symbol)=0;
    virtual void close(void)=0;
    virtual l3d_plugin_loader *clone(void)=0;
    virtual ~l3d_plugin_loader(void) {};
};

class l3d_plugin_loader_factory {
  public:
    virtual l3d_plugin_loader *create(void) = 0;
};

#endif
```

We also declare a class plugin_loader_factory, to protect application code from needing to create a concrete plug-in loader; application code need only deal with the abstract interface, allowing the factory to deal with the actual concrete type. (See Chapter 2 for an explanation of this factory design pattern.)

The concrete subclass l3d_plugin_loader_linux overrides the virtual methods in l3d_plugin_loader with the Linux-specific operating system calls necessary to realize dynamic loading of symbols. See Listings 7-9 and 7-10.

Listing 7-9: pl_linux.h

```
#ifndef __PL_LINUX_H
#define __PL_LINUX_H
#include "../../tool_os/memman.h"

#include "plugload.h"

class l3d_plugin_loader_linux : public l3d_plugin_loader {
  protected:
    void *handle;
  public:
    char filename[256];
    l3d_plugin_loader_linux(void);
    virtual ~l3d_plugin_loader_linux(void) {};
    void load(const char *filename);
    void *find_symbol(char *symbol);
    void close(void);
    l3d_plugin_loader *clone(void);
};

class l3d_plugin_loader_linux_factory : public l3d_plugin_loader_factory {
  public:
    l3d_plugin_loader *create(void);
};

#endif
```

Listing 7-10: pl_linux.cc

```
#include "pl_linux.h"
#include <dlfcn.h>
#include <stdio.h>
#include <stdlib.h>
#include <string.h>
#include <assert.h>
#include "../../tool_os/memman.h"

l3d_plugin_loader *l3d_plugin_loader_linux_factory::create(void) {
  return new l3d_plugin_loader_linux;
}

l3d_plugin_loader_linux::l3d_plugin_loader_linux(void) {
  filename[0] = '0';
  handle = 0;
}

void l3d_plugin_loader_linux::load(const char *filename) {

  strncpy(this->filename, filename, sizeof(this->filename));
  handle = dlopen(filename, RTLD_LAZY);
  if(!handle) {
    fputs(dlerror(),stderr);
  }
}
```

```
void *l3d_plugin_loader_linux::find_symbol(char *symbol) {

  return dlsym(handle, symbol);
}

void l3d_plugin_loader_linux::close(void) {

  if(handle) {
    dlclose(handle);
  }
}

l3d_plugin_loader * l3d_plugin_loader_linux::clone(void) {

  l3d_plugin_loader_linux *loader;
  loader = new l3d_plugin_loader_linux;
  strncpy(loader->filename, filename, sizeof(loader->filename));
  loader->load(loader->filename);
  return loader;
}
```

The overridden load method calls the Linux system function dlopen with the given filename parameter to open the dynamic library. We also pass a parameter of RTLD_LAZY to dlopen, which only has the effect of resolving undefined symbols as code from the library is executed (the other option, RTLD_NOW, forces resolution of undefined symbols to take place immediately). After loading the dynamic library, we save a handle to the library in the variable handle.

The overridden find_symbol method calls the Linux system function dlsym to search for the specified symbol (i.e., function name) within the previously loaded dynamic library. dlsym then returns a pointer to this symbol. Since dlsym must be compatible with all symbols in the library regardless of their type, it returns a void pointer; the calling routine must then cast the pointer to the correct type. Again, lack of type safety (perhaps we can call it "type danger"?) is the price we pay for dynamic symbol resolution.

The overridden close method calls dlclose to notify the operating system that we are finished using the dynamic library. If no other routines are using the dynamic library, it is freed at this point by the operating system; otherwise, it is only freed when all users of the library have called dlclose.

The overridden clone method creates a new Linux plug-in loader of type l3d_plugin_loader_linux, which references the same dynamic library file as the original.

A New Factory Manager for Plug-ins

Because application code accesses the plug-in loader through an abstract pointer, and because the concrete plug-in loader is created through a factory, we need to extend the factory manager of Chapter 2 to manage a plug-in loader factory as well. The class l3d_factory_manager_v_0_2 is the new version of the factory manager, shown in Listings 7-11 and 7-12.

Listing 7-11: fact0_2.h

```
#ifndef __FACTO_2_H
#define __FACTO_2_H
#include "../tool_os/memman.h"

#include "factorys.h"
```

```
#include "../raster/rast3.h"
#include "../dynamics/plugins/plugload.h"

class l3d_factory_manager_v_0_2 : public l3d_factory_manager_v_0_1 {
  public:
    l3d_factory_manager_v_0_2(void);
    virtual ~l3d_factory_manager_v_0_2(void);
    l3d_rasterizer_3d_imp_factory *ras_3d_imp_factory;
    l3d_plugin_loader_factory *plugin_loader_factory;
    int choose_factories(void);
};

extern l3d_factory_manager_v_0_2 factory_manager_v_0_2;

#endif
```

Listing 7-12: fact0_2.cc

```
#include "fact0_2.h"

#include "../tool_os/dis_x11.h"
#include "../tool_os/dis_mesa.h"
#include "../tool_2d/sc_x11.h"
#include "../tool_2d/sc_x11sh.h"
#include "../tool_2d/sc_mesa.h"
#include "../raster/ras3_sw.h"
#include "../raster/ras3_mes.h"
#include "../dynamics/plugins/pl_linux.h"

#include <stdio.h>
#include "../tool_os/memman.h"

l3d_factory_manager_v_0_2 factory_manager_v_0_2;

l3d_factory_manager_v_0_2::l3d_factory_manager_v_0_2(void) :
    l3d_factory_manager_v_0_1()
{
  ras_3d_imp_factory = NULL;
  plugin_loader_factory = NULL;
}

l3d_factory_manager_v_0_2::~l3d_factory_manager_v_0_2(void)
{
  if(should_delete_factories) {
    if (ras_3d_imp_factory) {
      delete ras_3d_imp_factory;
      ras_3d_imp_factory = NULL;
    }
    if (plugin_loader_factory) {
      delete plugin_loader_factory;
      plugin_loader_factory = NULL;
    }
  }
}

int l3d_factory_manager_v_0_2::choose_factories(void) {
  int i = l3d_factory_manager_v_0_1::choose_factories();

  switch(i) {
    case 1:
      ras_3d_imp_factory = new l3d_rasterizer_3d_sw_imp_factory;
```

```
      plugin_loader_factory = new l3d_plugin_loader_linux_factory;
      break;
    case 2:
      ras_3d_imp_factory = new l3d_rasterizer_3d_sw_imp_factory;
      plugin_loader_factory = new l3d_plugin_loader_linux_factory;
      break;
    case 3:
      ras_3d_imp_factory = new l3d_rasterizer_3d_mesa_imp_factory;
      plugin_loader_factory = new l3d_plugin_loader_linux_factory;
      break;
  }

  return i;
}
```

The new factory manager class declares an additional variable of type `l3d_plugin_loader_factory`, which is actually created in the overridden `choose_factories` method. Since we are running under Linux, we always create a Linux plug-in loader factory, which creates Linux plug-in loaders. Under another operating system, the factory manager would create and make available a different kind of plug-in loader factory, which would return a different kind of plug-in loader to the application code. The application code, of course, would not need to be changed in this case, since the factory design pattern shields the application code from the creation of new concrete types.

 NOTE The new factory manager also creates and maintains a 3D rasterizer implementation. The companion book *Advanced Linux 3D Graphics Programming* uses this member for more sophisticated rasterization of 3D polygons.

Summary of Using Plug-ins

The following list summarizes the steps for using plug-ins.

1. Write a plug-in conforming to the plug-in interface, and compile it into a `.so` dynamic library file.

2. In the l3d application program, create a plug-in loader by asking the plug-in loader factory to do so.

3. Create an empty instance of `l3d_object` with new. Call this object o.

4. Ask the plug-in loader to load the previously compiled `.so` file.

5. Ask the plug-in loader to find the symbol named "constructor." Assign the pointer which is returned to the function pointer `o.plugin_constructor`. Repeat this for symbols "update," "copy_data," and "destructor," assigning them to function pointers `o.plugin_update`, `o.plugin_copy_data`, and `o.plugin_destructor`.

6. The function pointers have now been bound to the actual executable code of the plug-in. Call `o.plugin_constructor(o, data)`. The pointer `data` is a pointer to any data which the `constructor` function, loaded from the plug-in file, needs in order to initialize o correctly. Therefore, the contents of the pointer `data` are completely dependent on the plug-in which is loaded; the plug-in `constructor` interprets the data in any way it wants. If the plug-in needs no data, simply pass NULL. Note that a plug-in will usually need at least some

data from the external environment in order to initialize itself correctly—the color depth of the screen, for instance.

7. Call `o.update`, as usual, to allow the object to update itself. The object automatically calls the `plugin_update` function if a plug-in is loaded, thus executing the plug-in's update code.

8. Destroy the object `o` with `delete`, as usual. The object's destructor automatically calls the `plugin_destructor` function if a plug-in is loaded.

The example programs in this chapter use both subclassing and plug-ins to implement dynamic behavior, so you'll get a chance to see both in action.

Grouping Objects into a World

We've now seen quite a bit about using 3D polygons to form objects, including specifications of geometry, transformations, and behavior. Thinking in terms of 3D objects (autonomous polygonal entities) increases the level of abstraction of our 3D programs, allowing us to speak of and think in terms of objects instead of one unmanageably large and unstructured set of polygons.

It is useful to introduce one more, higher level of abstraction: the concept of a *world*. Just as groups of 3D polygons form a 3D object, groups of 3D objects form a world. Class `l3d_world` is the class we use for storing worlds. See Listings 7-13 and 7-14. A world is a displayable, interactive 3D environment. It therefore contains 3D objects to populate the world, a camera to see the world, a rasterizer to plot pixels, and a screen to display the output.

For now, a world as implemented by `l3d_world` is really little more than a simple list of objects. In the companion book *Advanced Linux 3D Graphics Programming*, we subclass from `l3d_world` to perform more advanced visibility operations on our 3D objects, leading to a graph-like structure of objects connected via portals.

Listing 7-13: `world.h`

```
#ifndef __WORLD_H
#define __WORLD_H
#include "../../tool_os/memman.h"

#include "../../tool_os/dispatch.h"
#include "../../view/camera.h"
#include "../../tool_2d/screen.h"
#include "../object/object3d.h"

#define MAX_VISIBLE_FACETS 5000
#define MAX_OBJECTS 12000

class l3d_world {

  public:
    l3d_world(int xsize, int ysize);
    virtual ~l3d_world(void);

    l3d_screen *screen;
    l3d_rasterizer_3d *rasterizer;
    l3d_rasterizer_2d_imp *rasterizer_2d_imp;
```

```
    l3d_rasterizer_3d_imp *rasterizer_3d_imp;
    l3d_camera *camera;

    l3d_list<l3d_object *> objects;

    virtual void update_all(void);
    virtual void draw_all(void);

    static int compare_facet_zdepth(const void *key, const void *elem);

    int should_display_status;
    unsigned int framecount, first_tickcount, last_tickcount;
};

#endif
```

Listing 7-14: `world.cc`

```
#include "world.h"
#include <stdlib.h>
#include <string.h>

#include "../object/object3d.h"
#include "../polygon/polygon.h"
#include "../../tool_2d/screen.h"
#include "../../tool_os/dispatch.h"
#include "../../raster/rasteriz.h"
#include "../../tool_2d/scrinfo.h"
#include "../../system/fact0_2.h"
#include "../../tool_os/memman.h"

l3d_world::l3d_world(int xsize, int ysize) {

  screen =
    factory_manager_v_0_2.screen_factory->create(xsize,ysize);
  rasterizer_2d_imp =
    factory_manager_v_0_2.ras_2d_imp_factory->
    create(xsize,ysize,screen->sinfo);
  rasterizer_3d_imp =
    factory_manager_v_0_2.ras_3d_imp_factory->
    create(xsize,ysize,screen->sinfo);
  rasterizer = new l3d_rasterizer_3d(rasterizer_2d_imp, rasterizer_3d_imp);

  #ifdef DGROUP64K
  #define PI 3.14159265
  int i;
  for(i=0; i<360; i++) {
    cos_lu[i] = Float2MT(cos(i*PI/180.));
    sin_lu[i] = Float2MT(sin(i*PI/180.));
  }
  #endif

  screen->open_screen();

  camera = new l3d_camera;

  should_display_status = 0;
}

l3d_world::~l3d_world() {
```

```
    int i;

  //- clean up world database
  for(i=0; i<objects.num_items; i++) {
    delete objects[i];
  }

  delete screen;
  delete rasterizer_2d_imp;
  delete rasterizer_3d_imp;
  delete rasterizer;
  delete camera;
}

int l3d_world::compare_facet_zdepth(const void *key, const void *elem) {

  l3d_real zdif =
    ( (*((l3d_polygon_3d **)elem))->zvisible - (*((l3d_polygon_3d **)key))->zvisible );

  if (zdif>0) return 1;
  else if(zdif<0) return -1;
  else return 0;
}

void l3d_world::draw_all(void) {
  int iObj, iFacet;

  //- don't make this array into a l3d_list because we use qsort later
  l3d_polygon_3d *plist[MAX_VISIBLE_FACETS]; int pnum=0;

  rasterizer->clear_buffer();

  for(iObj=0; iObj<objects.num_items; iObj++) {

    //- reset object to its original position
    objects[iObj]->reset();

    //- position all vertices of object into world space
    if (objects[iObj]->num_xforms) {
      objects[iObj]->transform(objects[iObj]->modeling_xform);
    }

    //- transform polys to camera space
    objects[iObj]->camera_transform(camera->viewing_xform);

    //- clip polys to near-z
    l3d_polygon_3d_node *n;
    n = objects[iObj]->nonculled_polygon_nodes;
    while(n) {
      if(n->polygon->clip_near_z(camera->near_z))

      {
        //- polygon is not culled
      }else {

        //- take this polygon out of the list of nonculled_polygon_nodes
        if(n->prev) {
          n->prev->next = n->next;
        }else {
          objects[iObj]->nonculled_polygon_nodes = n->next;
```

```
        }

        if(n->next) {
          n->next->prev = n->prev;
        }
      }
      n = n->next;
    }

    //- perspective projection of vertices only of surviving polys
    objects[iObj]->apply_perspective_projection(*camera,
        screen->xsize, screen->ysize);

    n = objects[iObj]->nonculled_polygon_nodes;

    while(n) {
      if ( n->polygon->clip_to_polygon_2d(screen->view_win)) {

        //- polygon survived all culling tests and will be drawn.

        plist[pnum++] = n->polygon;

        //- Use the average of all z-values for depth sorting
        l3d_real zsum=int_to_l3d_real(0);
        register int ivtx;

        for(ivtx=0; ivtx<n->polygon->ivertices->num_items; ivtx++) {
          zsum += (**(n->polygon->vlist))[ (*n->polygon->ivertices)[ivtx].ivertex
].transformed_intermediates[1].Z_ ;
        }
        n->polygon->zvisible = l3d_divri(zsum, ivtx);
      }
      n = n->next;
    }
  }

  //- Sort the visible facets in decreasing order of z-depth
  qsort(plist, pnum, sizeof(l3d_polygon_3d *), compare_facet_zdepth);

  //- Display the facets in the sorted z-depth order (painter's algorithm)

  for(int i=0; i<pnum; i++) {
    plist[i]->draw(rasterizer);
  }

  if(should_display_status) {
    char msg[256];
    sprintf(msg,"%d polys drawn", pnum);
    rasterizer->draw_text(0,16,msg);
  }
}

void l3d_world::update_all(void) {
  register int i;

  for(i=0; i<objects.num_items; i++) {
    objects[i]->update();
  }
```

```
   //- camera is separate object not in objects[] so it is separately updated
   camera->update();
}
```

The World Database

The most important member of the class l3d_world is the *world database*, stored in the member variable objects. This is simply a list of pointers to l3d_object instances. The world class therefore manages the 3D objects contained within the world.

We call this list of objects a world database because this is standard graphics terminology, and because in the most general case, a 3D engine does deal with a database of objects which must be searched and traversed, not necessarily in simple linear order. For now, we do traverse the list of objects in linear order. In the companion book *Advanced Linux 3D Graphics Programming*, we see a visibility-based recursive portal traversal based on the current camera position.

Interaction with the Pipeline

As we saw in Chapter 2, l3d programs run in an event-based fashion: the dispatcher extracts events from the screen, and allows the pipeline to do its work, respond to input, and draw to the screen.

The idea behind l3d_world is that it should represent the entire interactive 3D environment. Since l3d programs do their processing in the pipeline class, we declare a subclass of l3d_pipeline, called l3d_pipeline_world, which does little more than forward update, keypress, and drawing events to the l3d_world for further processing. The l3d_world class provides appropriate functions to be called from the pipeline.

First, let's look at the l3d_pipeline_world class. See Listings 7-15 and 7-16.

Listing 7-15: pi_wor.h

```
#ifndef __PI_WOR_H
#define __PI_WOR_H
#include "../tool_os/memman.h"

#include "pipeline.h"
#include "../geom/world/world.h"

class l3d_pipeline_world : public l3d_pipeline {
  protected:
    l3d_world *world;
  public:

  l3d_pipeline_world(l3d_world *w) {world = w; }
    virtual ~l3d_pipeline_world(void) {};
    void key_event(int ch);
    void update_event(void);
    void draw_event(void);
};

#endif
```

Listing 7-16: pi_wor.cc

```
#include "pi_wor.h"

#include <sys/time.h>
#include <unistd.h>
```

```
#include <string.h>
#include "../tool_os/memman.h"

void l3d_pipeline_world::key_event(int c) {
  switch(c) {
    case 'q': done = 1;

      //- default keys for world->camera movement - full 360 degree movement
    case 'j': if(world->camera->rot_VUP_velocity>int_to_l3d_real(-95)) world->camera->rot_VUP_velocity
-= int_to_l3d_real(5); break;
    case 'l': if(world->camera->rot_VUP_velocity<int_to_l3d_real( 95)) world->camera->rot_VUP_velocity
+= int_to_l3d_real(5); break;
    case 'J': if(world->camera->rot_VFW_velocity<int_to_l3d_real( 95)) world->camera->rot_VFW_velocity
+= int_to_l3d_real(5); break;
    case 'L': if(world->camera->rot_VFW_velocity>int_to_l3d_real(-95)) world->camera->rot_VFW_velocity
-= int_to_l3d_real(5); break;
    case 'I': if(world->camera->rot_VRI_velocity<int_to_l3d_real( 95)) world->camera->rot_VRI_velocity
+= int_to_l3d_real(5); break;
    case 'K': if(world->camera->rot_VRI_velocity>int_to_l3d_real(-95)) world->camera->rot_VRI_velocity
-= int_to_l3d_real(5); break;
    case 'k': if(world->camera->VFW_velocity    >int_to_l3d_real(-90)) world->camera->VFW_velocity -=
world->camera->VFW_thrust; break;
    case 'i': if(world->camera->VFW_velocity    <int_to_l3d_real( 90)) world->camera->VFW_velocity +=
world->camera->VFW_thrust; break;
    case 's': if(world->camera->VRI_velocity    >int_to_l3d_real(-90)) world->camera->VRI_velocity -=
world->camera->VRI_thrust; break;
    case 'f': if(world->camera->VRI_velocity    <int_to_l3d_real( 90)) world->camera->VRI_velocity +=
world->camera->VRI_thrust; break;
    case 'd': if(world->camera->VUP_velocity    >int_to_l3d_real(-90)) world->camera->VUP_velocity -=
world->camera->VUP_thrust; break;
    case 'e': if(world->camera->VUP_velocity    <int_to_l3d_real( 90)) world->camera->VUP_velocity +=
world->camera->VUP_thrust; break;

      //- field-of-view modification
    case 'X': world->camera->fovx = world->camera->fovx + float_to_l3d_real(0.1); break;
    case 'x': world->camera->fovx = world->camera->fovx - float_to_l3d_real(0.1); break;
    case 'Y': world->camera->fovy = world->camera->fovy + float_to_l3d_real(0.1); break;
    case 'y': world->camera->fovy = world->camera->fovy - float_to_l3d_real(0.1); break;

      //- speed
    case 'v': case 'V':
      world->camera->VUP_thrust += int_to_l3d_real(1.0);
      if(world->camera->VUP_thrust  > 3.0) {
        world->camera->VUP_thrust  -= int_to_l3d_real(3.0);
      }
      world->camera->VFW_thrust = world->camera->VUP_thrust;
      world->camera->VRI_thrust = world->camera->VUP_thrust;
      break;

      //- display

    case 'n': case 'N':
      world->should_display_status = 1-world->should_display_status; //- toggle
      break;

  }

}

void l3d_pipeline_world::update_event() {
```

```
    world->update_all();
}

void l3d_pipeline_world::draw_event(void) {
  static int frame=0;
  static long last_sec, last_usec;
  long sec, usec;
  static float fps;
  static char str[80];

  struct timeval tv;
  struct timezone tz;
  tz.tz_minuteswest = -60;

  world->rasterizer->clear_buffer();
  world->draw_all();

  frame++;
  if((frame & 0x3F) == 0) {
    gettimeofday(&tv,&tz);
    fps = 64 * 1.0 / ( (tv.tv_sec + tv.tv_usec/1000000.0) - (last_sec + last_usec/1000000.0) );
    last_sec = tv.tv_sec;
    last_usec = tv.tv_usec;

  }

  if(world->should_display_status) {
    sprintf(str,"FPS: %f", fps);
    world->rasterizer->draw_text(0, 0, str);
  }

  world->screen->blit_screen();

}
```

The l3d_pipeline_world class is a pipeline which forwards its processing to an l3d_world object. The constructor for class l3d_pipeline_world requires a pointer to the world object with which it interacts; an l3d_pipeline_world cannot exist without a corresponding world object. The pointer to the world is then saved within the pipeline in variable world.

The overridden pipeline method key_event handles the typical keyboard input for the pipeline by modifying the position of the camera within the world. The handling of the keys is identical to that of programs camspikes or clipz; we have just moved the code into a common location so that we don't always have to rewrite the same code to handle the same keys in the same way. Notice that the keys x, Shift+x, y, and Shift+y modify the field of view terms, meaning that for all programs using this pipeline class, you can experiment with modifying the field of view interactively, as mentioned in Chapter 5. Also notice that the n key toggles the display of numeric statistics, such as the frames per second.

The overridden pipeline method update_event does nothing other than call the method update_all of the world, which we cover in the next section. Thus, the update processing is handed off to the world object.

The overridden pipeline method draw_event is similarly simple. It clears the world's rasterizer buffer, asks the world to draw itself by calling draw_all, and asks the world's screen to blit itself. It essentially forwards the drawing processing on to the world object. After the world has drawn itself, this method performs one new operation which we have not seen yet: it calculates the *frames per second*, also called *FPS* or *frame rate*. As our worlds increase in complexity, it can be interesting to see how the performance of the application holds up. FPS is one way of measuring this. To calculate FPS, we retrieve the physical system clock time every 64 frames. We use 64 frames instead of just one frame to get an average FPS value over several frames. We then subtract the current clock time from the clock time 64 frames ago. This gives us the elapsed seconds required to draw 64 frames. So, we divide 64 frames by the elapsed seconds to obtain the frames per second. The physical clock time is retrieved with the function `gettimeofday`, which takes a time zone structure as an input parameter and a time value structure as an output parameter. After the function call, the time value structure is filled with the current time of day. The fields `tv_sec` and `tv_usec` give the elapsed seconds and microseconds since 00:00:00 UTC January 1, 1970. We don't care about the actual values; what we care about is the difference between the current time and the time 64 frames ago. After computing the FPS, we display it by using the new `draw_text` method of the 3D rasterizer; this draws a text string into the rasterizer buffer as a series of pixels forming the characters.

So, the `l3d_pipeline_world` class essentially forwards the bulk of its processing to the world object. It calls two important functions of the world object: `update_all` and `draw_all`. These two functions form the interface between the pipeline object and the world object. Let's look at each one separately.

Updating the Entire World

Since a world consists of autonomous 3D objects, and since each object knows how to update itself through the method `l3d_object::update`, the world must allow each object to update itself by calling `update` on each object. This is exactly what the method `l3d_world::update_all` does. It loops through all objects in the world database and calls `update` for each object. It also calls `update` on the camera object of the world, since the camera is not in the objects list but also needs to be updated whenever the objects are updated. Note that if the world database consists of many objects, we might not want to allow all objects to update themselves every frame; instead, we might wish to define "active regions" of the world and "inactive regions," perhaps based on some criteria such as distance from the camera. We could then only update certain parts of the world—the active regions—for each frame, saving processing time, although with the slight oddity that the inactive regions of the world are "frozen in time." As the camera moves closer to inactive regions of the world, we could change them into active regions, simultaneously making some of the now more distant regions inactive.

Drawing the Entire World

The pipeline calls `l3d_world::draw_all` to allow the world to draw itself. We do this by looping through all objects in the world database. For each object, we reset its position, then transform it into world space using its composite `modeling_xform` array, and then transform it into camera space. In camera space, we clip all polygons of the object against the near *z* clip plane, removing a polygon from the linked list if it gets completely clipped away. For all surviving polygons, we apply the perspective projection, then clip the projected 2D polygon to the screen. All of this we have seen before, in the previous program `clipz`.

What is new is what happens to the surviving polygons which are ready to be displayed on screen. Instead of drawing them immediately, as we did in program `clipz`, we insert all surviving polygons for this object into a common array of polygons, and proceed to process the next object. The next object will also have zero or more surviving polygons, which are likewise inserted into the common array and not drawn immediately. Processing continues in this manner for all polygons of all objects.

After processing all objects, and before drawing anything, we then have an array containing pointers to all polygons that survived all clipping operations, both 2D and 3D, and are ready to be displayed on-screen. See Figure 7-22.

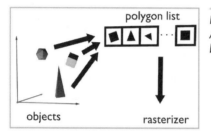

Figure 7-22: Processing all objects to find surviving polygons. All surviving polygons are inserted into one common list before being drawn.

Before drawing the polygons, we call `qsort` to sort the list of polygons. The `qsort` function can sort any array of homogeneous items, but needs a helper function which tells it how to compare items so that it knows which element comes before which. But what criteria should we use for sorting polygons, and why should we bother sorting polygons at all? This question scratches on the surface of the very broad area of visible surface determination or hidden surface removal, covered in more detail in the companion book *Advanced Linux 3D Graphics Programming*. If you look closely at the `clipz` program, you will notice some unusual drawing errors. In particular, objects which are nearer to you sometimes appear to be obstructed by smaller objects which are farther away. In reality, of course, this is impossible: the light rays coming from a farther object are blocked by the nearer object, meaning we see the nearer object in front of the farther object.

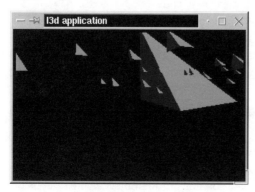

Figure 7-23: Drawing polygons in random order means that physically farther polygons might obstruct physically nearer polygons—a physical impossibility. Here, the large pyramid in the foreground should actually obscure all polygons behind it, but due to incorrect drawing order, polygons behind the large pyramid are drawn on top of it.

The reason for the odd drawing anomalies in `clipz` is that we didn't pay any attention to the physical distance of the polygons we were drawing. As soon as we found a polygon whose clipped and projected vertices were within the screen, we immediately drew the polygon to the screen, even if something was already on the screen at that position. We can liken the screen to a painter's canvas: if we draw in an area where something was already present, then we overwrite and obscure the previous contents. The problem with the `clipz` program is that the order in which we drew polygons was essentially random. Maybe we already drew some large, close-up polygons to the screen, but then we might later start to process some farther, smaller polygons. Since we draw a polygon to the screen as soon as it is deemed visible, a smaller polygon processed later will obscure a nearer polygon drawn earlier. Imagine a painter who first paints the house in the foreground, then paints the mountains in the background, blindly painting on top of the already painted house. The result is a background object obscuring a foreground object.

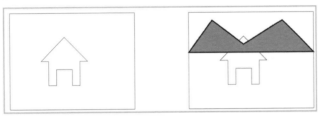

Figure 7-24: If a painter paints the foreground first, and then the background on top, the results are physically incorrect.

Continuing the painter's analogy leads to the *painter's algorithm*: first draw the background, then draw the foreground on top of the background.

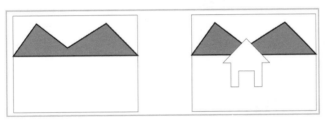

Figure 7-25: The painter's algorithm. First draw the background, then draw the foreground.

Returning to our array of polygons, we define the background polygons to be the ones with the largest z values in camera coordinates. Similarly, the foreground polygons are those with the smallest z values in camera coordinates. This reasoning therefore provides the sort criteria for the `qsort` routine: we sort all polygons from largest z to smallest z in the polygon array, and only then do we draw the polygons. The result is a far-to-near ordering of polygons, so that the nearest polygons are drawn last and obscure any farther polygons.

The `compare_facet_zdepth` function is the helper function for `qsort`, which sorts the polygons in order of decreasing z. The z value we use for sorting is the average of all the camera space z values of all vertices in the polygon. Conveniently, the class `l3d_object` saves the camera space coordinates of all its polygons in transformed intermediate number 1. So, all we need to do now is just retrieve the z component of the previously saved transformed intermediate coordinate number 1.

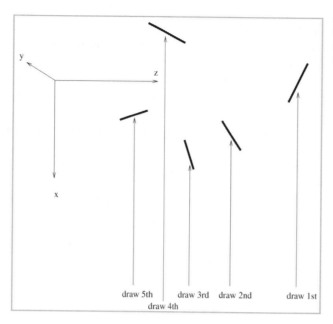

Figure 7-26: We sort polygons from farthest to nearest for the painter's algorithm.

draw 5th   draw 3rd   draw 2nd   draw 1st
     draw 4th

The painter's algorithm is one of the simplest and easiest to understand of the visible surface algorithms, returning mostly correct results most of the time, but it is not ideal in all cases. See the companion book *Advanced Linux 3D Graphics Programming* for a discussion of other techniques.

Finally, the world class uses the rasterizer routine `draw_text` to display a text message indicating the number of polygons sent to the rasterizer to be drawn. Toggle this display on and off by typing **n**.

Sample Program: fltsim

We've now seen a number of classes used for building worlds from 3D polygons. At the lowest level, we have an individual polygon, `l3d_polygon_3d`. At a higher level, we have 3D polygonal objects, `l3d_object`. Finally we have complete 3D worlds, `l3d_world`. Now, let's look at a sample program, `fltsim`, which uses these classes to make a 3D world. See Listings 7-17, 7-18, and 7-19. This program has the same keyboard controls as the program `camspikes`. It creates an `l3d_world` and populates the world with a number of 3D objects, both subclassed `l3d_objects` and plug-in `l3d_objects`. You can fly through the scene freely as in a flight simulator, hence the name `fltsim`, even if the landscape in this program is a bit on the simple side. The purpose of this program is mainly to illustrate the use of the world, object, and polygon classes. As an exercise, you might want to try writing a 3D object plug-in which draws a more interesting landscape.

When you run the program `fltsim`, you will see a long row of rotating pyramids. If you rotate the view slightly to the right (press **l** immediately after the program displays the 3D window), you will also see a more distant pyramid, rotating more slowly and around a different axis.

NOTE To execute this program, you must have compiled the plug-in files so that they can be loaded at run time. Execute **make -f makeall.lnx** in the $L3D directory to compile everything, including the plug-in files. See the Appendix for details. The plug-in files are located in directory `$L3D/binaries/linux_x/float/app/lib/dynamics/plugins`.

The long row of pyramids are all subclassed 3D objects. The more slowly rotating pyramid in the distance is a plug-in 3D object. We'll look at both of these next.

Listing 7-17: `main.cc`, the main program file for program `fltsim`

```
#include <stdlib.h>
#include <string.h>
#include <stdio.h>
#include <math.h>

#include "../lib/geom/object/object3d.h"
#include "../lib/geom/polygon/p3_flat.h"
#include "../lib/tool_2d/screen.h"
#include "../lib/tool_os/dispatch.h"
#include "../lib/raster/rast3.h"
#include "../lib/tool_2d/scrinfo.h"
#include "../lib/geom/world/world.h"
#include "../lib/system/fact0_2.h"
#include "../lib/pipeline/pi_wor.h"
#include "../lib/dynamics/plugins/plugenv.h"

#include "shapes.h"

#include <stdlib.h>
#include <string.h>
#include <stdio.h>
#include <math.h>
#include <stdarg.h>

class my_world:public l3d_world {
  public:
    my_world(void);
};

my_world::my_world(void)
    : l3d_world(640,400)
{
  l3d_screen_info *si = screen->sinfo;

  camera->VRP.set(0,0,-50,0);
  camera->near_z = float_to_l3d_real(5.5);
  camera->far_z = int_to_l3d_real(500);

  int i,j,k,onum=0;

  i=10; j=0; k=20;
  k=0;

  //- create some pyramid objects
  for(i=1; i<200; i+=20) {
    objects[onum=objects.next_index()] = new pyramid();
    l3d_screen_info_indexed *si_idx;
    l3d_screen_info_rgb *si_rgb;
```

```
        l3d_polygon_3d_flatshaded *p;
        for(int pnum=0; pnum<objects[onum]->polygons.num_items; pnum++) {
          p = dynamic_cast<l3d_polygon_3d_flatshaded *>(objects[onum]->polygons[pnum]);
          if(p) {
            p->final_color = si->ext_to_native
                             (rand()%si->ext_max_red,
                              rand()%si->ext_max_green,
                              rand()%si->ext_max_blue);
          }
        }

        if (objects[onum]==NULL) exit;
        objects[onum]->modeling_xforms[1].set
        ( int_to_l3d_real(1), int_to_l3d_real(0), int_to_l3d_real(0), int_to_l3d_real(i),
          int_to_l3d_real(0), int_to_l3d_real(1), int_to_l3d_real(0), int_to_l3d_real(1),
          int_to_l3d_real(0), int_to_l3d_real(0), int_to_l3d_real(1), int_to_l3d_real(1),
          int_to_l3d_real(0), int_to_l3d_real(0), int_to_l3d_real(0), int_to_l3d_real(1) );
        objects[onum]->modeling_xform =
          objects[onum]->modeling_xforms[1] |
          objects[onum]->modeling_xforms[0] ;
      }

      //- create a plugin object

      objects[onum=objects.next_index()] = new l3d_object(10);
      //- max 10 fixed vertices, can be overridden by plug-in if desired
      //- by redefining the vertex list

      objects[onum]->plugin_loader =
        factory_manager_v_0_2.plugin_loader_factory->create();
      objects[onum]->plugin_loader->load("../lib/dynamics/plugins/pyramid/pyramid.so");
      objects[onum]->plugin_constructor =
        (void (*)(l3d_object *, void *))
        objects[onum]->plugin_loader->find_symbol("constructor");
      objects[onum]->plugin_update =
        (void (*)(l3d_object *))
        objects[onum]->plugin_loader->find_symbol("update");
      objects[onum]->plugin_destructor =
        (void (*)(l3d_object *))
        objects[onum]->plugin_loader->find_symbol("destructor");
      objects[onum]->plugin_copy_data =
        (void (*)(const l3d_object *, l3d_object *))
        objects[onum]->plugin_loader->find_symbol("copy_data");

      l3d_plugin_environment *e = new l3d_plugin_environment
                                  (NULL, screen->sinfo, NULL, (void *)"");

      if(objects[onum]->plugin_constructor) {
        (*objects[onum]->plugin_constructor) (objects[onum],e);
      }

      screen->refresh_palette();
    }

main() {
  l3d_dispatcher *d;
  l3d_pipeline_world *p;
  my_world *w;

  factory_manager_v_0_2.choose_factories();
```

```
    d = factory_manager_v_0_2.dispatcher_factory->create();

    w = new my_world();
    p = new l3d_pipeline_world(w);
    d->pipeline = p;
    d->event_source = w->screen;

    d->start();

    delete d;
    delete p;
    delete w;
}
```

Listing 7-18: `shapes.h`, declaring a 3D object subclass for program `fltsim`

```
#include "../lib/geom/object/object3d.h"

class pyramid:public l3d_object {
    int xtheta;
  public:
    pyramid(void);
    virtual ~pyramid(void);
    int update(void);
};
```

Listing 7-19: `shapes.cc`, defining a 3D object subclass for program `fltsim`

```
#include "shapes.h"

#include <stdlib.h>
#include <string.h>

pyramid::pyramid(void) :
    l3d_object(4)
{
  (*vertices)[0].original.set
  (float_to_l3d_real(0.),
   float_to_l3d_real(0.),
   float_to_l3d_real(0.),
   float_to_l3d_real(1.));
  (*vertices)[1].original.set
  (float_to_l3d_real(10.0),
   float_to_l3d_real(0.),
   float_to_l3d_real(0.),
   float_to_l3d_real(1.));
  (*vertices)[2].original.set
  (float_to_l3d_real(0.),
   float_to_l3d_real(10.),
   float_to_l3d_real(0.),
   float_to_l3d_real(1.));
  (*vertices)[3].original.set
  (float_to_l3d_real(0.),
   float_to_l3d_real(0.),
   float_to_l3d_real(10.),
   float_to_l3d_real(1.));

  int pi;
  pi = polygons.next_index();
  polygons[pi] = new l3d_polygon_3d_flatshaded(3);
  printf("before: %p", polygons[pi]->vlist);
  polygons[pi]->vlist = &vertices;
```

```
    printf("after: %p", polygons[pi]->vlist);
    (*polygons[pi]->ivertices)[polygons[pi]->ivertices->next_index()].ivertex=0;
    (*polygons[pi]->ivertices)[polygons[pi]->ivertices->next_index()].ivertex=1;
    (*polygons[pi]->ivertices)[polygons[pi]->ivertices->next_index()].ivertex=3;
    polygons[pi]->compute_center();polygons[pi]->compute_sfcnormal();

    pi = polygons.next_index();
    polygons[pi] = new l3d_polygon_3d_flatshaded(3);
    polygons[pi]->vlist = &vertices;
    (*polygons[pi]->ivertices)[polygons[pi]->ivertices->next_index()].ivertex=2;
    (*polygons[pi]->ivertices)[polygons[pi]->ivertices->next_index()].ivertex=3;
    (*polygons[pi]->ivertices)[polygons[pi]->ivertices->next_index()].ivertex=1;
    polygons[pi]->compute_center();polygons[pi]->compute_sfcnormal();

    pi = polygons.next_index();
    polygons[pi] = new l3d_polygon_3d_flatshaded(3);
    polygons[pi]->vlist = &vertices;
    (*polygons[pi]->ivertices)[polygons[pi]->ivertices->next_index()].ivertex=0;
    (*polygons[pi]->ivertices)[polygons[pi]->ivertices->next_index()].ivertex=2;
    (*polygons[pi]->ivertices)[polygons[pi]->ivertices->next_index()].ivertex=1;
    polygons[pi]->compute_center();polygons[pi]->compute_sfcnormal();

    pi = polygons.next_index();
    polygons[pi] = new l3d_polygon_3d_flatshaded(3);
    polygons[pi]->vlist = &vertices;
    (*polygons[pi]->ivertices)[polygons[pi]->ivertices->next_index()].ivertex=3;
    (*polygons[pi]->ivertices)[polygons[pi]->ivertices->next_index()].ivertex=2;
    (*polygons[pi]->ivertices)[polygons[pi]->ivertices->next_index()].ivertex=0;
    polygons[pi]->compute_center();polygons[pi]->compute_sfcnormal();

    num_xforms = 2;
    xtheta=0;
    modeling_xforms[0] = l3d_mat_rotx(xtheta);
    modeling_xforms[1].set
    ( float_to_l3d_real(1.), float_to_l3d_real(0.), float_to_l3d_real(0.), float_to_l3d_real(0.),
      float_to_l3d_real(0.), float_to_l3d_real(1.), float_to_l3d_real(0.), float_to_l3d_real(0.),
      float_to_l3d_real(0.), float_to_l3d_real(0.), float_to_l3d_real(1.), float_to_l3d_real(0.),
      float_to_l3d_real(0.), float_to_l3d_real(0.), float_to_l3d_real(0.), float_to_l3d_real(1.) );

    modeling_xform=
      modeling_xforms[1] | modeling_xforms[0];
}

pyramid::~pyramid(void) {
  for(register int i=0; i<polygons.num_items; i++) {delete polygons[i]; }
}

int pyramid::update(void) {
  xtheta += 10; if (xtheta>359) xtheta-=360;
  modeling_xforms[0]=l3d_mat_rotx(xtheta);
  modeling_xform=
    modeling_xforms[1] | modeling_xforms[0];
}
```

The `main` function of the program is quite straightforward, choosing factories, creating a pipeline, and connecting the pipeline to the event dispatcher. The pipeline we create is of type `l3d_pipeline_world`. The main function therefore also declares a world, of type `my_world`, which is subclassed from `l3d_world`.

The class `my_world` is very small and makes only minimal additions to the standard `l3d_world` class. It declares no new member functions or variables; it only performs some extra initialization in the constructor. In particular, the constructor populates the 3D world by creating some objects of type `pyramid`, and inserting these objects into the world database. The class `pyramid` is a subclass of `l3d_object`, and defines custom geometry and behavior through the inheritance mechanism. The `my_world` class also creates and loads a plug-in object. Let's see how the sample program uses both subclassing and plug-ins to define custom objects.

A Subclassed 3D Object

Class `pyramid` is a subclassed 3D object which defines custom geometry and behavior.

The constructor defines the geometry. It calls the `l3d_object` base class constructor with a parameter of 4 to set the number of fixed vertices; then it defines these vertices. Next, the constructor defines a number of polygons based on the vertex list. Finally, it stores some modeling transformations in the `modeling_xforms` array, also immediately updating the composite `modeling_xform` matrix.

The overridden `update` method is responsible for the pyramid's behavior. In this case, the pyramid simply rotates itself. It does so by increasing an internal rotation variable representing the rotation angle in degrees, creating a rotation matrix based on the rotation angle, entering this rotation matrix into the `modeling_xforms` array, and updating the composite `modeling_xform` array.

That is actually all that is necessary to define an `l3d_object` subclass with custom geometry and behavior! Now, let's look at the other possibility to create customized 3D objects: plug-ins.

A Plug-in 3D Object

The following excerpt from the `my_world` constructor illustrates the creation of a plug-in 3D object.

```
//- create a plugin object

objects[onum=objects.next_index()] = new l3d_object(10);
//- max 10 fixed vertices, can be overridden by plug-in if desired
//- by redefining the vertex list

objects[onum]->plugin_loader =
  factory_manager_v_0_2.plugin_loader_factory->create();
objects[onum]->plugin_loader->load("../lib/dynamics/plugins/pyramid/pyramid.so");
objects[onum]->plugin_constructor =
  (void (*)(l3d_object *, void *))
  objects[onum]->plugin_loader->find_symbol("constructor");
objects[onum]->plugin_update =
  (void (*)(l3d_object *))
  objects[onum]->plugin_loader->find_symbol("update");
objects[onum]->plugin_destructor =
  (void (*)(l3d_object *))
  objects[onum]->plugin_loader->find_symbol("destructor");
objects[onum]->plugin_copy_data =
  (void (*)(const l3d_object *, l3d_object *))
  objects[onum]->plugin_loader->find_symbol("copy_data");
```

```
l3d_plugin_environment *e = new l3d_plugin_environment
                    (NULL, screen->sinfo, NULL, (void *)"");

if(objects[onum]->plugin_constructor) {
  (*objects[onum]->plugin_constructor) (objects[onum],e);
}
```

The code follows the steps outlined earlier for creating plug-in objects. First, we create an empty
`l3d_object`. Then, we create a plug-in loader and ask the plug-in loader to load a particular
dynamic library. In this case, we have hard-coded the name of the dynamic library into the program code, but we could just as well have read the plug-in name from a configuration file. (The
companion book *Advanced Linux 3D Graphics Programming* provides sample programs which
do exactly this.) Then we ask the plug-in loader to find the plug-in functions; we assign these functions to the plug-in function pointers in `l3d_object`. Finally we call the plug-in
`constructor` function.

The plug-in code itself is stored in a separate file. See Listing 7-20.

Listing 7-20: `pyramid.cc`, the plug-in for program `fltsim`

```
#include "../../../system/sys_dep.h"
#include "../../../geom/object/object3d.h"
#include "../../../geom/texture/texload.h"
#include "../../../geom/polygon/p3_ltex.h"
#include "../plugenv.h"
#include "../../../tool_os/memman.h"

class l3d_plugin_pyramid {
  public:
    l3d_plugin_environment *env;

    int xtheta;

    l3d_plugin_pyramid::l3d_plugin_pyramid(l3d_plugin_environment *e) {
      env = e;
    }
    l3d_plugin_pyramid::~l3d_plugin_pyramid(void) {
      delete env;
    }
};

extern "C" {

  void constructor(l3d_object *target, void *data) {
    l3d_plugin_pyramid *pyramid;

    target->plugin_data = pyramid =
                    new l3d_plugin_pyramid((l3d_plugin_environment *)data);

    int i;
    int vi;
    vi = 0;
    (*target->vertices)[vi].original.set(float_to_l3d_real(0.),float_to_l3d_real(0.),
                          float_to_l3d_real(0.),float_to_l3d_real(1.));
    vi++;
    (*target->vertices)[vi].original.set(float_to_l3d_real(10.0),float_to_l3d_real(0.),
                          float_to_l3d_real(0.),float_to_l3d_real(1.));
    vi++;
```

```
(*target->vertices)[vi].original.set(float_to_l3d_real(0.),float_to_l3d_real(10.),
                                     float_to_l3d_real(0.),float_to_l3d_real(1.));
vi++;
(*target->vertices)[vi].original.set(float_to_l3d_real(0.),float_to_l3d_real(0.),
                                     float_to_l3d_real(10.),float_to_l3d_real(1.));

l3d_polygon_3d_flatshaded *p;

i = target->polygons.next_index();
target->polygons[i] = p = new l3d_polygon_3d_flatshaded(3);
p->vlist = &target->vertices;
(*(p->ivertices))[p->ivertices->next_index()].ivertex=0;
(*(p->ivertices))[p->ivertices->next_index()].ivertex=1;
(*(p->ivertices))[p->ivertices->next_index()].ivertex=3;
p->compute_center();target->polygons[0]->compute_sfcnormal();
p->final_color = pyramid->env->sinfo->ext_to_native
                (rand()%pyramid->env->sinfo->ext_max_red,
                 rand()%pyramid->env->sinfo->ext_max_green,
                 rand()%pyramid->env->sinfo->ext_max_blue);

i = target->polygons.next_index();
target->polygons[i] = p = new l3d_polygon_3d_flatshaded(3);
p->vlist = &target->vertices;
(*(p->ivertices))[p->ivertices->next_index()].ivertex=2;
(*(p->ivertices))[p->ivertices->next_index()].ivertex=3;
(*(p->ivertices))[p->ivertices->next_index()].ivertex=1;
p->compute_center();p->compute_sfcnormal();
p->final_color = pyramid->env->sinfo->ext_to_native
                (rand()%pyramid->env->sinfo->ext_max_red,
                 rand()%pyramid->env->sinfo->ext_max_green,
                 rand()%pyramid->env->sinfo->ext_max_blue);

i = target->polygons.next_index();
target->polygons[i] = p = new l3d_polygon_3d_flatshaded(3);
p->vlist = &target->vertices;
(*(p->ivertices))[p->ivertices->next_index()].ivertex=0;
(*(p->ivertices))[p->ivertices->next_index()].ivertex=2;
(*(p->ivertices))[p->ivertices->next_index()].ivertex=1;
p->compute_center();p->compute_sfcnormal();
p->final_color = pyramid->env->sinfo->ext_to_native
                (rand()%pyramid->env->sinfo->ext_max_red,
                 rand()%pyramid->env->sinfo->ext_max_green,
                 rand()%pyramid->env->sinfo->ext_max_blue);

i = target->polygons.next_index();
target->polygons[i] = p = new l3d_polygon_3d_flatshaded(3);
p->vlist = &target->vertices;
(*(p->ivertices))[p->ivertices->next_index()].ivertex=3;
(*(p->ivertices))[p->ivertices->next_index()].ivertex=2;
(*(p->ivertices))[p->ivertices->next_index()].ivertex=0;
p->compute_center();p->compute_sfcnormal();
p->final_color = pyramid->env->sinfo->ext_to_native
                (rand()%pyramid->env->sinfo->ext_max_red,
                 rand()%pyramid->env->sinfo->ext_max_green,
                 rand()%pyramid->env->sinfo->ext_max_blue);

target->num_xforms = 3;

pyramid->xtheta=0;
target->modeling_xforms[0] = l3d_mat_rotz(pyramid->xtheta);
```

```
      target->modeling_xforms[1].set
      ( float_to_l3d_real(1.), float_to_l3d_real(0.), float_to_l3d_real(0.), float_to_l3d_real(70.),
        float_to_l3d_real(0.), float_to_l3d_real(1.), float_to_l3d_real(0.), float_to_l3d_real(0.),
        float_to_l3d_real(0.), float_to_l3d_real(0.), float_to_l3d_real(1.), float_to_l3d_real(0.),
        float_to_l3d_real(0.), float_to_l3d_real(0.), float_to_l3d_real(0.), float_to_l3d_real(1.) );
      target->modeling_xforms[2].set
      ( float_to_l3d_real(1.), float_to_l3d_real(0.), float_to_l3d_real(0.), float_to_l3d_real(0.),
        float_to_l3d_real(0.), float_to_l3d_real(1.), float_to_l3d_real(0.), float_to_l3d_real(0.),
        float_to_l3d_real(0.), float_to_l3d_real(0.), float_to_l3d_real(1.), float_to_l3d_real(50.),
        float_to_l3d_real(0.), float_to_l3d_real(0.), float_to_l3d_real(0.), float_to_l3d_real(1.) );

      target->modeling_xform=
        target->modeling_xforms[2] | (target->modeling_xforms[1] | target->modeling_xforms[0]);

    }


    void update(l3d_object *target) {
      l3d_plugin_pyramid *pyramid;
      pyramid = (l3d_plugin_pyramid *)target->plugin_data;
      pyramid->xtheta += 1; if (pyramid->xtheta>359) pyramid->xtheta-=360;
      target->modeling_xforms[0]=l3d_mat_rotz(pyramid->xtheta);
      target->modeling_xform=
        target->modeling_xforms[2] | target->modeling_xforms[1] | target->modeling_xforms[0];

    }


    void destructor(l3d_object *target) {
      delete (l3d_plugin_pyramid *) target->plugin_data;
    }

    void copy_data(l3d_object *target, l3d_object *copy_target) {
      l3d_plugin_pyramid *pyramid;
      pyramid = (l3d_plugin_pyramid *) target->plugin_data;

      l3d_plugin_environment *new_env;
      l3d_plugin_pyramid *new_pyramid;

      new_env = pyramid->env->clone();
      new_env->data = NULL;
      new_pyramid = new l3d_plugin_pyramid(new_env);
      new_pyramid->xtheta = pyramid->xtheta;

      copy_target->plugin_data = (void *) new_pyramid;
    }
  }
```

The plug-in code is almost identical to that of the subclassed 3D object: the `constructor` initializes the geometry, and `update` changes the transformation matrices. The main difference is that we have to access the 3D object through the `target` parameter, since the plug-in functions are C functions, not C++ member functions with a hidden `this` parameter. Also, we have chosen to make the plug-in pyramid rotate more slowly and around a different axis than the subclassed 3D object.

Notice that we declare a new class, `l3d_plugin_pyramid`, to hold plug-in specific data, and that we create an instance of this class in the `constructor` function. Importantly, we then save a pointer to this newly created object in the `target->plugin_data` member variable, where we can access it again later in the `update` function. This is similar to subclassing because we are associating arbitrary new data with an instance of l3d_object, but has the advantage that we don't actually need to declare and compile a new subclass. The disadvantage is the lack of type checking; all the extra data is passed around as a void pointer.

The last item of note with the plug-in 3D object is the use of the data parameter in the constructor function. The my_world code which creates the plug-in object also creates an object of type l3d_plugin_environment, and passes a pointer to this environment object to the constructor function. The constructor function then casts the void data pointer into a pointer of type l3d_plugin_environment, and extracts the environment data. As mentioned earlier, think of the data parameter as a means of passing arbitrary "arguments" to the plug-in constructor. The class l3d_plugin_environment is presented in Listing 7-21. It simply is a structure (without significant behavior) which holds information about the external environment that the plug-in needs to know in order to function properly. Two of the members of the class, the texture loader and the surface cache, are not used in this book and are relevant only for advanced polygon rendering algorithms, covered in the companion book *Advanced Linux 3D Graphics Programming*. The class offers a clone method to allow the environment object to clone itself, so that copying a plug-in object also copies the environment information.

Listing 7-21: plugenv.h

```
#ifndef __PLUGENV_H
#define __PLUGENV_H
#include "../../tool_os/memman.h"

#include "../../system/sys_dep.h"
#include "../../geom/object/object3d.h"
#include "../../geom/texture/texload.h"
#include "../../geom/polygon/p3_ltex.h"

class l3d_plugin_environment {
  public:
    l3d_texture_loader *texloader;
    l3d_screen_info *sinfo;
    l3d_surface_cache *scache;
    void *data;
    l3d_plugin_environment::l3d_plugin_environment(l3d_texture_loader *l,
        l3d_screen_info *sinfo,
        l3d_surface_cache *scache,
        void *data)
    {
      texloader = l;
      this->sinfo = sinfo;
      this->scache = scache;
      this->data = data;
    }

    virtual l3d_plugin_environment *clone(void) {
      l3d_plugin_environment *e = new l3d_plugin_environment
                                (texloader, sinfo, scache, NULL);
      return e;
    }
};

#endif
```

Planes in 3D

Until now we've been treating the concept of a plane in 3D rather informally. We have seen the near z clipping plane and the projection plane, both of which were oriented perfectly vertically, located a certain distance along the positive z axis. Now, let's see how we can generalize the notion of a plane to include arbitrary orientations. We need planes to perform 3D polygon clipping against arbitrary planes, collision detection, and several other operations in 3D graphics.

Defining a Plane

Geometrically, as we have mentioned before, you can think of a plane as an infinitely wide and high, flat, and infinitely thin 2D surface arbitrarily oriented in 3D space. We can define a plane with a normal vector and a point. The normal vector specifies the orientation of the plane. But there are an infinite number of planes with a particular orientation. This is the purpose of the point: to specify a particular point on the plane to distinguish it from all other planes with the same normal vector.

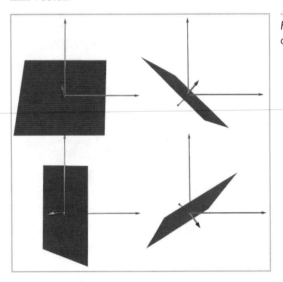

Figure 7-27: The normal vector specifies the orientation of a plane.

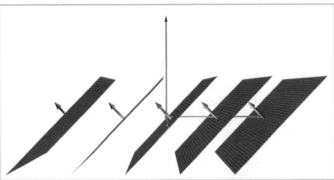

Figure 7-28: There are an infinite number of planes for a given normal vector. Thus we must specify a normal and a point on the plane to uniquely specify a particular plane.

Mathematically, the equation for a plane in 3D is as follows:

Equation 7-1 $Ax + By + Cz + D = 0$

This equation comes from the vector form of the equation:

Equation 7-2 $N \cdot P = N \cdot P_0$

In this equation, N is the known normal vector $[A,B,C,0]^T$ to the plane, P is a point of the form $[x,y,z,1]^T$, and P_0 is the known point $[x_0,y_0,z_0,1]^T$ on the plane. Taking the dot product of the normal vector with a point can be considered the same as taking the dot product of the normal vector with a vector going from the origin to the point (recall the discussion of the relationship between points and vectors in Chapter 5). Also, remember that the dot product of two vectors can be interpreted geometrically as the projection of the second vector onto the first vector. Therefore, the vector form of the equation says that all points lying on the plane must satisfy the constraint that the projection onto the normal vector of the vector going from the origin to the point must be a constant—specifically, the constant obtained by projecting the vector from the origin to the known point onto the plane's normal vector.

Put another way, in the non-vector form of the plane equation, the terms A, B, and C are the normal vector to the plane. Assuming the normal vector has been normalized, the term D is the signed distance from the plane to the origin, in the direction of the normal vector. A positive value of D means you travel D units in the direction of the normal vector to get from the plane to the origin; a negative value of D means you travel D units in the opposite direction of the normal vector to get from the plane to the origin.

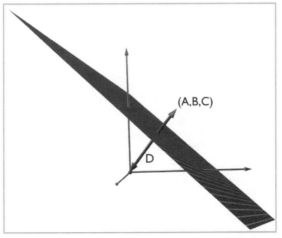

Figure 7-29: The meaning of A, B, C, and D in the plane equation.

Notice that if you expand the vector form of the equation, move all terms to the left-hand side of the equation, and denote all constant terms by the term D, you arrive at the non-vector form of the equation.

Sides of a Plane

A plane has two sides: a front side and a back side. Since a plane has infinite width and height, it divides the entire 3D space into two areas: the area in front of the plane and the area behind the plane. The front side of a plane is the same side in which the normal vector points; the back side is the other side.

Often, we have a given point and wish to determine whether the point is located in front of the plane or behind the plane. To do this, we simply evaluate the plane equation with the given point. If the point is (x_p, y_p, z_p), then we would calculate the value $Ax_p + By_p + Cz_p + D$. The result is a scalar number. The sign of this scalar number tells us the position of the point relative to the plane. If it is positive, the point is in front of the plane. If it is negative, the point is behind the plane. If it is neither positive nor negative, that is, if the result is exactly zero, then the point lies on the plane.

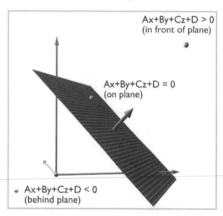

Figure 7-30: The front and back sides of a plane as evaluated by the plane equation.

The reason this method works can be understood by examining the vector form of the equation. For all points in front of the plane, the vector going from the origin to the point, projected onto the plane's normal vector, will be longer than the corresponding vector projection for points on the plane. Similarly, for all points behind the plane, the vector projection will be shorter. For all points on the plane, the vector projection will be identical. The term $Ax_p + By_p + Cz_p$ is the projection for the point being tested; by adding D, we are effectively subtracting the constant vector projection distance for all points on the plane. If the result of this subtraction is positive, then the vector projection for the point being tested is longer, meaning the point is in front of the plane; if the result is negative, the vector projection is shorter, and the point is behind the plane.

The l3d_plane Class

We use the class `l3d_plane` to represent a plane with arbitrary orientation.

Listing 7-22: `plane.h`

```
#ifndef __PLANE_H
#define __PLANE_H
#include "../../tool_os/memman.h"

#include "../../system/sys_dep.h"
#include "../../math/vector.h"
```

```
#include "../point/point.h"
#include "../../dynamics/collide.h"

#define EPSILON_PLANE float_to_l3d_real(0.001)
#define CROSS_FRONT_TO_BACK 1
#define CROSS_BACK_TO_FRONT -1

class l3d_plane
{
  public:
    l3d_real a,b,c,d;
    void align_with_point_normal(const l3d_point& point,
                                 const l3d_vector& normal);

    void align_with_points(const l3d_point& p0,
                           const l3d_point& p1,
                           const l3d_point& p2);

    l3d_real side_of_point(const l3d_point& p) const {
      return (l3d_mulrr(a,p.X_) +
              l3d_mulrr(b,p.Y_) +
              l3d_mulrr(c,p.Z_) +
              d);
    }

    l3d_real intersection_t;
    l3d_point intersection;
    int intersect_with_segment(const l3d_point& p0,
                               const l3d_point& p1);
};

#endif
```

Listing 7-23: `plane.cc`

```
#include "plane.h"
#include "../../tool_os/memman.h"

void l3d_plane::align_with_point_normal(const l3d_point& point,
                                        const l3d_vector& normal)
{

  a = normal.a[0];
  b = normal.a[1];
  c = normal.a[2];

  d = -a * point.X_ - b * point.Y_ - c * point.Z_;
}

void l3d_plane::align_with_points(const l3d_point& p0,
                                  const l3d_point& p1,
                                  const l3d_point& p2)
{
  align_with_point_normal(p0, normalized(cross(p1-p0, p2-p0)));
}

int l3d_plane::intersect_with_segment(const l3d_point& p0,
                                      const l3d_point& p1)
{
  l3d_real t_top, t_bottom,
```

```
        dx, dy, dz;

        t_bottom = (l3d_mulrr(a,(dx=p1.X_ - p0.X_)) +
                    l3d_mulrr(b,(dy=p1.Y_ - p0.Y_)) +
                    l3d_mulrr(c,(dz=p1.Z_ - p0.Z_)));
        if(l3d_abs(t_bottom) <= 0)
        {
          return 0;
        }

        t_top = -1*(d +
                    l3d_mulrr(a,p0.X_) +
                    l3d_mulrr(b,p0.Y_) +
                    l3d_mulrr(c,p0.Z_));

        intersection_t = l3d_divrr(t_top, t_bottom);

        intersection.X_ = l3d_mulrr(dx,intersection_t) + p0.X_;
        intersection.Y_ = l3d_mulrr(dy,intersection_t) + p0.Y_;
        intersection.Z_ = l3d_mulrr(dz,intersection_t) + p0.Z_;
        intersection.W_ = int_to_l3d_real(1);

        return (t_top>0 ? CROSS_BACK_TO_FRONT : CROSS_FRONT_TO_BACK);
      }
```

The member variables a, b, c, and d allow us to directly access and change the coefficients of the plane as seen in the plane equation. The method `align_with_point_normal` takes a point on the plane and a normal vector as parameters, and computes the appropriate a, b, c, and d coefficients. Similarly, the method `align_with_points` takes three points on the plane as parameters, and computes the plane coefficients based on these three points. It works by interpreting the three points as a clockwise specification of polygon vertices, computing the normal vector to this polygon by taking a cross product, and calling the `align_with_point_normal` method with the computed normal vector and one of the specified points.

The method `side_of_point` takes a point as a parameter and evaluates the plane equation with the given point. The returned real value is positive if the point is in front of the plane, negative if the point is behind the plane, or zero if the point is on the plane.

NOTE Due to the inherent numerical inaccuracy of finite precision computations in the computer, points on the plane may, when evaluated with `side_of_point`, return values close to but not exactly zero. The solution to this inaccuracy is usually to introduce an *epsilon* parameter, which has the effect of making the plane slightly "thick." All points whose `side_of_point` return values lie between –epsilon and epsilon are then considered to be on the plane.

The method `intersect_with_segment` intersects the plane with a line specified by two points p_0 and p_1. It returns 0 if no intersection could be found, 1 if an intersection was found and p_0 is on the front side of the plane, or –1 if an intersection was found and p_0 is on the back side of the plane. The intersection, if found, is stored in member variable `intersection`. The intersection time, a parametric value ranging from 0 to 1 and representing the percentage of displacement from p_0 to p_1, is stored in member variable `intersection_t`. The intersection of lines with planes is useful for polygon clipping against arbitrary planes (covered next) and collision detection (covered in the companion book *Advanced Linux 3D Graphics Programming*).

Let's look at how the method `intersect_with_segment` works. First of all, let us consider the parametric form of the line going from $p_0=(x_0,y_0,z_0)$ to $p_1=(x_1,y_1,z_1)$.

Equation 7-3
$$\begin{aligned} x &= x_0 + t(x_1 - x_0) \\ y &= y_0 + t(y_1 - y_0) \\ z &= z_0 + t(z_1 - z_0) \end{aligned}$$

As the parameter t varies from 0 to 1, the coordinates move from p_0 to p_1. Outside of this range, the coordinates move before p_0 or beyond p_1.

Next, we plug in the x, y, and z values from the line into the plane equation. This gives us an expression for the plane equation at the time of its intersection with the parametrically defined line.

Equation 7-4
$$A(x_0 + t(x_1 - x_0)) + B(y_0 + t(y_1 - y_0)) + C(z_0 + t(z_1 - z_0))$$

Solving the equation for t yields:

Equation 7-5
$$t = \frac{-(D + Ax_0 + By_0 + Cy_0)}{A(x_1 - x_0) + B(y_1 - y_0) + C(z_1 - z_0)}$$

Notice that if the denominator of t is zero, then the parametric line and the plane never intersect; the line runs "parallel" to the plane. After calculating t, we can then plug it into the parametric form of the line to obtain the exact intersection point between the line and the plane.

This method calculates the intersection between the infinitely long <u>line</u> defined by the two endpoints and the plane. To calculate the intersection between the finitely long line <u>segment</u> and the plane, we would simply need to ensure that the computed t value lies between 0 and 1; if not, then the intersection is somewhere along the infinitely long line, but outside of the finitely long line segment. The method `intersect_with_segment` does not make this test, but instead stores the intersection time t so that the calling routine can decide what to do—in some cases, we want to intersect with just the line segment; in other cases, with the entire line.

Clipping Polygons to an Arbitrary 3D Plane

With the capability of intersecting lines and arbitrarily oriented planes, we can now clip a polygon against an arbitrary 3D plane. We have already seen how to clip a polygon against the near z plane, which we defined by a single scalar value. Now, we know how to represent arbitrary planes and how to intersect line segments (i.e., polygon edges) with these planes. With this knowledge, clipping a polygon against an arbitrary plane is a simple implementation issue.

The l3d_polygon_3d_clippable Class

The class `l3d_polygon_3d_clippable` is a polygon in 3D which can be clipped against an arbitrary 3D plane. The member variable `plane` stores the 3D plane of the polygon itself and is updated by the overridden methods `init_transformed` and `transform`. The method `clip_to_plane` clips the polygon's geometry against an arbitrary plane, specified as the parameter `clip_plane`. This method works similarly to the near z clipping method we already saw, `clip_near_z`. We look for crossing edges by using the plane's `side_of_point` method. We intersect crossing edges with the plane by using the `intersect_with_segment` method. Then, as usual, we create a new list of clipped vertices, and swap this with the main list. The "inside side" of the plane is defined to be the front side of the plane; everything in front of the plane is kept, everything behind the plane is clipped away.

 CAUTION   Defining the front side of a plane to be the "inside side" is not necessarily universal for all situations; it is simply the naming convention we choose for the purposes of 3D clipping. For solid modeling purposes, discussed in the companion book *Advanced Linux 3D Graphics Programming*, we tend to view the front side of a plane as representing the "outside" of an object. When you see the term "inside side" of a plane, keep in mind in which context the "inside side" is meant.

Notice that the `clip_to_plane` method is virtual. This is because descendant polygon classes may need to clip other information in addition to the geometry. In particular, clipping a textured polygon in 3D requires us also to clip the texture coordinates at the vertices, as described in the companion book *Advanced Linux 3D Graphics Programming*. In this case, the textured polygon class, which inherits from the clippable polygon class, overrides this method.

Listing 7-24: `p3_clip.h`

```
#ifndef __P3_CLIP_H
#define __P3_CLIP_H
#include "../../tool_os/memman.h"

#define __ACTIVE__P3_CLIP_H

#include "poly3.h"
#include "../plane/plane.h"
#include "../../dynamics/collide.h"

class l3d_polygon_3d_clippable :
       virtual public l3d_polygon_3d
{
  public:
    l3d_polygon_3d_clippable(void) : l3d_polygon_3d() {};

    l3d_polygon_3d_clippable(int num_pts) :
    l3d_polygon_3d(num_pts),
    l3d_polygon_2d(num_pts)

  {};
    virtual ~l3d_polygon_3d_clippable(void) {};

    l3d_plane plane;
    virtual int clip_to_plane(l3d_plane& clip_plane);
    void init_transformed(void);
    void transform(const l3d_matrix &m, int count);

    l3d_polygon_3d_clippable(const l3d_polygon_3d_clippable &r);
    l3d_polygon_2d *clone(void);
};

#undef __ACTIVE__P3_CLIP_H

#endif
```

Listing 7-25: `p3_clip.cc`

```cpp
#include "p3_clip.h"
#include "../../tool_os/memman.h"

int l3d_polygon_3d_clippable::clip_to_plane(l3d_plane& clip_plane) {
  int idx0,idx1;
  int crossedge0_idx0,crossedge0_idx1,crossedge1_idx0,crossedge1_idx1;
  int newedge_ivertex0, newedge_ivertex1;
  int i;
  int dir;

  idx0=0;
  idx1=next_clipidx_right(idx0, clip_ivertices->num_items);

  temp_clip_ivertices->num_items = 0;
  int extends_behind_plane = 0;

  while(
    !( (clip_plane.side_of_point((**vlist)[ (*clip_ivertices)[idx0].ivertex ].transformed) >
EPSILON_PLANE
        && clip_plane.side_of_point((**vlist)[ (*clip_ivertices)[idx1].ivertex ].transformed) <
-EPSILON_PLANE)
        ||
        (clip_plane.side_of_point((**vlist)[ (*clip_ivertices)[idx0].ivertex ].transformed) <
-EPSILON_PLANE
        && clip_plane.side_of_point((**vlist)[ (*clip_ivertices)[idx1].ivertex ].transformed) >
EPSILON_PLANE)))

  {
    (*temp_clip_ivertices)[temp_clip_ivertices->next_index()].ivertex =
      (*clip_ivertices)[idx0].ivertex;
    idx0=idx1;
    if (clip_plane.side_of_point((**vlist)[ (*clip_ivertices)[idx0].ivertex ].transformed) <
-EPSILON_PLANE) {extends_behind_plane = 1; }

    if(idx0==0) {

      if (extends_behind_plane) {
        return 0;
      }

      else
      {
        return 1;
      }

    }

    idx1=next_clipidx_right(idx0, clip_ivertices->num_items);
  }

  if (clip_plane.side_of_point((**vlist)[ (*clip_ivertices)[idx0].ivertex ].transformed) >
EPSILON_PLANE
      && clip_plane.side_of_point((**vlist)[ (*clip_ivertices)[idx1].ivertex ].transformed) <
-EPSILON_PLANE)
    {dir = CROSS_FRONT_TO_BACK; }else {dir = CROSS_BACK_TO_FRONT; }

  crossedge0_idx0 = idx0;
  crossedge0_idx1 = idx1;
```

```
        idx0=idx1;
        idx1=next_clipidx_right(idx0, clip_ivertices->num_items);

        while(
          !( (dir==CROSS_FRONT_TO_BACK
             && clip_plane.side_of_point((**vlist)[ (*clip_ivertices)[idx1].ivertex ].transformed) >
EPSILON_PLANE)
             ||
             (dir==CROSS_BACK_TO_FRONT
             && clip_plane.side_of_point((**vlist)[ (*clip_ivertices)[idx1].ivertex ].transformed) <
-EPSILON_PLANE)
          )
        )
        {
          idx0=idx1;
          if(idx0==crossedge0_idx0) {
            fprintf(stderr,"shouldn't be here! can't find 2nd crossing edge");
            return 0;
          }

          idx1=next_clipidx_right(idx0, clip_ivertices->num_items);
        }

        crossedge1_idx0 = idx0;
        crossedge1_idx1 = idx1;

        int new_idx;
        clip_plane.intersect_with_segment(
          (**vlist)[(*clip_ivertices)[crossedge0_idx0].ivertex].transformed,
          (**vlist)[(*clip_ivertices)[crossedge0_idx1].ivertex].transformed);
        new_idx = newedge_ivertex0 = (*vlist)->next_varying_index();
        (**vlist)[ new_idx ].transform_stage = 0;
        (**vlist)[ new_idx ].original.X_ =
          (**vlist)[ new_idx ].transformed.X_ = clip_plane.intersection.X_;
        (**vlist)[ new_idx ].original.Y_ =
          (**vlist)[ new_idx ].transformed.Y_ = clip_plane.intersection.Y_;
        (**vlist)[ new_idx ].original.Z_ =
          (**vlist)[ new_idx ].transformed.Z_ = clip_plane.intersection.Z_;
        (**vlist)[ new_idx ].original.W_ =
          (**vlist)[ new_idx ].transformed.W_ = int_to_l3d_real(1);

        clip_plane.intersect_with_segment(
          (**vlist)[(*clip_ivertices)[crossedge1_idx0].ivertex].transformed,
          (**vlist)[(*clip_ivertices)[crossedge1_idx1].ivertex].transformed);
        new_idx = newedge_ivertex1 = (*vlist)->next_varying_index();
        (**vlist)[ new_idx ].transform_stage = 0;
        (**vlist)[ new_idx ].original.X_ =
          (**vlist)[ new_idx ].transformed.X_ = clip_plane.intersection.X_;
        (**vlist)[ new_idx ].original.Y_ =
          (**vlist)[ new_idx ].transformed.Y_ = clip_plane.intersection.Y_;
        (**vlist)[ new_idx ].original.Z_ =
          (**vlist)[ new_idx ].transformed.Z_ = clip_plane.intersection.Z_;
        (**vlist)[ new_idx ].original.W_ =
          (**vlist)[ new_idx ].transformed.W_ = int_to_l3d_real(1);

        {
          idx0=idx1; idx1=next_clipidx_right(idx0, clip_ivertices->num_items);
        }

        temp_clip_ivertices->num_items = 0;
```

```
  if(dir==CROSS_FRONT_TO_BACK) {
    (*temp_clip_ivertices)[temp_clip_ivertices->next_index()].ivertex =
      newedge_ivertex1;

    for(i=crossedge1_idx1;
        i!=crossedge0_idx0;
        i=next_clipidx_right(i,clip_ivertices->num_items))
    {
      (*temp_clip_ivertices)[temp_clip_ivertices->next_index()].ivertex =
        (*clip_ivertices)[i].ivertex;
    }
    (*temp_clip_ivertices)[temp_clip_ivertices->next_index()].ivertex =
      (*clip_ivertices)[crossedge0_idx0].ivertex;

    (*temp_clip_ivertices)[temp_clip_ivertices->next_index()].ivertex =
      newedge_ivertex0;

    swap_temp_and_main_clip_lists();
  }else {
    (*temp_clip_ivertices)[temp_clip_ivertices->next_index()].ivertex =
      newedge_ivertex0;

    for(i=crossedge0_idx1;
        i!=crossedge1_idx0;
        i=next_clipidx_right(i, clip_ivertices->num_items))
    {
      (*temp_clip_ivertices)[temp_clip_ivertices->next_index()].ivertex =
        (*clip_ivertices)[i].ivertex;

    }
    (*temp_clip_ivertices)[temp_clip_ivertices->next_index()].ivertex =
      (*clip_ivertices)[crossedge1_idx0].ivertex;

    (*temp_clip_ivertices)[temp_clip_ivertices->next_index()].ivertex =
      newedge_ivertex1;

    swap_temp_and_main_clip_lists();
  }

  return 1;
}

void l3d_polygon_3d_clippable::init_transformed(void) {
  l3d_polygon_3d::init_transformed();
  plane.align_with_point_normal(center.transformed,
                        normalized(sfcnormal.transformed- center.transformed));

}

void l3d_polygon_3d_clippable::transform(const l3d_matrix &m, int count) {
  l3d_polygon_3d::transform(m,count);
  plane.align_with_point_normal(center.transformed,
                        normalized(sfcnormal.transformed-center.transformed));
}

l3d_polygon_2d* l3d_polygon_3d_clippable::clone(void) {
  return new l3d_polygon_3d_clippable(*this);
}

l3d_polygon_3d_clippable::l3d_polygon_3d_clippable
```

```
(const l3d_polygon_3d_clippable &r)
    : l3d_polygon_3d(r)
{
  plane = r.plane;
}
```

The l3d_polygon_3d_flatshaded_clippable Class

Future polygon classes descend from `l3d_polygon_3d_clippable`, so that they can all be clipped against arbitrary planes. However, the existing flat-shaded 3D polygon class `l3d_polygon_3d_flatshaded` introduced earlier does not descend from `l3d_polygon_3d_clippable`. For this reason, we declare the `l3d_polygon_3d_flatshaded_clippable` class to allow for flat-shaded polygons which can also be clipped against arbitrary planes in 3D. The class only overrides the `clone` method to return a copy of itself; all other behavior is inherited.

Listing 7-26: `p_cflat.h`

```
#ifndef __P3_CFLAT_H
#define __P3_CFLAT_H
#include "../../tool_os/memman.h"

#include "p3_flat.h"
#include "p3_clip.h"

class l3d_polygon_3d_flatshaded_clippable :
    virtual public l3d_polygon_3d_flatshaded,
    virtual public l3d_polygon_3d_clippable
{
  public:
    l3d_polygon_3d_flatshaded_clippable(int num_faces) :
    l3d_polygon_2d(num_faces),
    l3d_polygon_2d_flatshaded(num_faces),
    l3d_polygon_3d(num_faces),
    l3d_polygon_3d_flatshaded(num_faces),
    l3d_polygon_3d_clippable(num_faces)
  {}

    l3d_polygon_3d_flatshaded_clippable
    (const l3d_polygon_3d_flatshaded_clippable &r);
    l3d_polygon_2d *clone(void);

};

#endif
```

Listing 7-27: `p_cflat.cc`

```
#include "p3_cflat.h"
#include "../../tool_os/memman.h"

l3d_polygon_2d* l3d_polygon_3d_flatshaded_clippable::clone(void) {
  return new l3d_polygon_3d_flatshaded_clippable(*this);
}

l3d_polygon_3d_flatshaded_clippable::l3d_polygon_3d_flatshaded_clippable
(const l3d_polygon_3d_flatshaded_clippable &r)
    : l3d_polygon_3d(r),
    l3d_polygon_2d_flatshaded(r),
```

```
l3d_polygon_3d_flatshaded(r),
l3d_polygon_2d(r),
l3d_polygon_3d_clippable(r)
{
}
}
```

The l3d_object_clippable Class

Since we can clip polygons against arbitrary planes, the next logical step is to clip entire objects of polygons against arbitrary planes. This is essentially nothing more than clipping each polygon of the object in turn. However, there is an additional catch which makes it worthwhile to encapsulate the code in a separate routine. Specifically, it is often the case that we wish to permanently clip an object against a plane. Until now, we have always regarded clipping as a temporary operation—the original definition of the vertices stayed constant, and for each frame we initialized the clip vertex lists to be the same as the original vertex lists, then did any clipping we needed for the frame. At the beginning of the next frame, we again began with the original vertex lists. But there are some cases where we wish to perform a clip operation, and then actually redefine the original geometry of the object to be the clipped version. Some of the visible surface schemes presented in the companion book *Advanced Linux 3D Graphics Programming* require such clipping operations. (Examples include the BSP tree and octree.)

Making clipped geometry permanent is easy, but tedious to implement. We must:

- Move the varying items in the vertex list into the non-varying part. These are the new vertices which were created during clipping.
- Set the `original` value of each vertex to be the same as the current `transformed` (i.e., clipped) value.
- Copy the clipped vertex index list into the original vertex index list.
- Create a new polygon list for the object, containing only those polygons which survived the clipping operation.
- Shrink the vertex list for the object by removing any vertices which are no longer referenced by any polygon, and rewrite all polygon definitions to use the new vertex indices in the new, smaller vertex list.

Because of the number of steps involved, we have implemented the object clipping routines in a class. The class `l3d_object_clippable` represents a 3D object which can be clipped as a whole against an arbitrary 3D plane. The method `clip_to_plane` clips each polygon of the object against the specified plane, removing any polygons which are completely clipped away from the object's non-culled polygon list. This implies that `init_nonculled_list` must have been called earlier, usually indirectly through a call to the object's `reset` method. The method `make_current_geometry_permanent` carries out the steps listed above to make the current clipped geometry permanent.

Listing 7-28: `oclip.h`

```
#ifndef __OCLIP_H
#define __OCLIP_H
#include "../../tool_os/memman.h"

#include "object3d.h"
```

```
#include "../polygon/p3_clip.h"

class l3d_object_clippable :
    virtual public l3d_object
{

  public:

    l3d_object_clippable(int num_fixed_vertices) :
    l3d_object(num_fixed_vertices) {};
    virtual ~l3d_object_clippable(void);

    int clip_to_plane(l3d_plane& clip_plane);
    void make_current_geometry_permanent(void);
};

#endif
```

Listing 7-29: `oclip.cc`

```
#include <stdio.h>
#include <stdlib.h>
#include "oclip.h"
#include "../../tool_os/memman.h"

l3d_object_clippable::~l3d_object_clippable() {}

int l3d_object_clippable::clip_to_plane(l3d_plane& clip_plane)
{
  l3d_polygon_3d_node *n = nonculled_polygon_nodes;
  while(n) {
    l3d_polygon_3d_clippable *pc;
    pc = dynamic_cast<l3d_polygon_3d_clippable*>(n->polygon);
    if(pc) {
      if(pc->clip_to_plane(clip_plane)) {
      }else {
        if(n->prev) {
          n->prev->next = n->next;
        }else {
          nonculled_polygon_nodes = n->next;
        }

        if(n->next) {
          n->next->prev = n->prev;
        }
      }
    }
    n = n->next;
  }
  if(nonculled_polygon_nodes) return 1; else return 0;
}

void l3d_object_clippable::make_current_geometry_permanent(void)
{
  vertices->num_fixed_items =
    vertices->num_fixed_items +
    vertices->num_varying_items;
  vertices->max_varying_items =
    vertices->max_varying_items -
    vertices->num_varying_items;
```

```
vertices->num_varying_items = 0;

int ivtx;
for(ivtx=0;
    ivtx<vertices->num_fixed_items;
    ivtx++)
{
  (*vertices)[ivtx].original = (*vertices)[ivtx].transformed;
}

l3d_polygon_3d_node *n = nonculled_polygon_nodes;
while(n) {
  *(n->polygon->ivertices) = *(n->polygon->clip_ivertices);
  n = n->next;
}

n = nonculled_polygon_nodes;
l3d_list<l3d_polygon_3d*> new_polygon_list;
while(n) {
  new_polygon_list[new_polygon_list.next_index()] = n->polygon;
  n=n->next;
}

for(int i=0; i<polygons.num_items; i++) {
  int found=0;

  for(int j=0; j<new_polygon_list.num_items; j++) {
    if(polygons[i] == new_polygon_list[j]) {found = 1; }
  }

  if(!found) {
    delete polygons[i];
  }
  delete ( & polygons[i] );
}
for(int i=polygons.num_items; i<polygons.max_items; i++) {
  delete ( & polygons[i] );
}
polygons.num_items = 0;
polygons.max_items = 0;

polygons = new_polygon_list;

//- clean up any unused vertices, and rewrite polygon definitions
//- to use new vertex indices

l3d_two_part_list<l3d_coordinate> *new_vlist;
new_vlist = new l3d_two_part_list<l3d_coordinate> (1);
*new_vlist = *vertices;
new_vlist->num_fixed_items = 0;
for(ivtx=0; ivtx<vertices->num_fixed_items; ivtx++) {
  int vtx_found = 0;
  for(int ipoly=0; ipoly<polygons.num_items && !vtx_found; ipoly++) {
    for(int ivtx_poly=0;
        ivtx_poly<polygons[ipoly]->ivertices->num_items && !vtx_found;
        ivtx_poly++)
    {
      if((*polygons[ipoly]->ivertices)[ivtx_poly].ivertex == ivtx) {
        //- vertex is used: keep it.
```

```
                vtx_found = 1;

                int new_ivtx = new_vlist->num_fixed_items;
                new_vlist->num_fixed_items++;

                (*new_vlist)[new_ivtx] = (*vertices)[ivtx];
                //- replace all occurrences in all polys of "ivtx" with "new_ivtx"
                for(int ipoly_repl=0; ipoly_repl<polygons.num_items; ipoly_repl++) {
                  for(int ivtx_poly_repl=0;
                      ivtx_poly_repl<polygons[ipoly_repl]->ivertices->num_items;
                      ivtx_poly_repl++)
                  {
                    if((*polygons[ipoly_repl]->ivertices)[ivtx_poly_repl].ivertex
                       == ivtx)
                    {
                      (*polygons[ipoly_repl]->ivertices)[ivtx_poly_repl].ivertex
                      = new_ivtx;
                    }
                  }
                }
              }
            }
          }
        }
      }

  new_vlist->num_varying_items = 0;
  new_vlist->max_varying_items = 0;

  for(int i=new_vlist->list->max_items - 1;
      i >= new_vlist->num_fixed_items;
      i--)
  {
    delete ( & (*new_vlist)[i] );
    new_vlist->list->max_items--;
  }

  new_vlist->list->num_items = new_vlist->num_fixed_items;

  l3d_two_part_list<l3d_coordinate> *old_vlist;

  old_vlist = vertices;
  vertices = new_vlist;

  delete old_vlist;

}
```

Sample Program: objcopy

The next sample program, objcopy, illustrates object clipping by splitting a pyramid object against a plane and animating the split part in a cyclic motion so that you can see exactly where the split occurred. Use the normal navigation keys of class l3d_pipeline_world to fly around the scene.

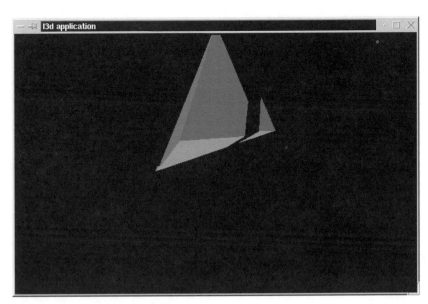

Figure 7-31:
Output from
sample program
objcopy.

NOTE To run this program, you must type **./objcopy** instead of just objcopy because of the system command named objcopy. The preceding dot and slash force the shell to execute the program in the current directory rather than the system command.

To "split" an object into two pieces, we create two identical copies of the object via the overridden assignment operator. Then, we clip the first copy of the object against the plane and make the clipping permanent. Next, we clip the second copy of the object against the other side of the plane and also make the clipping permanent. Clipping against the other side of the plane is done simply by negating the a, b, c, and d components of the plane—this has the effect of reversing the normal vector and the displacement of the plane, which essentially flips the front side and back side of the plane. By doing the clipping in this way, we end up with two parts of the object: one part which lies in front of the plane and another part which lies behind the plane. Thus, the object has been split by the plane into two pieces.

The main routine of interest in this program is the constructor for class my_world, which is where we create a pyramid object, copy it, and clip the two copies against different sides of the plane. The rest of the program is the typical object setup and pipeline initialization. The pyramid objects in this program have the ability to move back and forth in a cyclic motion, so that we can see the effect of the split more clearly (otherwise the two split pieces would still be located flush against one another, and no split would be visible).

Listing 7-30: main.cc, main file for program objcopy

```
#include <stdlib.h>
#include <string.h>
#include <stdio.h>
#include <math.h>

#include "../lib/geom/object/object3d.h"
#include "../lib/geom/polygon/p3_flat.h"
#include "../lib/tool_2d/screen.h"
```

```cpp
#include "../lib/tool_os/dispatch.h"
#include "../lib/raster/rast3.h"
#include "../lib/tool_2d/scrinfo.h"
#include "../lib/geom/world/world.h"
#include "../lib/pipeline/pi_wor.h"
#include "../lib/system/fact0_2.h"

#include "shapes.h"

#include <stdlib.h>
#include <string.h>
#include <stdio.h>
#include <math.h>
#include <stdarg.h>

class my_world:public l3d_world {
  public:
    my_world(void);
    void update_all(void);

};

main() {
  l3d_dispatcher *d;
  l3d_pipeline_world *p;
  my_world *w;

  factory_manager_v_0_2.choose_factories();
  d = factory_manager_v_0_2.dispatcher_factory->create();

  w = new my_world();
  p  = new l3d_pipeline_world(w);
  d->pipeline = p;
  d->event_source = w->screen;

  d->start();

  delete d;
  delete p;
  delete w;
}

void my_world::update_all(void) {
  l3d_world::update_all();
}

my_world::my_world(void)
    : l3d_world(640,400)
{

  l3d_screen_info *si = screen->sinfo;

  camera->VRP.set(0,0,-50,0);
  camera->near_z = float_to_l3d_real(5.5);
  camera->far_z = int_to_l3d_real(500);

  int i,j,k,onum=0, prev_onum;

  i=10; j=0; k=20;
```

```
    k=0;

    //- create a pyramid
    pyramid *orig_pyr;
    objects[onum=objects.next_index()] = orig_pyr = new pyramid();
    l3d_polygon_3d_flatshaded *p;
    for(int pnum=0; pnum<objects[onum]->polygons.num_items; pnum++) {
      p = dynamic_cast<l3d_polygon_3d_flatshaded *>
          (objects[onum]->polygons[pnum]);
      if(p) {
        p->final_color = si->ext_to_native
                          (rand()%si->ext_max_red,
                           rand()%si->ext_max_green,
                           rand()%si->ext_max_blue);
      }
    }
    orig_pyr->dx = 0;

    //- copy the pyramid
    pyramid *copy_pyr;
    prev_onum = onum;
    objects[onum=objects.next_index()] = copy_pyr =
                                          new pyramid();
    *objects[onum] = *objects[prev_onum];
    copy_pyr->dx = float_to_l3d_real(0.25);
    copy_pyr->maxx=int_to_l3d_real(5);
    copy_pyr->minx=int_to_l3d_real(0);

    //- define a clip plane
    l3d_plane clip_plane;
    clip_plane.a = int_to_l3d_real(-1);
    clip_plane.b = int_to_l3d_real(-1);
    clip_plane.c = int_to_l3d_real(-1);
    clip_plane.d = int_to_l3d_real(3);

    //- split the first copy on one side of the plane
    orig_pyr->reset();
    orig_pyr->clip_to_plane(clip_plane);
    orig_pyr->make_current_geometry_permanent();

    //- split the second copy on the other side of the plane
    clip_plane.a = -clip_plane.a;
    clip_plane.b = -clip_plane.b;
    clip_plane.c = -clip_plane.c;
    clip_plane.d = -clip_plane.d;
    copy_pyr->reset();
    copy_pyr->clip_to_plane(clip_plane);
    copy_pyr->make_current_geometry_permanent();

    screen->refresh_palette();
}
```

Listing 7-31: shapes.h, declaration of pyramid objects for program objcopy

```
#include "../lib/geom/object/oclip.h"

class pyramid:public l3d_object_clippable {
  public:
    l3d_real x;
    l3d_real dx;
    l3d_real maxx, minx;
```

```
    pyramid(void);
    virtual ~pyramid(void);
    int update(void);
};
```

Listing 7-32: shapes.cc, definition of pyramid objects for program objcopy

```
#include "shapes.h"

#include "../lib/geom/polygon/p3_cflat.h"
#include <stdlib.h>
#include <string.h>

pyramid::pyramid(void) :
    l3d_object(4),
    l3d_object_clippable(4)
{
  (*vertices)[0].original.set(float_to_l3d_real(0.),float_to_l3d_real(0.),float_to_l3d_real(0.),
                     float_to_l3d_real(1.));
  (*vertices)[1].original.set(float_to_l3d_real(10.0),float_to_l3d_real(0.),float_to_l3d_real(0.),
                     float_to_l3d_real(1.));
  (*vertices)[2].original.set(float_to_l3d_real(0.),float_to_l3d_real(10.),float_to_l3d_real(0.),
                     float_to_l3d_real(1.));
  (*vertices)[3].original.set(float_to_l3d_real(0.),float_to_l3d_real(0.),float_to_l3d_real(10.),
                     float_to_l3d_real(1.));

  int pi;
  pi = polygons.next_index();
  polygons[pi] = new l3d_polygon_3d_flatshaded_clippable(3);
  polygons[pi]->vlist = &vertices;
  (*polygons[pi]->ivertices)[polygons[pi]->ivertices->next_index()].ivertex=0;
  (*polygons[pi]->ivertices)[polygons[pi]->ivertices->next_index()].ivertex=1;
  (*polygons[pi]->ivertices)[polygons[pi]->ivertices->next_index()].ivertex=3;
  polygons[pi]->compute_center();polygons[pi]->compute_sfcnormal();

  pi = polygons.next_index();
  polygons[pi] = new l3d_polygon_3d_flatshaded_clippable(3);
  polygons[pi]->vlist = &vertices;
  (*polygons[pi]->ivertices)[polygons[pi]->ivertices->next_index()].ivertex=2;
  (*polygons[pi]->ivertices)[polygons[pi]->ivertices->next_index()].ivertex=3;
  (*polygons[pi]->ivertices)[polygons[pi]->ivertices->next_index()].ivertex=1;
  polygons[pi]->compute_center();polygons[pi]->compute_sfcnormal();

  pi = polygons.next_index();
  polygons[pi] = new l3d_polygon_3d_flatshaded_clippable(3);
  polygons[pi]->vlist = &vertices;
  (*polygons[pi]->ivertices)[polygons[pi]->ivertices->next_index()].ivertex=0;
  (*polygons[pi]->ivertices)[polygons[pi]->ivertices->next_index()].ivertex=2;
  (*polygons[pi]->ivertices)[polygons[pi]->ivertices->next_index()].ivertex=1;
  polygons[pi]->compute_center();polygons[pi]->compute_sfcnormal();

  pi = polygons.next_index();
  polygons[pi] = new l3d_polygon_3d_flatshaded_clippable(3);
  polygons[pi]->vlist = &vertices;
  (*polygons[pi]->ivertices)[polygons[pi]->ivertices->next_index()].ivertex=3;
  (*polygons[pi]->ivertices)[polygons[pi]->ivertices->next_index()].ivertex=2;
  (*polygons[pi]->ivertices)[polygons[pi]->ivertices->next_index()].ivertex=0;
  polygons[pi]->compute_center();polygons[pi]->compute_sfcnormal();

  num_xforms = 1;
  x=int_to_l3d_real(0);
```

```
    dx=int_to_l3d_real(0);
    modeling_xforms[0] = l3d_mat_translate
                        (dx,
                         int_to_l3d_real(0),
                         int_to_l3d_real(0));
    modeling_xform=
      modeling_xforms[0];
}

pyramid::~pyramid(void) {
}

int pyramid::update(void) {
  x += dx;
  if(x<=minx || x>=maxx) {
    dx = -dx;
  }
  modeling_xforms[0]=l3d_mat_translate
                      (x,
                       int_to_l3d_real(0),
                       int_to_l3d_real(0));
  modeling_xform=
    modeling_xforms[0];
}
```

Summary

In this chapter, we looked at the theoretical and practical side of using 3D polygons in our virtual environments. We saw l3d classes for handling 3D polygons, 3D objects, and 3D worlds. Some important topics we looked at were: normal vectors, vertex ordering, near z clipping, arbitrary plane clipping, dynamic behavior of 3D objects via subclassing or plug-ins, and the painter's algorithm.

We now have a pretty good handle on handling and drawing 3D polygons. But our sample programs have still been using fairly basic 3D objects: pyramids consisting of just a few triangles. Creating more complicated objects requires the use of a 3D modeling package. The next chapter covers using the free 3D modeling package Blender to create more interesting models for use in our 3D programs.

Chapter 8

Basic 3D Modeling with Blender

Overview

The previous chapters have emphasized the theoretical and algorithmic aspects of Linux 3D graphics. This chapter takes a break from the theory and looks at a completely different side of 3D graphics: 3D modeling. The term *3D modeling* refers to the use of a special software package to create, edit, and possibly animate 3D objects. In this book, we focus on 3D modeling from the standpoint of creating models for interactive 3D programs; the companion book *Advanced Linux 3D Graphics Programming* takes this one step further and shows how to model entire 3D worlds. 3D modeling in and of itself is a rich and varied field, and it is also possible to approach 3D modeling as a goal in its own right—to create visually attractive images or movies. For the purposes of this book, though, 3D modeling is a tool which makes it possible to create and to import interesting polygonal 3D objects into our 3D programs.

First of all, we look at the basics of 3D modeling packages in general, then proceed with a hands-on exercise using the freely available Blender modeler for Linux. To my knowledge, Blender is by far the most capable free 3D modeler available on any platform, and can definitely rival packages costing thousands of dollars. Blender 1.80 is included on the CD-ROM.

In this chapter we cover the following topics:

- Basics of 3D modeling
- The Blender user interface
- 3D polygonal modeling with Blender
- Exporting and importing 3D files

Basics of 3D Modeling

In order to create 3D models, a 3D modeling program must fulfill a few basic requirements. These include:

- Creation and placement in 3D of points, edges, polygons, surface normals, and meshes. A *mesh* is a group of 3D polygons sharing a common vertex list, just like the `l3d_object` class of Chapter 7.

- A selection of predefined primitive shapes (cube, sphere, pyramid) from which to build more complex objects.

- Viewing and changing the model from various viewpoints.

- Saving the polygonal data to a file for later import by a 3D engine.

Writing a simple 3D modeler is an instructive and to some extent enjoyable exercise; for some of my first experiments in 3D graphics, I used a 3D modeler that I wrote during my university studies. Based on the information from Chapters 1 through 7, you should be able to write your own 3D modeler. However, making a good 3D modeler—one which really saves time and enables complex models to be created and managed—is no small undertaking. Some of the features which a "good" 3D modeler should include are:

- Tools for changing meshes. Such tools work on groups of points instead of on individual points, which can greatly save time. Examples include a magnet tool, which allows proportional movement of several vertices within a given radius, and an extrusion tool for creating tubes from rings.

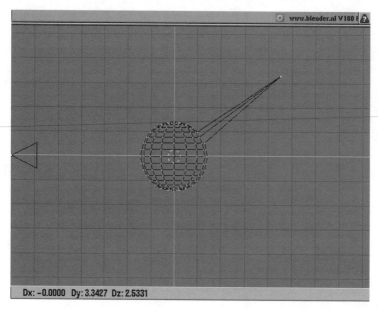

Figure 8-1: Editing one vertex without a magnet tool. Only the single vertex is moved. This makes larger scale changes very tedious; we must reposition each vertex individually.

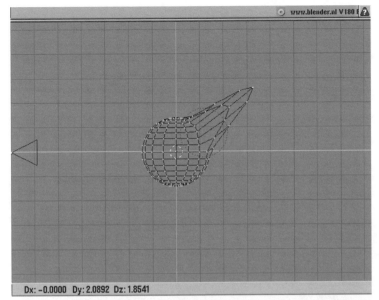

Figure 8-2: Editing a vertex with a magnet (or proportional editing) tool. The vertex and all surrounding vertices are magnetically pulled along with the selected vertex.

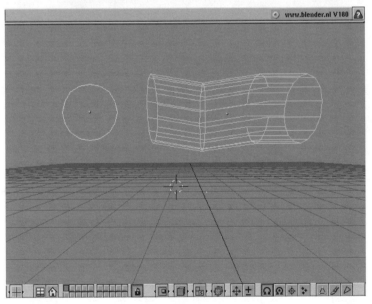

Figure 8-3: An extrusion tool. The ring shape, left, is extruded to create the tube shape on the right.

- Lighting capabilities to illuminate polygons.
- Texture mapping and texture coordinate assignment onto polygons.
- Animation of the objects within the scene.
- Layers for managing different, independent parts of the scene (background and foreground, for instance).
- Temporary hiding of some objects to make editing interior objects or parts of objects possible by temporarily hiding the exterior part. This is vital for dense or complex models.

Modelers which go beyond these requirements and offer some or more of the following features begin to fall in the professional category:

■ Scripting language and/or plug-ins for programmatically extending program functionality.

■ Key frame animation

■ Inverse kinematics for easy animation of jointed figures

■ Particle systems for creation of smoke, spark, or fire effects

■ Lattice deformation allowing the "bending" of an entire 3D mesh at once

■ Non-polygonal modeling with curved surfaces

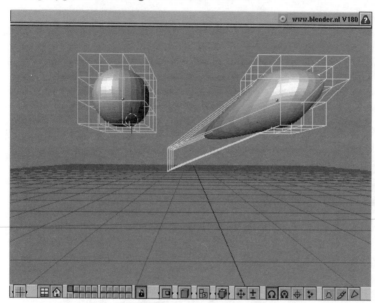

Figure 8-4: Lattice deformation of a spherical mesh. The sphere on the left has been assigned to a lattice, but the lattice has not been changed. The lattice for the sphere on the right has been changed by repositioning its vertices. This has the effect of deforming the underlying spherical mesh.

The free modeler Blender falls into the professional category, which is at first quite surprising, considering that it is a freely available tool. Let's first talk a bit about the history and philosophy of Blender, then take a tour of Blender and create some models.

Blender Background

Blender was originally the in-house modeling and animation tool for the Dutch animation company NeoGeo. Development of Blender took place internally in order to produce a better tool to create animations. Blender thus grew out of the real, day-to-day needs of 3D modelers and animators.

In May 1998, NeoGeo decided to go out of business. At this point, Ton Roosendaal, the primary architect and programmer of Blender, founded the company Not a Number (NaN) to support the further development of Blender as a product in its own right. Interestingly, NaN chose not to sell Blender, but rather to make it freely available for download. Blender was financed by the sale of user manuals and a special so-called C-key, which was a special license file which enabled the use of the newest Blender features. NaN's policy was always to let features migrate from the C-key version into the free version.

Today, the C-key has been discontinued, and all Blender features are freely available in Complete Blender, which is version 1.80. NaN now has financial backing from interested investors, and development continues on the much-awaited Blender version 2.0, which is currently available in a beta version for download on the Blender home page at `http://www.blender.nl`. Plans are to make Blender 2.0 also available as freeware. The official Blender user manuals are still available for purchase directly from NaN.

The unusual and generous business strategy of NaN has made it possible for countless individuals to enter the world of 3D modeling without needing to buy expensive 3D software, the prices of which usually start in the four-digit range. Blender is a powerful, freely available tool with which to do 3D modeling under Linux.

The Blender Philosophy

Blender has a very consistent, but somewhat unusual, user interface. This can be rather intimidating at first, but once you understand some basic principles, you will find that work with Blender is very efficient indeed.

Data, Visualize, Edit

Blender organizes 3D modeling around a three-part process: data, visualization, and editing. At the lowest level, data blocks form the basis for all Blender modeling activities. Blender scenes consist of many small data structures hierarchically linked together to form larger structures. For instance, the Blender mesh data structure defines the geometry of an object in 3D, containing vertices, polygons (also called *faces*), and normal vectors. The material data structure defines material properties of a surface, such as color, reflectivity, or transparency. The texture data defines a texture (i.e., an image) to be mapped onto a polygon or set of polygons. By linking a mesh with a material, and a material with a texture, we apply the texture to the mesh. This approach, which Blender terms an object-oriented approach to modeling, emphasizes the use and linking of several small data blocks, rather than a few monolithic data blocks, to create 3D objects and scenes.

Visualization of data blocks occurs within Blender's visualization and windowing system. The 3D data can be visualized in a number of ways, either in a high-quality 3D preview or in a simple wire-frame mode. Blender's windowing system allows for simultaneous viewing of the 3D data from various angles.

Editing of the data blocks occurs after the user selects some data to edit, typically by clicking on it with the mouse. Then, depending on the current selection, a number of different tools are available for changing the data. For instance, a mesh object offers tools for creating and repositioning vertices; a lamp object offers means of specifying light intensity and color. Editing occurs directly on the data itself, not on the visualization of the data. Then, the changed data is visualized once again, and the editing process continues in a loop.

The Keyboard and the Mouse

Blender typically offers both keyboard shortcuts and menu-based access to the same functions. However, to efficiently use Blender, you must take the time to learn several keyboard commands. During my visit to the NaN office, Ton explained that Blender's keyboard shortcuts were chosen so as to optimize work with the left hand on the keyboard and the right hand on the mouse. The right hand manipulates the mouse to select and position objects in the scene. The left hand presses single keys, which are more favorably located to the left side of the keyboard, to specify the desired tool for editing the selection. The alternative—always using the mouse to both choose commands from a menu and select parts of the 3D model—leads to a very tiring and repetitive movement of the mouse back and forth between menu and model. Once you get used to the system, you will like it!

The Learning Curve

Ton Roosendaal freely admits in the official Blender manual that Blender has a steep learning curve. It is not "easy to use" in the usual sense. Thus, please take the time to read slowly through the following few sections to understand the basics of Blender. Once you see how the system is constructed, you will find that all commands do indeed behave very consistently.

If you are fluent with the vi text editor, you can think of Blender as being similar for the area of 3D modelers. In vi, for instance, the command string **:.,$s/^/\/\/\/** puts a C++ comment delimiter at the beginning of every line from the current cursor position to the end of the file. With no knowledge of vi, the command looks cryptic, but with an understanding of regular expressions, the command is quite logical—indeed, simple. Learning Blender is similar to learning vi. At first, you fumble around trying to do the simplest of operations. Then, once you understand the system, you can learn the basic commands quickly. In the end, you can work very efficiently with the system.

So, it's now time to look at the Blender user interface and do some simple operations.

The Blender Interface

Start blender as follows: type **blender** at the shell prompt, and press **Enter**. (See the Appendix for instructions on installing Blender.) Immediately after starting, the Blender screen appears as in Figure 8-5. The same screen with added annotations appears in Figure 8-6. Later exercises in this chapter give you a chance to understand the various buttons and windows in a hands-on fashion, so don't worry if it all seems confusing now.

NOTE   The version of Blender described here is Blender 2.0 (also called the "Game Blender"). At the time of this writing, Blender 2.0 is currently in beta status, whereas Blender 1.80 (also called the "Complete Blender," and included on the CD-ROM) is the last stable release. A few features only work in 1.80 and not in 2.0, and vice versa. Therefore, at least for now, it is useful to use both Blender versions. The only differences in the interface between Blender 1.80 and Blender 2.0 are the location and appearance of some of the buttons; these differences are noted as appropriate in the remainder of the chapter.

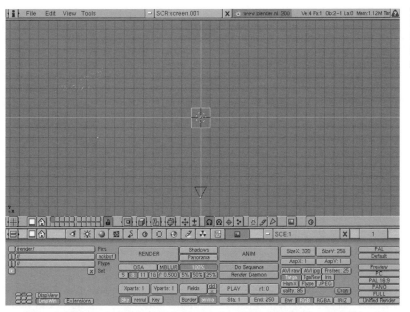

Figure 8-5: The Blender user interface immediately after starting.

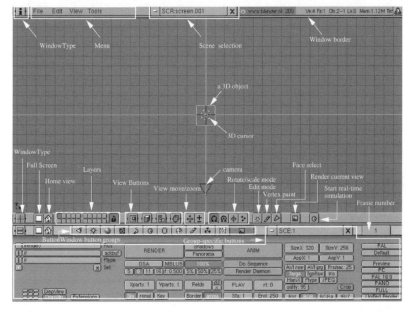

Figure 8-6: The Blender user interface, annotated.

The Window System

The first thing you will notice about Blender is that it fills the entire screen. Resizing the main Blender window depends on your window manager. The Blender user interface is drawn completely using OpenGL commands, not X Window System commands. This makes the interface portable to any OpenGL-capable operating system, but also means that the window handling depends on how your window manager deals with OpenGL windows.

To resize the main Blender window, using the KDE window manager:

1. Move the mouse cursor to one of the corners of the Blender screen.
2. Press and hold **Alt**.
3. Right-click the window corner, and drag the mouse cursor to resize the window.

To move the main Blender window:

1. Position the mouse cursor somewhere inside the Blender interface.
2. Press and hold **Alt**.
3. Left-click the Blender window, and drag the mouse cursor to reposition the window.

Under other window managers (for instance, IceWM under Debian), you can use the normal window manager commands to resize or move the main Blender window (drag the window corner to resize, drag the title bar to move).

Inside of its main window, Blender's user interface is completely under the control of Blender, and its behavior does not depend on the external window manager. The Blender interface consists of a number of non-overlapping, rectangular windows. A thin border separates windows at their edges. You can resize a window within Blender by dragging its border as follows:

1. Position the mouse cursor exactly over the border. The mouse cursor changes to a small two-sided arrow to indicate that the border can now be dragged. If the border is vertical, it can only be dragged horizontally; if it is horizontal, it can only be dragged vertically.
2. Click and hold the left mouse button, move the mouse cursor to a new position, and release the mouse button.

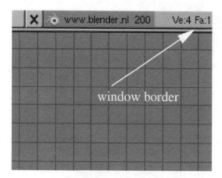

Figure 8-7: A window border.

Window Types

Each window in Blender has a *type*. The window type determines the appearance and functionality of the window. A unique feature of the Blender window system is that you can change the type of an existing window, rather than opening a new window of the desired type. Any window can assume every type. This means you can have multiple copies of the same window type, or you can even do all your work in one single window, changing the type of the window as necessary.

Each window has a header, which is a sort of miniature toolbar containing buttons for the most frequently used commands for the window type. The window header may be positioned either at the top or the bottom of the window. To change the positioning of the header:

1. Right-click on a blank area (between the buttons) in the header. A pop-up menu asks for confirmation.

2. Press **Enter**. The header changes position, from top to bottom or bottom to top.

NOTE If you try this out now, switch the header back to its original position when you are done. Otherwise, the appearance of your screen may no longer correspond to the figures and text.

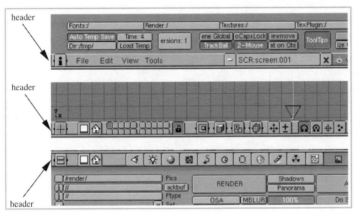

Figure 8-8: Various window headers in Blender. The leftmost button in the header indicates the window type.

A button at the very left of the window header indicates the current window type. This button is one of Blender's many custom button types—in this case, the button is of type ICONSLI. We cover Blender's button types later in this chapter. The window type button can take on one of a fixed number of "values," where each value is an icon specifying the window type. Figure 8-9 lists the possible window types, and Figure 8-10 shows a Blender interface with all window types open simultaneously.

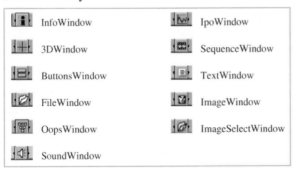

Figure 8-9: Window types in Blender.

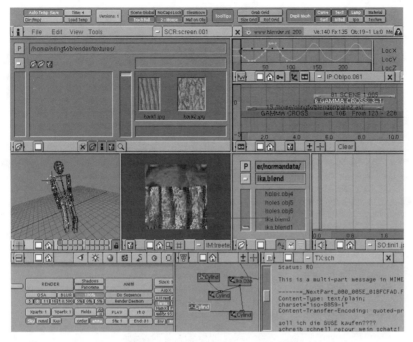

Figure 8-10: All window types open simultaneously.

In Blender 2.0, change the type of a window as follows:

1. Click on the ICONSLI button in the window header. Notice the vertical menu which pops up, where each entry in the menu is an icon representing a window type.

2. Click the desired entry in the menu. The current window changes to become a window of the selected type.

In Blender 1.80, the operation of the ICONSLI buttons was different. Thus, in Blender 1.80, change the type of a window as follows:

1. Position the mouse cursor over the leftmost ICONSLI button in the window header.

2. Left-click the ICONSLI button, keeping the left mouse button pressed.

3. Drag the mouse left or right to change the value of the button, and thus the window type, to the previous or next setting. Alternatively, left-click the left or right side of the button once to change to the immediately preceding or immediately following setting.

Let's now briefly go over each window type.

- InfoWindow: Contains global settings for the entire program, such as directory names.

- 3DWindow: Displays 3D objects and allows creation, positioning, and editing of these objects.

- ButtonsWindow: Edits properties of the current selection in the 3D window, or of global editing or rendering parameters.

- FileWindow: Selects files for loading and saving.

- OopsWindow: Displays the internal object-oriented programming structure (OOPS) of the currently selected scene, in a tree format. Editing is not allowed in this window.

- SoundWindow: Allows integration of sounds into interactive 3D environments created with Blender. In Blender 2.0 beta, this window type is not yet fully functional.

- IpoWindow: Displays and edits interpolators (IPOs), which are used for interpolating various object parameters over time. Blender has a very flexible interpolation system where many parameters can be interpolated and thus animated over time; interpolators can animate objects, vertices, textures, lamps, or sequences.

- SequenceWindow: Combines and mixes among various animation sequences. This window type is essentially a post-production video studio, where each animation sequence is represented as a horizontal strip with the length indicating the duration. Strips can be blended or combined with one another, allowing, for instance, smooth fades between different parts of a 3D animation. Another exciting possibility is the combination of Blender rendered animations with existing video footage from another source, such as a video camera.

- TextWindow: Edits a text file. Used primarily for creating script files for the built-in Python extension language.

- ImageWindow: Displays an image. Useful for previewing texture image files; also used for assigning specific texture coordinates to specific faces of a mesh.

- ImageSelectWindow: Selects an image file for loading or saving, displaying a thumbnail preview of each image file for easy differentiation.

The following sections cover in more detail the InfoWindow, 3DWindow, ButtonsWindow, and FileWindow, which are the main windows we need to perform basic 3D modeling. Unfortunately, a detailed coverage of all window types in Blender is beyond the scope of this book. Consult the Blender reference manual, available directly from NaN, for a comprehensive coverage of Blender functionality. Additionally, there are several excellent tutorials available online from enthusiastic Blender users. Many of these are linked directly from the Blender home page at `www.blender.nl`. After understanding the window system and the Blender mechanisms for moving and selecting objects, you should also be able to explore the other window types on your own.

Operations on Windows

We'll now look at some useful operations on windows: maximizing, restoring, splitting, and joining windows.

Maximizing a window causes it to fill the screen. Maximize a window as follows:

1. Move the mouse cursor into the window to be maximized.

2. Press **Ctrl+Up Arrow**. Pressing the same keys again undoes the maximization.

Splitting a window creates two windows in place of one, each of the same type as the previous window. You can only split a window at the borders. Split a window as follows:

1. Move the mouse cursor into the window to be split.

2. Move the mouse cursor towards the border until it changes shape into a two-sided arrow, indicating that the cursor is exactly on top of the border. If you overshoot the border and the mouse cursor lands in the next adjoining window, you must begin again at step 1; the window to be split is the window in which the mouse cursor was immediately before landing on the border.

3. Middle-click the border. A pop-up menu appears asking for confirmation of the action.

4. Press **Enter** to confirm the action, or **Esc** to cancel.

Joining two windows is the opposite of splitting them. To join two windows:

1. Move the mouse cursor into the window which should remain after the join operation.

2. Move the mouse cursor towards the border until it changes to a two-sided arrow, being careful again not to overshoot the border.

3. Right-click the border. A confirmation menu appears.

4. Press **Enter** to confirm the action, or **Esc** to cancel.

A final word about working with windows: the position of the mouse cursor determines which window may receive keyboard input. To work with a window, make sure that the mouse cursor is located somewhere within the borders of the desired window.

Button Types

Blender has a number of unique button types for setting options and entering data. Some are probably familiar to you, but some are almost certainly new or different than expected. Figure 8-11 illustrates the possible button types in Blender.

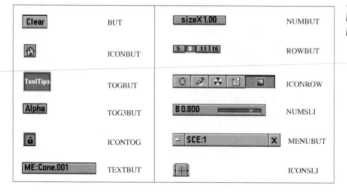

Figure 8-11: Button types in Blender.

A description of each button type follows.

- BUT: Executes a single action, such as save or load. Left-click the button once to invoke the action.
- ICONBUT: The same as type BUT, but with an iconic instead of a text caption.
- TOGBUT: Toggles a particular option on or off. Left-click the button once to change its status from off to on or vice versa. In the on status, the button appears depressed; on the off status, it appears to protrude.
- TOG3BUT: Toggles a particular option between three states: off, positive, or negative. In negative status, the text is displayed in yellow.
- ICONTOG: The same as type TOGBUT, but with an iconic instead of a text caption.

- TEXTBUT: Allows entry of text strings to name data blocks or specify other textual information. Left-click the button once to activate the text entry mode. Then, type the text. During text entry, press **Shift+Backspace** to delete the entire text; press **Shift+Left Arrow** or **Shift+Right Arrow** to move the cursor to the beginning or end of the text, respectively. Press **Enter** or left-click the button again to confirm the entry. Press **Esc** to cancel the entry.

- NUMBUT: Allows entry of numerical values. Left-click and drag the mouse left to decrease the value; drag the mouse right to increase the value. During dragging, press and hold **Ctrl** to change values in steps, or **Shift** to change the values in finer increments. Alternatively, left-click the left side of the button to decrease the value slightly; right-click to increase. Or, press and hold Shift, and left-click the button for approximately one second. The button then changes into a TEXTBUT, allowing direct keyboard entry of the desired numerical value.

- ROWBUT: Selects one of a number of mutually exclusive options. Only one button in the row can be active at any time.

- ICONROW: The same as type ROWBUT, but with iconic instead of text captions.

- NUMSLI: Allows visual entry of a numerical value, whose range is limited, via a slider. Left-click and drag the slider left or right to decrease or increase the value. The left side of the button functions exactly like a TEXTBUT and allows direct keyboard entry of the desired value.

- ICONSLI: The same as type ICONROW, but only the active button is displayed. The operation of this button is different between Blender 1.80 and Blender 2.0. In Blender 2.0, click the button to display a menu with the available options; then click on the desired selection. In Blender 1.80, left-click the button and drag the mouse left or right to see and activate the other available options. Alternatively, in Blender 1.80, left-click the left side of the button to select the previous option; left-click the right side of the button to select the next option.

- MENUBUT: Allows selection, creation, and deletion from a list of items. The middle part of the button is a TEXTBUT and displays the currently selected entry; if no entry is selected, this part is blank. Left-click and hold the left part of the button (displaying the hyphen) to display a pop-up menu containing the current list of items. Drag the mouse to the desired item and release the left mouse button to make a selection. Or, select the **ADD NEW** entry from the menu to create a new entry in the list. Edit the name of the new entry by using the TEXTBUT as described earlier. Left-click the X at the right side of the button to delete the currently selected entry from the list.

Now let's take a closer look at the windows we will need most frequently: the InfoWindow, the ButtonsWindow, the 3DWindow, and the FileWindow. Of these, the 3DWindow is the most important, because most of the 3D modeling work is done within this window.

The InfoWindow: Setting Global Parameters

The InfoWindow is initially located at the top of the Blender interface, with only one line visible. Resize this window by dragging its border downwards. Figure 8-10 shows a resized InfoWindow at the top.

Make sure that the ToolTips button is activated. This causes a brief explanatory text to appear either in the header of the InfoWindow (Blender 1.80) or next to the button (Blender 2.0) when the mouse is located over a button in the user interface. This makes understanding unknown features easier.

The Auto Temp Save button should also be activated, which causes your work to automatically be saved at regularly occurring intervals specified by the adjoining button Time. The automatically saved files are located in the directory specified by the underlying Dir button, and have the name `<pid>.blend`, where `<pid>` is the process number of the Blender program. After successfully exiting Blender, the file is renamed to `quit.blend`. This automatic save facility is very valuable; if for some reason your computer crashes, you will lose, at most, a few minutes of work.

TIP Make sure you understand the auto-save features of Blender to avoid losing work.

The header of the InfoWindow also contains some useful buttons. In particular, there are two buttons of type MENUBUT, one labeled "SCR," the other "SCE." The SCR button controls which screen is currently active. A Blender *screen* is a particular window configuration. By defining multiple screens, you can configure multiple work spaces for the same scene, each with a different window layout. For instance, one screen might contain a window layout ideal for editing 3D information, while another could contain a window layout optimized for editing video sequences. The SCE button controls which scene is currently active. (Starting with Blender 2.0, the SCE button is only accessible through the header of the ButtonsWindow, when the AnimButtons are active.) A *scene* is a complete set of 3D objects in Blender, typically separate from other scenes, although objects can be linked between scenes (with key Ctrl+l) so that changes to the object in one scene propagate to other scenes. Creating new scenes allows you to store several logically separate 3D scenes within one Blender file. Furthermore, you can copy the entire scene into a new scene, which allows you to freely experiment with making changes to the scene without the danger of destroying your original work.

Creation of new screens and new scenes occurs through the MENUBUT buttons and the entry ADD NEW. Creation of a new scene causes a pop-up menu to appear, where you can choose if the new scene should be empty, should contain links to the current scene, or should contain a complete and separate copy of the current scene. Creating links between the new scene and the old scene means that changing the positions of objects in the original scene also causes a change in position in the new scene; creating a complete and separate copy means that changes in one scene do not affect the other scene.

The ButtonsWindow: Properties of the Current Object

The ButtonsWindow is initially located at the bottom of the Blender interface, and provides information either about the currently active object in the 3DWindow (covered in the next section), or about globally applicable options such as rendering or radiosity parameters. A button of type ICONROW is in the middle of the window header; the current selection in this button determines the appearance of the rest of the window. See Figure 8-12.

Figure 8-12: The current selection in the ICONROW of the ButtonsWindow determines the appearance of the rest of the ButtonsWindow.

You may be familiar with contemporary visual programming environments for Rapid Application Development (RAD); such environments typically offer a window where you design dialog boxes, and a property editor with two tab sheets where you specify properties and events for the current selection in the design window. (Delphi is a good example of such an environment.) Think of Blender's ButtonsWindow as a property editor for the currently active object in the 3DWindow; instead of just having two categories of possible settings (properties and events), it has 12 categories of possible settings—the number of buttons in the ICONROW.

Each possible setting of the ICONROW button in the ButtonsWindow calls up a different set of buttons, each of which has a name. Figure 8-13 shows the name of the set of buttons which each setting causes to appear.

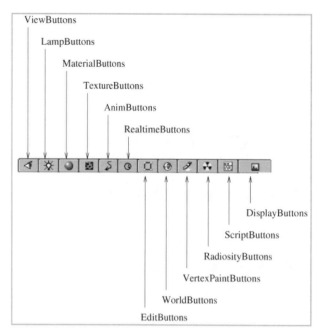

Figure 8-13: The possible settings of the ICONROW button in the ButtonWindow.

A description of each of these sets of buttons follows. Each set of buttons can also be called up with a single key combination. The following list shows the most important hotkeys in parentheses; see the Blender manual for the others.

- ViewButtons (Shift+F7): Control the view settings affecting this window. In order to use the ViewButtons, you must first change this window to be of type 3DWindow, then back to type ButtonsWindow, via the ICONSLI button in the window header (as described earlier). Having done this, you then see the ViewButtons. The settings in the ViewButtons then determine the viewing parameters for this window when it is of type 3DWindow. In a 3DWindow, press **Shift+F7** to display the ViewButtons; press **Shift+F5** to return to the 3DWindow. (Note that you can achieve the same effect by manually changing the window type.)

- LampButtons (F4): Control settings for the currently active lamp object in the 3DWindow. If no lamp object is active in the 3DWindow, then no LampButtons appear.

- MaterialButtons (F5): Control settings of the materials for the currently active object. A *material* is a set of parameters controlling the appearance of the surface of an object, and any textures mapped onto the surface; such parameters include color, specularity, reflection, and transparency. Up to 16 materials may be associated with an object. If the currently active object in the 3DWindow (such as a lamp) has no alterable material parameters, then no MaterialButtons appear.

- TextureButtons (F6): Control settings of the textures for the currently active object. Textures may be images, procedural textures, or plug-in textures. Up to eight textures may be associated with an object. If the currently selected object in the 3DWindow cannot be associated with a texture, then no TextureButtons appear.

- AnimButtons (F7): Control settings for animations consisting of moving objects. These buttons also allow for the creation of additional animation effects, such as particle systems.

- RealtimeButtons (F8): Control settings for the construction of real-time interactive environments within Blender. These buttons are only available starting with Blender 2.0, and are intended to allow the creation of interactive content within Blender by associating behavior with each object. Because of the complexity and amount of information which may be entered in these buttons for large real-time interactive simulations, these buttons may migrate into a new window type in a future version of Blender.

- EditButtons (F9): Control settings related to the editing of the currently active object in the 3DWindow. For instance, for a polygonal mesh object, the EditButtons offer functions to spin, extrude, or otherwise alter the positions or parameters of the vertices of the mesh; for a text object, the EditButtons allow the setting of the font and justification of the text.

- WorldButtons: Control settings of the current world. A *world* in Blender is a non-polygonal background image and settings above which the real 3D objects are rendered. For instance, modeling of skies and stars are usually done through the world.

- VertexPaintButtons: Control settings of VertexPaint mode. In VertexPaint mode, you can assign colors directly to the vertices of polygons in the 3DWindow, which are then interpolated across the polygon during rendering. This allows for custom lighting effects.

- RadiosityButtons: Control settings for the computation of radiosity lighting for the currently active object in the 3DWindow. Radiosity lighting in Blender creates a new, finely divided mesh with many more vertices, and assigns the newly computed light intensities to the new vertices. (An alternative, more often used in real-time graphics applications, would be to leave the original mesh intact, and to compute light maps for each of the polygons in the original mesh.)

- ScriptButtons: Control settings for either global or object-specific scripts. A Blender *script* is a small program in the Python programming language which can be executed manually or called automatically when certain events (such as a frame change in an animation) occur.

- DisplayButtons (F10): Control global settings for the display and rendering of images and animations.

Typically, you use the ButtonsWindow by making a certain object in the 3DWindow active, then by altering parameters of the active object in the ButtonsWindow. Thus, the ButtonsWindow and the 3DWindow interact closely. Let's now look at the 3DWindow.

The 3DWindow: Editing 3D Objects

The 3DWindow is the main part of the Blender interface, and is therefore, by default, the largest window. In the 3DWindow, you create and position vertices in 3D to form polygons and objects, and position objects in 3D to form complete 3D scenes. Typically, you do not begin creating a 3D polygonal object from scratch, but instead begin with one of Blender's predefined 3D primitives, such as a cube, a sphere, or a pyramid. Then, you change the model by scaling it, adding or deleting vertices and polygons, extruding it, and so forth.

Changing the Viewing Parameters

Initially, the 3DWindow displays an overhead view of the scene in parallel (also called *orthographic*) projection mode. Blender offers functions for changing the projection mode as well as the viewpoint. Let's cover each topic separately.

Perspective or Parallel Projection

As for the viewing mode, Blender offers two modes: a perspective projection mode and a parallel projection mode, as defined in Chapter 5. The viewing mode defines the appearance of the 3D objects within the 3DWindow. The default is the parallel projection mode. Typically, you perform modeling in the parallel projection mode, for precise positioning of the vertices. Precise modeling in perspective mode is difficult because of the convergence of parallel lines as they recede into the distance. However, perspective mode is useful after precise positioning in parallel mode, in order to see if the final model looks correct as it will be displayed later in the 3D program. Toggle the viewing mode between perspective and parallel by typing **5** on the numeric keypad.

Standard Viewpoints

Blender offers four standard viewpoints; alternatively, you can interactively change the viewpoint. Type any of the following keys, which must be typed from the numeric keypad, to change the viewpoint to one of the standard views:

- 1: Front view, parallel projection
- 3: Side view, parallel projection
- 7: Top view, parallel projection
- 0: Camera view, with projection mode being defined by the camera's parameters (typically perspective projection)

Notice that on the numeric keypad, the 7 key is above the 1 key, and the 3 key is beside the 1 key. This explains the choice of keys.

You can also interactively change the viewpoint in several ways, covered below.

Rotation

Rotation of the viewpoint allows you to see the scene from a different angle. Rotate the viewpoint with the mouse as follows:

1. Move the mouse cursor somewhere inside the 3DWindow.
2. Middle-click, and keep the mouse button pressed.
3. Drag the mouse cursor to change the viewpoint. The starting mouse location from step 1 determines the amount of rotation of the viewpoint.

Alternately, you can use the arrow keys on the numeric keypad (not the normal arrow keys) for rotating the viewpoint; the viewpoint rotates in the direction of the chosen arrow.

Typically, you only rotate the viewpoint in perspective mode, just to see how the model looks from various angles. Rotating the viewpoint in orthographic mode can be very confusing visually, because the lack of perspective foreshortening leads to confusion between the near side and far side of objects.

Zooming

Zooming the view allows you to see more or less of the scene. To zoom the view with the keyboard:

1. Press + on the numeric keypad to zoom in the view.
2. Press - on the numeric keypad to zoom out the view.

To zoom the view with the mouse:

1. Press and hold **Ctrl**.
2. Middle-click within the 3DWindow, and drag the cursor. Dragging up zooms the view in; dragging down zooms the view out.

Panning or Translating

Panning or translating the view allows you to move the viewpoint directly up, down, left, or right to see another part of the scene. To translate the view with the keyboard, press **Shift+Left Arrow**, **Shift+Right Arrow**, **Shift+Up Arrow**, or **Shift+Down Arrow** to translate the viewpoint directly left, right, up, or down. These arrow keys are the ones on the numeric keypad.

To translate the view with the mouse:

1. Press and hold **Shift**.
2. Middle-click within the 3DWindow, and drag the cursor. The viewpoint translates in the direction of the drag.

To zoom the view with the mouse:

1. Press and hold **Ctrl**.
2. Middle-click within the 3DWindow, and drag the cursor. Dragging up zooms the view in; dragging down zooms the view out.

Multiple Simultaneous Views

Blender's window system allows for several windows of the same type to be open simultaneously. This means that we can open several 3DWindows, each with a separate view of the scene. Blender automatically updates all 3DWindows simultaneously.

It can be useful, for instance, to have a top and side view of the scene open simultaneously. This makes modeling easy: in one 3DWindow, you model as seen from the top; in another, from the side. You can also open a 3DWindow with a perspective or camera view on the object to see, in real time, the object as it would appear in an l3d 3D application (since l3d applications use perspective projection).

The Home View

In large 3D scenes, it is possible to get "lost in space" by accidentally repositioning the viewpoint such that nothing more is visible. To recover from such a situation, left-click the Home button, displayed with a small house icon, in the header of the 3DWindow. This positions the viewpoint such that all objects are visible.

The 3D Cursor

The 3D cursor in Blender is shaped like a cross hair, and is initially located in the center of the screen. (Refer back to Figure 8-6.) It denotes the position, in 3D, where new objects or vertices will be added. It also plays a role in certain rotation and scaling operations. Therefore, knowing how to position the 3D cursor accurately is very important.

Fundamentally, a left-click in the 3DWindow causes the 3D cursor to be positioned at the location of the mouse cursor. Of course, this is an ambiguous problem: the mouse cursor position is specified by 2D screen coordinates, whereas the 3D cursor position is an arbitrary 3D location.

The fact that a left-click in the 3DWindow positions the 3D cursor, combined with the fact that the screen to 3D problem is ambiguous, means that we typically use two viewpoints to position the 3D cursor. For instance, first we switch to top view, then position the cursor from an overhead view. Then, we switch to side view, and additionally specify the vertical position of the cursor, as seen from the side. You can do this either by using one 3DWindow and switching the viewpoint as described above, or you can have two 3DWindows open simultaneously, each with a different viewpoint.

The Toolbox and Menus

The *ToolBox* is the main pop-up menu used for editing operations in the 3DWindow. Many of the functions in the ToolBox also have keyboard shortcuts.

Display the ToolBox by pressing Space. Select items in the ToolBox by moving the mouse cursor and left-clicking. The ToolBox is a multi-level menu: an entry followed by ">>" means that the entry has sub-entries; an entry preceded by ">" indicates that the entry is not at the top level of the menu, but is instead at some deeper level. Deeper levels of the ToolBox menu are not displayed in new menus, but instead use the same menu, where each entry is then preceded by a ">" character. To go back up to the higher level in the menu, simply move the mouse cursor to the left side of the menu.

Moving the mouse cursor outside of the boundaries of the ToolBox causes it to disappear, taking no action. The Esc key has the same effect. On the other hand, pressing **Enter** or left-clicking the desired entry accepts or executes the current selection within the menu.

The usage conventions described for the ToolBox apply not only to the ToolBox, but also to pop-up menus in general within the Blender interface.

Working with Objects

Now, with an understanding of the most important features of Blender's unique interface, we're ready to add and edit objects within the 3DWindow.

The following example adds a sphere to the scene. Other objects are added similarly, by selecting the corresponding entries from the ToolBox.

1. Position the 3D cursor to the desired location in 3D space where the new object should be added.

2. Press **Shift+a**. This brings up the ToolBox with the Add sub-menu already selected. Alternatively, you can display the ToolBox as normal with **Space**, then select **Add**.

3. Select item **Mesh** to add a polygonal mesh. The next deeper level of the menu appears.

4. Select item **UVsphere** to add a sphere defined by segments (vertical strips) and rings.

5. Notice the pop-up menu which asks for the number of segments. The entry is done in a button of type NUMBUT. Enter **16** and click **OK**.

6. Notice the pop-up menu which asks for the number of rings. Again, the entry is done in a button of type NUMBUT. Enter **16** and click **OK**.

7. Notice the sphere with 16 segments and 16 rings which is added. The Blender user interface now enters the EditMode, covered a bit later. For now, we just want to leave EditMode. Press **Tab** to leave EditMode.

At this point, you can reposition the 3D cursor and add other objects. Blender offers the following polygonal 3D primitives: plane, cube, circle, UVsphere, icosphere, cylinder, tube, cone, and grid. Of these, the plane, circle, and grid are actually flat 2D objects; the others are 3D. The 2D objects can then be extruded to form 3D objects, an operation which we see later in this chapter.

 NOTE Blender supports non-polygonal objects, such as NURBS curves and surfaces. We won't be using these directly, since we focus on polygonal 3D graphics in this book. However, non-polygonal objects can usually be converted to polygonal objects in Blender by activating the desired objected and pressing **Alt+c**.

Activating and Selecting Objects

Blender allows for selection of one or multiple objects in the 3DWindow. Although multiple objects may be selected at once, there may only be a maximum of one *active* object. The active object is the one for which the ButtonsWindow (and the IpoWindow, if one is open) show and allow editing of the data. However, most commands typically operate on all *selected* objects, such as scaling or deletion commands.

Selected objects are displayed in pink in the 3DWindow. The active object is displayed in a lighter color than the other selected objects.

Select an object and make it active by right-clicking it. This also automatically deselects any other objects. To select multiple objects, press and hold **Shift** while right-clicking the desired objects. In this selection mode, clicking an object which is already selected deselects the object. The last object clicked is the active object.

An alternative way of extending a current selection is to use the border selection mode. In this mode, you can either select or deselect all objects located within a rectangular region on the screen. Use border selection mode as follows:

1. Press **b** to enter border selection mode. Notice the large cross hair that appears within the 3DWindow.

2. Select a rectangular region of the screen by using the cross hair as follows. Move the mouse cursor to one corner of the desired selection rectangle. Left-click, drag the mouse cursor to the opposite corner of the desired rectangle, then release the left mouse button. The objects within the rectangle are selected.

3. Deselect a rectangular region in a similar manner, but using the right mouse button. Move the mouse cursor to one corner of the rectangle, right-click and drag to the opposite corner, then release the right mouse button. The objects within the rectangle are deselected.

Deleting Objects

Press **x** to delete the selected objects in the 3DWindow. A confirmation window appears; press **Enter** to confirm the deletion, or press **Esc** to cancel.

Translating, Rotating, and Scaling Objects

You can apply a transformation, as defined in Chapter 6, to the active and/or selected objects. The allowable transformations are translation, rotation, and scaling operations. All of these operations do not change the underlying geometry of the object; instead, they merely define an additional transformation to be applied to the object. Compare this with the array of transformation matrices stored with class `l3d_object`; transformations do not change the underlying geometry, which is defined in the vertex list. In Blender, applying a translation, rotation, or scaling operation to an object is similar to storing an additional transformation matrix in the transformations array. Changing the actual underlying geometry is done in EditMode, covered later in this chapter.

Use the following keys to translate, rotate, or scale the active and/or selected objects.

▪ Type **s** to scale the current selection. Then, move the cursor closer to the object's center to scale down or away from the object's center to scale up. While moving the cursor, press and hold **Ctrl** to scale in fixed increments; press and hold **Shift** to scale in very fine increments. Left-click or press **Enter** to accept the scaling, or **Esc** to cancel. While scaling, you can middle-click to limit the scaling to just the *x*, *y*, or *z* axis (thus creating a non-uniform scaling); Blender computes the appropriate axis based on the already initiated mouse movement. Middle-click again to return to normal uniform scaling mode. To completely undo a previously applied scaling operation, press **Alt+s**; a pop-up menu appears. Confirm your choice by pressing **Enter**.

▪ Type **r** to rotate the current selection. Then, move the cursor around the 3D object to rotate it, and press **Enter** to accept. The **Ctrl** and **Shift** keys also work as described above. Type **Alt+r** to clear a previously applied rotation.

▪ Type **g** to translate (grab) the current selection. Then, move the cursor to reposition the object, and press **Enter** to accept. The **Ctrl** and **Shift** keys also work as described above. Type **Alt+g** to clear a previously applied translation.

 TIP   Notice that in general, whenever a numerical value is being changed within the Blender interface, the Ctrl and Shift keys work as modifiers to allow changing the value in fixed increments or in extremely fine increments. You can begin now to see what we mean when we say that the Blender user interface is unique, but consistent.

While scaling, rotating, or translating an object, you can also use the arrow keys (the normal ones, not the ones on the numeric keypad) to move the mouse cursor in pixel increments. This is convenient for "nudging" an object very slightly in a particular direction.

Duplicating Objects

Duplicating an object, which we equivalently refer to as copying an object, allows you to make a second, identical copy of an object. Blender offers two duplicate functions: a normal and a linked duplicate function. The normal duplicate function creates a completely separate and independent copy of the original. On the other hand, the linked duplicate function creates a copy of the original which may be independently transformed, but whose underlying geometrical shape is linked with that of the original. With a linked duplicate, changes to the geometry (which are done in EditMode, covered a bit later) of one of the objects automatically causes the same change in all of the linked objects. This is useful for identical objects which must be positioned or oriented differently. For instance, you might want to model the four wheels of a car as linked duplicates. This way, if you change the shape of one of the wheels, all four wheels automatically reflect the new shape. With separate duplicates, you would have to update each of the wheels individually, and could not be completely sure that all of the wheels were completely identical.

Create duplicates in Blender as follows.

1. Select the object or objects to be duplicated by right-clicking them. You may duplicate several objects at once by selecting several objects (**Shift+right-click**).

2. Press **Shift+d** to create a normal (separate) duplicate, or press **Alt+d** to create a linked duplicate. Blender immediately creates duplicates of the selected objects, places them at the same location as the original objects, selects only the newly created duplicate objects, then enters grab mode to allow you to move the newly created objects to a new location.

3. Move the mouse or use the arrow keys to position the duplicate objects at the desired position. Left-click to finish the operation.

 CAUTION   You cannot cancel the duplicate operation by pressing Esc; instead, you must delete the duplicate objects afterwards if you wish to cancel the operation.

Note that Blender immediately duplicates the objects after pressing Shift+d or Alt+d. If you press Esc to try and cancel the operation, you actually cancel the grab operation which Blender automatically invokes after the duplication; the duplicate objects have already been created at this point. To delete the duplicate objects—and effectively cancel the duplicate operation—press **x**. Remember, Blender automatically selects just the duplicate objects after a duplicate operation, so pressing x deletes just the duplicate objects. If you don't press x to delete the duplicate objects, but instead just press Esc, the duplicate objects remain in the 3DWindow, positioned exactly on top of the original objects. This can lead to great confusion later because what looks like one object in the 3DWindow would in this case actually be two exactly overlapping objects. So, make sure to either reposition or delete the duplicate objects after executing a duplicate operation.

In some cases, you may have made a linked duplicate which you then wish to separate from its linked siblings, so that the duplicate object is then completely separate from all others and can be modified without affecting any others. Remove the linked relationship as follows:

1. Select the object you wish to unlink.

2. Press **l**, which invokes the Make Local command. A menu appears asking which objects should be made local.

3.   Select **Selected** from the menu and press **Enter**.

The selected object is now completely separate from all other objects, just as if it were duplicated with the Shift+d instead of Alt+d duplicate command.

Hierarchical Objects

Sometimes, it can be useful to link objects together in a hierarchy, so that transformations applied to the parent object also apply to the child objects. For instance, if modeling a car, it can be useful to make the car body the parent of the wheel objects. This way, any transformation of the parent object, the car body, also propagates to the child objects, the wheels. Or, if modeling an arm consisting of a top limb and a bottom limb, you can make the top limb the parent of the bottom limb. This way, moving the top part of the arm (the parent) also moves the rest of the arm (the child) along with it, but the bottom part of the arm still has its own local transformation matrix and can thus be rotated (or less commonly, translated) relative to the top of the arm.

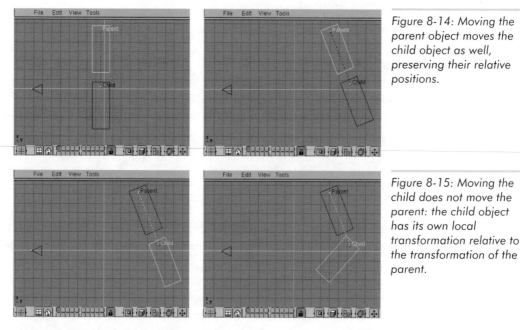

Figure 8-14: Moving the parent object moves the child object as well, preserving their relative positions.

Figure 8-15: Moving the child does not move the parent: the child object has its own local transformation relative to the transformation of the parent.

To make such a hierarchical link between objects, proceed as follows:

1.   Select all child objects.

2.   Select the parent object. Make sure the parent object is active, as shown by its lighter color than the other selected objects.

3.   Press **Ctrl+p** to make the active object the parent. A confirmation menu appears; press **Enter**.

From this point on, all transformations applied to the parent object also apply to the child objects. A broken line is drawn between the child and parent objects to indicate the hierarchical relationship.

To clear the hierarchical relationship, select the child object, and press **Alt+p**. A confirmation menu appears. Select **Clear Parent** to separate the child object from its parent. This, however, also clears any transformation which the parent may have applied to the child, which might cause the child object to have a different location, rotation, or size after the parent has been cleared. To maintain the same relative transformation between parent and child even after clearing the parent relationship, select **...and keep transform** from the confirmation menu. As the name suggests, this clears the parent relationship, but keeps the same transformation so that the child object appears identical after clearing the relationship.

 TIP   You can use the OopsWindow, mentioned earlier, to view the hierarchical relationships among objects.

Layers

Blender allows objects to be stored within different layers. A *layer* is a collection of objects whose visibility may be toggled between visible and invisible. Using layers allows you to organize your work into logical areas and selectively make certain layers visible or invisible, so that you can focus just on certain parts of the scene. Another use of layers is to temporarily move an object into a different, invisible layer, which effectively makes the object temporarily invisible. Later, you can move the object back into the original layer to make it visible again.

Blender offers 20 layers. The following keys control the use of layers:

- 1 through 0: Switch the currently visible layer to be a layer between 1 and 10.
- Alt+1 through Alt+0: Switch the current layer between layers 11 and 20.
- Shift+1 through Shift+0: Toggle visibility of layers 1 through 10, allowing multiple selection of layers.
- Shift+Alt+1 through Shift+Alt+0: Toggle visibility of layers 11 through 20.
- m: Move the currently selected objects to another layer. After pressing m, a menu appears. Type a digit from 1 through 0 or from Alt+1 through Alt+0 to choose the layer into which the selected objects should be moved, and press **Enter**. The objects are moved into the specified layer. If the specified layer is visible, then no change appears to take place; if the specified layer is invisible, then the objects appear to disappear. Switch to the other layer to see the objects again.

The currently visible layers are displayed in the layer buttons in the header of the 3DWindow. The layer buttons are a group of 20 small toggle buttons, where any number may be simultaneously activated. If the layer's button is activated, then the objects in the layer are visible; otherwise, they are invisible. You activate layers either by using the number keys, as described above, or by clicking directly on the appropriate layer buttons with the mouse.

Figure 8-16: The layer buttons.

EditMode

We have now seen how to create primitive polygonal 3D objects, such as cubes, spheres, or cones. We know how to place these objects in 3D space, how to view these objects from different viewpoints, how to transform these objects, how to copy these objects, and how to use layers to organize these objects.

There is a limit, however, to the types of modeling we can achieve only by using primitive objects like cubes and spheres. Although we can theoretically use extremely large numbers of extremely small primitives to create models of arbitrary complexity, this strategy approaches a voxel representation rather than a polygonal one, meaning that we lose the efficiency of polygonal representation. To create more interesting and efficient polygonal 3D models, we need to define and change our 3D objects at the vertex and polygon level.

Blender clearly distinguishes between the object-level operations, which we have been performing so far, and the vertex-level operations, which allow us to exactly define the vertices and polygons forming an object. To perform vertex-level operations, you must switch Blender into a special mode, the EditMode. Conversely, to return to object-level operations, you must exit out of EditMode. EditMode operates only on one object at a time, the currently active object.

Switch into EditMode by pressing **Tab**. The currently active object is then displayed with its edges drawn in black, instead of the usual light pink color. The individual vertices of the object are drawn in pink, to indicate that they, in EditMode, may be directly manipulated. Exit EditMode by pressing **Tab** again.

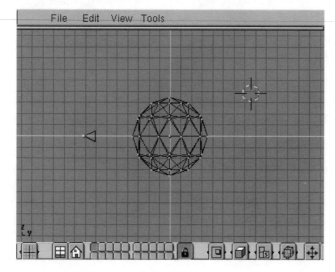

Figure 8-17: An object in EditMode.

The EditButtons allow you to set some options which make editing easier. In particular, Blender can draw the faces and normal vectors belonging to an object. (Normally, only the edges of the faces are drawn, and the normal vectors are not drawn.) This is quite useful in many cases, but can clutter the display when many faces are present, which is why Blender's default is not to activate these options. But, for beginning modeling, it is better to turn these options on. Turn on Blender's face and normal vector drawing as follows:

1. Activate any polygonal mesh object in the 3DWindow by right-clicking it.
2. Display the EditButtons for the polygonal mesh in the ButtonsWindow: press **F9** or click on the EditButtons icon.
3. Notice the two buttons of type TOGBUT in the lower-right corner of the mesh EditButtons, labled "Draw Normals" and "Draw Faces." Activate both of these buttons.

From this point on, all polygonal mesh objects will be drawn with faces and normal vectors when in EditMode.

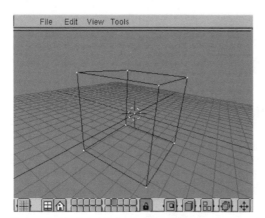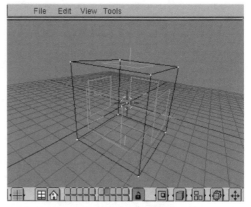

Figure 8-18: EditMode without faces and normal vectors drawn (left), and with faces and normal vectors drawn (right).

Now, let's see what we can do in EditMode; the following sections all assume that Blender is already in EditMode. First, we see how to manipulate existing vertices and faces; then, we see how to add new vertices and faces to an existing polygonal mesh.

Working with Existing Vertices and Faces

Working with vertices in EditMode is similar to working with objects when you are not in EditMode. The following are the most important operations:

■ Selection. Select a vertex by right-clicking it; select multiple vertices by pressing **Shift+right-click**. Selected vertices are displayed by Blender in yellow; non-selected vertices are displayed in pink. Type **b** to enable border selection mode of vertices; then, just as with objects, dragging the cross hair with the left or right mouse button selects or deselects all vertices within the dragged region. Type **a** to toggle selection of all vertices in the object. Selecting a polygonal face is done by selecting all of its corresponding vertices; the selected face is then displayed in yellow.

■ Transformation. Type **g**, **r**, or **s** to grab (translate), rotate, or scale the selected vertices. The transformations work very similarly to translating, rotating, or scaling complete objects; moving the mouse after pressing the appropriate transformation key allows you to control the amount of the transformation. The modifier keys Ctrl or Shift may be held down while moving the mouse to allow finer control of the transformation, just as before. Press the arrow keys after pressing the appropriate translation key to "nudge" the selected vertices slightly in a particular direction.

■ Deletion. Type **x** to delete the selected vertices. Since selection of vertices and faces are essentially equivalent in EditMode, Blender cannot immediately know whether you wish to delete just the faces (leaving the vertices in place) or both the vertices and the faces. Thus, a menu appears, asking you to specify what exactly you wish to delete. The allowable options are to delete the vertices, edges, faces, all, edges and faces, or only faces.

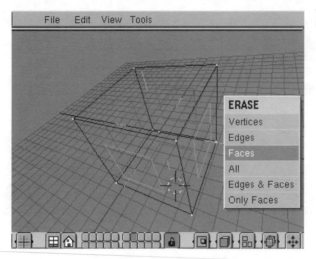

Figure 8-19: Deletion of faces.

■ Alignment. Type **Shift+s** to snap (align) the selected vertices to certain positions. A pop-up menu then allows you to snap the selected vertices to the nearest grid point or to the current location of the 3D cursor. The second operation is generally only recommended when only one vertex is selected, since with multiple selected vertices a snap to the cursor causes all the selected vertices to overlap, which is usually undesirable (but overlapping vertices can be removed with the Rem Doubles button in the EditButtons). Additionally, the pop-up menu for the snap operation allows you to snap the cursor, instead of the selection, to the nearest grid point or to the location of the selection (the center of the selection is used if multiple vertices are selected).

TIP The snap commands can also be applied to entire objects outside of EditMode.

■ Hiding. A very useful feature in EditMode is the temporary hiding of certain parts of the geometry so that other parts are visible. Type **h** to hide the selected vertices temporarily; press **Alt+h** to show all vertices again. Leaving EditMode also causes all vertices to be displayed.

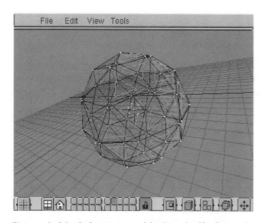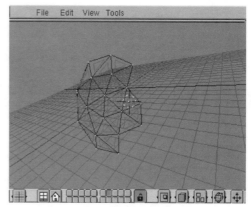

Figure 8-20: Selecting and hiding half of an object's vertices.

Adding New Vertices and Faces

In addition to merely manipulating existing vertices, you can also add new vertices and faces to an object in EditMode. Add new vertices as follows:

1. Move the mouse cursor to the desired location for the new vertex.
2. Press and hold **Ctrl**, and left-click. A new vertex appears at the location of the mouse cursor. If previously a vertex was selected, an edge is automatically created between the previously selected vertex and the newly created one; otherwise, the new vertex appears alone and unconnected to any other vertex. The new vertex is automatically selected after creation, meaning that a series of connected edges may be created by a series of Ctrl+left-click operations.

Creating faces requires an additional step. Faces (polygons) in Blender all have either three or four vertices—no more. To create a face:

1. Select exactly three or four vertices which you wish to belong to a face.
2. Type **f**. Blender creates a face from the selected vertices. Assuming that face drawing mode is enabled, as described above, the outline of the new face is also drawn.

Tips for Effectively Using EditMode

When you are dealing with moderate to large meshes, working in EditMode can sometimes get confusing due to the large number of vertices and faces present. In particular, sometimes it is not clear which vertices or faces have been selected, because things appear to overlap so much. Here are a few tips for dealing with complex models in EditMode.

■   Hide vertices which are obstructing your view (press **Alt+h**).

■   Change the viewpoint interactively (middle-click and drag in the 3DWindow). Often, vertices may appear to overlap, so what appears to be a selected vertex or face may in fact be a vertex or face behind the intended one.

- Switch between orthogonal and perspective viewpoints (type **5** on the numeric keypad). Orthogonal mode is best for modeling, but perspective is good for getting a spatial sense of the model.

- Temporarily start, then cancel a grab operation (type **g**, then press **Esc**). This allows you to temporarily move the selected vertices to see which ones they actually are. This technique is quite useful for discovering duplicate, overlapping vertices, edges, or faces. The Rem Doubles button in the EditButtons removes overlapping vertices automatically should you discover any unwanted duplicates.

- Use border select mode to select all of a set of apparently overlapping vertices. (Apparently overlapping vertices refers to the fact that the vertices simply appear to overlap from the current viewpoint, though they may or may not actually overlap in 3D space.) Without border selection mode, clicking on the vertex will only randomly select one of the overlapping vertices. Border select mode selects them all.

- Activate the TOGBUT Draw Faces in the EditButtons if you want to be able to see which faces are selected.

Undoing Changes in EditMode

We saw earlier that transformations made to objects outside of EditMode are easily undone; Alt+g clears a translation, Alt+r clears a rotation, and Alt+s clears a scaling transformation on an object. The reason that such changes are so easily undone, as explained earlier, is that these transformations do not affect the underlying geometry of the object, but are instead simply additional matrices which are applied to the underlying geometry.

Changes in EditMode, however, are indeed permanent and affect the intrinsic geometry of the object. For this reason, changes in EditMode are not easily undone. Blender offers a limited undo mechanism. As soon as you enter EditMode, the current geometry (i.e., the position of all vertices and the definitions of all faces) is saved. While in EditMode, and after having made any number of changes to the vertices and faces, you can revert the object back to its original state by pressing **u**.

However, as soon as you leave EditMode, you can no longer undo your changes. Therefore, before you make any changes to an object which you might wish to undo, it is useful to leave and then enter EditMode, so that you can revert to the original state of the object. Additionally, you may find it useful to make a separate copy of the object (Shift+d, outside of EditMode) before making any major modifications, so that you still have the original in case something goes wrong. You may also want to store the original in another, invisible layer, so that it does not clutter the current scene. Finally, you can also create an unlimited number of scenes (by using the scene button in the InfoWindow, described earlier) to store progressively more complicated versions of your work so that going back to a previous state simply requires you to switch to a previously created scene.

The FileWindow: Saving, Loading, and Exporting Files

Saving and loading files occurs in the FileWindow. Blender supports a number of different file formats, including native Blender, VRML, DXF, and a simple ASCII file format called Videoscape. We focus on the native Blender file format and the Videoscape format. The native

Blender file format is the usual format you should use to save your work; it saves all objects, all layers, all scenes, and even the window layout and any global parameters set in the InfoWindow. Therefore, loading a file previously saved in native Blender format completely restores your working environment to be the way it was at the time of the save. The native Blender file format, however, is extremely complex internally (it is in fact a sort of self-contained file system) and is not documented. Therefore, to save our 3D models into files which can be read by other programs, we need to use one of the other file formats supported by Blender. In this book, we use the Videoscape format, which is a very simple ASCII file format, described below.

Save a file in native Blender format as follows:

1. Press **F2**. The current window changes to become type FileWindow. Notice the window header displays the caption "SAVE FILE." The top line of the FileWindow displays the current directory. The next line displays the current filename. Beneath these two lines is a list of directories and files accessible from the current directory.

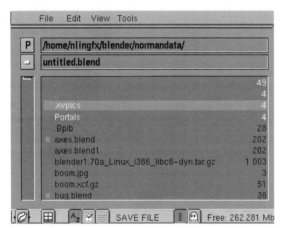

Figure 8-21: Saving a file.

2. Type a filename into the second line of the FileWindow and press **Enter**. Or, middle-click on a filename within the list to select an existing file. Left-click a directory name in the list to change to that directory; this also refreshes the directory listing.

 NOTE Blender filenames end with the string ".blend." If you do not specify ".blend" as the filename extension, it will be appended automatically to the filename you specify.

3. If the specified file already exists, a confirmation menu appears asking if you wish to save over the existing file. Press **Enter** to confirm, or **Esc** to cancel.

Load a file as follows:

 CAUTION Even if you have unsaved changes in the current file, Blender will load a new file without asking you to save your previous changes. So make sure you have saved any changes before loading a new file.

1. Press **F1**. The current window changes to become type FileWindow.

2. Type a filename into the second line of the FileWindow and press **Enter**. Or, middle-click an existing filename in the list.

You can append an existing file to the current file by pressing Shift+F1, clicking on the button APPEND in the window header, and specifying a filename.

Save objects in the Videoscape file format as follows:

1. Select the objects to be saved in the 3DWindow by right-clicking them.

2. Press **Alt+w**. The current window changes to become type FileWindow. Notice the window header displays the caption "SAVE VIDEOSCAPE."

3. Type a filename into the second line of the FileWindow and press **Enter**. Or, middle-click on a filename within the list to select an existing file. Videoscape files end with the string ".obj"; if you do not specify this extension, it will be appended automatically to the filename you specify.

Blender then saves each 3D object into a separate file. The separate files have sequentially numbered filenames; that is, each file has a filename of the form `xxx.obj`, `xxx.obj1`, `xxx.obj2`, and so forth.

Loading Videoscape files is done with the F1 key, just as with normal native Blender files. Selecting one of the sequentially numbered Videoscape files causes that Videoscape file and all sequentially following files to be loaded. So, if you choose the first `xxx.obj` Videoscape file, all files `xxx.obj`, `xxx.obj1`, `xxx.obj2`, and so forth will be loaded. If you choose `xxx.obj1`, then only all files with a number of 1 or higher will be loaded.

A Videoscape file looks as follows:

```
3DG1
number
X Y Z
X Y Z
...
nr index1 index2 index3 ... color
nr index1 index2 index3 ... color
```

 NOTE This is the Videoscape file format for polygonal meshes. Blender also supports curves and surfaces, as mentioned earlier. The Videoscape export formats for these objects is different than these for polygonal meshes, but we only use polygonal meshes in this book.

The lines of the file are interpreted as follows:

▪ `3DG1`: The header for a Videoscape file.

▪ `number`: The total number of vertices.

▪ `X Y Z`: A vertex, represented as a 3D (x,y,z) location. This line type appears within the file as many times as the total number of vertices.

▪ `nr index1 index2 index3 ... color`: A polygonal face definition. This line type appears within the file as many times as there are polygonal faces. The term `nr` is the number of vertex indices within this face. The terms `index1`, `index2`, and so forth are integer vertex indices, starting at 0, that refer to vertices in the vertex list specified earlier in the file. The vertices define the polygon and are specified in counterclockwise order looking at the front side of the polygon, which is exactly the opposite of the convention we have been using so far. (We use a left-handed system for our computations; Blender uses a right-handed system. We see later how to convert from the right-handed to the left-handed system.) The term color is a 24-bit hexadecimal number specifying the color of the face in blue, green, red format (the highest 8 bits blue, the middle 8 bits green, and the lowest 8 bits red.

At this point, we know enough about Blender to create some models and import them into our programs. We haven't looked at all of Blender's features, but will touch upon some other of Blender's capabilities in the course of exploring a practical example. So now, let's look at a hands-on tutorial with Blender.

Tutorial: Creating and Exporting a Spaceship

In this tutorial, we create a simple spaceship consisting of two identically shaped side thrusters and a main body. Begin by starting Blender. Then, press **Ctrl+x, Enter** to clear the entire scene.

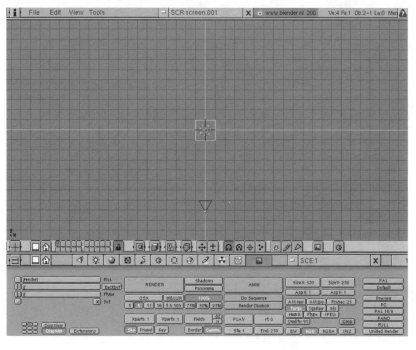

Figure 8-22: The default Blender configuration after clearing the entire scene.

Create and Link a Thruster Object

The first step is to create the thruster objects as follows:

1. Type **1** on the numeric keypad to switch to front view. Left-click somewhere in the upper-left corner of the 3DWindow to position the 3D cursor.

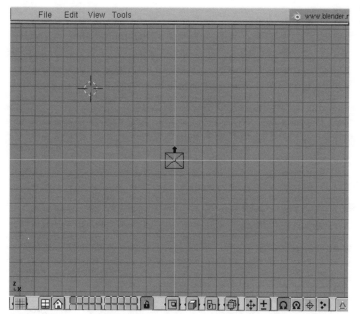

Figure 8-23

2. Type **3** on the numeric keypad to change to side view. Left-click the 3DWindow approximately seven grid lines to the right of the middle line to position the 3D cursor further back.

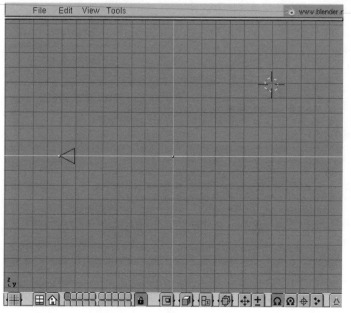

Figure 8-24

3. Press **Shift+a**, and select **Mesh** then **Cone** from the Toolbox. A menu appears asking the number of vertices in the cone.

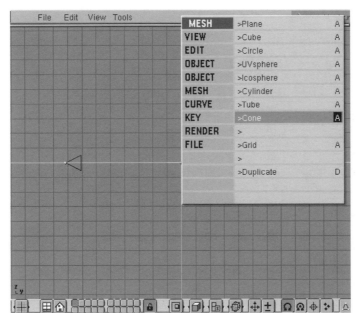

Figure 8-25

4. Enter **5** in the NUMBUT and press **Enter**. A cone appears at the 3D cursor position, viewed from the front, and Blender switches into EditMode.

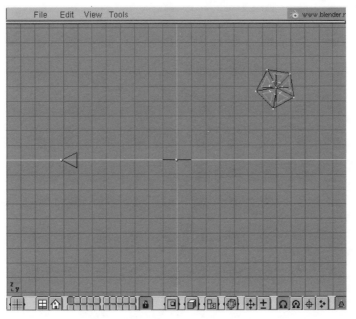

Figure 8-26

5. Type **7** on the numeric keypad to change to top view. Notice that from the top, the cone is now clearly recognizable.

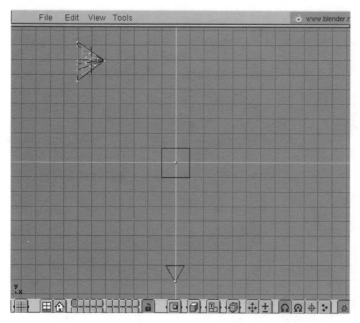

Figure 8-27

6. Press **Tab** to exit EditMode.
7. Press **Alt+d** to create a linked duplicate of the cone. Blender enters grab mode automatically. Move the duplicate cone somewhere to the right of the square plane object in the middle of the screen, and left-click to place the object.

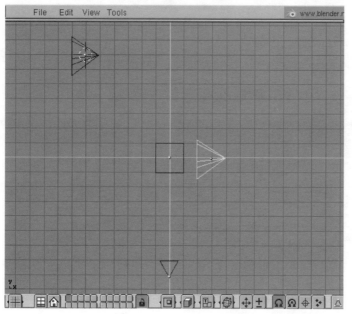

Figure 8-28

8. Type **r** and rotate the cone about 70 degrees so that the tip points upwards and slightly away from the square plane object. Left-click to finish.

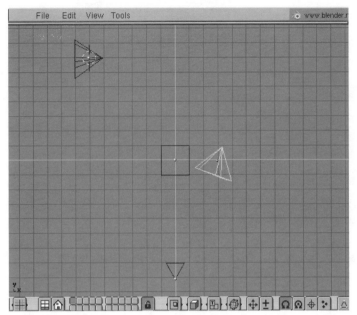

Figure 8-29

9. Press **Alt+d** to create another linked duplicate of the cone, and position it similarly on the left side of the square plane object. Rotate it as well, so that it points towards the upper left. The left and right cones should now be mirror images of one another, one on each side of the plane object.

10. Right-click the first cone object, located at the upper-left corner of the screen. Press **Tab** to enter EditMode, right-click the tip vertex of the cone, press **g**, and move the vertex a few units to the right so that the cone is longer, and left-click to finish. Notice that all cone objects change shape simultaneously, because they are all linked. Also notice that we are using the upper-left cone object as a "help" object, whose simple horizontal orientation makes changes in length easier than direct manipulation of the oddly oriented (with 70 degree rotations) objects actually forming the geometry of our model.

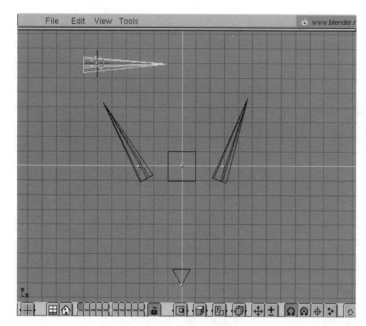

Figure 8-30

11. Press **a** to deselect all vertices. Press **b** and use border selection mode to select all vertices forming the base of the cone. Press **s** to scale all of these vertices. Move the mouse cursor slightly closer to the center of the cone to cause a scale-down operation of the selected vertices. Left-click to finish.

12. Press **Tab** to exit EditMode.

At this point, we have a help object which forms the basic shape of the thruster, and two linked thruster objects which are linked to the help object's shape and which are positioned correctly in the model.

Create the Main Body

Next, we create the main body. For this, we make use of the default plane object which Blender has already placed in the center of the screen.

NOTE Blender's "plane" object is actually simply a finite, square polygon. This is in contrast to the mathematically infinite planes we defined in Chapter 7; do not confuse these notions.

First of all, let's temporarily hide the thruster objects by moving them to a different, invisible layer.

1. Select all thruster objects (**Shift+right click**).

2. Type **m**, **2** and press **Enter**. All selected objects are moved into layer 2 and are no longer visible.

3. Type **2** to switch to layer 2. Notice that only the thruster objects are in layer 2.

4. Type **1** to switch back to layer 1. Notice that only the plane object is visible.

Now that we have removed some of the surrounding clutter, we can work on creating the main body from the plane object. To do this, we use the extrude function, which, as we mentioned earlier, creates tube-like forms out of ring-like forms. In this case, the ring-like form is the square formed by the plane object. By extruding a square, we produce a box. More specifically, extruding a flat polygonal shape causes a duplicate of the shape to be created, all vertices to be linked, and new faces to be formed.

Create the main body using extrusion as follows:

1. Select the plane object.
2. Type **3** on the numeric keypad to switch to side view.
3. Press **Tab** to enter EditMode.
4. Type **a** to select all vertices.
5. Type **e** and press **Enter** to begin the extrusion operation. Blender automatically duplicates the selected vertices and enters grab mode, allowing you to position the newly copied vertices.

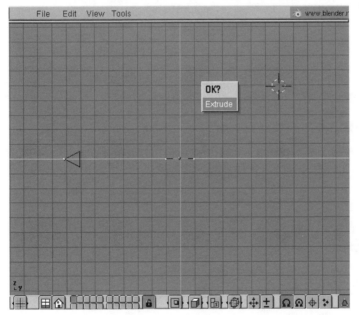

Figure 8-31

6. Press **Up Arrow** a few times to move the new vertices up about two units on the grid, and press **Enter**.

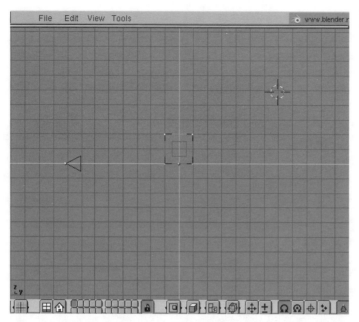

Figure 8-32

7. Now, check your work to see what the extrusion operation has just done. Press **5** on the numeric keypad to change the view from orthographic to perspective. Middle-click and drag the mouse cursor to rotate the view. Notice that the plane has now been extruded to become a box.

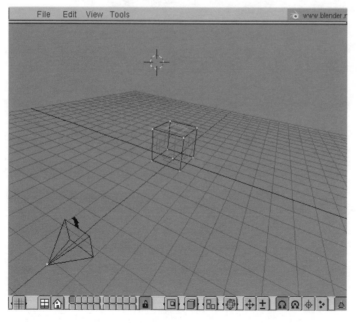

Figure 8-33

8. Return to the side orthographic view: type **5, 3** on the numeric keypad.

9. Type **a** to deselect all vertices, then type **b** and use border select mode to select all vertices on the right-hand side of the box. Type **g** to grab the vertices, move them a few units to the right, and left-click to finish.

10. Type **s** to scale the selected vertices, move the mouse cursor towards the center of the object to scale down slightly, and left-click to finish.

11. Press **Tab** to exit EditMode.

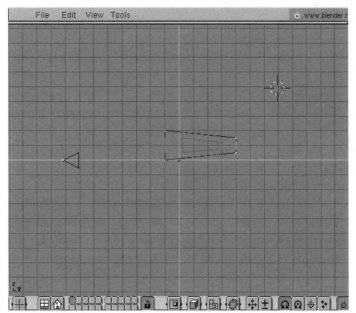

Figure 8-34

Now, we have finished the main body. It's time to move the thruster objects back from the invisible layer 2 into layer 1.

1. Type **2** to switch to layer 2.

2. Type **a** to select all objects.

3. Type **m, 1** and press **Enter** to move all objects in layer 2 back into layer 1.

4. Type **1** to switch back to layer 1.

5. Press **7** on the numeric keypad to switch to top view. Notice that all objects are now again located in layer 1.

With the main body and thrusters now modeled, position the thrusters so that they are located at the same height as the main body:

1. Select the two thruster objects to the left and right of the main body.

2. Press **3** on the numeric keypad to switch to side view.

3. Type **g** to grab the selected thruster objects, use the mouse to position them vertically at the same height as the main body, and left-click to finish.

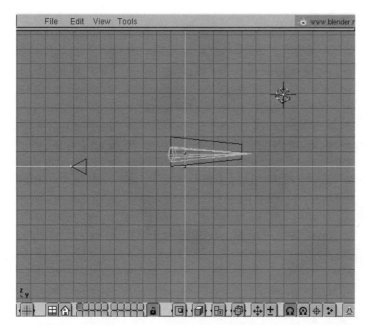

Figure 8-35

To complete our modeling, let's join the thruster and body objects into one mesh so that we can export the entire spaceship as one combined object (instead of as separate body and thruster objects). Join the thrusters and body as follows:

1. Select only the main body and the two side thrusters. Do not select the "help" thruster object in the upper-left corner of the screen.

2. Type **l**, select **Selected** from the pop-up menu, and press **Enter** to break the link between the thrusters and the help thruster object.

3. Press **Ctrl+j** and press **Enter** to join the selected meshes.

At this point, the entire spaceship is one polygonal mesh. The help object, which we used earlier to set the length of the thrusters, is no longer needed and can be deleted. In fact, the help object no longer has links to the thruster objects, since we joined the thrusters with the main spaceship body; this means that the help object indeed cannot be used any further, since it has no more influence on the shape of the now merged thruster objects. In general, this implies that after joining meshes, any help objects which you may have used will generally become useless.

Checking the Normal Vectors

After creating the model, you should generally check to make sure that all normal vectors are pointing in the correct directions; if they are not, then faces will be pointing the wrong way when you import the models into l3d. Check the normal vectors as follows:

1. Ensure that the TOGBUT Draw Normals in EditButtons is activated.

2. Set the value in the NUMBUT Nsize (short for "Normal size") to be approximately 0.6.

3. Select the model in the 3DWindow (**right-click**) and enter EditMode (**Tab**).

4. Notice the normal vectors drawn in blue. They should all be pointing outward, since the visible surface of the model is on the outside. Rotate the model to see it from various angles, and verify that the normals are pointing in the right direction.

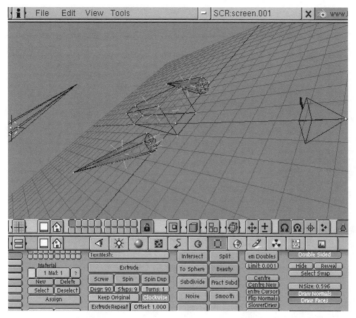

Figure 8-36

  NOTE For a room object, where the camera is located inside the object, the normal vectors should point inward, not outward, since the visible surface of the object is, in this case, the inside of the object. For normal objects viewed from outside of the object itself, the normal vectors should point outward.

5. If any normal vectors are pointing the wrong way, correct this in EditMode as follows: select the face (by selecting all of its vertices). Press **Ctrl+n** to recalculate the normal vector of the face to point outward; press **Ctrl+Shift+n** to recalculate the normal vector of the face to point inward. A pop-up menu appears asking for confirmation; press **Enter**, and the normal vector is recalculated and redisplayed. To correct all normal vectors at once, select all faces (**a**), then press **Ctrl+n** or **Ctrl+Shift+n**.

After ensuring that the normal vectors are all pointing in the correct direction, we are ready to make a test rendering of our model within Blender to see how it looks.

Rendering Our Creation

Let's now make Blender draw a rendering of our 3D model so that we can see approximately how it will look when it is imported into a 3D program.

Positioning the Camera

To draw a rendering with Blender, we first must position the camera so that it has a good view of the scene. Blender allows us to interactively position the camera in real time. Position the camera as follows.

1. Split the 3DWindow into two vertical halves: middle-click the top border of the 3DWindow, click **Split**, position the new vertical window border approximately in the middle of the screen, and left-click to finish.

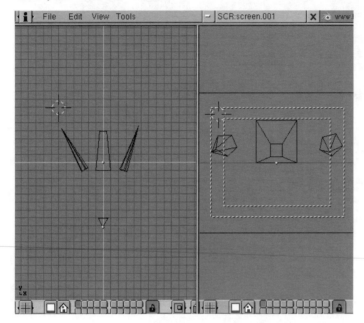

Figure 8-37

2. In the right window, press **0** on the numeric keypad to shift to the camera view.

3. In the left window, press **7** on the numeric keypad to switch to top view.

4. Right-click the camera object. It is the pyramid-shaped object located (as seen from the top view) slightly beneath the center of the window.

5. Move the camera by grabbing and rotating it (with keys **g** and **r**). Notice that the view in the right window updates automatically to show the view from the current camera position. Position the camera so that the entire spaceship is visible. Since from the top view you can only move the camera around in two dimensions, you probably will also want to change to side view to control the position of the camera in the third dimension.

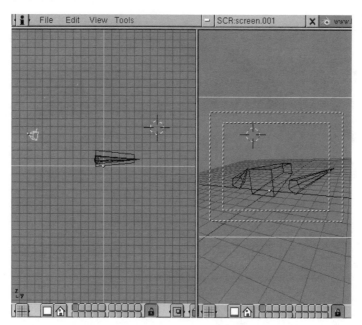

Figure 8-38

 NOTE Blender actually allows several camera objects to be present within one scene, to allow for the definition of multiple viewpoints. Only one camera, however, is the current camera whose view actually gets rendered. You can add additional cameras through the Toolbox, and make an active camera object the current camera by pressing Ctrl+0 on the numeric keypad.

Adding a Light

The next step in rendering our model is to add a light object. Otherwise, our scene would be pitch black, and we would see nothing. Add a light to the scene as follows:

1. Position the 3D cursor slightly above and behind the main body of the spaceship. To do this, you must use both the top and side views in the 3DWindow.

2. Press **Shift+a**, and select **Lamp** from the Toolbox. A lamp appears at the position of the 3D cursor.

3. Verify in the top and side views that the lamp is indeed positioned correctly, slightly above and behind the spaceship.

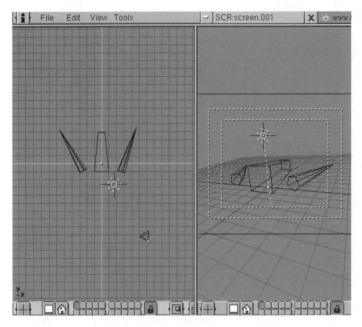

Figure 8-39

Rendering the Scene

To render the scene, press **F12**. This is the one exception where Blender actually opens a new window separate from the main Blender window. Blender renders the scene in the new window. Toggle the visibility of the render window by pressing **F11**; this allows you to quickly hide or recall a previously rendered image.

If you have positioned the camera and the light correctly, you should see a gray spaceship on a black background, from the viewpoint you selected earlier.

Figure 8-40: The spaceship rendered within Blender.

For a more interesting rendering, go to the WorldButtons (F8), and add a new world via the MENUBUT in the header of the ButtonsWindow. By default this adds a fading blue sky to the scene. Activate the TOGBUT labeled "Stars." Render the scene again. The spaceship then appears to be located in a starry blue sky. The settings in the WorldButtons do not affect the polygonal model, and therefore are only of interest for creating pretty pictures. As mentioned at the beginning of this chapter, we are more interested in using Blender to create polygonal models rather than pretty pictures—although creating good images can also be a goal in itself.

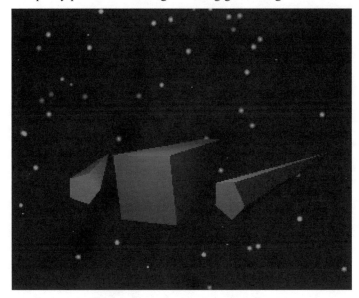

Figure 8-41: The spaceship rendered with a more interesting background, created via the WorldButtons.

You can now reposition the camera, add more lights, or alter the model, and render the scene again, until you are satisfied with the model.

Saving and Exporting the Spaceship

Next, save the Blender file in native Blender format, so that you can load and change the model later if desired. Save the entire workspace with the F2 key, as described earlier.

Then, export the spaceship mesh as a Videoscape file. Remember, the Blender file format is very complex, whereas the Videoscape file format is quite simple and ideal for importing into our own programs. To export in Videoscape, select the spaceship, press **Alt+w**, specify a filename of `spaceship.obj`, and press **Enter**. This creates the file `spaceship.obj` in Videoscape format. Take a glance at the contents of the file and compare it with the Videoscape file description presented earlier. Notice how simple and straightforward the file format is: it contains vertices and polygons defined in terms of indices into a common vertex list. Conveniently, this is exactly the same way that l3d stores polygonal objects. So, let's see how to import the Videoscape file into an l3d program.

Reading a Videoscape File into l3d

We use a plug-in to read the Videoscape file into l3d. The code for the plug-in is shown in Listings 8-1 and 8-2.

Listing 8-1: `vidflat.h`

```
#include "../../../dynamics/plugins/plugenv.h"
#include "../../../tool_os/memman.h"

class l3d_plugin_videoscape_flatshaded_mesh {
  public:
    l3d_plugin_environment *plugin_env;

    l3d_plugin_videoscape_flatshaded_mesh(l3d_plugin_environment *env);
    virtual ~l3d_plugin_videoscape_flatshaded_mesh(void);
    char mesh_fname[1024];
};
```

Listing 8-2: `vidflat.cc`

```
#include "../../../system/sys_dep.h"
#include "../../../geom/object/object3d.h"
#include "../../../geom/polygon/p3_cflat.h"
#include "../../../dynamics/plugins/plugenv.h"
#include "../../../tool_2d/si_idx.h"
#include "../../../tool_2d/si_rgb.h"
#include <stdlib.h>
#include <string.h>
#include "vidflat.h"
#include "../../../tool_os/memman.h"

l3d_plugin_videoscape_flatshaded_mesh::l3d_plugin_videoscape_flatshaded_mesh
(l3d_plugin_environment *env)
{
  plugin_env = env;
}

l3d_plugin_videoscape_flatshaded_mesh::~l3d_plugin_videoscape_flatshaded_mesh(void) {
  delete plugin_env;
}

extern "C" {

  void constructor(l3d_object *target, void *data) {
    l3d_plugin_environment *env = (l3d_plugin_environment *)data;
    l3d_plugin_videoscape_flatshaded_mesh *mesh;

    target->plugin_data = mesh = new l3d_plugin_videoscape_flatshaded_mesh(env);

    char rest_parms[4096];
    strncpy(rest_parms, (char *)env->data, sizeof(rest_parms));
    char *tok;

    float posx,posy,posz;
    float xaxis_x, xaxis_y, xaxis_z,
    yaxis_x, yaxis_y, yaxis_z,
    zaxis_x, zaxis_y, zaxis_z;
    l3d_matrix position, orientation;
    strcpy(mesh->mesh_fname,"");
    position.set(int_to_l3d_real(1),
```

```
                    int_to_l3d_real(0),
                    int_to_l3d_real(0),
                    int_to_l3d_real(0),
                    int_to_l3d_real(0),
                    int_to_l3d_real(1),
                    int_to_l3d_real(0),
                    int_to_l3d_real(0),
                    int_to_l3d_real(0),
                    int_to_l3d_real(0),
                    int_to_l3d_real(1),
                    int_to_l3d_real(0),
                    int_to_l3d_real(0),
                    int_to_l3d_real(0),
                    int_to_l3d_real(0),
                    int_to_l3d_real(1));
orientation = position;

tok = strtok(rest_parms, " ");  if(tok) {sscanf(tok, "%f", &posx); }
tok = strtok(NULL, " ");  if(tok) {sscanf(tok, "%f", &posy); }
tok = strtok(NULL, " ");  if(tok) {sscanf(tok, "%f", &posz); }
tok = strtok(NULL, " ");  if(tok) {sscanf(tok, "%f", &xaxis_x); }
tok = strtok(NULL, " ");  if(tok) {sscanf(tok, "%f", &yaxis_x); }
tok = strtok(NULL, " ");  if(tok) {sscanf(tok, "%f", &zaxis_x); }
tok = strtok(NULL, " ");  if(tok) {sscanf(tok, "%f", &xaxis_y); }
tok = strtok(NULL, " ");  if(tok) {sscanf(tok, "%f", &yaxis_y); }
tok = strtok(NULL, " ");  if(tok) {sscanf(tok, "%f", &zaxis_y); }
tok = strtok(NULL, " ");  if(tok) {sscanf(tok, "%f", &xaxis_z); }
tok = strtok(NULL, " ");  if(tok) {sscanf(tok, "%f", &yaxis_z); }
tok = strtok(NULL, " ");  if(tok) {sscanf(tok, "%f", &zaxis_z); }

tok = strtok(NULL, " ");
if(tok) {strncpy(mesh->mesh_fname, tok, sizeof(mesh->mesh_fname)); }

FILE *fp;
fp = fopen(mesh->mesh_fname, "rt");

char line[4096];
if(fp) {
  fgets(line, sizeof(line), fp);
  fgets(line, sizeof(line), fp);

  int num_vert;
  sscanf(line, "%d", &num_vert);
  int i;

  delete target->vertices;
  target->vertices =
    new l3d_two_part_list<l3d_coordinate> ( num_vert );

  for(i=0; i<num_vert; i++) {
    fgets(line, sizeof(line), fp);
    float x,y,z;
    sscanf(line, "%f %f %f", &x, &y, &z);

    //- change from blender's right-handed +z-up system to a
    //- left-handed +y-up system
    (*target->vertices)[i].original.set
    (float_to_l3d_real(x),
     float_to_l3d_real(z),
     float_to_l3d_real(y),
```

```
    float_to_l3d_real(1.));
}

while(!feof(fp)) {
  fgets(line, sizeof(line), fp);
  if(feof(fp)) break;

  char *tok;

  int numv;
  tok = strtok(line, " ");
  sscanf(tok, "%d", &numv);

  l3d_polygon_3d_flatshaded_clippable *p;
  int polygon_idx = target->polygons.next_index();
  target->polygons[polygon_idx] =
    p =
    new l3d_polygon_3d_flatshaded_clippable(numv);
  target->polygons[polygon_idx]->vlist = &target->vertices;

  int r,g,b;

  unsigned long col;
  l3d_screen_info_indexed *si_idx;
  l3d_screen_info_rgb *si_rgb;
  if (si_idx = dynamic_cast<l3d_screen_info_indexed *>( env->sinfo )) {
    col = rand() % si_idx->get_palette_size();
  }else if (si_rgb = dynamic_cast<l3d_screen_info_rgb *>(env->sinfo)) {

    r = rand() % ((si_rgb->red_mask) > (si_rgb->red_shift));
    g = rand() % ((si_rgb->green_mask) > (si_rgb->green_shift));
    b = rand() % ((si_rgb->blue_mask) > (si_rgb->blue_shift));

    col =  r<si_rgb->red_shift |
           g<si_rgb->green_shift |
           b<si_rgb->blue_shift;
  }
  p->final_color = col;

  for(i=0; i<numv; i++) {
    int cur_iv=0;

    tok = strtok(NULL," ");
    if(tok) {
      int ivtx;
      sscanf(tok,"%d", &ivtx);
      cur_iv=target->polygons[polygon_idx]->ivertices->next_index();
      (*(target->polygons[polygon_idx]->ivertices)) [cur_iv].ivertex
      = ivtx;

    }
  }

  //- now reverse the list IN-PLACE; for this we need one temp swap
  //- variable, which we allocate (virtually from the list, i.e. we
  //- let the type of the temp object be allocated by the list itself)
  //- here:

  l3d_polygon_ivertex *
  swap_iv =
```

```
         &((*(target->polygons[polygon_idx]->ivertices))
          [target->polygons[polygon_idx]->ivertices->next_index()]);

      for(i=0; i<numv/2; i++) {
        *swap_iv = (*(target->polygons[polygon_idx]->ivertices))[i];
        (*(target->polygons[polygon_idx]->ivertices))[i] =
          (*(target->polygons[polygon_idx]->ivertices))[numv-1 - i];
        (*(target->polygons[polygon_idx]->ivertices))[numv-1 - i] =
          *swap_iv;

      }

      target->polygons[polygon_idx]->ivertices->num_items =
        target->polygons[polygon_idx]->ivertices->num_items - 1;

      target->polygons[polygon_idx]->compute_center();
      target->polygons[polygon_idx]->compute_sfcnormal();

      p->plane.align_with_point_normal(p->center.original, normalized(p->sfcnormal.original -
p->center.original));

    }
    target->num_xforms = 2;

    orientation.set
    (float_to_l3d_real(xaxis_x),
     float_to_l3d_real(yaxis_x),
     float_to_l3d_real(zaxis_x),
     int_to_l3d_real(0),
     float_to_l3d_real(xaxis_y),
     float_to_l3d_real(yaxis_y),
     float_to_l3d_real(zaxis_y),
     int_to_l3d_real(0),
     float_to_l3d_real(xaxis_z),
     float_to_l3d_real(yaxis_z),
     float_to_l3d_real(zaxis_z),
     int_to_l3d_real(0),
     int_to_l3d_real(0),
     int_to_l3d_real(0),
     int_to_l3d_real(0),
     int_to_l3d_real(1));

    target->modeling_xforms[0] =
      orientation;

    position.set(int_to_l3d_real(1),
                 int_to_l3d_real(0),
                 int_to_l3d_real(0),
                 float_to_l3d_real(posx),
                 int_to_l3d_real(0),
                 int_to_l3d_real(1),
                 int_to_l3d_real(0),
                 float_to_l3d_real(posy),
                 int_to_l3d_real(0),
                 int_to_l3d_real(0),
                 int_to_l3d_real(1),
                 float_to_l3d_real(posz),
                 int_to_l3d_real(0),
                 int_to_l3d_real(0),
                 int_to_l3d_real(0),
```

```
                    int_to_l3d_real(1));

        target->modeling_xforms[1] = position;
        target->modeling_xform = target->modeling_xforms[1]   |
                            target->modeling_xforms[0];


    }

    if(fp) fclose(fp);
}

void update(l3d_object *target) {
  l3d_plugin_videoscape_flatshaded_mesh *mesh;
  mesh = (l3d_plugin_videoscape_flatshaded_mesh *)target->plugin_data;

}

void destructor(l3d_object *target) {
  delete (l3d_plugin_videoscape_flatshaded_mesh *) target->plugin_data;
}

void copy_data(l3d_object *target, l3d_object *copy_target) {
  l3d_plugin_videoscape_flatshaded_mesh *mesh;
  mesh = (l3d_plugin_videoscape_flatshaded_mesh *) target->plugin_data;

  l3d_plugin_environment *new_env;
  l3d_plugin_videoscape_flatshaded_mesh *new_mesh;

  new_env = mesh->plugin_env->clone();
  new_env->data = mesh->plugin_env->data;
  new_mesh = new l3d_plugin_videoscape_flatshaded_mesh(new_env);

  strcpy(new_mesh->mesh_fname, mesh->mesh_fname);

  copy_target->plugin_data = (void *)new_mesh;
}
}
```

The structure of the plug-in is as defined in Chapter 7: a constructor, an update function, a copy function, and a destructor. The constructor is the function of interest. The data parameter passed to the constructor is a plug-in environment object, as introduced in Chapter 7, so that the plug-in knows something about its calling environment. The environment object, in turn, stores another data parameter. In the case of the Videoscape plug-in, this data parameter is a pointer to a character string containing a list of additional parameters needed to load the Videoscape file.

The Videoscape parameter string in the environment object has the following form:

```
x y z A B C D E F G H I mesh.obj
```

The entries are interpreted as follows:

- x y z: Floating-point numbers indicating the origin of the object's local coordinate system. In other words, this is the location of the object.

- A B C D E F G H I: Nine floating-point numbers representing the object's orientation as a 3×3 rotation matrix. The numbers are in row-major order (i.e., A B C is the first row of the matrix, D E F the second row, G H I the last row). Recalling the discussion in Chapter 6 about matrices and coordinate systems, this means that the vector (A,D,G) (the first row of the matrix) is the x axis of the object's local coordinate system, (B,E,H) is the y axis, and (C,F,I) is the z axis.

■ `mesh.obj`: The filename of the Videoscape file containing the geometry of the object.

The plug-in constructor first parses the parameter string to get the position, orientation, and required filename for the Videoscape object to be loaded. Next, it opens the mesh file and reads in the vertices and faces. The Videoscape format stores coordinates in a right-handed system, with the z axis going up; l3d uses a left-handed system with the y axis going up. To convert between these two systems, we need to do two things: swap the y and the z values as we read them from the Videoscape file, and reverse the ordering of the vertices in a face definition to preserve the front/back orientation of the face after the vertex swap. After converting the coordinates in this manner, the constructor then initializes each polygon by computing its center, surface normal, and containing plane. At this point, the polygon is also assigned a random color.

After reading in all vertices and faces, the constructor then defines two transformation matrices, one for rotating the object according to the rotation matrix specified within the parameter string, and a second matrix for translating the object to the specified position. These matrices are concatenated together and stored in the object as a composite transformation.

The program `vidflat`, in Listing 8-3, creates a Videoscape plug-in object with the appropriate parameters by creating an environment object, storing the parameter string within the `data` member of the environment object, and passing the environment itself to the plug-in constructor. Calling the plug-in constructor then causes loading of the Videoscape file.

Listing 8-3: File `main.cc` of program `vidflat`

```
#include <stdlib.h>
#include <string.h>
#include <stdio.h>
#include <math.h>

#include "../lib/geom/object/object3d.h"
#include "../lib/geom/polygon/p3_flat.h"
#include "../lib/tool_2d/screen.h"
#include "../lib/tool_os/dispatch.h"
#include "../lib/raster/rast3.h"
#include "../lib/tool_2d/scrinfo.h"
#include "../lib/geom/world/world.h"
#include "../lib/system/fact0_2.h"
#include "../lib/pipeline/pi_wor.h"
#include "../lib/dynamics/plugins/plugenv.h"

#include <stdlib.h>
#include <string.h>
#include <stdio.h>
#include <math.h>
#include <stdarg.h>

class my_world:public l3d_world {
  public:
    my_world(void);
    virtual ~my_world(void);
};

my_world::my_world(void)
    : l3d_world(400,300)
```

```
   {
     l3d_screen_info *si = screen->sinfo;

     camera->VRP.set(0,0,-50,0);
     camera->near_z = float_to_l3d_real(5.5);
     camera->far_z = int_to_l3d_real(500);

     //- for mesa rasterizer's reverse projection
     rasterizer_3d_imp->fovx = &(camera->fovx);
     rasterizer_3d_imp->fovy = &(camera->fovy);
     rasterizer_3d_imp->screen_xsize = &(screen->xsize);
     rasterizer_3d_imp->screen_ysize = &(screen->ysize);

     int i,j,k,onum=0;

     i=10; j=0; k=20;
     k=0;

     //- create a plugin object

     objects[onum=objects.next_index()] = new l3d_object(10);
     //- max 10 fixed vertices, can be overridden by plug-in if desired
     //- by redefining the vertex list

     objects[onum]->plugin_loader =
       factory_manager_v_0_2.plugin_loader_factory->create();
     objects[onum]->plugin_loader->load("../lib/dynamics/plugins/vidflat/vidflat.so");
     objects[onum]->plugin_constructor =
       (void (*)(l3d_object *, void *))
       objects[onum]->plugin_loader->find_symbol("constructor");
     objects[onum]->plugin_update =
       (void (*)(l3d_object *))
       objects[onum]->plugin_loader->find_symbol("update");
     objects[onum]->plugin_destructor =
       (void (*)(l3d_object *))
       objects[onum]->plugin_loader->find_symbol("destructor");
     objects[onum]->plugin_copy_data =
       (void (*)(const l3d_object *, l3d_object *))
       objects[onum]->plugin_loader->find_symbol("copy_data");

     l3d_plugin_environment *e =
       new l3d_plugin_environment
         (NULL, screen->sinfo, NULL,
          (void *)"0 0 0 1 0 0 0 1 0 0 0 1 spaceship.obj");

     if(objects[onum]->plugin_constructor) {
       (*objects[onum]->plugin_constructor) (objects[onum],e);
     }

     screen->refresh_palette();
   }

   my_world::~my_world(void) {
   }

   main() {
     l3d_dispatcher *d;
     l3d_pipeline_world *p;
     my_world *w;
```

```
factory_manager_v_0_2.choose_factories();
d = factory_manager_v_0_2.dispatcher_factory->create();

w = new my_world();
p  = new l3d_pipeline_world(w);
d->pipeline = p;
d->event_source = w->screen;

d->start();

delete d;
delete p;
delete w;
}
```

The glorious output of program vidflat is shown in Figure 8-42—the model we created in Blender has now been successfully imported into our program, where we can manipulate it at will. You can navigate around the scene with the usual `l3d_world` navigation keys.

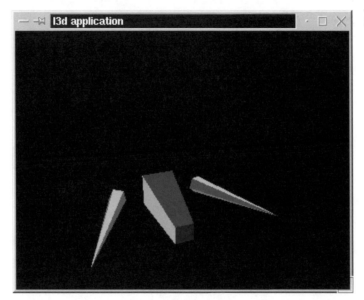

Figure 8-42

Notice that each polygon has a random color assigned to it, since the Videoscape plug-in assigns a random color to each flat-shaded polygon as it is created from the data in the Videoscape file. Instead of assigning random colors to the polygons, it would be possible to assign colors to the polygons in Blender, then to export these polygons with color information to a Videoscape file. When reading the polygons into l3d, the plug-in would then create the polygons and assign them a color according to the information in the Videoscape file. The practical problem with this approach is that the Videoscape format saves colors per vertex, not per polygon, which makes a coloring scheme somewhat complex. A better solution is to associate an entire bitmap image with each polygon. This makes for much more interesting polygonal displays, since in this case each polygon then appears to be "colored" with an entire image instead of with just one single color.

This technique is called texture mapping, and is covered in detail in the companion book *Advanced Linux 3D Graphics Programming*.

Summary

In this chapter, we took a break from 3D theory—indeed, there wasn't a single equation in this chapter—and looked at the artistic side of 3D graphics. We looked at the basics of 3D modeling in general, then looked at the specifics of the quite unique software package Blender. We then got hands-on experience creating a model in Blender and learned a number of useful modeling techniques.

We then imported the Blender model into our l3d programs, using the Videoscape file format. We used a Videoscape plug-in object to read the Videoscape file. We also saw how to convert Videoscape's right-handed coordinates into l3d's left-handed coordinates.

Having come this far in the book, you now know quite a bit about Linux 3D graphics programming—both theoretical and practical aspects. With the free compilers and 3D modeling tools available for Linux, you can put all of this knowledge to work by practicing writing 3D programs and creating interesting 3D models for use in these programs.

The next and final chapter takes a brief look at some of the 3D techniques specific to creating larger, more interesting, more interactive environments.

Chapter 9

Advanced Topics

We've almost reached the end of this book. Regrettably, the space between the covers of a book is limited. Much as I would have liked to, it is simply not feasible to include in this book much more information on Linux 3D graphics programming. There is still much more material left to cover.

The purpose of this chapter is to provide a brief overview of other advanced topics in Linux 3D graphics programming. Space considerations force me to treat each subject at a very high level of abstraction; I focus mainly on the important concepts, with little attention to implementation details. If you have carefully read the previous chapters, and have understood and adopted the geometrical and mathematical style of inquiry which I have tried to emphasize in this book, then you should be able to derive the details and come up with working implementations for yourself.

But you don't have to.

All of these topics are covered at much greater length in the companion volume to this book, titled *Advanced Linux 3D Graphics Programming*. If this chapter whets your appetite, I encourage you to read the advanced volume. It discusses all of the following topics in the same geometrical and incremental explanatory philosophy I have tried to apply in this book. Numerous code examples also accompany the advanced volume, building on the l3d library.

In this chapter, we look at the following topics:

- Morphing in 3D
- Computing and rendering the effects of light
- Texture mapping, light mapping, and shadows
- Visible surface determination (back-face culling, frustum culling, *z* buffer, BSP trees, octrees, portals)
- More complex modeling with Blender (textured models, jointed models with inverse kinematics, editing entire interactive 3D worlds)
- Special effects, such as smoke, particle systems, water, and lens flare
- Non-graphical elements (digital sound, networking, physics, collision detection)
- High-level 3D content creation systems on Linux (World Foundry, Game Blender)

3D Morphing

In Chapter 3, we looked at a sample program that performed morphing in 2D through the use of a vertex interpolator. The idea was to start with one source polygon and one destination polygon, both with equal numbers of vertices. Each vertex in the source polygon corresponds to a particular vertex in the destination polygon. Then, over a fixed number of frames, we interpolate the position of each vertex from its starting location to its destination location.

We can extend this idea easily into 3D. Instead of morphing one polygon's shape into another polygon's shape, in 3D we can morph an entire polygonal object, of type l3d_object, from one shape into another. For instance, you could morph a cube into a palm tree.

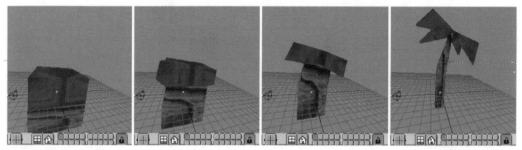

Figure 9-1: Morphing in 3D. Here, a cube is morphed into a palm tree.

To morph in 3D, we start with two objects of type l3d_object: a source and a destination object. Both objects should have the same number of total vertices. Remember that a 3D object of type l3d_object stores one common vertex list which is shared by all polygons in the object. This means that to morph one 3D object into another, we merely need to morph the vertices in the object's vertex list into the vertices in the destination object's vertex list. By changing the values in the object's vertex list, all polygons in that object change shape accordingly.

Computing Lighting Effects

Displaying polygons with physically realistic lighting effects can greatly enhance the visual appearance of a program. In Chapter 2, when we developed the classes for accessing the 2D raster display under Linux, we introduced the concept of a lighting table. The idea was that each color should also be displayable in a range of intensities. Each intensity value in the lighting table corresponds to an intensity of light. The lighting table therefore allows us to show any color at any light intensity.

The question remains as to how we compute the light intensity in the first place. One simple lighting model is the *Lambertian* or *diffuse* lighting model. In this model, the intensity of light falling on a surface is calculated by taking the dot product of two normalized vectors N and L. Vector N is the surface normal vector, and vector L is a normalized vector pointing from the surface to the light source. Assuming the surface is facing the light, the dot product yields a value between zero and one, which can be thought of as the percent of light energy reaching the surface based on the angle that the light strikes the surface. We can then multiply the result of the dot product, which is a scalar, with an arbitrary light intensity measured in arbitrary units. The dot product either allows the full light intensity to illuminate the surface (if the light is striking the surface head-on), or scales the light intensity down (if the light strikes the surface at an angle).

As it turns out, for diffusely reflective surfaces, the amount of light energy seen from a surface is independent of the location of the viewer. Therefore, once we know the amount of light striking the surface, we know the amount of light seen by the viewer.

To summarize: take the dot product between the surface normal and a vector from the surface to the light source. Multiply this by the light intensity to obtain the light striking the surface. Since the lighting model assumes diffuse reflection, use the light striking the surface as the amount of light seen by the viewer. Use this light value as a look-up value in the lighting table, and alter the color of the surface accordingly.

How often you compute the light is another issue. You can compute light intensities for each pixel, which results in the highest quality but is the slowest. You can calculate a light value just once for each entire polygon. This gives surfaces a definite faceted, computer-like appearance. You can compute light at each vertex, and interpolate the values during rasterization, which is a compromise between the above two extremes. Or you can compute the light at regularly spaced points along the polygon, a technique called *light mapping*, discussed in the next section.

Texture Mapping, Light Mapping, and Shadows

We've briefly mentioned the topic of texture mapping at a number of points in this book. Texture mapping is the process of applying a *texture*, or an image, to a polygon. When we draw the polygon, it then appears that the texture image is "glued onto" or otherwise mapped onto the surface of the polygon. This, like lighting, allows us to create more engaging 3D images.

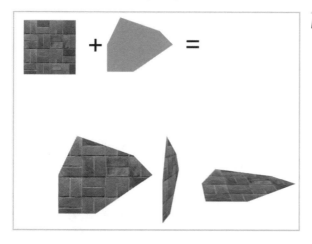

Figure 9-2: Texture mapping.

Texture mapping is a subject too complex to cover in depth here. Nevertheless, I can summarize the important points, should you wish to try to implement your own texture mapping routines. Again, as with all topics in this chapter, if you are interested in learning more, I suggest you read the companion book *Advanced Linux 3D Graphics Programming*, where we have much more space to discuss these topics at length.

Texture mapping can be conceptually thought of as "stretching" an image to fit across a polygon. For simplicity, let us assume we have a square texture image and a square polygon. To map the texture to the polygon, we associate each vertex of the polygon with a location in the texture image. For instance, we could associate the first polygon vertex with the upper-left corner (0,0) of the texture image, the second polygon vertex with the lower-left corner (0,64) of the texture, and so forth. Then, to draw the polygon, we first project it from 3D into 2D (as discussed in Chapter 5). Assuming the projected polygon is not clipped to the 2D screen, we then have four projected screen-space coordinates corresponding to the original four 3D vertices of the polygon, which in turn are associated with four locations in the texture image.

We rasterize the polygon by starting at the topmost vertex, and proceeding downward on-screen along the polygon's left and right edges (see Chapter 3). A key observation is that the rasterization loop always proceeds from vertex to vertex in the polygon; the polygon "edges" that are traversed during rasterization are defined by their end vertices. At each vertex we know the corresponding location in the texture map; this location is called a *texture coordinate*. This means we can interpolate texture coordinates between vertices as we draw the polygon. For each pixel being rasterized in the polygon, we draw the color of the pixel found in the texture map at the interpolated texture coordinate.

Consider the projected image of a square polygon. Depending on the orientation of the polygon with respect to the viewer, the polygon may appear tilted on-screen, but, assuming it is not clipped, it will still have four vertices. Think of the texture as a square piece of rubber with the texture image printed on it. The above description of texture mapping corresponds to pinning each corner of the rubber square onto each corner of the projected polygon, resulting in the image on the square getting stretched onto the surface of the projected polygon.

The above description of texture mapping is mathematically incorrect for polygons displayed with perspective projection. The reason is that the image on the texture is not foreshortened, as it should be; the texture stretching is a purely 2D operation which fails to account for the 3D effects of perspective. Let us use the terminology (u,v) to denote a texture coordinate associated with a polygon vertex. Instead of storing and directly interpolating the texture coordinates u and v across the projected polygon surface during rasterization, a perspective-correct scheme must interpolate the values u/z, v/z, and $1/z$ across the polygon surface. This means that each vertex of the polygon is associated with a u/z, v/z, and $1/z$ value. The z value is the camera space z coordinate of the polygon vertex. We interpolate these values during rasterization, and for each pixel, we divide the interpolated u/z value by the interpolated $1/z$ value to obtain the perspective-correct u value for the pixel. Similarly, we divide the interpolated v/z value by the interpolated $1/z$ value to obtain the perspective-correct v value for the pixel. This gives us a perspective-correct (u,v) texture coordinate for the pixel, which we then use to find the appropriate pixel from the texture image, whose color is displayed for the pixel currently being rasterized.

This description is admittedly very terse. I strongly encourage the interested reader to read the discussion of texture mapping in the companion book *Advanced Linux 3D Graphics Programming*, where the topic of texture mapping is given much more thorough treatment, complete with diagrams, equations, and sample programs. Texture mapping is actually a change in coordinate system, as discussed in Chapter 6, but with the added twist that a perspective projection has eliminated one dimension, which needs to be recovered.

Light mapping is similar to texture mapping. Instead of mapping an image onto a polygon, as is the case with texture mapping, light mapping maps an *intensity grid* onto a polygon. This intensity grid, which actually is called a *light map*, is a rectangular array of values, where each entry represents the light intensity falling on that particular area of the polygon. Light maps are often combined with texture maps.

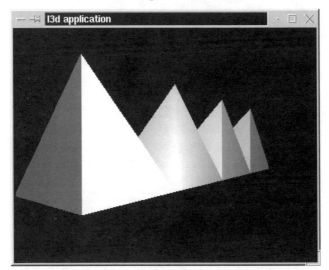

Figure 9-3: Light mapping.

If a light map represents the light intensity falling on a polygon, then it follows that dark areas of the light map are those areas of the polygon which are in shadow. Computing shadowed areas requires that we not illuminate any elements of the light map which are blocked from the light source. An element in the light map is blocked from the light source if there exists any object obstructing a ray from the light source to the 3D location of the light map element. This corresponds with physical reality: if an opaque object lies between a light ray and a part of a target object, then that part of the target object is in shadow.

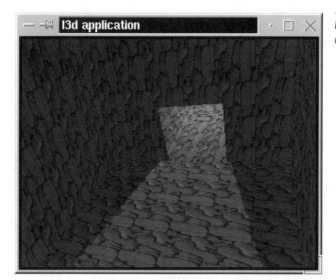

Figure 9-4: Light mapping, texture mapping, and shadows.

Visible Surface Determination

Chapter 7 mentioned the topic of visual surface determination (VSD), also known as hidden surface removal (HSR). The main issue with VSD schemes is to ensure a correct display of all surfaces which should be visible to the viewer. This also means eliminating, as much as possible, any unnecessary processing of surfaces which are not visible to the viewer. VSD schemes therefore address correctness and efficiency issues.

The VSD scheme covered in Chapter 7 was the painter's algorithm. This algorithm is easy to understand and implement, and gives acceptable results most of the time. Nevertheless, there are several more sophisticated VSD algorithms worth mentioning, which effectively attack both the correctness and efficiency issues. The following list summarizes some of the most important algorithms.

- Back-face culling culls polygons which are not facing the camera, since they are never seen in closed, convex polyhedra.

- View frustum culling culls polygons which are outside of the field of view, or which are too far away. The scheme can be hierarchically applied.

- The z buffer algorithm computes surface visibility per-pixel and is very accurate, but is also potentially slow and memory intensive. Graphics acceleration hardware often includes a z buffer, making it a very viable choice for solving many (but by no means all) VSD problems in the presence of appropriate hardware.

- BSP trees, octrees, and regular spatial partitioning schemes all use a "divide and conquer" approach to VSD. In these schemes, space is partitioned into separate, disjoint areas to allow spatial sorting of these areas with respect to the viewpoint, thereby allowing a correct display for the given viewpoint.

■ Portals and cells are another way of spatially partitioning and sorting which require explicit specification of the spatial regions and specification of a connectivity graph between regions. Portal schemes can quickly eliminate very large invisible portions of the world from further processing, but are generally only easily applicable in indoor environments.

Advanced 3D Modeling with Blender

We saw in Chapter 8 some of the features of the Blender 3D modeling package. Blender has many other features which we didn't get to cover. There are also some useful tips and tricks for achieving specific effects. Blender techniques relevant to programming interactive Linux 3D applications include:

■ Creating compatible morph targets. Generally, you do this by starting with one mesh, and deforming it in Blender to the other mesh. In this way both meshes have the same number of vertices and faces.

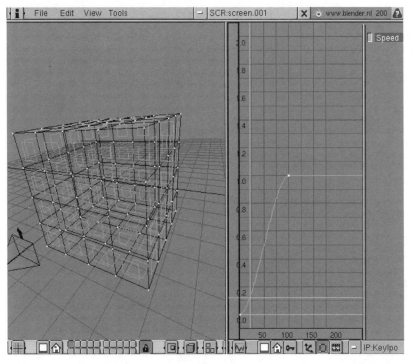

Figure 9-5:
Using a
subdivided
cube to create
compatible
morph targets.

■ Applying textures and texture coordinates to polygons. We saw in Chapter 8 how to export a simple spaceship model, but the model included only geometry. We can also use Blender to associate textures and texture coordinates with our polygonal models. Doing so requires us to use Blender's texture edit mode (activated with the "f" key and using the ImageWindow to select a texture) and the VRML export feature of Blender to extract the texture coordinates. We also need a new custom Videoscape plug-in to read in the texture image and coordinates.

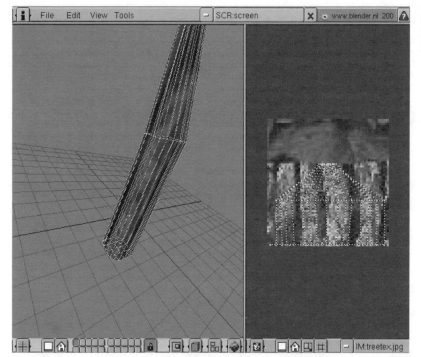

Figure 9-6:
Using Blender's
texture editor.

Using inverse kinematics (IK) to create animated, jointed figures. Blender allows you to create Ika chains, which are limb-like structures connected by joints. (Add an Ika by selecting Add-Ika from the Blender Toolbox.) By moving the tip of the Ika chain, the entire limb repositions itself in a very natural manner. For instance, you can control the position of an entire jointed arm, including the intermediate elbow joint, just by positioning the hand. IK allows you to easily pose humanoid models simply by positioning the "hands" and "feet" in the appropriate locations. Combined with animation, this is a very powerful technique.

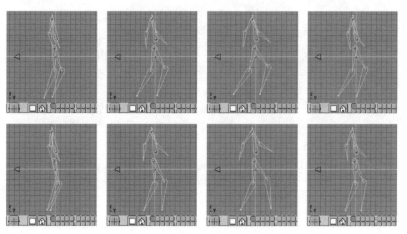

Figure 9-7:
Using IK to
animate a
humanoid
figure.

Special Effects

There are a few special effects we can use to increase the visual realism or impact of our 3D programs. Here is a brief list of some important techniques.

■ Environment mapping. This is a form of dynamic texture mapping where the image mapped onto a polygon's surface is a reflection of the surrounding environment. For instance, a silvered, highly reflective cylinder placed within a forest will reflect the surrounding trees. As the cylinder moves through the environment, it also reflects different parts of the environment off of its surface. OpenGL provides functions for realizing environment mapping (you must enable automatic texture coordinate generation by calling `glTexGeni` with a parameter of `GL_SPHERE_MAP`).

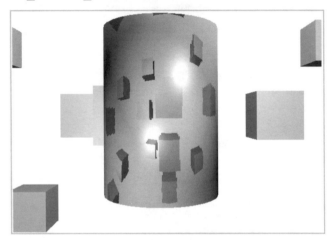

Figure 9-8: Environment mapping. The reflective cylinder reflects the surrounding cubes.

■ Billboards. A *billboard* is a special texture-mapped polygon which is always drawn such that it is facing the screen. You can think of a billboard as a sort of 2D "sticker" placed on top of a 3D image. Imagine viewing the world through a pair of glasses. Then, imagine putting a flat, 2D sticker, with an image of a tree, on the surface of the glasses. You would then appear to see the tree on top of the 3D scene you see through the glasses, although the tree is actually a flat 2D image. This is the idea behind billboarding. Billboarding allows us to simulate complex geometry with very few polygons.

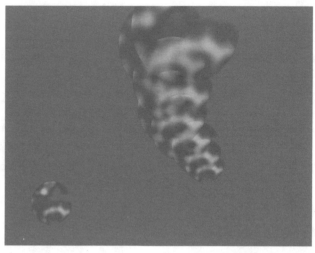

Figure 9-9: Using billboard images of smoke puffs to simulate smoke. The single billboard image appears in the lower left of the image.

■ Particle systems. A *particle system* is a system of many small objects, called *particles*, all of which are set into motion and controlled by some algorithm specific to the system. Any effect which can be viewed as a collection of particles can be modeled with a particle system. Examples of systems which can be modeled with particle systems are explosions, fire, smoke, a swarm of insects, or a school of swimming fish. Programming particle systems requires you to define a large number of particles and a set of rules controlling the behavior of the particles. The behavior of one particle may depend on the behavior of neighboring particles, as is the case with a school of fish. The optical effect of a particle system can be very convincing.

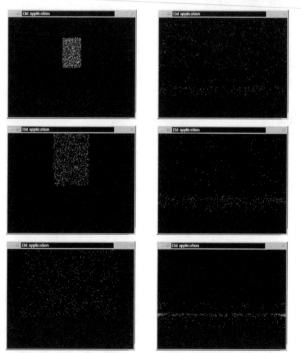

Figure 9-10: An exploding particle system.

Non-Graphical Elements

It can be useful to incorporate a number of non-graphical elements into 3D graphics programs. These elements all add to the overall immersive effect of a 3D environment.

- Digital sound. Sound is controlled on Linux systems by the character special file `/dev/audio`. Also, ready-made sound server programs exist, such as RPlay.

- TCP/IP networking. Networking is useful when multiple 3D programs running on different machines must communicate with one another to allow for multi-user virtual worlds. TCP/IP networking is done via sockets under Linux, and enables both local network communications inside a LAN, as well as worldwide communication with other Internet-connected machines.

- Collision detection. Detecting if solid objects are about to move through one another (and preventing this situation) is the goal of collision detection (and collision response, respectively). By implementing collision detection and response, a program conveys a sense of physical reality. Objects appear solid and impenetrable, just as they are in real life. Absence of collision detection allows objects within a virtual environment to float unhindered through one another, which distracts from the illusion of reality such environments usually attempt to create. Simple collision detection can be done with bounding spheres, where a collision is detected if the distance between two objects' centers is less than the sum of their bounding spheres' radii.

- Physics. As with collision detection, a realistic physical response system acting in accordance with Newtonian laws of physics can contribute to the sense of reality of a 3D program. Objects can appear to fall, tumble, bounce, roll, or crash realistically, as we would expect them to in real life. Implementing physics requires some sort of numerical integration scheme to solve Newtonian equations of motion.

Content Development Systems

The term *3D content development system* refers to a visual 3D environment which allows the creation of interactive content with a minimum of programming. Such systems show us the direction that future 3D development might take. Two existing and exciting content development systems for Linux are Blender 2.0 (also known as Game Blender), and World Foundry.

Game Blender is a free, proprietary product available for download at `http://www.blender.nl`. It integrates the creation of interactive content, such as games, into Blender's already powerful modeling and animation facilities. This means that all game development activity, from modeling to texturing to scripting, can take place within Blender.

World Foundry is an open source (GPL) package, originally developed as a commercial product, that enables non-programmers to create 3D environments and games. It combines a powerful 3D engine with an external level editing system and an internal scripting system. The system is extremely modular, and, through its scripting capabilities, the engine is capable of very varied behavior without changing the engine itself. This gives game designers a large amount of flexibility. There is also a sophisticated, unique camera-handling model, allowing for dramatic camera motion during game scenes.

Figure 9-11: Some of the types of worlds possible with World Foundry.

 TIP The companion book *Advanced Linux 3D Graphics Programming* contains tutorials on using both Game Blender and World Foundry.

Summary

In this chapter, we took a quick look at some more advanced topics relating to Linux 3D graphics programming. We skimmed over geometrical techniques (3D morphing), visual techniques (lighting, texture mapping, special effects), VSD schemes, advanced Blender modeling (texturing and IK), and non-graphical elements (sound, networking, physics). Finally we mentioned two 3D content development systems for Linux, which provide an interesting glance into the possible future of interactive 3D graphics programming.

A Look Ahead

This concludes the content for this book, *Linux 3D Graphics Programming*. Congratulations on making it to the end! You now have a wealth of knowledge and code for creating realistic, interactive Linux 3D applications. Hopefully your mind is buzzing with ideas you want to try out. I encourage you to try them out, and to have fun and continue to learn in the process. Also, check out this book's WWW site at `http://www.linux3dgraphicsprogramming.org` for additional resources and information pertaining to the book, the code, and Linux 3D programming in general.

You might still have some questions about topics we didn't have time to cover properly, like the topics in this last chapter. Not to fear—the journey isn't over yet! The companion book, *Advanced Linux 3D Graphics Programming*, picks up right here where this book leaves off. Texture mapping, shadows, fog, *z* buffering, portals, BSP trees, view frustum culling, IK modeling, particle systems, collision detection, digital sound, and more—it's all in the next volume, complete with explanations, images, equations, and working sample code. Excited? I certainly am!

I sincerely hope that this book has helped you to learn and experience the wonderful world of Linux 3D graphics programming, and that you will join me on the continued journey in *Advanced Linux 3D Graphics Programming*. All aboard!

Appendix

CD Installation

The first part of this appendix explains what is on the companion CD-ROM and how to install it.

License

The source code in this book was written by myself, Norman Lin, and is Copyright © 2000 Norman Lin. This version of the source code has been released under the GNU General Public License (GPL). Please read the file `book/l3d/COPYING` on the CD-ROM. The other software packages on the CD-ROM, located in directory `book/software`, were written by other individuals or companies and may be subject to other licenses; read the documentation for each software package carefully.

Essentially, the GPL allows you to use this software in your own projects, but also requires you to make the source code to such projects available under the GPL. The GPL therefore encourages the sharing of information and source code among software developers. The GNU/Linux operating system was written in this spirit; developing the code in this book would not have been possible without the availability of free, open source, high-quality software and tools. Releasing my code under the GPL is my way of giving something back to the community. Check out this book's Web site, `http://www.linux3dgraphicsprogramming.org`, to find the latest source code and related information. You can also download or submit your own source code improvements to l3d (via a common CVS repository), leave your comments, discuss the material with others, or join an open source project. I encourage you to do all of these things.

Note that the GPL permits you to sell your programs for a fee, even if those programs are based off of l3d or other GPL source code. The "free" in free software refers to freedom, not price. The purpose of requiring you to provide source code is not to try to prevent you from earning money based on the sale of your software; the purpose is to ensure that users of your program receive the same freedoms that you receive when you choose to use GPL source code as a basis for your own code. You must therefore make the source code to your software available so that others have the freedom to analyze, modify, improve, and use your software, just as you have the freedom to analyze, modify, improve, or use the software in this book.

Contents of the CD-ROM

Here is a brief list of some of the more important software and files included on the CD-ROM. There is, in reality, much more software on the CD-ROM (since the Linux operating system and tools are included), but here the focus is on the software and files relevant to 3D graphics programming.

- l3d library and sample programs
- Color versions of all the figures from the book
- Animated videos of 3D concepts to supplement the static 2D figures, in AVI format
- Xanim: Video file player to play the AVI files
- The GNU/Linux operating system, based on Debian GNU/Linux 2.2
- gcc: C++ compiler and tools for Linux
- Blender 1.80: Complete 3D modeling and animation suite
- Cygnus gcc: C++ compiler and tools for Microsoft Windows (can be used to port l3d to Windows)
- GIMP: GNU Image Manipulation Program, for editing 2D images
- Mesa: OpenGL compatible library
- GLUT: Mark Kilgard's GL Utility Toolkit
- XFree86 4.0: Free X Window System with support for 3D hardware acceleration in a window
- Glide: 3D library for communicating with 3DFX graphics hardware (used indirectly through Mesa)

For those software packages or libraries distributed under the GPL, you can obtain the source code by following the links on this book's Web page, `http://www.linux3dgraphicspro-gramming.org`.

Quick Start Guide

This section describes the essential information to install the software on the CD-ROM. It reviews the locations of files on the CD-ROM and basic installation instructions, including the order in which the various software packages should be installed.

This section assumes you already have a working Linux installation with the X Window System (XFree86) installed. If this is not the case, first install Linux and the X Window System, both included on the CD-ROM. Instructions appear in the section, "Installing Linux from the CD-ROM."

Directories

The directories on the CD-ROM are organized as follows:

- `debian/`: Contains release 2.2 of the Debian distribution of the GNU/Linux operating system. Also contains hundreds of software libraries and packages in the `.deb` package format.
- `book/`: Contains all software written for or mentioned in the book.

- ■ `book/l3d`: Contains all of the example programs in the book and the l3d library, in `.tar.gz` format.
- ■ `book/software`: Contains all of the third-party software and extra libraries used by the book, including Blender, GIMP, Mesa, and XFree86 4.0.
- ■ `book/figures`: Contains color versions of all of the figures and equations in the book, in PCX format.
- ■ `book/videos`: Contains animated 3D videos illustrating 3D concepts, to supplement the flat 2D pictures in the book.

The CD-ROM is bootable. Booting from the CD-ROM starts the installation process for the Debian GNU/Linux operating system. You do not need to boot from the CD-ROM if you only want to install the l3d programs; you only need to boot from the CD-ROM if you want to install the included Linux operating system.

Installing the Sample Programs and Other Software

1. Install Linux from the CD-ROM by booting from the CD-ROM and following the instructions provided by the menu-driven Debian GNU/Linux installation program. Alternatively, use an existing Linux installation. The installed Linux distribution must include the following software packages: gcc 2.95, an X Server (e.g., XFree86 3.3.5), Mesa, and GLUT. Almost all Linux distributions, including the one on the CD-ROM, include these libraries. If your Linux distribution does not include some of these packages, you must find them from another source (e.g., download from the Internet) and install them manually.

2. Mount the CD-ROM to make it accessible: **mount /cdrom**.

3. Type **export LD_LIBRARY_PATH=/usr/local/lib**. This allows the supplementary libraries, installed into this directory in the next step, to be located by other programs during the installation process.

4. Install each of the following supplementary libraries in the following order: `glib-1.2.8.tar.gz`, `gtk+-1.2.8.tar.gz`, `libsigc++-1.0.1.tar.gz`, `gtkmm-1.2.1.tar.gz`, and `rplay-3.2.0b5.tgz`. All of these libraries are located in `/cdrom/book/software`. The first four are needed by the Blender attributes editor program of Chapter 8; the last library is the RPlay sound server described in Chapter 9.

4a. Make a temporary directory to contain the files during installation. For instance, to install the glib library, type **mkdir glib_work**. Change to the directory you just created: **cd glib_work**.

4b. Unpack the files into the current work directory. Type **tar xzvf /cdrom/book/software/ LIB.tgz**, where LIB is the name of the library being installed (e.g., `glib-1.2.8.tar.gz`). This should create a new subdirectory, such as `glib-1.2.8`. Change to this directory: type **cd glib-1.2.8**.

4c. If desired, read the documentation for the software package.

4d. Compile the library. Type **./configure; make**. (Though all of the libraries listed above require the configuration step with **configure**, in general not all software requires this step, in which case you would simply type **make**.) Compilation should complete without errors. If an error occurs, carefully examine the output of the command to determine the reason for failure, correct this, and try again. One possible reason for failure is the absence of other libraries required by the library being compiled. In this case, you must install the prerequisite libraries first.

4e. After successful compilation, install the library. Type **su** and press **Enter**, enter the root password, and press **Enter**. You are now the superuser. Type **make install** to install the compiled binaries into the proper locations on the system. Type **exit** to end the superuser session.

4f. Remove the temporary work directory. Assuming the temporary work directory was glib_work, then type **cd ../..** to change to the original top-level directory from which you started the installation. Then, type **rm -rf glib_work** to remove the work directory.

4g. Repeat this process for each of the supplemental libraries to be installed.

5. Install the l3d sample programs as follows.

5a. Choose a directory where you want to install the sample programs, create it, and change to it. For instance, type **mkdir l3d;cd l3d**.

5b. Set the L3D environment variable to point to the l3d directory, which is the current directory into which you are about to unpack the sample programs. Type **export L3D=`pwd`** and press **Enter**. Note that the quotation marks are single back-quotes, not normal quotes.

5c. Unpack the sample programs: **tar xzvf /cdrom/book/l3d/l3d-0.5.tar.gz**.

NOTE It is recommended that you recompile the sample programs as described in the steps below. However, the CD-ROM also contains precompiled binary versions of the programs. To run the precompiled sample programs under the included Debian distribution, you should first execute the following command as the root user: **ln -s /usr/lib/libstdc++-libc6.1-2.so.3 /usr/lib/libstdc++-libc6.1-1.so.2**. This command "tricks" the system into using a newer version of the dynamically linked C++ library even if an older version is requested. This trick is necessary because the C++ library version in the included Debian distribution is a newer version than the C++ library version which was used to compile the precompiled sample programs on the CD-ROM.

5d. Edit the file Makefile.vars to set up the proper directory names for your system. The defaults work for the Debian GNU/Linux system, but may need to be changed for other Linux distributions. In particular, the variable GLIDEDIR should be set to the directory containing the Glide libraries, in case you are using Glide for 3DFX hardware acceleration. MESAINCLUDEDIR should point to the directory containing the Mesa include files. MESALIBDIR should point to the directory containing the Mesa binary library files libGL.a, libGLU.a, and libglut.a. The standard values should be correct for most systems.

5e. Type **make -f makeall.lnx** to build all of the sample programs. Remember, compiling the blend_at program requires that the following libraries be installed: glib 1.2.8, gtk+ 1.2.8, libsigc++ 1.0.1, and gtkmm 1.2.1.

6. Install Blender. Blender installation is different than installation of the other packages because Blender is distributed without source code in a precompiled binary form. Install Blender as follows.

6a. Make a directory to store the Blender files, and change to it. For instance, type **mkdir blender1.80; cd blender1.80**.

6b. Unpack the Blender executable files into the current directory. Type **tar zxvf /cdrom/book/software/blender/blender1.80-linux-glibc2.1.2-i386.tar.gz**. This creates a new subdirectory. Change to this subdirectory: type **cd blender1.80-linux-glibc2.1.2-i386**.

6c. Set the Blender environment variable to point to the current directory containing the Blender files. Type **export BLENDERDIR=`pwd`**. Note the back-quotes.

6d. To start Blender, type **./blender** in the Blender directory.

To install any other programs or libraries in the directory `book/software`, unpack each `.tar.gz` file into a separate directory, and read the installation instructions for each package.

Installing Linux from the CD-ROM

The CD-ROM includes the Debian 2.2 distribution of the GNU/Linux operating system. If you do not yet have Linux installed on your computer, you can install it from the CD-ROM. Simply boot from the CD-ROM and follow the instructions in the menu-driven interface. Note that you must have at least one free partition available on your hard drive to install Linux. It is recommended that the boot partition for Linux be located within the first 1024 cylinders (approximately 524 megabytes) of the hard drive; your computer might not be able to boot from a partition located beyond cylinder 1024. If you only have a free partition past cylinder 1024, and you don't want to repartition, then you can also create a boot floppy, and boot from it to access Linux. Full installation instructions appear on the CD-ROM in the file `debian/doc/install/index.html`, which is in HTML format; view it with your favorite WWW browser.

CAUTION   Always back up all of your data before attempting to install Linux or any other operating system. One false move could destroy all of the data on your hard drive. Of course, you should run regular backups anyway.

TIP   The key rule when installing Debian is: if you don't know the answer to a question, just press Enter. The default settings for almost all of the questions asked during installation are correct.

After installation, the system will reboot from the hard drive. You should remove the CD-ROM from the drive before restarting the system. If the system does not boot from the hard drive automatically (possible causes include a boot partition lying beyond the 1024th cylinder), then reboot from the CD-ROM again, and at the first boot prompt, type **rescue root=/dev/XXXX**, where XXXX is the name of the partition where you installed Linux. For instance, if you installed Linux on the second partition of an IDE hard drive, you would use `/dev/hda2`. Alternatively, you can use the rescue boot disk that you should have created during the installation process. This method of rebooting from external media allows you to access your newly installed system, and to repeat the steps necessary to correct the setup for hard drive booting. See the Debian installation documentation for more information.

After the reboot, the installation process continues by asking you which software you wish to install. You can choose either the simple or the advanced installation method. I suggest that you use both procedures as follows:

1. Use the simple method during initial installation to quickly obtain a basic running system. You should install the following packages: C++ development, and X Window System (complete). Allow the X Window System installation to automatically detect your video card, and also install the `icewm` window manager.

2. After basic installation, run `dselect` (as the root user) to install the following additional Debian packages not installed by the simple method: `mesag3`, `mesag-dev`, `glutg3`, and `glutg3-dev`. This installs the Mesa and GLUT libraries from the prepackaged Debian package files.

3. Finally, manually install the other software (e.g., Blender, l3d, and so forth) as described in the Quick Start section.

After installing the operating system, the X server may or may not automatically start. You can choose to configure this during installation. If the X server does not start immediately (i.e., you see a text screen rather than a graphics screen after booting the system), then you should log in and start the X server with the following command: **startx -- -bpp 32**. The 32 indicates the color depth of the X server. You can also use 16- or 8-bit mode if you wish, which are slightly faster (because less data must be transmitted for each pixel), but also have lower visual quality.

If for some reason your configuration of the X server during the initial setup is incorrect, you can run XF86Setup (as the root user) to reconfigure X. Also, note that the program gpm (which allows text selection with the mouse in a text console) may interfere with the mouse movement under X. The mouse file /dev/mouse must exist and be a symbolic link to the proper device file (such as /dev/psaux for a PS/2 style mouse) in order for the mouse to work under X, or at all. The documentation in directory /usr/doc/HOWTO provides additional notes on getting your mouse to work.

If you want to reinstall the packages or review your selections after the installation process has completed, then become the root user and run `tasksel` to install logical groups of packages (e.g., "Games," or "C++ programming"). Alternatively, use `dselect` to install individual packages, such as one particular programming utility or one particular library such as Mesa. Note that these are Debian-specific commands; for another Linux distribution, consult the documentation for the appropriate commands.

Please note that it is not possible for me or the publisher to provide support related to installation of the Linux operating system. The CD-ROM contains ample documentation on the installation and configuration process. Furthermore, the documentation lists Internet addresses where you can look up more information or ask questions to the Debian community at large. Also, see this book's Web site http://www.linux3dgraphicsprogramming.org for a discussion board where you can post questions or share your experiences with other members of the community.

Using an Existing Linux Distribution

You do not have to install the included Debian distribution of Linux in order to run the programs; if you have an existing Linux installation from another source, you can almost certainly use it as well. It is important that your Linux installation has the following software:

- gcc compiler version 2.95 or greater, to compile the C++ code
- An X server, such as XFree86 version 3.3.5 or greater, to display the 3D graphics output in an X window
- The Mesa library, an OpenGL-compatible graphics library, to take advantage of OpenGL features and hardware acceleration
- GLUT, Mark Kilgard's GL Utility Toolkit library, for use with OpenGL

You will probably also want to install the following software. Most Linux distributions come pre-packaged with these software packages; you just need to select them during the installation process.

- GIMP, the Gnu Image Manipulation Program, for editing 2D images such as texture maps
- The PPM utilities for converting PPM files to other formats from the command line.

All of this software is included on the CD-ROM in the Debian package format (`.deb`). Also, the following software is provided in `.tar.gz` format: Mesa, GLUT, Blender.

Basic Linux Configuration and Commands

This section assumes that you have successfully installed Linux and have the X server working. We now look at a few basic commands which you need in order to correctly configure your Linux system for using the software in this book.

After starting X, a terminal window, also called a command shell, should either appear automatically or can be started via a menu. This depends on the exact window manager you use. Typically, the menu can be invoked by clicking on a starting button at the lower left of the desktop, or by clicking on the desktop itself. Many important commands under Linux must be executed from a command shell, so make sure you can start one.

The most important part of using the X Window System is to ensure that the DISPLAY environment variable is set correctly. An environment variable is a variable set within the command shell, which can then be queried by all programs started from within that environment. The DISPLAY environment variable is used by all X programs to find the network address of the computer on which the program should display its output.

You ordinarily want to display graphics on your local monitor. First, check to see if the DISPLAY variable is already set. Type **printenv DISPLAY** and press **Enter**. If a line such as "0:0" or "localhost:0.0" is displayed, then the DISPLAY variable is already correctly set. If you see nothing, then you need to set the DISPLAY variable.

To set the DISPLAY variable, type the following command in the shell and press **Enter**:

```
export DISPLAY=127.0.0.1:0.0
```

This sets the display to be the local host (127.0.0.1), using screen 0 and display 0. This assumes you are using the command shell `bash`, which is standard on Linux systems.

NOTE If you are using a csh variant as your command shell (as opposed to sh or bash), then you must type **setenv DISPLAY 127.0.0.1:0.0** to set the environment variable. This syntax applies to setting all environment variables in csh, not just the DISPLAY variable.

To test your DISPLAY variable, type **xterm&** and press **Enter**. A new command shell window should appear. If this occurs, your DISPLAY environment is set correctly. If you get an error such as Can't open display, then the DISPLAY variable is not correctly set. If you get an error such as Client is not authorized to connect to Server, then for some reason the X program was not allowed to connect to the specified X server. In the case of a local X server, one reason for this can be if you started the X server as one user, but then tried to start X applications as another user. To solve this, start X programs as the same user that started the X server.

If you're new to Linux, the following are some useful shell commands to get you started.

- mount /cdrom makes the files on the CD-ROM available in directory /cdrom.
- cd directory_name changes to a particular directory.
- ls lists the contents of the current directory. ls -l shows more information.
- pwd prints the current directory.
- less filename displays the contents of a file. Press **q** to exit less.
- printenv VARIABLE and setenv VARIABLE=value print and set environment variables.

Simply type the name of a program in the current directory, such as **program_name**, to execute it. If that doesn't work, then type **./program_name**. Whether or not it works without the leading dot depends on whether or not the current directory (denoted by the dot character ".") is in your PATH environment variable. This setting is different among the various Linux distributions.

With these basic commands, you will be able to navigate around a Linux system and find other documentation to read. See Chapter 1 for more information on how to access the online documentation on a Linux system with the man command.

Troubleshooting the Sample Programs

If you have problems running the sample programs, here are some tips for finding the problem.

- Ensure that the DISPLAY environment variable is set correctly and that you can start other X programs from the command line.
- Ensure that all required libraries (Mesa, GLUT) have been installed. Under Debian, run dselect to install the Mesa and GLUT packages.
- Ensure that any data files needed by the program are accessible or in the current directory. Such files include object mesh files and plug-in shared library files.
- Ensure that mesh files contain no invalid polygons. An example of an invalid polygon would be one with only two vertices, since a valid polygon must contain at least three vertices.
- If all else fails, try compiling the sample code with debugging. Edit the file Makefile.vars, uncomment the line containing "DEBUG=-g", and comment out all other lines referencing "DEBUG." (In Makefiles, the comment character is the pound sign #.) Then, type **cd $L3D;make clean;make -f makeall.lnx** to recompile all programs with

debugging. Finally, execute the program in question with the debugger, as described in Chapter 1, to determine exactly where the program crashes and why.

Some Comments on the Sample Programs

The source code on the CD-ROM has additional comments within the C++ source code which, for space reasons, were omitted in the listings in the book. This removal of comments was done via an automated Perl program, so you can be sure that the code contents of the listings in the book are identical to those on the CD-ROM. The only difference is that there are ample comments in the code on the CD-ROM.

Again, see this book's Web site `http://www.linux3dgraphicsprogramming.org` to see the latest version of the l3d code.

Hardware Acceleration

As covered in Chapter 2, l3d programs can all take advantage of hardware acceleration by using OpenGL as the rasterization layer. This means that OpenGL must be configured to use hardware acceleration in order for l3d programs to use hardware acceleration.

There are two ways for you to use hardware acceleration. The first way requires a 3DFX graphics card, the Glide library, and a Mesa distribution compiled with Glide support. This means that you need to manually install Glide and compile Mesa; see the Mesa documentation for more information. There are many versions of the Glide library, for different generations of 3DFX hardware. I have included two versions of Glide on the CD-ROM, which should work with Voodoo and Voodoo3 cards. If you have a different 3DFX card, check out the Web site `http://linux.3dfx.com` to download the proper version of Glide for yourself. After installing Glide and compiling Mesa to use Glide, you must edit the file `$L3D/Makefile.vars` to point to the correct directories. Variable `GLIDEDIR` should point to the directory containing the Glide library; `MESAINCLUDEDIR` should point to the directory containing the include files used to compile Mesa, and `MESALIBDIR` should point to the directory containing the new, 3DFX-enabled Mesa libraries. Also, you must uncomment the line starting with GLIDE_LIBS to cause l3d programs to be linked with the Glide library. After following these steps, you can use 3DFX/Glide hardware acceleration as described in Chapter 2.

The second way of using hardware acceleration involves using XFree86 4.0 and the Direct Rendering Infrastructure (DRI). This requires you to compile the XFree86 4.0 system (included on the CD-ROM) with support for your 3D graphics card, and for you to use the special DRI Mesa/OpenGL libraries, which use the DRI to communicate directly with the underlying graphics hardware. This is similar to using Mesa to access 3DFX hardware through Glide, but with broader support for various hardware, and with the ability to display accelerated 3D graphics within a window, as opposed to full-screen. Using the DRI for hardware acceleration does not require you to change the file `Makefile.vars`. However, you do need to ensure that the DRI OpenGL libraries, which use hardware acceleration, are dynamically linked to your executable program. To test this, type **ldd PROGRAM**, where PROGRAM is the name of the executable program which should use hardware acceleration. You should see a line indicating that the `libGL.so` file is dynamically linked with the `libGL.so` file from the XFree86 4.0 directory. If some other `libGL.so` file is linked, then this other OpenGL library will most likely be unable to use the DRI hardware acceleration. To control which directories are searched during dynamic linking, set the environment variable `LD_LIBRARY_PATH`. See the man page on the dynamic linker `ld.so` for more information. The XFree86 4.0 documentation also provides information on troubleshooting the DRI.

TIP The Utah-GLX project contains drivers for some 3D cards which are not yet supported by the DRI. Eventually, the Utah-GLX drivers will be integrated into the DRI, but before this happens, you may still find it useful to use the Utah-GLX drivers directly. The home page for the Utah-GLX project is `http://utah-glx.sourceforge.net`.

Integer, Floating-Point, and Fixed-Point Math

Throughout this book, we have made reference to fixed-point math. The type `l3d_real` is a sort of facade allowing either fixed-point or floating-point variables to be used throughout the code just by changing a `#define`. We also explicitly used fixed-point in the software texture mapping routines. This section discusses exactly what fixed-point math is.

Motivation

When dealing with numbers in a programming language, a fundamental distinction is made between integer values and fractional values. Integer values are whole numbers with no fractional portion and are represented in memory directly as byte values in two's complement format. Integer values which are too large to be stored in one byte must span multiple bytes, in which case, byte ordering or "endian-ness" becomes an issue. Fractional values are represented either in a *fixed-point* or, more frequently, a *floating-point* representation. The latter part of this section describes fixed-point in detail. With a floating-point representation, the total number of bits of precision is limited, but the precision can "float" to the range of interest. For instance, a typical 10-digit pocket calculator uses a floating-point system: you have 10 digits, but these 10 digits can represent a 10-digit number with no decimal places, an eight-digit number with two decimal places, a four-digit number with six decimal places, and so forth. The decimal point—or generalizing to other number bases, the "fraction point"—floats to accommodate the desired range of precision; hence the term "floating-point."

In computer memory, integer and floating-point numbers are internally represented and processed differently. Hardware support for mathematical operations on integers has always been present, since the processor itself requires integer mathematics in order to fetch the next instruction from the correct address in memory. Thus, integer math has always been relatively fast.

Historically, hardware support for floating-point numbers had lagged behind that for integers. Originally, floating-point coprocessors, also known as *floating-point units* or FPUs, were a rarity in the consumer PC scene. High-end number-crunching workstations might have boasted an FPU, but the average PC had to emulate floating-point operations in software. Thus, operations on floating-point numbers were, in earlier PC generations, noticeably slower than equivalent operations on integers.

3D graphics deals conceptually with fractional values. Thus, conceptually speaking, integers are insufficient for modeling 3D graphics. On the other hand, without an FPU, using floating-point would have been too slow for interactive 3D applications in earlier PC generations. The solution was to use a sort of hybrid representation—the so-called fixed-point system. This system encodes a fractional value within an integer, offering simultaneously fractional precision and integer speed.

Recently, FPUs have become widespread. This makes it quite possible to write a real-time 3D program completely using floating-point. Fixed-point has decreased in significance as a result. So, why should anyone worry about fixed-point anymore? There are two reasons:

1. You may wish to develop 3D graphics programs for platforms that have no floating-point coprocessor. For instance, a friend recently asked me if I could program a wireframe tank simulation for his palmtop computer, which had no FPU.

2. Conversion between floating-point and integer values is slower than conversion between fixed-point and integer values. This is particularly an issue with rasterization, since sub-pixel accuracy requires computations using sub-integer precision, but actually plotting the pixel requires conversion to an integer coordinate.

So, although due to the spread of FPUs the need for fixed-point has diminished, it is still a technique which can be used to your advantage. Let's now examine fixed-point math in detail.

Concepts

The idea behind fixed-point math is actually quite simple. We restrict our numbers to have a fixed amount of precision before the decimal point and a fixed amount of precision after the decimal point. In a decimal (base 10) system, this could mean, for instance, that we have five digits before the decimal point, and five digits after the decimal point. Then, if we artificially move the decimal point five places to the right, and remember that the actual value requires us to move the decimal point back five places to the left, then we have effectively devised a scheme for storing fractional values in integers. For instance, we could store the fractional number 47213.46325 as the whole number 4721346325. The five rightmost, or least significant, digits represent the fractional part of the number, and the five leftmost, or most significant, digits represent the whole part of the number.

In a binary system, we don't deal with digits, but instead with bits. This means that we have a certain number of bits for the whole part (before the decimal point) and a certain number of bits for the fractional part (after the decimal point). The l3d library by default uses 32-bit signed integers, with 14 bits of precision (the least significant or rightmost 14 bits) for the fractional part of the number.

Overflow and Underflow

As we mentioned earlier in this book, adding and subtracting fixed-point numbers can be done with normal C addition and subtraction operators. However, multiplication and division requires us to use the macros `l3d_mulrr`, `l3d_mulri`, `l3d_divrr`, or `l3d_divri`, as we saw earlier. When using fixed-point math, these macros are mapped to the macros `fixfixmul`, `fixintmul`, `fixfixdiv`, and `fixintdiv`. Each of these macros defines a special way of multiplying or dividing fixed-point numbers with integers or other fixed-point numbers.

The reason we need to use special routines to deal with multiplication of fixed-point numbers is due to the unfortunate and rather annoying topic of *overflow*. By converting fractional numbers into integers, we are essentially merely multiplying the fractional numbers by a constant in order to scale them to be larger integers. For instance, with 14 bits of fractional precision, we multiply a fractional value by 2^{14} to arrive at the corresponding integer value.

The problem is that when multiplying two fixed-point values, we effectively multiply by the square of the scaling factor. For instance, say we have fractional values x and y. To represent these in fixed-point as integers, we store these as $x*2^{14}$ and $y*2^{14}$. If we multiply these two values together, we arrive at the value $x*y*(2^{14})*(2^{14})$. However, the desired result is the scaled value of the product, in other words, $x*y*(2^{14})$. Therefore, conceptually, we can perform fixed-point multiplication by multiplying the numbers, then dividing by the scaling factor to cancel out the second scaling factor. However, practically, it isn't quite this simple. After performing the multiplication but before the corrective division, the maximum possible size of the temporary result is much larger—2^{14} or 16,384 times larger, to be exact—than the actual desired result. This large result will very likely not fit into the number of bits (32, in this case) allocated for our fixed-point numbers, meaning that after the multiplication, overflow has occurred and the higher bits of the result have been irrevocably lost. This means that after performing the corrective division, it's too late—overflow has already occurred and the corrective division cannot recover the lost digits. A similar problem, underflow, plagues division of fixed-point numbers; in this case, we lose fractional precision in the lower (instead of the higher) bits.

The only solution to this quandary is to perform the multiplication or division operations with higher precision so that the larger temporary results do not overflow or underflow. There are generally two ways to do this. One is to use algebraic manipulation to explicitly partition the multiplication operation into a series of smaller multiplications, all of which can fit into the space of a single integer, then combining the results. The other way is to use assembler instructions to call processor-specific higher-precision integer multiplication and division routines. The algebraic solution is more portable, but is slower because it requires several operations to perform just one multiplication or division. The assembler solution is less portable, but is faster.

The l3d library illustrates both techniques of implementing fixed-point multiplication and division, but by default the assembler solution is used. As we saw earlier, since we use macros to perform the multiplications and divisions, we often need to nest macros to perform complex operations. For instance, $x*(y/z)$ would be expressed in code as:

```
fixfixmul(x,fixfixdiv(y,z))
```

Even after eliminating the inherent overflow problem by reformulating the multiplication and division operators, overflow still comes back to haunt us again and again with fixed-point math. This is because many operations, such as matrix multiplication, cross product and dot product computation, distance calculations, and so forth, require multiplying large numbers by other large numbers. Eventually, these numbers usually get scaled down again by a division, but if at any intermediate point during the computation an intermediate result is too large, then overflow occurs and the entire computation returns an invalid result. For instance, say that the maximum whole value you can represent in the whole part of your fixed-point numbers is 131072. Then, say that you have two objects located at the edge of the universe, with x coordinates of 131071 and 131070. Assume you wish to compute the distance between these two objects. Doing so requires a dot product, which multiplies the two x coordinates together. We multiply 131071 by 131070, which exceeds our maximum allowable value of 131072—overflow has struck again.

This means that you always need to be extremely careful when formulating complex fixed-point computations to ensure that even intermediate results can never overflow. The l3d library has some built-in assertions to assist in this process, as described in the next section. Another useful technique (currently not implemented in l3d) is to define an operator which performs a multiplication immediately followed by a division, because this is a typically recurring operation in 3D graphics. By performing the multiplication and division with extended precision in an assembler routine and only returning the scaled-down result, we can avoid overflow by judicious use of this operator.

Classes and Fixed-Point Math

One last comment on fixed-point math is in order. The use of macros leads to somewhat unnatural nested invocation of two-argument macros. The problem seems to lend itself readily to a C++ class with overloaded operators for the necessary mathematical operations (+, −, *, /). This approach, while conceptually correct, has a major drawback: it creates and destroys temporary objects on the fly. This can be quite expensive in terms of execution time. Consider the expression $(x*y) + ((y/z) / (x*z))$. Using overloaded operators, five temporary objects are created and destroyed. Why? Because this natural, mathematical form of expression is recursive in nature. At the highest level, the expression is the sum of one term plus another. Each term is, in turn, another complete subexpression. When evaluating this expression, the computer needs to save each of the intermediate results, which, in turn, requires invocation of an object constructor and shortly thereafter the destructor. Even if we use a global pool of pre-allocated objects (as we did in Chapter 4 for matrices), we still have an overhead of fetching a temporary object, updating a global counter to point to the next free object, and so forth.

One could argue that clarity of expression afforded through overloaded operators outweighs the performance penalty. In general, this is true, but in the case of fixed-point math, we must keep overhead to an absolute minimum. The fundamental fixed-point mathematical operations could be performed hundreds of thousands of times per frame, multiplying every small inefficiency by orders of magnitude.

You might wonder, "If the overloaded-operator version creates temporaries, doesn't the nested-function version also create temporaries?" The answer is yes, but the overloaded-operator version creates temporary _objects_, whereas the nested-function version creates temporary _integers_. The former requires calling a constructor and a destructor, or at the very least requires fetching of a pre-allocated object from a global pool. The latter only requires allocation of an intrinsic data type. This is the reason for the difference in performance. It should be noted that the overloaded-operator version can be optimized somewhat by using an inline constructor/destructor combined with a peephole optimization phase after compilation, which can theoretically reduce the overhead to be the same as that of integers. However, the compiler may not be able to store a class within a register (even if it fits), whereas integers are more likely to be able to be stored in registers with the `register` keyword. The only way to check this for sure is to examine the assembler output of the compiler.

Compiling Fixed-Point Examples

At one earlier point in time, the l3d library supported both fixed-point and floating-point versions of the code. Currently, only the floating-point versions have been maintained; most of the fixed-point versions do not currently run as they stand. Nevertheless, the entire infrastructure for fixed-point math is present. If you define the symbol `FIXED_POINT_MATH` before compilation, the `l3d_mulXX` and `l3d_divXX` macros will be mapped to their fixed-point versions. Furthermore, an entire directory tree is devoted to the binary files for the fixed-point versions of the programs, and contains appropriate Makefiles defining `FIXED_POINT_MATH`. All programs do at least compile in the fixed-point directory, but they need extra work to actually run.

The most annoying part about getting fixed-point programs to work is, as we mentioned earlier, overflow. You must use algebraic manipulation to break up computations into parts which cannot overflow the size of the fixed-point numbers.

To make porting the code to fixed-point a less tedious affair, the l3d macros for fixed-point multiplication and division include an assertion which checks that the result of the operation is the same as the result when performed with floating-point numbers. If the results differ, then the program aborts execution and prints the offending line number. If the program is compiled with the symbol `NDEBUG` defined, then the assertions are removed by the compiler and incur zero run-time overhead (but then, of course, cannot catch any overflow errors).

So, to convert a particular program to use fixed-point, follow this general procedure:

1. Change to the fixed-point directory, such as
   `$L3D/binaries/linux_x/fixed/app/fltsim`.

2. Copy any data files from the corresponding floating-point directory into the fixed-point directory.

3. Edit file `$L3D/Makefile.vars`. Turn on debugging (set `DEBUG=-g`). This also turns off optimization and enables assertion checking.

4. Compile and run the l3d library and the program. Notice and correct any overflow assertion violations.

5. Manually scan the source code for floating-point variables or multiplications, and replace these with appropriate calls to `l3d_mulXX` or `l3d_divXX`. For instance, if there are three variables of type `l3d_real` named x, y, and z, and there is a line reading x=y*z, then you should replace this with x=`l3d_mulrr(y,z)`. Again, every such change you make is a potential source of an overflow error and needs to be carefully checked. Note that changing the code to use `l3d_mulXX` and `l3d_divXX` variables still allows the floating-point version of the code to work, since with floating-point, the macros map to ordinary C floating-point multiplication and division operators.

Program Listings for Fixed-Point Math

The following code is the l3d code implementing fixed-point math. Remember, the use of these macros is controlled by the #define FIXED_POINT_MATH. If this symbol is not defined, then the l3d_mulXX and l3d_divXX macros map to ordinary C floating-point operators; otherwise, the operators are defined as shown in the following listings. (This differentiation takes place in sys_dep.h.)

Listing A-1: math_fix.h

```c
#ifndef __MATH_FIX_H
#define __MATH_FIX_H
#include "../tool_os/memman.h"

#include "../system/sys_dep.h"
#include <assert.h>

//- We perform fixed point math by using 32-bit integers, which
//- we assume are signed. Since we assume they are signed,
//- fixed point multiplication does not do sign extension, for speed
//- reasons.

typedef long l3d_fixed;  //- this must be 32 bits, and MUST BE SIGNED

//- Now we define how many bits we use to store the fractional part, and
//- the remainder we use to store the integer part.
//-
//- FX_PRECIS is the # of precision bits, which we set to 14
//- FX_PRECIS_QUOT is the # of precision bits for the divisor AND quotient
//-
//- 14 bits means we can represent up to 2^-16384 precision = 4 dec places
//- implies 32 - 14 - 1(sign bit) = 17 bits for whole part = max 131072
//- implies 32 - 14 -1(sign) whole bits after int multiplication = max 131072
//- implies 32 - (14+14) -1(sign) whole bits after fix*fix mult. = max 8
//-    but we can express fix*fix mult as a series of fix*int mult's; slower
//- implies FX_PRECIS_QUOT bits of precision for divisor AND quotient
//-
//- summarizing:
//- addition/subtraction of fixed points: +/- 131072.0000
//- mult of fixed*int:                   : +/- 131072.0000
//- mult of fixed*fixed:                 : +/- 8.00000000
//- slower mult of fixed*fixed           : +/- 131072.0000
//- div of fixed/fixed                   : +/- 131072.00
//- div of fixed/int                     : +/- 131072.0000

#ifndef FX_PRECISION_ALREADY_DEFINED
#define FX_PRECISION_ALREADY_DEFINED
#include "fix_prec.h"
#endif

extern int fm_whole;
extern long fm_localdata;
extern float fm_sign;

//- conversion routines between fixed and floating/integer and vice-versa

#define float2fix(aFloat) ((long)((aFloat)*FX_PRECIS_MAX))
```

```
#define int2fix(aInt) ((long)(aInt) < FX_PRECIS)

#define fix2float(aFixed) ((double)((aFixed) / FX_PRECIS_MAX))

#define fix2int(aFixed) ( (aFixed) > FX_PRECIS)

//- right shift for whole, discard frac. part

//- routines for fixed*fixed and fixed*int multiplication
//-
//- general notes for multiplication:
//- 1. ensure operands are in correct format (sign-extending if necessary)
//- 2. ensure result is in correct format (sign-extending if necessary)
//-
//- #2 automatically taken care of IF fixed-type is signed
//- thus we just worry about #1, for FixIntMul

//-
//- just treat a as a regular signed long and b as a regular signed int
//- proof:
//-     f1_fixed = Int(f1*SHIFT)
//-     f1_fixed * x = Int(f1*SHIFT) * x;
//-     f1_fixed * x = Int(f1*x*SHIFT);
//-
//- the result is properly shifted.
//-
//- sign extension is unnecessary if we assume a is signed; this means
//- we do not need sign-extending code such as
//-     if(b<0) {
//-         return a * ( ((long)(-b)^FX_ALLBITS_MASK) + 1 ) ;
//-     }
//-

#define fixintmul(a,b) ( {\
assert((fix2float(a)*(b)-fix2float((a)*(b)) > -0.2) && \
       (fix2float(a)*(b)-fix2float((a)*(b)) <  0.2) || \
       (printf("fixintmul %f %d = %f, should be %f", \
               fix2float(a),b,fix2float((a)*(b)),fix2float(a)*(b))\
       &&0)); \
(a)*(b); })

//- a=fixed, b=int

#define FIX_ASM
#ifdef FIX_ASM

#define fixfixmul(a,b) \
  ( {long __result = (a), __arg = (b); \
      asm("imul %2;" \
          "shrd %3,%2,%0;" \
          : "=a" (__result) \
          : "0" (__result), "d" (__arg) , "I" (FX_PRECIS) ); \
      assert( \
          ((fix2float(__result) - fix2float(a)*fix2float(b) > -0.2) \
           && \
           (fix2float(__result) - fix2float(a)*fix2float(b) <  0.2)) \
           || \
           (printf("fixfixmul %f %f = %f, should be %f", \
              fix2float(a),fix2float(b),fix2float(__result), \
              fix2float(a)*fix2float(b)) \
```

```
                  && 0) \
                ); \
        _result; \
      }\
  )


#else


//-
//- if we were to use a formula of the form
//-     return ((a*b) > FX_PRECIS) ;
//- then we would have only
//-    32 - (14+14) -1(sign) whole bits after fix*fix mult. = max 8
//- as the maximum after a fixed*fixed multiplication.
//-
//- proof:
//-    f1_fixed = Int(f1*SHIFT)
//-    f2_fixed = Int(f2*SHIFT)
//-    f1_fixed- f2_fixed = Int(f1*SHIFT)- Int(f2*SHIFT)
//-                       = Int(f1*f2*SHIFT*SHIFT)
//-                          so we shift TWICE = 2*SHIFT bits taken up by
//-                          fractional part; = TOTAL_BITS - 2*SHIFT -1(sign)
//-                          for whole part   = 32 - 2*14 - 1 = 3; 2^3=8 !
//-
//- Instead we recast the fixed*fixed multplication as follows:
//-
//- fixed1- fixed2 = (f1_whole + f1_frac)- (f2_whole + f2_frac)
//-               =    f1_whole*f2_whole
//-                  + f1_frac*f2_frac
//-                  + f1_whole*f2_frac
//-                  + f1_frac*f2_whole
//- note that if fixed1 is negative, BOTH f1_whole and f1_frac are negative
//- particularly important is f1_frac, since if we try to access the
//- fractional part with &FX_SIGN_MASK we lose the sign if it's negative.
//- thus if a # is negative we access its fractional part by first
//- making it positive, &'ing with FX_SIGN_MASK, and -ating the result.
//-

(
  /* if */ ( ((b) & FX_SIGN_MASK) ^ ((a) & FX_SIGN_MASK) ) ? /* dift signs */ \
  /* if */ ( ((b) & FX_SIGN_MASK) ^ ((a) & FX_SIGN_MASK) ) ? /* dift signs */ \
  /* if */  ((b) & FX_SIGN_MASK) ?  /* a +ve, b -ve */ \
  - ( \
      ( (((a)>FX_PRECIS) * ((-(b))>FX_PRECIS)) < FX_PRECIS ) + \
      ( ((a) & FX_PRECIS_MASK) * ((-(b)) & FX_PRECIS_MASK) > FX_PRECIS ) + \
      ( ((a)>FX_PRECIS) * ((-(b)) & FX_PRECIS_MASK) ) + \
      ( ((-(b))>FX_PRECIS) * ((a) & FX_PRECIS_MASK) ) \
    ) \
  /* else */ : /* a -ve, b +ve */ \
  - ( \
      ((((-(a))>FX_PRECIS) * ((b)>FX_PRECIS)) < FX_PRECIS ) + \
      (((-(a)) & FX_PRECIS_MASK) * ((b) & FX_PRECIS_MASK) > FX_PRECIS )+\
      (((-(a))>FX_PRECIS) * ((b) & FX_PRECIS_MASK) ) + \
      (((b)>FX_PRECIS) * ((-(a)) & FX_PRECIS_MASK) ) \
    ) \
  /* else */ : /* same signs */ \
     /* if */ ((b) & FX_SIGN_MASK) ?  /* a -ve, b -ve */ \
      ( \
        ((((-(a))>FX_PRECIS) * ((-(b))>FX_PRECIS)) < FX_PRECIS ) + \
        (((-(a)) & FX_PRECIS_MASK) * ((-(b)) & FX_PRECIS_MASK) > FX_PRECIS )+\
```

```
            (((-(a))>FX_PRECIS) * ((-(b)) & FX_PRECIS_MASK) ) + \
            (((-(b))>FX_PRECIS) * ((-(a)) & FX_PRECIS_MASK) ) \
          ) \
          /* else */ : /* a +ve, b+ve */ \
          ( \
            ((((a)>FX_PRECIS) * ((b)>FX_PRECIS)) < FX_PRECIS ) + \
            (((a & FX_PRECIS_MASK) * ((b) & FX_PRECIS_MASK) > FX_PRECIS ) + \
            (((a)>FX_PRECIS) * ((b) & FX_PRECIS_MASK) ) + \
            (((b)>FX_PRECIS) * ((a) & FX_PRECIS_MASK) ) \
          ) \
        )

#endif

//- routines for fixed/int and fixed/fixed division

//- NOTES: fixed division – each bit you take OUT of the divisor is
//- a bit of precision you RECEIVE in the quotient.  If you take NO
//- bits out of the divisor (i.e. divisor is not right-shifted and
//- has full precision), quotient has NO fractional precision!
//- proof:
//-    f1_fixed = Int(f1 SHIFT)
//-    f2_fixed = Int(f2 SHIFT)
//-    f1_fixed/f2_fixed = Int(f1*SHIFT) div Int(f2*SHIFT)
//-                      = Int((f1*SHIFT)/(f2*SHIFT))
//-                      = Int(f1/f2)
//-                      = no fractional precision at all
//-                        a final shift of SHIFT is necessary to cvt 2 fixed

//- taking bits out of the divisor means doing a reverse-shift on the
//- divisor and yields:
//-    f1_fixed/f2_fixed = Int(f1*SHIFT) div Int(f2*SHIFT/RSHIFT)
//-                      = Int( (f1*SHIFT)/(f2*SHIFT/RSHIFT) )
//-                      = Int( f1*RSHIFT / f2 )
//-                      = gained RSHIFT bits of precision in result
//-                        final shift of SHIFT-RSHIFT is needed to cvt 2 fixed

//- This is solved in HW by making dividend twice as large, but here we
//- must simply make our divisor less accurate. We make our divisor
//- less accurate by FX_PRECIS_QUOT (=RSHIFT) bits. We normally
//- shift by FX_PRECIS (=SHIFT) bits.

//- general notes for division:
//- 1. ensure operands are both positive (negating – based on the
//-    type of the operand – as necessary)
//- 2. ensure result has correct sign (negating, based on the representation
//-    of Tfixed, as necessary)

#ifdef FIX_ASM

#define fixfixdiv(a,b) \
   ( {long __result = (a), __arg = (b); \
       asm("xor %1,%1;" \
           "shrd %4,%3,%1;" \
           "sar  %4,%3;" \
           "idiv %2" \
          : "=a" (__result) \
          : "0" (0), "b" (__arg) , "d"(a) , "I" (32-FX_PRECIS) ); \
       assert( \
             (fix2float(__result) - fix2float(a)/fix2float(b) > -0.2) \
```

```
                && \
                (fix2float(__result) - fix2float(a)/fix2float(b) <  0.2) \
                || \
                (printf("fixfixdiv %f %f = %f, should be %f", \
                  fix2float(a),fix2float(b),fix2float(__result), \
                  fix2float(a)/fix2float(b)) \
                && 0) \
              ); \
          __result; \
        }\
    )

#else

(\
 /* NEGATIVE RESULT */ \
 \
 /* if */ ( ((b) & FX_SIGN_MASK) ^ ((a) & FX_SIGN_MASK)) ? /* dift signs */ \
 /* if */ ((b)&FX_SIGN_MASK) ?  /* a+ve, b-ve */ \
 /* do a negative/positive division and negate (2's comp.) result */ \
 ~ (((a)/((~(b)+1)>FX_PRECIS_QUOT)) < (FX_PRECIS-FX_PRECIS_QUOT)) \
 + 1 \
 /* else */ : /* a-ve, b+ve */ \
 /* do a positive/positive division and negate (2's comp.) result */ \
 ~ (((~(a)+1)/((b)>FX_PRECIS_QUOT)) < (FX_PRECIS - FX_PRECIS_QUOT)) \
 + 1\
 \
 /* POSITIVE RESULT */ \
 \
 /* else */ : \
 /* if */ ((b)&FX_SIGN_MASK) ?  /* a-ve, b-ve */ \
 \
 /* do a positive/positive division instead of a -ve/-ve division */ \
 ((~(a)+1) / ((-(b))>FX_PRECIS_QUOT)) < (FX_PRECIS - FX_PRECIS_QUOT) \
 /* else */ : /* a+ve, b+ve */ \
 \
 /* easiest case: a positive/positive division */ \
 ((a) / ((b)>FX_PRECIS_QUOT)) < (FX_PRECIS - FX_PRECIS_QUOT)
)

#endif

//- just treat a as a regular signed long and b as a regular signed int
//- proof:
//-    f1_fixed = Int(f1*SHIFT)
//-    f1_fixed / x = Int(f1*SHIFT) / x;
//-    f1_fixed / x = Int(f1/x*SHIFT);

//- the result is properly shifted.

#define fixintdiv(a,b) ( {\
assert((fix2float(a)/(b)-fix2float((a)/(b)) > -0.2) && \
      (fix2float(a)/(b)-fix2float((a)/(b)) <  0.2) || \
      (printf("fixintdiv %f %d = %f, should be %f", \
              fix2float(a),b,fix2float((a)/(b)),fix2float(a)/(b))\
      &&0)); \
(a)/(b); })
/* a fix, b int */

#endif
```

Listing A-2: `math_fix.cc`

```
/*****************************************************************************
 * Global temporary variables for fixed math. We declare these once instead
 * of allowing each inline fixed math function to have its own copy (which
 * would be wasteful of space)
 *****************************************************************************/

int   fm_whole;
long  fm_localdata;
float fm_sign;
```

Porting the Code to Microsoft Windows

The l3d code has been designed so that it can be easily ported to other operating systems, such as Microsoft Windows. With a few exceptions, the sample programs in this book compile and run under Windows. However, support for Windows has not been a primary concern for l3d, since it was written to illustrate graphics programming under Linux, and since I have neither installed nor need any Microsoft products whatsoever on my main computer. Under the (not necessarily true) assumption that Microsoft and Windows continue to maintain some short-term market relevance, it might be interesting for you to make your programs available under Microsoft Windows as well.

To compile the code under Microsoft Windows, you can use the Cygnus GCC compiler, included on the CD-ROM in directory `book/software/ms-win`. This is a free C++ compiler and debugger which runs under Microsoft Windows and which can be used to compile the l3d code. Be sure also to read and install the OpenGL header files and libraries included with the Cygnus GCC compiler. The OpenGL files are located in the archive file `opengl-1.2.1-1.tar.gz` on the CD-ROM.

The file `makecyg.bat` is a batch file which compiles all of the examples for Microsoft Windows by using the Cygnus GCC compiler. The following are Windows-specific source code files, which you should use as a starting point for understanding the ported code:

- `fwin.cc`, `fwin.h`: factory classes for creating Microsoft Windows factories.
- `sc_mswin.h`, `sc_mswin.cc`: screen classes for creating a 2D output window using a device-independent bitmap (DIB) section.
- `dis_mswin.h`, `dis_mswin.cc`: dispatcher classes for event handling under Microsoft Windows.
- `sc_wogl.h`, `sc_wogl.cc`, `sc_wzogl.h`, `sc_wzogl.cc`: screen classes for creating an output window using OpenGL under Windows.

The binaries directory for Windows object and executable files is `$L3D/binaries/cygwin`. The porting was performed by duplicating the directory structure from the Linux directory and by editing the Makefiles as necessary.

By default the Windows code is compiled with both a software renderer and an OpenGL-based renderer. This means that you should have OpenGL and the GLUT libraries installed on your system. OpenGL libraries should come standard with the operating system, and are also distributed as specialized drivers with any modern 3D graphics card. The GLUT library (file `GLUT32.DLL`) is included in the file `opengl-1.2.1-1.tar.gz` included with the Cygnus GCC compiler on the CD-ROM. If your OpenGL driver supports hardware acceleration, then the l3d programs will also run with hardware acceleration under Microsoft Windows. In the unlikely event that you do not have any OpenGL libraries at all installed on your system, you can change the Makefiles to compile and link without the OpenGL-specific files; in other words, it is also possible to compile l3d using purely software rendering under Windows.

Plug-ins do not yet work with the Microsoft Windows version of the code. There appears to be some difficulty in using Linux-style plug-ins with Cygnus GCC. For this reason, any programs using plug-ins will not currently work under Windows. Currently, the code is relying on an emulation of the Linux `dlopen` system call to load the libraries. However, windows has its own dynamic library loading mechanism, `LoadLibrary`, which could be used instead.

NOTE   Using a scripting language for dynamic behavior instead of plug-ins would avoid the problems of system-specific dynamic library conventions, but with a possibly slower run-time performance.

Be sure to check this book's Web site `http://www.linux3dgraphicsprogram-ming.org` to see the status of the Microsoft Windows l3d code and to download the latest version. Alternatively, you can choose to abandon Microsoft Windows entirely, which for the long term may be a better solution.

Tools Used to Prepare This Book

At the suggestion of my technical editor, Kevin Seghetti, I'll now briefly go over the tools used to prepare this book.

This book was written using exclusively Linux tools. The Linux distribution was SuSE 6.3, though I am currently in the process of migrating to Debian, because of Debian's clear commitment to the free software community.

The text was prepared using Corel WordPerfect 8 for Linux. I would have preferred to have written the text in LyX, which is a front end to the LaTeX document preparation system often used in academic circles. However, at the time of this writing, there exists no reliable way of converting LyX/LaTeX files to the proprietary word processing format required by my publisher. Sure, there were several tools which could do most of the conversion (`latex2html`, for instance), but after trying around five different packages, I found no solution which preserved fonts, lists, indentation, headers, and so forth. So I used WordPerfect, which could export files in exactly the format needed by the publisher.

The program listings were stored separately from the text, as subdocuments. A Perl script stripped extraneous comments from all source code files and converted the ASCII source code files into RTF files. The RTF files were then linked into the master document. The code snippets within the text were delimited by specially formatted comments in the code; another Perl script then extracted these regions, and again created RTF files which could be bound into the master document. The scripts are in the l3d distribution, as files `make_clean.sh`, `no_dou-ble_space.pl`, and `snippets.pl`. Whenever I needed to update the source code, I would then merely run my scripts again, and the updated source code was automatically rebound into the master document.

The 2D figures were generated using Xfig, a very flexible object-based (as opposed to bitmap) drawing program. The class diagrams were generated manually with TCM, the Toolkit for Conceptual Modeling. Other promising class diagram tools include Argo/UML (which I did not use because it focuses on Java) and doxygen (which automatically produces excellent documentation from uncommented C++ code, and which I will probably use in the future). The 3D figures were generated with Blender. The animations on the CD-ROM were also created with Blender. Post-processing work on the figures was done with GIMP.

The equations were generated using LyX, an almost WYSIWYG environment for LaTeX. I created one LyX file containing all equations for a particular chapter. Next, I exported the LyX file as a LaTeX file. Then, I used latex2html to convert the LaTeX code into HTML; latex2html has the wonderful feature that it automatically converts LaTeX equations into bitmap image files. These bitmap image files were then renamed into the `eqnxx-xx` files on the CD-ROM.

To manage the large number of figures and equations for each chapter, I again wrote a Perl script which read an input file containing a list of all the figures for the chapter, in order. These figures were then converted into the format needed by the publisher and assigned sequential filenames. This way, I could work on the figures separately, with different file formats, and not worry about their exact order. If a figure got added or deleted, I simply made the appropriate change to the list of figures, and all the figures got assigned the correct numbers during the next run of the script. The PBM utilities were used within the script file to convert the varying image file formats into one common format.

Resources

The following is a list of some printed and online resources which may be of use to you as you continue to explore, and hopefully advance the state of, Linux 3D graphics. The next section is a comprehensive list of the specific literature referenced in this book.

Blender v1.5 Manual by Ton Roosendaal. This is the definitive guide to using Blender. See also `http://www.blender.nl`.

Computer Graphics, Principles and Practice by James Foley, Andries van Dam, Steven Feiner, and John Hughes. Regarded by many as a classic in the field, this book covers an extremely broad range of topics relevant to 2D and 3D graphics programmers. Practically every important topic is covered, even if only briefly. This book has a somewhat mathematical slant to it.

The C++ Programming Language by Bjarne Stroustrup. This is, of course, the definitive reference on the C++ language.

Das Blender Buch by Carsten Wartmann. This book provides a practical introduction and guide to using Blender, with several hands-on tutorials. (In German.)

Data Structures and Program Design by Robert Kruse. This introduction to data structures describes many of the fundamental structures of computer science that are essential in programs of all kinds, including 3D programs.

Design Patterns: Elements of Reusable Object-Oriented Software by Erich Gamma, Richard Helm, Ralph Johnson, and John Vlissides. This landmark book documented for the first time the concept of a "design pattern," presented a catalog of reusable patterns, and encouraged the use of this technique for object-oriented development.

Digital Character Animation 2, Volume 1—Essential Techniques by George Maestri. This platform-independent book illustrates the fundamentals of character animation with plenty of exercises and illustrations to help you understand and master the difficulties.

Drawing on the Right Side of the Brain by Betty Edwards. This book deals with developing the visual skills to become a good 2D artist. While it doesn't directly deal with computer graphics, the visual skills you can learn from this book are very effective for all types of visual expression, including 3D modeling.

The Guitar Handbook by Ralph Denyer. I have found that good programmers are often also good artists—musically, visually, or otherwise. If you write interactive 3D programs such as games, you might also need to write music to accompany these programs. This book, while focusing on the guitar, provides a good treatment of music theory as well.

Keys to Drawing by Bert Dodson. This book, too, does not deal directly with computer graphics, but offers a number of useful tips or "keys" to creating effective 2D art.

Looking Good in 3D by Andrew Reese. This practice-oriented book explains basic principles of 3D imagery and illustrates which 3D graphics techniques to use in order to create effective presentations.

Object-Oriented Software Construction by Bertrand Meyer. This book is a comprehensive treatment of the subject of object orientation and how it improves software quality. The book is very readable, yet also provides rigorous treatment of what object orientation actually is, and its relationship to other software methodologies and to the field of scientific study as a whole. While much literature attempts to make object orientation appear easy, this book does not shy away from showing the true, subtle, real-world difficulties of software construction, and how object orientation attacks these problems head-on.

OpenGL Programming Guide by Mason Woo, Jackie Neider, and Tom Davis. This is the definitive guide to programming with OpenGL.

Real-Time Rendering by Tomas Möller and Eric Haines. This book contains numerous algorithms and concepts required for rendering high-quality graphics in real time. It is currently (March 2001) one of the more up-to-date books in the field, and is a good collection of the most useful contemporary techniques.

University Physics by Francis W. Sears, Mark W. Zemansky, and Hugh D. Young. This undergraduate-level text provides a useful introduction to the field of physics, some of which can be applied to computer simulations.

The X Window System: Programming and Applications with Xt by Douglas Young and John Pew. This book provides an introduction to programming the X Window System.

`http://mesa3d.sourceforge.net`. The Mesa home page provides news and the latest version of the Mesa library, which is effectively compatible with OpenGL.

`http://sunsite.auc.dk/linuxgames`. The Linux Games Development Center provides articles and news for developers of games under Linux.

`http://www.blender.nl`. This is the official home page of the Blender 3D rendering, animation, and game development suite.

`http://www.debian.org`. This is the home page for the Debian GNU/Linux distribution of the Linux operating system.

`http://www.flipcode.com`. This site offers many tutorials and columns relevant to programming real-time 3D graphics and games.

`http://www.gnu.org`. This is the home page of the GNU project, which is a pivotal proponent of free software ("free" as in "freedom"), and whose software forms a large and important part of the GNU/Linux operating system. The GNU project is the source of the GNU General Public License, or GPL, under which much Linux software has been released.

`http://www.graphicspapers.com`. This site contains a very large searchable database of academic papers dealing with 3D graphics.

`http://www.linux3dgraphicsprogramming.org`. This is the home page for the book, and provides links to many other resources, as well as discussion forums, hourly updated Linux 3D news, tutorials, articles, code repositories, and more. Check it out!

`http://www.opengl.org`. The OpenGL home page provides news, links, and sample code dealing with OpenGL.

`http://www.worldfoundry.org`. This is the home page for the World Foundry system described in Chapter 9, a game development kit allowing creation of sophisticated, multi-platform 3D games with no programming.

References

FOLE92   Foley, James, Andries van Dam, Steven Feiner, John Hughes. *Computer Graphics: Principles and Practice*. New York: Addison-Wesley, 1992.

GAMM95   Gamma, Erich, Richard Helm, Ralph Johnson, and John Vlissides. *Design Patterns: Elements of Reusable Object-Oriented Software*. Reading (Massachusetts): Addison-Wesley, 1995.

HECK97   Hecker, Chris. "Physics." A four-part series of articles for *Game Developer*, 1995-1997. `http://www.d6.com`.

MEYE97   Meyer, Bertrand. *Object-Oriented Software Construction*. New Jersey: Prentice Hall PTR, 1997.

MOEL99   Möller, Tomas, and Eric Haines. *Real-Time Rendering*. A K Peters, 1999.

SUTH74   Sutherland, I.E., and G.W. Hodgman. "Reentrant Polygon Clipping." *Communications of the ACM* 17(1), 32-42, January 1974.

WOO97   Woo, Mason, Jackie Neider, Tom Davis. *OpenGL Programming Guide, Second Edition*. Reading (Massachusetts): Addison-Wesley, 1997.

Index

An asterisk indicates the reference includes code segments.

CAUTION Opening the CD package makes this book nonreturnable.

NOTE See the Appendix for information about the companion CD-ROM.